SOCIALISM

T0124936

The Liberty Fund Library of the Works of Ludwig von Mises

EDITED BY BETTINA BIEN GREAVES

The Anti-capitalistic Mentality
Bureaucracy
Economic Freedom and Interventionism: An Anthology of Articles and Essays
Economic Policy: Thoughts for Today and Tomorrow
Epistemological Problems of Economics
Human Action: A Treatise on Economics
Interventionism: An Economic Analysis
Liberalism: The Classical Tradition
Money, Method, and the Market Process: Essays by Ludwig von Mises
Nation, State, and Economy: Contributions to the Politics and History of Our Time
Notes and Recollections: With The Historical Setting of the Austrian School of Economics
Omnipotent Government: The Rise of the Total State and Total War
On the Manipulation of Money and Credit: Three Treatises on Trade-Cycle Theory
Planning for Freedom: Let the Market System Work; A Collection of Essays and Addresses
Socialism: An Economic and Sociological Analysis
Theory and History: An Interpretation of Social and Economic Evolution
The Theory of Money and Credit
The Ultimate Foundation of Economic Science: An Essay on Method

EDITED BY RICHARD M. EBELING

Selected Writings of Ludwig von Mises

Volume 1: Monetary and Economic Policy Problems Before, During, and After the Great War
Volume 2: Between the Two World Wars: Monetary Disorder, Interventionism, Socialism, and the Great Depression
Volume 3: The Political Economy of International Reform and Reconstruction

LUDWIG VON MISES

SOCIALISM

An Economic and Sociological Analysis

by
LUDWIG VON MISES

Translated
by
J. KAHANE B.Sc. (Econ.)

Liberty Fund

This book is published by Liberty Fund, Inc., a foundation established to encourage study of the ideal of a society of free and responsible individuals.

The cuneiform inscription that serves as the design motif for our endpapers is the earliest-known written appearance of the word "freedom" (*amagi*), or "liberty." It is taken from a clay document written about 2300 B.C. in the Sumerian city-state of Lagash.

This edition of *Socialism* follows the text, with correction and enlargement of footnotes, of the Jonathan Cape Ltd., edition published in London in 1969. The edition was based on the 1951 edition by Yale University Press which slightly enlarged the first English edition published by Jonathan Cape in 1936, translated from the German by J. Kahane.

© 1981 by Bettina Bien Greaves

All rights reserved. Published 1981.

Photograph of Ludwig von Mises used by permission of the Ludwig von Mises Institute, Auburn, Alabama.

Printed in the United States of America.

10 22 23 24 25 C 12 11 10 9 8
23 24 25 26 27 P 16 15 14 13 12

Library of Congress Cataloging in Publication Data

Von Mises, Ludwig, 1881–1973.
Socialism.

Translation of the 2d ed. (1932) of Die Gemeinwirtschaft.
Includes index.
1. Socialism. I. Title
HX276. V562 1979 335 79-21701
ISBN 0-913966-62-2
ISBN 0-913966-63-0 pbk.

Liberty Fund, Inc.
11301 North Meridian Street
Carmel, Indiana 46032
libertyfund.org

CONTENTS

PART I
LIBERALISM AND SOCIALISM

III. *Particular Forms of Socialism and Pseudo-Socialism*

PART III
THE ALLEGED INEVITABILITY OF SOCIALISM

I. *Social Evolution*

PART IV
SOCIALISM AS A MORAL IMPERATIVE

EPILOGUE

PUBLISHER'S PREFACE TO THE LIBERTY FUND EDITION

Socialism, by Ludwig von Mises, was originally published in German under the title *Die Gemeinwirtschaft: Untersuchungen über den Sozialismus* (Jena: Gustav Fischer, 1922). A few paragraphs and the appendix were added to the second German edition, published by the same firm in 1932, and a few more paragraphs were included in the first English translation—*Socialism: An Economic and Sociological Analysis*, translated by J. Kahane (London: Jonathan Cape, 1936).

An enlarged edition of the Kahane translation was published in 1951 (New Haven: Yale University Press). This edition included an epilogue originally published (and still available) under the title *Planned Chaos* (Irvington, New York: Foundation for Economic Education, 1947). This enlarged edition was reprinted by Jonathan Cape (London) in 1969, and is here reprinted again, in 1981, by Liberty Fund (Indianapolis).

This edition leaves the text as translated by Kahane in 1936 and added to by Mises in 1951 undisturbed. The present publisher has, however, undertaken to add certain features to aid the contemporary reader. Translations have been provided for all non-English expressions left untranslated in the Jonathan Cape edition. These translations appear in parentheses after the expressions or passages in question. Chapters have been numbered consecutively throughout the book.

All footnotes have been checked against the second German edition. When works in languages other than English are cited by Mises, information concerning versions in English has been provided when such versions could be located. The corresponding page references in the English versions are also provided insofar as location of these was possible. Complete information concerning the English version is provided at the first citation of a given work. Only the page references in the English are provided in later citations, but full information is easily located in the Index to Works Cited. All bibliographical information added to the footnotes is clearly labeled as a publisher's note.

Having been written in 1922 in Austria and ranging over many fields of learning, *Socialism* contains a number of references to individuals and events with which many readers will not be familiar. Brief explanations of such references are provided by asterisked footnotes printed below Mises' notes and clearly labeled as being added by the publisher. Such notes also offer explanations quoted from Mises of his special use of a few English terms.

In order to facilitate study of the book, two new indexes have been provided. An Index to Works Cited lists all books and authors cited in *Socialism*. This index also provides English versions of works cited by Mises in German. In cases where no English version has been found, a literal translation of the title has been provided. A general Subject and Name Index is also provided.

Socialism has been available in English for more than forty years and references to it abound in the scholarly literature. Since Liberty Fund editions are set in new type, the pagination of this new edition differs from the earlier ones. We have, therefore, indicated the pagination of the expanded edition of 1951 in the margins of the Liberty Fund edition.

The pagination of all previous English language editions was the same from pages 15 through 521. In the enlarged edition of 1951, a Preface was added as pages 13–14, and the Epilogue was added as pages 522–592. By placing the pagination of the 1951 edition in the margins of our edition, we provide a guide to the location of citations of all earlier English editions.

The publisher wishes to acknowledge with thanks the aid of several persons who helped with this edition. The many aids to study and understanding offered in this edition are due primarily to the work of Bettina Bien Greaves of the Foundation for Economic Education. She performed the monumental task of checking the footnotes against the second German edition. She also undertook the equally difficult task of providing most of the citations to English language versions of works cited in German. She provided most of the material for the asterisked explanations of unfamiliar references. She also did most of the work of preparing the new indexes. If this edition is more easily studied by contemporary readers, most of the credit should go to Mrs. Greaves.

For aid with translations from Greek, the publisher acknowledges the help of Professors Perry E. Gresham and Burton Thurston of Bethany College. For help with Latin translations, Professor Gresham must be acknowledged again along with Father Laut of Wheeling College. Percy L. Greaves, Jr., of Dobbs Ferry, New York, provided translations from French. Professor H. D. Brueckner of Pomona College provided aid with locating translations and citations of Kant.

FOREWORD

By F. A. Hayek

When *Socialism* first appeared in 1922, its impact was profound. It gradually but fundamentally altered the outlook of many of the young idealists returning to their university studies after World War I. I know, for I was one of them.

We felt that the civilization in which we had grown up had collapsed. We were determined to build a better world, and it was this desire to reconstruct society that led many of us to the study of economics. Socialism promised to fulfill our hopes for a more rational, more just world. And then came this book. Our hopes were dashed. *Socialism* told us that we had been looking for improvement in the wrong direction.

A number of my contemporaries, who later became well known but who were then unknown to each other, went through the same experience: Wilhelm Röpke in Germany and Lionel Robbins in England are but two examples. None of us had initially been Mises' pupils. I had come to know him while working for a temporary Austrian government office which was entrusted with the implementation of certain clauses of the Treaty of Versailles. He was my superior, the director of the department.

Mises was then best known as a fighter against inflation. He had gained the ear of the government and, from another position as financial adviser to the Vienna Chamber of Commerce, was immensely busy urging the government to take the only path by which a complete collapse of the currency could still be prevented. (During the first eight months I served under him, my nominal salary rose to two hundred times the initial amount.)

As students during the early 1920's, many of us were aware of Mises as the somewhat reclusive university lecturer who, a decade or so earlier, had published a book[1] known for its successful application of the Austrian marginal utility analysis theory of money—a book Max Weber described as the most acceptable work on the subject. Perhaps we ought to have known that in 1919 he had also published a thoughtful and farseeing study on the wider aspects of social philosophy, concerning the nation, the state, and the economy.[2] It never became widely known, however, and I discovered it only when I was his subordinate at the government office in Vienna. At any rate, it was a great surprise to me when this book, *Socialism,* was first published.[3] For all I knew, he could hardly have had much free time for academic pursuits during the preceding (and extremely busy) ten years. Yet this was a major treatise on social philosophy, giving every evidence of independent thought and reflecting, through Mises' criticism, an acquaintance with most of the literature on the subject.

For the first twelve years of this century, until he entered military service, Mises studied economic and social problems. He was, as was my generation nearly twenty years later, led to these topics by the fashionable concern with *Sozialpolitik,* similar in outlook to the "Fabian" socialism of England. His first book,[4] published while he was still a young law student at the University of Vienna, was in the spirit of the predominant German "historical school" of economists who devoted themselves mainly to problems of "social policy." He later even joined one of those organizations which prompted a German satirical weekly to define economists as persons who went around measuring workingmen's dwellings and saying they were too small. But in the course of this process, when he was taught political economy as part of his law studies, Mises discovered economic theory in the shape of the *Grundsätze der Volkswirtschaftslehre (Principles of Economics)* of Carl Menger,[5] then about to retire as a professor at the university. As Mises says in his fragment of an autobiography,[6] this book made him an economist. Having gone through the same experience, I know what he means.

---

[1] Ludwig von Mises, *Theorie des Geldes und der Umlaufsmittel* (Munich and Leipzig: Duncker & Humblot, 1912). Publisher's Note: This has been translated into English as *The Theory of Money and Credit* (Indianapolis: Liberty*Classics*, 1981).

[2] Ludwig von Mises, *Nation, Staat und Wirtschaft: Beiträge zur Politik und Geschichte der Zeit* (Vienna: Manz'sche Verlags und Universitäts-Buchhandlung, 1919).

[3] Ludwig von Mises, *Die Gemeinwirtschaft: Untersuchungen über den Sozialismus* (Jena: Gustav Fischer, 1922).

[4] Ludwig von Mises, *Die Entwicklung des gutsherrlichbäuerlichen Verhältnisses in Galizien, 1772–1848* (Vienna and Leipzig: Franz Deuticke, 1902).

[5] Carl Menger, *Principles of Economics* (New York: New York University Press, 1981).

[6] Ludwig von Mises, *Notes and Recollections;* foreword by Margit von Mises, translation and postscript by Hans F. Sennholz (South Holland, Ill.: Libertarian Press, 1978); p. 33.

Mises' initial interests had been primarily historical, and to the end he retained a breadth of historical knowledge rare among theoreticians. But, finally, his dissatisfaction with the manner in which historians and particularly economic historians interpreted their material led him to economic theory. His chief inspiration came from Eugen von Böhm-Bawerk, who had returned to a professorship at the University of Vienna after serving as Austrian Minister of Finance. During the decade before the war, Böhm-Bawerk's seminar became the great center for the discussion of economic theory. Its participants included Mises, Joseph Schumpeter, and the outstanding theoretician of Austrian Marxism, Otto Bauer, whose defense of Marxism long dominated the discussion. Böhm-Bawerk's ideas on socialism during this period appear to have developed a good deal beyond what is shown by the few essays he published before his early death. There is no doubt that the foundations of Mises' characteristic ideas on socialism were laid then, though almost as soon as he had published his first major work, *The Theory of Money and Credit* (1912), the opportunity for further systematic pursuit of this interest vanished with Mises' entry into service for the duration of World War I.

Most of Mises' military service was spent as an artillery officer on the Russian front, but during the last few months he served in the economic section of the Ministry of War. It must be assumed that he started on *Socialism* only after his release from military duty. He probably wrote most of it between 1919 and 1921—the crucial section on economic calculation under socialism was in fact provoked by a book by Otto Neurath published in 1919, from which Mises quotes. That under the prevailing conditions he found time to concentrate and to pursue a comprehensive theoretical and philosophical work has remained a wonder to one who at least during the last months of this period saw him almost daily at his official work.

As I suggested before, *Socialism* shocked our generation, and only slowly and painfully did we become persuaded of its central thesis. Mises continued, of course, thinking about the same range of problems, and many of his further ideas were developed in the "private seminar" which began about the time *Socialism* was published. I joined the seminar two years later, upon my return from a year of postgraduate study in the United States. Although there were few unquestioning followers at first, he gained interest and admiration among a younger generation and attracted those who were concerned with problems of the borderline of social theory and philosophy. Reception of the book by the profession was mostly either indifferent or hostile. I remember but one review that showed any recognition of *Socialism*'s importance and that was by a surviving liberal statesman of the preceding century. The tactics of his opponents were generally to represent him as an extremist whose views no one else shared.

Mises' ideas ripened during the next two decades, culminating in the first (1940) German version of what became famous as *Human Action*.[7] But to those of us who experienced its first impact, *Socialism* will always be his decisive contribution. It challenged the outlook of a generation and altered, if only slowly, the thinking of many. The members of Mises' Vienna group were not disciples. Most of them came to him as students who had completed their basic training in economics, and only gradually were they converted to his unconventional views. Perhaps they were influenced as much by his disconcerting habit of rightly predicting the ill consequences of current economic policy as by the cogency of his arguments. Mises hardly expected them to accept all his opinions, and the discussions gained much from the fact that the participants were often only gradually weaned from their different views. It was only later, after he had developed a complete system of social thought, that a "Mises School" developed. The very openness of his system enriched his ideas and enabled some of his followers to develop them in somewhat different directions.

Mises' arguments were not always easily apprehended. Sometimes personal contact and discussion were required to understand them fully. Though written in a pellucid and deceptively simple prose, they tacitly presuppose an understanding of economic processes—an understanding not shared by all his readers. We see this most clearly in his crucial argument on the impossibility of an economic calculation under socialism. When one reads Mises' opponents, one gains the impression that they did not really see why such calculation was necessary. They treat the problem of economic calculation as if it were merely a technique to make the managers of socialist plants accountable for the resources entrusted to them and wholly unconnected with the problem of what they should produce and how. Any set of magic figures appeared to them sufficient to control the honesty of those still indispensable survivors of a capitalist age. They never seemed to comprehend that it was not a question of playing with some set of figures, but one of establishing the only indicators those managers could have for deciding the role of their activities in the whole structure of mutually adjusted activities. As a result, Mises became increasingly aware that what separated him from his critics was his wholly different intellectual approach to social and economic problems, rather than mere differences of interpretation of particular facts.

---

[7] Ludwig von Mises, *Nationalökonomie: Theorie des Handelns und Wirtschaftens* (Geneva: Éditions Union, 1940).

To convince them, he would have to impress on them the necessity of an altogether different methodology. This of course became his central concern.

Publication in 1936 of the English translation was largely the result of the efforts of Professor Lionel C. Robbins (now Lord Robbins). He found a highly qualified translator in a former fellow student at the London School of Economics, Jacques Kahane (1900–1969), who had remained an active member of a circle of academic economists of that generation, although he himself had not remained in the profession. After many years of service with one of the great firms of grain dealers in London, Kahane concluded his career with the United Nations Food and Agricultural Office at Rome and the World Bank at Washington. The typescript of Kahane's translation was the last form in which I had read the entire text of *Socialism*, before doing so again in preparation for writing this introduction.

This experience necessarily makes one reflect on the significance of some of Mises' arguments after so long a period. Much of the work now inevitably sounds much less original or revolutionary than it did in its early years. It has in many ways become one of those "classics" which one too often takes for granted and from which one expects to learn but little that is new. I must admit, however, that I was surprised at not only how much of it is still highly relevant to current disputes, but how many of its arguments, which I initially had only half accepted or regarded as exaggerated and one-sided, have since proved remarkably true. I still do not agree with all of it, nor do I believe that Mises would. He certainly was not one to expect that his followers receive his conclusions uncritically and not progress beyond them. In all, though, I find that I differ rather less than I expected.

One of my differences is over a statement of Mises on page 463 of the 1951 edition (page 418 of this edition). I had always felt a little uneasy about that statement of basic philosophy, but only now can I articulate why I was uncomfortable with it. Mises asserts in this passage that liberalism "regards all social cooperation as an emanation of rationally recognized utility, in which all power is based on public opinion, and can undertake no course of action that would hinder the free decision of thinking men." It is the first part of this statement only which I now think is wrong. The extreme rationalism of this passage, which as a child of his time he could not escape from, and which he perhaps never fully abandoned, now seems to me factually mistaken. It certainly was not rational insight into its general benefits that led to the spreading of the market economy. It seems to me that the thrust of Mises' teaching is to show that we have *not* adopted freedom because we understood what benefits it would bring: that we have *not* designed, and certainly were not intelligent enough to design, the order which we now have learned partly to understand long after we had plenty of opportunity to see how it worked. Man has *chosen* it only in the sense that he has learned to prefer something that already operated, and through greater understanding has been able to improve the conditions for its operation.

It is greatly to Mises' credit that he largely emancipated himself from that rationalist-constructivist starting point, but that task is still to be completed. Mises as much as anybody has helped us to understand something which we have not designed.

There is another point about which the present-day reader should be cautioned. It is that half a century ago Mises could still speak of liberalism in a sense which is more or less the opposite of what the term means today in the United States, and increasingly elsewhere. He regarded himself as a liberal in the classical, nineteenth-century meaning of the term. But almost forty years have now elapsed since Joseph Schumpeter was constrained to say that in the United States the enemies of liberty, "as a supreme but unintended compliment, have thought it wise to appropriate this label."

In the epilogue, which was written in the United States twenty-five years after the original work, Mises reveals his awareness of this and comments on the misleading use of the term "liberalism." An additional thirty years have only confirmed these comments, as they have confirmed the last part of the original text, "Destructionism." That shocked me for its inordinate pessimism when first I read it. Yet, on rereading it, I am awed rather by its foresight than by its pessimism. In fact, most readers today will find that *Socialism* has more immediate application to contemporary events than it had when it first appeared in its English version just over forty years ago.

August 1978

PREFACE TO THE SECOND ENGLISH EDITION

The world is split today into two hostile camps, fighting each other with 13
the utmost vehemence, Communists and anti-Communists. The magniloquent rhetoric to which these factions resort in their feud obscures the fact that they both perfectly agree in the ultimate end of their programme for mankind's social and economic organization. They both aim at the abolition of private enterprise and private ownership of the means of production and at the establishment of socialism. They want to substitute totalitarian government control for the market economy. No longer should individuals by their buying or abstention from buying determine what is to be produced and in what quantity and quality. Henceforth the government's unique plan alone should settle all these matters. 'Paternal' care of the 'Welfare State' will reduce all people to the status of bonded workers bound to comply, without asking questions, with the orders issued by the planning authority.

Neither is there any substantial difference between the intentions of the self-styled 'progressives' and those of the Italian Fascists and the German Nazis. The Fascists and the Nazis were no less eager to establish all-round regimentation of all economic activities than those governments and parties which flamboyantly advertise their anti-Fascist tenets. And Mr. Peron in Argentina tries to enforce a scheme which is a replica of the New Deal and the Fair Deal and like these will, if not stopped in time, result in full socialism.

The great ideological conflict of our age must not be confused with the mutual rivalries among the various totalitarian movements. The real issue is not who should run the totalitarian apparatus. The real problem is whether or not socialism should supplant the market economy.

It is this subject with which my book deals.

World conditions have changed considerably since the first edition of my

essay was published. But all these disastrous wars and revolutions, heinous mass murders and frightful catastrophes have not affected the main issue:
14 the desperate struggle of lovers of freedom, prosperity and civilization against the rising tide of totalitarian barbarism.

In the *Epilogue* I deal with the most important aspects of the events of the last decades. A more detailed study of all the problems involved is to be found in three books of mine published by the Yale University Press:

Omnipotent Government, the Rise of the Total State and Total War;[1]
Bureaucracy;[2]
Human Action, a Treatise on Economics.[3]

LUDWIG VON MISES

New York, July 1950

---

[1] French translation by M. de Hulster, Librairie de Médicis, Paris; Spanish translation by Pedro Elgoibar, Editorial Hermes, México.

[2] British edition by William Hodge & Company Limited, London; French translation by R. Florin and P. Barbier, Librairie de Médicis, Paris.

[3] British edition by William Hodge & Company Limited, London.

TRANSLATOR'S NOTE

The following work is translated from the second German edition (published 1932) of the author's *Die Gemeinwirtschaft* (originally published in 1922). The author, who has lent assistance at every stage, has inserted certain additions, notably on the problem of economic calculation and on unemployment (pp. 137 ff., 485 ff.), which are not to be found in the German edition, and certain changes have been made in terminology to meet the convenience of English readers.

PREFACE TO THE SECOND GERMAN EDITION

It is a matter of dispute whether, prior to the middle of the nineteenth 15
century, there existed any clear conception of the socialist idea—by which is understood the socialization of the means of production with its corollary, the centralized control of the whole of production by one social or, more accurately, state organ. The answer depends primarily upon whether we regard the demand for a centralized administration of the means of production throughout the world as an essential feature in a considered socialist plan. The older socialists looked upon the autarky of small territories as 'natural' and on any exchange of goods beyond their frontiers as at once 'artificial' and harmful. Only after the English Free-Traders had proved the advantages of an international division of labour, and popularized their views through the Cobden movement, did the socialists begin to expand the ideas of village and district Socialism into a national and, eventually, a world Socialism. Apart from this one point, however, the basic conception of Socialism had been quite clearly worked out in the course of the second quarter of the nineteenth century by those writers designated by Marxism as "Utopian Socialists." Schemes for a socialist order of society were extensively discussed at that time, but the discussion did not go in their favour. The Utopians had not succeeded in planning social structures that would withstand the criticisms of economists and sociologists. It was easy to pick holes in their schemes; to prove that a society constructed on such principles must lack efficiency and vitality, and that it certainly would not come up to expectations. Thus, about the middle of the nineteenth century, it seemed that the ideal of Socialism had been disposed of. Science had demonstrated its worthlessness by means of strict logic and its supporters were unable to produce a single effective counter-argument.

It was at this moment that Marx appeared. Adept as he was in Hegelian dialectic—a system easy of abuse by those who seek to dominate thought by arbitrary flights of fancy and metaphysical verbosity—he was not slow in finding a way out of the dilemma in which socialists found themselves.
16 Since Science and Logic had argued against Socialism, it was imperative to devise a system which could be relied on to defend it against such unpalatable criticism. This was the task which Marxism undertook to perform. It had three lines of procedure. First, it denied that Logic is universally valid for all mankind and for all ages. Thought, it stated, was determined by the class of the thinkers; was in fact an "ideological superstructure" of their class interests. The type of reasoning which had refuted the socialist idea was "revealed" as "bourgeois" reasoning, an apology for Capitalism. Secondly, it laid it down that the dialectical development led of necessity to Socialism; that the aim and end of all history was the socialization of the means of production by the expropriation of the expropriators—the negation of negation. Finally, it was ruled that no one should be allowed to put forward, as the Utopians had done, any definite proposals for the construction of the Socialist Promised Land. Since the coming of Socialism was inevitable, Science would best renounce all attempt to determine its nature.

At no point in history has a doctrine found such immediate and complete acceptance as that contained in these three principles of Marxism. The magnitude and persistence of its success is commonly underestimated. This is due to the habit of applying the term Marxist exclusively to formal members of one or other of the self-styled Marxist parties, who are pledged to uphold word for word the doctrines of Marx and Engels as interpreted by their respective sects and to regard such doctrines as the unshakable foundation and ultimate source of all that is known about Society and as constituting the highest standard in political dealings. But if we include under the term "Marxist" all who have accepted the basic Marxian principles—that class conditions thought, that Socialism is inevitable, and that research into the being and working of the socialist community is unscientific—we shall find very few non-Marxists in Europe east of the Rhine, and even in Western Europe and the United States many more supporters than opponents of Marxism. Professed Christians attack the materialism of Marxists, monarchists their republicanism, nationalists their internationalism; yet they themselves, each in turn, wish to be known as Christian Socialists, State Socialists, National Socialists. They assert that their particular brand of Socialism is the only true one—that which "shall" come, bringing with it happiness and contentment. The Socialism of others, they say, has not the genuine class-
17 origin of their own. At the same time they scrupulously respect Marx's

prohibition of any inquiry into the institutions of the socialist economy of the future, and try to interpret the working of the present economic system as a development leading to Socialism in accordance with the inexorable demand of the historical process. Of course, not Marxists alone, but most of those who emphatically declare themselves anti-Marxists, think entirely on Marxist lines and have adopted Marx's arbitrary, unconfirmed and easily refutable dogmas. If and when they come into power, they govern and work entirely in the socialist spirit.

The incomparable success of Marxism is due to the prospect it offers of fulfilling those dream-aspirations and dreams of vengeance which have been so deeply embedded in the human soul from time immemorial. It promises a Paradise on earth, a Land of Heart's Desire full of happiness and enjoyment, and—sweeter still to the losers in life's game—humiliation of all who are stronger and better than the multitude. Logic and reasoning, which might show the absurdity of such dreams of bliss and revenge, are to be thrust aside. Marxism is thus the most radical of all reactions against the reign of scientific thought over life and action, established by Rationalism. It is against Logic, against Science and against the activity of thought itself—its outstanding principle is the prohibition of thought and inquiry, especially as applied to the institutions and workings of a socialist economy. It is characteristic that it should adopt the name "Scientific Socialism" and thus gain the prestige acquired by Science, through the indisputable success of its rule over life and action, for use in its own battle against any scientific contribution to the construction of the socialist economy. The Bolshevists persistently tell us that religion is opium for the people. Marxism is indeed opium for those who might take to thinking and must therefore be weaned from it.

In this new edition of my book, which has been considerably revised, I have ventured to defy the almost universally respected Marxian prohibition by examining the problems of the socialist construction of society on scientific lines, i.e., by the aid of sociological and economic theory. While gratefully recalling the men whose research has opened the way for all work, my own included, in this field, it is still a source of gratification to me to be in a position to claim to have broken the ban placed by Marxism on the scientific treatment of these problems. Since the first publication of this book, problems
previously ignored have come into the foreground of scientific interest; the 18
discussion of Socialism and Capitalism has been placed on a new footing. Those who were formerly content to make a few vague remarks about the blessings which Socialism would bring are now obliged to study the nature of the socialist society. The problems have been defined and can no longer be ignored.

As might be expected, socialists of every sort and description, from the most radical Soviet Bolshevists to the *"Edelsozialisten"** of western civilization, have attempted to refute my reasonings and conclusions. But they have not succeeded, they have not even managed to bring forward any argument that I had not already discussed and disproved. At the present time, scientific discussion of the basic problems of Socialism follows the line of the investigation of this book.

The arguments by which I demonstrated that, in a socialist community, economic calculation would not be possible have attracted especially wide notice. Two years before the appearance of the first edition of my book I published this section of my investigations in the *Archiv für Sozialwissenschaft* (Vol. XLVII, No. I),** where it is worded almost exactly as in both editions of the present work. The problem, which had scarcely been touched before, at once roused lively discussion in German-speaking countries and abroad. It may truly be said that the discussion is now closed; there is today hardly any opposition to my contention.

Shortly after the first edition appeared, Heinrich Herkner, chief of the Socialists of the Chair (*"Kathedersozialisten"*) in succession to Gustav Schmoller, published an essay which in all essentials supported my criticism of Socialism.[1] His remarks raised quite a storm amongst German socialists and their literary followings. Thus there arose, in the midst of the catastrophic struggle in the Ruhr and the hyper-inflation, a controversy which speedily became known as the crisis of the "Social Reform Policy." The result of the controversy was indeed meagre. The "sterility" of socialist thought, to which an ardent socialist had drawn attention, was especially apparent on this occasion.[2] Of the good results that can be obtained by an unprejudiced
19 scientific study of the problems of Socialism there is proof in the admirable works of Pohle, Adolf Weber, Röpke, Halm, Sulzbach, Brutzkus, Robbins, Hutt, Withers, Benn, and others.

---

[1] Herkner, "Sozialpolitische Wandlungen in der wissenschaftlichen Nationalökonomie" (*Der Arbeitgeber*, vol. 13, p. 35).

[2] Cassau, "Die sozialistische Ideenwelt vor und nach dem Kriege" in *Die Wirtschaftswissenschaft nach dem Kriege, Festgabe für Lujo Brentano zum 80. Geburtstag* (Munich, 1925), vol. 1, pp. 149 ff.

* "Edelsozialisten" means pure, or intellectual, socialists, "parlour socialists" of the world of culture, as one would say in colloquial English (Pub.).

** "Die Wirtschaftsrechnung im sozialistischen Gemeinwesen." This article was translated under the title "Economic Calculation in the Socialist Commonwealth" from the German by S. Adler and into English. It is included in the anthology edited by F. A. Hayek, *Collectivist Economic Planning* (London: Routledge and Kegan, 1935), on pp. 87–130. This collection was reprinted in 1967 by Augustus M. Kelley Publishers of New Jersey (Pub.).

But scientific inquiry into the problems of Socialism is not enough. We must also break down the wall of prejudice which at present blocks the way to an unbiased scrutiny of these problems. Any advocate of socialistic measures is looked upon as the friend of the Good, the Noble, and the Moral, as a disinterested pioneer of necessary reforms, in short, as a man who unselfishly serves his own people and all humanity, and above all as a zealous and courageous seeker after truth. But let anyone measure Socialism by the standards of scientific reasoning, and he at once becomes a champion of the evil principle, a mercenary serving the egotistical interests of a class, a menace to the welfare of the community, an ignoramus outside the pale. For the most curious thing about this way of thinking is that it regards the question, whether Socialism or Capitalism will better serve the public welfare, as settled in advance—to the effect, naturally, that Socialism is considered as good and Capitalism as evil—whereas in fact of course only by a scientific inquiry could the matter be decided. The results of economic investigations are met, not with arguments, but with that "moral pathos," which we find in the invitation to the Eisenach Congress* in 1872 and on which Socialists and Etatists always fall back, because they can find no answer to the criticism to which science subjects their doctrines.

The older Liberalism, based on the classical political economy, maintained that the material position of the whole of the wage-earning classes could only be permanently raised by an increase of capital, and this none but capitalist society based on private ownership of the means of production can guarantee to find. Modern subjective economics has strengthened and confirmed the basis of the view by its theory of wages. Here modern Liberalism agrees entirely with the older school. Socialism, however, believes that the socialization of the means of production is a system which would bring wealth to all. These conflicting views must be examined in the light of sober science: righteous indignation and jeremiads take us nowhere.

It is true that Socialism is today an article of faith for many, perhaps for most of its adherents. But scientific criticism has no nobler task than to shatter false beliefs.

To protect the socialist ideal from the crushing effects of such criticism,
attempts have recently been made to improve upon the accepted definition 20
of the concept "Socialism." My own definition of Socialism, as a policy which

* The Eisenach Congress of German Economists was called by Gustav Schmoller and some of his German Historical School colleagues. This Congress led to the founding of the Verein für Sozialpolitik (Society for Social Policy), which advocated government intervention in economic affairs. "Socialists of the chair" who were members of this organization had considerable influence on German policy (Pub.).

aims at constructing a society in which the means of production are socialized, is in agreement with all that scientists have written on the subject. I submit that one must be historically blind not to see that this and nothing else is what has stood for Socialism for the past hundred years, and that it is in this sense that the great socialist movement was and is socialistic. But why quarrel over the wording of it! If anyone likes to call a social ideal which retains private ownership in the means of production socialistic, why, let him! A man may call a cat a dog and the sun the moon if it pleases him. But such a reversal of the usual terminology, which everyone understands, does no good and only creates misunderstandings. The problem which here confronts us is the socialization of ownership in the means of production, i.e. the very problem over which a worldwide and bitter struggle has been waged now for a century, the problem κατ' ἐξοχὴν (above all others) of our epoch.

One cannot evade this defining of Socialism by asserting that the concept Socialism includes other things besides the socialization of the means of production: by saying, for example, that we are actuated by certain special motives when we are socialists, or that there is a second aim—perhaps a purely religious concept bound up with it. Supporters of Socialism hold that the only brand worthy the name is that which desires socialization of the means of production for "noble" motives. Others, who pass for opponents of Socialism, will have it that nationalization of the means of production desired from "ignoble" motives only, has to be styled Socialism also. Religious socialists say that genuine Socialism is bound up with religion; the atheistical socialist insists on abolishing God along with private property. But the problem of how a socialistic society could function is quite separate from the question of whether its adherents propose to worship God or not and whether or not they are guided by motives which Mr. X from his private point of view would call noble or ignoble. Each group of the great socialist movement claims its own as the only true brand and regards the others as heretical; and naturally tries to stress the difference between its own particular ideal and those of other parties. I venture to claim that in the course of my researches I have brought forward all that need be said about these claims.

21 In this emphasizing of the peculiarities of particular socialist tendencies, the bearing which they may have on the aims of democracy and dictatorship obviously plays a significant part. Here, too, I have nothing to add to what I have said on the subject in various parts of this book (Chapter 3, Chapter 15, and Chapter 31). It suffices here to say that the planned economy which the advocates of dictatorship wish to set up is precisely as socialistic as the Socialism propagated by the self-styled Social Democrats.

Capitalist society is the realization of what we should call economic democracy, had not the term—according I believe, to the terminology of Lord Passfield and Mrs. Webb—come into use and been applied exclusively to a system in which the workers, as producers, and not the consumers themselves, would decide what was to be produced and how. This state of affairs would be as little democratic as, say, a political constitution under which the government officials and not the whole people decided how the state was to be governed—surely the opposite of what we are accustomed to call democracy. When we call a capitalist society a consumers' democracy we mean that the power to dispose of the means of production, which belongs to the entrepreneurs and capitalists, can only be acquired by means of the consumers' ballot, held daily in the market-place. Every child who prefers one toy to another puts its voting paper in the ballot-box, which eventually decides who shall be elected captain of industry. True, there is no equality of vote in this democracy; some have plural votes. But the greater voting power which the disposal of a greater income implies can only be acquired and maintained by the test of election. That the consumption of the rich weighs more heavily in the balance than the consumption of the poor—though there is a strong tendency to overestimate considerably the amount consumed by the well-to-do classes in proportion to the consumption of the masses—is in itself an 'election result', since in a capitalist society wealth can be acquired and maintained only by a response corresponding to the consumers' requirements. Thus the wealth of successful business men is always the result of a consumers' plebiscite, and, once acquired, this wealth can be retained only if it is employed in the way regarded by consumers as most beneficial to them. The average man is both better informed and less corruptible in the decisions he makes as a consumer than as a voter at political elections. There are said to be voters who, faced with a decision between
Free Trade and Protection, the Gold Standard and Inflation, are unable to 22
keep in view all that their decision implies. The buyer who has to choose between different sorts of beer or makes of chocolate has certainly an easier job of it.

The socialist movement takes great pains to circulate frequently new labels for its ideally constructed state. Each worn-out label is replaced by another which raises hopes of an ultimate solution of the insoluble basic problem of Socialism—until it becomes obvious that nothing has been changed but the name. The most recent slogan is "State Capitalism." It is not commonly realized that this covers nothing more than what used to be called Planned Economy and State Socialism, and that State Capitalism, Planned Economy, and State Socialism diverge only in non-essentials from the "classic" ideal of egalitarian Socialism. The criticisms in this book are aimed impartially at all the conceivable forms of the socialistic community.

Only Syndicalism, which differs fundamentally from Socialism, calls for special treatment (Chapter 16, Section 4).

I hope that these remarks will convince even the cursory and superficial reader that my investigation and criticisms do not apply solely to Marxian Socialism. As, however, all socialistic movements have been strongly stimulated by Marxism I devote more space to Marxian views than to those of other varieties of Socialism. I think I have passed in review everything bearing essentially on these problems and made an exhausting criticism of the characteristic features of non-Marxist programmes too.

My book is a scientific inquiry, not a political polemic. I have analysed the basic problems and passed over, as far as possible, all the economic and political struggles of the day and the political adjustments of governments and parties. And this will, I believe, prove the best way of preparing the foundation of an understanding of the politics of the last few decades and years: above all, of the politics of tomorrow. Only a complete critical study of the ideas of Socialism will enable us to understand what is happening around us.

The habit of talking and writing about economic affairs without having probed relentlessly to the bottom of their problems has taken the zest out of public discussions on questions vital to human society and diverted politics into paths that lead directly to the destruction of all civilization. The pro-
23 scription of economic theory, which began with the German historical school, and today finds expression notably in American Institutionalism, has demolished the authority of qualified thought on these matters. Our contemporaries consider that anything which comes under the heading of Economics and Sociology is fair game to the unqualified critic. It is assumed that the trade union official and the entrepreneur are qualified by virtue of their office alone to decide questions of political economy. "Practical men" of this order, even those whose activities have, notoriously, often led to failure and bankruptcy, enjoy a spurious prestige as economists which should at all costs be destroyed. On no account must a disposition to avoid sharp words be permitted to lead to a compromise. It is time these amateurs were unmasked.

The solution of every one of the many economic questions of the day requires a process of thought, of which only those who comprehend the general interconnection of economic phenomena are capable. Only theoretical inquiries which get to the bottom of things have any real practical value. Dissertations on current questions which lose themselves in detail are useless, for they are too much absorbed in the particular and the accidental to have eyes for the general and the essential.

It is often said that all scientific inquiry concerning Socialism is useless, because none but the comparatively small number of people who are able to follow scientific trains of thought can understand it. For the masses, it is said, they will always remain incomprehensible. To the masses the catchwords of Socialism sound enticing and the people impetuously desire Socialism because in their infatuation they expect it to bring full salvation and satisfy their longing for revenge. And so they will continue to work for Socialism, helping thereby to bring about the inevitable decline of the civilization which the nations of the West have taken thousands of years to build up. And so we must inevitably drift on to chaos and misery, the darkness of barbarism and annihilation.

I do not share this gloomy view. It may happen thus, but it need not happen thus. It is true that the majority of mankind are not able to follow difficult trains of thought, and that no schooling will help those who can hardly grasp the most simple proposition to understand complicated ones. But just because they cannot think for themselves the masses follow the lead of the people we call educated. Once convince these, and the game is won. But I do not want to repeat here what I have already said in the first edition 24
of this book, at the end of the last chapter.[3]

I know only too well how hopeless it seems to convince impassioned supporters of the Socialist Idea by logical demonstration that their views are preposterous and absurd. I know too well that they do not want to hear, to see, or above all to think, and that they are open to no argument. But new generations grow up with clear eyes and open minds. And they will approach things from a disinterested, unprejudiced standpoint, they will weigh and examine, will think and act with forethought. It is for them that this book is written.

Several generations of economic policy which was nearly liberal have enormously increased the wealth of the world. Capitalism has raised the standard of life among the masses to a level which our ancestors could not have imagined. Interventionism and efforts to introduce Socialism have been working now for some decades to shatter the foundations of the world economic system. We stand on the brink of a precipice which threatens to engulf our civilization. Whether civilized humanity will perish forever or whether the catastrophe will be averted at the eleventh hour and the only possible way of salvation retraced—by which we mean the rebuilding of a

[3] pp. 459 ff. of this edition.

society based on the unreserved recognition of private property in the means of production—is a question which concerns the generation destined to act in the coming decades, for it is the ideas behind their actions that will decide it.

Vienna, January 1932

INTRODUCTION

1

The Success of Socialist Ideas

Socialism is the watchword and the catchword of our day. The socialist 25
idea dominates the modern spirit. The masses approve of it. It expresses the thoughts and feelings of all; it has set its seal upon our time. When history comes to tell our story it will write above the chapter "The Epoch of Socialism."

As yet, it is true, Socialism has not created a society which can be said to represent its ideal. But for more than a generation the policies of civilized nations have been directed towards nothing less than a gradual realization of Socialism.[1] In recent years the movement has grown noticeably in vigour and tenacity. Some nations have sought to achieve Socialism, in its fullest sense, at a single stroke. Before our eyes Russian Bolshevism has already accomplished something which, whatever we believe to be its significance, must by the very magnitude of its design be regarded as one of the most remarkable achievements known to world history. Elsewhere no one has yet achieved so much. But with other peoples only the inner contradictions of Socialism itself and the fact that it cannot be completely realized have frustrated socialist triumph. They also have gone as far as they could under the given circumstances. Opposition in principle to Socialism there is none. Today no influential party would dare openly to advocate Private Property in the Means of Production. The word "Capitalism" expresses, for our age, the sum of all evil. Even the opponents of Socialism are dominated by socialist ideas. In seeking to combat Socialism from the standpoint of their special

[1] "It may now fairly be claimed that the socialist philosophy of today is but the conscious and explicit assertion of principles of social organization which have been already in great part unconsciously adopted. The economic history of the century is an almost continuous record of the progress of Socialism." (Sidney Webb, *Fabian Essays* [1889], p. 30.)

class interest these opponents—the parties which particularly call themselves "bourgeois" or "peasant"—admit indirectly the validity of all the essentials of socialist thought. For if it is only possible to argue against the socialist
26 programme that it endangers the particular interests of one part of humanity, one has really affirmed Socialism. If one complains that the system of economic and social organization which is based on private property in the means of production does not sufficiently consider the interests of the community, that it serves only the purposes of single strata, and that it limits productivity; and if therefore one demands with the supporters of the various "social-political" and "social-reform" movements, state interference in all fields of economic life, then one has fundamentally accepted the principle of the socialist programme. Or again, if one can only argue against socialism that the imperfections of human nature make its realization impossible, or that it is inexpedient under existing economic conditions to proceed at once to socialization, then one merely confesses that one has capitulated to socialist ideas. The nationalist, too, affirms socialism, and objects only to its Internationalism. He wishes to combine Socialism with the ideas of Imperialism and the struggle against foreign nations. He is a national, not an international socialist; but he, also, approves of the essential principles of Socialism.[2]

The supporters of Socialism therefore are not confined to the Bolshevists and their friends outside Russia or to the members of the numerous socialist parties: all are socialists who consider the socialistic order of society economically and ethically superior to that based on private ownership of the means of production, even though they may try for one reason or another to make a temporary or permanent compromise between their socialistic ideal and the particular interests which they believe themselves to represent. If we define Socialism as broadly as this we see that the great majority of people are with Socialism today. Those who confess to the principles of Liberalism*

---

[2] Foerster points out particularly that the labour movement has attained its real triumph "in the hearts of the possessing classes"; through this "the moral force for resistance has been taken away from these classes." (Foerster, *Christentum und Klassenkampf* [Zurich, 1908], p. 111 ff.) In 1869 Prince-Smith had noted the fact that the socialist ideas had found supporters among employers. He mentions that amongst business men, "however strange this may sound, there are some who understand their own activity in the national economy with so little clarity that they hold the socialist ideas as more or less founded, and, consequently, have a bad conscience really, as if they had to admit to themselves that their profits were actually made at the cost of their workmen. This makes them timid and even more muddled. It is very bad. For our economic civilization would be seriously threatened if its bearers could not draw, from the feeling of complete justification, the courage to defend its foundations with the utmost resolution." (Prince-Smith's *Gesammelte Schriften* [Berlin, 1877], vol. 1, p. 362.) Prince-Smith, however, would not have known how to discuss the socialist theories critically.

* The term "liberalism" is used by Mises "in the sense attached to it everywhere in the nineteenth century and still today in the countries of continental Europe. This usage is imperative because

and who see the only possible form of economic society in an order based 27
on private ownership of the means of production are few indeed.

One striking fact illustrates the success of socialist ideas: namely, that we have grown accustomed to designating as Socialism only that policy which aims to enact the socialist programme immediately and completely, while we call by other names all the movements directed towards the same goal with more moderation and reserve, and even describe these as the enemies of Socialism. This can only have come about because few real opponents of Socialism are left. Even in England, the home of Liberalism, a nation which has grown rich and great through its liberal policy, people no longer know what Liberalism really means. The English "Liberals" of today are more or less moderate socialists.[3] In Germany, which never really knew Liberalism and which has become impotent and impoverished through its anti-liberal policy, people have hardly a conception of what Liberalism may be.

It is on the complete victory of the socialist idea in the last decades that the great power of Russian Bolshevism rests. What makes Bolshevism strong is not the Soviets' artillery and machine-guns but the fact that the whole world receives its ideas sympathetically. Many socialists consider the Bolshevists' enterprise premature and look to the future for the triumph of Socialism. But no socialist can fail to be stirred by the words with which the Third International summons the peoples of the world to make war on Capitalism. Over the whole earth is felt the urge towards Bolshevism. Among the weak and lukewarm sympathy is mixed with horror and with the admiration which the courageous believer always awakens in the timid opportunist. But bolder and more consistent people greet without hesitation the dawn of a new epoch.

2

The Scientific Analysis of Socialism

The starting-point of socialist doctrine is the criticism of the bourgeois order of society. We are aware that socialist writers have not been very

there is simply no other term available to signify the great political and intellectual movement that substituted free enterprise and the market economy for the precapitalistic methods of production; constitutional representative government for the absolutism of kings or oligarchies; and freedom of all individuals for slavery, serfdom, and other forms of bondage." Mises, *Human Action: A Treatise on Economics*, 3rd ed. (Chicago: Regnery, 1966), p. v. (Pub.).

[3] This is shown clearly in the programme of present-day English Liberals: *Britain's Industrial Future, being the Report of the Liberal Industrial Inquiry* (London, 1928).

successful in this respect. We know that they have misconceived the working
28 of the economic mechanism, and that they have not understood the function of the various institutions of the social order which is based on division of labour and on private ownership of the means of production. It has not been difficult to show the mistakes socialistic theorists have made in analysing the economic process: critics have succeeded in proving their economic doctrines to be gross errors. Yet to ask whether the capitalist order of society is more or less defective is hardly a decisive answer to the question whether Socialism would be able to provide a better substitute. It is not sufficient to have proved that the social order based on private ownership of the means of production has faults and that it has not created the best of all possible worlds; it is necessary to show further that the socialistic order is better. This only a few socialists have tried to prove, and these have done so for the most part in a thoroughly unscientific, some even in a frivolous, manner. The science of Socialism is rudimentary, and just that kind of Socialism which calls itself "Scientific" is not the last to be blamed for this. Marxism has not been satisfied to present the coming of Socialism as an inevitable stage of social evolution. Had it done only this it could not have exerted that pernicious influence on the scientific treatment of the problems of social life which must be laid to its charge. Had it done nothing except describe the socialistic order of society as the best conceivable form of social life it could never have had such injurious consequences. But by means of sophistry it has prevented the scientific treatment of sociological problems and has poisoned the intellectual atmosphere of the time.

According to the Marxist conception, one's social condition determines one's way of thought. His membership of a social class decides what views a writer will express. He is not able to grow out of his class or to free his thoughts from the prescriptions of his class interests.[4] Thus the possibility of a general science which is valid for all men, whatever their class, is contested. It was only another step for Dietzgen to proceed to the construction of a special proletarian logic.[5] But truth lies with the proletarian science only: "the ideas of proletarian logic are not party ideas, but the consequences of
29 logic pure and simple."[6] Thus Marxism protects itself against all unwelcome

[4] "Science exists only in the heads of the scientists, and they are products of society. They cannot get out of it and beyond it" (Kautsky, *Die soziale Revolution*, 3rd ed. [Berlin, 1911], vol. 2, p. 39). Publisher's Note: In English, see *The Social Revolution*, trans. J. B. Askew (London, 1907).

[5] Dietzgen, "Briefe über Logik, speziell demokratisch-proletarische Logik," *Internationale Bibliothek*, 2d ed. (Stuttgart, 1903), vol. 22, p. 112: "Finally logic deserves the epithet 'proletarian' also for the reason that to understand it one must have overcome all the prejudices which hold the bourgeoisie."

[6] *Ibid*, p. 112.

criticism. The enemy is not refuted: enough to unmask him as a bourgeois.[7] Marxism criticizes the achievements of all those who think otherwise by representing them as the venal servants of the bourgeoisie. Marx and Engels never tried to refute their opponents with argument. They insulted, ridiculed, derided, slandered, and traduced them, and in the use of these methods their followers are not less expert. Their polemic is directed never against the argument of the opponent, but always against his person. Few have been able to withstand such tactics. Few indeed have been courageous enough to oppose Socialism with that remorseless criticism which it is the duty of the scientific thinker to apply to every subject of inquiry. Only thus is to be explained the fact that supporters and opponents of Socialism have unquestioningly obeyed the prohibition which Marxism has laid on any closer discussion of the economic and social conditions of the socialist community. Marxism declares on the one hand that the socialization of the means of production is the end towards which economic evolution leads with the inevitability of a natural law; on the other hand it represents such socialization as the aim of its political effort. In this way he expounded the first principle of socialist organization. The purpose of the prohibition to study the working of a socialist community, which was justified by a series of threadbare arguments, was really intended to prevent the weaknesses of Marxist doctrines from coming clearly to light in discussions regarding the creation of a practicable socialist society. A clear exposition of the nature of socialist society might have damped the enthusiasm of the masses, who sought in Socialism salvation from all earthly ills. The successful suppression of these dangerous inquiries, which had brought about the downfall of all earlier socialistic theories, was one of Marx's most skillful tactical moves. Only
because people were not allowed to talk or to think about the nature of the 30
socialist community was Socialism able to become the dominant political movement of the late nineteenth and early twentieth centuries.

These statements can hardly be illustrated better than by a quotation from the writings of Hermann Cohen, one of those who, in the decades imme-

[7] It is a fine irony of history that even Marx suffered this fate. Untermann finds that "even the mental life of typical proletarian thinkers of the Marxist school" contains "remains of past epochs of thought, if only in rudimentary form. These rudiments will appear all the stronger the more the thought stages lived through before the thinker became Marxist were passed in a bourgeois or feudal milieu. This was notoriously so with Marx, Engels, Plekhanov, Kautsky, Mehring, and other prominent Marxists" (Untermann, *Die logischen Mängel des engeren Marxismus* [Munich, 1910], p. 125). And De Man believes that to understand "the individuality and variety of the theories" one would have to consider, besides the thinker's general social background, also his own economic and social life—a "bourgeois" life . . . "in the case of the college-trained Marx" (De Man, *Zur Psychologie des Sozialismus*, new ed. [Jena, 1927], p. 17).

diately preceding the world war,* exerted the strongest influence on German thought. "Today," says Cohen, "no want of understanding prevents us from recognizing the kernel of the social question and therefore, even if only furtively, the necessity of social reform policy, but only the evil, or the not sufficiently good, will. The unreasonable demand that it should unveil the picture of the future state for the general view, with which attempts are made to embarrass party Socialism, can be explained only by the fact that such defective natures exist. The state presupposes law, but these people ask what the state would look like rather than what are the ethical requirements of law. By thus reversing the concepts one confuses the ethics of Socialism with the poesy of the Utopias. But ethics are not poetry and the idea has truth without image. Its image is the reality which is only to arise according to its prototype. The socialist idealism can to-day be looked upon as a general truth of public consciousness, though as one which is still, nevertheless, an open secret. Only the egoism implicit in ideals of naked covetousness, which is the true materialism, denies it a faith."[8] The man who wrote and thought thus was widely praised as the greatest and most daring German thinker of his time, and even opponents of his teaching respected him as an intellect. Just for that reason it is necessary to stress that Cohen not only accepts without criticism or reserve the demands of Socialism and acknowledges the prohibition against attempts to examine conditions in the socialist community, but that he represents as a morally inferior being anyone who tries to embarrass "party-Socialism" with a demand for light upon the problems of socialist economies. That the daring of a thinker whose criticism otherwise spares nothing should stop short before a mighty idol of his time is a phenomenon which may be observed often enough in the history of thought—even Cohen's great exemplar, Kant, is accused of this.[9]
31 But that a philosopher should charge with ill-will, defective disposition, and naked covetousness not merely all those of a different opinion but all who even touch on a problem dangerous to those in authority—this, fortunately, is something of which the history of thought can show few examples.

Anyone who failed to comply unconditionally with this coercion was proscribed and outlawed. In this way Socialism was able from year to year to win more and more ground without anyone being moved to make a fundamental investigation of how it would work. Thus, when one day

---

[8] Cohen, *Einleitung mit kritischem Nachtrag zur neunten Auflage der Geschichte des Materialismus von Friedrich Albert Lange*, 3rd extended ed. (Leipzig, 1914), p. 115. Also Natorp, *Sozialpädagogik*, 4th ed. (Leipzig, 1920), p. 201.

[9] Anton Menger, *Neue Sittenlehre* (Jena, 1905), pp. 45, 62.

* World War I (Pub.).

Marxian Socialism assumed the reins of power, and sought to put its complete programme into practice, it had to recognize that it had no distinct idea of what, for decades, it had been trying to achieve.

A discussion of the problems of the socialist community is therefore of the greatest importance, and not only for understanding the contrast between liberal and socialist policy. Without such a discussion it is not possible to understand the situations which have developed since the movement towards nationalization and municipalization commenced. Until now economics—with a comprehensible but regrettable onesidedness—has investigated exclusively the mechanism of a society based on private ownership of the means of production. The gap thus created must be filled.

The question whether society ought to be built up on the basis of private ownership of the means of production or on the basis of public ownership of the means of production is political. Science cannot decide it; Science cannot pronounce a judgment on the relative values of the forms of social organization. But Science alone, by examining the effects of institutions, can lay the foundations for an understanding of society. Though the man of action, the politician, may sometimes pay no attention to the results of this examination, the man of thought will never cease to inquire into all things accessible to human intelligence. And in the long run thought must determine action.

3

Alternative Modes of Approach to the Analysis of Socialism

There are two ways of treating the problems which Socialism sets to Science.

The cultural philosopher may deal with Socialism by trying to place it in 32
order among all other cultural phenomena. He inquires into its intellectual derivation, he examines its relation to other forms of social life, he looks for its hidden sources in the soul of the individual, he tries to understand it as a mass phenomena. He examines its effects on religion and philosophy, on art and literature. He tries to show the relation in which it stands to the natural and mental sciences of the time. He studies it as a style of life, as an utterance of the psyche, as an expression of ethical and aesthetic beliefs. This is the cultural-historical-psychological way. Ever trodden and retrodden, it is the way of a thousand books and essays.

We must never judge a scientific method in advance. There is only one touchstone for its ability to achieve results: success. It is quite possible that the cultural-historical-psychological method will also contribute much towards a solution of the problems which Socialism has set to Science. That its results have been so unsatisfactory is to be ascribed not only to the incompetence and political prejudices of those who have undertaken the work, but above all to the fact that the sociological*-economical treatment of the problems must precede the cultural-historical-psychological. For Socialism is a programme for transforming the economic life and constitution of society according to a defined ideal. To understand its effects in other fields of mental and cultural life one must first have seen clearly its social and economic significance. As long as one is still in doubt about this it is unwise to risk a cultural-historical-psychological interpretation. One cannot speak of the ethics of Socialism before one has cleared up its relation to other moral standards. A relevant analysis of its reactions on religion and public life is impossible when one has only an obscure conception of its essential reality. It is impossible to discuss Socialism at all without having first and foremost examined the mechanism of an economic order based on public ownership of the means of production.

This comes out clearly at each of the points at which the cultural-historical-psychological method usually starts. Followers of this method regard Socialism as the final consequences of the democratic idea of equality without having decided what democracy and equality really mean or in what relation they stand to each other, and without having considered whether Socialism is essentially or only generally concerned with the idea of equality. Sometimes they refer to Socialism as a reaction of the psyche to the spiritual desolation created by the rationalism inseparable from Capitalism; sometimes again
33 they assert that Socialism aims at the highest rationalization of material life, a rationalization which Capitalism could never attain.[10] Those who engulf their cultural and theoretical exposition of Socialism in a chaos of mysticism and incomprehensible phrases need not be discussed here.

---

[10] Muckle, *Das Kulturideal des Sozialismus* (Munich, 1918) even expects of socialism that it will bring about both "the highest rationalization of economic life" and "redemption from the most terrible of all barbarisms: capitalist rationalism."

* Throughout the 1920s, Mises continued to refer to the science of human action as "sociology." However, he later came to prefer the term "praxeology," derived from the Greek *praxis*, meaning action, habit or practice. In his "Foreword" to *Epistemological Problems of Economics* (Princeton: Van Nostrand, 1960; New York: NYU Press, 1981), he commented on his use of the term "sociology" in a 1929 essay included in that volume: ". . . in 1929, I still believed that it was unnecessary to introduce a new term to signify the general theoretical science of human action as distinguished from the historical studies dealing with human action performed in the past. I thought that it would be possible to employ for this purpose the term *sociology*, which in the opinion of some authors was designed to signify such a general theoretical science. Only later did I realize that this was not expedient and adopted the term praxeology." (Pub.)

The researches of this book are to be directed above all to the sociological and economic problems of Socialism. We must treat these before we can discuss the cultural and psychological problems. Only on the results of such research can we base studies of the culture and psychology of Socialism. Sociological and economic research alone can provide a firm foundation for those expositions—so much more attractive to the great public—which present a valuation of Socialism in the light of the general aspirations of the human race.

PART I
LIBERALISM AND SOCIALISM

CHAPTER 1

Ownership

1

The Nature of Ownership

Regarded as a sociological category ownership appears as the power to 37
use economic goods. An owner is he who disposes of an economic good.

Thus the sociological and juristic concepts of ownership are different. This, of course, is natural, and one can only be surprised that the fact is still sometimes overlooked. From the sociological and economic point of view, ownership is the *having* of the goods which the economic aims of men require.[1] This *having* may be called the natural or original ownership, as it is purely a physical relationship of man to the goods, independent of social relations between men or of a legal order. The significance of the legal concept of property lies just in this—that it differentiates between the physical *has* and the legal *should have*. The Law recognizes owners and possessors who lack this natural *having*, owners who do not have, but ought to have. In the eyes of the Law 'he from whom has been stolen' remains owner, while the thief can never acquire ownership. Economically, however, the natural *having* alone is relevant, and the economic significance of the legal *should have* lies only in the support it lends to the acquisition, the maintenance, and the regaining of the natural *having*.

To the Law ownership is a uniform institution. It makes no difference whether goods of the first order or goods of higher order form its subject, or whether it deals with durable consumption goods or non-durable consumption goods. The formalism of the Law, divorced as it is from any

[1] Böhm-Bawerk, *Rechte und Verhältnisse vom Standpunkte der volkswirtschaftlichen Güterlehre* (Innsbruck, 1881), p. 37. Publisher's Note: This has been translated into English by George D. Huncke as "Whether Legal Rights and Relationships Are Economic Goods," in *Shorter Classics of Böhm-Bawerk* (South Holland, Ill.: Libertarian Press, 1962), vol. 1, pp. 25–138. Passage cited here is on page 58 of this edition.

economic basis, is clearly expressed in this fact. Of course, the Law cannot
38 isolate itself completely from economic differences which may be relevant. The peculiarity of land as a means of production is, partly, what gives the ownership of real property its special position in the Law. Such economic differences are expressed, more clearly than in the law of property itself, in relationships which are sociologically equivalent to ownership but juristically allied to it only, e.g., in servitudes and, especially, in usufruct. But on the whole, in Law formal equality covers up material differences.

Considered economically, ownership is by no means uniform. Ownership in consumption goods and ownership in production goods differ in many ways, and in both cases, again, we must distinguish between durable goods and goods that are used up.

Goods of the first order, the consumption goods, serve the immediate satisfaction of wants. In so far as they are goods that are used up, goods, that is, which in their nature can be used but once, and which lose their quality as goods when they are used, the significance of ownership lies practically in the possibility of consuming them. The owner may also allow his goods to spoil unenjoyed or even permit them to be destroyed intentionally, or he may give them in exchange or give them away. In every case he disposes of their use, which cannot be divided.

The position is a little different with goods of lasting use, those consumption goods that can be used more than once. They may serve several people successively. Here, again, those are to be regarded as owners in the economic sense who are able to employ for their own purposes the uses afforded by the goods. In this sense, the owner of a room is he who inhabits it at the time in question; the owners of the Matterhorn, as far as it is part of a natural park, are those who set foot on it to enjoy the landscape; the owners of a picture are those who enjoy looking at it.[2] The *having* of the uses which these goods afford is divisible, so that the natural ownership of them is divisible also.

Production goods serve enjoyment only indirectly. They are employed in the production of consumption goods. Consumption goods emerge finally from the successful combination of production goods and labour. It is the ability to serve thus indirectly for the satisfaction of wants which qualifies a thing as a production good. To dispose of production goods is to *have* them
39 naturally. The *having* of production goods is of economic significance only because and in so far as it leads finally to a *having* of consumption goods.

Goods to be used up, which are ripe for consumption, can be *had* but

[2] Fetter, *The Principles of Economics*, 3rd ed. (New York, 1913), p. 408.

once—by the person who consumes them. Goods of lasting use, which are ripe for consumption, may be *had*, in temporal succession, by a number of people; but simultaneous use will disturb the enjoyment of others, even though this enjoyment is not quite excluded by the nature of the commodity. Several people may simultaneously look at a picture, even though the proximity of others, who perhaps keep him from the most favorable viewpoint, may disturb the enjoyment of any individual in the group; but a coat cannot be worn simultaneously by two people. In the case of consumption goods the *having* which leads to the satisfaction of wants by the goods cannot be further divided than can the uses which arise from the goods. This means that with goods to be used up, natural ownership by one individual completely excludes ownership by all others, while with durable goods ownership is exclusive at least at a given point of time and even in regard to the smallest use arising from it. For consumption goods, any economically significant relationship other than that of the natural *having* by individuals is unthinkable. As goods to be used up absolutely and as durable goods, at least to the extent of the smallest use arising from them, they can be in the natural ownership of one person only. Ownership here is also *private* ownership, in the sense that it deprives others of the advantages which depend upon the right of disposing of the goods.

For this reason, also, it would be quite absurd to think of removing or even of reforming ownership in consumption goods. It is impossible in any way to alter the fact that an apple which is enjoyed is used up and that a coat is worn out in the wearing. In the natural sense consumption goods cannot be the joint property of several or the common property of all. In the case of consumption goods, that which one usually calls joint property has to be shared before consumption. The joint ownership ceases at the moment a commodity is used up or employed. The *having* of the consumer must be exclusive. Joint property can never be more than a basis for the appropriation of goods out of a common stock. Each individual partner is owner of that part of the total stock which he can use for himself. Whether he is already owner legally, or owner only through the division of the stock, or whether 40
he becomes legal owner at all, and whether or not a formal division of the stock precedes consumption—none of these questions is economically material. The fact is that even without division he is owner of his lot.

Joint property cannot abolish ownership in consumption goods. It can only distribute ownership in a way which would not otherwise have existed. Joint property restricts itself, like all other reforms which stop short at consumption goods, to effecting a different distribution of the existing stock of consumption goods. When this stock is exhausted its work is done. It cannot refill the empty storehouses. Only those who direct the disposal of production goods and labour can do this. If they are not satisfied with what they are offered, the flow of goods which is to replenish stocks ceases. Therefore, any attempt to alter the distribution of consumption goods must in the last resort depend on the power to dispose of the means of production.

The *having* of production goods, contrary to that of consumption goods, can be divided in the natural sense. Under conditions of isolated production the conditions of sharing the *having* of production goods are the same as the conditions of sharing consumption goods. Where there is no division of labour the *having* of goods can only be shared if it is possible to share the services rendered by them. The having of non-durable production goods cannot be shared. The having of durable production goods can be shared according to the divisibility of the services they provide. Only one person can *have* a given quantity of grain, but several may *have* a hammer successively; a river may drive more than one water wheel. So far, there is no peculiarity about the *having* of production goods. But in the case of production with division of labour there is a two-fold *having* of such goods. Here in fact the *having* is always two-fold: there is a physical *having* (direct), and a social *having* (indirect). The physical *having* is his who holds the commodity physically and uses it productively; the social *having* belongs to him who, unable to dispose physically or legally of the commodity, may yet dispose indirectly of the effects of its use, i.e. he who can barter or buy its products or the services which it provides. In this sense natural ownership in a society which divides labour is shared between the producer and those for whose wants he produces. The farmer who lives self-sufficiently outside exchange society can call his fields, his plough, his draught animals his own, in the sense that
41 they serve only him. But the farmer whose enterprise is concerned with trade, who produces for and buys in the market, is owner of the means of production in quite a different sense. He does not control production as the self-supporting peasant does. He does not decide the purpose of his production; those for whom he works decide it—the consumers. They, not the producer, determine the goal of economic activity. The producer only directs production towards the goal set by the consumers.

But further owners of the means of production are unable in these conditions to place their physical *having* directly into the service of production. Since all production consists in combining the various means of production, some of the owners of such means must convey their natural ownership to others, so that the latter may put into operation the combinations of which production consists. Owners of capital, land, and labour place these factors at the disposal of the entrepreneur, who takes over the immediate direction of production. The entrepreneurs, again, conduct production according to the direction set by the consumers, who are no other than the owners of the means of production: owners of capital, land, and labour. Of the product, however, each factor receives the share to which he is economically entitled, according to the value of his productive contribution in the yield.

In essence, therefore, natural ownership of production goods is quite different from natural ownership of consumption goods. To have production goods in the economic sense, i.e. to make them serve one's own economic purposes, it is not necessary to have them physically in the way that one must have consumption goods if one is to use them up or to use them lastingly. To drink coffee I do not need to own a coffee plantation in Brazil, an ocean steamer, and a coffee roasting plant, though all these means of production must be used to bring a cup of coffee to my table. Sufficient that others own these means of production and employ them for me. In the society which divides labour no one is exclusive owner of the means of production, either of the material things or of the personal element, capacity to work. All means of production render services to everyone who buys or sells on the market. Hence if we are disinclined here to speak of ownership as shared between consumers and owners of the means of production, we should have to regard consumers as the true owners in the natural sense and describe those who are considered as the owners in the legal sense as 42
administrators of other people's property.[3] This, however, would take us too far from the accepted meaning of the words. To avoid misinterpretation it is desirable to manage as far as possible without new words and never to employ, in an entirely different sense, words habitually accepted as conveying a particular idea. Therefore, renouncing any particular terminology, let us only stress once more that the essence of the ownership of the means of

---

[3] See the verses of Horace:

> Si proprium est quod quis libra mercatus et aere est,
> quaedam, si credis consultis, mancipat usus:
> qui te pascit ager, tuus est; et vilicus Orbi
> cum segetes occat tibi mox frumenta daturas,
> te dominum sentit, das nummos: accipis uvam
> pullos ova, cadum temeti.[2. *Epistol.*, 2, 158–163]

(If that which one buys with formal purchase is one's own,
If usage confers title to things, as the lawyers maintain;
Then the farm which feeds you is yours; and the farmer,
when he cultivates the field which soon will give you grain, feels you are his master.
You pay your money: you get in return grapes, chickens, eggs, a jar of wine.)

The attention of economists was first drawn to this passage by Effertz (*Arbeit und Boden*, new ed. [Berlin, 1897], vol. 1, pp. 72, 79).

production in a society which divides labour differs from that found where the division of labour does not take place; and that it differs essentially from the ownership of consumption goods in any economic order. To avoid any misunderstanding we will henceforth use the words, 'ownership of the means of production' in the generally accepted sense, i.e. to signify the immediate power of disposal.

2

Violence and Contract

The physical *having* of economic goods, which economically considered constitutes the essence of natural ownership, can only be conceived as having originated through Occupation. Since ownership is not a fact independent of the will and action of man, it is impossible to see how it could have begun except with the appropriation of ownerless goods. Once begun ownership continues, as long as its object does not vanish, until either it is given up voluntarily or the object passes from the physical *having* of the owner against his will. The first happens when the owner voluntarily gives up his property; the latter when he does it involuntarily—e.g. when cattle stray into the wilds—or when some other person forcibly takes the property from him.

All ownership derives from occupation and violence. When we consider
43 the natural components of goods, apart from the labour components they contain, and when we follow the legal title back, we must necessarily arrive at a point where this title originated in the appropriation of goods accessible to all. Before that we may encounter a forcible expropriation from a predecessor whose ownership we can in its turn trace to earlier appropriation or robbery. That all rights derive from violence, all ownership from appropriation or robbery, we may freely admit to those who oppose ownership on considerations of natural law. But this offers not the slightest proof that the abolition of ownership is necessary, advisable, or morally justified.

Natural ownership need not count upon recognition by the owners' fellow men. It is tolerated, in fact, only as long as there is no power to upset it and it does not survive the moment when a stronger man seizes it for himself. Created by arbitrary force it must always fear a more powerful force. This the doctrine of natural law has called the war of all against all. The war ends when the actual relation is recognized as one worthy to be maintained. Out of violence emerges law.

The doctrine of natural law has erred in regarding this great change, which

lifts man from the state of brutes into human society, as a conscious process; as an action, that is, in which man is completely aware of his motives, of his aims and how to pursue them. Thus was supposed to have been concluded the social contract by which the State and the community, the legal order, came into existence. Rationalism could find no other possible explanation after it had disposed of the old belief which traced social institutions back to divine sources or at least to the enlightenment which came to man through divine inspiration.[4] Because it led to present conditions, people regarded the development of social life as absolutely purposeful and rational; how then could this development have come about, except through conscious choice in recognition of the fact that it was purposeful and rational? Today we have other theories with which to explain the matter. We talk of natural selection in the struggle for existence and of the inheritance of acquired characteristics, though all this, indeed, brings us no nearer to an understanding of ultimate riddles than can the theologian or the rationalist. We can 'explain' the birth 44
and development of social institutions by saying that they were helpful in the struggle for existence, by saying that those who accepted and best developed them were better equipped against the dangers of life than those who were backward in this respect. To point out how unsatisfactory is such an explanation nowadays would be to bring owls* to Athens. The time when it satisfied us and when we proposed it as a final solution of all problems of being and becoming is long since past. It takes us no further than theology or rationalism. This is the point at which the individual sciences merge, at which the great problems of philosophy begin—at which all our wisdom ends.

No great insight, indeed, is needed to show that Law and the State cannot be traced back to contracts. It is unnecessary to call upon the learned apparatus of the historical school to show that no social contract can anywhere be established in history. Realistic science was doubtless superior to the Rationalism of the seventeenth and eighteenth centuries in the knowledge that can be gained from parchments and inscriptions, but in sociological insight it lagged far behind. For however we may reproach a social philosophy of Rationalism we cannot deny that it has done imperishable work in showing us the effects of social institutions. To it we owe above all our first knowledge of the functional significance of the legal order and of the State.

---

[4] Etatistic social philosophy, which carries all these institutions back to the "state," returns to the old theological explanation. In it the state assumes the position which the theologians assign to God.

* In Greek mythology, the owl was the favorite bird, and a frequent companion of, Athena, the Goddess of Athens (Pub.).

Economic action demands stable conditions. The extensive and lengthy process of production is the more successful the greater the periods of time to which it is adapted. It demands continuity, and this continuity cannot be disturbed without the most serious disadvantages. This means that economic action requires peace, the exclusion of violence. Peace, says the rationalist, is the goal and purpose of all legal institutions; but we assert that peace is their result, their function.[5] Law, says the rationalist, has arisen from contracts; we say that Law is a settlement, and end to strife, an avoidance of strife. Violence and Law, War and Peace, are the two poles of social life; but its content is economic action.

All violence is aimed at the property of others. The person—life and health—is the object of attack only in so far as it hinders the acquisition of property. (Sadistic excesses, bloody deeds which are committed for the sake
45 of cruelty and nothing else, are exceptional occurrences. To prevent them one does not require a whole legal system. Today the doctor, not the judge, is regarded as their appropriate antagonist.) Thus it is no accident that it is precisely in the defence of property that Law reveals most clearly its character of peacemaker. In the two-fold system of protection according to *having*, in the distinction between ownership and possession, is seen most vividly the essence of the law as peacemaker—yes, peacemaker at any price. Possession is protected even though it is, as the jurists say, no title. Not only honest but dishonest possessors, even robbers and thieves, may claim protection for their possession.[6]

Some believe that ownership as it shows itself in the distribution of property at a given time may be attacked by pointing out that it has sprung illegally from arbitrary acquisition and violent robbery. According to this view all legal rights are nothing but time-honoured illegality. So, since it conflicts with the eternal, immutable idea of justice, the existing legal order must be abolished and in its place a new one set which shall conform to that idea of justice. It should not be the task of the State "to consider only the condition of possession in which it finds its citizens, without inquiring into the legal grounds of acquisition." Rather it is "the mission of the State first to give everyone his own, first to put him into his property, and only then to protect him in it."[7] In this case one either postulates an eternally valid idea of justice which it is the duty of the State to recognize and realize; or else one finds the origin of true Law, quite in the sense of the contract theory, in the social

---

[5] J.S. Mill, *Principles of Political Economy*, People's ed. (London, 1867), p, 124.
[6] Dernburg, *Pendekten*, 6th ed. (Berlin, 1900), vol. 1, pt. 2, p. 12.
[7] Fichte, *Der geschlossene Handelsstaat*, edited by Medicus (Leipzig, 1910), p. 12.

contract, which contract can only arise through the unanimous agreement of all individuals who in it divest themselves of a part of their natural rights. At the basis of both hypotheses lies the natural law view of the "right that is born with us." We must conduct ourselves in accordance with it, says the former; by divesting ourselves of it according to the conditions of the contract the existing legal system arises, says the latter. As to the source of absolute justice, that is explained in different ways. According to one view, it was the gift of Providence to Humanity. According to another, Man created it with his Reason. But both agree that Man's ability to distinguish between justice and injustice is precisely what marks him from the animal; that this is his "moral nature."

Today we can no longer accept these views, for the assumptions with
which we approach the problem have changed. To us the idea of a human 46
nature which differs fundamentally from the nature of all other living creatures seems strange indeed; we no longer think of man as a being who has harboured an idea of justice from the beginning. But if, perhaps, we offer no answer to the question how Law arose, we must still make it clear that it could not have arisen legally. Law cannot have begot itself of itself. Its origin lies beyond the legal sphere. In complaining that Law is nothing more or less than legalized injustice, one fails to perceive that it could only be otherwise if it had existed from the very beginning. If it is supposed to have arisen once, then that which at that moment became Law could not have been Law before. To demand that Law should have arisen legally is to demand the impossible. Whoever does so applies to something standing outside the legal order a concept valid only within the order.

We who only see the effect of Law—which is to make peace—must realize that it could not have originated except through a recognition of the existing state of affairs, however that has arisen. Attempts to do otherwise would have renewed and perpetuated the struggle. Peace can come about only when we secure a momentary state of affairs from violent disturbance and make every future change depend upon the consent of the person involved. This is the real significance of the protection of existing rights, which constitutes the kernel of all Law.

Law did not leap into life as something perfect and complete. For thousands of years it has grown and it is still growing. The age of its maturity—the age of impregnable peace—may never arrive. In vain have the systematicians of Law sought dogmatically to maintain the division between private and public Law which doctrine has handed down to us and which in practice they think it cannot do without. The failure of these attempts—which indeed has led many to abandon the distinction—must not surprise us. The division is not,

as a matter of fact, dogmatic; the system of Law is uniform and cannot comprehend it. The division is historical, the result of the gradual evolution and accomplishment of the idea of Law. The idea of Law is realized at first in the sphere in which the maintenance of peace is most urgently needed to assure economic continuity—that is, in the relations between individuals. Only for the further development of the civilization which rises on this
47 foundation does the maintenance of peace in a more advanced sphere become essential. This purpose is served by Public Law. It does not formally differ from Private Law. But it is felt to be something different. This is because only later does it attain the development vouchsafed earlier to Private Law. In Public Law the protection of existing rights is not yet as strongly developed, as it is in Private Law.[8] Outwardly the immaturity of Public Law can most easily be recognized perhaps in the fact that it has lagged behind Private Law in systematization. International Law is still more backward. Intercourse between nations still recognizes arbitrary violence as a solution permissible under certain conditions whereas, on the remaining ground regulated by Public Law, arbitrary violence in the form of revolution stands, even though not effectively suppressed, outside the Law. In the domain of Private Law this violence is wholly illegal except as an act of defence, when it is permitted under exceptional circumstances as a gesture of legal protection.

The fact that what became Law was formerly unjust or, more precisely expressed, legally indifferent, is not a defect of the legal order. Whoever tries juristically or morally to justify the legal order may feel it to be such. But to establish this fact in no way proves that it is necessary or useful to abolish or alter the system of ownership. To endeavour to demonstrate from this fact that the demands for the abolition of ownership were legal would be absurd.

3

The Theory of Violence and the Theory of Contract

It is only slowly and with difficulty that the idea of Law triumphs. Only slowly and with difficulty does it rebut the principle of violence. Again and again there are reactions; again and again the history of Law has to start

[8] Liberalism tried to extend the protection of acquired rights by developing the subjective public rights and extending legal protection through the law courts. Etatism and socialism, on the contrary, try to restrict increasingly the sphere of private law in favor of public law.

once more from the beginning. Of the ancient Germans Tacitus relates: *"Pigrum quin immo et iners videtur sudore adquirere quod possis sanguine parare."*[9] (It seems feckless, nay more, even slothful, to acquire something by toil and sweat which you could grab by the shedding of blood.) It is a far cry from this view to the views that dominate modern economic life.

This contrast of view transcends the problems of ownership, and embraces our whole attitude to life. It is the contrast between a feudal and a bourgeois way of thought. The first expresses itself in romantic poetry, whose beauty delights us, though its view of life can carry us away only in passing moments and while the impression of the poetry is fresh.[10] The second is developed in the liberal social philosophy into a great system, in the construction of which the finest minds of all ages have collaborated. Its grandeur is reflected in classical literature. In Liberalism humanity becomes conscious of the powers which guide its development. The darkness which lay over the paths of history recedes. Man begins to understand social life and allows it to develop consciously. 48

The feudal view did not achieve a similarly closed systematization. It was impossible to think out, to its logical conclusion, the theory of violence. Try to realize completely the principle of violence, even only in thought, and its anti-social character is unmasked. It leads to chaos, to the war of all against all. No sophistry can evade that. All anti-liberal social theories must necessarily remain fragments or arrive at the most absurd conclusions. When they accuse Liberalism of considering only what is earthly, of neglecting, for the petty struggles of daily life, to care for higher things, they are merely picking the lock of an open door. For Liberalism has never pretended to be more than a philosophy of earthly life. What it teaches is concerned only with earthly action and desistance from action. It has never claimed to exhaust the Last or Greatest Secret of Man. The anti-liberal teachings promise everything. They promise happiness and spiritual peace, as if man could be thus blessed from without. Only one thing is certain, that under their ideal social system the supply of commodities would diminish very considerably. As to the value of what is offered in compensation opinions are at least divided.[11]

The last resort of the critics of the liberal ideal of society is to attempt to destroy it with the weapons it itself provides. They seek to prove that it serves and wants to serve only the interests of single classes; that the peace,

---

[9] Tacitus, *Germania*, p. 14.

[10] A fine poetic mockery of the romantic longing, "Where thou art not, there is happiness," is to be found in the experience of Counselor Knap in Andersen's "The Galoshes of Fortune." Publisher's Note: (New York: Doubleday, 1974).

[11] Wiese, *Der Liberalismus in Vergangenheit und Zukunft* (Berlin, 1917), pp. 58 ff.

for which it seeks, favours only a restricted circle and is harmful to all others. Even the social order, achieved in the constitutional modern state, is based
49 on violence. The free contracts on which it pretends to rest are really, they say, only the conditions of a peace dictated by the victors to the vanquished, the terms being valid as long as the power from which they sprang continues, and no longer. All ownership is founded on violence and maintained by violence. The free workers of the liberal society are nothing but the unfree of feudal times. The entrepreneur exploits them as a feudal lord exploited his serfs, as a planter exploited his slaves. That such and similar objections can be made and believed will show how far the understanding of liberal theories has decayed. But these objections in no way atone for the absence of a systematic theory for the movement against Liberalism.

The liberal conception of social life has created the economic system based on the division of labour. The most obvious expression of the exchange economy is the urban settlement, which is only possible in such an economy. In the towns the liberal doctrine has been developed into a closed system and it is here that it has found most supporters. But the more and the quicker wealth grew and the more numerous therefore were the immigrants from the country into the towns, the stronger became the attacks which Liberalism suffered from the principle of violence. Immigrants soon find their place in urban life, they soon adopt, externally, town manners and opinions, but for a long time they remain foreign to civic thought. One cannot make a social philosophy one's own as easily as a new costume. It must be earned—earned with the effort of thought. Thus we find, again and again in history, that epochs of strongly progressive growth of the liberal world of thought, when wealth increases with the development of the division of labour, alternate with epochs in which the principle of violence tries to gain supremacy—in which wealth decreases because the division of labour decays. The growth of the towns and of the town life was too rapid. It was more extensive than intensive. The new inhabitants of the towns had become citizens superficially, but not in ways of thought. And so with their ascendancy civic sentiment declined. On this rock all cultural epochs filled with the bourgeois spirit of Liberalism have gone to ruin; on this rock also our own bourgeois culture, the most wonderful in history, appears to be going to ruin. More menacing than barbarians storming the walls from without are the seeming citizens within—those who are citizens in gesture, but not in thought.

50 Recent generations have witnessed a mighty revival of the principle of violence. Modern Imperialism, whose outcome was the World War with all its appalling consequences, develops the old ideas of the defenders of the principle of violence under a new mask. But of course even Imperialism has

not been able to set in opposition to liberal theory a complete system of its own. That the theory according to which struggle is the motive power of the growth of society should in any way lead to a theory of co-operation is out of the question—yet every social theory must be a theory of co-operation. The theory of modern Imperialism is characterized by the use of certain scientific expressions such as the doctrine of the struggle for existence and the concept of the race. With these it was possible to coin a multitude of slogans, which have proved themselves effective for propaganda but for nothing else. All the ideas paraded by modern Imperialism have long since been exploded by Liberalism as false doctrines.

Perhaps the strongest of the imperialist arguments is an argument which derives from a total misconception of the essence of the ownership of the means of production in a society dividing labour. It regards as one of its most important tasks the provision of the nation with its own coal mines, own sources of raw material, own ships, own ports. It is clear that such an argument proceeds from the view that natural ownership in these means of production is undivided, and that only those benefit from them who *have* them physically. It does not realize that this view leads logically to the socialist doctrine with regard to the character of ownership in the means of production. For if it is wrong that Germans do not possess their own German cotton plantations, why should it be right that every single German does not possess *his* coal mine, *his* spinning mill? Can a German call a Lorraine iron ore mine *his* any more when a German citizen possesses it than when a French citizen possesses it?

So far the imperialist agrees with the socialist in criticism of bourgeois ownership. But the socialist has tried to devise a closed system of a future social order and this the imperialist could not do.

4

Collective Ownership of the Means of Production

The earliest attempts to reform ownership and property can be accurately described as attempts to achieve the greatest possible equality in the distri- 51
bution of wealth, whether or not they claimed to be guided by considerations of social utility or social justice. All should possess a certain minimum, none more than a certain maximum. All should possess about the same amount—that was, roughly, the aim. The means to this end were always the same.

Confiscation of all or part of the property was usually proposed, followed by redistribution. A world populated only by self-sufficient agriculturists, leaving room for at most a few artisans—that was the ideal society towards which one strove. But today we need not concern ourselves with all these proposals. They become impracticable in an economy dividing labour. A railway, a rolling mill, a machine factory cannot be distributed. If these ideas had been put into practice centuries or millenniums ago, we should still be at the same level of economic development as we were then—unless, of course, we had sunk back into a state hardly distinguishable from that of brutes. The earth would be able to support but a small fraction of the multitudes it nourishes today, and everyone would be much less adequately provided for than he is, less adequately even than the poorest member of an industrial state. Our whole civilization rests on the fact that men have always succeeded in beating off the attack of the re-distributors. But the idea of re-distribution enjoys great popularity still, even in industrial countries. In those countries where agriculture predominates the doctrine calls itself, not quite appropriately, Agrarian Socialism, and is the end-all and be-all of social reform movements. It was the main support of the great Russian revolution, which against their will temporarily turned the revolutionary leaders, born Marxists, into the protagonists of its ideal. It may triumph in the rest of the world and in a short time destroy the culture which the effort of millenniums has built up. For all this, let us repeat, one single word of criticism is superfluous. Opinions on the matter are not divided. It is hardly necessary to prove today that it is impossible to found on a "land and homestead communism" a social organization capable of supporting the hundreds of millions of the white race.

A new social ideal long ago supplanted the naive fanaticism for equality of the distributors, and now not distribution but common ownership is the slogan of Socialism. To abolish private property in the means of production, to make the means of production the property of the community, that is the whole aim of Socialism.

52 In its strongest and purest form the socialistic idea has no longer anything in common with the idea of re-distribution. It is equally remote from a nebulous conception of common ownership in the means of consumption. Its aim is to make possible for everyone an adequate existence. But it is not so artless as to believe that this can be achieved by the destruction of the social system which divides labour. True, the dislike of the market, which characterizes enthusiasts of re-distribution, survives; but Socialism seeks to abolish trade otherwise than by abolishing the division of labour and re-

turning to the autarky of the self-contained family economy or at least to the simpler exchange organization of the self-sufficient agricultural district.

Such a socialistic idea could not have arisen before private property in the means of production had assumed the character which it possesses in the society dividing labour. The interrelation of separate productive units must first reach the point at which production for external demand is the rule, before the idea of common property in the means of production can assume a definite form. The socialist ideas could not be quite clear until the liberal social philosophy had revealed the character of social production. In this sense, but in no other, Socialism may be regarded as a consequence of the liberal philosophy.

Whatever our view of its utility or its practicability, it must be admitted that the idea of Socialism is at once grandiose and simple. Even its most determined opponents will not be able to deny it a detailed examination. We may say, in fact, that it is one of the most ambitious creations of the human spirit. The attempt to erect society on a new basis while breaking with all traditional forms of social organization, to conceive a new world plan and foresee the form which all human affairs must assume in the future—this is so magnificent, so daring, that it has rightly aroused the greatest admiration. If we wish to save the world from barbarism we have to conquer Socialism, but we cannot thrust it carelessly aside.

5

Theories of the Evolution of Property

It is an old trick of political innovators to describe that which they seek to realize as Ancient and Natural, as something which has existed from the 53
beginning and which has been lost only through the misfortune of historical development; men, they say, must return to this state of things and revive the Golden Age. Thus natural law explained the rights which it demanded for the individual as inborn, inalienable rights bestowed on him by Nature. This was no question of innovation, but of the restoration of the "eternal rights which shine above, inextinguishable and indestructible as the stars themselves." In the same way the romantic Utopia of common ownership as an institution of remote antiquity has arisen. Almost all peoples have known this dream. In Ancient Rome it was the legend of the Golden Age

of Saturn, described in glowing terms by Virgil, Tibullus, and Ovid, and praised by Seneca.[12] Those were the carefree, happy days when none had private property and all prospered in the bounty of a generous Nature.[13] Modern Socialism, of course, imagines itself beyond such simplicity and childishness, but its dreams differ little from those of the Imperial Romans.

Liberal doctrine had stressed the important part played in the evolution of civilization by private property in the means of production. Socialism might have contented itself with denying the use of maintaining the institution of ownership any longer, without denying at the same time the usefulness of this ownership in the past. Marxism indeed does this by representing the epochs of simple and of capitalistic production as necessary stages in the development of society. But on the other hand it joins with other socialist doctrines in condemning with a strong display of moral indignation all private property that has appeared in the course of history. Once upon a time there were good times when private property did not exist; good times will come again when private property will not exist.

In order that such a view might appear plausible the young science of Economic History had to provide a foundation of proof. A theory demonstrating the antiquity of the common land system was constructed. There was a time, it was said, when all land had been the common property of all members of the tribe. At first all had used it communally; only later, while the common ownership was still maintained, were the fields distributed to
54 individual members for separate use. But there were new distributions continually, at first every year, then at longer intervals of time. Private property according to this view was a relatively young institution. How it arose was not quite clear. But one had to assume that it had crept in more or less as a habit through omission in re-distributions—that is, if one did not wish to trace it back to illegal acquisition. Thus it was seen that to give private ownership too much credit in the history of civilization was a mistake. It was argued that agriculture had developed under the rule of common ownership with periodic distribution. For a man to till and sow the fields one needs only to guarantee him the produce of his labour, and for this purpose annual possession suffices. We are told that it is false to trace the origin of ownership in land to the occupation of ownerless fields. The unoccupied land was not for a single moment ownerless. Everywhere, in early times as nowadays, man had declared that it belonged to the State or the community;

[12] Poehlmann, *Geschichte der sozialen Frage und des Sozialismus in der antiken Welt,* 2nd ed. (Munich, 1912), vol. 2, pp. 577 ff.

[13] *"Ipsaque tellus omnia liberius nullo poscente ferebat"* (Virgil, *Georgica,* I, 127 ff.) ["And the land itself provided everything spontaneously with a liberal hand."]

consequently in early times as little as today the seizing of possession could not have taken place.[14]

From these heights of newly-won historical knowledge it was possible to look down with compassionate amusement at the teachings of liberal social philosophy. People were convinced that private property had been proved an historical-legal category *only*. It had not existed *always*, it was nothing more than a not particularly desirable outgrowth of culture, and therefore it could be abolished. Socialists of all kinds, but especially Marxists, were zealous in propagating these ideas. They have brought to the writings of their champions a popularity otherwise denied to researches in Economic History.

But more recent researches have disproved the assumption that common ownership of the agricultural land was an essential stage with all peoples, that it was the primeval form of ownership (*"Ureigentum"*). They have demonstrated that the Russian Mir arose in modern times under the pressure of serfdom and the head-tax, that the Hauberg co-operatives* of the Siegen district are not found before the sixteenth century, that the Trier Gehöferschaften** evolved in the thirteenth, perhaps only in the seventeenth and eighteenth centuries, and that the South Slav Zadruga came about through the introduction of the Byzantine system of taxation.[15] The earliest German agricultural history has still not been made sufficiently clear; here, 55
in regard to the important questions, unanimous opinion has not been possible. The interpretation of the scanty information given by Caesar and Tacitus presents special difficulties. But in trying to understand them one must never overlook the fact that the conditions of ancient Germany as described by these two writers had this characteristic feature—good arable land was so abundant that the question of land ownership was not yet economically relevant. *"Superest ager,"* (Arable land abounds.) that is the basic fact of German agrarian conditions at the time of Tacitus.[16]

In fact, however, it is not necessary to consider the proofs adduced by Economic History, which contradict the doctrine of the "Ureigentum," in order to see that this doctrine offers no argument against private property in the means of production. Whether or not private property was everywhere

[14] Laveleye, *Das Ureigentum*, trans. by Bücher from French (Leipzig, 1879), pp. 514 ff.

[15] Below, *Probleme der Wirtschaftsgeschichte* (Tübingen, 1920), pp. 13 ff.

[16] *Germania*, 26.

* *Hauberg cooperatives* were associations of workers in lumbering (Hauberg) and tanning enterprises (Pub.).

** Trier Gehöferschaften (German) were rural hereditary associations dating from the Middle Ages, set up to cultivate the lands lying outside the manorial freeholds and maintained until recently in the vicinity of Trier in southwestern Germany (Pub.).

preceded by common property is irrelevant when we are forming a judgment as to its historical achievement and its function in the economic constitution of the present and the future. Even if one could demonstrate that common property was once the basis of land law for all nations and that all private property had arisen through illegal acquisition, one would still be far from proving that rational agriculture with intensive cultivation could have developed without private property. Even less permissible would it be to conclude from such premises that private property could or should be abolished.

CHAPTER 2

Socialism

1

The State and Economic Activity

It is the aim of Socialism to transfer the means of production from private 56
ownership to the ownership of organized society, to the State.[1] The socialistic State owns all material factors of production and thus directs it. This transfer need not be carried out with due observance of the formalities elaborated for property transfers according to the law set up in the historical epoch which is based on private property in the means of production. Still less important in such a process of transfer is the traditional terminology of Law. Ownership is power of disposal, and when this power of disposal is divorced from its traditional name and handed over to a legal institution which bears a new name, the old terminology is essentially unimportant in the matter. Not the word but the thing must be considered. Limitation of the rights of owners as well as formal transference is a means of socialization. If the State takes the power of disposal from the owner piecemeal, by extending its influence over production; if its power to determine what direction production shall take and what kind of production there shall be, is increased, then the owner is left at last with nothing except the empty name of ownership, and property has passed into the hands of the State.

People often fail to perceive the fundamental difference between the liberal and the anarchistic idea. Anarchism rejects all coercive social organizations, and repudiates coercion as a social technique. It wishes in fact to abolish the State and the legal order, because it believes that society could do better without them. It does not fear anarchical disorder because it believes that

[1] The term "Communism" signifies just the same as "Socialism." The use of these two words has repeatedly changed during the past decades, but always the question that separated socialists from communists was only political tactics. Both aim to socialize the means of production.

without compulsion men would unite for social co-operation and would behave in the manner that social life demands. Anarchism as such is neither
57 liberal nor socialistic: it moves on a different plane from either. Whoever denies the basic idea of Anarchism, whoever denies that it is or ever will be possible to unite men without coercion under a binding legal order for peaceful co-operation, will, whether liberal or socialist, repudiate anarchistic ideals. All liberal and socialist theories based on a strict logical connection of ideas have constructed their systems with due regard to coercion, utterly rejecting Anarchism. Both recognize the necessity of the legal order, though for neither is it the same in content and extent. Liberalism does not contest the need of a legal order when it restricts the field of State activity, and certainly does not regard the State as an evil, or as a necessary evil. Its attitude to the problem of ownership and not its dislike of the "person" of the State is the characteristic of the liberal view of the problem of the State. Since it desires private ownership in the means of production it must, logically, reject all that conflicts with this ideal. As for Socialism, as soon as it has turned fundamentally from Anarchism, it must necessarily try to extend the field controlled by the compulsory order of the State, for its explicit aim is to abolish the "anarchy of production." Far from abolishing State and compulsion it seeks to extend governmental action to a field which Liberalism would leave free. Socialistic writers, especially those who recommend Socialism for ethical reasons, like to say that in a socialistic society public welfare would be the foremost aim of the State, whereas Liberalism considers only the interests of a particular class. Now one can only judge of the value of a social form of organization, liberal or socialistic, when a thorough investigation has provided a clear picture of what it achieves. But that Socialism alone has the public welfare in view can at once be denied. Liberalism champions private property in the means of production because it expects a higher standard of living from such an economic organization, not because it wishes to help the owners. In the liberal economic system more would be produced than in the socialistic. The surplus would not benefit only the owners. According to Liberalism therefore, to combat the errors of Socialism is by no means the particular interest of the rich. It concerns even the poorest, who would be injured just as much by Socialism. Whether or not one accepts this, to impute a narrow class interest to Liberalism is erroneous. The systems, in fact, differ not in their aims but in the means by which they wish to pursue them.

2 58

The "Fundamental Rights" of Socialist Theory

The programme of the liberal philosophy of the State was summarized in a number of points which were put forward as the demands of natural law. These are the Rights of Man and of Citizens, which formed the subject of the wars of liberation in the eighteenth and nineteenth centuries. They are written in brass in the constitutional laws composed under the influence of the political movements of this time. Even supporters of Liberalism might well ask themselves whether this is their appropriate place, for in form and diction they are not so much legal principles—fit subject matter for a law of practical life—as a political programme to be followed in legislation and administration. At any rate it is obviously insufficient to include them ceremoniously in the fundamental laws of states and constitutions; their spirit must permeate the whole State. Little benefit the citizen of Austria has had from the fact that the Fundamental Law of the State gave him the right "to express his opinion freely by word, writing, print, or pictorial representation within the legal limits." These legal limits prevented the free expression of opinion as much as if that Fundamental Law had never been laid down. England has no Fundamental Right of the free expression of opinion; nevertheless in England speech and press are really free because the spirit which expresses itself in the principle of the freedom of thought permeates all English legislation.

In imitation of these political Fundamental Rights some antiliberal writers have tried to establish basic economic rights. Here their aim is twofold: on the one hand they wish to show the insufficiency of a social order which does not guarantee even these alleged natural Rights of Man; on the other hand they wish to create a few easily remembered, effective slogans to serve as propaganda for their ideas. The view that it might be sufficient to establish these basic rights legally in order to establish a social order corresponding to the ideals they express, is usually far from the minds of their authors. The majority indeed, especially in recent years, are convinced that they can get what they want only by the socialization of the means of production. The economic basic rights were elaborated only to show what requirements a social order had to satisfy, a critique rather than a programme. Considered from this point of view they give us an insight into what, according to the 59
opinion of its advocates, Socialism should achieve.

According to Anton Menger, Socialism usually assumes three economic basic rights—the right to the full produce of labour, the right to existence, and the right to work.[2]

All production demands the co-operation of the material and personal factors of production: it is the purposeful union of land, capital, and labour. How much each of these has contributed physically to the result of production cannot be ascertained. How much of the value of the product is to be attributed to the separate factors is a question which is answered daily and hourly by buyers and sellers on the market, though the scientific explanation of this process has achieved satisfactory results only in very recent years, and these results are still far from final. The formation of market prices for all factors of production attributes to each a weight that corresponds to its part in production. Each factor receives in the price the yield of its collaboration. The labourer receives in wages the full produce of his labour. In the light of the subjective theory of value therefore that particular demand of Socialism appears quite absurd. But to the layman it is not so. The habit of speech with which it is expressed derives from the view that value comes from labour alone. Whoever takes this view of value will see in the demand for the abolition of private ownership in the means of production a demand for the full produce of labour for the labourer. At first it is a negative demand—exclusion of all income not based on labour. But as soon as one proceeds to construct a system on this principle insurmountable obstacles arise, difficulties which are the consequence of the untenable theories of the formation of value which have established the principle of the right to the full produce of labour. All such systems have been wrecked on this. Their authors have had to confess finally that what they wanted was nothing else than the abolition of the income of individuals not based on labour, and that only socialization of the means of production could achieve this. Of the right to the full produce of labour, which had occupied minds for decades, nothing remains but the slogan—effective for propaganda, of course—demanding that "unearned" non-labour income should be abolished.

60 The Right to Existence can be defined in various ways. If one understands by this the claim of people, without means and unfit for work and with no relation to provide for them, to subsistence, then the Right to Existence is a harmless institution which was realized in most communities centuries ago. Certainly the manner in which the principle has been carried into practice may leave something to be desired, as for reasons that arise from

[2] Anton Menger, *Das Recht auf den vollen Arbeitsertrag in geschichtlicher Darstellung*, 4th ed. (Stuttgart and Berlin, 1910), p. 6. Publisher's Note: For an English translation, see *Right to the Whole Produce of Labor*, with an introduction by Foxwell, 1899.

its origin in charitable care of the poor, it gives to the necessitous no title recoverable by law. By "Right to Existence," however, the socialists do not mean this. Their definition is: "that each member of society may claim that the goods and services necessary to the maintenance of his existence shall be assigned to him, according to the measure of existing means, before the less urgent needs of others are satisfied."[3] The vagueness of the concept, "maintenance of existence," and the impossibility of recognizing and comparing how urgent are the needs of different persons from any objective standpoint, make this finally a demand for the utmost possible equal distribution of consumption goods. The form which the concept sometimes takes—that no one should starve while others have more than enough—expresses that intention even more clearly. Plainly, this claim for equality can be satisfied, on its negative side, only when all the means of production have been socialized and the yield of production is distributed by the State. Whether on its positive side it can be satisfied at all is another problem with which the advocates of the Right to Existence have scarcely concerned themselves. They have argued that Nature herself affords to all men a sufficient existence and only because of unjust social institutions is the provisioning of a great part of humanity insufficient; and that if the rich were deprived of all they are allowed to consume over and above what is "necessary," everyone would be able to live decently. Only under the influence of the criticism based on the Malthusian Law of Population[4] has socialist doctrine been amended. Socialists admit that under non-socialist production not enough is produced to supply all in abundance, but argue that Socialism would so enormously increase the productivity of labour that it would be possible to create an earthly paradise for an unlimited number of persons.
Even Marx, otherwise so discreet, says that the socialist society would make 61
the wants of each individual the standard measure of distribution.[5]

This much is certain, however: the recognition of the Right to Existence, in the sense demanded by the socialist theorists, could be achieved only by the socialization of the means of production. Anton Menger has, it is true, expressed the opinion that private property and the Right to Existence might well exist side by side. In this case claims of citizens of the State to what was

[3] *Ibid.*, p. 9

[4] Malthus, *An Essay on the Principle of Population*, 5th ed. (London, 1817), vol. 3, pp. 154 ff.

[5] Marx, *Zur Kritik des sozialdemokratischen Parteiprogramms von Gotha*, ed. Kreibich (Reichenberg, 1920), p. 17. Publisher's Note: For an English translation of this passage, see *Critique of the Gotha Programme* (New York: International Publishers, 1938), p. 10, or pp. 2–7 of Marx, *Capital, the Communist Manifesto and Other Writings*, ed. and introd. Max Eastman (New York: Random House, Modern Library, 1932). The passage referred to here concludes: "From each according to his abilities, to each according to needs!"

necessary for existence would have to be considered a mortgage on the national income, and these claims would have to be met before favoured individuals received an unearned income. But even he has to confess that were the Right to Existence admitted completely, it would absorb such an important part of the unearned income and would strip so much benefit from private ownership that all property would soon be collectively owned.[6] If Menger had seen that the Right to Existence necessarily involved a right to the equal distribution of consumption goods, he would not have asserted that it was fundamentally compatible with private ownership in the means of production.

The Right to Existence is very closely connected with the Right to Work.[7] The basis of the idea is not so much a Right to Work as a duty. The laws which allow the unemployable a sort of claim to maintenance exclude the employable from a like favour. He has only a claim to the allotment of work. Naturally the socialist writers and with them the older socialist policy have a different view of this right. They transform it, more or less clearly, into a claim to a task which is agreeable to the inclinations and abilities of the worker, and which yields a wage sufficient for his subsistence needs. Beneath the Right to Work lies the same idea, that engendered the Right to Existence—the idea that in "natural" conditions—which we are to imagine existing before and outside the social order based on private property but which is to be restored by a socialist constitution when private property has been abolished—every man would be able to procure a sufficient income through work. The bourgeois society which has destroyed this satisfactory state of
62 affairs owes to those thus injured the equivalent of what they have lost. This equivalent is supposed to be represented just by the Right to Work. Again we see the old illusion of the means of subsistence which Nature is supposed to provide irrespective of the historical development of society. But the fact is that Nature grants no rights at all, and just because she dispenses only the scantiest means of subsistence and because wants are practically unlimited, man is forced to take economic action. This action begets social collaboration; its origin is due to the realization that it heightens productivity and improves the standard of living. The notion, borrowed from the most naive theories of natural law, that in society the individual is worse off than "in the freer primitive state of Nature" and that society must first, so to speak, buy his

[6] Anton Menger, *op. cit.*, p. 10.

[7] *Ibid.*, pp. 10 ff. Also Singer-Sieghart, *Das Recht auf Arbeit in geschichtlicher Darstellung* (Jena, 1895), pp. 1 ff.; Mutasoff, *Zur Geschichte des Rechts auf Arbeit mit besonderer Rücksicht auf Charles Fourier* (Berne, 1897), pp. 4 ff.

toleration with special rights, is the cornerstone of expositions upon the Right to Work as well as upon the Right to Existence.

Where production is perfectly balanced there is no unemployment. Unemployment is a consequence of economic change, and where production is unhindered by the interferences of authorities and trade unions, it is always only a phenomenon of transition, which the alteration of wage rates tends to remove. By means of appropriate institutions, by the extension, for example, of labour exchanges, which would evolve out of the economic mechanism in the unimpeded market—i.e. where the individual is free to choose and to change his profession and the place where he works—the duration of separate cases of unemployment could be so much shortened that it would no longer be considered a serious evil.[8] But the demand that every citizen should have a right to work in his accustomed profession at a wage not inferior to the wage rates of other labour more in demand is utterly unsound. The organization of production cannot dispense with a means of forcing a change of profession. In the form demanded by the socialist, the Right to Work is absolutely impracticable, and this is not only the case in a society based on private ownership in the means of production. For even the socialist community could not grant the worker the right to be active only in his wonted profession; it, also, would need the power to move labour to the places where it was most needed.

The three basic economic rights—whose number incidentally could easily
be increased—belong to a past epoch of social reform movements. Their 63
importance today is merely, though effectively, propagandistic. Socialization
of the means of production has replaced them all.

3

Collectivism and Socialism

The contrast between realism and nominalism which runs through the history of human thought since Plato and Aristotle is revealed also in social philosophy.[9] The difference between the attitude of Collectivism and Indi-

---

[8] My works: *Kritik des Interventionismus* (Jena, 1929), pp. 12 ff.; *Die Ursachen der Wirtschaftskrise* (Tübingen, 1931), pp. 15 ff. Publisher's Note: These references are now available in English. See *A Critique of Interventionism*, trans. Hans F. Sennholz (New Rochelle, N.Y.: Arlington House, 1977), pp. 26 ff.; "The Causes of the Economic Crisis," in *On the Manipulation of Money and Credit*, trans. Bettina Bien Greaves and ed. Percy L. Greaves, Jr. (Dobbs Ferry, N.Y.: Free Market Books, 1978), pp. 186 ff.

[9] Pribram, *Die Entstehung der individualistischen Sozialphilosophie* (Leipzig, 1912), pp. 3 ff.

vidualism to the problem of social associations, is not different from the attitude of Universalism and Nominalism to the problem of the concept of species. But in the sphere of social science this contrast—to which in philosophy the attitude towards the idea of God has given a significance which extends far beyond the limits of scientific research—has the highest importance. The powers which are in existence and which do not want to succumb, find in the philosophy of Collectivism weapons for the defence of their rights. But even here Nominalism is a restless force seeking always to advance. Just as in the sphere of philosophy it dissolves the old concepts of metaphysical speculation, so here it breaks up the metaphysics of sociological Collectivism.

The political misuse of the contrast is clearly visible in the teleological form which it assumes in Ethics and Politics. The problem here is stated otherwise than in Pure Philosophy. The question is whether the individual or the community shall be the purpose.[10] This presupposes a contrast between the purposes of individuals and those of the social whole, a contrast which only the sacrifice of the one in favour of the other can overcome. A quarrel over the reality or nominality of the concepts becomes a quarrel over the precedence of purposes. Here there arises a new difficulty for Collectivism. As there are various social *collectiva,* whose purposes seem to conflict just as much as those of the individuals contrast with those of the *collectiva,* the
64 conflict of their interests must be fought out. As a matter of fact, practical Collectivism does not worry much about this. It feels itself to be only the apologist of the ruling classes and serves, as it were, as scientific policeman, on all fours with political police, for the protection of those who happen to be in power.

But the individualist social philosophy of the epoch of enlightenment disposed of the conflict between Individualism and Collectivism. It is called individualistic because its first task was to clear the way for subsequent social philosophy by breaking down the ideas of the ruling Collectivism. But it has not in any way replaced the shattered idols of Collectivism with a cult of the individual. By making the doctrine of the harmony of interests the starting point of sociological thought, it founded modern social science and showed that the conflict of purposes upon which the quarrel turned did not exist in reality. For society is only possible on these terms, that the individual finds therein a strengthening of his own ego and his own will.

The collectivist movement of the present day derives its strength not from an inner want on the part of modern scientific thought but from the political

[10] Thus Dietzel ("Individualismus," *Handwörterbuch der Staatswissenschaften,* 3rd ed., vol. 5, p. 590) formulates the contrast of the individual principle and the social principle. Similarly Spengler, *Preussentum und Sozialismus* (Munich, 1920), p. 14.

will of an epoch which yearns after Romanticism and Mysticism. Spiritual movements are revolts of thought against inertia, of the few against the many; of those who because they are strong in spirit are strongest alone against those who can express themselves only in the mass and the mob, and who are significant only because they are numerous. Collectivism is the opposite of all this, the weapon of those who wish to kill mind and thought. Thus it begets the "New Idol," "the coldest of all cold monsters," the State.[11] By exalting this mysterious being into a sort of idol, decking it out in the extravagance of fantasy with every excellence and purifying it of all dross,[12] and by expressing a readiness to sacrifice everything on its altar, Collectivism seeks consciously to cut every tie that unites sociological with scientific thought. This is most clearly discernible in those thinkers who exerted the keenest criticism to free scientific thought from all teleological elements, whilst in the field of social cognition they not only retained traditional ideas and teleological ways of thinking but even, by endeavouring to justify this, barred the way by which sociology could have won for itself the liberty of 65
thought already achieved by natural science. No god and no ruler of Nature lives for Kant's theory of cognition of nature, but history he regards "as the execution of a hidden plan of nature in order to bring about a state-constitution perfect inwardly—and, for this purpose, outwardly as well—as the only condition in which she can develop all her abilities in humanity."[13] In the words of Kant we can see with especial clearness the fact that modern Collectivism has nothing more to do with the old realism of concepts but rather, having arisen from political and not from philosophical needs, occupies a special position outside science which cannot be shaken by attacks based on the theory of cognition. In the second part of his *Ideen zu einer Philosophie der Geschichte der Menschheit* (*Ideas to a Philosophy of the History of Humanity*) Herder violently attacked the critical philosophy of Kant, which

[11] Nietzsche, "Also Sprach Zarathustra," vol. 6, *Werke* (Krönersche Klassikerausgabe), p. 69. Publisher's Note: In English, see *Thus Spake Zarathustra*, pp. 103–439 in *The Portable Nietzsche*, ed. Walter Kaufman (New York: Viking Press, 1954). Reference here is to No. 11, "On the New Idol."

[12] *"L'État étant conçu comme un être ideal, on le pare de toutes les qualités que l'on rêve et on le dépouille de toutes les faiblesses que l'on hait"* ("The state, being conceived as an ideal being, is endowed with all the qualities of our dreams and stripped of all those qualities we hate") (P. Leroy-Beaulieu, *L'État moderne et ses fonctions*, 3rd ed. [Paris, 1900], p. 11); also, Bamberger, *Deutschland und der Sozialismus* [Leipzig, 1878], pp. 86 ff.

[13] Kant, *Idee zu einer allgemeinen Geschichte in weltbürgerlicher Absicht*, vol. 1, *Sämtliche Werke*, Inselausgabe (Leipzig, 1912), p. 235. Publisher's Note: In English, "Idea for a Universal History from a Cosmopolitan Point of View" (Complete Works, Insel Edition). In *On History*. Immanuel Kant, ed. Lewis White Beck and trans. Lewis White Beck, Robert E. Anchor and Emil L. Fackenheim (Indianapolis: Bobbs-Merrill, 1963), p. 21.

appeared to him as "Averroic" hypostasization of the general. Anyone who sought to maintain that the race, and not the individual, was the subject of education and civilization, would be speaking incomprehensibly, "as race and species are only general concepts, except in so far as they exist in the individual being." Even if one attributed to this general concept all the perfections of humanity—culture and highest enlightenment—which an ideal concept permits, one would have "said just as little about the true history of our race, as I would if, speaking of animality, stoneness, metalness, in general, I were to ascribe to them the most glorious, but in single individuals self-conflicting, attributes."[14] In his reply to this Kant completes the divorce of ethical-political Collectivism from the philosophical concept-realism. "Whoever said that no single horse has horns but the species of horses is nevertheless horned would be stating a downright absurdity. For then species means nothing more than the characteristic in which all individuals must agree. But if the meaning of the expression 'the human species' is—and this is generally the case—the *whole* of a series of generations going into the infinite (indefinable), and it is assumed that this series is continuously nearing the line of its destiny, which runs alongside of it, then it is no contradiction to say, that in all its parts it is asymptotic to it, yet on the whole meets it—
66 in other words, that no link of all the generations of the human race but only the species attains its destiny completely. Mathematicians can elucidate this. The philosopher would say: the destiny of the human race as a whole is continuous progress, and the completion of this is a mere idea—but in all intention a useful idea—of the aim towards which we, according to the plan of Providence, have to direct our exertions."[15] Here the teleological character of Collectivism is frankly admitted, and there opens up an unbridgeable chasm between it and the way of thought of pure cognition. The cognition of the hidden intentions of Nature lies beyond all experience and our own thought gives us nothing upon which to form a conclusion as to whether it exists or what it contains. Such behaviour of individual man and of social systems as we are able to observe provides no basis for a hypothesis. No logical connection can be forged between experience and that which we shall or may suppose. We are to believe—because it cannot be proved—that

[14] Herder, *Ideen zu einer Philosophie der Geschichte der Menschheit*, vol. 13, *Sämtliche Werke*, ed. Suphan (Berlin, 1887) pp. 345 ff.

[15] Kant, *Rezension zum zweiten Teil von Herders Ideen zur Philosophie der Geschichte der Menschheit*, vol. 1. *Werke*, p. 267. On this, see Cassirer, *Freiheit und Form* (Berlin, 1916), pp. 504 ff. Publisher's Note: In English, "Review on the Second Part of Herder's Ideas for a Philosophy on the History of Mankind." In *On History*. Immanuel Kant, ed. Lewis White Beck (Indianapolis: Bobbs-Merrill, 1963), p. 51.

against his will man does that which is ordained by Nature, who knows better; that he does what profits the race, not the individual.[16] This is not the customary technique of science.

The fact is that Collectivism is not to be explained as a scientific necessity. Only the needs of politics can account for it. Therefore it does not stop, as conceptual realism stopped, at affirming the real existence of social associations—calling them organisms and living beings in the proper sense of the words—but idealizes them and makes them Gods. Gierke explains quite openly and unequivocally that one must hold fast to the "idea of the real unity of the community," because this alone makes possible the demand that the individual should stake strength and life for Nation and State.[17] Lessing has said that Collectivism is nothing less than "the cloak of tyranny."[18]

If the conflict between the common interests of the whole and the particular interests of the individual really existed, men would be quite incapable of collaborating in society. The natural intercourse between human beings would be the war of all against all. There could be no peace or mutual sufferance, but only temporary truce, which lasted no longer than the wear- 67
iness of one or all the parts made necessary. The individual would, at least potentially, be in constant revolt against each and all, in the same way as he finds himself in unceasing war with beasts of prey and bacilli. The collective view of history, which is thoroughly asocial, cannot therefore conceive that social institutions could have arisen in any way except through the intervention of a "world shaper" of the Platonic δημιουργὸς (one who works for the people). This operates in history through its instruments, the heroes, who lead resistant man to where it wants him. Thus the will of the individual is broken. He who wants to live for himself alone is forced by the representatives of God on earth to obey the moral law, which demands that he shall sacrifice his well-being in the interests of the Whole and its future development.

The science of society begins by disposing of this dualism. Perceiving that the interests of separate individuals within society are compatible and that these individuals and the community are not in conflict, it is able to understand social institutions without calling gods and heroes to its aid. We can dispense with the Demiurge, which forces the individual into the Collectivism against his will, as soon as we realize that social union gives him more than it takes away. Even without assuming a "hidden plan of nature" we can

[16] Kant, *Idee zu einer allgemeinen Geschichte* . . . p. 228. Publisher's Note: In English this is page 16 of *Idea for a Universal History* . . . as cited above.

[17] Gierke, *Des Wesen der menschlichen Verbände* (Leipzig, 1902), pp. 34 ff.

[18] In "Ernst und Falk," *Gespräche für Freimaurer*, vol. 5. *Werke* (Stuttgart, 1873), p. 80.

understand the development to a more closely-knit form of society when we see that every step on this way benefits those who take it, and not only their distant great-grandchildren.

Collectivism had nothing to oppose to the new social theory. Its continually reiterated accusation, that this theory does not apprehend the importance of the collectiva, especially those of State and Nation, only shows that it has not observed how the influence of liberal sociology has changed the setting of the problem. Collectivism no longer attempts to construct a complete theory of social life; the best it can produce against its opponents is witty aphorism, nothing more. In economics as well as in general sociology it has proved itself utterly barren. It is no accident that the German mind, dominated by the social theories of classical philosophy from Kant to Hegel, for a long time produced nothing important in economics, and that those who have broken the spell, first Thünen and Gossen, then the Austrians Carl Menger, Böhm-Bawerk, and Wieser, were free from any influence of the collectivist philosophy of the State.

68 How little Collectivism was able to surmount the difficulties in the way of amplifying its doctrine is best shown by the manner in which it has treated the problem of social will. To refer again and again to the Will of the State, to the Will of the People, and to the Convictions of the People is not in any way to explain how the collective will of the social associations comes into being. As it is not merely different from the will of separate individuals but, in decisive points, is quite opposed to the latter, the collective will cannot originate as the sum or resultant of individual wills. Every collectivist assumes a different source for the collective will, according to his own political, religious and national convictions. Fundamentally it is all the same whether one interprets it as the supernatural powers of a king or priest or whether one views it as the quality of a chosen class or people. Friedrich Wilhelm IV and Wilhelm II were quite convinced that God had invested them with special authority, and this faith doubtless served to stimulate their conscientious efforts and the development of their strength. Many contemporaries believed alike and were ready to spend their last drop of blood in the service of the king sent to them by God. But science is as little able to prove the truth of this belief as to prove the truth of a religion. Collectivism is political, not scientific. What it teaches are judgments of value.

Collectivism is generally in favour of the socialization of the means of production because this lies nearer to its world philosophy. But there are collectivists who advocate private ownership in the means of production because they believe that the well-being of the social whole is better served by this system.[19] On the other hand, even without being influenced by collectivist ideas it is possible to believe that private ownership in the means of production is less able than common ownership to accomplish the purposes of humanity.

---

[19] Huth, *Soziale und individualistische Auffassung im 18. Jahrhundert, vornehmlich bei Adam Smith und Adam Ferguson* (Leipzig, 1907), p. 6.

CHAPTER 3

The Social Order and the Political Constitution

1

The Policy of Violence and the Policy of Contract

69 The domination of the principle of violence was naturally not restricted to the sphere of property. The spirit which put its trust in might alone, which sought the fundamentals of welfare, not in agreement, but in ceaseless conflict, permeated the whole of life. All human relations were settled according to the "Law of the Stronger," which is really the negation of Law. There was no peace; at best there was a truce.

Society grows out of the smallest associations. The circle of those who combined to keep the peace among themselves was at first very limited. The circle widened step by step through millennia, until the community of international law and the union of peace extended over the greatest part of humanity, excluding the half savage peoples who lived on the lowest plane of culture. Within this community the principle of contract was not everywhere equally powerful. It was most completely recognized in all that was concerned with property. It remained weakest in fields where it touched the question of political domination. Into the sphere of foreign policy it has so far penetrated no further than to limit the principle of violence by setting up rules of combat. Apart from the process of arbitration, which is a recent development, disputes between states are still, in essentials, decided by arms, the most usual of ancient judicial processes; but the deciding combat, like the judicial duels of the most ancient laws, must conform to certain rules. All the same, it would be false to maintain that in the intercourse of states, fear of foreign violence is the one factor that keeps the sword in its sheath.[1] Forces which have been active in the foreign policy of states through millennia have set the value of peace above the profit of victorious war. In our time

[1] As, for instance, Lasson maintains (*Prinzip und Zukunft des Völkerrechts*, Berlin, 1871), p. 35.

even the mightiest war lord cannot isolate himself completely from the influence of the legal maxim that wars must have valid reasons. Those who 70
wage war invariably endeavour to prove that theirs is the just cause and that they fight in defence or at least in preventive-defence; this is a solemn recognition of the principle of Law and Peace. Every policy which has openly confessed to the principle of violence has brought upon itself a world-coalition, to which it has finally succumbed.

In the Liberal Social Philosophy the human mind becomes aware of the overcoming of the principle of violence by the principle of peace. In this philosophy for the first time humanity gives itself an account of its actions. It tears away the romantic nimbus with which the exercise of power had been surrounded. War, it teaches, is harmful, not only to the conquered but to the conqueror. Society has arisen out of the works of peace; the essence of society is peacemaking. Peace and not war is the father of all things. Only economic action has created the wealth around us; labour, not the profession of arms, brings happiness. Peace builds, war destroys. Nations are fundamentally peaceful because they recognize the predominant utility of peace. They accept war only in self-defence; wars of aggression they do not desire. It is the princes who want war, because thus they hope to get money, goods, and power. It is the business of the nations to prevent them from achieving their desire by denying them the means necessary for making war.

The love of peace of the liberal does not spring from philanthropic considerations, as does the pacifism of Bertha Suttner* and of others of that category. It has none of the woebegone spirit which attempts to combat the romanticism of blood lust with the sobriety of international congresses. Its predilection for peace is not a pastime which is otherwise compatible with all possible convictions. It is *the* social theory of Liberalism. Whoever maintains the solidarity of the economic interests of all nations, and remains indifferent to the extent of national territories and national frontiers, whoever has so far overcome collectivist notions that such an expression as "Honour of the State" sounds incomprehensible to him, that man will nowhere find a valid cause for wars of aggression. Liberal pacificism is the offspring of the Liberal Social Philosophy. That Liberalism aims at the protection of property and that it rejects war are two expressions of one and the same principle.[2]

---

* Bertha Suttner (1843–1914) was an Austrian author, pacifist, and 1905 Nobel Peace Prize recipient (Pub.).

[2] In their efforts to debit capitalism with all evil, the socialists have tried to describe even modern imperialism and thus world war as products of capitalism. It is probably unnecessary to deal more fully with this theory, put forward for the unthinking masses. But it is not inappropriate to recall that Kant represented the facts correctly when he expected the growing influence of

71 ## 2

The Social Function of Democracy

In internal politics Liberalism demands the fullest freedom for the expression of political opinion and it demands that the State shall be constituted according to the will of the majority; it demands legislation through representatives of the people, and that the government, which is a committee of the people's representatives, shall be bound by the Laws. Liberalism merely compromises when it accepts a monarchy. Its ideal remains the republic or at least a shadow-principality of the English type. For its highest political principle is the self-determination of peoples as of individuals. It is idle to discuss whether one should call this political ideal democratic or not. The more recent writers are inclined to assume a contrast between Liberalism and Democracy. They seem to have no clear conceptions of either; above all, their ideas as to the philosophical basis of democratic institutions seem to be derived exclusively from the ideas of natural law.

Now it may well be that the majority of liberal theories have endeavoured to recommend democratic institutions on grounds which correspond to the theories of natural law with regard to the inalienable right of human beings to self-determination. But the reasons which a political movement gives in justification of its postulates do not always coincide with the reasons which force them to be uttered. It is often easier to act politically than to see clearly the ultimate motives of one's actions. The old Liberalism knew that the democratic demands rose inevitably from its system of social philosophy. But it was not at all clear what position these demands occupied in the system. This explains the uncertainty it has always manifested in questions of ultimate principle; it also accounts for the measureless exaggeration which certain pseudo-democratic demands have enjoyed at the hands of those who
72 ultimately claimed the name democrat for themselves alone and who thus became contrasted with liberals who did not go so far.

The significance of the democratic form of constitution is not that it represents more nearly than any other the natural and inborn rights of man; not

---

"money power" would gradually diminish warlike tendencies. "It is the spirit of commerce," he says, "which cannot exist side by side with war" (Kant, "Zum ewigen Frieden," vol. 5, *Sämtliche Werke*, p. 688); see also Sulzbach, *Nationales Gemeinschaftsgefühl und wirtschaftliches Interesse* (Leipzig, 1929), pp. 80 ff. Publisher's Note: In English, "Perpetual Peace." In *On History*. Immanuel Kant, ed. Lewis White Beck (Indianapolis: Bobbs-Merrill, 1963), p. 114.

that it realizes, better than any other kind of government, the ideas of liberty and equality. In the abstract it is as little unworthy of a man to let others govern him as it is to let someone else perform any kind of labour for him. That the citizen of a developed community feels free and happy in a democracy, that he regards it as superior to all other forms of government, and that he is prepared to make sacrifices to achieve and maintain it, this, again, is not to be explained by the fact that democracy is worthy of love for its own sake. The fact is that it performs functions which he is not prepared to do without.

It is usually argued that the essential function of democracy is the selection of political leaders. In the democratic system the appointment to at least the most important public offices is decided by competition in all the publicity of political life, and in this competition, it is believed, the most capable are bound to win. But it is difficult to see why democracy should necessarily be luckier than autocracy or aristocracy in selecting people for directing the state. In nondemocratic states, history shows, political talents have frequently won through, and one cannot maintain that democracy always puts the best people into office. On this point the enemies and the friends of democracy will never agree.

The truth is that the significance of the democratic form of constitution is something quite different from all this. Its function is to make peace, to avoid violent revolutions. In non-democratic states, too, only a government which can count on the backing of public opinion is able to maintain itself in the long run. The strength of all governments lies not in weapons but in the spirit which puts the weapons at their disposal. Those in power, always necessarily a small minority against an enormous majority, can attain and maintain power only by making the spirit of the majority pliant to their rule. If there is a change, if those on whose support the government depends lose the conviction that they must support this particular government, then the ground is undermined beneath it and it must sooner or later give way. Persons and systems in the government of non-democratic states can be
changed by violence alone. The system and the individuals that have lost 73
the support of the people are swept away in the upheaval and a new system and other individuals take their place.

But any violent revolution costs blood and money. Lives are sacrificed, and destruction impedes economic activity. Democracy tries to prevent such material loss and the accompanying psychical shock by guaranteeing accord between the will of the state—as expressed through the organs of the state—and the will of the majority. This it achieves by making the organs of the state legally dependent on the will of the majority of the moment. In internal policy it realizes what pacifism seeks to realize in external policy.[3]

That this alone is the decisive function of democracy becomes clearly evident when we consider the argument which opponents of the democratic principle most frequently adduce against it. The Russian conservative is undoubtedly right when he points out that Russian Tsarism and the policy of the Tsar was approved by the great mass of the Russian people, so that even a democratic state form could not have given Russia a different system of government. Russian democrats themselves have had no delusions about this. As long as the majority of the Russian people or, better, of that part of the people which was politically mature and which had the opportunity to intervene in policy—as long as this majority stood behind tsardom, the empire did not suffer from the absence of a democratic form of constitution. This lack became fatal, however, as soon as a difference arose between public opinion and the political system of tsardom. State will and people's will could not be adjusted pacifically; a political catastrophe was inevitable. And what is true of the Russia of the Tsar is just as true of the Russia of the Bolshevists; it is just as true of Prussia, of Germany, and of every other state. How disastrous were the effects of the French Revolution, from which France has psychically never quite recovered! How enormously England has benefited from the fact that she has been able to avoid revolution since the seventeenth century!

Thus we see how mistaken it is to regard the terms democratic and
74 revolutionary as synonymous or even as similar. Democracy is not only not revolutionary, but it seeks to extirpate revolution. The cult of revolution, of violent overthrow at any price, which is peculiar to Marxism, has nothing whatever to do with democracy. Liberalism, recognizing that the attainment of the economic aims of man presupposes peace, and seeking therefore to eliminate all causes of strife at home or in foreign politics, desires democracy. The violence of war and revolutions is always an evil to liberal eyes, an evil which cannot always be avoided as long as man lacks democracy. Yet even when revolution seems almost inevitable Liberalism tries to save the people from violence, hoping that philosophy may so enlighten tyrants that they will voluntarily renounce rights which are opposed to social development. Schiller speaks with the voice of Liberalism when he makes the Marquis de

[3] In some sense it is, perhaps, not altogether an accident that the writer who, at the threshold of the Renaissance, first raised the democratic demand for legislation by the people—Marsilius of Padua—called his work *Defensor Pacis* (Atger, *Essai sur l'Histoire des Doctrines du Contrat Social* [Paris, 1906], p. 75; Scholz, "Marsilius von Padua und die Idee der Demokratie" [*Zeitschrift fur Politik*, 1908], vol. 1, pp. 66 ff.

Posa implore the king for liberty of thought; and the great night of August 4th, 1789, when the French feudal lords voluntarily renounced their privileges, and the English Reform Act of 1832, show that these hopes were not quite vain. Liberalism has no admiration to spare for the heroic grandiosity of Marxism's professional revolutionaries, who stake the lives of thousands and destroy values which the labour of decades and centuries has created. Here the economic principle holds good: Liberalism wants success at the smallest price.

Democracy is self-government of the people; it is autonomy. But this does not mean that all must collaborate equally in legislation and administration. Direct democracy can be realized only on the smallest scale. Even small parliaments cannot do all their work in plenary assemblies; committees must be chosen, and the real work is done by individuals; by the proposers, the speakers, the rapporteurs, and above all by the authors of the bills. Here then is final proof of the fact that the masses follow the leadership of a few men. That men are not all equal, that some are born to lead and some to be led is a circumstance which even democratic institutions cannot alter. We cannot all be pioneers: most people do not wish to be nor have they the necessary strength. The idea that under the purest form of democracy people would spend their days in council like the members of a parliament derives from the conception we had of the ancient Greek city State at its period of decay; but we overlook the fact that such communities were not in fact democracies at all, since they excluded from public life the slaves and all who did not possess full citizen rights. Where all are to collaborate, the "pure" ideal of direct democracy becomes impracticable. To want to see 75
democracy realized in this impossible form is nothing less than pedantic natural law doctrinairianism. To achieve the ends for which democratic institutions strive it is only necessary that legislation and administration shall be guided according to the will of the popular majority and for this purpose indirect democracy is completely satisfactory. The essence of democracy is not that everyone makes and administers laws but that lawgivers and rulers should be dependent on the people's will in such a way that they may be peaceably changed if conflict occurs.

This defeats many of the arguments, put forward by friends and opponents of popular rule, against the possibility of realizing democracy.[4] Democracy is not less democracy because leaders come forth from the masses to devote

---

[4] See, on the one hand, especially the writings of the advocates of the Prussian authoritarian state; on the other, above all, the syndicalists (Michels, *Zur Soziologie des Parteiwesens in der modernen Demokratie*, 2nd ed. [Leipzig, 1925]), pp. 463 ff.

themselves entirely to politics. Like any other profession in the society dividing labour, politics demand the entire man; dilettante politicians are of no use.[5] As long as the professional politician remains dependent on the will of the majority, so that he can carry out only that for which he has won over the majority, the democratic principle is satisfied. Democracy does not demand, either that parliament shall be a copy, on a reduced scale, of the social stratification of the country, consisting, where peasant and industrial labourers form the bulk of the population, mainly of peasants and industrial labourers.[6] The gentleman of leisure who plays a great role in the English parliament, the lawyer and journalist of the parliaments of the Latin countries probably represent the people better than the trade union leaders and peasants who have brought spiritual desolation to the German and Slav parliaments. If members of the higher social ranks were excluded from parliaments, those parliaments and the governments emanating from them could not
76 represent the will of the people. For in society these higher ranks, the composition of which is itself the result of a selection made by public opinion, exert on the minds of the people an influence out of all proportion to their mere numbers. If one kept them from parliament and public administration by describing them to the electors as men unfit to rule, a conflict would have arisen between public opinion and the opinion of parliamentary bodies, and this would make more difficult, if not impossible, the functioning of democratic institutions. Non-parliamentary influences make themselves felt in legislation and administration, for the intellectual power of the excluded cannot be stifled by the inferior elements which lead in parliamentary life. Parliamentarism suffers from nothing so much as from this; we must seek here the reason for its much deplored decline. For democracy is not mob rule, and to do justice to its tasks, parliament should include the best political minds of the nation.

Grave injury has been done to the concept of democracy by those who, exaggerating the natural law notion of sovereignty, conceived it as limitless rule of the *volonté générale* (general will). There is really no essential difference

[5] Max Weber, *Politik als Beruf* (Munich and Leipzig, 1920), pp. 17 ff.

[6] The natural-law theories of democracy, which fail to appreciate the essentials of the division of labor, cling to the idea of the "representation" of electors by elected. It was not difficult to show how artificial was this concept. The member of parliament who makes laws for me and controls for me the administration of the postal system, no more "represents" me than the doctor who heals me or the cobbler who makes shoes for me. What differentiates him essentially from the doctor and the cobbler is not that he fulfills services of a different kind for me but that if I am dissatisfied with him I cannot withdraw the care of my affairs from him in the same simple way I can dismiss a doctor or a cobbler. To get that influence in government which I have over my doctor and shoemaker I want to be an elector.

between the unlimited power of the democratic state and the unlimited power of the autocrat. The idea that carries away our demagogues and their supporters, the idea that the state can do whatever it wishes, and that nothing should resist the will of the sovereign people, has done more evil perhaps than the caesar-mania of degenerate princelings. Both have the same origin in the notion of a state based purely on political might. The legislator feels free of all limitations because he understands from the theory of law that all law depends on his will. It is a small confusion of ideas, but a confusion with profound consequences, when he takes his formal freedom to be a material one and believes himself to be above the natural conditions of social life. The conflicts which arise out of this misconception show that only within the framework of Liberalism does democracy fulfil a social function. Democracy without Liberalism is a hollow form.

3

The Ideal of Equality

Political democracy necessarily follows from Liberalism. But it is often said
that the democratic principle must eventually lead beyond Liberalism. Carried 77
out strictly, it is said, it will require economic as well as political rights of equality. Thus logically Socialism must necessarily evolve out of Liberalism, while Liberalism necessarily involves its own destruction.

The ideal of equality, also, originated as a demand of natural law. It was sought to justify it with religious, psychological, and philosophical arguments; but all these proved to be untenable. The fact is that men are endowed differently by nature; thus the demand that all should be equally treated cannot rest on any theory that all are equal. The poverty of the natural law argument is exposed most clearly when it deals with the principle of equality.

If we wish to understand this principle we must start with an historical examination. In modern times, as earlier, it has been appealed to as a means of sweeping away the feudal differentiation of individuals' legal rights. So long as barriers hinder the development of the individual and of whole sections of the people, social life is bound to be disturbed by violent upheavals. People without rights are always a menace to social order. Their common interest in removing such barriers unites them; they are prepared to resort to violence because by peaceable means they are unable to get what they want. Social peace is attained only when one allows all members of society to participate in democratic institutions. And this means equality of All before the Law.

Another consideration too urges upon Liberalism the desirability of such equality. Society is best served when the means of production are in the possession of those who know how to use them best. The gradation of legal rights according to accident of birth keeps production goods from the best managers. We all know what role this argument has played in liberal struggles, above all in the emancipation of the serfs. The soberest reasons of expediency recommend equality to Liberalism. Liberalism is fully conscious, of course, that equality before the Law can become extremely oppressive for the individual under certain circumstances, because what benefits one may injure another; the liberal idea of equality is however based on social considerations, and where these are to be served the susceptibilities of individuals must give way. Like all other social institutions, the Law exists for social purposes. The individual must bow to it, because his own aims can be served only in and with society.

78 The meaning of legal institutions is misunderstood when they are conceived to be anything more than this, and when they are made the basis of new claims which are to be realized at whatever cost to the aim of social collaboration. The equality Liberalism creates is equality before the Law; it has never sought any other. From the liberal point of view, therefore, criticism which condemns this equality as inadequate—maintaining that true equality is full equality of income through equal distribution of commodities—is unjustified.

But it is precisely in this form that the principle of equality is most acclaimed by those who expect to gain more than they lose from an equal distribution of goods. Here is a fertile field for the demagogue. Whoever stirs up the resentment of the poor against the rich can count on securing a big audience. Democracy creates the most favourable preliminary conditions for the development of this spirit, which is always and everywhere present, though concealed.[7] So far all democratic states have foundered on this point. The democracy of our own time is hastening towards the same end.

It is a strange fact that just that idea of equality should be called unsocial which considers equality only from the point of view of the interests of society as a whole, and which wants to see it achieved only in so far as it helps society to attain its social aims; while the view which insists that

[7] To this extent one can say with Proudhon: "*La democratie c'est l'envie*" ("Democracy is envy") (Poehlmann, *Geschichte der sozialen Frage und des Sozialismus in der antiken Welt*, vol. 1, p. 317, fn. 4).

equality, regardless of the consequences, implies a claim to an equal quota of the national income is put forward as the only view inspired by consideration for society. In the Greek city State of the fourth century the citizen considered himself lord of the property of all the subjects of the State and he demanded his part imperiously, as a shareholder demands his dividends. Referring to the practice of distributing common property and confiscated private property, Aeschines made the following comment: "The Athenians come out of the Ecclesia not as out of a political assembly but as from the meeting of a company in which the surplus profit has been distributed."[8] It cannot be denied that even to-day the common man is inclined to look on the State as a source from which to draw the utmost possible income.

But the principle of equality in this form by no means follows necessarily 79
from the democratic idea. It should not be recognized as valid *a priori* any more than any other principle of social life. Before one can judge it, its effects must be clearly understood. The fact that it is generally very popular with the masses and therefore finds easy recognition in a democratic state neither makes it a fundamental principle of democracy nor protects it from the scrutiny of the theorist.

4

Democracy and Social-Democracy

The view that democracy and Socialism are inwardly related spread far and wide in the decades which preceded the Bolshevist revolution. Many came to believe that democracy and Socialism meant the same thing, and that democracy without Socialism or Socialism without democracy would not be possible.

This notion sprang principally from a combination of two chains of thought, both of which sprang originally from the Hegelian philosophy of history. For Hegel world history is "progress in the consciousness of freedom." Progress takes place in this way: ". . . the Orientals only knew that *one* is free, the Greek and Roman world that *some* are free, but we know that *all* men are free as such, that man is free as man."[9] There is no doubt that the freedom of which Hegel spoke was different from that for which the radical

---

[8] *Ibid.*, vol. 1, p. 333

[9] Hegel, *Vorlesungen über die Philosophie der Weltgeschichte*, ed. Lasson (Leipzig, 1917), vol. 1, p. 40.

politicians of his day were fighting. Hegel took ideas which were common to the political doctrines of the epoch of enlightenment and intellectualized them. But the radical young Hegelians read into his words what appealed to them. For them it was certain that the evolution to Democracy was a necessity in the Hegelian sense of this term. The historians follow suit. Gervinus sees "by and large in the history of humanity," as "in the internal evolution of the states," "a regular progress . . . from the spiritual and civil freedom of the single individual to that of the Several and the Many."[10]

80 The materialist conception of history provides the idea of the "liberty of the many" with a different content. The Many are the proletarians; they must necessarily become socialists because consciousness is determined by the social conditions. Thus evolution to democracy and evolution to Socialism are one and the same thing. Democracy is the means towards the realization of Socialism, but at the same time Socialism is the means towards the realization of democracy. The party title, "Social Democracy," most clearly expresses this co-ordination of Socialism and democracy. With the name democracy the socialist workers' party took over the spiritual inheritance of the movements of Young Europe. All the slogans of the pre-March[11] radicalism are to be found in the Social-Democratic Party programmes. They recruit, for the party, supporters who feel indifferent to or are even repulsed by the demands of Socialism.

The relation of Marxist Socialism to the demand for democracy was determined by the fact that it was the Socialism of the Germans, the Russians, and the smaller nations which lived under the Austro-Hungarian monarchy and the empire of the Tsars. Every opposition party in these more or less autocratic states had to demand democracy first of all, so as to create the conditions that must precede the development of political activity. For the Social Democrats this practically excluded democracy from discussion; it would never have done to cast a doubt on the democratic ideology *pro foro externo*.

But the question of the relation between the two ideas expressed in its double name could not be completely suppressed within the party. People began by dividing the problem into two parts. When they spoke of the coming socialist paradise they continued to maintain the interdependence of the terms and even went a little farther and said that they were ultimately one. Since one continued to regard democracy as in itself a good thing, one could not—as a faithful socialist awaiting absolute salvation in the paradise-to-be—arrive at any other conclusion. There would be something wrong

[10] Gervinus, *Einleitung in die Geschichte des neunzehnten Jahrhunderts* (Leipzig, 1853), p. 13.
[11] i.e., German radicalism before the revolution of 1848 (Trans.).

with the land of promise if it were not the best imaginable from a political point of view. Thus socialist writers did not cease to proclaim that only in a socialist society could true democracy exist. What passed for democracy in the capitalist states was a caricature designed to cover the machinations of exploiters.

But although it was seen that Socialism and democracy must meet at the goal, nobody was quite certain whether they were to take the same road. 81
People argued over the problem whether the realization of Socialism—and therefore, according to the views just discussed, of democracy too—was to be attempted through the instrumentality of democracy or whether in the struggle one should deviate from the principles of democracy. This was the celebrated controversy about the dictatorship of the proletariat; it was the subject of academic discussion in Marxist literature up to the time of the Bolshevist revolution and has since become a great political problem.

Like all other differences of opinion which divide Marxists into groups, the quarrel arose from the dualism which cuts right through that bundle of dogmas called the Marxist system. In Marxism there are always two ways at least of looking at anything and everything, and the reconciliation of these views is attained only by dialectic artificialities. The commonest device is to use, according to the needs of the moment, a word to which more than one meaning may be attached. With these words, which at the same time serve as political slogans to hypnotize the mass psyche, a cult suggestive of fetishism is carried on. The Marxist dialectic is essentially word-fetishism. Every article of the faith is embodied in a word fetish whose double or even multiple meaning makes it possible to unite incompatible ideas and demands. The interpretation of these words, as intentionally ambiguous as the words of the Delphic Pythia, eventually brings the different parties to blows, and everyone quotes in his favour passages from the writings of Marx and Engels to which authoritative importance is attached.

"Revolution" is one of these words. By "industrial revolution" Marxism means the gradual transformation of the pre-capitalist way of production into the capitalist. "Revolution" here means the same as "development," and the contrast between the terms "evolution" and "revolution" is almost extinguished. Thus the Marxist is able, when it pleases him, to speak of the revolutionary spirit as contemptible *"putschism"* ("insurrectionism"). The revisionists were quite right when they called many passages in Marx and Engels to their support. But when Marx calls the workers' movement a revolutionary movement and says that the working class is the only true revolutionary class, he is using the term in the sense that suggests barricades and street fights. Thus syndicalism is also right when it appeals to Marx.

Marxism is equally obscure in the use of the word State. According to

82 Marxism, the State is merely an instrument of class domination. By acquiring political power the proletariat abolishes class conflict and the State ceases to exist. "As soon as there is no longer any social class to be kept in suppression, and as soon as class domination and the struggle for individual existence based on the hitherto existing anarchy of production are removed, along with the conflicts and excesses which arise from them, then there will be nothing more to repress and nothing that would make necessary a special repressive power, a state. The first act in which the State really appears as representative of the whole society—the taking possession of the means of production in the name of society—is simultaneously its last independent act as a state. The intervention of state power in social affairs becomes superfluous in one field after another until at last it falls asleep of its own accord."[12] However obscure or badly thought out may be its view of the essence of political organization, this statement is so positive in what it says of the proletarian rule that it would seem to leave no room for doubt. But it seems much less positive when we remember Marx's assertion that between the capitalist and the communist societies must lie a period of revolutionary transformation, in addition to which there will be a corresponding "political period of transition whose state can be no other than the revolutionary dictatorship of the proletariat."[13] If we assume, with Lenin, that this period is to endure until that "higher phase of communist society" is reached, in which "the enslaving subordination of individuals under the division of labour has vanished, and with it the contrast of mental and physical work," in which "work will have become not only a means to life but itself the first necessity of life," then of course we come to a very different conclusion with regard to Marxism's attitude to democracy.[14] Obviously the socialist community will have no room for democracy for centuries to come.

Although it occasionally comments on the historical achievements of Liberalism, Marxism entirely overlooks the importance of liberal ideas. It is at

---

[12] Engels, *Herrn Eugen Dührings Umwälzung der Wissenschaft*, 7th ed. (Stuttgart, 1910), p. 302. Publisher's Note: in English, see *Anti-Dühring: Herr Eugen Dühring's Revolution in Science* (Moscow: Foreign Languages Publishing House, 1954), p. 389.

[13] Marx, *Zur Kritik des sozialdemokratischen Parteiprogramms von Gotha*, ed. Kreibich (Reichenberg, 1920), p. 23. Publisher's Note: In English, see *Critique of the Gotha Programme*, rev. trans. (New York: International Publishers, 1938), p. 18, or in *Capital, the Communist Manifesto and Other Writings*, ed. and introd. Max Eastman (New York: Random House, Modern Library, 1932). p. 355.

[14] Ibid., p. 17; also V. I. Lenin, *Staat und Revolution* (Berlin, 1918), p. 89. Publisher's Note: In English, see Marx, *Critique of the Gotha Programme*, p. 10. or p. 7 in the Eastman anthology; also Lenin, "The State and Revolution," in *Selected Work in Two Volumes* (Moscow: Foreign Languages Publishing House, 1952), vol. 2, pt. 1, pp. 199–325. The reference cited here is p. 290 in this English translation.

a loss when it comes to deal with the liberal demands for liberty of conscience and expression of opinion, for the recognition on principle of every opposition 83
party and the equal rights of all parties. Wherever it is not in power, Marxism claims all the basic liberal rights, for they alone can give it the freedom which its propaganda urgently needs. But it can never understand their spirit and will never grant them to its opponents when it comes into power itself. In this respect it resembles the Churches and other institutions which rest on the principle of violence. These, too, exploit the democratic liberties when they are fighting their battle, but once in power they deny their adversaries such rights. So, plainly, the democracy of Socialism exposes its deceit. "The party of the communists," says Bukharin, "demands no sort of liberties for the bourgeois enemies of the people. On the contrary." And with remarkable cynicism he boasts that the communists, before they were in power, advocated the liberty of expression of opinion merely because it would have been "ridiculous" to demand from the capitalists liberty for the workers' movement in any other way than by demanding liberty in general.[15]

Always and everywhere Liberalism demands democracy at once, for it believes that the function which it has to fulfil in society permits of no postponement. Without democracy the peaceful development of the state is impossible. The demand for democracy is not the result of a policy of compromise or of a pandering to relativism in questions of world-philosophy,[16] for Liberalism asserts the absolute validity of its doctrine. Rather, it is the consequence of the Liberal belief that power depends upon a mastery over mind alone and that to gain such a mastery only spiritual weapons are effective. Even where for an indefinite time to come it may expect to reap only disadvantages from democracy, Liberalism still advocates democracy. Liberalism believes that it cannot maintain itself against the will of the majority; and that in any case the advantages which might accrue from a liberal regime maintained artificially and against the feeling of the people would be infinitesimal compared to the disturbances that would stay the quiet course of state development if the people's will were violated.

The Social Democrats would certainly have continued to juggle with the 84
catchword democracy, but, by an historical accident, the Bolshevist revolution has compelled them prematurely to discard their mask, and to reveal the violence which their doctrine implies.

---

[15] Bukharin, *Das Programm der Kommunisten (Bolschewiki)* (Zurich, 1918), pp. 24 ff. Publisher's Note: For an English translation, see *Program of the Communists, Bolshevists*, 1918.

[16] As is the opinion of Kelsen, "Vom Wesen und Wert der Demokratie," in *Archiv für Sozialwissenschaft und Sozialpolitik*, vol. 47, p. 84; also Menzel, "Demokratie und Weltanschauung," in *Zeitschrift für öffentliches Recht*, vol. 2, pp. 701 ff.

5

The Political Constitution of Socialist Communities

Beyond the dictatorship of the proletariat lies the paradise, the "higher phase of the communist society," in which, "with the all round development of individuals, the productive forces will also have increased, and all the springs of social wealth will flow more freely."[17] In this land of promise "there will remain nothing to repress, nothing which would necessitate a special repressive power, a state . . . In place of the government over persons comes the administration of things and the direction of productive processes."[18] An epoch will have begun in which "a generation, grown up in new, free social conditions, will be able to discard the whole lumber of State."[19] The working class will have gone, thanks to "long struggles, a whole series of historical processes," by which "the men, like the conditions, were completely transformed."[20] Thus society is able to exist without coercion, as once it did in the Golden Age. Of this Engels has much to relate, much that is beautiful and good.[21] Only we have read it all before, all better and more beautifully expressed in Virgil, Ovid, and Tacitus!

> Aurea prima sata est aetas, quae vindice nullo,
> sponte sua, sine lege fidem rectumque colebat.
> Poena metusque aberant, nec verba minantia fixo
> aere legebantur [22]

(The first golden age flourished, which begat truth and justice spontaneously;
No laws of formal guarantees were needed. Punishment and fear were unheard of; no savage, restrictive decrees were carved on bronze tablets.)

It follows from all this that the Marxists have no occasion to occupy themselves with problems concerned with the political constitution of the

---

[17] Marx, *op. cit.*, p. 17. Publisher's Note: In English, see *Critique of the Gotha Programme*, rev. trans. (New York: International Publishers, 1938), p. 10, or Marx, *Capital, the Communist Manifesto and Other Writings*, ed. and introd. Max Eastman (New York: Random House, Modern Library, 1932), p. 7.

[18] Engels, *op. cit.*, p. 302. Publisher's Note: In the English, *op. cit.*, p. 389.

[19] Engels, Preface to Marx, *Der Bürgerkrieg in Frankreich*, Politische Aktions-Bibliothek (Berlin, 1919), p. 16. Publisher's Note: In English, see Engels, "Introduction to the German Edition" of Marx's "The Civil War in France" (1871), in Marx, *Capital, the Communist Manifesto and Other Writings*, ed. and introd. Max Eastman (New York: Random House, Modern Library, 1932), p. 381.

[20] Marx, *Der Bürgerkrieg*, p. 54. Publisher's Note: In English, see p. 408 of Eastman anthology cited in fn. 19.

[21] Engels, *Der Ursprung der Familie, des Privateigentums und des Staates*, 20th ed. (Stuttgart, 1921), pp. 163 ff. Publisher's Note: In English, see Engels, *The Origin of the Family, Private Property and the State* (New York: International Publishers, 1972), pp. 162 ff.

[22] Ovid, *Metamorphoses*, I, pp. 89 ff.; also Virgil, *Aeneid*, VII, pp. 203 ff.; Tacitus, *Annal*, III, p. 26; Poehlmann, *Geschichte der sozialen Frage und des Sozialismus in der antiken Welt*, vol. 2, pp. 583 ff.

socialist community. In this connection they perceive no problems at all 85
which cannot be dismissed by saying nothing about them. Yet even in the socialist community the necessity of acting in common must raise the question of how to act in common. It will be necessary to decide how to form that which is usually called, metaphorically, the will of the community or the will of the people. Even if we overlooked the fact that there can be no administration of goods which is not administration of men—i.e. the bending one human will to another—and no direction of productive processes which is not the government over persons—i.e. domination of one human will by another [23]—even if we overlooked this we should still have to ask who is to administer the goods and direct the productive processes, and on what principles. Thus, once again we are beset by all the political problems of the legally regulated social community.

All historical attempts to realize the socialist ideal of society have a most pronounced authoritarian character. Nothing in the Empire of the Pharaohs or of the Incas, and nothing in the Jesuit State of Paraguay was suggestive of democracy, of self-determination by the majority of the people. The Utopias of all the older kinds of socialists were equally undemocratic. Neither Plato nor Saint-Simon were democrats. One finds nothing in history or in the literary history of socialist theory which shows an internal connection between the socialist order of society and political democracy.

If we look closer we find that the ideal of the higher phase of communist society, ripening only in remote distances of the future, is, as the Marxists view it, thoroughly undemocratic.[24] Here, too, the socialist intends that eternal peace shall reign—the goal of all democratic institutions. But the means by which this peace is to be gained are very different from those employed by the democrats. It will not rest on the power to change peacefully rulers and ruling policy, but on the fact that the regime is made permanent, and that rulers and policy are unchangeable. This, too, is peace; not the peace of progress which Liberalism strives to attain but the peace of the
graveyard. It is not the peace of pacifists but of pacifiers, of men of violence 86
who seek to create peace by subjection. Every absolutist makes such peace by setting up an absolute domination, and it lasts just as long as his domination can be maintained. Liberalism sees the vanity of all this. It sets itself, therefore, to make a peace which will be proof against the perils which threaten it on account of man's inextinguishable yearning for change.

---

[23] Bourguin, *Die sozialistischen Systeme und die wirtschaftliche Entwicklung*, trans. Katenstein (Tübingen, 1906), pp. 70 ff.; Kelsen, *Sozialismus und Staat*, 2nd ed. (Leipzig, 1923), p. 105.

[24] Also Bryce, *Moderne Demokratien*, trans. Loewenstein and Mendelssohn Bartholdy (Munich, 1926), vol. 3, pp. 289 ff. Publisher's Note: In English, see James Bryce, *Modern Democracies* (New York: Macmillan, 1921), 2 vols.

CHAPTER 4

The Social Order and the Family

1

Socialism and the Sexual Problem

87 Proposals to transform the relations between the sexes have long gone hand in hand with plans for the socialization of the means of production. Marriage is to disappear along with private property, giving place to an arrangement more in harmony with the fundamental facts of sex. When man is liberated from the yoke of economic labour, love is to be liberated from all the economic trammels which have profaned it. Socialism promises not only welfare—wealth for all—but universal happiness in love as well. This part of its programme has been the source of much of its popularity. It is significant that no other German socialist book was more widely read or more effective as propaganda than Bebel's *Woman and Socialism,* which is dedicated above all to the message of free love.

It is not strange that many should feel the system of regulating sexual relations under which we live to be unsatisfactory. This system exerts a far reaching influence in diverting those sexual energies, which are at the bottom of so much human activity, from their purely sexual aspect to new purposes which cultural development has evolved. Great sacrifices have been made to build up this system and new sacrifices are always being made. There is a process which every individual must pass through in his own life if his sexual energies are to cast off the diffuse form they have in childhood and take their final mature shape. He must develop the inner psychic strength which impedes the flow of undifferentiated sexual energy and like a dam alters its direction.

A part of the energy with which nature has endowed the sexual instinct is in this way turned from sexual to other purposes. Not everyone escapes unscathed from the stress and struggle of this change. Many succumb, many

become neurotic or insane. Even the man who remains healthy and becomes a useful member of society is left with scars which an unfortunate accident 88
may re-open.[1] And even though sex should become the source of his greatest happiness, it will also be the source of his deepest pain; its passing will tell him that age has come, and that he is doomed to go the way of all transient, earthly things. Thus sex, which seems ever and again to fool man by giving and denying, first making him happy and then plunging him back into misery, never lets him sink into inertia. Waking and dreaming man's wishes turn upon sex. Those who sought to reform society could not have overlooked it.

This was the more to be expected since many of them were themselves neurotics suffering from an unhappy development of the sexual instinct. Fourier, for example, suffered from a grave psychosis. The sickness of a man whose sexual life is in the greatest disorder is evident in every line of his writings; it is a pity that nobody has undertaken to examine his life history by the psycho-analytic method. That the crazy absurdities of his books should have circulated so widely and won the highest commendation is due entirely to the fact that they describe with morbid fantasy the erotic pleasures awaiting humanity in the paradise of the "phalanstère."

Utopianism presents all its ideals for the future as the reconstruction of a Golden Age which humanity has lost through its own fault. In the same way it pretends that it is demanding for sexual life only a return to an original felicity. The poets of antiquity are no less eloquent in their praises of marvellous, bygone times of free love than when they speak of the saturnian ages when property did not exist.[2] Marxism echoes the older Utopians.

Marxism indeed seeks to combat marriage just as it seeks to justify the abolition of private property, by attempting to demonstrate its origin in history; just as it looked for reasons for abolishing the State in the fact that the State had not existed "from eternity," that societies had lived without a vestige of "State and State power."[3] For the Marxist, historical research is merely a means of political agitation. Its use is to furnish him with weapons against the hateful bourgeois order of society. The main objection to this method is not that it puts forward frivolous, untenable theories without

[1] Freud, *Drei Abhandlungen zur Sexualtheorie*, 2nd ed. (Leipzig and Vienna, 1910), pp. 38 ff. Publisher's Note: In English, see Freud, "Three Essays on the Theory of Sexuality," in *The Standard Edition of the Complete Psychological Works of Sigmund Freud* (New York: Avon Books, 1965). This citation is found on pp. 53 ff.

[2] Poehlmann, *Geschichte der sozialen Frage und des Sozialismus in der antiken Welt*, vol. 2, p. 576.

[3] Engels, *Der Ursprung der Familie, des Privateigentums und des Staates*, p. 182. Publisher's Note: In English, see Engels, *The Origin of the Family, Private Property and the State* (New York: International Publishers, 1972), p. 232.

89 thoroughly examining the historical material, but that he smuggles an evaluation of this material into an exposition which pretends to be scientific. Once upon a time, he says, there was a golden age. Then came one which was worse, but supportable. Finally, Capitalism arrived, and with it every imaginable evil. Thus Capitalism is damned in advance. It can be granted only a single merit, that thanks to the excess of its abominations, the world is ripe for salvation by Socialism.

2

Man and Woman in the Age of Violence

Recent ethnographical and historical research has provided a wealth of material on which to base a judgment of the history of sexual relations, and the new science of psycho-analysis has laid the foundations for a scientific theory of sexual life. So far sociology has not begun to understand the wealth of ideas and material available from these sources. It has not been able to restate the problems in such a way that they are adjusted to the questions that should be its first study today. What it says about exogamy and endogamy, about promiscuity, not to mention matriarchy and patriarchy, is quite out of touch with the theories one is now entitled to put forward. In fact, sociological knowledge of the earliest history of marriage and the family is so defective that one cannot draw on it for an interpretation of the problems which occupy us here. It is on fairly secure ground where it is dealing with conditions in historical times but nowhere else.

Unlimited rule of the male characterizes family relations where the principle of violence dominates. Male aggressiveness, which is implicit in the very nature of sexual relations, is here carried to the extreme. The man seizes possession of the woman and holds this sexual object in the same sense in which he *has* other goods of the outer world. Here woman becomes completely a thing. She is stolen and bought; she is given away, sold away, ordered away; in short, she is like a slave in the house. During life the man is her judge; when he dies she is buried in his grave along with his other possessions.[4] With almost absolute unanimity the older legal sources of

[4] Westermarck, *Geschichte der menschlichen Ehe*, trans. Katscher and Grazer, 2nd ed. (Berlin, 1902), p. 122; Weinhold, *Die deutschen Frauen in dem Mittelalter*, 3rd ed. (Vienna, 1897), vol. 2, pp. 9 ff. Publisher's Note: The Westermarck book first appeared in English as *The History of Human Marriage* (1891).

almost every nation show that this was once the lawful state of affairs. 90
Historians usually try, especially when dealing with the history of their own nations, to soften the painful impression which a description of these conditions leaves on a modern mind. They point out that practice was milder than the letter of the law, that the harshness of the law did not cloud the relations between the married couple. For the rest, they get away as quickly as possible from a subject which does not seem to fit too well into their system, by dropping a few remarks about the ancient severity of morals and purity of family life.[5] But these attempts at justification, to which their nationalist point of view and a predilection for the past seduce them, are distorted. The conception afforded by the old laws and law books of the relations between man and woman is not a theoretical speculation of unworldly dreamers. It is a picture direct from life and reproduces exactly what men, and women too, believed of marriage and intercourse between the sexes. That a Roman woman who stood in the "manus" of the husband or under the guardianship of the clan, or an ancient German woman who remained subject to the "munt" all her life, found this relation quite natural and just, that they did not revolt against it inwardly, or make any attempt to shake off the yoke—this does not prove that a broad chasm had developed between law and practice. It only shows that the institution suited the feeling of women; and this should not surprise us. The prevailing legal and moral views of a time are held not only by those whom they benefit but by those, too, who appear to suffer from them. Their domination is expressed in that fact—that the people from whom they claim sacrifices also accept them. Under the principle of violence, woman is the servant of man. In this she too sees her destiny. She shares the attitude to which the New Testament has given the most terse expression:

> Neither was the man created for the woman; but the woman for the man.[6]

The principle of violence recognizes only the male. He alone possesses power, hence he alone has rights. Woman is merely a sexual object. No
woman is without a lord, be it father or guardian, husband or employer. 91
Even the prostitutes are not free; they belong to the owner of the brothel. The guests make their contracts, not with them, but with him. The vagabond woman is free game, whom everyone may use according to his pleasure. The right to choose a man herself does not belong to the woman. She is given to the husband and taken by him. That she loves him is her duty,

---

[5] For example, Weinhold, *op. cit.*, pp. 7 ff.
[6] I Cor xi.9.

perhaps also her virtue; the sentiment will sharpen the pleasure which a man derives from marriage. But the woman is not asked for her opinion. The man has the right to repudiate or divorce her; she herself has no such right.

Thus in the age of violence, belief in man's lordship triumphs over all older tendencies to evolve equal rights between the sexes. Legend preserves a few traces of a time when woman enjoyed a greater sexual freedom—the character of Brünhilde, for example—but these are no longer understood. But the dominion of man is so great that it has come into conflict with the nature of sexual intercourse and for sheer sexual reasons man must, in his own interest, eventually weaken this dominion.

For it is against nature that man should take woman as a will-less thing. The sexual act is a mutual give and take, and a merely suffering attitude in the woman diminishes man's pleasure. To satisfy himself he must awaken her response. The victor who has dragged the slave into his marriage bed, the buyer who has traded the daughter from her father must court for that which the violation of the resisting woman cannot give. The man who outwardly appears the unlimited master of his woman is not so powerful in the house as he thinks; he must concede a part of his rule to the woman, even though he ashamedly conceals this from the world.

To this is added a second factor. The sexual act gradually becomes an extraordinary psychic effort which succeeds only with the assistance of special stimuli. This becomes more and more so in proportion as the individual is compelled by the principle of violence, which makes all women owned women and thus renders more difficult sexual intercourse, to restrain his impulses and to control his natural appetites. The sexual act now requires a special psychic attitude to the sexual object. This is love, unknown to primitive man and to the man of violence, who use every opportunity to possess, without selection. The characteristic of love, the overvaluation of
92 the object, cannot exist when women occupy the position of contempt which they occupy under the principle of violence. For under this system she is merely a slave, but it is the nature of love to conceive her as a queen.

Out of this contrast arises the first great conflict in the relations of the sexes which we can perceive in the full light of history. Marriage and love become contradictory. The forms in which this contrast appears vary, but in essence it always remains the same. Love has entered the feelings and thoughts of men and women and becomes ever more and more the central point of psychic life, giving meaning and charm to existence. But at first it has nothing to do with marriage and the relations between husband and wife. This inevitably leads to grave conflicts, conflicts which are indeed revealed to us in the epic and lyric poetry of the age of chivalry. These conflicts are familiar to us because they are immortalized in imperishable works of art and because they are still treated by epigones and by that art which takes its themes from such primitive conditions as persist at the present day. But we moderns cannot grasp the essence of the conflict. We cannot understand what is to prevent a solution which would satisfy all parties, why the lovers must remain separated and tied to those they do not love. Where love finds love, where man and woman desire nothing except to be allowed to remain forever devoted to each other, there, according to our view of the matter everything should be quite simple. The kind of poetry which deals with no other situation than this can, under the circumstances of present day life, do nothing less than bring Hansel and Gretel* into each other's arms, a denouement which is no doubt calculated to delight the readers of novels, but which is productive of no tragic conflict.

If, without knowledge of the literature of the age of chivalry, and basing our judgment merely on information about the relations of the sexes derived from other sources, we tried to picture for ourselves the psychic conflict of chivalric gallantry, we should probably imagine a situation in which a man is torn between two women: one his wife, to whom is bound the fate of his children; the other the lady to whom belongs his heart. Or we should delineate the position of a wife neglected by her husband, who loves another. Yet nothing would lie farther from an age dominated by the principle of violence. The Greek who divided his time between the *hetaeras* (prostitutes or courtesans) and love-boys by no means felt that his relationship with his
wife was a psychic burden, and she herself did not see in the love given to 93
the courtesan any encroachment on her own rights. Neither the troubadour who devoted himself wholly to the lady of his heart nor his wife who waited patiently at home suffered under the conflict between love and marriage. Both Ulrich von Lichtenstein** and his good housewife found the chivalrous "Minnedienst" just as it should be. In fact, the conflict in chivalrous love was of an altogether different nature. When the wife granted the utmost favours to another the rights of the husband were injured. However eagerly he himself set out to win the favours of other women, he would not tolerate interference in *his* property rights, he would not hear of anyone possessing *his* woman. This is a conflict based on the principles of violence. The husband is offended, not because the love of his wife is directed away from him, but

* The German edition refers to "Hans und Grete," not Hansel and Gretel, the brother and sister in the Grimm fairy tale. Most likely these names were merely like "John and Mary." (Pub.)

** Ulrich von Lichtenstein, a thirteenth-century poet, caricatured the form of chivalry of a knight's homage to his mistress, "Minnedienst," in his *Frauendienst* (1255).

because her body, which he owns, is to belong to others. Where, as so often in antiquity and the orient, the love of man sought not the wives of others but prostitutes, female slaves, and love-boys, all standing outside society, a conflict could not arise. Love forces the conflict only from the side of male jealousy. The man alone, as owner of his wife, can claim to possess completely. The wife has not the same right over her husband. In the essentially different judgment bestowed upon the adultery of a man and the adultery of a woman and in the different manner in which husband and wife regard the adultery of one another, we see today the remnants of that code, which is otherwise already incomprehensible to us.

Under such circumstances, as long as the principle of violence rules, the impulse to love is denied an opportunity to develop. Banished from the homely hearth it seeks out all manner of hiding places, where it assumes queer forms. Libertinage grows rampant, perversions of the natural instincts become more and more common. Conditions are conducive to the spread of venereal diseases. Whether syphilis was indigenous to Europe or whether it was introduced after the discovery of America is a questionable point. Whatever the truth, we know that it began to ravage Europe like an epidemic about the beginning of the sixteenth century. With the misery it brought, the love play of chivalric romanticism was at an end.

94 3

Marriage Under the Influence of the Idea of Contract

Nowadays only one opinion is expressed about the influence which the "economic" has exercised on sexual relations; it is said to have been thoroughly bad. The original natural purity of sexual intercourse has, according to this view, been tainted by the interference of economic factors. In no field of human life has the progress of culture and the increase of wealth had a more pernicious effect. Prehistoric men and women paired in purest love; in the pre-capitalist age, marriage and family life were simple and natural, but Capitalism brought money marriages and *mariages des convenances* on the one hand, prostitution and sexual excesses on the other. More recent historical and ethnographic research has demonstrated the fallacy of this argument and has given us another view of sexual life in primitive times and of primitive races. Modern literature has revealed how far from the realities of rural life was our conception, even only a short while ago, of the simple morals of the countryman. But the old prejudices were too deep-rooted to have been seriously shaken by this. Besides, socialistic literature, with the assistance of its peculiarly impressive rhetoric, sought to popularize the legend by giving it a new pathos. Thus today few people do not believe that the modern view of marriage as a contract is an insult to the essential spirit of sexual union and that it was Capitalism which destroyed the purity of family life.

For the scientist it is difficult to know what attitude he should take to a method of treating such problems which is founded on high-minded sentiments rather than on a discernment of the facts.

What is Good, Noble, Moral, and Virtuous the scientist as such is not able to judge. But he must at least correct the accepted view on one important point. The ideal of sexual relations of our age is utterly different from that of early times, and no age has come nearer to attaining its ideal than ours. The sexual relations of the good old times seem thoroughly unsatisfactory when measured by this, our, ideal; therefore, this ideal must have arisen from just that evolution which is condemned by the current theory as being responsible for the fact that we have failed to attain our ideal completely. Hence it is clear that the prevailing doctrine does not represent the facts;
that, indeed, it turns the facts upside down and is entirely valueless in an 95
attempt to understand the problem.

Where the principle of violence dominates, polygamy is universal. Each man has as many wives as he can defend. Wives are a form of property, of which it is always better to have more than few. A man endeavours to own more wives, just as he endeavours to own more slaves or cows; his moral attitude is the same, in fact, for slaves, cows, and wives. He demands fidelity from his wife; he alone may dispose of her labour and her body, himself remaining free of any ties whatever. Fidelity in the male implies monogamy.[7] A more powerful lord has the right to dispose also of the wives of his subjects.[8] The much discussed Jus Primae Noctis was an echo of these conditions, of which a final development was the intercourse between father-in-law and daughter-in-law in the "joint-family" of the Southern Slavs.

Moral reformers did not abolish polygamy, neither did the Church at first combat it. For centuries Christianity raised no objections to the polygamy of the barbarian kings. Charlemagne kept many concubines.[9] By its nature polygamy was never an institution for the poor man; the wealthy and the

---

[7] Weinhold, *op. cit.*, 1st ed. (Vienna, 1851), pp. 292 ff.

[8] Westermarck, *op. cit.*, pp. 74 ff.; Weinhold, *op. cit.*, 3rd ed. (Vienna), vol. 1, p. 273.

[9] Schröder, *Lehrbuch der deutschen Rechtsgeschichte*, 3rd ed. (Leipzig, 1898), pp. 70, 110; Weinhold, *op. cit.*, vol. 2, pp. 12 ff.

aristocratic could alone enjoy it.[10] But with the latter it became increasingly complex according to the extent to which women entered marriage as heiresses and owners, were provided with rich dowries, and were endowed with greater rights in disposing of the dowry. Thus monogamy has been gradually enforced by the wife who brings her husband wealth and by her relatives—a direct manifestation of the way in which capitalist thought and calculation has penetrated the family. In order to protect legally the property of wives and their children a sharp line is drawn between legitimate and illegitimate connection and succession. The relation of husband and wife is acknowledged as a contract.[11]

As the idea of contract enters the Law of Marriage, it breaks the rule of the male, and makes the wife a partner with equal rights. From a one-sided relationship resting on force, marriage thus becomes a mutual agreement;
96 the servant becomes the married wife entitled to demand from the man all that he is entitled to ask from her. Step by step she wins the position in the home which she holds today. Nowadays the position of the woman differs from the position of the man only in so far as their peculiar ways of earning a living differ. The remnants of man's privileges have little importance. They are privileges of honour. The wife, for instance, still bears her husband's name.

This evolution of marriage has taken place by way of the law relating to the property of married persons. Woman's position in marriage was improved as the principle of violence was thrust back, and as the idea of contract advanced in other fields of the Law of Property it necessarily transformed the property relations between the married couple. The wife was freed from the power of her husband for the first time when she gained legal rights over the wealth which she brought into marriage and which she acquired during marriage, and when that which her husband customarily gave her was transformed into allowances enforceable by law.

Thus marriage, as we know it, has come into existence entirely as a result of the contractual idea penetrating into this sphere of life. All our cherished ideals of marriage have grown out of this idea. That marriage unites one man and one woman, that it can be entered into only with the free will of both parties, that it imposes a duty of mutual fidelity, that a man's violations of the marriage vows are to be judged no differently from a woman's, that the rights of husband and wife are essentially the same—these principles

[10] Tacitus, *Germania*, c. 17.

[11] Marianne Weber, *Ehefrau und Mutter in der Rechtsentwicklung* (Tübingen, 1907), pp. 53 ff., 217 ff.

develop from the contractual attitude to the problem of marital life. No people can boast that their ancestors thought of marriage as we think of it today. Science cannot judge whether morals were once more severe than they are now. We can establish only that our views of what marriage should be are different from the views of past generations and that their ideal of marriage seems immoral in our eyes.

When panegyrists of the good old morality execrate the institution of divorce and separation they are probably right in asserting that no such things existed formerly. The right to cast off his wife which man once possessed in no way resembles the modern law of divorce. Nothing illustrates more clearly the great change of attitude than the contrast between these two institutions. And when the Church takes the lead in the struggle against divorce, it is well to remember that the existence of the modern marriage ideal of monogamy—of husband and wife with equal rights—in the defence 97
of which the Church wishes to intervene, is the result of capitalist, and not ecclesiastical, development.

4

The Problems of Married Life

In the modern contractual marriage, which takes place at the desire of husband and wife, marriage and love are united. Marriage appears morally justified only when it is concluded for love; without love between the bridal couple it seems improper. We find strange those royal weddings which are arranged at a distance, and in which, as in most of the thinking and acting of the ruling Houses, the age of violence is echoed. The fact that they find it necessary to represent these marriages to the public as love marriages shows that even royal families have not been able to escape the bourgeois marriage ideal.

The conflicts of modern married life spring first of all from the necessarily limited duration of passion in a contract concluded for life. *"Die Leidenschaft flieht, die Liebe muss bleiben"* ("Passion flies, love must remain"), says Schiller, the poet of bourgeois married life. In most marriages blessed with children, married love fades slowly and unnoticeably; in its place develops a friendly affection which for a long time is interrupted ever and again by a brief flickering of the old love; living together becomes habitual, and in the children, in whose development they relive their youth, the parents find consolation for the renunciation they have been forced to make as old age deprives them of their strength.

But this is not so for all. There are many ways by which man may reconcile himself to the transience of the earthly pilgrimage. To the believer, religion brings consolation and courage; it enables him to see himself as a thread in the fabric of eternal life, it assigns to him a place in the imperishable plan of a world creator, and places him beyond time and space, old age and death, high in the celestial pastures. Others find satisfaction in philosophy. They refuse to believe in a beneficent providence, the idea of which conflicts with experience; they disdain the easy solace to be derived from an arbitrary structure of fantasies, from an imaginary scheme designed to create the
98 illusion of a world order different from the order they are forced to recognize around them. But the great mass of men takes another way. Dully and apathetically they succumb to everyday life; they never think beyond the moment, but become slaves of habit and the passions. Between these, however, is a fourth group, consisting of men who do not know where or how to find peace. Such people can no longer believe because they have eaten of the tree of knowledge; they cannot smother their rebellious hearts in apathy; they are too restless and too unbalanced to make the philosophic adjustment to realities. At any price they want to win and hold happiness. With all their might they strain at the bars which imprison their instincts. They will not acquiesce. They want the impossible, seeking happiness not in the striving but in the fulfillment, not in the battle but in victory.

Such natures cannot tolerate marriage when the wild fire of the first love has begun to die. They make the highest demands upon love itself and they exaggerate the overvaluation of the sexual object. Thus they are doomed, if only for physiological reasons, to experience sooner than more moderate people disappointment in the intimate life of marriage. And this disappointment can easily change to revulsion. Love turns to hate. Life with the once beloved becomes a torment. He who cannot content himself, who is unwilling to moderate the illusions with which he entered a marriage of love, who does not learn to transfer to his children, in sublimated form, those desires which marriage can no longer satisfy—that man is not made for marriage. He will break away from the bonds with new projects of happiness in love, again and again repeating the old experience.

But all this has nothing to do with social conditions. These marriages are not wrecked because the married couple live in the capitalist order of society and because the means of production are privately owned. The disease germinates not without, but within; it grows out of the natural disposition of the parties concerned. It is fallacious to argue that because such conflicts

were lacking in precapitalist society, wedlock must then have provided what is deficient in these sick marriages. The truth is that love and marriage were separate and people did not expect marriage to give them lasting and unclouded happiness. Only when the idea of contract and consent has been imposed on marriage does the wedded couple demand that their union shall satisfy desire permanently. This is a demand which love cannot possibly
meet. The happiness of love is in the contest for the favours of the loved one 99
and in fulfillment of the longing to be united with her. We need not discuss whether such happiness can endure when physiological satisfaction is denied. But we know for certain that desire gratified, cools sooner or later and that endeavours to make permanent the fugitive hours of romance would be vain. We cannot blame marriage because it is unable to change our earthly life into an infinite series of ecstatic moments, all radiant with the pleasures of love. We should be equally wrong to blame the social environment.

The conflicts that social conditions cause in married life are of minor importance. It would be wrong to assume that loveless marriages made for the dowry of the wife or the wealth of the husband, or that marriages made miserable by economic factors are in any way as important an aspect of the question as the frequency with which literature treats of them would suggest. There is always an easy way out if people will only look for it.

As a social institution marriage is an adjustment of the individual to the social order by which a certain field of activity, with all its tasks and requirements, is assigned to him. Exceptional natures, whose abilities lift them far above the average, cannot support the coercion which such an adjustment to the way of life of the masses must involve. The man who feels within himself the urge to devise and achieve great things, who is prepared to sacrifice his life rather than be false to his mission, will not stifle his urge for the sake of a wife and children. In the life of a genius, however loving, the woman and whatever goes with her occupy a small place. We do not speak here of those great men in whom sex was completely sublimated and turned into other channels—Kant, for example—or of those whose fiery spirit, insatiable in the pursuit of love, could not acquiesce in the inevitable disappointments of married life and hurried with restless urge from one passion to another. Even the man of genius whose married life seems to take a normal course, whose attitude to sex does not differ from that of other people, cannot in the long run feel himself bound by marriage without violating his own self. Genius does not allow itself to be hindered by any consideration for the comfort of its fellows—even of those closest to it. The ties of marriage become intolerable bonds which the genius tries to cast off or at least to loosen so as to be able to move freely. The married couple must

100 walk side by side amid the rank and file of humanity. Whoever wishes to go his own way must break away from it. Rarely indeed is he granted the happiness of finding a woman willing and able to go with him on his solitary path.

All this was recognized long ago. The masses had accepted it so completely that anyone who betrayed his wife felt himself entitled to justify his action in these terms. But the genius is rare and a social institution does not become impossible merely because one or two exceptional men are unable to adjust themselves to it. No danger threatened marriage from this side.

The attacks launched against it by the Feminism of the Nineteenth Century seemed much more serious. Its spokesmen claimed that marriage forced women to sacrifice personality. It gave man space enough to develop his abilities, but to woman it denied all freedom. This was imputed to the unchangeable nature of marriage, which harnesses husband and wife together and thus debases the weaker woman to be the servant of the man. No reform could alter this; abolition of the whole institution alone could remedy the evil. Women must fight for liberation from this yoke, not only that she might be free to satisfy her sexual desires but so as to develop her individuality. Loose relations which gave freedom to both parties must replace marriage.

The radical wing of Feminism, which holds firmly to this standpoint, overlooks the fact that the expansion of woman's powers and abilities is inhibited not by marriage, not by being bound to man, children, and household, but by the more absorbing form in which the sexual function affects the female body. Pregnancy and the nursing of children claim the best years of a woman's life, the years in which a man may spend his energies in great achievements. One may believe that the unequal distribution of the burden of reproduction is an injustice of nature, or that it is unworthy of woman to be child-bearer and nurse, but to believe this does not alter the fact. It may be that a woman is able to choose between renouncing either the most profound womanly joy, the joy of motherhood, or the more masculine development of her personality in action and endeavour. It may be that she has no such choice. It may be that in suppressing her urge towards motherhood she does herself an injury that reacts through all other functions of her being. But whatever the truth about this, the fact remains that when she becomes a mother, with or without marriage, she is prevented from leading
101 her life as freely and independently as man. Extraordinarily gifted women may achieve fine things in spite of motherhood; but because the functions of sex have the first claim upon woman, genius and the greatest achievements have been denied her.

So far as Feminism seeks to adjust the legal position of woman to that of man, so far as it seeks to offer her legal and economic freedom to develop and act in accordance with her inclinations, desires, and economic circumstances—so far it is nothing more than a branch of the great liberal movement, which advocates peaceful and free evolution. When, going beyond this, it attacks the institutions of social life under the impression that it will thus be able to remove the natural barriers, it is a spiritual child of Socialism. For it is a characteristic of Socialism to discover in social institutions the origin of unalterable facts of nature, and to endeavour, by reforming these institutions, to reform nature.

5

Free Love

Free love is the socialist's radical solution for sexual problems. The socialistic society abolishes the economic dependence of woman which results from the fact that woman is dependent on the income of her husband. Man and woman have the same economic rights and the same duties, as far as motherhood does not demand special consideration for the woman. Public funds provide for the maintenance and education of the children, which are no longer the affairs of the parents but of society. Thus the relations between the sexes are no longer influenced by social and economic conditions. Mating ceases to found the simplest form of social union, marriage and the family. The family disappears and society is confronted with separate individuals only. Choice in love becomes completely free. Men and women unite and separate just as their desires urge. Socialism desires to create nothing that is new in all this, but "would only recreate on a higher level of culture and under new social forms what was universally valid on a more primitive cultural level and before private ownership dominated society."[12]

The arguments, sometimes unctuous and sometimes venomous, which 102
are put forward by theologians and other moral teachers, are entirely inadequate as a reply to this programme. And most of the writers who have occupied themselves with the problems of sexual intercourse have been dominated by the monastic and ascetic ideas of the moral theologians. To

[12] August Bebel, *Die Frau und der Sozialismus*, 16th ed. (Stuttgart, 1892), p. 343. Publisher's Note: English, see Bebel, *Women and Socialism*, auth. trans. Meta L. Stern (New York: Socialist Literature, 1910), p. 467.

them the sexual instinct is the absolute evil, sensuality is sin, voluptuousness is a gift of the devil, and even the thought of such things is immoral. Whether or not we uphold this condemnation of the sexual instinct depends entirely on our inclination and scale of values. The moralist's endeavour to attack or defend it from the scientific point of view is wasted labour. The limits of scientific method are misconceived when one attributes to it the role of judge and valuer; the nature of scientific method is misunderstood when it is expected to influence action not merely by showing the effectiveness of means to ends but also by determining the relative value of the ends themselves. The scientist treating ethical problems should, however, point out that we cannot begin by rejecting the sexual instinct as evil in itself and then go on to give, under certain conditions, our moral approval or toleration to the sexual act. The usual dictum condemning sensual pleasure in sexual intercourse but declaring nevertheless that the dutiful fulfillment of the *debitum conjugale* (conjugal duty) for the purpose of begetting successors is quite moral, springs from poverty-stricken sophistry. The married couple act in sensuality; no child has ever yet been begotten and conceived out of dutiful consideration for the State's need of recruits or taxpayers. To be quite logical, an ethical system which branded the act of procreation as shameful would have to demand complete and unconditional abstinence. If we do not wish to see life become extinct we should not call the source from which it is renewed a sink of vice. Nothing has poisoned the morals of modern society more than this ethical system which by neither condemning logically nor approving logically blurs the distinction between good and evil and bestows on sin a glittering allurement. More than anything it is to blame for the fact that the modern man vacillates aimlessly in questions of sexual morality, and is not even capable of properly appreciating the great problems of the relations between the sexes.

It is clear that sex is less important in the life of man than of woman.
103 Satisfaction brings him relaxation and mental peace. But for the woman the burden of motherhood begins here. Her destiny is completely circumscribed by sex; in man's life it is but an incident. However fervently and wholeheartedly he loves, however much he takes upon himself for the woman's sake, he remains always above the sexual. Even women are finally contemptuous of the man who is utterly engrossed by sex. But woman must exhaust herself as lover and as mother in the service of the sexual instinct. Man may often find it difficult, in the face of all the worries of his profession, to preserve his inner freedom and so to develop his individuality, but it will not be his sexual life which distracts him most. For woman, however, sex is the greatest obstacle.

Thus the meaning of the feminist question is essentially woman's struggle for personality. But the matter affects men not less than women, for only in co-operation can the sexes reach the highest degree of individual culture. The man who is always being dragged by woman into the lower spheres of psychic bondage cannot develop freely in the long run. To preserve the freedom of inner life for the woman, this is the real problem of women; it is part of the cultural problem of humanity.

It was failure to solve this problem which destroyed the Orient. There woman is an object of lust, a childbearer and nurse. Every progressive movement which began with the development of personality was prematurely frustrated by the women, who dragged men down again into the miasma of the harem. Nothing separates East and West more decisively today than the position of women and the attitude towards woman. People often maintain that the wisdom of the Orientals has understood the ultimate questions of existence more profoundly than all the philosophy of Europe. At any rate the fact that they have never been able to free themselves in sexual matters has sealed the fate of their culture.

Midway between Orient and Occident the unique culture of the Greeks grew up. But antiquity also failed to raise woman to the level on which it had placed man. Greek culture excluded the married woman. The wife remained in the woman's quarters, apart from the world, nothing more than the mother of the man's heirs and the steward of his house. His love was for the *hetaera* alone. Eventually he was not satisfied even here, and turned to homosexual love. Plato sees the love of boys transfigured by the spiritual union of the lovers and by joyful surrender to the beauty of soul and body. To him the love of woman was merely gross sensual satisfaction. 104

To Western man woman is the companion, to the Oriental she is the bedfellow. European woman has not always occupied the position she occupies today. She has won it in the course of evolution from the principle of violence to the principle of contract. And now man and woman are equal before the law. The small differences that still exist in private law are of no practical significance. Whether, for example, the law obliges the wife to obey her husband is not particularly important; as long as marriage survives one party will have to follow the other and whether husband or wife is stronger is certainly not a matter which paragraphs of the legal code can decide. Nor is it any longer of great significance that the political rights of women are restricted, that women are denied the vote and the right to hold public office. For by granting the vote to women the proportional political strength of the political parties is not on the whole much altered; the women of those parties which must suffer from the changes to be expected (not in any case important ones) ought in their own interests to become opponents of women's suffrage rather than supporters. The right to occupy public office is denied women less by the legal limitations of their rights than by the peculiarities of their sexual character. Without underestimating the value of the feminists' fight to extend woman's civil rights, one can safely risk the assertion that neither women nor the community are deeply injured by the slights to women's legal position which still remain in the legislation of civilized states.

The misconception to which the principle of equality before the law is exposed in the field of general social relationships is to be found in the special field of the relations between those sexes. Just as the pseudo-democratic movement endeavours by decrees to efface natural and socially conditioned inequalities, just as it wants to make the strong equal to the weak, the talented to the untalented, and the healthy to the sick, so the radical wing of the women's movement seeks to make women the equal of men.[13] Though they cannot go so far as to shift half the burden of motherhood on to men, still they would like to abolish marriage and family life so that women may have at least all that liberty which seems compatible with
105 childbearing. Unencumbered by husband and children, woman is to move freely, act freely, and live for herself and the development of her personality.

But the difference between sexual character and sexual destiny can no more be decreed away than other inequalities of mankind. It is not marriage which keeps woman inwardly unfree, but the fact that her sexual character demands surrender to a man and that her love for husband and children consumes her best energies. There is no human law to prevent the woman who looks for happiness in a career from renouncing love and marriage. But those who do not renounce them are not left with sufficient strength to master life as a man may master it. It is the fact that sex possesses her whole personality, and not the facts of marriage and family, which enchains woman. By "abolishing" marriage one would not make woman any freer and happier; one would merely take from her the essential content of her life, and one could offer nothing to replace it.

Woman's struggle to preserve her personality in marriage is part of that struggle for personal integrity which characterizes the rationalist society of the economic order based on private ownership of the means of production. It is not exclusively to the interest of woman that she should succeed in this struggle; to contrast the interests of men and women, as extreme feminists try to do, is very foolish. All mankind would suffer if woman should fail to

[13] To examine how far the radical demands of feminism were created by men and women whose sexual character was not normally developed would go beyond the limits set to these expositions.

develop her ego and be unable to unite with man as equal, freeborn companions and comrades.

To take away a woman's children and put them in an institution is to take away part of her life; and children are deprived of the most far-reaching influences when they are torn from the bosom of the family. Only recently Freud, with the insight of genius, has shown how deep are the impressions which the parental home leaves on the child. From the parents the child learns to love, and so comes to possess the forces which enable it to grow up into a healthy human being. The segregated educational institution breeds homosexuality and neurosis. It is no accident that the proposal to treat men and women as radically equal, to regulate sexual intercourse by the State, to put infants into public nursing homes at birth and to ensure that children and parents remain quite unknown to each other should have originated with Plato; he saw only the satisfaction of a physical craving in the relations between the sexes.

The evolution which has led from the principle of violence to the contractual 106
principle has based these relations on free choice in love. The woman may deny herself to anyone, she may demand fidelity and constancy from the man to whom she gives herself. Only in this way is the foundation laid for the development of woman's individuality. By returning to the principle of violence with a conscious neglect of the contractual idea, Socialism, even though it aims at an equal distribution of the plunder, must finally demand promiscuity in sexual life.

6

Prostitution

The *Communist Manifesto* declares that the "complement" of the "bourgeois family" is public prostitution. "With the disappearance of capital" prostitution would also disappear.[14] A chapter in Bebel's book on woman is headed "Prostitution, a necessary social institution of the bourgeois world." Here is amplified the theory that prostitution is as necessary to bourgeois

[14] Marx and Engels, *Das Kommunistische Manifest*, 7th German ed. (Berlin, 1906), p. 35. Publisher's Note: In English, see "The Communist Manifesto," in Marx, *Capital, the Communist Manifesto and Other Writings*, ed. and introd. Max Eastman (New York: Random House, Modern Library, 1932), pp. 315–355. The reference to prostitution is on page 340 of this English edition.

society as "police, standing army, church, entrepreneurs, etc."[15] Since its appearance the view that prostitution is a product of Capitalism has gained ground enormously. And as, in addition, preachers still complain that the good old morals have decayed, and accuse modern culture of having led to loose living, everyone is convinced that all sexual wrongs represent a symptom of decadence peculiar to our age.

In answer to this it is sufficient to point out that prostitution is an extremely ancient institution, unknown to hardly any people that has ever existed.[16] It is a remnant of ancient morals, not a symptom of the decay of higher culture. The most powerful influence against it today—the demand for man's abstinence outside marriage—is one of the principles involved in equal moral rights for man and woman, and is therefore altogether an ideal of the capitalist age. The age of the principle of violence demands sexual purity only from the bride, not from the bridegroom also. All those factors which favour prostitution today have nothing whatever to do with private property and
107 Capitalism. Militarism, which keeps young men from marriage longer than they wish, is anything but a product of peace-loving Liberalism. The fact that government and other officials can only marry when they are rich, as otherwise they would not be able to keep up appearances, is, like all other caste fetishes, a vestige of pre-capitalist thought. Capitalism does not recognize caste or caste customs; under Capitalism everyone lives according to his income.

Some women prostitute themselves because they want men, some because they want food. With many both motives operate. One may admit without further discussion that in a society where incomes were equal the economic temptation to prostitution would cease completely or dwindle to a minimum. But it would be idle to speculate whether or not, in a society without inequalities of income, other new social sources of prostitution could not arise. At any rate one cannot merely *assume* that the sexual morality of a socialist society would be more satisfactory than that of capitalist society.

It is in the study of the relations between sexual life and property, more than in any other field of social knowledge, that our ideas must be clarified and remodelled. Contemporary treatment of this problem is riddled with prejudices of all kinds. But the eyes with which we look at the matter must not be those of the dreamer envisioning a lost paradise, who sees the future in a blaze of rose-coloured light, and condemns all that goes on around us.

---

[15] Bebel, *op. cit.*, pp. 141 ff. Publisher's Note: In the English edition cited earlier, see pp. 174 ff.

[16] Marianne Weber, *op. cit.*, pp. 6 ff.

PART II
THE ECONOMICS OF A SOCIALIST COMMUNITY

SECTION 1

THE ECONOMICS OF AN ISOLATED SOCIALIST COMMUNITY

CHAPTER 5

The Nature of Economic Activity

1

A Contribution to the Critique of the Concept "Economic Activity"

Economic Science originated in discussion of the money price of goods 111
and services. Its first beginnings are to be found in inquiries about coinage, which developed into investigations of price movements. Money, money prices, and everything concerned with calculation in terms of money—these form the problems in the discussion of which the science of Economics emerged. Those attempts at economic inquiry, which are discernible in works on household management and the organization of production—particularly agricultural—did not develop further in this direction. They became merely the starting point for various departments of technology and natural science. And this was no accident. Only through the rationalization inherent in economic calculation based on the use of money could the human mind come to understand and trace the laws of its action.

The earlier economists did not ask themselves what the "economic" and "economic activity" really were. They had enough to do with the great tasks presented by the particular problems with which they were then concerned. They were not concerned with methodology. It was quite late before they began to grapple with the methods and ultimate aims of economics, and its place in the general system of knowledge. And then an obstacle was encountered which seemed to be insurmountable—the problem of defining the subject matter of economic activity.

All theoretical inquiries—those of the classical economists, equally with those of the moderns—start from the economic principle. Yet, as was necessarily soon perceived, this provides no basis for clearly defining the subject matter of economics. The economic principle is a general principle of rational
action, and not a specific principle of such action as forms the subject of 112

economic inquiry.[1] The economic principle directs all rational action, all action capable of becoming the subject matter of a science. It seemed absolutely unserviceable for separating the "economic" from the "non-economic," so far as the traditional economic problems were concerned.[2]

But, on the other hand, it was equally impossible to divide up rational actions according to the immediate end to which they were directed, and to regard as the subject matter of economics only those actions which were directed to providing mankind with the commodities of the external world. Against such a procedure it is a decisive objection that, in the last analysis, the provision of material goods serves not only those ends which are usually termed economic, but also many other ends.

Such a division of the motives of rational action involves a dual conception of action—action from economic motives, on the one side, action from non-economic motives, on the other—which is absolutely irreconcilable with the necessary unit of will and action. A theory of rational action must conceive such action as unitary.

2

Rational Action

Action based on reason, action therefore which is only to be understood by reason, knows only *one* end, the greatest pleasure of the acting individual. The attainment of pleasure, the avoidance of pain—these are its intentions. By this, of course, we do not mean "pleasure" and "pain" in the sense in which these terms used to be used. In the terminology of the modern economist, pleasure is to be understood as embracing all those things which men hold to be desirable, all that they want and strive for. There can therefore be no longer any contrast between the "noble" ethics of duty and the vulgar
113 hedonistic ethics. The modern concept of pleasure, happiness, utility, satisfaction and the like includes all human ends, regardless of whether the motives of action are moral or immoral, noble or ignoble, altruistic or egotistical.[3]

---

[1] It was left to the empirical-realistic school, with its terrible confusion of all concepts, to explain the economic principle as a specific of production under a money economy, *e.g.*, Lexis, *Allgemeine Volkswirtschaftslehre* (Berlin and Leipzig, 1910), p. 15.

[2] Amonn, *Objekt und Grundbegriffe der theoretischen Nationalökonomie* (Vienna and Leipzig, 1927), p. 185.

[3] Mill, *Das Nützlichkeitsprinzip.* Trans. Wahrmund, *Gesammelte Werke,* German ed. Th. Gomperz (Leipzig, 1869), vol, 1, pp. 125-200. Publisher's Note: This is a German translation of *Utilitarianism.*

In general men act only because they are not completely satisfied. Were they always to enjoy complete happiness, they would be without will, without desire, without action. In the land of the lotus-eaters there is no action. Action arises only from need, from dissatisfaction. It is purposeful striving towards something. Its ultimate end is always to get rid of a condition which is conceived to be deficient—to fulfil a need, to achieve satisfaction, to increase happiness. If men had all the external resources of nature so abundantly at their disposal that they were able to obtain complete satisfaction by action, then they could use them heedlessly. They would only have to consider their own powers and the limited time at their disposal. For, compared with the sum of their needs, they would still have only a limited strength and a limited life-time available. They would still have to economize time and labour. But to economy of materials they would be indifferent. In fact, however, materials are also limited, so that they too have to be used in such a way that the most urgent needs are satisfied first, with the least possible expenditure of materials for each satisfaction.

The spheres of rational action and economic action are therefore co-incident. All rational action is economic. All economic activity is rational action. All rational action is in the first place individual action. Only the individual thinks. Only the individual reasons. Only the individual acts. How society arises from the action of individuals will be shown in a later part of our discussion.

3

Economic Calculation

All human action, so far as it is rational, appears as the exchange of one condition for another. Men apply economic goods and personal time and labour in the direction which, under the given circumstances, promises the highest degree of satisfaction, and they forgo the satisfaction of lesser needs 114
so as to satisfy the more urgent needs. This is the essence of economic activity—the carrying out of acts of exchange.[4]

Every man who, in the course of economic activity, chooses between the satisfaction of two needs, only one of which can be satisfied, makes judgments

[4] Schumpeter, *Das Wesen und der Hauptinhalt der theoretischen Nationalökonomie*, (Leipzig, 1908), pp. 50, 80.

of value.[5] Such judgments concern firstly and directly the satisfactions themselves; it is only from these that they are reflected back upon goods. As a rule anyone in possession of his senses is able at once to evaluate goods which are ready for consumption. Under very simple conditions he should also have little difficulty in forming a judgment upon the relative significance to him of the factors of production. When, however, conditions are at all complicated, and the connection between things is harder to detect, we have to make more delicate computations if we are to evaluate such instruments. Isolated man can easily decide whether to extend his hunting or his cultivation. The processes of production he has to take into account are relatively short. The expenditure they demand and the product they afford can easily be perceived as a whole. But to choose whether we shall use a waterfall to produce electricity or extend coal-mining and better utilize the energy contained in coal, is quite another matter. Here the processes of production are so many and so long, the conditions necessary to the success of the undertaking so multitudinous, that we can never be content with vague ideas. To decide whether an undertaking is sound we must calculate carefully.

But computation demands units. And there can be no unit of the subjective use-value of commodities. Marginal utility provides no unit of value. The worth of two units of a given commodity is not twice as great as one—although it is necessarily greater or smaller than one. Judgments of value do not measure: they arrange, they grade.[6] If he relies only on subjective valuation, even isolated man cannot arrive at a decision based on more or less exact computations in cases where the solution is not immediately evident. To aid his calculations he must assume substitution relations between commodities. As a rule he will not be able to reduce all to a common unit.
115 But he may succeed in reducing all elements in the computation to such commodities as he can evaluate immediately, that is to say, to goods ready for consumption and the disutility of labour and then he is able to base his decision upon this evidence. It is obvious that even this is possible only in very simple cases. For complicated and long processes of production it would be quite out of the question.

In an exchange economy, the objective exchange value of commodities

[5] The following remarks reproduce parts of my essay "Die Wirtschaftsrechnung im sozialistischen Gemeinwesen" (*Archiv für Sozialwissenschaft*, Vol. XLVII, pp. 86-121). Publisher's Note: Mises' essay was translated into English by S. Adler and included in *Collectivist Economic Planning: Critical Studies on the Possibilities of Socialism* by N. G. Pierson, Ludwig von Mises, Georg Halm, and Enrico Barone; edited, with an Introduction and a Concluding Essay by F. A. Hayek. London: Routledge & Kegan Paul Ltd., 1935. 293 pp. bibl. Mises' essay, titled "Economic Calculation in the Socialist Commonwealth" in English, appears on pages 87–130.

[6] Čuhel, *Zur Lehre von den Bedürfnissen* (Innsbruck, 1907), p. 198.

becomes the unit of calculation. This involves a threefold advantage. In the first place we are able to take as the basis of calculation the valuation of all individuals participating in trade. The subjective valuation of one individual is not directly comparable with the subjective valuation of others. It only becomes so as an exchange value arising from the interplay of the subjective valuations of all who take part in buying and selling. Secondly, calculations of this sort provide a control upon the appropriate use of the means of production. They enable those who desire to calculate the cost of complicated processes of production to see at once whether they are working as economically as others. If, under prevailing market prices, they cannot carry through the process at a profit, it is a clear proof that others are better able to turn to good account the instrumental goods in question. Finally, calculations based upon exchange values enable us to reduce values to a common unit. And since the higgling of the market establishes substitution relations between commodities, any commodity desired can be chosen for this purpose. In a money economy, money is the commodity chosen.

Money calculations have their limits. Money is neither a yardstick of value nor of prices. Money does not *measure* value. Nor are prices measured in money: they are amounts of money. And, although those who describe money as a "standard of deferred payments" naively assume it to be so, as a commodity it is not stable in value. The relation between money and goods perpetually fluctuates not only on the "goods side," but on the "money side" also. As a rule, indeed, these fluctuations are not too violent. They do not too much impair the economic calculus, because under a state of continuous change of all economic conditions, this calculus takes in view only comparatively short periods, in which "sound money" at least does not change its purchasing power to any very great extent.

The deficiencies of money calculations arise for the most part, not because 116
they are made in terms of a general medium of exchange, money, but because they are based on exchange values rather than on subjective use-values. For this reason all elements of value which are not the subject of exchange elude such computations. If, for example, we are considering whether a hydraulic power-works would be profitable we cannot include in the computation the damage which will be done to the beauty of the waterfalls unless the fall in values due to a fall in tourist traffic is taken into account. Yet we must certainly take such considerations into account when deciding whether the undertaking shall be carried out.

Considerations such as these are often termed "non-economic." And we may permit the expression for disputes about terminology gain nothing. But not all such considerations should be called irrational. The beauty of a place or of a building, the health of the race, the honour of individuals or nations, even if (because they are not dealt with on the market) they do not enter into exchange relations, are just as much motives of rational action, provided people think them significant, as those normally called economic. That they cannot enter into money calculations arises from the very nature of these calculations. But this does not in the least lessen the value of money calculations in ordinary economic matters. For all such moral goods are goods of the first order. We can value them directly; and therefore have no difficulty in taking them into account, even though they lie outside the sphere of money computations. That they elude such computations does not make it any more difficult to bear them in mind. If we know precisely how much we have to pay for beauty, health, honour, pride, and the like, nothing need hinder us from giving them due consideration. Sensitive people may be pained to have to choose between the ideal and the material. But that is not the fault of a money economy. It is in the nature of things. For even where we can make judgments of value without money computations we cannot avoid this choice. Both isolated man and socialist communities would have to do likewise, and truly sensitive natures will never find it painful. Called upon to choose between bread and honour, they will never be at a loss how to act. If honour cannot be eaten, eating can at least be forgone for honour. Only such as fear the agony of choice because they secretly know that they could not forgo the material, will regard the necessity of choice as a profanation.

117 Money computations are only significant for purposes of economic calculation. Here they are used in order that the disposal of commodities may conform to the criterion of economy. And such calculations take account of commodities only in the proportions in which, under given conditions, they exchange for money. Every extension of the sphere of money calculation is misleading. It is misleading when in historical researches, it is employed as a measure of past commodity values. It is misleading when it is employed to evaluate the capital or national income of nations. It is misleading when it is employed to estimate the value of things which are not exchangeable as, for instance, when people attempt to estimate the loss due to emigration or war.[7] All these are dilettantisms—even when they are undertaken by the most competent economists.

But within these limits—and in practical life they are not overstepped—money calculation does all that we are entitled to ask of it. It provides a

---

[7] Wieser, *Über den Ursprung und die Hauptgesetze des wirtschaftlichen Wertes*, Vienna, 1884, pp. 185 ff.

guide amid the bewildering throng of economic possibilities. It enables us to extend judgments of value which apply directly only to consumption goods—or at best to production goods of the lowest order—to all goods of higher orders. Without it, all production by lengthy and roundabout processes would be so many steps in the dark.

Two things are necessary if computations of value in terms of money are to take place. First, not only goods ready for consumption but also goods of higher orders must be exchangeable. If this were not so, a system of exchange relationships could not emerge. It is true that if an isolated man is "exchanging" labour and flour for bread within his own house, the considerations he has to take into account are not different from those which would govern his actions if he were to exchange bread for clothes on the market. And it is, therefore, quite correct to regard all economic activity, even the economic activity of isolated man, as exchange. But no single man, be he the greatest genius ever born, has an intellect capable of deciding the relative importance of each one of an infinite number of goods of higher orders. No individual could so discriminate between the infinite number of alternative methods of production that he could make direct judgments of their relative value without auxiliary calculations. In societies based on the division of labour, the dis- 118
tribution of property rights effects a kind of mental division of labour, without which neither economy nor systematic production would be possible.

In the second place, there must be a general medium of exchange, a money, in use. And this must serve as an intermediary in the exchange of production goods equally with the rest. If this were not so, it would be impossible to reduce all exchange relationships to a common denominator.

Only under very simple conditions is it possible to dispense with money calculations. In the narrow circle of a closed household, where the father is able to supervise everything, he may be able to evaluate alterations in methods of production without having recourse to money reckoning. For, in such circumstances, production is carried on with relatively little capital. Few roundabout methods of production are employed. As a rule production is concerned with consumption goods, or goods of higher orders not too far removed from consumption goods. Division of labour is still in its earliest stages. The labourer carries through the production of a commodity from beginning to end. In an advanced society all this is changed. It is impossible to argue from the experience of primitive societies that under modern conditions we can dispense with money.

In the simple conditions of a closed household, it is possible to survey the whole process of production from beginning to end. It is possible to judge whether one particular process gives more consumption goods than another.

But, in the incomparably more complicated conditions of our own day, this is no longer possible. True, a socialistic society could see that 1000 litres of wine were better than 800 litres. It could decide whether or not 1000 litres of wine were to be preferred to 500 litres of oil. Such a decision would involve no calculation. The will of some man would decide. But the real business of economic administration, the adaptation of means to ends only begins when such a decision is taken. And only economic calculation makes this adaptation possible. Without such assistance, in the bewildering chaos of alternative materials and processes the human mind would be at a complete loss. Whenever we had to decide between different processes or different centres of production, we would be entirely at sea.[8]

119 To suppose that a socialist community could substitute calculations in kind for calculations in terms of money is an illusion. In a community that does not practice exchange, calculations in kind can never cover more than consumption goods. They break down completely where goods of higher order are concerned. Once society abandons free pricing of production goods rational production becomes impossible. Every step that leads away from private ownership of the means of production and the use of money is a step away from rational economic activity.

It was possible to overlook all this because such Socialism as we know at first hand exists only, one might say, in socialistic oases in what, for the rest, is a system based upon free exchange and the use of money. To this extent, indeed, we may agree with the otherwise untenable socialist contention—it is only employed for propagandist purposes—that nationalized and municipalized undertakings within an otherwise capitalist system are not Socialism. For the existence of a surrounding system of free pricing supports such concerns in their business affairs to such an extent that in them the essential peculiarity of economic activity under Socialism does not come to light. In State and municipal undertakings it is still possible to carry out technical improvements, because it is possible to observe the effects of similar improvements in similar private undertakings at home and abroad. In such concerns it is still possible to ascertain the advantages of reorganization because they are surrounded by a society which is still based upon private ownership in the means of production and the use of money. It is still possible for them to keep books and make calculations which for similar concerns in a purely socialist environment would be entirely out of the question.

[8] Gottl-Otthlienfeld, "Wirtschaft und Technik," *Grundriss der Sozialökonomik*, II (Tübingen, 1914), p. 216.

Without calculation, economic activity is impossible. Since under Socialism economic calculation is impossible, under Socialism there can be no economic activity in our sense of the word. In small and insignificant things rational action might still persist. But, for the most part, it would no longer be possible to speak of rational production. In the absence of criteria of rationality, production could not be consciously economical.

For some time possibly the accumulated tradition of thousands of years
of economic freedom would preserve the art of economic administration from
complete disintegration. Men would preserve the old processes, not because
they were rational, but because they were sanctified by tradition. In the 120
meantime, however, changing conditions would make them irrational. They
would become uneconomical as the result of changes brought about by the
general decline of economic thought. It is true that production would no
longer be "anarchical." The command of a supreme authority would govern
the business of supply. Instead of the economy of "anarchical" production
the senseless order of an irrational machine would be supreme. The wheels
would go round, but to no effect.

Let us try to imagine the position of a socialist community. There will be hundreds and thousands of establishments in which work is going on. A minority of these will produce goods ready for use. The majority will produce capital goods and semi-manufactures. All these establishments will be closely connected. Each commodity produced will pass through a whole series of such establishments before it is ready for consumption. Yet in the incessant press of all these processes the economic administration will have no real sense of direction. It will have no means of ascertaining whether a given piece of work is really necessary, whether labour and material are not being wasted in completing it. How would it discover which of two processes was the more satisfactory? At best, it could compare the quantity of ultimate products. But only rarely could it compare the expenditure incurred in their production. It would know exactly—or it would imagine it knew—what it wanted to produce. It ought therefore to set about obtaining the desired results with the smallest possible expenditure. But to do this it would have to be able to make calculations. And such calculations must be calculations of value. They could not be merely "technical," they could not be calculations of the objective use-value of goods and services; this is so obvious that it needs no further demonstration.

Under a system based upon private ownership in the means of production, the scale of values is the outcome of the actions of every independent member of society. Everyone plays a two-fold part in its establishment first as a consumer, secondly as producer. As consumer, he establishes the valuation

of goods ready for consumption. As producer, he guides production-goods into those uses in which they yield the highest product. In this way all goods of higher orders also are graded in the way appropriate to them under the existing conditions of production and the demands of society. The interplay of these two processes ensures that the economic principle is observed in
121 both consumption and production. And, in this way, arises the exactly graded system of prices which enables everyone to frame his demand on economic lines.

Under Socialism, all this must necessarily be lacking. The economic administration may indeed know exactly what commodities are needed most urgently. But this is only half the problem. The other half, the valuation of the means of production, it cannot solve. It can ascertain the value of the totality of such instruments. That is obviously equal to the value of the satisfactions they afford. If it calculates the loss that would be incurred by withdrawing them, it can also ascertain the value of single instruments of production. But it cannot assimilate them to a common price denominator, as can be done under a system of economic freedom and money prices.

It is not necessary that Socialism should dispense altogether with money. It is possible to conceive arrangements permitting the use of money for the exchange of consumers goods. But since the prices of the various factors of production (including labour) could not be expressed in money, money could play no part in economic calculations.[9]

Suppose, for instance, that the socialist commonwealth was contemplating a new railway line. Would a new railway line be a good thing? If so, which of many possible routes should it cover? Under a system of private ownership we could use money calculations to decide these questions. The new line would cheapen the transportation of certain articles, and, on this basis, we could estimate whether the reduction in transport charges would be great enough to counterweigh the expenditure which the building and running of the line would involve. Such a calculation could be made only in money. We could not do it by comparing various classes of expenditure and savings in kind. If it is out of the question to reduce to a common unit the quantities of various kinds of skilled and unskilled labour, iron, coal, building materials of different kinds, machinery and the other things which the building and upkeep of railways necessitate, then it is impossible to make them the subject

[9] Neurath too admitted this. (*Durch die Kriegswirtschaft zur Naturalwirtschaft* [Munich, 1919], pp. 216 ff.) He asserts that every complete administrative economy (planned economy) is ultimately a natural economy (barter system). "To socialize therefore means to advance the natural economy." Neurath, however, did not recognize the insurmountable difficulties economic calculation would encounter in the socialist community.

of economic calculation. We can make systematic economic plans only when
all the commodities which we have to take into account can be assimilated 122
to money. True, money calculations are incomplete. True, they have profound deficiencies. But we have nothing better to put in their place. And under sound monetary conditions they suffice for practical purposes. If we abandon them, economic calculation becomes absolutely impossible.

This is not to say that the socialist community would be entirely at a loss. It would decide for or against the proposed undertaking and issue an edict. But, at best, such a decision would be based on vague valuations. It could not be based on exact calculations of value.

A stationary society could, indeed, dispense with these calculations. For there, economic operations merely repeat themselves. So that, if we assume that the socialist system of production were based upon the last state of the system of economic freedom which it superseded, and that no changes were to take place in the future, we could indeed conceive a rational and economic Socialism. But only in theory. A stationary economic system can never exist. Things are continually changing, and the stationary state, although necessary as an aid to speculation, is a theoretical assumption to which there is no counterpart in reality. And, quite apart from this, the maintenance of such a connection with the last state of the exchange economy would be out of the question, since the transition to Socialism with its equalization of incomes would necessarily transform the whole "set" of consumption and production. And then we have a socialist community which must cross the whole ocean of possible and imaginable economic permutations without the compass of economic calculation.

All economic change, therefore, would involve operations the value of which could neither be predicted beforehand nor ascertained after they had taken place. Everything would be a leap in the dark. Socialism is the renunciation of rational economy.

4

The Capitalist Economy

The terms "Capitalism" and "Capitalistic Production" are political catchwords. They were invented by socialists, not to extend knowledge, but to
carp, to criticize, to condemn. Today, they have only to be uttered to conjure 123
up a picture of the relentless exploitation of wage-slaves by the pitiless rich.

They are scarcely ever used save to imply a disease in the body-politic. From a scientific point of view, they are so obscure and ambiguous that they have no value whatever. Their users agree only in this, that they indicate the characteristics of the modern economic system. But wherein these characteristics consist is always a matter of dispute. Their use, therefore, is entirely pernicious, and the proposal to extrude them altogether from economic terminology, and to leave them to the matadors of popular agitation, deserves serious consideration.[10]

If, nevertheless, we do desire to discover for them a precise application, we should start from the idea of capital calculations. And since we are concerned only with the analysis of actual economic phenomena, and not with economic theory—where "capital" is often used in a sense specially extended for particular purposes—we must first ask what significance is attached to the term in business practice. There we find it used only for purposes of economic calculation. It serves to bring the original properties of a concern under one denomination, whether they consisted of money or were only expressed in money.[11] The object of its computations is to enable us to ascertain how much the value of this property has altered in the course of business operations. The concept of capital is derived from economic calculation. Its true home is accountancy—the chief instrument of commercial rationality. Calculation in terms of money is an essential element of the concept of capital.[12]

If the term capitalism is used to designate an economic system in which production is governed by capital calculations, it acquires a special significance for defining economic activity. Understood thus, it is by no means misleading to speak of Capitalism and capitalistic methods of production, and expressions such as the capitalistic spirit and the anti-capitalistic disposition acquire a rigidly circumscribed connotation. Capitalism is better suited to be the antithesis of Socialism than Individualism, which is often used in this way. As a rule those who contrast Socialism with Individualism
124 proceed on the tacit assumption that there is a contradiction between the interests of the individual and the interest of society, and that, while Socialism takes the public welfare as its object, individualism serves the interests of particular people. And since this is one of the gravest sociological fallacies

[10] Passow, *Kapitalismus, eine begrifflich-terminologische Studie* (Jena, 1918), pp. 1 ff. In the 2nd edition, published 1927, Passow expressed the opinion (p. 15, note 2), in view of the most recent literature, that the term "Capitalism" might in time gradually lose the moral colouring.

[11] Carl Menger, "Zur Theorie des Kapitals" (*Jahrbücher für Nationalökonomie und Statistik*, Vol. XVII), p. 41.

[12] Passow, *op. cit.* (2nd edition), pp. 49 ff.

we must avoid carefully any form of expression which might allow it secretly to creep in.

According to Passow, where the term Capitalism is used correctly, the association it is intended to convey is usually bound up with the development and spread of large scale undertakings.[13] We may admit this—even if it is rather difficult to reconcile with the fact that people customarily speak of "*Grosskapital*" and "*Grosskapitalist*" and then of "*Kleinkapitalisten*." But, if we recollect that only capital calculation made the growth of giant enterprise and undertakings possible, this does not in any way invalidate the definitions we propose.

5

The Narrower Concept of the "Economic"

The common habit of economists of distinguishing between "economic" or "purely economic" and "non-economic" action is just as unsatisfactory as the old distinction between ideal and material goods. For willing and acting are unitary. All ends conflict among themselves and it is this conflict which ranges them in one scale. Not only the satisfaction of wishes, desires and impulses that can be attained through interaction with the external world, but the satisfaction also of ideal needs must be judged by one criterion. In life we have to choose between the "ideal" and the "material." It is, therefore, just as essential to make the former subject to a unitary criterion of values as the latter. In choosing between bread and honour, faith and wealth, love and money, we submit both alternatives to one test.

It is, therefore, illegitimate to regard the "economic" as a definite sphere of human action which can be sharply delimited from other spheres of action. Economic activity is rational activity. And since complete satisfaction is impossible, the sphere of economic activity is coterminous with the sphere of rational action. It consists firstly in valuation of ends, and then in the valuation of the means leading to these ends. All economic activity depends,
therefore, upon the existence of ends. Ends dominate economy and alone *125*
give it meaning.

Since the economic principle applies to all human action, it is necessary to be very careful when distinguishing, within its sphere, between "purely

[13] Passow, *op. cit.* (2nd edition), pp. 132 ff.

economic" and other kinds of action. Such a division is indeed indispensable for many scientifc purposes. It singles out one particular end and contrasts it with all others. This end—at this point we need not discuss whether it is ultimate or not—is the attainment of the greatest possible product measured in money. It is, therefore, impossible to assign it a specially delimited sphere of action. It is true that for each individual it has such a delimited sphere, but this varies in extent according to the general outlook of the individual concerned. It is one thing for the man to whom honour is dear. It is another for him who sells his friend for gold. Neither the nature of the end nor the peculiarity of the means is what justifies the distinction, but merely the special nature of the methods employed. Only the fact that it uses exact calculation distinguishes "purely economic" from other action.

The sphere of the "purely economic" is nothing more and nothing less than the sphere of money calculation. The fact that in a certain field of action it enables us to compare means with minute exactitude down to the smallest detail means so much both for thought and action that we tend to invest this kind of action with special importance. It is easy to overlook the fact that such a distinction is only a distinction in the *technique* of thought and action and in no way a distinction in the ultimate end of action—which is unitary. The failure of all attempts to exhibit the "economic" as a special department of the rational and within that to discover still another sharply defined department, the "purely economic," is no fault of the analytical apparatus employed. There can be no doubt that great subtlety of analysis has been concentrated on this problem, and the fact that it has not been solved clearly indicates that the question is one to which no satisfactory answer can be given. The sphere of the "economic" is plainly the same as the sphere of the rational: and the sphere of the "purely economic" is nothing but the sphere in which money calculation is possible.

In the last resort the individual can acknowledge one end, and one end only: the attainment of the greatest satisfaction. This expression includes the satisfying of all kinds of human wants and desires, regardless of whether
126 they are "material" or immaterial (moral). In the place of the word "satisfaction" we could employ the word "happiness," had we not to fear the misunderstandings, for which the controversy on Hedonism and Eudaemonism was responsible.

Satisfaction is subjective. Modern social philosophy has emphasized this so sharply in contrast to former theories that there is a tendency to forget that the physiological structure of mankind and the unity of outlook and emotion arising from tradition create a far-reaching similarity of views regarding wants and the means to satisfy them. It is precisely this similarity of views which makes society possible. Because they have common aims, men are able to live together. Against this fact that the majority of ends (and those the most important) are common to the great mass of mankind, the fact that some ends are only entertained by a few is of subordinate importance.

The customary division between economic and non-economic motives is, therefore, invalidated by the fact that on the one hand, the end of economic activity lies outside the range of economics, and on the other, that all rational activity is economic. Nevertheless, there is good justification for separating "purely economic" activities (that is to say, activity susceptible of valuation in money) from all other forms of activity. For, as we have already seen, outside the sphere of money calculation there remain only intermediate ends which are capable of evaluation by immediate inspection: and once this sphere is left, it is necessary to have recourse to such judgments. It is the recognition of this necessity which provides the occasion for the distinction we have been discussing.

If, for example, a nation desires to make war, it is illegitimate to regard the desire as necessarily irrational because the motive for making war lies outside those customarily considered as "economic"—as might be the case, e.g. with wars of religion. If the nation decides on the war with complete knowledge of all the facts because it judges that the end in view is more important than the sacrifice involved, and because it regards war as the most suitable means of obtaining it, then war cannot be regarded as irrational. It is not necessary at this point to decide whether this supposition is ever true or if it ever can be true. It is precisely this which has to be examined when one comes to choose between war and peace. And it is precisely with a view to introducing clarity into such an examination that the distinction we have been discussing has been introduced.

It is only necessary to remember how often wars or tariffs are recommended 127
as being "good business" from the "economic" point of view to realize how often this is forgotten. How much clearer would have been the political discussions of the last century if the distinction between the "purely economic" and the "non-economic" grounds of action had been kept in mind.

CHAPTER 6

The Organization of Production Under Socialism

1

The Socialization of the Means of Production

128 Under Socialism all the means of production are the property of the community. The community alone disposes of them and decides how to use them in production. The community produces, the products accrue to the community, and the community decides how those products are to be used.

Modern socialists, espcially those of the Marxian persuasion, lay great emphasis on designating the socialist community as Society, and therefore on describing the transfer of the means of production to the control of the community as the "Socialization of the means of production." In itself the expression is unobjectionable but in the connection in which it is used it is particularly designed to obscure one of the most important problems of Socialism.

The word "society," with its corresponding adjective "social," has three separate meanings. It implies, first, the abstract idea of social interrelationships, and secondly, the concrete conception of a union of the individuals themselves. Between these two sharply different meanings, a third has been interposed in ordinary speech: the abstract society is conceived as personified in such expressions as "human society," "civil society."

Now Marx uses the term with all these meanings. This would not matter as long as he made the distinction quite clear. But he does just the opposite. He interchanges them with a conjurer's skill whenever it appears to suit him. When he talks of the social character of capitalistic production he is using social in its abstract sense. When he speaks of the society which suffers during crises he means the personified society of mankind. But when he speaks of the society which is to expropriate the expropriators and socialize

the means of production he means an actual social union. And all the meanings are interchanged in the links of his argument whenever he has to prove the unprovable. The reason for all this is in order to avoid using the 129
term State or its equivalent, since this word has an unpleasant sound to all those lovers of freedom and democracy, whose support the Marxian does not wish to alienate at the outset. A programme which would give the State the general responsibility and direction of all production has no prospect of acceptance in these circles. It follows that the Marxist must continually find a phraseology which disguises the essence of the programme, which succeeds in concealing the unbridgeable abyss dividing democracy and Socialism. It does not say much for the perception of men who lived in the decades immediately preceding the World War that they did not see through this sophistry.

The modern doctrine of the state understands by the word "State" an authoritative unit, an apparatus of compulsion characterized not by its aims but by its form. But Marxism has arbitrarily limited the meaning of the word State, so that it does not include the Socialistic State. Only those states and forms of state organization are called the State which arouse the dislike of the socialist writers. For the future organization to which they aspire the term is rejected indignantly as dishonourable and degrading. It is called "Society." In this way the Marxian social democracy could at one and the same time contemplate the destruction of the existing State machine, fiercely combat all anarchistic movements, and pursue a policy which led directly to an all powerful state.[1]

Now it does not matter in the least what particular name is given to the coercive apparatus of the socialistic community. If we use the word "State" we have a term in common use, except in the quite uncritical Marxian literature, an expression which is generally understood and which evokes the idea it is intended to evoke. But there is no disadvantage in avoiding this term if we wish, since it arouses mixed feelings in many people, and in substituting the expression "community." The choice of terminology is purely a matter of style, and has no practical importance.

What is important is the problem of the organization of this socialistic State or community. When dealing with the concrete expression of the will of the State, the English language provides a more subtle distinction by permitting us to use the term government instead of the term state. Nothing is better designed to avoid the mysticism which in this connection has been fostered 130

[1] See the critique of Kelsen, "Staat und Gesellschaft," in *Sozialismus und Staat* (Leipzig, 1923), pp. 11 ff. and pp. 20 ff.

by Marxian usages to the highest degree. For the Marxists talk glibly about expressing the will of society, without giving the slightest hint how 'society' can proceed to will and act. Yet of course the community can only act through organs which it has created.

Now it follows from the very conception of the socialistic community that the organ of control must be unitary. A socialist community can have only one ultimate organ of control which combines all economic and other governmental functions. Of course this organ can be subdivided and there can be subordinate offices to which definite instructions are transmitted. But the unitary expression of the common will, which is the essential object of the socialization of the means of production and of production, necessarily implies that all offices entrusted with the supervision of different affairs shall be subordinate to one office. This office must have supreme authority to resolve all variations from the common purpose and unify the executive aim. How it is constituted, and how the general will succeeds in expressing itself in and by it, is of minor importance in the investigation of our particular problem. It does not matter whether this organ is an absolute prince or an assembly of all citizens organized as a direct or indirect democracy. It does not matter how this organ conceives its will and expresses it. For our purpose we must consider this as accomplished and we need not spend any time over the question how it can be accomplished, whether it can be accomplished or whether Socialism is already doomed because it cannot be accomplished.

At the outset of our inquiry we must postulate that the socialistic community is without foreign relations. It embraces the whole world and its inhabitants. If we conceive it as limited, so that it comprises only a part of the world and the inhabitants therein, we must assume that it has no economic relations with the territories and peoples outside its boundaries. We are to discuss the problem of the isolated socialistic community. The implications of the contemporaneous existence of several socialistic communities will be dealt with when we have surveyed the problem in complete generality.

131

2

Economic Calculation in the Socialist Community

The theory of economic calculation shows that in the socialistic community economic calculation would be impossible.

In any large undertaking the individual works or departments are partly independent in their accounts. They can reckon the cost of materials and labour, and it is possible at any time for an individual group to strike a separate balance and to sum up the results of its activity in figures. In this way it is possible to ascertain with what success each separate branch has been operated and thereby to make decisions concerning the reorganization, limitations or extension of existing branches or the establishment of new ones. Some mistakes are of course unavoidable in these calculations. They arise partly from the difficulty of allocating overhead costs. Other mistakes again arise from the necessity of calculating from insufficiently determined data, as, e.g. when in calculating the profitability of a certain process, depreciation of the machinery employed is determined by assuming a certain working life for the machine. But all such errors can be confined within certain narrow limits which do not upset the total result of the calculation. Whatever uncertainty remains is attributed to the uncertainty of future conditions inevitable in any imaginable state of affairs.

It seems natural then to ask why individual branches of production in a socialistic community should not make separate accounts in the same manner. But this is impossible. Separate accounts for a single branch of one and the same undertaking are possible only when prices for all kinds of goods and services are established in the market and furnish a basis of reckoning. Where there is no market there is no price system, and where there is no price system there can be no economic calculation.

Some may think that it is possible to permit exchange between the different groups of undertakings so as to establish a system of exchange relations (prices) and in this way create a basis for economic calculation in the socialistic community. Thus within a framework of a unitary economic system which does not recognize private property in the means of production, individual branches of industry with separate administration could be set up, subject
of course, to the supreme economic authority, but able to transfer to each 132
other goods and services for a consideration reckoned in a common medium of exchange. This, roughly, is how people conceive the productive organization of socialistic industry when they speak nowadays of complete socialization and the like. But here again the decisive point is evaded. Exchange relations in productive goods can only be established on the basis of private property in the means of production. If the Coal Syndicate delivers coal to the Iron Syndicate a price can be fixed only if both syndicates own the means of production in the industry. But that would not be Socialism but Syndicalism.

For those socialist writers who accept the labour theory of value the problem is, of course, quite simple.

"As soon," says Engels, "as Society has taken possession of the means of production and applies them to direct social production the labour of everyone, however different its specific use may be, will immediately become direct social labour. The amount of social labour inherent in any product does not require to be ascertained in any roundabout way: everyday experience will show how much of it on the average is necessary. Society can easily reckon how many hours of labour inhere in a steam engine, in a hectolitre of wheat of the last harvest, in a hundred square metres of cloth of a certain quality. Of course society will have to find out how much work is required for the manufacture of every article of consumption. It will have to base its plans on a consideration of the means of production at its disposal—and of course the labour force falls into this category. The utility of the different objects of consumption weighed against one another and against the labour necessary for their production will finally determine the plan. The people will decide everything quite easily without the intervention of the much-vaunted value."[2]

It is not part of our business here to restate the critical arguments against the labour theory of value. They interest us at this point only in so far as they enable us to judge the possibility of making labour the basis of economic calculation in a socialistic community.

At first sight it would appear that calculations based on labour take into account the natural conditions of production, as well as conditions arising
133 from the human element. The Marxian concept of the socially necessary labour time takes the law of diminishing returns into consideration in so far as it results from different natural conditions of production. If the demand for a commodity increases and less favourable natural conditions have to be exploited, then the average socially necessary time for the production of a unit also increases. If more favourable conditions of production are discovered then the necessary quantum of social labour declines.[3] But this is not enough. Computation of changes in marginal labour costs only take account of natural conditions in so far as they influence labour costs. Beyond that, the "labour"

---

[2] Engels, *Herrn Eugen Dührings Umwälzung der Wissenschaft,* pp. 335 ff. Publisher's Note: In the English edition, *Anti-Dühring: Herrn Eugen Dühring's Revolution in Science,* pp. 429 ff.

[3] Marx, *Das Kapital,* Vol. 1, pp. 5 ff. Publisher's Note: In English, see Marx, Karl. *Capital: A Critique of Political Economy.* 3 volumes. Vol. I. The Process of Capitalist Production. Translated from the 3rd German edition by Samuel Moore and Edward Aveling. Edited by Frederick Engels. Revised and amplified according to the 4th German edition by Ernest Untermann. Chicago: Charles H. Kerr & Co., 1906. (Note: This Volume I also reprinted by Random House as a Modern Library Giant, with same paging as the Kerr edition.) Vol. II. The Process of Circulation of Capital. Vol.III. The Process of Capitalist Production as a Whole. Both Volumes II and III were translated by Ernest Untermann and edited by Frederick Engels. Both were published by the same Charles H. Kerr & Co. of Chicago in 1909. In this footnote, pp. 5 ff. refers to pp. 45 ff. in the English Vol. I.

calculation breaks down. It leaves, for instance, the consumption of material factors of production entirely out of account. Suppose the socially necessary labour time for producing two commodities P and Q is ten hours, and that the production of a unit both of P and of Q requires material A, one unit of which is produced by one hour of socially necessary labour, and that the production of P involves two units of A and eight hours of labour, and of Q one unit of A and nine hours of labour. In a calculation based on labour time P and Q are equivalent, but in a calculation based on value P must be worth more than Q. The former calculation is false. Only the latter corresponds to the essence and object of economic calculation. It is true that this surplus by which the value of P exceeds that of Q, this material substratum, "is furnished by nature without the help of man,"[4] but provided it is present only in such quantities that it becomes an economic factor it must also in some form enter into economic calculation.

The second deficiency of the labour calculation theory is that it disregards differences in the quality of labour. For Marx all human labour is economically homogeneous, because it is always the "productive expenditure of human brain, muscles, nerves, hands, etc." "Skilled labour is only intensified, or rather multiplied simple labour, so that a small quantity of skilled labour equals a larger quantity of simple labour. Experience shows that this resolution of skilled into simple constantly happens. A commodity may be the product of highly skilled labour, but its value equates it to the product of simple labour and represents only a certain quantity of simple labour."[5] Böhm-Bawerk was justified in describing this argument as a masterpiece of
astounding naivety.[6] In criticizing it one may conveniently leave undecided 134
whether one can discover a unitary physiological measure of all human labour, physical as well as "mental." For it is certain that between men themselves there are differences of capability and skill which result in differing qualities of the goods and services produced. What is ultimately decisive for the solution of the problem of the feasibility of using labour as a basis of economic calculation is the question whether one can assimilate different kinds of work to a common denominator without a valuation of the products by the consumer. It is clear that the argument which Marx brings to bear on this point has failed. Experience does indeed show that commodities enter

[4] *Ibid.*, pp. 9 ff. Publisher's Note: pp. 50 ff. in English translation.
[5] *Ibid.*, pp. 10 ff. Publisher's Note: pp. 51–52 in English translation.
[6] Böhm-Bawerk, *Kapital und Kapitalzins*, Vol. I, 3rd ed. (Innsbruck, 1914), p. 531. Publisher's Note: Böhm-Bawerk's three volume work in English is: Böhm-Bawerk, Eugen von. *Capital and Interest*. 3 volumes. (South Holland, Illinois: Libertarian Press, 1959.) Volume I. *History and Critique of Interest Theories*. Translated by George D. Huncke and Hans F. Sennholz.

into exchange regardless of the question whether they are the products of skilled or simple labour. But this would only prove that a definite quantity of simple labour is equal to a definite quantity of skilled labour if it were proved that labour is the source of exchange value. But not only is this unproven; it is exactly what Marx originally set out to prove. The fact that in exchange a substitute relation between simple and skilled labour has arisen in the form of wage rates—a point to which Marx does not here allude—is not in the least a proof of this homogeneity. This process of equating is a result of the working of the market, not its presupposition. Calculations based on labour cost rather than on monetary values would have to establish a purely arbitrary relation by which to resolve skilled into simple labour, and this would make them useless as an instrument for the economic organization of resources.

It was long thought that the labour theory of value provided a necessary ethical basis for the demand to socialize the means of production. We know now that this was an error. Although the majority of socialists have adopted this view and although even Marx with his professedly non-ethical standpoint could not shake it off, it is clear that, on the one hand, the political demands for the introduction of the socialistic method of production neither need nor receive support from the labour theory of value, and, on the other hand, that those who hold different views on the nature and cause of value can also have socialistic tendencies. But from another point of view, the labour
135 theory of value is still an essential dogma for the advocates of the socialistic method of production. For socialistic production in a society based on division of labour seems practicable only if there is an objective recognizable unit of value which would enable economic calculations to be made in an exchangeless and moneyless community and labour seems the only thing to serve this purpose.

3

Recent Socialist Doctrines and the Problems of Economic Calculation

The problem of economic calculation is the fundamental problem of Socialism. That for decades people could write and talk about Socialism without touching this problem only shows how devastating were the effects of the

Marxian prohibition on scientific scrutiny of the nature and working of a socialist economy.[7]

To prove that economic calculation would be impossible in the socialist community is to prove also that Socialism is impracticable. Everything brought forward in favour of Socialism during the last hundred years, in thousands of writings and speeches, all the blood which has been spilt by the supporters of Socialism, cannot make socialism workable. The masses may long for it ever so ardently, innumerable revolutions and wars may be fought for it, still it will never be realised. Every attempt to carry it out will lead to syndicalism or, by some other route, to chaos, which will quickly dissolve the society, based upon the division of labour, into tiny autarkous groups.

The discovery of this fact is clearly most inconvenient for the socialist parties, and socialists of all kinds have poured out attempts to refute my arguments and to invent a system of economic calculation for Socialism. They have not been successful. They have not produced a single new 136
argument which I have not already taken account of.[8] Nothing has shaken the proof that under Socialism economic calculation is impossible.[9]

The attempt of the Russian Bolsheviks to transfer Socialism from a party

---

[7] We may point out here that as early as 1854 Gossen knew "that only through private property is the measure found for determining the quantity of each commodity which it would be best to produce under given conditions. Therefore, the central authority, proposed by the communists, for the distribution of the various tasks and their reward, would very soon find that it had taken on a job the solution of which far surpasses the abilities of individual men." (Gossen, *Entwicklung der Gesetze des menschlichen Verkehrs*, new ed., [Berlin, 1889] p. 231.) Pareto (*Cours d'Économie Politique*, Vol. II, Lausanne, 1897, pp. 364 ff.) and Barone ("Il Ministro della Produzione nello Stato Coletivista" in *Giornale degli Economisti*, Vol. XXXVII, 1908, pp. 409 ff.) did not penetrate to the core of the problem. Pierson clearly and completely recognized the problem in 1902. See his *Das Wertproblem in der sozialistischen Gesellschaft* (German translation by Hayek, *Zeitschrift für Volkswirtschaft*, New Series, Vol. IV, 1925, pp. 607 ff.) Publisher's Note: Both the Barone article ("The Ministry of Production in the Collectivist State," pp. 245–290) and the Pierson article ("The Problem of Value in the Socialist Society," pp. 41–85) are included in the Hayek edited *Collectivist Economic Planning*.

[8] I have briefly discussed the most important of these replies in two short essays—"Neue Beiträge zum Problem der sozialistischen Wirtschaftsrechnung" (*Archiv für Sozialwissenschaft*, Vol. LI, pp. 488–500) and "Neue Schriften zum Problem der sozialistischen Wirtschaftsrechnung" (*Ibid.*, Vol. LX, pp. 187–90. Publisher's Note: "Neue Beiträge zum Problem der sozialistischen Wirtschaftsrechnung" appears in part as the Appendix of this book on p. 473. The second essay mentioned by Mises in this footnote was published in 1928 and has not been translated into English. The essay was a review of recent literature on economic calculations under socialism.

[9] In scientific literature there is no more doubt about this. See Max Weber, "Wirtschaft und Gesellschaft" (*Grundriss der Sozialökonomik*, Vol. III), Tübingen, 1922, pp. 45–59; Adolf Weber, *Allgemeine Volkswirtschaftslehre*, 4th ed., Munich and Leipzig, 1932, Vol. II, pp. 369 ff.; Brutzkus,

programme into real life has not encountered the problem of economic calculation under Socialism, for the Soviet Republics exist within a world which forms money prices for all means of production. The rulers of the Soviet Republics base the calculations on which they make their decisions on these prices. Without the help of these prices their actions would be aimless and planless. Only so far as they refer to this price system, are they able to calculate and keep books and prepare their plans. Their position is the same as the position of the state and municipal Socialism of other countries: the problem of socialist economic calculation has not yet arisen for them. State and municipal enterprises calculate with those prices of the means of production and of consumption goods which are formed on the market. Therefore it would be precipitate to conclude from the fact that municipal and state enterprises exist, that socialist economic calculation is possible.

We know indeed that socialist enterprises in single branches of production are practicable only because of the help they get from their non-socialist environment. State and municipality can carry on their own enterprises because the taxes which capitalist enterprises pay, cover their losses. In a similar manner Russia, which left to herself would long ago have collapsed, has been supported by finance from capitalist countries. But incomparably more important than this material assistance, which the capitalist economy gives to socialist enterprises, is the mental assistance. Without the basis for calculation which Capitalism places at the disposal of Socialism, in the shape of market prices, socialist enterprises would never be carried on, even within single branches of production or individual countries.

137 Socialist writers may continue to publish books about the decay of Capitalism and the coming of the socialist millennium: they may paint the evils of Capitalism in lurid colours and contrast with them an enticing picture of the blessings of a socialist society; their writings may continue to impress the thoughtless—but all this cannot alter the fate of the socialist idea.[10] The attempt to reform the world socialistically might destroy civilization. It would never set up a successful socialist community.

Die Lehren des Marxismus im Lichte der russischen Revolution, Berlin, 1928, pp. 21 ff.; C. A. Verrijn Stuart, "Winstbejag versus behoeftenbevrediging" *(Overdruk Economist*, Vol, 76 No. 1), pp. 18 ff.; Pohle-Halm, *Kapitalismus und Sozialismus*, 4th ed., Berlin, 1931, pp. 237 ff.

[10] Characteristic of this branch of literature is the recently published work of C. Landauer, *Planwirtschaft und Verkehrswirtschaft* (Munich and Leipzig, 1931). Here the writer deals with the problem of economic calculation quite naively, at first by asserting that in a socialist society "the individual enterprises . . . could buy from each other, just as capitalist enterprises buy from each other" (p. 114). A few pages on he explains that "besides this" the socialist state will "have to set up a control accountancy in kind"; the state will be "the only one able to do this because in

4

The Artificial Market as the Solution of the Problem of Economic Calculation

Some of the younger socialists believe that the socialist community could solve the problem of economic calculation by the creation of an artificial market for the means of production. They admit that it was an error on the part of the older socialists to have sought to realize Socialism through the suspension of the market and the abolition of pricing for goods of higher orders; they hold that it was an error to have seen in the suppression of the market and of the price system the essence of the socialistic ideal. And they contend that if it is not to degenerate into a meaningless chaos in which the whole of our civilization would disappear, the socialist community equally with the capitalistic community, must create a market in which all goods and services may be priced. On the basis of such arrangements, they think, the socialist community will be able to make its calculations as easily as the capitalist entrepreneurs.

Unfortunately the supporters of such proposals do not see (or perhaps *will* not see) that it is not possible to divorce the market and its functions in regard to the formation of prices from the working of a society which is based on private property in the means of production and in which, subject to the rules of such a society, the landlords, capitalists and entrepreneurs can dispose of their property as they think fit. For the motive force of the whole process which gives rise to market prices for the factors of production is the ceaseless search on the part of the capitalists and the entrepreneurs to 138
maximize their profits by serving the consumers' wishes. Without the striving of the entrepreneurs (including the shareholders) for profit, of the landlords for rent, of the capitalists for interest and the labourers for wages, the successful functioning of the whole mechanism is not to be thought of. It is only the prospect of profit which directs production into those channels in which the demands of the consumer are best satisfied at least cost. If the prospect of profit disappears the mechanism of the market loses its mainspring, for it is only this prospect which sets it in motion and maintains it in operation. The market is thus the focal point of the capitalist order of society; it is the essence of Capitalism. Only under Capitalism, therefore, is it possible; it cannot be "artificially" imitated under Socialism.

---

contrast to Capitalism it controls production itself" (p. 122). Landauer cannot understand that—and why—one is not permitted to add and subtract figures of different denominations. Such a case is, of course, beyond help.

The advocates of the artificial market, however, are of the opinion that an artificial market can be created by instructing the controllers of the different industrial units to act *as if* they were entrepreneurs in a capitalistic state. They argue that even under Capitalism the managers of joint stock companies work not for themselves but for the companies, that is to say, for the shareholders. Under Socialism, therefore, it would be possible for them to act in exactly the same way as before, with the same circumspection and devotion to duty. The only difference would be that under socialism the product of the manager's labours would go to the community rather than to the shareholders. In such a way, in contrast to all socialists who have written on the subject hitherto, especially the Marxians, they think it would be possible to construct a decentralized, as opposed to a centralized, Socialism.

In order to judge properly such proposals, it is necessary in the first place to realize that these controllers of individual industrial units would have to be appointed. Under Capitalism the managers of the joint stock companies are appointed either directly or indirectly by the shareholders. In so far as the shareholders give to the managers power to produce by the means of the company's (i.e. the shareholders') stock they are risking their own property or a part of their own property. The speculation (for it is necessarily a speculation) may succeed and bring profit; it may, however, misfire and
139 bring about the loss of the whole or a part of the capital concerned. This committing of one's own capital to a business whose outcome is uncertain and to men whose future ability is still a matter of conjecture whatever one may know of their past, is the essence of joint stock company enterprise.

Now it is a complete fallacy to suppose that the problem of economic calculation in a socialist community relates solely to matters which fall into the sphere of the daily business routine of managers of joint stock companies. It is clear that such a belief can only arise from exclusive concentration on the idea of a stationary economic system—a conception which no doubt is useful for the solution of many theoretical problems but which has no counterpart in fact and which, if exclusively regarded, can even be positively misleading. It is clear that under stationary conditions the problem of economic calculation does not really arise. When we think of the stationary society, we think of an economy in which all the factors of production are already used in such a way as, under the given conditions, to provide the maximum of the things which are demanded by consumers. That is to say, under stationary conditions there no longer exists a problem for economic calculation to solve. The essential function of economic calculation has *by hypothesis* already been performed. There is no need for an apparatus of calculation. To use a popular but not altogether satisfactory terminology we can say that the problem of economic calculation is of economic dynamics: it is no problem of economic statics.

The problem of economic calculation is a problem which arises in an economy which is perpetually subject to change, an economy which every day is confronted with new problems which have to be solved. Now in order to solve such problems it is above all necessary that capital should be withdrawn from particular lines of production, from particular undertakings and concerns and should be applied in other lines of production, in other undertakings and concerns. This is not a matter for the managers of joint stock companies, it is essentially a matter for the capitalists—the capitalists who buy and sell stocks and shares, who make loans and recover them, who make deposits in the banks and draw them out of the banks again, who speculate in all kinds of commodities. It is these operations of speculative capitalists which create those conditions of the money market, the stock
exchanges and the wholesale markets which have to be taken for granted by 140
the manager of the joint stock company, who, according to the socialist writers we are considering, is to be conceived as nothing but the reliable and conscientious servant of the company. It is the speculative capitalists who create the data to which he has to adjust his business and which therefore gives direction to his trading operations.

It follows therefore that it is a fundamental deficiency of all these socialistic constructions which invoke the "artificial market" and artificial competition as a way out of the problem of economic calculation, that they rest on the belief that the market for factors of production is affected only by producers buying and selling commodities. It is not possible to eliminate from such markets the influence of the supply of capital from the capitalists and the demand for capital by the entrepreneurs, without destroying the mechanism itself.

Faced with this difficulty, the socialist is likely to propose that the socialist state as owner of all capital and all means of production should simply direct capital to those undertakings which promise the highest return. The available capital, he will contend, should go to those undertakings which offer the highest rate of profit. But such a state of affairs would simply mean that those managers who were less cautious and more optimistic would receive capital to enlarge their undertakings while more cautious and more skeptical managers would go away empty-handed. Under Capitalism, the capitalist decides to whom he will entrust *his own* capital. The beliefs of the managers of joint stock companies regarding the future prospects of their undertakings and the hopes of project-makers regarding the profitability of their plans are not in any way decisive. The mechanism of the money market and the capital market decides. This indeed is its main task: to serve the economic system as a whole, to judge the profitability of alternative openings and not blindly to follow what the managers of particular concerns, limited by the narrow horizon of their own undertakings, are tempted to propose.

To understand this completely, it is essential to realise that the capitalist does not just invest his capital in those undertakings which offer high interest or high profit; he attempts rather to strike a balance between his desire for profit and his estimate of the risk of loss. He must exercise foresight. If he does not do so then he suffers losses—losses that bring it about that his
141 disposition over the factors of production is transferred to the hands of others who know better how to weigh the risks and the prospects of business speculation.

Now if it is to remain socialistic, the socialist State cannot leave to other hands that disposition over capital which permits the enlargement of existing undertakings, the contraction of others and the bringing into being of undertakings that are completely new. And it is scarcely to be assumed that socialists of whatever persuasion would seriously propose that this function should be made over to some group of people who would "simply" have the business of doing what capitalists and speculators do under capitalistic conditions, the only difference being that the product of their foresight should not belong to them but to the community. Proposals of this sort may well be made concerning the managers of joint stock companies. They can never be extended to capitalists and speculators, for no socialist would dispute that the function which capitalists and speculators perform under Capitalism, namely directing the use of capital goods into that direction in which they best serve the demands of the consumer, is only performed because they are under the incentive to preserve their property and to make profits which increase it or at least allow them to live without diminishing their capital.

It follows therefore that the socialist community can do nothing but place the disposition over capital in the hands of the State or to be exact in the hands of the men who, as the governing authority, carry out the business of the State. And that signifies elimination of the market, which indeed is the fundamental aim of Socialism, for the guidance of economic activity by the market implies organization of production and a distribution of the product according to that disposition of the spending power of individual members of society which makes itself felt on the market; that is to say, it implies precisely that which it is the goal of Socialism to eliminate.

If the socialists attempt to belittle the significance of the problem of eco-

nomic calculation in the Socialist community, on the ground that the forces of the market do not lead to ethically justifiable arrangements, they simply show that they do not understand the real nature of the problem. It is not a question of whether there shall be produced cannons or clothes, dwelling houses or churches, luxuries or subsistence. In any social order, even under Socialism, it can very easily be decided which kind and what number of
consumption goods should be produced. No one has ever denied that. But 142
once this decision has been made, there still remains the problem of ascertaining how the existing means of production can be used most effectively to produce these goods in question. In order to solve this problem it is necessary that there should be economic calculation. And economic calculation can only take place by means of money prices established in the market for production goods in a society resting on private property in the means of production. That is to say, there must exist money prices of land, raw materials, semimanufactures; that is to say, there must be money wages and interest rates.

Thus the alternative is still *either* Socialism or a market economy.

5

Profitability and Productivity

The economic activity of the socialist community is subject to the same external conditions as govern an economic system based on private property in the means of production or indeed any conceivable economic system. The economic principle applies to it in the same way as to any and to all economic systems: that is to say it recognizes an hierarchy of ends, and must therefore strive to achieve the more important before the less important. This is the essence of economic activity.

It is obvious that the production activities of the socialist community will involve not only labour but also material instruments of production. According to a very widespread custom, these material instruments of production are called capital. Capitalist production is that which adopts wise roundabout methods in contrast with a non-capitalistic production which goes directly to its end in a hand to mouth manner.[11] If we adhere to this

[11] Böhm-Bawerk, *Kapital und Kapitalzins*, Vol. II, 3rd ed. (Innsbruck, 1912), p. 21. Publisher's Note: The page in the English (Sennholz/Huncke) translation of Böhm-Bawerk, referred to here is page 14 in Volume II. Böhm-Bawerk, Eugen von. *Capital and Interest*. 3 volumes. South Holland, Illinois:

terminology, we must admit that the socialist community must also work with capital and will therefore produce capitalistically. Capital conceived as the intermediate products, which arise at the different stages of production
143 by indirect methods, would not, at any rate at first[12] be abolished by Socialism. It would merely be transferred from individual to common possession.

But if, as we have suggested above, we wish to understand by capitalistic production that economic system in which money-calculation is employed, so that we can summarize under the term capital a set of goods devoted to production and evaluated in terms of money, and can attempt to estimate the results of economic activity by the variations in the value of capital, then it is clear that socialist methods of production cannot be termed capitalistic. In quite another sense than the Marxians we can distinguish between socialistic and capitalistic methods of production, and between Socialism and Capitalism.

The characteristic feature of the capitalistic method of production, as it appears to socialists, is that the producer works to obtain a profit. Capitalistic production is production for profit, socialist production will be production for the satisfaction of needs. That capitalistic production aims at profit is quite true. But to achieve a profit, that is a result greater in value than the costs, must also be the aim of the socialist community. If economic activity is rationally directed, that is if it satisfies more urgent before less urgent needs, it has already achieved profits, since the cost, i.e. the value of the most important of the unsatisfied needs, is less than the result attained. In the capitalistic system profits can only be obtained if production meets a comparatively urgent demand. Whoever produces without attending to the relation between supply and demand fails to achieve the result at which he is aiming. To direct production towards profit simply means to direct it to satisfy other people's demand: in this sense it may be contrasted with isolated man's production for personal needs. But he also is working for profit in the sense used above. Between production for profit and production for needs there is no contrast.[13]

Libertarian Press, 1959. [Information re Vol. I above.] Volume II. *Positive Theory of Capital*. Translated by George D. Huncke; Hans F. Sennholz, Consulting Economist. Volume III. *Further Essays on Capital and Interest*. Translated by Hans F. Sennholz.

[12] The limitation comprised in the words "at first" is not intended to mean that Socialism will later on, say after attaining a "higher stage of the communist society," intentionally set about abolishing capital in the sense used here. Socialism can never plan the return to the life from hand to mouth. Rather do I want to point out here that Socialism must, by inner necessity, lead to the gradual consumption of capital.

[13] Pohle-Halm, *Kapitalismus und Sozialismus*, pp. 12 ff.

The contrasting of production for profit and production for needs is closely connected with the common practice of contrasting productivity and profitability or the "social" and "private" economic point of view. An economic action is said to be profitable if in the capitalist system it yields an excess of receipts over costs. An economic action is said to be productive when, seen from the point of view of a hypothetical socialist community, the yield exceeds the cost involved. Now in some cases productivity and profitability
do not coincide. Some economic acts which are profitable are not productive 144
and, vice versa, some are productive but not profitable. For those naively biased in favour of Socialism, as is the case even with most economists, this fact is sufficient to condemn the capitalistic order of society. Whatever a socialist community would do seems to them undisputably good and reasonable: that anything different can happen in a capitalistic society is, in their opinion, an abuse which cannot be tolerated. But an examination of the cases in which profitability and productivity are alleged not to coincide will show that this judgment is purely subjective, and that the scientific cloak with which it is invested is a sham.[14]

In the majority of cases in which it is usually assumed that there is a contrast between profitability and productivity no such contrast exists. This is true, for example, of profits from speculation. Speculation in the capitalist system performs a function which must be performed in any economic system however organized: it provides for the adjustment of supply and demand over time and space. The source of the profit of speculation is enhanced value which is independent of any particular form of economic organization. When the speculator purchases at a low price products which come on the market in comparatively large quantities and sells them at a higher price when the demand has again increased, his gains represent, from a business and from the economic point of view, an increase of value. That in a socialist order the community and not the individual would get this much grudged and maligned profit we do not deny. But that is not the significance of the problem in which we are interested. The point which concerns us here is that the alleged contrast between profitability and productivity does not exist in this case. Speculation performs an economic service which cannot conceivably be eliminated from any economic system. If it is eliminated, as socialists intend to do, then some other organization must take over its functions: the community itself must become a speculator. Without speculation there can be no economic activity reaching beyond the immediate present.

---

[14] On Monopoly see pp. 344 ff. and on "uneconomic" consumption see p. 401 ff.

A contrast between profitability and productivity is sometimes supposed to be discovered by picking out a particular process and considering it by itself. People may perhaps characterize as unproductive certain features
145 peculiar to the constitution of the capitalistic organization of industry, e.g. selling expenses, advertising costs and the like are characterized as unproductive. This is not legitimate. We must consider the result of the complete process, not the individual stages. We must not consider the constituent expenses without setting against them the result to which they contribute.[15]

6

Gross and Net Product

The most ambitious attempt to contrast productivity and profitability derives from the examination of the relationship between gross product and net product. It is clear that every entrepreneur in the capitalist system aims at achieving the largest net product. But it is asserted that rightly considered the object of economic activity should be to achieve not the largest *net* product but the largest gross product.

This belief, however, is a fallacy based upon primitive speculations regarding valuation. But judged by its widespread acceptance even today it is a very popular fallacy. It is implicit when people say that a certain line of production is to be recommended because it employs a large number of workers, or when a particular improvement in production is opposed because it may deprive people of a living.

If the advocates of such views were logical they would have to admit that the gross product principle applies not only to labour but also to the material instruments of production. The entrepreneur carries production up to the point where it ceases to yield a net product. Let us assume that production beyond this point requires material instruments only and not labour. Is it in the interest of society that the entrepreneur should extend production so as to obtain a larger gross product? Would society do so if it had the control of production? Both questions must be answered with a decided NO. The fact that further production does not pay shows that the instruments of production could be applied to a more urgent purpose in the economic system. If, nevertheless, they are applied to the unprofitable line then they will be

[15] See pp. 140 ff., 160 ff.

lacking in places where they are more urgently needed. This is true under both Capitalism and Socialism. Even a socialist community, supposing it 146
acted rationally, would not push certain lines of production indefinitely and neglect others. Even a socialist community would discontinue a particular line of production when further production would not cover the expense, that is to say, at the point where further production would mean failure to satisfy a more urgent need elsewhere.

But what is true of the increased use of material instruments is true exactly in the same way of the increased use of labour. If labour is devoted to a particular line of production to the point where it only increases the gross product while the net product declines, it is being withheld from some other line where it could perform more valuable service. And here, again, the only result of neglecting the principle of net product is that more urgent wants remain unsatisfied whilst less urgent ones are met. It is this fact, and no other which is made evident in the mechanism of the capitalist system by the decline in the net product. In a socialist community it would be the duty of the economic administration to see that similar misapplications of economic activity did not occur. Here, therefore, is no discrepancy between profitability and productivity. Even from the socialist standpoint, the largest possible net product and not the largest possible gross product must be the aim of economic activity.

Nevertheless, people continue to maintain the contrary, sometimes of production in general, sometimes of labour alone and sometimes of agricultural production. That capitalist activity is directed solely toward the attainment of the largest net product is adversely criticized and State intervention is called for to redress the alleged abuse.

This discussion has a lengthy ancestry. Adam Smith maintained that different lines of production should be regarded as more or less productive according to the greater or smaller amount of labour which they set in motion.[16] For this he was adversely criticized by Ricardo who pointed out that welfare of the people increased only through an enlargement of the net product and not of the gross product.[17] For this Ricardo was severely attacked. Even J. B. Say misunderstood him and accused him of an utter disregard for the welfare of so many human beings.[18] While Sismondi, who was fond of 147

[16] A. Smith, *An Inquiry into the Nature and Causes of the Wealth of Nations*, Book II, Chap. V (London 1776, Vol. I, pp. 437 ff.).

[17] Ricardo, *Principles of Political Economy and Taxation*, Chap. XXVI (*Works*, ed. MacCulloch, 2nd ed. [London 1852] pp. 210 ff.).

[18] Say, in his Notes to Constancio's French Edition of Ricardo's works, Vol. II (Paris, 1819), pp. 222 ff.

meeting economic arguments by sentimental declamations, thought he could dispose of the problem by witticism: he said that a king who could produce net product by pressing a button would, according to Ricardo, make the nation superfluous.[19] Bernhardi followed Sismondi on this point.[20] Proudhon went as far as to epitomize the contrast between socialistic and private enterprise in the formula: that although society must strive for the largest gross product the aim of the entrepreneur is the largest net product.[21] Marx avoids committing himself on this point, but he fills two chapters of the first book of *Das Kapital* with a sentimental exposition in which the transition from intensive to extensive agricultural methods is depicted in the darkest colour as, in the words of Sir Thomas More, a system "where sheep eat up men," and manages in the course of this discussion to confuse the large expropriations achieved by the political power of the nobility, which characterized European agrarian history in the first centuries of modern times, with the changes in the methods of cultivation initiated later on by the landowners.[22]

Since then declamations on this scheme have formed the stock equipment of the controversial writings and speeches of the socialists. A German agricultural economist, Freiherr von der Goltz, has tried to prove that the attainment of the largest possible gross product is not only productive from the social point of view but is also profitable from the individual point of view. He thinks that a large gross product naturally presupposes a large net product, and to that extent the interests of the individuals whose main object
148 is to achieve a large net product coincide with those of the State which desires a large gross product.[23] But he can offer no proof of this.

[19] Sismondi, *Nouveaux Principes d'Économie Politique* (Paris, 1819), Vol. II, p. 331 footnote.

[20] Bernhardi, *Versuch einer Kritik der Gründe, die für grosses und kleines Grundeigentum angeführt werden* (Petersburg, 1849), pp. 367 ff.; also Cronbach, *Das landwirtschaftliche Betriebsproblem in der deutschen Nationalökonomie bis zur Mitte des 19. Jahrhunderts* (Vienna, 1907), pp. 292 ff.

[21] *"La société recherche le plus grand produit brut, par conséquent la plus grande population possible, parce que pour elle produit brut et produit net son identiques. Le monopole, au contraire, vise constamment au plus grand produit net, dût-il ne l'obtenir qu'au prix de l'extermination du genre humain."* ("Society seeks the largest *gross* product and thus the largest possible population, because for it gross product and net product are the same thing. On the other hand, monopoly continually aims at the highest *net* product which it can obtain only at the price of exterminating the human race.") Proudhon, *Système des contradictions économiques ou philosophie de la misère* (Paris, 1846), Vol. I, p. 270. In Proudhon's language "Monopoly" means the same as Private Property. *Ibid.*, Vol. I, p. 236; also Landry, *L'utilité sociale de la propriété individuelle* (Paris, 1901), p. 76.

[22] Marx, *Das Kapital*, Vol. I, pp. 613–726. The arguments about "the theory of compensation for the workers displaced by machinery" (*ibid.*, pp. 403–12) are vain in view of the Marginal Utility Theory. Publisher's Note: The page references cited here are pp. 738–821 and 478–488, respectively, in the English edition.

[23] Goltz, *Agrarwesen und Agrarpolitik*, 2nd ed. (Jena, 1904), p. 53; also Waltz, *Vom Reinertrag in der Landwirtschaft* (Stuttgart and Berlin, 1904), pp. 27 ff. Goltz contradicts himself in his arguments,

Much more logical than these efforts to overcome the apparent contrast between social and private interests by ignoring obvious facts of agricultural accountancy, is the position taken up by followers of the romantic school of economic thought, particularly the German etatists, viz. that the agriculturist has the status of a civil servant, and is therefore obliged to work in the public interest. Since this is said to require the largest possible gross product it follows that the farmer, uninfluenced by commercial spirit, ideas or interests, and regardless of the disadvantages, which may be entailed, must devote himself to the attainment of this end.[24] All these writers take it for granted that the interests of the community are served by the largest gross product. But they do not go out of their way to prove it. When they do try, they only argue from the point of view of *Machtpolitik* (power politics) or *Nationalpolitik* (national policy). The State has an interest in a strong agricultural population since the agricultural population is conservative; agriculture supplies the largest number of soldiers; provision must be made for feeding the population in time of war and so on.

In contrast to this an attempt to justify the gross product principle by economic reasoning has been made by Landry. He will only admit that the effort to attain the greatest net product is socially advantageous in so far as the costs which no longer yield a profit arise from the use of material instruments of production. When the application of labour is involved he thinks quite otherwise. Then, from the economic point of view the application of labour costs nothing: social welfare is not thereby diminished. Wage economies which result in a diminution of the gross product are harmful.[25] He arrives at this conclusion by assuming that the labour force thus released could find no employment elsewhere. But this is absolutely wrong. The need of society for labour is never satisfied as long as labour is not a "free good." The released workers find other employment where they have to supply work more urgent from the economic point of view. If Landry were right it 149
would have been better if all the labour-saving machinery had never existed, and the attitude of those workers who resist all technical innovations which economize labour and who destroy such machinery would be justified. There is no reason why there should be a distinction between the employment of material instruments and of labour. That, in view of the price of the material

for, to the assertion mentioned above, he adds immediately: "Nevertheless the amount remaining as net profit from the gross product after deducting costs varies considerably. On the average it is greater with extensive than with intensive cultivation."

[24] See Waltz, *op. cit.* pp. 19 ff. on Adam Müller, Bülow-Cummerow and Phillipp *v.* Arnim, and pp. 30 ff. on Rudolf Meyer and Adolf Wagner.

[25] Landry, *L'utilité sociale de la propriété individuelle*, pp. 109, 127 ff.

instruments and the price of their products, an increase of production in the same line is not profitable, is due to the fact that the material instruments are required in some other line to satisfy more urgent needs. But this is equally true of labour. Workers who are employed in unprofitably increasing the gross product are withheld from other lines of production in which they are more urgently required. That their wages are too high for an increase in production involving a larger gross product to be profitable, results indeed from the fact that the marginal productivity of labour in general is higher than in the particular line of production in question, where it is applied beyond the limits determined by the net product principle. There is no contrast whatever here between social and private interests: a socialist organization would not act differently from an entrepreneur in the capitalist organization.

Of course there are plenty of other arguments which can be adduced to show that adherence to the net product principle may be harmful. They are common to all nationalist-militarist thinking, and are the well-known arguments used to support every protectionist policy. A nation must be populous because its political and military standing in the world depends upon numbers. It must aim at economic self-sufficiency or at least it must produce its food at home and so on. In the end Landry has to fall back on such arguments to support his theory.[26] To examine such arguments would be out of place in a discussion of the isolated socialist community.

But if the arguments we have examined are untrue it follows that the socialist community must adopt net product and not gross product as the guiding principle of economic activity. The socialist community equally with the capitalist society will also transform arable into grass land, if it is possible to put more productive land under the plough elsewhere. In spite of Sir Thomas More, "sheep will eat up men" even in Utopia, and the rulers of the socialist community will act no differently from the Duchess of Sutherland,
150 that "economically instructed person," as Marx once jeeringly called her.[27]

The net product principle is true for every line of production. Agriculture is no exception. The dictum of Thaer, the German pioneer of modern agriculture, that the aim of the agriculturist must be a high net yield "even from the standpoint of the public welfare" still holds good.[28]

---

[26] Landry, *L'utilité sociale de la propriété individuelle*, pp. 109, 127 ff.

[27] Marx, *Das Kapital*, Vol. I, p. 695.

[28] Quoted by Waltz, *Vom Reinertrag in der Landwirtschaft*, p. 29.

CHAPTER 7

The Distribution of Income

1

The Nature of Distribution Under Liberalism and Socialism

On logical grounds, treatment of the problem of income should properly 151
come at the end of any investigation into the life of the socialist community. Production must take place before distribution is possible, therefore, logically, the former should be discussed before the latter. But the problem of distribution is so prominent a feature of Socialism as to suggest the earliest possible discussion of the question. For fundamentally, Socialism is nothing but a theory of "just" distribution; the socialist movement is nothing but an attempt to achieve this ideal. All socialist schemes start from the problem of distribution and all come back to it. For Socialism the problem of distribution is *the* economic problem.

The problem of distribution is moreover peculiar to socialism. It arises only in a socialist economy. It is true, we are in the habit of speaking of distribution in an economic society based on private property, and economic theory deals with the problem of income and the determination of the prices of the factors of production under the heading "Distribution." This terminology is traditional, and it is so firmly established that the substitution of another would be unthinkable. Nevertheless, it is misleading and does not indicate the nature of the theory which it is meant to describe. Under Capitalism incomes emerge as a result of market transactions which are indissolubly linked up with production. We do not first produce things and afterwards distribute them. When products are supplied for use and consumption, incomes for the greater part have already been determined, since they arise during the process of production and are indeed derived from it. Workers, landowners, and capitalists and a large number of the entrepreneurs contributing to production have already received their share before the product is ready for

consumption. The prices which are obtained for the final product on the
152 market decide only the income which a section of entrepreneurs obtain from the process of production. (The influence which these prices have on the income of other classes has already been exerted via the anticipations of the entrepreneurs.) As thus in the capitalistic order of society the aggregation of individual incomes to form a total social income is only a theoretical conception, the concept of distribution is only figurative. The reason that this expression has been adopted, instead of the simple and more suitable term formation of income, is that the founders of scientific economics, the Physiocrats and the English classical school, only gradually learned to free themselves from the etatistic outlook of mercantilism. Although precisely this analysis of income formation as a result of market transactions was their principal achievement, they adopted the practice—fortunately without any harm to the content of their teachings—of grouping the chapters dealing with the different kinds of income under the heading "distribution."[1]

Only in the socialist community is there any distribution of consumable goods in the true sense of the word. If in considering capitalistic society we use the term distribution in any but a purely figurative sense then an analogy is being made between the determination of income in a socialist and in a capitalist community. The conception of any actual process of distribution of income must be kept out of any investigation of the mechanism of capitalist society.

2

The Social Dividend

According to the fundamental idea of Socialism only goods which are ripe for consumption are eligible for distribution. Goods of a higher order remain the property of the community for purposes of further production; they must not be distributed. Goods of the first order, on the contrary, are without exception destined to be distributed: they constitute indeed the net social dividend. Since in considering the socialist society we cannot quite get rid of ideas which are only appropriate to the capitalist order, it is usual to say that the society will retain a part of the consumers' goods for public con-

[1] Cannan, *A History of the Theories of Production and Distribution in English Political Economy from 1776 to 1848*, 3rd ed. (London, 1917), pp. 183 ff. Also p. 294 of *Socialism*.

sumption. We are really thinking of that part of consumption which in the capitalistic society is usually called public expenditure. Where the principle 153
of private property is rigidly applied this public expenditure consists exclusively of the cost of maintaining the apparatus which assures the undisturbed course of things. The only task of the strictly Liberal state is to secure life and property against attacks both from external and internal foes. It is a producer of security, or, as Lassalle mockingly termed it, a night watchman's state. In a socialist community there will be the corresponding task of securing the socialist order and the peaceful course of socialistic production. Whether the apparatus of coercion and violence which serves this purpose will still be known as the state or be called by some other name, and whether it will be legally given a separate status among the other functions incumbent upon the socialist community, is a matter of complete indifference to us. We have only to make it clear that all expenditure devoted to this end will appear in the socialist community as general costs of production. So far as they involve the use of labour for the purposes of distributing the social dividend, they must be reckoned in such a way that the workers employed get their share.

But public expenditure includes other outlays. Most states and municipalities provide their citizens with certain utilities in kind, sometimes gratuitously, sometimes at a charge which covers only a part of the expense. As a rule this happens in the case of single services which are yielded by durable commodities. Thus parks, art galleries, public libraries, places of worship, are made available for those who wish to use them. Similarly, roads and streets are accessible to everyone. Moreover, direct distribution of consumption goods takes place, as for example, when medicine and diet are given to the sick and educational apparatus to pupils; personal service is also supplied when medical treatment is given. All this is not Socialism, it is not production on the basis of common ownership of the means of production. Distribution, indeed, occurs here, but what is distributed is first collected by taxation from the citizens. Only so far as this distribution deals with products of state or municipal production can it be described as a piece of Socialism within the framework of an otherwise liberal order of society. We need not stop to inquire how far this branch of state and municipal activity is due to views which have been influenced by the socialist critics of capitalist society and how far it is due to the special nature of certain particularly durable consumption goods which yield almost unlimited service. For us it is only important that in the case of this public expenditure, even 154
in an otherwise capitalistic society, a distribution in the actual sense of the word takes place.

Moreover, the socialist community will not make a physical distribution of all consumers' goods. It is not likely to present a copy of every new book to every citizen, but rather to place the books in public reading rooms for the general use. It will do the same with its schools and teaching, its public gardens, playgrounds and assembly halls. The expenditure which all these arrangements necessitate is not deducted from the social dividend; on the contrary, it is a part of the social dividend.

This part of the social dividend exhibits this one peculiarity, that without prejudice to the principles which determine the distribution of consumable consumers' goods and part of durable goods, special principles of distribution can be applied to it corresponding to the special nature of the services involved. The way in which art collections and scientific publications are made available for general use is quite independent of the rules which are otherwise applied to the distribution of goods of the first order.

3

The Principles of Distribution

The socialist community is characterized by the fact that in it there is no connection between production and distribution. The magnitude of the share which is assigned for the use of each citizen is quite independent of the value of the service he renders. It would be fundamentally impossible to base distribution on the imputation of value because it is an essential feature of socialistic methods of production that the shares of the different factors of production in the result cannot be ascertained; and any arithmetical test of the relations between effort and result is impossible.

It would therefore not be possible to base even a part of distribution on an economic calculation of the contribution of the different factors, e.g. by first granting the worker the full product of his labour which under the capitalist system he would receive in the form of wages, and then applying a special form of distribution in the case of the shares which are attributed to the material factors of production and to the work of the entrepreneur. On the whole socialists lack any clear conception of this fact. But a faint
155 suspicion of them pervades the Marxian doctrine that under Socialism the categories wages, profit, and rent would be unthinkable.

There are four different principles upon which socialistic distribution can conceivably be based: equal distribution per head, distribution according to service rendered to the community, distribution according to needs, and distribution according to merit. These principles can be combined in different ways.

The principle of equal distribution derives from the old doctrine of natural law of the equality of all human beings. Rigidly applied it would prove absurd. It would permit no distinction between adults and children, between the sick and the healthy, between the industrious and the lazy, or between good and bad. It could be applied only in combination with the other three principles of distribution. It would at least be necessary to take into account the principle of distribution according to needs, so that shares might be graded according to age, sex, health and special occupational needs; it would be necessary to take into account the principle of distribution according to services rendered, so that distinction could be made between industrious and less industrious, and between good and bad workers; and finally, some account would have to be taken of merit, so as to make reward or punishment effective. But even if the principle of equal distribution is modified in these ways the difficulties of socialistic distribution are not removed. In fact, these difficulties cannot be overcome at all.

We have already shown the difficulties raised by applying the principle of distribution according to value of services rendered. In the capitalist system the economic subject receives an income corresponding to the value of his contribution to the general process of production. Services are rewarded according to their value. It is precisely this arrangement which Socialism wishes to change and to replace by one under which the shares attributed to the material factors of production and to the entrepreneur would be so distributed that no property owner and no entrepreneur would have a standing fundamentally different from that of the rest of the community. But this involves a complete divorce of distribution from economic imputation of value. It has nothing to do with the value of the individual's service to the community. It could be brought into external relation with the service rendered only if the service of the individual were made the basis of distribution
according to some external criteria. The most obvious criterion appears to be 156
the number of hours worked. But the significance to the social dividend of any service rendered is not to be measured by the length of working time. For, in the first place, the value of the service differs according to its use in the economic scheme. The results will differ according to whether the service is used in the right place, that is to say, where it is most urgently required, or in the wrong place. In the socialist organization, however, the worker cannot be made ultimately responsible for this, but only those who assign him the work. Secondly, the value of the service varies according to the quality of the work and according to the particular capability of the worker;

it varies according to his strength and his zeal. It is not difficult to find ethical reasons for equal payments to workers of unequal capabilities. Talent and genius are the gifts of God, and the individual is not responsible for them, as is often said. But this does not solve the problem whether it is expedient or practicable to pay all hours of labour the same price.

The third principle of distribution is according to needs. The formula of each according to his needs is an old slogan of the unsophisticated communist. It is occasionally backed up by referring to the fact that the Early Christians shared all goods in common.[2] Others again regard it as practicable because it is supposed to form the basis of distribution within the family. No doubt it could be made universal if the disposition of the mother, who hungers gladly rather than that her children should go without, could be made universal. The advocates of the principle of distribution according to needs overlook this. They overlook much more besides. They overlook the fact that so long as any kind of economic effort is necessary only a part of our needs can be satisfied, and a part must remain unsatisfied. The principle of "to each according to his needs" remains meaningless so long as it is not defined to what extent each individual is allowed to satisfy his needs. The formula is illusory since everyone has to forgo the complete satisfaction of all his
157 needs.[3] It could indeed be applied within narrow limits. The sick and suffering can be assigned special medicine, care, and attendance, better attention and special treatment for their special needs, without making this consideration for exceptional cases the general rule.

Similarly it is quite impossible to make the merit of the individual the general principle of distribution. Who is to decide on merits? Those in power have often had very strange views on the merits or demerits of their contemporaries. And the voice of the people is not the voice of God. Who would the people choose today as the best of their contemporaries? It is not unlikely that the choice would fall on a film star, or perhaps on a prize-fighter. Today the English people would probably be inclined to call Shakespeare the greatest Englishman. Would his contemporaries have done so? And how would they esteem a second Shakespeare if he were among them today? Moreover, why should those be penalized in whose lap Nature has not placed the great gifts

---

[2] Acts of the Apostles, II. 45.

[3] See Pecqueur's criticism of this formula of distribution in *Théorie nouvelle d'Économie sociale et politique* (Paris, 1842), pp. 613 ff. Pecqueur shows himself superior to Marx, who unhesitatingly indulges in the illusion that "In a higher stage of the communist society . . . the narrow bourgeois legal horizon could be completely surpassed and society could write on its banners: From each according to his abilities, to each according to his needs!" Marx, *Zur Kritik des sozialdemokratischen Parteiprogramms von Gotha*, p. 17.

of talent and genius? Distribution according to the merits of the individual would open the door wide to mere caprice and leave the individual defenseless before the oppression of the majority. Conditions would be created which would make life unbearable.

As far as the economics of the problem are concerned it is a matter of indifference which principle or which combination of different people is made a basis for distribution. Whatever principle is adopted the fact remains that each individual will receive an allocation from the community. The citizen will receive a bundle of claims which can be exchanged within a certain time for a definite amount of different goods. In this way he will procure his daily meals, fixed shelter, occasional pleasures, and from time to time new clothing. Whether the satisfaction of needs which he obtains in this way is great or small will depend upon the productivity of the efforts of the community.

4

The Process of Distribution

It is not necessary that each individual should himself consume the whole share allotted to him. He can let some go to waste, give some away, or, as far as the commodity permits, put some aside for later consumption. Some, 158
however, he can exchange. The beer drinker will readily forgo his share of non-alcoholic drink to obtain more beer. The abstainer will be prepared to forgo his claim to spirits if he can acquire other commodities instead. The aesthete will surrender a visit to the cinema for the sake of more opportunities to hear good music; the lowbrow will willingly exchange tickets to art galleries for more congenial pleasures. Everyone will be ready to exchange, but the exchange will be confined to consumers' goods. Producers' goods will be *res extra commercium* (things beyond commerce).

Such exchange need not be confined to direct barter: it can also take place indirectly within certain narrow limits. The same reasons which have led to indirect exchange in other types of society will make it advantageous to those exchanging in the socialistic community. It follows that even here there will be opportunity for the use of a general medium of exchange—money.

The role of money in the socialist economy will be fundamentally the same as in a free economic system—that of a general facilitator of exchange. But the significance of this role will be quite different. In a society based on the collective ownership of the means of production, the significance of the role of money will be incomparably narrower than in a society based on private property in the means of production. For in the socialist commonwealth, exchange itself has a much narrower significance, since it is confined to consumers' goods only. There cannot be money prices of producers' goods since these do not enter into exchange. The accounting function which money exercises in production in a free economic order will no longer exist in a socialist community. Money calculations of value will be impossible.

Nevertheless the central administration of production and distribution cannot leave out of consideration the exchange relations which arise in this sort of traffic. Clearly it would have to take them into account if it desired to make different commodities mutually substitutable when assessing the distribution of the social dividend.

Thus if in the process of exchange the relation of one cigar to five cigarettes was established, the administration could not arbitrarily lay it down that one cigar equalled three cigarettes, so that it might be able on this basis to give one individual only cigars and another only cigarettes. If the tobacco allowance has not been equally distributed, partly in cigars and partly in cigarettes,
159 that is to say, if some—either according to their wishes or by order of the government—received only cigars and others only cigarettes, the exchange relations already established could not be ignored. Otherwise all those who received cigarettes would be unfairly treated, compared with those receiving cigars, since the person who had received a cigar could exchange it for five cigarettes whilst he had obtained it as the equivalent of three cigarettes.

Alterations of exchange relationships in this traffic among the citizens would consequently compel the administration to make corresponding changes in the substitution ratios of the various commodities. Every such change will indicate that the relations between the various needs of the citizens and their satisfaction had altered, that people now wanted some commodities more than before, others less. The economic administration would presumably endeavor to adjust production to this change. It would endeavour to produce more of the more desired commodity and less of the less desired. But one thing, however, it would not be able to do: it would not be able to permit the individual citizens to redeem their tobacco tickets arbitrarily in cigars or cigarettes. If individuals were allowed free choice of cigars or cigarettes they might demand more cigars or more cigarettes than had been produced, or, on the other hand, cigars or cigarettes might be left on hand at the distributing centers because no one demanded them.

The labour theory of value appears to offer a simple solution of this problem. For an hour of labour a citizen receives a token which entitles him to the product of one hour of labour, with a deduction to defray the general obligation of the community, e.g. support of the disabled, expenditure on cultural purposes. Allowing for this deduction to cover the expenditure borne by the community as a whole, every worker who has worked one hour will have the right to obtain products on which one hour of labour has been expended. Any one who is ready to pay by giving to the community his own working time corresponding to the working time used to produce them can draw from the supply centers consumers' goods and services and apply them to his own use.

But such a principle of distribution would not work, since labour is not uniform or homogeneous. There are qualitative differences between the different forms of labour which, taken in conjunction with variations in the supply and demand of the resulting products, lead to different values. *Ceteris* 160
paribus the supply of pictures cannot be increased without the quality of the work suffering. The worker who has supplied an hour of simple labour cannot be granted the right to consume the product of an hour of work of a higher quality: and it would be impossible in a socialist community to establish any connection between the importance of work done for the community and the share in the yield of communal production given for the work. Payment for work would be quite arbitrary. For the methods of calculating value used in a free economic society based on private ownership of the means of production would be inaccessible to it since, as we have seen, such imputation is impossible in a socialistic society. Economic facts would clearly limit the power of society to reward the labourer arbitrarily; in the long run the wage total can in no circumstances exceed the income of society. Within this limit, however, the community is free to act. It can decide to pay all work equally, regardless of quality; it can just as easily make a distinction between the various hours of work, according to the quality of the work rendered. But in both cases it must reserve the right to decide the particular distribution of the products.

Even if we abstract from differences in the quality of labour and its product and accept the possibility of determining how much labour inheres in any product, the community would never allow the individual who had rendered an hour of labour to consume the product of an hour's labour. For all economic goods entail material costs apart from labour. A product for which more raw material is required must not be made equivalent to a product requiring less raw material.

5

The Costs of Distribution

Socialistic criticism of the capitalist system devotes much space to complaints about the high costs of what can be called the apparatus of distribution. They include under this the cost of all national and political institutions, including expenditure on military purposes and war. They also include the expense to society arising from free competition. All the expenditure on advertisement and the activities of persons involved in the competitive struggle such as agents, commercial travellers, etc., and the costs entailed
161 by the efforts of firms to remain independent instead of amalgamating into larger units or joining cartels which make possible specialization and thereby the cheapening of production, are debited to the distributive process of the capitalist system. The socialistic society will, so the critics think, save enormously by putting an end to this waste.

The expectation that the socialist community will save that outlay which can properly be termed state expenditure is derived from the doctrine, peculiar to many anarchists and to Marxian socialists, that state compulsion would be superfluous in a society not based on private property in the means of production. They argue that in the socialist community "obedience to the simple fundamental rules governing any form of social life will very soon become of necessity a habit," but this is backed up by a hint that "evasion of regulation and control enforced by the whole people will undoubtedly be enormously difficult," and will incur "swift and severe punishment," since "the armed workers" would not be "sentimental intellectuals" nor "let themselves be mocked."[4] All this is merely playing with words. Control, Arms, Punishment, are not these "a special repressive authority," and thus according to Engels' own words a "State"?[5] Whether the compulsion is exercised by armed workers—who cannot work while they bear arms—or by the workers' sons clad in police uniforms, will make no difference to the costs which the compulsion entails.

But the State is a coercive apparatus not only to its own inhabitants: it applies coercion externally. Only a state comprising the whole universe would need to exert no external coercion and then only because in that event there would be no foreign land, no foreigners and no foreign states. Liberalism, with its fundamental antagonism to warfare, wants to give the whole

[4] Lenin, *Staat und Revolution*, p. 96. Publisher's Note: pp. 305–306 in the English edition.

[5] Engels, *Herrn Eugen Dührings Umwälzung der Wissenschaft*, p. 302. Publisher's Note: p. 389 in the English edition.

world some state form of organization. If this can be achieved it is inconceivable without a coercive apparatus. If all the armies of the individual states were abolished we could not dispense with a world apparatus of coercion, a world police to ensure world peace. Whether Socialism unites all states into a single one or whether it leaves them independent of each other, in any case it too will not be able to do without a coercive apparatus.

The socialist apparatus of coercion too will entail some expense. Whether 162
this will be greater or less than the expense of the state apparatus of the capitalist society naturally we cannot say. We merely need to see that the social dividend will be reduced by the amount involved.

As for the wastes of distribution under Capitalism, little need be said. Since in capitalist society there is no distribution in the real sense of the word there are no costs of distribution. Trading expenses and similar costs cannot be called distribution costs, not only because they are not the costs of a distribution, which is a special process in itself, but also because the effects of the services devoted to these purposes extend far beyond the mere distribution of goods. Competition is not confined to distribution: that is only a part of its service. It serves equally the process of production, indeed it is essential for any organization of production which is to ensure high productivity. It is not enough therefore to compare these costs with the costs incurred by the apparatus of distribution and management in a socialist community. If socialist methods of production reduce productivity—and we shall speak of this later—it matters little that it saves the work of commercial travellers, brokers and advertisers.

CHAPTER 8

The Socialist Community Under Stationary Conditions

1

Stationary Conditions

163 To assume stationary economic conditions is a theoretical expedient and not an attempt to describe reality. We cannot dispense with this line of thought if we wish to understand the laws of economic change. In order to study movement we must first imagine a condition where it does not exist. The stationary condition is that point of equilibrium to which we conceive all forms of economic activity to be tending and which would actually be attained if new factors did not, in the meantime, create a new point of equilibrium. In the imaginary state of equilibrium all the units of the factors of production are employed in the most economic way, and there is no reason to contemplate any changes in their number or their disposition.

Even if it is impossible to imagine a living—that is to say a *changing*—socialist economic order, because economic activity without economic calculation seems inconceivable, it is quite easy to postulate a socialist economic order under stationary conditions. We need only avoid asking how this stationary condition is achieved. If we do this there is no difficulty in examining the statics of a socialist community. All socialist theories and Utopias have always had only the stationary condition in mind.

2

The Disutilities and Satisfactions of Labour

Socialist writers depict the socialist community as a land of heart's desire. Fourier's sickly fantasies go farthest in this direction. In Fourier's state of the future all harmful beasts will have disappeared, and in their places will be

animals which will assist man in his labours—or even do his work for him. An anti-beaver will see to the fishing; an anti-whale will move sailing ships 164
in a calm; an anti-hippopotamus will tow the river boats. Instead of the lion there will be an anti-lion, a steed of wonderful swiftness, upon whose back the rider will sit as comfortably as in a well-sprung carriage. "It will be a pleasure to live in a world with such servants."[1] Godwin even thought that men might be immortal after property had been abolished.[2] Kautsky tells us that under the socialist society "a new type of man will arise . . . a superman . . . an exalted man."[3] Trotsky provides even more detailed information: "Man will become incomparably stronger, wiser, finer. His body more harmonious, his movements more rhythmical, his voice more musical . . . The human average will rise to the level of an Aristotle, a Goethe, a Marx. Above these other heights new peaks will arise."[4] And writers of this sort of stuff are continually being reprinted and translated into other tongues, and made the subject of exhaustive historical theses!

Other socialist writers are more circumspect in their pronouncements but they proceed on essentially similar assumptions. Tacitly underlying Marxian theory is the nebulous idea that the natural factors of production are such that they need not be economized. Such a conclusion indeed follows inevitably from a system that reckons labor as the only element in costs, that does not accept the law of diminishing returns, rejects the Malthusian law of population and loses itself in obscure fantasies about the unlimited possibility of increasing productivity.[5] We need not go further into these matters. It is sufficient to recognize that even in a socialist community the natural factors of production would be limited in quantity and would therefore have to be economized.

The second element which would have to be economized is labour. Even if we ignore differences in quality it is obvious that labour is available only 165
to a limited extent: the individual can only perform a certain amount of labour. Even if labour were a pure pleasure it would have to be used economically, since human life is limited in time, and human energy is not inexhaustible. Even the man who lives at his leisure, untrammelled by monetary considerations, has to dispose of his time, i.e. choose between different possible ways of spending it.

---

[1] Fourier, *Oeuvres complètes*, Vol. IV, 2nd ed. (Paris, 1841), pp. 254 ff.

[2] Godwin, *Das Eigentum*, Bahrfeld's translation of that part of *Political Justice* which deals with the problem of property (Leipzig, 1904), pp. 73 ff.

[3] Kautsky, *Die soziale Revolution*, 3rd ed., (Berlin, 1911), II, p. 48.

[4] Trotsky, *Literatur und Revolution* (Vienna, 1924), p. 179.

[5] "Today all enterprises . . . are first and foremost a question of profitability . . . A socialist society

It is clear, therefore, that in the world as we know it, human behaviour must be governed by economic considerations. For while our wants are unlimited, the goods of the first order bestowed by nature are scarce; and, with a given productivity of labour, goods of a higher order can serve to increase the satisfaction of needs only by increasing labour. Now, quite apart from the fact that labour cannot be increased beyond a certain point, an increase of labour is accompanied by increasing disutility.

Fourier and his school regard the disutility of labour as a result of perverse social arrangements. These alone in their view are to blame for the fact that in accepted usage the words "labour" and "toil" are synonymous. Labour in itself is not unpleasant. On the contrary, all men need to be active. Inactivity entails intolerable boredom. If labour is to be made attractive it must be carried on in healthy, clean workplaces; the joy of labour must be aroused by a happy feeling of union among the workers and cheerful competition between them. The chief cause of the repugnance which labour arouses is its continuity. Even pleasures pall if they last too long. Therefore the workers must be allowed to interchange their occupations at will; work will then be a pleasure and no longer create aversion.[6]

It is not difficult to expose the error contained in this argument, though it is accepted by socialists of all schools. Man feels the impulse to activity. Even if need did not drive him to work he would not always be content to roll in the grass and bask in the sun. Even young animals and children whose nourishment is provided by their parents kick their limbs, dance, jump and run so as to exercise powers yet unclaimed by labour. To be stirring is a physical and mental need. Thus, in general, purposeful labour gives satisfaction. Yet only up to a certain point; beyond this it is only toil. In the
166 following diagram the line o x along which the product of labour is measured, marks the dividing line between the disutility of labour and the satisfaction the exercise of our powers affords, which may be called immediate satisfaction due to labour. The curve, *a*, *b*, *c*, *p* represents labour disutility and immediate labour satisfaction in relation to the product. When labour commences it is

---

knows no other question than of sufficient labour forces, and if it has these the work . . . is done." (Bebel, *Die Frau und der Sozialismus*, p. 308. Publisher's Note: p. 427 in the English edition.) "Everywhere it is the social institution and the *methods of production and distribution* connected with these which produce want and misery, and *not the number* of people." (*Ibid.*, p. 368. Publisher's Note: p. 492 in the English edition.) "We suffer *not from a lack but from a superfluity of foodstuffs*, just as we have a superfluity of industrial products." (*Ibid.*, p. 368, p. 429 in the English. Also Engels, *Herrn Eugen Dührings Umwälzung der Wissenschaft*, p. 305. Publisher's Note: pp. 390–391 in the English edition.) "We have . . . *not too many but rather too few people.*" (Bebel, *op. cit.*, p. 370; p. 494 in the English edition.)

[6] Considerant, *Exposition abrégee du Système Phalanstérien de Fourier*, 4th Impression, 3rd ed. (Paris, 1846), pp. 29 ff.

found disagreeable. After the first difficulties have been overcome and body and mind are better adapted, then the disagreeableness declines. At *b* neither disagreeableness nor satisfaction predominates. Between *b* and *c* direct satisfaction prevails. After *c* disagreeableness recommences. With other forms of labour the curve may run differently, as in $o\,c_1\,p_1$ or op_2. That depends on the nature of the work and the personality of the workers. It is different for ditchdiggers and for jockeys: it is different for dull and for energetic men.[7]

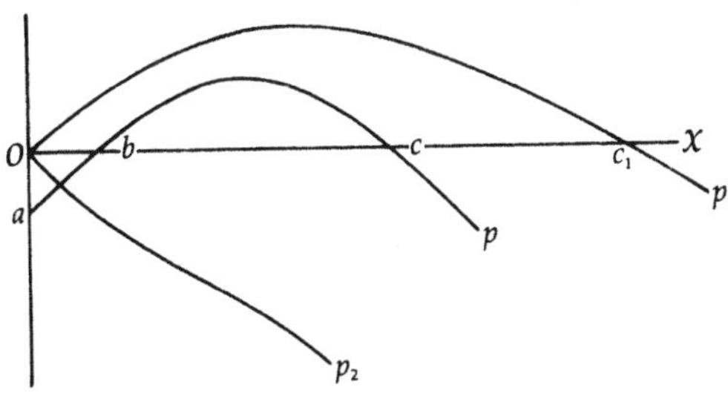

Why is labour continued when the disutility which its continuance occasions exceeds the direct satisfaction deriving from it? Because something else beside direct labour satisfaction comes into account, namely the satisfaction afforded by the product of the labour; we call this indirect labour satisfaction. Labour will be continued so long as the dissatisfaction which it arouses is counterbalanced by the pleasure derived from its product. Labour will only be discontinued at the point at which its continuation would give rise to more disutility than utility.

The methods by which Fourier wished to deprive labour of its unattractiveness were indeed based upon correct observations, but he greatly overrated the bearing of his argument. It is clear that the amount of work which 167
affords direct labour satisfaction supplies such a small fraction of the needs which men consider imperative that they readily undergo the hardship of performing irksome work. But it is a mistake to assume that any significant change would take place if workers were allowed to change occupations at short intervals. For in the first place the product of labour would be reduced because of the diminished skill acquired by the individual as a result of diminished practice in each of his various occupations; also because every changeover would cause loss of time, and labour would be expended in the shuffling. And in the second place only a very slight part of the excess of labour disutility over direct labour satisfaction is due to weariness with the

[7] Jevons, *The Theory of Political Economy*, 3rd ed. (London, 1888), pp. 169, 172 ff.

particular job in hand. Hence the capacity to derive direct satisfaction from another form of labour is not what it would have been if the first job had not been performed. Clearly the greater part of the disutility is due to general fatigue of the organism and to a desire to be released from any further constraint. The man who has worked for hours at a desk will prefer to chop wood for an hour rather than spend another hour at the desk. But what made his labour unpleasant was not only the need for change but rather the length of the work. If the product is not to be diminished the length of the working day can be reduced only by increased productivity. The widespread opinion that there is labour which only tires the body and labour which only tires the mind is incorrect, as everyone can prove for himself. All labour affects the whole organism. We deceive ourselves on this point because in observing other forms of occupation we see only the direct labour satisfaction. The clerk envies the coachman, because he would like a little recreation in driving: but his envy would last only as long as the satisfaction exceeded the pain. Similarly hunting and fishing, mountain climbing, riding and driving are undertaken for sport. But sport is not work in the economic sense. It is the hard fact that men cannot subsist on the small amount of labour yielding direct labour satisfaction which compels them to suffer the irksomeness of toil, not the bad organization of labour.

It is obvious, that improvements in the conditions under which labour is performed may increase the product with unchanged irksomeness or lessen the irksomeness for the same product. But it would be impossible to improve
168 these conditions more than actually occurs under capitalism without rising cost. That labour is less irksome when performed in company has been known from of old, and where it seems possible to let workers work together without reducing output, it is done.

There are, of course, exceptional natures that rise above the common level. The great creative genius who perpetuates himself in immortal works and deeds does not when working distinguish the pain from the pleasure. For such men creation is at once the greatest joy and the bitterest torment, an inner necessity. What they create has no value to them as a product: they create for the sake of creation, not for the result. The product costs them nothing because, when working, they forgo nothing dearer to them than their work. And their product only costs society what they could have produced by other labour. In comparison to the value of the service this cost is nothing. Genius is truly a gift of God.

Now the life history of great men is familiar to all. Thus the social reformer is easily tempted to regard what he has heard of them as common attributes. We continually find people inclined to regard the mode of life of the genius as the typical way of living of a simple citizen of a socialist community. But not every one is a Sophocles or a Shakespeare, and standing behind a lathe is not the same thing as writing Goethe's poems or founding the Empire of Napoleon.

It is therefore easy to see the nature of the illusions entertained by Marxians with regard to the satisfactions and toil of the inhabitants of the socialist community. Here, as in everything else it has to say about the socialist community, Marxism moves along the lines set out by the Utopians. With express reference to Fourier's and Owen's ideas of restoring to work "the attractiveness lost through division of labour," by arranging for each form of work to be performed for a short time only, Engels sees in Socialism an organization of production "in which productive labour will be not a means for enslaving but for liberating mankind, which will give every individual the opportunity to develop and to exercise all his capabilities, bodily and mental, in all directions, and will transform a bane into a boon."[8] And Marx talks of "a higher phase of communist society after having done away with the slavish subjection of the individual under the division of labour, a society
in which the contrast between mental and physical work has disappeared" 169
and "labour has become not only a means of life but the first need of life itself."[9] Max Adler promises that the socialist society will "at the very least" not assign to anyone any work "which must cause him pain."[10] These statements distinguish themselves from the utterances of Fourier and his school only by the fact that there is nowhere any attempt to provide them with a basis of proof.

Fourier and his school, however, had another device, apart from changes of occupation, for rendering work more attractive: competition. Men would be capable of the highest achievement if inspired by *un sentiment de rivalité joyeuse ou de noble émulation* (a feeling of joyous rivalry or noble emulation). Here for once they recognize the advantages of competition, which everywhere else they describe as pernicious. If the workers show a deficiency in achievement it will be sufficient to divide them into groups: immediately a fierce competition will blaze up between the groups, which will double the energy of the individual and suddenly arouse in all *un acharnement passioné au travail* (A passionate tenacity for work).[11]

---

[8] Engels, *Herrn Eugen Dührings Umwälzung der Wissenschaft,* p. 317. Publisher's Note: p. 408 in the English edition.

[9] Marx, *Zur Kritik des sozialdemokratischen Parteiprogramms von Gotha,* p. 17. Publisher's Note: This passage can be found on p. 7 of the Eastman edited Modern Library edition and p. 10 of the International Publishers edition.

[10] Max Adler, *Die Staatsauffassung des Marxismus* (Vienna, 1922), p. 287.

[11] Considerant, *Exposition abrégée du Système Phalanstérien de Fourier,* p. 33.

The observation that competition makes for greater accomplishment is of course correct enough, but it is superficial. Competition is not in itself a human passion. The efforts put forth by men in competition are not made for the sake of the competition but for the end attained thereby. The fight is waged not for its own sake, but for the prize which beckons the victor. But what prizes would spur to emulation the workers in a socialist community? Experience shows that titles and rewards of honour are not estimated too highly. Material goods to increase the satisfaction of wants could not be given as prizes since the principle of distribution would be independent of individual performance, and the increase per head through the increased effort of a single worker would be so insignificant that it would not count. The simple satisfaction from duty performed would not suffice: it is precisely because this incentive cannot be trusted that we seek others. And even if it were so, labour would still be irksome. It would not thereby become attractive in itself.

The Fourier school, as we have seen, regards it as the main point of their
170 solution of the social problem that work will be made a joy instead of a toil.[12]
But unfortunately the means which it provides for this are quite impracticable. If Fourier had really been able to show the way to make work attractive he would have deserved the divine honours bestowed on him by his followers.[13]

---

[12] Considerant, "Studien über einige Fundamentalprobleme der sozialen Zukunft" (contained in *Fouriers System der sozialen Reform*, translated by Kaatz, Leipzig 1906), pp. 55 ff. Fourier has the distinction of having introduced the fairies into social science. In his future state the children, organized in *"Petites Hordes"* (small groups), will perform what the adults do not do. To them will be entrusted, amongst other things, maintenance of the roads. *"C'est à leur amour propre que l'Harmonie sera redevable d'avoir, par toute la terre, des chemins plus somptueux que les allées de nos parterres. Ils seront entretenus d'arbres et d'arbustes, même de fleurs, et arrosés au trottoir. Les Petites Hordes courent frénétiquement au travail, qui est exécuté comme œuvre pie, acte de charité envers la Phalange, service de Dieu et de l'Unité."* (It is to their own self-esteem that "Harmony" will be indebted for having, everywhere, roads more magnificent than the walks in our flower gardens. They will be maintained with trees, shrubs, even flowers, and they will be irrigated along the footpaths. The small groups run frantically to their work, which will be carried out as a pious duty, an act of love [charity] for the Phalanx [community], a service for God and Unity.) By three o'clock in the morning they are up, cleaning the stables, attending to the cattle and horses, and working in the slaughter houses, where they take care that no animal is ever treated cruelly, killing always in the most humane manner. *"Elles ont la haute police du règne animal."* (They are the eminent police of the animal kingdom.) When their work is done they wash themselves, dress themselves, and appear triumphantly at the breakfast table. See Fourier, *Oeuvres complètes*, Vol. V, 2nd Edition (Paris, 1841), pp. 141, 159.

[13] Fabre des Essarts, *Odes Phalanstériennes*, Montreuil-sous-Bois 1900. Béranger and Victor Hugo also venerated Fourier. The first dedicated to him a poem, reprinted in Bebel (*Charles Fourier*, Stuttgart 1890, pp. 294 ff.).

But his much lauded doctrines are nothing but the fantasies of a man who was incapable of seeing clearly the world as it really is.

Even in a socialist community work will arouse feelings of pain and not of pleasure.[14]

3

The "Joy of Labour"

If this is recognized, one of the main supports of socialist structure of thought collapses. It is therefore only too easy to understand why socialists try stubbornly to maintain that there is in man an innate impulse and striving to work, that work gives satisfaction *per se* and that only the unsatisfactory conditions under which work is performed in capitalist society could restrict this natural joy of labour and transform it into toil.[15]

In proof of this assertion they assiduously collect statements made by 171
workers in modern factories on the pleasurability of the labour. They ask the workers leading questions and are extraordinarily satisfied when the answers are of the kind they want to hear. But because of their prepossession they omit to notice that between the actions and replies of those whom they cross-examine there is a contradiction which demands solution. If work gives satisfaction *per se* why is the worker paid? Why does he not reward the employer for the pleasure which the employer gives him by allowing him to work? Nowhere else are people paid for the pleasure given to them, and the fact that pleasures are rewarded ought at least to give pause for reflection. By common definition, labour cannot give satisfaction directly. We define labour as just that activity which does not give any direct pleasurable sensations, which is performed only because the produce of the labour yields indirectly pleasurable sensations sufficient to counterbalance the primary sensations of pain.[16]

[14] Socialist writers are still far from knowing this. Kautsky (*Die soziale Revolution*, II, pp. 16 ff.) considers that the main task of a proletarian regime is "to make work, which today is a burden, into a pleasure, so that people will enjoy working and the workers go joyfully to work." He admits that "this is not such a simple matter" and concludes that "it will hardly be possible to make work in factories and mines attractive quickly." But he cannot naturally bring himself to abandon completely Socialism's fundamental illusion.

[15] Veblen, *The Instinct of Workmanship* (New York, 1922), pp. 31 ff.; De Man, *Zur Psychologie des Sozialismus*, pp. 45 ff.; De Man, *Der Kampf um die Arbeitsfreude* (Jena, 1927), pp. 149 ff.

[16] We here disregard the above-mentioned pleasure in beginning work, in practice unimportant. See p. 145.

The so-called "joy of labour" which is generally adduced in support of the view that labour awakens feelings of satisfaction, not of pain, is attributable to three quite separate sensations.

There is first the pleasure which can be obtained from the perversion of work. When the public official abuses his office, often while performing his function in a manner which is formally quite correct, so as to satisfy the instincts of power, or to give free rein to sadistic impulses, or to pander to erotic lusts (and in this one need not always think merely of things condemned by law or morals), the pleasures that follow are undoubtedly not pleasures of work but pleasures derived from certain accompanying circumstances. Similar considerations apply also to other kinds of work. Psychoanalytic literature has repeatedly pointed out how extensively matters of this sort influence the choice of occupation. In so far as these pleasures counterbalance the pain of labour they are reflected also in the rates of pay; the larger supply of labour in the occupations offering the greatest scope for this kind of perversion tending to lower the rate of pay. The worker pays for the "pleasure" with an income lower than he otherwise could have earned.

By "joy of labour" people mean also the satisfaction of completing a task.
172 But this is pleasure in being free of work rather than pleasure in the work itself. Here we have a special kind of pleasure, which can be shown to exist everywhere, in having got rid of something difficult, unpleasant, painful, the pleasure of "I've done it." Socialist Romanticism and romantic socialists praise the Middle Ages as a time when joy of labour was unrestricted. As a matter of fact we have no reliable information from medieval artisans, peasants, and their assistants about the "joy of labour," but we may presume that their joy was in having performed their work and begun the hours of pleasure and repose. Medieval monks, who in the contemplative peace of their monasteries copied manuscripts, have bequeathed us remarks which are certainly more genuine and reliable than the assertions of our romantics. At the end of many a fine manuscript we read: *Laus tibi sit Christe, quoniam liber explicit iste.*[17] (Praise be to you, O Christ, for this book is completed.) Not because the work itself has given pleasure.

But we must not forget the third and most important source of the joy of labour—the satisfaction the worker feels because his work goes so well that through it he can earn a living for himself and his family. This joy of labour is clearly rooted in the pleasure of what we have called the indirect enjoyment of labour. The worker rejoices because in his ability to work and in his skill

[17] Wattenbach, *Das Schriftwesen in Mittelalter*, 3rd ed. (Leipzig, 1896), p. 500. Amongst the many similiar sayings and verses quoted by Wattenbach is the still more drastic: *Libro completo saltat scriptor pede laeto* (Once the book is finished, the author dances with joy).

he sees the basis of his existence and of his social position. He rejoices because he has attained a position better than that of others. He rejoices because he sees in his ability to work the guarantee of future economic success. He is proud because he can do something "good," that is, something society values and consequently pays for on the labour market. Nothing raises self-respect higher than this feeling, which indeed is often exaggerated to the ridiculous belief that one is indispensable. To the healthy man, however, it gives the strength to console himself for the unalterable fact that he is able to satisfy his wants only by toil and pain. As people say: he makes the best of a bad job.

Of the three sources of that which we may call the "joy of labour" the first, arising from perversion of the true ends of the work, will undoubtedly exist in the socialist community. As under capitalist society it will naturally be restricted to a narrow circle. The other two sources of the joy of labour will presumably dry up completely. If the connection between the yield of
labour and the income of the labourer is dissolved, as it must be in socialist 173
society, the individual will always labour under the impression that proportionately *too much work* has been piled on him. The over-heated, neurasthenic dislike of work will develop which nowadays we can observe in practically all government offices and public enterprises. In such concerns where the pay depends upon rigid schedules, everyone thinks he is overburdened, that just *he* is being given too much to do and things which are too unpleasant—that his achievements are not duly appreciated and rewarded. Out of these feelings grows a sullen hate of work which stifles even the pleasure in completing it.

The socialist community cannot count on the "joy of labour."

4

The Stimulus to Labour

It is the duty of the citizen of the socialist commonwealth to work for the community according to his powers and his ability: in return he has a claim against the community for a share in the social dividend. He who unjustifiably omits to perform his duty will be recalled to obedience by the usual methods of state coercion. The economic administration would exercise so great a power over individual citizens that it is inconceivable that anyone could permanently withstand it.

It is not sufficient however that citizens should arrive at their tasks punctually and spend the prescribed number of hours at their posts. They must really work while they are there.

In the capitalist system the worker receives the value of the product of his labour. The static or natural wage-rate tends to such a level that the worker receives the value of the product of his labour: i.e. all that is attributable to his work.[18] The worker himself is therefore concerned that his productivity should be as great as possible. This does not apply to work done for piece rates only. The level of time rates is also dependent upon the marginal productivity of the particular kind of work concerned. The technical form of wage payment which is customary does not alter the level of wages in the long run. The wage rate has always a tendency to return to its static level, and time rates are no exception.

174 But even so work done for time wages gives us an opportunity of observing how work is carried on when the worker feels that he is not working for himself, because there is no connection between his output and his remuneration. Under time wages the more skilful worker has no inducement to do more than the minimum expected from every worker. Piece wages are an incentive to the maximum activity, time wages to the minimum. Under Capitalism the graduation of time wages for different kinds of work greatly mitigates these social effects of the system of payment by time. The worker has a motive in finding a position where the minimum work required is as great as he can perform, because the wage increases with the rise in the minimum requirements.

Only when we depart from the principle of graduating time wages according to the work required does the time wage begin to affect production adversely. This is particularly noticeable in the case of state and municipal employment. Here, in the last few decades, not only has the minimum required from the individual workers been continually reduced, but every incentive to better work—for example, different treatment of the various grades and rapid promotion of industrious and capable workers to better-paid posts—has been removed. The result of this policy has clearly vindicated the principle that the worker only puts forth his best efforts when he knows that he stands to gain by it.

Under Socialism the usual connection between work performed and its remuneration cannot exist. All attempts to ascertain what the work of the individual has produced and thereby to determine the wage rate, must fail because of the impossibility of calculating the productive contributions of

[18] Clark, *Distribution of Wealth* (New York, 1907), pp. 157 ff.

the different factors of production. The socialist community could probably make distribution dependent upon certain external aspects of the work performed. But any such differentiation would be arbitrary. Let us suppose that the minimum requirement is determined for each branch of production. Let us suppose this is done on the basis of Rodbertus' proposal for a "normal working day." For each industry there is laid down the time which a worker with average strength and effort can continue to work and the amount of work which an average worker of average skill and industry can perform in
this time.[19] We will completely ignore the technical difficulties in the way of 175
deciding, in any particular concrete example the question whether this minimum has been achieved or not. Nevertheless it is obvious that any such general determination can only be quite arbitrary. The workers of the different industries would never be made to agree on this point. Everyone would maintain that he had been overtasked and would strive for a reduction of the amount set to him. Average quality of the worker, average skill, average strength, average effort, average industry—these are all vague conceptions that cannot be exactly determined.

Now it is evident that the minimum performance calculated for the worker of average quality, skill, and strength will be achieved only by a part—say one-half—of the workers. The others will do less. How can the authorities ascertain whether a performance below the minimum is due to laziness or incapacity? Either the unfettered decision of the administration must be allowed free play, or certain general criteria must be established. Doubtless, as a result, the amount of work performed would be continually reduced.

Under Capitalism everybody who takes an active part in business life is concerned that labour should be paid the whole product. The employer who dismisses a worker who is worth his wage harms himself. The foreman who discharges a good worker and retains a bad one, adversely affects the business results of the department under his charge, and thereby indirectly himself. Here we do not need formal criteria to limit the decisions of those who have to judge the work performed. Under Socialism such criteria would have to be established, because otherwise the powers entrusted to persons in charge could be arbitrarily misused. And so then the worker would have no further interest in the actual performance of work. He would only be concerned to do as much as is prescribed by the formal criteria in order to avoid punishment.

---

[19] Rodbertus, Johann Karl, *Briefe und sozialpolitische Aufsätze*, ed. R. Meyer (Berlin, 1881), pp. 553 ff. We shall not enter here into Rodbertus' other proposals for the normal working day. They are throughout based on the untenable view Rodbertus has formed about the problem of value.

What kind of results will be achieved by workers, who are not directly interested in the product of the work, can be learnt from the experience of a thousand years of slave labour. Officials and employees of state and municipal undertakings provide new examples. An attempt may be made to weaken the argumentative force of the first example by contending that these workers had no interest in the result of their labour because they did not share in the distribution; in the socialist community everyone would realize that he was working for himself and that would spur him on to the
176 highest activity. But this is just the problem. If the worker exerts himself more at the work then he has so much the more labour disutility to overcome. But he will receive only an infinitesimal fraction of the result of his increased effort. The prospect of receiving a two thousand millionth part of the result of his increased effort will scarcely stimulate him to exert his powers any more than he needs.[20]

Socialist writers generally pass over these ticklish questions in silence or with a few inconsequential remarks. They only bring forward a few moralistic phrases and nothing else.[21] The new man of Socialism will be free from base self-seeking; he will be morally infinitely above the man of the frightful age of private property and from a profound knowledge of the coherency of things and from a noble perception of duty he will devote all his powers to the general welfare.

But closer examination shows that these arguments lead to only two conceivable alternatives: free obedience to the moral law with no compulsion save that of the individual conscience, or enforced service under a system of reward and punishment. Neither will achieve the end. The former supplies no sufficient incentive to persist in overcoming the disutility of labour even though it is publicly extolled on every possible occasion and proclaimed in all schools and churches; the latter can only lead to a formal performance of duty, never to performance with the expenditure of all one's powers.

The writer who has occupied himself most thoroughly with this problem is John Stuart Mill. All subsequent arguments are derived from his. His ideas are to be encountered everywhere in the literature of the subject and in everyday political discussion; they have even become popular catchwords. Everyone is familiar with them even if he is totally unacquainted with the author.[22] They have provided for decades one of the main props of the

---

[20] Schäffle, *Die Quintessenz des Sozialismus*, 18th ed. (Gotha, 1919), pp. 30 ff.

[21] Degenfeld-Schonburg, *Die Motive des volkswirtschaftlichen Handelns und der deutsche Marxismus* (Tübingen, 1920), p. 80.

[22] J. S. Mill, *Principles*, pp. 126 ff. We cannot here examine how far Mill took over these ideas from

socialist idea, and have contributed more to its popularity than the hate-inspired and frequently contradictory arguments of socialist agitators.

One of the main objections, says Mill, that could be urged against the practicability of the socialist idea, is that each person would be incessantly 177
occupied in evading his fair share of work. But those who urge this objection forget to how great an extent the same difficulty exists under the system under which nine-tenths of the business of society is now conducted. The objection supposes that honest and efficient labour is only to be had from those who are themselves individually to reap the benefit of their own exertions. But under the present system only a small fraction of all labour can do this. Time rates or fixed salaries are the prevailing forms of remuneration. Work is performed by people who have less personal interest in the execution of the task than the members of a socialist community, since, unlike the latter, they are not working for an enterprise in which they are partners. In the majority of cases they are not personally superintended and directed by people whose own interests are bound up with the results of the enterprise. For employees paid by time carry out even the supervisory, managing and technical work. It may be admitted that labour would be more productive in a system in which the whole or a large share of the product of extra exertion belongs to the labourer, but under the present system it is precisely this incentive which is lacking. Even if communistic labour might be less vigorous than that of a peasant proprietor, or a workman labouring on his own account, it would probably be more energetic than that of a labourer for hire, who has no personal interest in the matter at all.

One can easily see the cause of Mill's mistake. The last representative of the classical school of economists, he did not survive to see the transformation of economics by the subjective theory of value, and he did not know the connection between wage rates and the marginal productivity of labour. He does not perceive that the worker has an interest in doing his utmost because his income depends upon the value of the work which he performs. Without the light of modern economic thought he sees only on the surface and not into the heart of things. Doubtless the individual working for a time wage has no interest in doing more than will keep his job. But if he can do more, if his knowledge, capability and strength permit, he seeks for a post where more is wanted and where he can thus increase his income. It may be that he fails to do this out of laziness, but this is not the fault of the system. The system does all that it can to incite everyone to the utmost diligence, since

others. Their wide diffusion they owe to the brilliant exposition in which Mill has presented them in his much read work.

it ensures to everyone the fruits of his labour. That Socialism cannot do this is the great difference between Socialism and Capitalism.

178 In the extreme case of obstinate perseverance in not performing a due share of work, the socialist community, Mill thinks, would have reserve powers which society now has at its disposal: it could submit the workers to the rules of a coercive institution. Dismissal, the only remedy at present, is no remedy when no other labourer who can be engaged does any better than his predecessor. The power to dismiss only enables an employer to obtain from his workman the customary amount of labour; but that customary labour may be of any degree of inefficiency.

The fallacy of this argument is plain. Mill does not realize that the wage rate is adjusted according to this customary amount of labour, and that the worker who wishes to earn more must do more. It may be admitted straight away that wherever the time wage prevails the individual worker is obliged to seek elsewhere for a job in which the customary amount of labour is greater because he has no chance of increasing his income by doing more work if he remains where he is. In the circumstances he must change over to piece work, take up another occupation, or even emigrate. In this way millions have emigrated from those European countries, where the customary amount of labour is low, to Western Europe or to the United States, where they have to work more but earn more. The inferior workers remain behind, and are content to work less for less wages.

If this is kept in mind it is also easy to understand the case of supervisory and managerial work performed by employees. Their activities, too, are paid according to the value of the service: they, too, must do as much as they can if they wish to obtain the highest possible income. They can and must be given authority in the name of the entrepreneur to take on and dismiss workers without any fear that they will abuse the power. They perform the social task incumbent upon them of securing that the worker obtains only as much wages as his work is worth, apart from any other consideration whatever.[23] The system of economic calculation supplies a sufficient test of the efficacy of their work. This distinguishes their work from the kind of control which could be exercised under Socialism. They harm themselves if from revengeful motives they treat a worker worse than he deserves. (Nat-
179 urally "deserves" is not used here in any ethical sense.) This authority to dismiss workers and fix their wages which the employer possesses and delegates to subordinates, is considered by socialists to be dangerous in the hands of private individuals. But the socialists overlook the fact that the

[23] Competition between the entrepreneurs sees to it that wages do not fall below this level.

employer's ability to exercise this power is limited, that he cannot dismiss and mistreat arbitrarily because the result would be harmful to himself. In endeavouring to purchase labour as cheaply as possible the employer is fulfilling one of his most important social tasks.

Mill admits that in the present state of society the neglect by the uneducated classes of labourers for hire of the duties which they engage to perform is flagrant. This, he thinks, can only be attributed to a low level of education. Under Socialism, with universal education, all citizens would undoubtedly fulfill their duty towards society as zealously as the majority of those members of the upper and middle classes who are in receipt of salaries, perform it today. It is clear that Mill's thought repeatedly involves the same error. He does not see that in this case too, there is a correspondence between payment and performance. Finally he is compelled to admit that, there can be no doubt that remuneration by fixed salaries does not produce the maximum of zeal in any class of functionaries. To this extent, Mill says, objection could reasonably be made against the socialist organization of labour. It is, however, according to Mill, by no means certain that this inferiority will continue in a socialist community as is assumed by those whose imaginations are little used to range beyond the state of things with which they are familiar. It is not impossible that under Socialism the public spirit will be so general that disinterested devotion to the common welfare will take the place of self seeking. Here Mill lapses into the dreams of the Utopians and conceives it possible that public opinion will be powerful enough to incite the individual to increased zeal for labour, that ambition and self-conceit will be effective motives, and so on.

It need only be said that unfortunately we have no reason to assume that human nature will be any different under Socialism from what it is now. And nothing goes to prove that rewards in the shape of distinctions, material gifts, or even the honourable recognition of fellow citizens, will induce the workers to do more than the formal execution of the tasks allotted to them. Nothing can completely replace the motive to overcome the irksomeness of labour which is given by the opportunity to obtain the full value of that labour.

Many socialists of course think that this argument can be refuted by appeal 180
to the labour which in the past has been performed without the incentive of a wage payment. They instance the case of the labours of scientists and artists, of the doctor who exhausts himself at the sickbed, the soldier who dies the death of a hero, the statesman who sacrifices all for his idea. But the artist and the scientist find their satisfaction in the work itself, and in the recognition which they hope to gain at some time, if only from posterity,

even though material gains are not forthcoming. The doctor and the professional soldier are in the same position as many other workers whose work is associated with danger. The supply of workers for these professions reflects their lesser attractiveness, and the wage is adapted correspondingly. But if, in spite of the danger, a man enters the profession for sake of the higher remuneration and other advantages and honours, he cannot evade the dangers without the greatest prejudice to himself. The professional soldier who turned tail, the doctor who refused to treat an infectious case, would endanger their future careers to such an extent that they have virtually no choice in the matter. It cannot be denied that there are doctors who are concerned to do their utmost in cases where no one would detect remissness, and that there are professional soldiers who incur danger when no one would reproach them for avoiding it. But in these exceptional cases, as in the case of the staunch statesman who is ready to die for his principles, man raises himself, as is given to few to do, to the highest peak of manhood, to complete union of will and deed. In his exclusive devotion to a single purpose which sets aside all other desires, thoughts and feelings, removes the instinct of self-preservation and makes him indifferent to pain and suffering, such a man forgets the world, and nothing remains except the one thing to which he sacrifices himself and his life. Of such men it used to be said, according to the estimate set on their aims, that the spirit of the Lord moved them, or that they were possessed of the devil—so incomprehensible were their motives to the ordinary run of mankind.

It is certain that mankind would not have risen above the beasts if it had not had such leaders; but it is certain that mankind does not in the main consist of such men. The essential social problem is to make useful members of society out of the general masses.

Socialist writers have for a long time ceased to exercise their ingenuity on
181 this insoluble problem. Kautsky can tell us nothing more than that habit and discipline will provide incentives to work in the future. "Capital has so accustomed the modern labourer to work day in and day out that he cannot endure to be without his work. There are even people who are so accustomed to work that they do not know what to do with their leisure time and are unhappy when they cannot work." Kautsky does not seem to fear that this habit could be shaken off more easily than other habits such as eating and sleeping but he is not prepared to rely on this incentive alone, and freely admits that "it is the weakest." He therefore recommends discipline. Naturally not "military discipline" nor "blind obedience to an authority imposed from above," but "democratic discipline—the free subjection to elected leadership." But then doubts arise and he endeavours to dispel them with the

idea that under Socialism labour will be so attractive "that it will be a pleasure to work," but finally admits that this will not be sufficient at first, and at last arrives at the conclusion that besides the attractiveness of the work some other incentive must be brought to bear, "that of the wages of labour."[24]

Thus even Kautsky, after many limitations and considerations, arrives at this result, that the irksomeness of labour will only be overcome if the product of labour, and only the product of his own labour, accrues to the worker, in so far as he is not also an owner or an employer. But this is to deny the feasibility of socialistic organization of labour, since private property in the means of production cannot be abolished without abolishing at the same time the possibility of remunerating the labourer according to the product of his labour.

5

The Productivity of Labour

The old "distributivist" theories were based on the assumption that it only needed equal distribution for everyone to have if not riches, at least a comfortable existence. This seemed so obvious, that hardly any trouble was taken to prove it. At the beginning Socialism took over this assumption in its entirety, and expected that comfort for all would be achieved by an equal distribution of the social income. Only when the criticisms of their opponents 182
drew their attention to the fact that equal distribution of the income obtained by the whole economic society would scarcely improve the conditions of the masses at all, did they set up the proposition that capitalist methods of production restrict the productivity of labour, and that Socialism would remove these limitations and multiply production to ensure for everyone a life in comfortable circumstances. Without troubling about the fact that they had not succeeded in disproving the assertion of the liberal school that productivity under Socialism would sink so low that want and poverty would be general, socialist writers began to promulgate fantastic assertions about the increase in productivity to be expected under Socialism.

Kautsky mentions two ways of achieving increased production by a transition from capitalistic to socialistic methods of production. One is the concentration of all production in the best concerns and the closing down of the

[24] Kautsky, *Die soziale Revolution*, II, pp. 15 ff.

less efficient.[25] That this is a means of increasing production cannot be denied, but it is a means which operates most effectively under the regime of an exchange-economy. Competition ruthlessly eliminates all inferior productive undertakings and concerns. That it does so is a constant source of complaint from those involved, and because of it the weaker undertakings demand State subsidies, special consideration in public contracts, and in general restriction of freedom of competition in every possible way. Kautsky is forced to admit that trusts formed by private enterprise exploit these means to the utmost, so as to obtain higher productivity, and in fact he frankly regards them as the forerunners of the social revolution. It is more than questionable whether the socialist State would feel the same necessity to carry out similar improvements in production. Would it not continue an unprofitable undertaking rather than provoke local prejudice by its discontinuance? The private entrepreneur closes down without much ado undertakings that no longer pay; and in this way he compels the worker to change his locality and sometimes even his occupation. Undoubtedly this involves initial hardships for the people concerned, but it is to the general advantage, since it makes possible a cheaper and better provisioning of the market. Would the Socialist State do likewise? Would it not, on the contrary, be constrained for political reasons to avoid local discontent? On most state railways all reforms of this
183 kind are frustrated by the attempt to avoid the harm to particular districts which would result from the elimination of superfluous branch offices, workshops, and power stations. Even the army administration has encountered parliamentary opposition when for military reasons it has been desired to withdraw a garrison from a particular place.

His second method of achieving increased production, viz., "economies of every description," on his own admission, Kautsky already finds operating under the trust of today. He particularly mentions economies of materials, transport charges, advertisements and publicity costs.[26] As far as economies in materials and transport are concerned, experience shows that nothing is operated with less economy and with more waste of labour and material of every kind than public services and undertakings. Private enterprise on the other hand naturally induces the owner to work with the greatest economy in his own interest.

Of course the Socialist state would save all advertising expenses, all the costs of commercial travellers and agents. But it is more than probable that it would employ many more persons in the service of the apparatus of

[25] Kautsky, *Die soziale Revolution*, II, pp. 21 ff.

[26] Kautsky, *Die soziale Revolution*, II, p. 26.

distribution. Wartime experience has taught us how cumbrous and expensive the social apparatus of distribution can be. Were the costs of bread, flour, meat, sugar, and other cards really less than the costs of advertisement? Has the enormous personnel required to run a rationing system been cheaper than the expenditure on commercial travellers and agents?

Socialism would eliminate the small retailers. But in their place it must set up distributive centers which would not be cheaper. Co-operative stores do not employ less hands than the retail stores organized on modern lines, and many of them, because of their large expenses, could not compete with the latter if they were not granted privileges of exemption from taxation.

Speaking generally, it must be said that it is inadmissible to pick out special costs in capitalist society, and then at once to infer from the fact that they would disappear in a socialist society, that the productivity of the latter would surpass that of the former. It is necessary to compare the *total* costs and the *total* yields of both systems. The fact that the electromobile needs no gasoline is no proof that it is cheaper to run than the gasoline-powered car.

The weakness of Kautsky's argument is evident, when he asserts that "by *184*
the application of these two methods a proletarian regime could raise production to such a high level that it would be possible to increase wages considerably and at the same time reduce the hours of labour." Here he is making an assertion for which he offers no proof whatever.[27]

And it is no better with the other arguments that are often brought forward to prove the supposed higher productivity of a socialistic society. When for example people argue that under Socialism everyone capable of work will have to work, they are sadly mistaken as to the number of idlers under Capitalism.

So far as can be judged there is no convincing reason for supposing that labour under Socialism would be more productive than under Capitalism. On the contrary it can be asserted that under a system which provides no incentive to the worker to overcome the irksomeness of labour and to strive his utmost, the productivity of labour must inevitably decline. But the prob-

---

[27] In the years of controlled economy we heard quite often of frozen potatoes, rotten fruit, spoiled vegetables. Did such things not happen formerly? Certainly. But they happened less often. The merchant whose fruit spoiled suffered monetary loss, and that made him careful in the future. If he did not take better care he was ruined at last. He ceased to direct production and was removed to a place in economic life where he could do no more harm. But it is otherwise with the goods which the state deals in. Here there is no individual interest behind the commodities. Here officials trade, whose responsibility is so divided that no one gets particularly excited about a small misfortune.

lem of productivity cannot be dealt with only within the limits of a study of static conditions. Incomparably more important than the question whether the transition to Socialism would increase productivity is the question whether, given the existence of a socialistic order, it would be able further to increase production and to achieve economic progress. This leads us to the problem of dynamics.

CHAPTER 9

The Position of the Individual Under Socialism

1

Selection of Personnel and Choice of Occupation

The Socialist Community is a great authoritarian association in which 185
orders are issued and obeyed. This is what is implied by the words "planned economy" and the "abolition of the anarchy of production." The inner structure of a socialist community is best understood if we compare it with the inner structure of an army. Many socialists indeed prefer to speak of the "army of labour." As in an army, so under Socialism, everything depends on the orders of the supreme authority. Everyone has a place to which he is appointed. Everyone has to remain in his place until he is moved to another. It follows that men become pawns of official action. They rise only when they are promoted. They sink only when they are degraded. It would be waste of time to describe such conditions. They are the common knowledge of every citizen of a bureaucratic state.

It is obvious that, in a state of this sort, all appointments should be based upon personal capacity. Each position should be held by the individual best fitted to hold it—always provided that he is not required for more important work elsewhere. Such is the fundamental principle of all systematically ordered authoritarian organizations—of the Chinese Mandarinate equally with modern bureaucracies.

In giving effect to this principle the first problem that arises is the appointment of the supreme authority. There are two ways to the solution of this problem, the oligarchical-monarchical and the democratic, but there can be only one solution—the charismatic solution. The supreme rulers (or ruler) are chosen in virtue of the grace with which they are endowed by divine dispensation. They have superhuman powers and capacities lifting them above the other mortals. To resist them is not only to resist the powers that
be; it is to defy the commandments of the Deity. Such is the basis of 186

theocracies—of clerical aristocracies of realms of "the Lord's anointed." But it is equally the basis of the Bolshevist dictatorship in Russia. Summoned by history to the performance of their sublime task, the Bolsheviks pose as the representatives of humanity, as the tools of necessity, as the consummators of the great scheme of things. Resistance to them is the greatest of all crimes. But against their adversaries they may resort to any expedients. It is the old aristocratic-theocratic idea in a new form.

Democracy is the other method of solving the problem. Democracy places everything in the hands of the majority. At its head is a ruler, or rulers, chosen by a majority decision. But the basis of this is as charismatic as any other. Only in this case grace is regarded as being granted in equal proportions to all and sundry. Everyone is endowed with it. The voice of the people is the voice of God. This is to be seen especially clearly in Tommaso Campanella's *City of the Sun*. The Regent chosen by the national assembly is also priest and his name is "Hoh," that means "metaphysics."[1] In authoritarian ideology, democracy is valued not for its social functions, but only as a means for the ascertainment of the absolute.[2]

According to charismatic theory, in appointing officials the supreme authority transmits to them the grace it possesses itself. An official appointment raises ordinary mortals above the level of the masses. They count for more than others. When on duty their status is especially enhanced. No doubt of their capacity, or of their fitness for office, is permissible. Office makes the man.

Apart from their polemical value, all these theories are purely formal. They do not tell us anything about how such appointments actually work. They are indifferent to origins. They do not inquire whether the dynasties and the aristocracies concerned attained to power by the chance of war. They give no idea of the mechanism of the party system which brings the leaders of a democracy to the helm. They tell nothing of the actual machinery for selecting officials.

But since only an omniscient ruler could do without them, special arrangements for the appointment of the officials must be made. Since the supreme authority cannot do everything, appointment to lesser positions at least must
187 be left to subordinate authorities. To prevent this power from degenerating into mere license, it must be hedged about by regulations. In this way selection comes to be based not on genuine capacity but on compliance with certain forms, the passing of certain examinations, attendance at certain

[1] Georg Adler, *Geschichte des Sozialismus und Kommunismus* (Leipzig, 1899), pp. 185 ff.
[2] On the social-dynamic functions of democracy see p. 60 of *Socialism*.

schools, having spent a certain number of years in a subordinate position, and so on. Of the shortcomings of such methods there can be only one opinion. The successful conduct of business demands qualities quite other than those necessary for passing examinations—even if the examinations deal with subjects bearing on the work of the position in question. A man who has spent a certain time in a subordinate capacity is far from being, for that reason, fitted for a higher post. It is not true that one learns to command by first learning to obey. Age is no substitute for personal capacity. In short, the system is deficient. Its only justification is that nothing better is known to put in its place.

Attempts have recently been made to invoke the aid of experimental psychology and physiology, and many promise therefrom results of the highest importance to Socialism. There can be no doubt that under Socialism, something corresponding to medical examination for military service would have to be employed on a larger scale and with more refined methods. Those who feigned bodily deformities to escape difficult and uncongenial work would have to be examined, as would those who attempted work for which they were not properly developed. But the warmest advocates of such methods could scarcely pretend that they could do more than impose a very loose curb upon the grossest abuses of officialdom. For all those kinds of work demanding something more than mere muscular strength and a good development of particular senses they are not applicable at all.

2

Art and Literature, Science and Journalism

Socialist society is a society of officials. The way of living prevailing in it, and the mode of thinking of its members, are determined by this fact. People who are always expecting promotion, people who had always a "chief" on
whom they depend, people who, because they receive a fixed salary, never *188*
understand the connection between production and their own consumption—the last ten years has witnessed the rise of this type everywhere in Europe. It is in Germany, however, where it is especially at home. The whole psychology of our time derives from it.

Socialism knows no freedom of choice in occupation. Everyone has to do what he is told to do and to go where he is sent. Anything else is unthinkable. We shall discuss later and in another connection how this will affect the productivity of labour. Here we have to discuss the position of art and science, literature and the press under such conditions.

Under Bolshevism in Russia and Hungary, the artists, scientists and writers, who were recognized as such by the selectors appointed for this purpose, were exempted from the general obligation to work and given a definite salary. All such as were not recognized remained subject to the general obligation to work and received no support for other activity. The press was nationalized.

This is the simplest solution of the problem, and one which harmonizes completely with the general structure of socialist society. Officialdom is extended to the sphere of the spirit. Those who do not please the holders of power are not allowed to paint or to sculpt or to conduct an orchestra. Their works are not printed or performed. And if the decision does not depend directly upon the free judgment of the economic administration but is referred to the advice of an expert council the case is not materially altered. On the contrary, expert councils, which are inevitably composed of the old and the established, must be admitted to be even less competent than laymen to assist the rise of young talent with different views and perhaps greater mastery than their own. Even if the choice were referred to the whole nation the rise of independent spirits setting themselves against traditional technique and accepted opinions would not be facilitated. Such methods can only foster a race of epigones.

In Cabet's *Icaria,* only such books which please the republic are to be printed (*les ouvrages préférés* [the preferred or favored works]). Writings of pre-socialistic times are to be examined by the Republic. Those which are partially useful are to be revised. Those which are regarded as dangerous or useless are to be burnt. The objection, that this would be to do what Omar did by burning the Alexandrian Library, Cabet held to be quite untenable.
189 For, said he, "*nous faisons en faveur de l'humanité ce que ces oppresseurs faisaient contre elle. Nous avons fait du feu pour brûler les méchants livres, tandis que des brigands ou des fanatiques allumaient les bûchers pour brûler d'innocents hérétiques.*" ("We do on behalf of society what oppressors do against it. We make fires to burn the evil books, while the brigands or fanatics light fires to burn innocent heretics at the stake.")[3] From a point of view such as this, solution of the problem of toleration is impossible. Mere opportunists excepted, everyone is convinced of the rightness of his opinions. But, if such a conviction by itself were a justification for intolerance, then everyone would have a

[3] Cabet, *Voyage en Icarie* (Paris, 1848), p. 127.

right to coerce and persecute everyone else of another way of thinking.[4] In these circumstances, the demand for toleration can only be a prerogative of the weak. With power comes the exercise of intolerance. In such a case there must always be war and enmity between men. Peaceful co-operation is out of the question. It is because it desires peace that Liberalism demands toleration for all opinions.

Under Capitalism the artist and the scientist have many alternatives open to them. If they are rich they can follow their own inclinations. They can seek out rich patrons. They can work as public officials. They can attempt to live on the sale of their creative work. Each of these alternatives has its dangers, in particular the two latter. It may well be that he who gives new values to mankind, or who is capable of so giving, suffers want and poverty. But there is no way to prevent this effectively. The creative spirit innovates necessarily. It must press forward. It must destroy the old and set the new in its place. It could not conceivably be relieved of this burden. If it were it would cease to be a pioneer. Progress cannot be organized.[5] It is not difficult to ensure that the genius who has completed his work shall be crowned with laurel; that his mortal remains shall be laid in a grave of honour and monuments erected to his memory. But it is impossible to smooth the way that 190
he must tread if he is to fulfil his destiny. Society can do nothing to aid progress. If it does not load the individual with quite unbreakable chains, if it does not surround the prison in which it encloses him with quite unsurmountable walls, it has done all that can be expected of it. Genius will soon find a way to win its own freedom.

The nationalization of intellectual life, which must be attempted under Socialism, must make all intellectual progress impossible. It is possible to deceive oneself about this because, in Russia, new kinds of art have become the fashion. But the authors of these innovations were already working,

[4] Luther urged the Princes of his party not to tolerate the monastic system and the Mass. According to him it would be irrelevant to answer that, as the Emperor Charles was convinced that the Papist doctrine was true, he would act justly, from his point of view, in destroying the Lutheran teachings as heresy. For we know "that he is not certain of this, nor can he be certain, because we know that he errs and fights against the Gospels. For it is not our duty to believe that he is certain, because he goes without God's Word and we go with God's Word; rather it is his duty to recognize God's Word and to advance it, like us, with all his power." Dr. Martin Luther's *Briefe, Sendschreiben und Bedenken*, ed. de Wette, Part IV (Berlin, 1827), pp. 93 ff.; Paulus, *Protestantismus und Toleranz im 16. Jahrhundert* (Freiburg, 1911), p. 23.

[5] "It is misleading to say: Progress should be organized. What is really productive cannot be put into forms made in advance; it flourishes only in unrestricted freedom. The followers may then organize themselves, which is also called 'forming a school'." Spranger, *Begabung und Studium* (Leipzig, 1917), p. 8. See also Mill, *On Liberty*, 3rd ed. (London, 1864), pp. 114 ff.

when the Soviet came into power. They sided with it because, not having been recognized hitherto, they entertained hopes of recognition from the new regime. The great question, however, is whether later innovators will be able to oust them from the position they have now gained.

In Bebel's Utopia only physical labour is recognized by society. Art and science are relegated to leisure hours. In this way, thinks Bebel, the society of the future "will possess scientists and artists of all kinds in countless numbers." These, according to their several inclinations, will pursue their studies and their arts in their spare time.[6] Thus Bebel allows himself to be swayed by the manual labourer's philistine resentment against all those who are not hewers of wood and drawers of water. All mental work he regards as mere dilettantism, as can be seen from the fact that he groups it with "social intercourse."[7] But nevertheless we must inquire whether under these conditions the mind would be able to create that freedom without which it cannot exist.

Obviously all artistic and scientific work which demands time, travel, technical education and great material expenditure, would be quite out of the question. But we will assume that it is possible to devote oneself to writing or to music, after the day's work is done. We will assume further
191 that such activities will not be hindered by malicious intervention on the part of the economic administration—by transferring unpopular authors to remote localities, for instance—so that with the aid perhaps of devoted friends, an author or a composer is able to save enough to pay the fee demanded by the state printing works for the publication of a small edition. In this way he may even succeed in bringing out a little independent periodical—perhaps even in procuring a theatrical production.[8] But all this would have to overcome the overwhelming competition of the officially supported arts, and the economic administration could at any time suppress it. For we must not forget that as one could not ascertain the cost of printing, the

[6] Bebel, *Die Frau und der Sozialismus*, p. 284. Publisher's Note: p. 395 in the English edition. See Index to Works Cited for complete citation.

[7] How Bebel pictured to himself life in a socialist community is shown by the following: "Here she (Woman) is active under the same conditions as the man. At one moment a practical worker in some industry she is in the next hour educator, teacher, nurse; in the third part of the day she exercises some art or cultivates a science; and in the fourth part she fulfils some administrative function. She enjoys studies, pleasures and amusement with her like or with men, just as she wishes and as the opportunity offers. In love choice she is free and unfettered like the man. She woos or lets herself be wooed, etc." (Bebel, *op. cit.*, p. 342). Publisher's Note: pp. 466–467 in English edition.

[8] This corresponds to Bellamy's ideas. (*Ein Rückblick*, translated by Hoops in Meyers Volksbücher, pp. 130 ff.) Publisher's Note: In English, *Looking Backward: If Socialism Comes, 2000–1887* (Boston, 1889); chapter 15; and (W. Foulsham, London), pp. 92–99.

economic administration would be free to decide the business conditions under which publication could take place. No censor, no emperor, no pope, has ever possessed the power to suppress intellectual freedom which would be possessed by a socialist community.

3

Personal Liberty

It is customary to describe the position of the individual under Socialism by saying that he would be unfree, that the socialist community would be a "prison state." This expression contains a judgment of value which, as such, lies outside the sphere of scientific thought. Science cannot decide whether freedom is a good or an evil or a mere matter of indifference. It can only inquire wherein freedom consists and where freedom resides.

Freedom is a sociological concept. It is meaningless to apply it to conditions outside society: as can be well seen from the confusions prevailing everywhere in the celebrated free-will controversy. The life of man depends upon natural conditions that he has no power to alter. He lives and dies under these conditions and, because they are not subject to his will, he must subordinate himself to them. Everything he does is subject to them. If he throws a stone it follows a course conditioned by nature. If he eats and drinks the processes within his body are similarly determined. We attempt to exhibit this de-
pendence of the process of events upon definite and permanent functional 192
relationship, by the idea of the conformity of all natural occurrences to unerring and unchangeable laws. These laws dominate man's life; he is completely circumscribed by them. His will and his actions are only conceivable as taking place within their limits. Against nature and within nature there is no freedom.

Social life, too, is a part of nature and, within it, unalterable laws of nature hold their sway. Action, and the results of action, are conditioned by these laws. If, with the origin of action in will, and its working out in societies, we associate an idea of freedom, this is not because we conceive that such action takes place independently of natural laws: the meaning of this concept of freedom is quite different.

It is not here a question of the problem of internal freedom. It is the problem of external freedom with which we are concerned. The former is a problem of the origin of willing, the latter of the working out of action. Every man is dependent upon the attitude of his fellow men. He is affected by their actions in a multitude of ways. If he has to suffer them to treat him as if he had no will of his own, if he cannot prevent them from riding roughshod over his wishes, he must feel a one-sided dependence upon them and will say that he is unfree. If he is weaker, he must accommodate himself to coercion by them.

Under the social relations that arise from co-operation in common work this one-sided dependence becomes reciprocal. In so far as each individual acts as a member of society he is obliged to adapt himself to the will of his fellows. In this way no one depends more upon others than others depend upon him. This is what we understand by external freedom. It is a disposition of individuals within the framework of social necessity involving, on the one side, limitation of the freedom of the individual in relation to others, and, on the other, limitation of the freedom of others in relation to him.

An example should make this clear. Under Capitalism the employer appears to have great power over the employee. Whether he engages a man, how he employs him, what wages he gives him, whether he dismisses him—all depend upon his decision. But this freedom on his part and the corresponding unfreedom of the other are only apparent. The conduct of the employer to the employee is part of a social process. If he does not deal with the employee in a manner appropriate to the social valuation of the employee's service, then there arise consequences which he himself has to bear.
193 He can, indeed, deal badly with the employee, but he himself must pay the costs of his arbitrary behaviour. To this extent therefore the employee is dependent upon him. But this dependence is not greater than the dependence of each one of us upon our neighbour. For even in a state where the laws are enforced everybody of course who is willing to bear the consequences of his action, is free to break our windows or do us bodily harm.

Strictly speaking, of course, on this view there can be no social action which is entirely arbitrary. Even the oriental despot, who to all appearances is free to do what he likes with the life of the enemy he captures, must consider the results of his action. But there are differences of degree in the way in which the costs of arbitrary action are related to the satisfactions arising therefrom. No laws can afford us protection against the assaults of men whose enmity is such that they are willing to bear all the consequences of their action. But if the laws are sufficiently severe to ensure that, as a general rule, our peace is not disturbed, then we feel ourselves independent of the evil intentions of our fellows, at any rate to a certain extent. The historical relaxation of the penal laws is to be attributed, not to an amelioration of morals, or to decadence on the part of legislators, but simply to the fact that so far as men have learnt to check resentment by considering the consequences of action it has been possible to abate the severity of punishments without weakening their deterrent power. To-day the menace of a short term of imprisonment is more effective protection against crimes against the person than the gallows were at one time.

There is no place for the arbitrary, where exact money reckoning enables us completely to calculate action. If we allow ourselves to be carried away by the current laments over the stony-heartedness of an age which reckons everything in terms of shillings and pence, we overlook that it is precisely this linking up of action with considerations of money profit which is society's most effective means of limiting arbitrary action. It is precisely arrangements of this kind which make the consumer, on the one hand, the employer, the capitalist, the landowner and the worker on the other—in short, all concerned in producing for demands other than their own—dependent upon social cooperation. Only complete failure to understand this reciprocity of relationship can lead anyone to ask whether the debtor is dependent on the creditor, or
the creditor on the debtor. In fact, each is dependent on the other, and the 194
relationship between buyer and seller, employer and employee, is of the same nature. It is customary to complain that, nowadays, personal considerations are banished from business life and that money rules everything. But what really is here complained of is simply that, in that department of activity which we call purely economic, whims and favours are banished and only those considerations are valid which social co-operation demands.

This, then, is freedom in the external life of man—that he is independent of the arbitrary power of his fellows. Such freedom is no natural right. It did not exist under primitive conditions. It arose in the process of social development and its final completion is the work of mature Capitalism. The man of pre-capitalistic days was subject to a "gracious lord" whose favour he had to acquire. Capitalism recognizes no such relation. It no longer divides society into despotic rulers and rightless serfs. All relations are material and impersonal, calculable and capable of substitution. With capitalistic money calculations freedom descends from the sphere of dreams to reality.

When men have gained freedom in purely economic relationships they begin to desire it elsewhere. Hand in hand with the development of Capitalism, therefore, go attempts to expel from the State all arbitrariness and all personal dependence. To obtain legal recognition of the subjective rights of citizens, to limit the arbitrary action of officials to the narrowest possible field—this is the aim and object of the liberal movement. It demands not grace but rights. And it recognizes from the outset that there is no other way of realizing this demand than by the most rigid suppressing of the powers of the State over the individual. Freedom, in its view, is freedom from the State.

For the State—the coercive apparatus worked by the persons forming the government—is scathless to freedom only when its actions have to conform to certain clear, unequivocal, universal norms, or when they obey the principles governing all work for profit. The former is the case when it functions judicially; for the judge is bound by laws allowing small play for personal opinion. The latter is the case when under Capitalism the State functions as an entrepreneur working under the same conditions and subject to the same principles as other entrepreneurs working for a profit. What it does beyond
195 this can neither be determined by law or in any other way limited sufficiently to guard against arbitrary action. The individual then has no defence against the decision of officials. He cannot calculate what consequences his actions will have because he cannot tell how they will be regarded by those on whom he depends. This is the negation of freedom.

It is customary to regard the problem of external freedom as a problem of the greater or less dependence of the individual upon society.[9] But political freedom is not the whole of freedom. In order that a man may be free it is not sufficient that he may do anything unharmful to others without hindrance from the government or from the repressive power of custom. He must also be in the position to act without fearing unforeseen social consequences. Only Capitalism guarantees this freedom by explicitly referring all reciprocal relations to the cold impersonal principle of exchange *du ut des* (I give as you give, or colloquially, give and take).

Socialists usually attempt to refute the argument for freedom by contending that under Capitalism only the possessor is free. The proletarian is unfree because he must work for his livelihood. It is impossible to imagine a cruder conception of freedom. That man must work, because his desire to consume is greater than that of the beasts of the field, is part of the nature of things. That the possessor is able to live without conforming to this rule is a gain derived from the existence of society which injures no one—not even the possessionless. And the possessionless themselves benefit from the existence of society, in that co-operation makes labour more productive. Socialism could only lessen the dependence of the individual upon natural conditions by increasing this productivity. If it cannot do that, if on the contrary it diminishes productivity, then it will diminish freedom.

---

[9] Similarly formulated by J. S. Mill, *On Liberty*, p. 7.

CHAPTER 10

Socialism Under Dynamic Conditions

1

The Nature of the Dynamic Forces

The idea of a stationary state is an aid to theoretical speculation. In the 196
world of reality there is no stationary state, for the conditions under which economic activity takes place are subject to perpetual alterations which it is beyond human capacity to limit.

The influences which maintain this perpetual change in the economic system can be grouped into six great classes. First and foremost come changes in external Nature. Under this heading must be classified not only all those changes in climate and other specifically natural conditions which take place independent of human actions, but also changes arising from operations carried out within these conditions, such as exhaustion of the soil, or consumption of standing timber or mineral deposits. Secondly come changes in the quantity and quality of the population, then changes in the quantity and quality of capital goods, then changes in the technique of production, then changes in the organization of labour, and finally changes in demand.[1]

Of all these causes of change the first is the most fundamentally important. For the sake of argument let us assume that a socialist community might be able so to regulate the growth of population and demand for commodities as to avert danger to the economic equilibrium from these factors. Were that so, there are other causes of change that could be avoided. But the socialist community would never be able to influence the natural conditions of economic activity. Nature does not adapt itself to man. Man must adapt himself to Nature. Even the socialist community will have to reckon with changes in external nature; it will have to take account of the consequences of elemental disturbances. It will have to take account of the fact that the natural

[1] Clark, *Essentials of Economic Theory* (New York, 1907), pp. 131 ff.

197 powers and resources at its disposal are not inexhaustible. Disturbances from without will intrude on its peaceful running. No more than Capitalism will it be able to remain stationary.

2

Changes in Population

For the naive socialist there is quite enough in the world to make everybody happy and contented. The dearth of goods is only the result of a perverse social order which, on the one hand limits the extension of productive powers, and on the other, by unequal distribution, lets too much go to the rich and thus too little to the poor.[2]

The Malthusian Law of Population and the Law of Diminishing Returns put an end to these illusions. *Ceteris Paribus* the increase of population beyond a certain point is not accompanied by a proportional increase of wealth: if this point is passed, production per head diminishes. The question whether at any given time production has reached this point is a question of fact which must not be confused with the question of general principle.

In the light of this knowledge, socialists have adopted various attitudes. Some have simply rejected it. During the whole of the nineteenth century scarcely any author was so vigorously attacked as Malthus. The writings of Marx, Engels, Dühring, and many others, bristle with abuse of "parson" Malthus.[3] But they do not refute him. Today, discussion of the Law of Population may be regarded as closed. The Law of Diminishing Returns is not contested nowadays; it is therefore not necessary to deal with those authors who either deny the doctrine or ignore it.

Other socialists imagine that it is possible to undermine such considerations by pointing to the unprecedented increase in productivity which will take place once the means of production are socialized. It is not necessary at this point to discuss whether in fact such an increase would take place; for even granted that it would, this would not alter the fact that at any given time

---

[2] Bebel, *Die Frau und der Sozialismus*, p. 340. Bebel quotes therewith the well-known verse of Heine. Publisher's Note: p. 463 in the English edition.

[3] Heinrich Soetbeer, *Die Stellung der Sozialisten zur Malthusschen Bevölkerungslehre* (Berlin, 1886), pp. 33 ff.; 52 ff.; 85 ff.

there is a definite optimal size of population beyond which any increase in numbers must diminish production per head. If it is desired to deny the 198
effectiveness of the Laws of Population and Diminishing Returns under Socialism, then it must be proved that every child born into the world beyond the existing optimum will at the same time bring with it so great an increase of productivity that production per head will not be diminished by its coming.

A third group of writers content themselves with the reflection that with the spread of civilization and rational living, with the increase of wealth and the desire for a higher standard of life, the growth of population is slackening. But this is to overlook the fact that the birth-rate does not fall because the standard of life is higher but only because of "moral restraint," and that the incentive to the individual to refrain from procreation disappears the moment it is possible to have a family without economic sacrifice because the children are maintained by society. This is fundamentally the same error that entrapped Godwin when he thought that there was "a principle in human society" which kept the population permanently within the limits set by the means of subsistence. Malthus exhibited the nature of this mysterious "principle."[4]

Without coercive regulation of the growth of population, a socialist community is inconceivable. A socialist community must be in a position to prevent the size of the population from mounting above or falling below certain definite limits. It must attempt to maintain the population always at that optimal number which allows the maximum production per head. Equally with any other order of society it must regard both under- and over-population as an evil. And since in it those motives, which in a society based on private ownership of the means of production harmonize the number of births with the limitations of the means of subsistence, would not exist, it will be obliged to regulate the matter itself. How it will accomplish this need not be here discussed. Nor is it relevant to our purpose to inquire whether its measures will serve eugenic or ethnological ideas. But it is certain that even if a socialist community may bring "free love," it can in no way bring free birth. The right to existence of every person born can be said to exist only when undesirable births can be prevented. In the socialist community as in any other, there will be those for whom "at the great banquet of Nature 199
no place has been laid" and to whom the order must be given to withdraw themselves as soon as may be. No indignation that these words of Malthus may arouse can alter this fact.

[4] Malthus, *An Essay on the Principle of Population*, 5th ed. (London, 1817), Vol. II, pp. 245 ff.

3

Changes in Demand

It follows from the principles which the socialist community must necessarily observe in the distribution of consumption goods, that alterations of demand cannot be allowed free play. If economic calculation and therewith even an approximate ascertainment of the costs of production were possible, then within the limits of the total consumption-units assigned to him, each individual citizen could be allowed to demand what he liked; each would choose what was agreeable to him. It would indeed be possible that as a result of malicious intent on the part of the directors of production certain commodities might be priced higher than they need be. Either they might be made to bear too high a proportion of overhead costs, or they might be made dearer by uneconomic methods of production; and the citizens who suffered would have no defence, except political agitation, against the government. So long as they remained in the minority they themselves would not be able either to rectify the accounts or to improve the methods of production. But at any rate the fact that at least the greater number of the factors concerned could be measured and that, as a result of this, the whole question could be relatively clearly put, would be some support for their point of view.

Since, under Socialism, no such calculations are possible, all such questions of demand must necessarily be left to the government. The citizens as a whole will have the same influence on them as on other acts of government. The individual will exercise this influence only in so far as he contributes to the general will. The minority will have to bow to the will of the majority. The system of proportional representation, which by its very nature is suitable only for elections and can never be used for decisions with regard to particular acts, will not protect them.

The general will, i.e. the will of those who happen to be in power, will
200 take over those functions which in a free economic system are discharged by demand. Not individuals but the government would decide which needs are the most urgent and must therefore be satisfied first.

For this reason demand will be much more uniform, much less changeable than under Capitalism. The forces which under Capitalism are continually bringing about alterations in demand will be lacking under Socialism. How will innovations, ideas deviating from those traditionally accepted, obtain recognition? How will innovators succeed in getting inert masses out of the rut? Will the majority be willing to forsake the well beloved customs of their forefathers for something better, which is yet unknown to them? Under Capitalism where each individual within the limits of his means can decide what he is to consume, it is sufficient for one individual, or a few, to be brought to recognize that the new methods satisfy their needs better than the old. Others will gradually follow their example. This progressive adoption of new modes of satisfaction is especially facilitated by the fact that incomes are not equal. The rich adopt novelties and become accustomed to their use. This sets a fashion which others imitate. Once the richer classes have adopted a certain way of living, producers have an incentive to improve the methods of manufacture so that soon it is possible for the poorer classes to follow suit. Thus luxury furthers progress. Innovation "is the whim of an *élite* before it becomes a need of the public. The luxury of today is the necessity of tomorrow."[5] Luxury is the roadmaker of progress: it develops latent needs and makes people discontented. In so far as they think consistently, moralists who condemn luxury must recommend the comparatively desireless existence of the wild life roaming in the woods as the ultimate ideal of civilized life.

4

Changes in the Amount of Capital

The capital goods employed in production are sooner or later used up. This is true, not only of those goods which constitute circulating capital, but
also of those which constitute fixed capital. Those, too, sooner or later are 201
consumed in production. In order that capital may be maintained in the same proportions, or that it may be increased, constant effort is necessary on the part of those who supervise production. Care must be taken that the capital goods used up in the process of production are replaced; and, beyond that, that new capital is created. Capital does not reproduce itself.

In a completely stationary economic system, this operation demands no particular foresight. Where everything remains unchanged, it is not very difficult to ascertain what becomes used up, and what must therefore be put

[5] Tarde, *Die Sozialen Gesetze*, German translation by Hammer (Leipzig, 1908), p. 99. Also the numerous examples in Roscher, *Ansichten der Volkswirtschaft vom geschichtlichen Standpunkt*, 3rd ed. (Leipzig, 1878), Vol. I, pp. 112 ff. Publisher's Note: The Tarde book in English is *Social Laws*. Translated by Howard C. Warren, with preface by James Mark Baldwin (New York: Macmillan, 1899).

aside to replace it. Under changing conditions, it is quite otherwise. Here the direction of production and the different processes involved are continually changing. Here it is not enough to replace the used-up plant and the semi-manufactured products consumed in similar qualities and quantities: others—better or at least better corresponding to the new conditions of demand—have to take their place; or the replacement of capital goods used in one branch of production has to be restricted in order that another branch of production may be extended or commenced. In order to carry out such complicated operations, it is necessary to calculate. Without economic calculations capital calculations are impossible. Thus in the face of one of the most fundamental problems of economic activity, the socialist community—which has no means of economic calculation—must be quite helpless. With the best will in the world it will be quite unable to carry out the operations necessary to bring production and consumption into such a balance, that value of capital is at least maintained and only what is obtained over and above this is consumed.

But apart from this, in itself quite unsurmountable difficulty, the carrying out of a rational economic policy in a socialist community would encounter other difficulties.

To maintain and accumulate capital involves costs. It involves sacrificing present satisfactions in order that greater satisfactions may be obtained in the future. Under Capitalism the sacrifice that has to be made by the possessors of the means of production, and those who, by limiting consumption, are on the way to being possessors of the means of production. The advantage which they thereby procure for the future does indeed not entirely accrue
202 to them. They are obliged to share it with those whose incomes are derived from work, since other things being equal, the accumulation of capital increases the marginal productivity of labour and therewith wages. But the fact that, in the main, the gain of not living beyond their means (i.e. not consuming capital) and saving (i.e. increasing capital) does pay them is a sufficient stimulus to incite them to maintain and extend it. And this stimulus is the stronger the more completely their immediate needs are satisfied. For the less urgent are those present needs, which are not satisfied when provision is made for the future, the easier it is to make the sacrifice. Under Capitalism the maintenance and accumulation of capital is one of the functions of the unequal distribution of property and income.

Under Socialism the maintenance and accumulation of capital are tasks for the organized community—the State. The utility of a rational policy is the same here as under Capitalism. The advantages will be the same for all members of the community: the costs will be the same also. Decisions upon matters of capital policy will be made by the community—immediately by the economic administration, ultimately by all the citizens. They will have to decide whether more production goods or more consumption goods shall be produced—whether methods of production which are shorter but which yield a smaller product or whether methods of production which are longer but which yield a greater product shall be employed. It is impossible to say how these majority decisions will work out. It would be senseless to conjecture. The conditions under which decisions will have to be made are different from what they are under Capitalism. Under Capitalism the decision whether saving shall take place is the concern of the thrifty and the well-to-do. Under Socialism it is the concern of everybody, without distinction—therefore also of the idler and the spendthrift. Moreover, it must be remembered that here the incentive which provides a higher standard of life in return for saving will not be present. The door would therefore be open to demagogues. The opposition will always be ready to prove that more could be assigned to immediate satisfactions, and the government will not be disinclined to maintain itself longer in power by lavish spending. *Après nous le déluge* (After us, the deluge) is an old maxim of government.

Experience of the capital policy of public bodies does not inspire much hope of the thriftiness of future socialist governments. In general, new capital
is created only when the necessary sums have been raised by loans—that is 203
from the savings of private citizens. It is very seldom that capital is accumulated out of taxes or special public income. On the other hand, numerous examples can be adduced of cases in which the means of production owned by public bodies have depreciated in value, because in order that present costs may be relieved as much as possible, insufficient care has been taken for the maintenance of capital.

It is true that the governments of the socialist or half-socialist communities existing today are anxious to restrict consumption for the sake of an expenditure which is generally considered as investment and formation of new capital. Both the Soviet Government in Russia and the Nazi Government in Germany are spending great sums for the construction of works of a military character and for the construction of industrial plants whose purpose it is to make the country independent of foreign imports. A part of the capital wanted for this purpose has been provided by foreign loans; but the greater part has been provided by a restriction both of home consumption and of investment of such a type which could serve for the production of consumption goods wanted by the people. Whether we may consider this policy as a policy of saving and forming new capital, or not, depends on the way in which we judge a policy whose aim it is to increase a country's military equipment and to make its economic system independent of foreign imports. The fact alone that consumption is restricted for the sake of constructing big plants of different kinds is not evidence that new capital is created. These plants will have to prove in the future whether they will contribute to the better supply of commodities wanted for the improvement of the economic situation of the country.

5

The Element of Change in the Socialist Economy

It should be already sufficiently clear from what has been said, that under Socialism, as under any other system, there could be no perfectly stationary state. Not only incessant changes in the natural conditions of production
204 would make this impossible; quite apart from these, incessant dynamic forces would be at work, in changes in the size of the population, in the demand for commodities, and in the quantity of capital goods. One cannot conceive these factors eliminated from the economic system. It is thus unnecessary to inquire whether these changes would also involve changes in the organization of labour and the technical processes of production. For, once the economic system ceases to be in perfect equilibrium it is a matter of indifference whether actual innovations are thought of and put into practice. Once everything is in a state of flux, everything which happens is an innovation. Even when the old is repeated, it is an innovation because, under new conditions, it will have different effects. It is an innovation in its consequences.

But this is not in the least to say that the socialist system will be a progressive system. Economic change and economic progress are by no means one and the same thing. That an economic system is not stationary is no proof that it is progressing. Economic change is necessitated by the fact of changes in the conditions under which economic activity takes place. When conditions change the economic system must change also. Economic progress, however, consists only in change which takes place in a quite definite direction, towards the goal of all economic activity, e.g. the greatest possible wealth. (This conception of progress is quite free from implications of subjective judgment.) When more, or the same number of people are better provided for, then the economic system is progressive. That the difficulties of measuring value make it impossible to measure progress exactly, and that it is by no means certain that it makes men "happier," are matters which do not concern us here.

Progress can take place in many ways. Organization can be improved. The technique of production can be made more efficient, the quantity of capital can be increased. In short, many paths lead to this goal.[6] Would socialist society be able to follow them?

We may assume that it would entrust the most suitable people to direct production. But, however, talented they were, how would they be able to act rationally if they were unable to reckon, to make calculations? On this difficulty alone Socialism must surely founder.

6 205

Speculation

In any economic system which is in process of change all economic activity is based upon an uncertain future. It is therefore bound up with risk. It is essentially speculation.

The great majority of people, not knowing how to speculate successfully, and socialist writers of all shades of opinion, speak very ill of speculation. The literateur and the bureaucrat, both alien to an atmosphere of business activity, are filled with envy and rage when they think of fortunate speculators and successful entrepreneurs. To their resentment we owe the efforts of many writers on economics to discover subtle distinctions between speculation on the one hand and "legitimate trade," "value creating production," etc., on the other.[7] In reality all economic activity outside the stationary state

---

[6] On the difficulties a socialist economy must put in the way of the invention and, even more, of the realization of technical improvements, see Dietzel, *Technischer Fortschritt und Freiheit der Wirtschaft* (Bonn and Leipzig, 1922), pp. 47 ff.

[7] See the pertinent criticism of these efforts which are evidence of good intentions rather than of scientific sharpness of thought, in Michaelis, *Volkswirtschaftliche Schriften* (Berlin, 1873), Vol. II, pp. 3 ff., and by Petritsch, *Zur Lehre von der Überwälzung der Steuern mit besonderer Beziehung auf den Börsenverkehr* (Graz, 1903), pp. 28 ff. Of Adolf Wagner, Petritsch says that "although he likes to call economic life an 'organism' and wants to have it considered as such, and although he always stresses the interest of the community against that of individuals, yet in concrete economic problems he does not get beyond the individuals and their more or less moral aims, and wilfully overlooks the organic connection between these and other economic phenomena. Thus he ends where, strictly speaking, should be the starting point, not the end, of every economic investigation" (p. 59). The same is true of all writers who have thundered against speculation.

is speculation. Between the work of the humble artisan who promises to deliver a pair of shoes within a week at a fixed price, and the sinking of a coal mine based upon conjectures with regard to the disposal of its products years hence, there is only a difference of degree. Even those who invest in gilt-edged fixed-interest-bearing securities speculate—quite apart from the risk of the debtor's inability to pay. They buy money for future delivery—just as speculators in cotton buy cotton for future delivery. Economic activity is necessarily speculative because it is based upon an uncertain future. Speculation is the link that binds isolated economic action to the economic activity of society as a whole.

It is customary to attribute the notoriously low productivity of government undertakings to the fact that the persons employed are not sufficiently interested in the success of their labours. If once it were possible to lift each
206 citizen to such a plane that he could realize the connection between his own efforts and the social income, part of which belongs to him, if once his character could be so strengthened that he would remain steadfast in the face of all temptations to idle, then government undertakings would not be less productive than those of the private entrepreneur. The problem of socialization appears thus to be a problem of ethics. To make Socialism possible it is only necessary to raise men sufficiently above the state of ignorance and immorality to which they have been degraded during the terrible epoch of Capitalism. Until this plane has been reached bonuses and so on must be employed to make men more diligent.

It has already been shown that, under Socialism, the lack of an adequate stimulus to the individual to overcome the disutility of labour must have the effect of lowering productivity. This difficulty would arise even in a stationary state. Under dynamic conditions there arises another, the difficulty of speculation.

In an economic system based upon private ownership of the means of production, the speculator is interested in the result of his speculation in the highest possible degree. If it succeeds, then, in the first instance, it is *his* gain. If it fails, then, *he* is the first to feel the loss. The speculator works for the community, but he himself feels the success or failure of his action proportionately more than the community. As profit or loss, they appear much greater in proportion to his means than to the total resources of society. The more successfully he speculates the more means of production are at his disposal, the greater becomes his influence on the business of society. The less successfully he speculates the smaller becomes his property, the less becomes his influence in business. If he loses everything by speculation he disappears from the ranks of those who are called to the direction of economic affairs.

Under Socialism it is quite different. Here the leader of industry is interested in profit and loss only in so far as he participates in them as a citizen—one among millions. On his actions depends the fate of all. He can lead the nation to riches. He can just as well lead it to poverty and want. His genius can bring prosperity to the race. His incapacity, or his indifference, can bring it to destruction and decay. In *his* hands lie happiness and misery as in the hands of a god. And he must indeed be god-like to accomplish what he has to do. His vision must include everything which is of significance to the community. His judgment must be unfailing; he must be able rightly to 207
weigh the conditions of distant parts and future centuries.

That Socialism would be immediately practicable if an omnipotent and omniscient Deity were personally to descend to take in hand the government of human affairs, is incontestable. But so long as this event cannot definitely be counted upon, it is not to be expected that men will be ready freely to grant such a position to any one out of their midst. One of the fundamental facts of all social life, which all reformers must take into account, is that men have their own thoughts and their own wills. It is not to be supposed that they would suddenly, of their own free will, make themselves for all time the passive tools of *anyone* out of their midst—even though he were the wisest and best of them all.

But so long as the possibility of a single individual permanently planning the direction of affairs is excluded, it is necessary to fall back upon the majority decisions of committees, general assemblies and, in the last resort, the whole enfranchised population. But therewith arises the danger on which all collectivist undertakings inevitably come to grief—the crippling of initiative and the sense of responsibility. Innovations are not introduced because the majority of the members of the governing body cannot be induced to consent to them.

Things would not be made any better by the fact that the impossibility of leaving all decisions to a single man, or a single committee, would lead to the creation of innumerable sub-committees by which decisions would be taken. All such sub-committees would only be delegates of the one supreme authority which, as an economic system working according to a unitary plan, is implied by the very nature of Socialism. They would necessarily be bound by the instructions of the supreme authority and this, in itself, would breed irresponsibility.

We all know the appearance of the apparatus of socialist administration: a countless multitude of office holders, each zealously bent on preserving his position and preventing anybody from intruding on his sphere of activity—yet at the same time anxiously endeavouring to throw all responsibility of action on to somebody else.

For all its officiousness, such a bureaucracy offers a classic example of human indolence. Nothing stirs when no external stimulus is present. In the
208 nationalized concerns, existing within a society based for the most part on private ownership of the means of production, all stimulus to improvements in process comes from those entrepreneurs who as contractors for semi-manufactured articles and machines hope to make a profit by them. The heads of the concern itself seldom, if ever, make innovations. They content themselves with imitating what goes on in similar privately-owned undertakings. But where all concerns are socialized there will be hardly any talk of reforms and improvements.

7

Joint Stock Companies and the Socialist Economy

One of the current fallacies of socialism is that joint stock companies are a preliminary stage of the socialist undertaking. The heads of joint stock companies—it is argued—are not owners of the means of production, and yet the undertakings flourish under their direction. If, in place of the shareholders, society should assume the function of ownership, things would not be altered. The directors would not work worse for society than they would for the shareholders.

This notion, that in the joint stock company the entrepreneur-function is solely the shareholder's and that all the organs of the company are active only as the shareholders' employees, pervades also legal theory, and it has been attempted to make it the basis of Company Law. It is responsible for the fact that the business idea, which underlies the creation of the joint stock company, has been falsified, and that up to today people have been unable to find for the joint stock company a legal form which would enable it to work without friction, and that the company system everywhere suffers from grave abuses.

In fact there have never and nowhere been prosperous joint stock companies corresponding to the ideal etatistic jurists have created. Success has always been attained only by those companies whose directors have predominant personal interest in the prosperity of the company. The vital force and the effectiveness of the joint stock company lie in a partnership between the company's real managers—who generally have power to dispose over part, if not the majority, of the share-capital—and the other shareholders. Only where these directors have the same interest in the prosperity of the
209 undertaking as every owner, only where their interests coincide with the

shareholder's interests, is the business carried on in the interests of the joint stock company. Where the directors have interests other than those of a part, or of the majority, or of all of the shareholders, business is carried on against the company's interests. For in all joint stock companies that do not wither in bureaucracy, those who really are in power always manage business in their own interests, whether this coincides with the shareholders' interests or not. It is an unavoidable presupposition of the prosperity of the companies, that those in power shall receive a large part of the profits of the enterprise and that they shall be primarily affected by the misfortunes of the enterprise. In all flourishing joint stock companies, such men, immaterial of what their legal status is, wield the decisive influence. The type of man to whom joint stock companies owe their success is not the type of general manager who resembles the public official in his ways of thought, himself often an ex-public servant whose most important qualification is good connection with those in political power. It is the manager who is interested himself through his shares, it is the promoter and the founder—these are responsible for prosperity.

Socialist-etatistic theory of course will not admit this. It endeavours to force the joint stock company into a legal form in which it must languish. It refuses to see in those who guide the company anything except officials, for the etatist wants to think of the whole world as inhabited only by officials. It is allied with the organized employees and workers in their resentment-ridden fight against high sums paid to the management, believing that the profits of the business arise of themselves and are reduced by whatever is paid to the men in charge. Finally, it turns also against the shareholder. The latest German doctrine does not want, "in view of the evolution of the concept of fair play," to let the shareholder's self-interest decide, but rather "the interest and well-being of the enterprise, itself, namely its own economic, legal and sociological value, independent of transient majorities of transient shareholders." It wants to create for the administration of the companies a position of power, which should make them independent of the will of those who have put up the majority of the share-capital.[8]

That "altruistic motives" or the like are ever decisive in the administration 210
of successful joint stock companies is a fable. Such attempts to model Company Law after the illusory ideal of etatistic politicians, have not succeeded in making the joint stock company a piece of the illusory "functional economy"; they have however damaged the joint stock company form of enterprise.

---

[8] See the criticism of these theories and movements in Passow, *Der Strukturwandel der Aktiengesellschaft im Lichte der Wirtschaftsenquete* (Jena, 1930), pp. 1 ff.

CHAPTER 11

The Impracticability of Socialism

1

The Fundamental Problems of a Socialist Economy Under Conditions of Change

211 The preceding investigations have shown the difficulties confronting the establishment of a socialist order of society. In a socialist community the possibility of economic calculations is lacking: it is therefore impossible to ascertain the cost and result of an economic operation or to make the result of the calculation the test of the operation. This in itself would be sufficient to make Socialism impracticable. But, quite apart from that, another insurmountable obstacle stands in its way. It is impossible to find a form of organization which makes the economic action of the individual independent of the co-operation of other citizens without leaving it open to all the risks of mere gambling. These are the two problems, and without their solution the realization of Socialism appears impracticable unless in a completely stationary state.

Too little attention has hitherto been given to these fundamental questions. The first has generally been almost ignored. The reason for this is that people have not been able to get rid of the idea that labour time can afford an efficient measure of value. But even many of those who recognize that the labour theory of value is untenable continue to believe that value can be measured. The frequent attempts which have been made to discover a standard of value prove this. To understand the problem of economic calculation it was necessary to recognize the true character of the exchange relations expressed in the prices of the market.

The existence of this important problem could be revealed only by the methods of the modern subjective theory of value. In actual practice although the tendency has been all in the direction of Socialism, the problem has not become so urgent as to attract general attention.

It is quite otherwise with the second problem. The more communal enterprise extends, the more attention is drawn to the bad business results of nationalized and municipalized undertakings. It is impossible to miss the cause of the difficulty: a child could see where something was lacking. So that it cannot be said that this problem has not been tackled. But the way in which it has been tackled has been deplorably inadequate. Its organic connection with the essential nature of socialist enterprise has been regarded as merely a question of better selection of persons. It has not been realized that even exceptionally gifted men of high character cannot solve the problems created by socialist control of industry. 212

2

Attempted Solutions

As far as most socialists are concerned, recognition of these problems is obstructed, not only by their rigid adherence to the labour theory of value but also by their whole conception of economic activity. They fail to realize that industry must be constantly changing: their conception of the socialist community is always static. As long as they are criticizing the capitalist order they deal throughout with the phenomena of a progressive economy and they paint in glaring colours the friction caused by economic change. But they seem to regard all change and not only the friction caused by it, as a peculiar attribute of the capitalist order. In the happy kingdom of the future everything will develop without movement or friction.

We can see this best if we think of the picture of the entrepreneur which is generally drawn by socialists. In such a picture the entrepreneur is characterized only by the special way he derives his income. Clearly any analysis of the capitalist order must take as its central point not capital nor the capitalists but the entrepreneur. But Socialism, including Marxian Socialism, sees in the entrepreneur someone alien to the process of production, someone whose whole work consists in the appropriation of surplus value. It will be sufficient to expropriate these parasites to bring about a socialist society. The recollection of the liberation of the peasants and the abolition of slavery hovers vaguely in Marx's mind and even more so in the minds of many other
socialists. But they fail to see that the position of the feudal lord was quite 213
different from that of the entrepreneur. The feudal lord had no influence on

production. He stood outside the process of production: only when it was finished did he step in with a claim to a share in the yield. But in so far as the lord of the manor and the slave owner were also leaders of production they retained their position even after the abolition of serfdom and slavery. The fact that henceforward they had to give the workers the value of their labour did not change their economic function. But the entrepreneur fulfils a task which must be performed even in a socialist community. This the Socialist does not see; or at least refuses to see.

Socialism's misunderstanding of the entrepreneur degenerates into idiosyncrasy whenever the word speculator is mentioned. Even Marx, unmindful of the good resolutions which animated him, proceeds entirely along "petty bourgeois" lines in this connection and his school has even surpassed him. All socialists overlook the fact that even in a socialist community every economic operation must be based on an uncertain future, and that its *economic* consequence remains uncertain even if it is *technically* successful. They see in the uncertainty which leads to speculation a consequence of the anarchy of production, whilst in fact it is a necessary result of changing economic conditions.

The great mass of people are incapable of realizing that in economic life nothing is permanent except change. They regard the existing state of affairs as eternal; as it has been so shall it always be. But even if they were in a position to envision the πάντα 'ρεῖ (everything simple or all so easy) they would be baffled by the problems to be solved. To see and to act in advance, to follow new ways, is always the concern only of the few, the leaders. Socialism is the economic policy of the crowd, of the masses, remote from insight into the nature of economic activity. Socialist theory is the precipitate of their views on economic matters—it is created and supported by those who find economic life alien, and do not comprehend it.

Among socialists only Saint-Simon realized to some extent the position of the entrepreneurs in the capitalistic economy. As a result he is often denied the name of Socialist. The others completely fail to realize that the functions of entrepreneurs in the capitalist order must be performed in a socialist community also. This is reflected most clearly in the writings of Lenin.
214 According to him the work performed in a capitalist order by those whom he refused to designate as "working" can be boiled down to "Auditing of Production and Distribution" and "keeping the records of labour and products." This could easily be attended to by the armed workers, "by the whole of the armed people."[1] Lenin quite rightly separates these functions of the

[1] Lenin, *Staat und Revolution*, p. 94. Publisher's Note: p. 304 in the English edition.

"capitalists and clerks" from the work of the technically trained higher personnel, not however missing the opportunity to take a side thrust at scientifically trained people by giving expression to that contempt for all highly skilled work which is characteristic of Marxian proletarian snobbishness. "This recording, this exercise of audit," he says, "Capitalism has simplified to the utmost and has reduced to extremely simple operations of superintendence and book-entry within the grasp of anyone able to read and write. To control these operations a knowledge of elementary arithmetic and the drawing of correct receipts is sufficient."[2] It is therefore possible straightway to enable all members of society to do these things for themselves.[3] This is all, absolutely all that Lenin had to say on this problem; and no socialist has a word more to say. They have no greater perception of the essentials of economic life than the errand boy, whose only idea of the work of the entrepreneur is that he covers pieces of paper with letters and figures.

It was for this reason that it was quite impossible for Lenin to realize the causes of the failure of his policy. In his life and his reading he remained so far removed from the facts of economic life that he was as great a stranger to the work of the bourgeoisie as a Hottentot to the work of an explorer taking geographical measurements. When he saw that his work could proceed no further on the original lines he decided to rely no longer on references to "armed workers" in order to compel the "bourgeois" experts to co-operate: instead they were to receive "high remuneration" for "a short transition period" so that they could set the socialist order going and thus render themselves superfluous. He even thought it possible that this would take place within a year.[4]

Those socialists who do not think of the socialist community as the strongly centralized organization conceived by their more clearheaded brethren and which alone is logically conceivable, believe that the difficulties confronting 215
the management of industry can be solved by democratic institutions inside undertakings. They believe that individual industries could be allowed to conduct their operations with a certain degree of independence without endangering the uniformity and the correct co-ordination of industry. If every enterprise were placed under the control of a workers' committee, no further difficulties could exist. In all this there is a whole crop of fallacies and errors. The problem of economic management with which we are here concerned lies much less in the work of individual industries than in harmonizing the work of individual concerns in the whole economic system. It

[2] *Ibid.*, p. 95. Publisher's Note: pp. 304–305 in the English edition.

[3] *Ibid.*, p. 96. Publisher's Note: p. 305 in the English edition.

[4] Lenin, *Die nächsten Aufgaben der Sowjetmacht* (Berlin, 1918), pp. 16 ff.

deals with such questions as dissolving, extending, transforming and limiting existing undertakings and establishing new undertakings—matters which can never be decided by the workers of one industry. The problems of conducting an industry stretch far beyond the individual concern.

State and municipal Socialism have supplied enough unfavourable experience to compel the closest attention to the problem of economic control. But etatists in general have treated this problem no less inadequately than those who have dealt with it in Bolshevik Russia. General opinion seems to regard the main evil of communal undertakings to be due to the fact that they are not run on "business" lines. Now rightly understood this catchword could lead to a correct view on the problem. Communal enterprise does indeed lack the spirit of the business man, and the very problem for Socialism here is to create something to put in its place. But the catchword is not understood in this way at all. It is an offspring of the bureaucratic mind: that is to say it comes from people for whom all human activity represents the fulfilment of formal official and professional duties. Officialdom classifies activity according to the capacity for undertaking it formally acquired by means of examinations and a certain period of service. "Training" and "length of service" are the only things which the official brings to the "job." If the work of a body of officials appears unsatisfactory, there can be only one explanation: the officials have not had the right training, and future appointments must be made differently. It is therefore proposed that a different training should be required of future candidates. If only the officials of the communal undertaking came with a *business* training, the undertaking would be more *business-like.* But for the official who cannot enter into the spirit of
216 capitalist industry this means nothing more than certain external manifestations of business technique: prompter replies to inquiries, the adoption of certain technical office appliances, which have not yet been sufficiently introduced into the departments, such as typewriters, copying machines, etc., the reduction of unnecessary duplication, and other things. In this way "the business spirit" penetrates into the offices of communal enterprise. And people are greatly surprised when these men trained on these lines, also fail, fail even worse than the much-maligned civil servants, who in fact, show themselves superior at least in formal schooling.

It is not difficult to expose the fallacies inherent in such notions. The attributes of the business man cannot be divorced from the position of the entrepreneur in the capitalist order. "Business" is not in itself a quality innate in a person; only the qualities of mind and character essential to a business man can be inborn. Still less is it an accomplishment which can be acquired by study, though the knowledge and the accomplishments needed by a business man can be taught and learned. A man does not become a business man by passing some years in commercial training or in a commercial institute, nor by a knowledge of book-keeping and the jargon of commerce, nor by a skill in languages and typing and shorthand. These are things which the clerk requires. But the clerk is not a business man, even though in ordinary speech he may be called a "trained business man."

When these obvious truths became clear in the end the experiment was tried of making entrepreneurs, who had worked successfully for many years, the managers of public enterprises. The result was lamentable. They did no better than the others; furthermore they lacked the sense for formal routine which distinguishes the life-long official. The reason was obvious. An entrepreneur deprived of his characteristic role in economic life ceases to be a business man. However much experience and routine he may bring to his new task he will still only be an official in it.

It is just as useless to attempt to solve the problem by new methods of remuneration. It is thought that if the managers of public enterprises were better paid, competition for these posts would arise and make it possible to select the best men. Many go even further and believe that the difficulties will be overcome by granting the managers a share in the profits. It is significant that these proposals have hardly ever been put in practice, although they appear quite practicable as long as public undertakings exist 217
alongside private enterprises, and as long as the possibility of economic calculation permits the ascertainment of the result achieved by the public enterprise which is not the case under pure Socialism. But the problem is not nearly so much the question of the manager's share in the profit, as of his share in the losses which arise through his conduct of business. Except in a purely moral sense the property-less manager of a public undertaking can be made answerable only for a comparatively small part of the losses. To make a man materially interested in profits and hardly concerned in losses simply encourages a lack of seriousness. This is the experience, not only of public undertakings but also of all private enterprises, which have granted to comparatively poor employees in managerial posts rights to a percentage of the profits.

It is an evasion of the problem to put one's faith in the hope that the moral purification of mankind, which the socialists expect to occur when their aims are realized, will of itself make everything perfectly right. Whether Socialism will or will not have the moral effect expected from it may here be conveniently left undecided. But the problems with which we are concerned do not arise from the moral shortcomings of humanity. They are problems of the logic of will and action which must arise at all times and in all places.

3

Capitalism the Only Solution

But let us disregard the fact that up to now all socialist efforts have been baffled by these problems, and let us attempt to trace out the lines on which the solution ought to be sought. Only by making such an attempt can we throw any light on the question whether such a solution is possible in the framework of a socialist order of society.

The first step which would be necessary would be to form sections inside the socialist community to which the management of definite branches of business would be entrusted. As long as the industry of a socialist community is directed by one single authority which makes all arrangements and bears all the responsibility, a solution of the problems is inconceivable, because all the other workers are only acting instruments without independent delimited
218 spheres of operation and consequently without any special responsibility. What we must aim at is precisely the possibility not only of supervising and controlling the whole process, but of considering and judging separately the subsidiary processes which take place within a narrower sphere.

In this respect at least, our procedure runs parallel to all past attempts to solve our problem. It is clear to everyone that the desired aim can be achieved only if responsibility is built up from below. We must therefore start from a single industry or from a single branch of industry. It makes no difference whether the unit with which we start is large or small since the same principle which we have once used for our division can be again used when it is necessary to divide too large a unit. Much more important than the question where and how often the division shall be made is the question how in spite of the division of industry into parts we can preserve that unity of cooperation without which a social economy is impossible.

We imagine then the economic order of the socialist community to be divided into any number of parts each of which is put in the charge of a particular manager. Every manager of a section is charged with the full responsibility for his operations. This means that the profit or a very considerable part of the profit accrues to him; on the other hand the burden of losses falls upon him, insomuch as the means of production which he squanders through bad measures will not be replaced by society. If he squanders all the means of production under his care he ceases to be manager of a section and is reduced to the ranks of the masses.

If this personal responsibility of the section manager is not to be a mere sham, then his operations must be clearly marked off from that of other

managers. Everything he receives from other section managers in the form of raw materials or partly manufactured goods for further working or for use as instruments in his section and all the work which he gets performed in his section will be debited to him; everything he delivers to other sections or for consumption will be credited to him. It is necessary, however, that he should be left free choice to decide what machines, raw materials, partly manufactured goods, and labour forces he will employ in his section and what he will produce in it. If he is not given this freedom he cannot be burdened with any responsibility. For it would not be his fault if at the 219
command of the supreme controlling authority he had produced something for which, under existing conditions, there was no corresponding demand, or if his section was handicapped because it received its material from other sections in an unsuitable condition, or, what comes to the same thing, at too high a charge. In the first event, the failure of his section would be attributable to the dispositions of the supreme control, in the latter to the failures of the sections which produced the material. But on the other hand the community must also be free to claim the same rights which it allows to the section manager. This means that it takes the products which he has produced only according to its requirements, and only if it can obtain them at the lowest rate of charge, and it charges him with the labour, which it supplies to him at the highest rate it is in a position to obtain: that is to say it supplies the labour to the highest bidder.

Society as a production community now falls into three groups. The supreme direction forms one. Its function is merely to supervise the orderly course of the process of production as a whole, the execution of which is completely detailed to the section managers. The third group is the citizens who are not in the service of the supreme administration and are not section managers. Between the two groups stand the section managers as a special group: they have received from the community once and for all at the beginning of the regime an allotment of the means of production for which they have had to pay nothing, and they continue to receive from it the labour force of the members of the third group, who are assigned to the highest bidders amongst them. The central administration which has to credit each member of the third group with everything it has received from the section managers for his labour power, or, in case it employs him directly in its own sphere of operation, with everything which it might have received from the section managers for his labour power, will then distribute the consumption goods to the highest bidders amongst the citizens of all three groups. The proceeds will be credited to the section managers who have delivered the products.

By such an arrangement of the community, the section manager can be made fully responsible for his doings. The sphere for which he bears responsibility is sharply delimited from that for which others bear the respon-
220 sibility. Here we are no longer faced with the total result of the economic activity of the whole industrial community in which the contribution of one individual cannot be distinguished from that of another. The "productive contribution" of each individual section manager is open to separate judgment, as is also that of each individual citizen in the three groups.

It is clear that the section managers must be permitted to change, extend or contract their section according to the prevailing course of demand on the part of the citizens as indicated in the market for consumption goods. They must therefore be in a position to sell those means of production in their section which are more urgently required in other sections, to these other sections: and they ought to demand as much for them as they can obtain under the existing conditions. . . .

But we need not carry the analysis further. For what are we confronted with but the capitalist order of society—the only form of economy in which strict application of the principle of the personal responsibility of every individual citizen is possible. Capitalism is that form of social economy in which all the deficiencies of the socialist system described above are made good. Capitalism is the only conceivable form of social economy which is appropriate to the fulfilment of the demands which society makes of any economic organization.

PART II
THE ECONOMICS OF A SOCIALIST COMMUNITY

SECTION 2

THE FOREIGN RELATIONS OF A SOCIALIST COMMUNITY

CHAPTER 12

National Socialism and World Socialism

1

The Spatial Extent of the Socialist Community

Early Socialism is marked by its predilection for a return to the simpler 223
modes of production of primitive times. Its ideal is the self-sufficing village, or, at most, the self-sufficing province—a town around which a number of villages are grouped. Being averse to all trade and commerce, its protagonists regard foreign trade as something entirely evil which must be abolished. Foreign Trade introduces superfluous commodities into the country. Since it was once possible to do without them, it is obvious that they are unnecessary, and that only the extreme ease with which they can be procured is responsible for the unnecessary expenditure upon them. Foreign Trade undermines morality and introduces foreign ideas and customs. In Utopia the stoic ideal of self-mastery was transmuted into the economic ideal of self-sufficiency. Plutarch found it an admirable thing in Lycurgusan Sparta—as romantically conceived in his day—that no merchant ship ever entered her harbours.[1]

This attachment to the ideal of economic self-sufficiency, and their complete incapacity to understand the nature of trade and commerce, led the Utopians to overlook the problem of the territorial limits of the ideal state. Whether the borders of fairyland are to be wider or narrower in extent does not enter into their considerations. In the tiniest village there is space enough to realize their plans. In this way it was possible to think of realizing Utopia tentatively in small instalments. Owen founded the New Harmony community in Indiana. Cabet founded a small Icaria in Texas. Considerant founded a model phalanstery in the same state. "Duodecimo editions of the New Jerusalem," jeers the Communist Manifesto.

[1] Poehlmann, *Geschichte der sozialen Frage und des Sozialismus in der antiken Welt*, Vol. I, pp. 110 ff.; 123 ff.

224 It was only gradually that socialists came to perceive that the self-sufficiency of a small area could provide no foundation for Socialism. Thompson, a disciple of Owen, remarked that the realization of equality among the members of one community was far from signifying the realization of equality between the members of different communities. Under the influence of this discovery, he turned to centralized Socialism.[2] Saint-Simon and his school were thorough centralizers. Pecqueur's schemes of reform claimed to be national and universal.[3]

Thus emerges a problem peculiar to Socialism. Can Socialism exist within limited areas of the earth's surface? Or is it necessary that the entire inhabited world should constitute a unitary socialistic community?

2

Marxian Treatment of this Problem

For the Marxian, there can be only one solution of this problem—the ecumenical solution.

Marxism, indeed, proceeds from the assumption that by an inner necessity, Capitalism has already set its mark upon the whole world. Even to-day Capitalism is not limited to a single nation or to a small group of nations. Even today it is international and cosmopolitan. "Instead of the old local and national isolation and self-sufficiency, world trade has developed and the interdependence of nations." The cheapness of their commodities is the "heavy artillery" of the bourgeoisie. With the aid of this it compels all nations, on pain of extinction, to adopt bourgeois methods of production. "It forces them to adopt so-called civilization, i.e. to become bourgeois. In a word, it creates a world after its own image." And this is true not only of material but also of intellectual production. "The intellectual productions of one nation become the common property of all. National narrowness and exclusiveness become daily more impossible, and out of the many national and local literatures a world literature arises."[4]

---

[2] Tugan-Baranowsky, *Der moderne Sozialismus in seiner geschichtlichen Entwicklung* (Dresden, 1908), p. 136.

[3] Pecqueur, *Théorie nouvelle d'Économie sociale et politique*, p. 699.

[4] Marx-Engels, *Das Kommunistische Manifest*, p. 26. Publisher's Note: p. 325 of the Eastman anthology edition.

It follows, therefore, from the logic of the materialist interpretation of history that Socialism too can be no national, but only an international 225
phenomenon. It is a phase not merely in the history of a single nation, but in the history of the whole human race. In the logic of Marxism the question whether this or that nation is "ripe" for Socialism cannot even be asked. Capitalism makes *the world* ripe for Socialism, not a single nation or a single industry. The expropriators, through whose expropriation the last step towards Socialism must be taken, must not be conceived save as major capitalists whose capital is invested throughout the whole world. For the Marxian, therefore, the socialistic experiments of the "Utopians" are just as senseless as Bismarck's facetious proposal to introduce Socialism experimentally into one of the Polish districts of the Prussian State.[5] Socialism is an historical process. It cannot be tested in a retort or anticipated in miniature. For the Marxian, therefore, the problem of the autarky of a socialist community cannot even arise. The only socialist community he can conceive comprehends the entire human race and the entire surface of the globe. For him the economic administration of the world *must* be unitary.

Later Marxians have, indeed, recognized that, at any rate for a time, the existence of many independent socialist communities side by side must be anticipated.[6] But, once this is conceded one must go further and also take into account the possibility of one or more socialist communities existing within a world which, for the most part, is still capitalistic.

3

Liberalism and the Problem of the Frontiers

When Marx and, with him, the majority of recent writers on Socialism consider Socialism only as realized in a unitary world state, they overlook powerful forces that work against economic unification.

The levity with which they dispose of all these problems may not unreasonably be attributed to what, as we shall see, was an entirely unjustifiable acceptance of an attitude with regard to the future political organization of the world, which was prevalent at the time when Marxism was taking form. 226

[5] Bismarck's speech in the German Reichstag, on February 19, 1878 (*Fürst Bismarcks Reden,* edited by Stein, Vol. VII, p. 34).

[6] Bauer, *Die Nationalitätenfrage und die Sozialdemokratie* (Vienna, 1907), p. 519.

At that time, liberals held that all regional and national divisions could be regarded as political atavisms. The liberal doctrine of free trade and protection had been propounded—irrefutable for all time. It had been shown that all limitations on trade were to the disadvantage of all concerned: and, arguing from this, it had been attempted with success to limit the functions of the state to the production of security. For Liberalism the problem of the frontiers of the state does not arise. If the functions of the state are limited to the protection of life and property against murder and theft, it is no longer of any account to whom this or that land belongs. Whether the state extended over a wider or a narrower territory, seemed a matter of indifference to an age which was shattering tariff barriers and assimilating the legal and administrative systems of single states to a common form. In the middle of the nineteenth century, optimistic liberals could regard the idea of a League of Nations, a true world-state, as practicable in the not too far distant future.

The liberals did not sufficiently consider that greatest of hindrances to the development of universal free trade—the problem of races and nationalities. But the socialists overlooked completely that this constituted an infinitely greater hindrance to the development of a socialistic society. Their incapacity to go beyond Ricardo in all matters of economics, and their complete failure to understand all questions of nationalism, made it impossible for them even to conceive this problem.

CHAPTER 13

The Problem of Migration Under Socialism

1

Migration and Differences in National Conditions

If trade were completely free, production would only take place under the 227
most suitable conditions. Raw materials would be produced in those parts which, taking everything into account, would yield the highest product. Manufacture would be localized where the transport charges, including those necessary to place the commodities in the hands of the ultimate consumer, were at a minimum. As labour settles around the centres of production, the geographical distribution of population would necessarily adapt itself to the natural conditions of production.

Natural conditions, however, are unchanging only in a stationary economic system. The forces of change are continually transforming them. In a changing economy men migrate continually from the places where conditions are less favourable to places where they are more favourable for production. Under Capitalism the stress of competition tends to direct labour and capital to the most suitable places. In a closed socialist community the same result would have to be achieved by administrative decree. In both cases the principle would be the same: men would have to go where the conditions of life were most favourable.[1]

---

[1] See my *Nation, Staat und Wirtschaft* (Vienna, 1919), pp. 45 ff., and *Liberalismus* (Jena, 1927), pp. 93 ff. Publisher's Note: *Nation, Staat und Wirtschaft* is not in English. *Liberalismus* is in English as *The Free and Prosperous Commonwealth: An Exposition of the Ideas of Classical Liberalism.* Translated by Ralph Raico. Edited by Arthur Goddard (Princeton, N.J.: D. Van Nostrand, 1962). This book was republished in 1978 under the title *Liberalism: A Socio-Economic Exposition.* Foreword to the Second Edition by Louis M. Spadaro. (Kansas City: Sheed Andrews and McMeel, Inc., 1978). The pages in the German work referred to here (93 ff.) are pp. 105 ff. in both English editions.

These migrations have the closest bearing upon the condition of the different nations. They cause citizens of one nation, the natural conditions of which are less favourable, to move into the territory of other nations more favourably endowed. If the conditions under which migration takes place
228 are such that the immigrants are assimilated to their new surroundings then the nation from which they came is, to that extent, weakened in numbers. If they are such that the immigrants preserve their nationality in their new home—still more if they assimilate the original inhabitants—then the nation receiving them will find immigration a menace to its national position.

To be a member of a national minority involves multitudinous political disadvantages.[2] The wider the functions of the political authority the more burdensome are these disadvantages. They are smallest in the state which is founded upon purely liberal principles. They are greatest in the state which is founded upon Socialism. The more they are felt, the greater become the efforts of each nation to protect its members from the fate of belonging to a national minority. To wax in numbers, to be a majority in rich and extensive territories these become highly desirable political aims. But this is nothing but Imperialism.[3] In the last decades of the nineteenth century, and the first decades of the twentieth, the favourite weapons of Imperialism were commercial weapons—protective tariffs, prohibitions of imports, premiums on exports, freight discriminations, and the like. Less attention was paid to the use of another powerful imperialistic weapon—limitations on emigration and immigration. This is becoming more significant now. The *ultima ratio* of imperialism is, however, war. Beside war, all other weapons that it may use appear merely insufficient auxiliaries.

Nothing justifies us in assuming that under Socialism the disadvantages of belonging to a national minority would be diminished. On the contrary. The more the individual depended on the State—the more importance political decisions had for the life of the individual—the more would the national minority feel the political impotence to which it was condemned.

But when we are considering migration under Socialism we need not give special attention to the friction which would arise thereform between nations. For under Socialism there must arise, even between members of one and the same nation, points of difference which make the division of the surface of the earth—which is a matter of indifference to Liberalism—a problem of cardinal importance.

---

[2] *Nation, Staat und Wirtschaft*, pp. 37 ff.

[3] *Ibid.*, pp. 63 ff.; *Liberalismus*, p. 107 ff. Publisher's Note: pp. 121 ff. in both the 1962 and 1978 English editions of this work.

2 229

The Tendency Towards Decentralization Under Socialism

Under Capitalism, capital and labour move until marginal utilities are everywhere equal. Equilibrium is attained when the marginal productivity of all capital and labour is the same.

Let us leave the movement of capital on one side and consider first the movement of labour. The migrating workers depress the marginal productivity of labour wherever they betake themselves. The fact that wages, their income, sink, directly damages the workers who were employed in centres of migration before the incursion of new workers took place. They regard the "immigrants" as the enemy of high wages. The particular interest would be served by a prohibition of "immigration." It becomes a cardinal point of the particularist policy of all such particular groups of workers to keep newcomers out.

It has been the task of Liberalism to show who bear the costs of such a policy. The first to be injured are the workers in the less favourably situated centres of production, who, on account of the lower marginal productivity of their labour in those centres, have to content themselves with lower wages. At the same time, the owners of the more favourably situated means of production suffer through not being able to obtain the product which they might obtain could they employ a larger number of workers. But this is not the end of the matter. A system that protects the immediate interests of particular groups limits productivity in general and, in the end, injures everybody—even those whom it began by favouring. How protection finally affects the individual, whether he gains or loses, compared with what he would have got under complete freedom of trade, depends on the degrees of protection to him and to others. Although, under protection, the total produce is lower than it would have been under free trade, so that the average income is necessarily lower, it is still quite possible that certain individuals may do better than they would under free trade. The greater the protection afforded to particular interests, the greater the damage to the community as a whole, and to that extent the smaller the probability that single individuals gain thereby more than they lose.

As soon as it is possible to forward private interests in this way and to
obtain special privileges, a struggle for pre-eminence breaks out among those 230
interested. Each tries to get the better of the other. Each tries to get more privileges so as to reap the greater private gain. The idea of perfectly equal protection for all is the fantasy of an ill-thought out theory. For, if all particular interests were equally protected, nobody would reap any advantage: the

only result would be that all would feel the disadvantage of the curtailment of productivity equally. Only the hope of obtaining for himself a degree of protection, which will benefit him as compared with the less protected, makes protection attractive to the individual. It is always demanded by those who have the power to acquire and preserve especial privileges for themselves.

In exposing the effects of protection, Liberalism broke the aggressive power of particular interests. It now became obvious that, at best, only a few could gain absolutely by protection and privileges and that the great majority must inevitably lose. This demonstration deprived such systems of the support of the masses. Privilege fell because it lost popularity.

In order to rehabilitate protection, it was necessary to destroy Liberalism. This was attempted by a double attack: an attack from the point of view of nationalism, and an attack from the point of view of those special interests of the middle and working classes which were menaced by Capitalism. The one served to mature the movement towards territorial exclusiveness, the other the growth of special privileges for such employers and workmen as are not equal to the stress of competition. Once Liberalism has been completely vanquished, however, and no longer menaces the protective system, there remains nothing to oppose the extension of particular privilege. It was long thought that territorial protection was limited to national areas, that the re-imposition of internal tariffs, limitation of internal migration, and so on, was no longer conceivable. And this is certainly true so long as any regard at all is preserved for Liberalism. But, during the war, even this was abandoned in Germany and Austria, and there sprang up overnight all kinds of regional barriers. In order to secure a lower cost of living for their own population, the districts producing a surplus of agricultural produce cut themselves off from the districts that could support their population only by importing foodstuffs. The cities and industrial areas limited immigration in
231 order to counteract the rise in the price of foodstuffs and rents. Regional particularism broke up that unity of economic area on which national neo-mercantilism had based all its plans.

Even granting that Socialism is at all practicable, the development of a unitary world socialism would encounter grave difficulties. It is quite possible that the workers in particular districts, or particular concerns, or particular factories, would take the view that the instruments of production which happened to lie within their area were their own property, and that no outsider was entitled to profit by them. In such a case World Socialism would split up into numerous self-independent socialist communities—if, indeed, it did not become completely syndicalized. For Syndicalism is nothing less than the principle of decentralization consistently applied.

CHAPTER 14

Foreign Trade Under Socialism

1

Autarky and Socialism

A socialist community, which did not include the whole of mankind, 232
would have no reason to remain isolated from the rest of the world. It is true, that it might be disquieting for the rulers of such a state that foreign ideas would come over the frontiers with foreign products. They might fear for the permanence of their system, if their subjects were able to compare their position with that of foreigners who were not citizens of a socialist community. But these are political considerations, and do not apply if the foreign states are also socialistic. Moreover, a statesman who is convinced of the desirability of Socialism must expect that intercourse with foreigners will make them also socialists: he will not fear lest it undermine the socialism of his own compatriots.

The theory of Free Trade shows how the closing of the frontiers of a socialist community against the import of foreign commodities would injure its inhabitants. Capital and labour would have to be applied under relatively unfavourable conditions yielding a lower product than otherwise would have been obtained. An extreme example will make this clear. At the expense of an enormous outlay of capital and labour a socialist Germany could grow coffee in greenhouses. But it would obviously be more advantageous to procure it from Brazil in exchange for products for whose production conditions in Germany were more favourable.[1]

---

[1] It is superfluous to dispute with the autarky plans, which have been most zealously argued by the naive *litterateurs* of the "Tat" circle (Fried, *Das Ende des Kapitalismus,* Jena 1931). Autarky would probably depress the standard of life of the German people incomparably more than could the Reparations burden multiplied a hundred-fold.

2

Foreign Trade Under Socialism

Such considerations indicate the principles on which a socialist community
233 would have to base its commercial policy. In so far as it aspired to let its actions be guided *purely* by economic considerations it would have to aim at securing just what under complete freedom of trade would be secured by the unrestricted play of economic forces. The socialist community would limit its activities to the production of those commodities it could produce under comparatively more favourable conditions than existed abroad, and it would exploit each single line of production only so far as this relative advantage justified. It would procure all other commodities from abroad by way of exchange.

This fundamental principle holds good whether or not trade with abroad is carried out by recourse to a general medium of exchange—by recourse to money—or not. In foreign trade, just as in internal trade—there is no difference between them—no rational production could proceed without money reckoning and the formation of prices for the means of production. On this point, we have nothing to add to what we have said already. But here we wish to consider a socialist community, existing in a world not otherwise socialistic. This community could estimate and compute in money in exactly the same way as a state railway, or a city waterworks, existing in a society otherwise based upon private ownership of the means of production.

3

Foreign Investment

No one can regard what his neighbour does as a matter of mere indifference. Everyone is interested in raising the productivity of labour by the widest division of labour possible under given circumstances. I too am injured if some people maintain a state of economic self-sufficiency: for, if they were to relax their isolation, the division of labour could be made even more comprehensive. If the means of production are in the hands of relatively inefficient agents, the damage is universal.

Under Capitalism the profit-seeking of individual entrepreneurs harmonizes the interests of the individual with those of the community. On the one hand, the entrepreneur is always seeking for new markets, and under-

selling with cheaper and better wares the dearer and inferior products of less rationally organized production. On the other, he is always seeking 234
cheaper and more productive sources of raw materials and opening up more favourable sites for production. This is the true nature of that expansive tendency of Capitalism, which neo-Marxian propaganda so completely misrepresents as the "Verwertungsstreben des Kapitals" ("the drive of capital for profit"), and so amazingly involves into an explanation of modern Imperialism.

The old colonial policy of Europe was mercantilistic, militaristic, and imperialistic. With the defeat of mercantilism by liberal ideas, the character of colonial policy completely changed. Of the old colonial powers, Spain, Portugal and France had lost the greater part of their former possessions. England, who had become the greatest of the colonial powers, managed her possessions according to the principles of free trade theory. It was not cant for English free traders to speak of England's vocation to evaluate backward people to a state of civilization. England has shown by acts that she has regarded her position in India, in the Crown Colonies, and in the Protectorates, as a general mandatory of European civilization. It is not hypocrisy when English liberals speak of England's rule in the colonies as being not less useful for the inhabitants and for the rest of the world than it is for England. The mere fact that England preserved Free Trade in India shows that she conceived her colonial policy in a spirit quite different from that of the states who entered, or re-entered the sphere of colonial policy in the last decades of the nineteenth century—France, Germany, the United States, Japan, Belgium and Italy. The wars waged by England during the era of Liberalism to extend her colonial empire and to open up territories which refused to admit foreign trade, laid the foundations of the modern world economy.[2] To measure the true significance of these wars one has only to imagine what would have happened if India and China and their hinterland had remained closed to world commerce. Not only each Chinese and each

[2] In judging the English policy for opening up China, people constantly put in the foreground the fact that it was the opium trade which gave the direct, immediate occasion for the outbreak of war complications. But in the wars which the English and French waged against China between 1839 and 1860 the stake was the general freedom of trade and not only the freedom of the opium trade. That from the Free Trade point of view no barriers ought to be put in the way even of the trade in poisons, and that everyone should abstain by his own impulse from enjoyments harmful to his organism, is not so base and mean as socialist and anglophobe writers tend to represent. Rosa Luxemburg, *Die Akkumulation des Kapitals* (Berlin, 1913), pp. 363 ff. reproaches the English and French that it was no heroic act to defeat with European weapons the Chinese, who were provided only with out of date arms. Ought the French and English also to have taken the field only with ancient guns and spears?

235 Hindu, but also each European and each American, would be considerably worse off. Were England to lose India today, and were that great land, so richly endowed by nature, to sink into anarchy, so that it no longer offered a market for international trade—or no longer offered so large a market—it would be an economic catastrophe of the first order.

Liberalism aims to open all doors closed to trade. But it no way desires to compel people to buy or to sell. Its antagonism is confined to those governments which, by imposing prohibition and other limitations on trade, exclude their subjects from the advantages of taking part in world commerce, and thereby impair the standard of life of all mankind. The Liberal policy has nothing in common with Imperialism. On the contrary, it is designed to overthrow Imperialism and expel it from the sphere of international trade.

A socialist community would have to do the same. It, too, would not be able to allow areas lavishly endowed by nature to be permanently shut off from international trade, nor whole nations to refrain from exchange. But here Socialism would encounter a problem which can only be solved under Capitalism—the problem of ownership of capital abroad.

Under Capitalism, as Free Traders would have it, frontiers would be without significance. Trade would flow over them unhindered. They would prohibit neither the movement of the most suitable producers towards immobile means of production, nor the investment of mobile means of production in the most suitable places. Ownership of the means of production would be independent of citizenship. Foreign investment would be as easy as investment at home.

Under Socialism the situation would be different. It would be impossible for a socialist community to possess means of production lying outside its own borders. It could not invest capital abroad even if it would yield a higher product there. A socialist Europe must remain helpless, while a socialist India exploits its resources inefficiently, and thereby brings fewer goods to the world market than it would otherwise have done. New supplies of capital must be utilized under less favourable conditions in Europe, while in India, for want of new capital, more favourable conditions of production are not fully exploited. Thus independent socialist communities existing side by side and exchanging commodities only, would achieve a nonsensical position. Quite apart from other considerations the very fact of their independence would lead to a state of affairs under which productivity would necessarily diminish.

These difficulties could not be overcome so long as independent socialist communities existed side by side. They could only be surmounted by the amalgamation of the separate communities into a unitary socialist state comprehending the whole world.

PART II
THE ECONOMICS OF A SOCIALIST COMMUNITY

SECTION 3

PARTICULAR FORMS OF SOCIALISM AND PSEUDO-SOCIALISM

CHAPTER 15

Particular Forms of Socialism

1

The Nature of Socialism

The essence of Socialism is this: All the means of production are in the 239
exclusive control of the organized community. This and this alone is Socialism. All other definitions are misleading.

It is possible to believe that Socialism can only be brought about under quite definite political and cultural conditions. Such a belief however is no justification for confining the term to one particular form of Socialism and withholding it from all other conceivable ways of realizing the socialist ideal. Marxian socialists have been very zealous in commending their own particular brand of Socialism as the only true Socialism and in insisting that all other socialist ideals and methods of realizing Socialism have nothing to do with genuine Socialism. Politically this attitude of the socialists has been extremely astute. It would have greatly increased the difficulties of their campaign if they had been prepared to admit that their ideal had anything in common with the ideals advocated by the leaders of other parties. They would never have rallied millions of discontented Germans to their banners if they had openly admitted that their aims were not fundamentally different from those of the governing classes of the Prussian state. If a Marxian had been asked before October 1917 in what way his Socialism differed from the Socialism of other movements, especially from that of the Conservatives, he would have replied that under Marxian Socialism, Democracy and Socialism were indissolubly united, and moreover that Marxian Socialism was a stateless Socialism because it intended to abolish the State.

We have seen already how much these arguments are worth, and as a matter of fact, since the victory of the Bolsheviks, they have rapidly disappeared from the list of Marxian commonplaces. At any rate the conceptions of democracy and statelessness which the Marxians hold today are quite different from those which they held previously.

240 But the Marxians might have answered the question another way. They might have said that their Socialism was revolutionary, as opposed to the reactionary and conservative Socialism of others. Such an answer leads much sooner to a recognition of the difference between Marxian social democracy and other socialist movements. For to a Marxian, revolution does not merely signify a forcible alteration of the existing state of affairs, but, as befits his peculiar fatalism, a process which brings mankind nearer the fulfilment of its destiny.[1] For him the impending social revolution which will bring about Socialism is the last step to eternal salvation. Revolutionaries are those whom history has chosen to be the instruments for the realization of its plan. The revolutionary spirit is the sacred fire which has descended upon them and enables them to accomplish this great work. In this sense the Marxian socialist regards it as the most notable characteristic of his party that it is a revolutionary party. In this sense he regards all other parties as a single, uniform, reactionary mass because they are opposed to his methods of achieving ultimate bliss.

It is obvious that all this has nothing to do with the sociological concept of the socialist community. It is certainly a remarkable thing that a group of persons should claim to be the only people elected to bring us to salvation; but when these persons know of no other road to salvation than one which many others have believed in, the assertion that they exclusively are ordained for the task is not sufficient to differentiate their aim fundamentally from that of others.

2

State Socialism

To understand the concept of State Socialism it is not sufficient to explain the term etymologically. The history of the word reflects only the fact that State Socialism was the Socialism professed by the authorities of the Prussian and other German states. Because they identified themselves with the State and with the form taken by the State and with the idea of the State generally, it suggested calling the Socialism which they adopted State Socialism. The

---

[1] On the other meanings which the term Revolution has for the Marxists see pp. 69 ff.

more Marxian teaching about the class character of the State and the decay 241
of the State obscured the fundamental idea of the State, the easier it became to use the term.

Marxian Socialism was vitally concerned in making a distinction between nationalization and socialization of the means of production. The slogans of the Social Democratic party would never have become popular if they had represented nationalization of the means of production as the ultimate aim of socialist change. For the state known to the people among whom Marxism found its widest acceptance was not such as to inspire much hope from its incursions into economic activity. The German, Austrian and Russian disciples of Marxism lived in open feud with the powers which to them represented the State. In addition they had the opportunity of gauging the results of nationalization and municipalization; and, with the best will in the world, they could not overlook the great shortcomings of state and municipal enterprise. It was quite impossible to arouse enthusiasm for a programme aiming at nationalization. A party of opposition was bound above all things to attack the hated authoritarian state; only in this way could it win over the discontented. From this need of political agitation arose the Marxian doctrine of the withering away of the state. The liberals had demanded the limitation of the authority of the state and the transfer of government to the representatives of the people; they had demanded the free state. Marx and Engels tried to outbid them by unscrupulously adopting the anarchistic doctrine of the abolition of all state authority regardless of the fact that Socialism would not mean the abolition, but rather the unrestricted expansion of the power of the state.

Equally untenable and absurd as the doctrine of the withering away of the state under Socialism is the academic distinction between nationalization and socialization which is closely bound up with it. The Marxians themselves are so conscious of the weakness of their line of argument that they usually avoid discussing this point and confine themselves to talking of the socialization of the means of production, without any further elaboration of the idea, so as to create the impression that socialization is something different from the nationalization with which everybody is acquainted. When they cannot avoid discussing this ticklish point they are obliged to admit that the
nationalization of undertakings is a "preliminary stage in the acquisition of 242
all productive powers by society itself"[2] or "the natural jumping-off point in the process leading to the socialist community."[3]

[2] Engels, *Herrn Eugen Dührings Umwälzung der Wissenschaft*, p. 299. Publisher's Note: p. 385 in the English edition.

[3] Kautsky, *Das Erfurter Programm*, 12th ed. (Stuttgart, 1914), p. 129.

Thus Engels finally contents himself with entering a caveat against accepting without further ado "*every*" form of nationalization as socialistic. He would not in the first place describe as "steps towards Socialism," nationalization carried out for purposes of state finance, such as might be adopted "chiefly to provide new sources of revenue independent of Parliamentary sanction." Nevertheless for these reasons nationalization would also mean, in the Marxian language, that in one branch of production, the appropriation of surplus value by the capitalist was abolished. The same is true of nationalization carried out for political or military reasons which Engels also refused to accept as socialistic. He regards it as the criterion of socialistic nationalization that the means of production and trade taken over "should have actually out-grown the direction by joint stock companies, so that nationalization has become economically inevitable." This necessity arises first in the case of "the large scale communications: posts, telegraphs and railways."[4] But it is precisely the largest railways in the world—the North American—and the most important telegraph lines—the deep sea cables—that have not been nationalized, whilst small unimportant lines in the etatistic countries have long been nationalized. The nationalization of the postal service moreover was primarily for political reasons and that of the railways for military ones. Can it be said that these nationalizations were "economically inevitable?" And what on earth does "economically inevitable" mean?

Kautsky, too, contents himself with rejecting the view "that every nationalization of an economic function or of an economic enterprise is a step towards Socialism and that this can be brought about by a general nationalization of the whole economic machine without the need for a fundamental change in the nature of the State."[5] But no one has ever disputed that the fundamental nature of the State would be greatly changed if it were transformed into a socialist community through the nationalization of the whole economic apparatus. Thus Kautsky is unable to say anything more than that
243 "as long as the possessing classes are the governing classes" complete nationalization is impossible. It will be achieved when "the workers become the governing classes in the state." Only when the proletariat has seized political power will it "transform the state into a great fundamentally self-sufficient economic society."[6] The main question—the question which alone needs an answer—whether complete nationalization carried out by another party than the socialist one would also constitute Socialism, Kautsky carefully avoids.

---

[4] Engels, *Herrn Eugen Dührings Umwälzung der Wissenschaft*, pp. 298 ff. Publisher's Note: p. 385n in the English edition.

[5] Kautsky, *Das Erfurter Programm*, p. 129.

[6] Kautsky, *Das Erfurter Programm*, p. 130.

There is, of course, a fundamental distinction of the highest importance between the nationalization or municipalization of individual undertakings which are publicly or communally run in a society otherwise maintaining the principle of private property in the means of production, and the complete socialization which tolerates no private ownership by individuals in the means of production alongside that of the socialist community. As long as only a few undertakings are run by the State, prices for the means of production will be established in the market, and it is thus still possible for State undertakings to make calculations. How far the conduct of the undertakings would be based on the results of these calculations is another question; but the very fact that to a certain extent the results of operations can be quantitatively ascertained provides the business administration of such undertakings with a gauge which would not be available to the administration of a purely socialist community. The way in which State undertakings are run may justifiably be called bad business but it is still business. In a socialist community, as we have seen, economy in the strict sense of the word, cannot exist.[7]

Nationalization of all the means of production involves complete Socialism. Nationalization of some of the means of production is a step towards complete Socialism. Whether we are to remain satisfied with the first step or whether we desire to proceed further does not alter its fundamental character. In the same way, if we wish to transfer all undertakings to the ownership of the organized community we cannot do otherwise than nationalize every single undertaking, simultaneously or successively.

The obscurity thrown by Marxism on the idea of socialization was strikingly illustrated in Germany and Austria when the Social Democrats came into 244
power in November 1918. A new and hitherto almost unheard slogan became popular overnight: Socialization (*Sozialisierung*) was the solution. This was merely the paraphrasing of the German word *Vergesellschaftung* into a fine-sounding foreign word. The idea that *Sozialisierung* was nothing more than nationalization or municipalization could not occur to anybody; anyone who maintained this was simply believed to know nothing about it, since it was thought that between the two things yawned an abysmal gap. The Socialization Commissions set up soon after the Social Democrats acquired power were set the problem of defining *Sozialisierung* in such a way that, ostensibly at least, it could be distinguished from the nationalization and municipalization of the previous regime.

The first report issued by the German commission dealt with the socialization of the coal industry, and in rejecting the idea of achieving this by the

[7] See, pp. 102 ff.

nationalization of the coal mines and the coal trade it emphasized in a striking manner the shortcomings of a national coal industry. But nothing was said as to how socialization differed actually from nationalization. The report professed the opinion that "an isolated nationalization of the coal industry cannot be considered as socialization while capitalist enterprise continues in other branches of production: it would only mean the replacement of one employer by another." But it left open the question whether an isolated "socialization" such as it intended and proposed could mean anything else under the same conditions.[8] It would have been understandable if the commission had gone on to say that in order to fulfil the happy results of a socialist order of society it was not sufficient to nationalize one branch of production, and had recommended that the State should take over all undertakings at one blow, as the Bolsheviks in Russia and Hungary had done and as the Spartacists in Germany wanted to do. But it did not do this. On the contrary, it elaborated proposals for socialization which advocated the isolated nationalization of various branches of production, beginning with coal production and distribution. That the commission avoided using the term nationalization makes no difference. It was mere juristic hair-splitting
245 when the commission proposed that the owners of the socialized German coal industry should not be the German State but a "German public coal trust" and when it went on to assert that this ownership should be conceived "only in a formal juristic sense," but that "the material position of the private employer and thereby the possibility of exploiting workers and consumers" is denied to this public trust,[9] the commission was using the emptiest of gutter catchwords. Indeed the whole report is nothing but a collection of all the popular fallacies about the evils of the capitalist system. The only way in which the coal industry, socialized in accordance with the proposals of the majority, would differ from other public undertakings is the composition of its directorate. At the head of the coal mines there should be no single official but a committee constituted in a certain way. *Parturiunt montes, nascetur ridiculus mus!* (The mountain labors and a ridiculous mouse is born!)

State Socialism, therefore, is not distinguished by the fact that the State is the pivot of the communal organization, since Socialism is quite inconceivable otherwise. If we wish to understand its nature we must not look to the term itself. This would take us no further than would an attempt to grasp the concept of metaphysics from an examination of the meaning of the parts that make up the word. We must ask ourselves what ideas have been

[8] *Bericht der Sozialisierungskommission über die Frage der Sozialisierung des Kohlenbergbaues vom 31 Juli 1920*, with appendix: *Vorläufiger Bericht vom 15 Februar 1919* 2nd ed. (Berlin, 1920), pp. 32 ff.

[9] *Bericht der Sozialisierungskommission über die Frage der Sozialisierung des Kohlenbergbaues vom 31 Juli, 1920*, with appendix: *Vorläufiger Bericht vom 15 Februar 1919*, 2nd ed. (Berlin, 1920), p. 37.

associated with the expression by those who are generally regarded as the followers of the state socialistic movements, that is, the out-and-out etatists.

Etatistic Socialism is distinguished from other socialist systems in two ways. In contradistinction to many other socialist movements which contemplate the greatest possible measure of equality in the distribution of the social income between individuals, Etatistic Socialism makes the basis of distribution the merit and rank of the individual. It is obviously superfluous to point out that judgment of merit is purely subjective and cannot in any way be tested from a scientific view of human relations. Etatism has quite definite views about the ethical value of individual classes in the community. It is imbued with a high esteem for the monarchy, the nobility, big landowners, the clergy, professional soldiers, especially the officer class, and officials. With certain reservations it also allots a privileged position to savants and to artists. Peasants and small tradesmen are in a special class and below them
come the manual labourers. At the bottom are the unreliable elements which 246
are discontented with the sphere of action and the income allotted to them by the etatist plan and strive to improve their material position. The etatist mentally arranges a hierarchy of the members composing his future state. The more noble will have more power, more honours and more income than the less noble. What is noble and what is ignoble will be decided above all by tradition. To the etatist the worst feature of the capitalist system is that it does not assign income according to his valuation of merit. That a milk dealer or a manufacturer of trouser buttons should draw a larger income than the sprig of a noble family, than a privy councillor or a lieutenant, strikes him as intolerable. In order to remedy this state of affairs the capitalist system must be replaced by the etatistic.

This attempt on the part of the etatists to maintain the traditional social order of rank and the ethical valuation of different classes, in no way contemplates transferring all property in the means of production to the formal ownership of the State. This indeed, in the etatistic view, would be a complete subversion of all historical rights. Only the large undertakings would be nationalized, and even then an exception would be made in favour of large scale agriculture, especially inherited family property. In agriculture and in small and medium-sized industries private property is to continue in name at least. In the same way the free professions will be allowed scope, with certain limitations. But all enterprises must become essentially state undertakings. The agriculturist will retain the name and title of owner, but he will be forbidden "egotistically to look merely to mercantile profit"; he has the "duty to execute the aims of the State."[10] For agriculture, according

[10] Philipp v. Arnim, *Ideen zu einer vollständigen landwirtschaftlichen Buchhaltung*, 1805, p. vi (quoted by Waltz, *Vom Reinertrag in der Landwirtschaft*, p. 20).

to the etatist, is a public office. "The agriculturist is a state official and must cultivate for the needs of the State according to his best knowledge and conscience, or according to state orders. If he gets his interest and sufficient to maintain himself he has everything he is entitled to demand."[11] The same applies to the artisan and the trader. For the independent entrepreneur with
247 free control over the means of production there is as little room in State Socialism as in any other Socialism. The authorities control prices and decide what and how much shall be produced and in what way. There will be no speculation for "excessive" profit. Officials will see to it that no one draws more than the appropriate "fair income," that is to say an income ensuring him a standard of life appropriate to his rank. Any excess will be "taxed away."

Marxian writers are also of the opinion that to bring Socialism about, small undertakings need not necessarily be transferred directly to public ownership. Indeed they have regarded this as quite impossible; the only way in which socialization can be carried out for these small undertakings is to leave them in the formal possession of their owners and simply subject them to the all-embracing supervision of the State. Kautsky himself says that "no socialist worthy of serious consideration has ever demanded that peasants should be expropriated, let alone their property confiscated."[12] Neither does Kautsky propose to socialize small producers by expropriating their property.[13] The peasant and the craftsman will be fitted into the machinery of the socialist community in such a way that their production and the valuation of their products will be regulated by the economic administration whilst nominally the property will remain theirs. The abolition of the free market will transform them from independent owners and entrepreneurs into functionaries of the socialist community, distinguished from other citizens only by the form of the remuneration.[14] It cannot therefore be regarded as a peculiarity of the etatistic socialist scheme that in this way remnants of private property in the means of production formally persist. The only characteristic peculiarity is the extent to which this method of arranging the social conditions of production is applied. It has already been said that etatism in general proposes in the same way to leave the large landowners—with the exception perhaps

[11] Philipp v. Arnim, *Ideen zu einer vollständigen landwirtschaftlichen Buchhaltung*, 1805, p. 2 (quoted in Waltz, *op. cit.*, p. 21). See also Lenz, *Agrarlehre und Agrarpolitik der deutschen Romantik*, Berlin, 1912, p. 84. See similar remarks of Prince Alois Liechtenstein, a leader of the Austrian Christian Socialists, quoted in Nitti, *Le Socialisme Catholique* (Paris, 1894), pp. 370 ff.

[12] Kautsky, *Die Soziale Revolution*, II, p. 33.

[13] *Ibid.*, p. 35.

[14] Bourguin, *Die sozialistischen Systeme*, pp. 62 ff.

of the latifundia owners—in formal possession of their property. What is still more important is that it proceeds upon the assumption that the greater part of the population will find work in agriculture and small concerns, and that comparatively few will enter the direct service of the State as employees in large undertakings. Not only is etatism opposed to orthodox Marxists, as 248
represented by Kautsky, through its theory that small scale agriculture is not less productive than large scale agriculture, but it is also of the opinion that in industry too, small scale undertakings have a great scope for operation at the side of the large concerns. This is the second peculiarity which distinguishes State Socialism from other socialist systems, especially social-democracy.

It is perhaps unnecessary further to elaborate the picture of the ideal State drawn by the state socialists. Over a large part of Europe it has been for decades the tacit ideal of millions, and everyone knows it even if no one has clearly defined it. It is the Socialism of the peaceful loyal civil servant, of the land-owner, the peasant, the small producer and of countless workers and employees. It is the Socialism of the professors, the famous "socialists of the chair"—the *Kathedersozialismus*—it is the Socialism of artists, poets, writers in an epoch of the history of art plainly bearing all the signs of decay. It is the Socialism supported by the churches of all denominations. It is the Socialism of Caesarism and of Imperialism, the ideal of the so-called "social monarchy." It is this that the policy of most European states, especially the German states, envisaged as the distant goal of man's endeavours. It is the social ideal of the age which prepared the Great War* and perished with it.

A Socialism which allots the shares of individuals in the social dividend according to merit and rank can be conceived only in the form of State Socialism. The hierarchy on which it bases its distribution is the only one popular enough not to arouse overwhelming opposition. Although it is less able to withstand rationalist criticism than many others that might be suggested, nevertheless it has the sanction of age. In so far as State Socialism attempts to perpetuate this hierarchy and to prevent any change in the scale of social relationships, the description "conservative socialism," sometimes applied to it, is justified.[15] In fact it is imbued more than any other form of Socialism with ideas that credit the possibility of complete crystallization and changelessness of economic conditions: its followers regard every economic innovation as superfluous and even harmful. And corresponding to this

---

[15] Andler, *Les Origines du Socialisme d'Etat en Allemagne*, 2nd ed. (Paris, 1911), p. 2, specially stresses this character of state Socialism.

* World War I.

attitude is the method by which Etatism wishes to attain its ends. If Marxian
249 Socialism is the social ideal of those who expect nothing except through a radical subversion of the existing order by bloody revolutions, State Socialism is the ideal of those who call in the police at the slightest sign of trouble. Marxism relies upon the infallible judgment of a proletariat filled with the revolutionary spirit, Etatism upon the infallibility of the reigning authority. They both agree in belief in a political absolutism which does not admit the possibility of error.

In contrast to State Socialism, Municipal Socialism presents no special form of the socialist ideal. The municipalization of undertakings is not regarded as a general principle on which to base a new arrangement of economic life. It would affect only undertakings with a market limited in space. In a rigorous system of State Socialism the municipal undertakings would be subordinated to the chief economic administration and would be no freer to develop than the agricultural and industrial undertakings nominally remaining in private hands.

3

Military Socialism

Military Socialism is the Socialism of a state in which all institutions are designed for the prosecution of war. It is a State Socialism in which the scale of values for determining social status and the income of citizens is based exclusively or preferably on the position held in the fighting forces. The higher the military rank the greater the social value and the claim on the national dividend.

The military state, that is the state of the fighting man in which everything is subordinated to war purposes, cannot admit private ownership in the means of production. Standing preparedness for war is impossible if aims other than war influence the life of individuals. All warrior castes whose members have been supported by the assignment of manorial rights or of grants of land, or even by industries based on a supply of unfree labour, have in time lost their warlike nature. The feudal lord became absorbed in economic activity and acquired other interests than waging war and reaping military honours. All over the world the feudal system demilitarized the warrior. The knights were succeeded by the *Junkers*. Ownership turns the fighting man into the economic man. Only the exclusion of private property

can maintain the military character of the State. Only the warrior, who has 250
no other occupation apart from war than preparation for war, is always ready for war. Men occupied in affairs may wage wars of defence but not long wars of conquest.

The military state is a state of bandits. It prefers to live on booty and tribute. Compared with this source of income the product of economic activity plays only a subordinate role; often it is completely lacking. And if booty and tribute accrue from abroad it is clear that they cannot go direct to individuals but only to the common treasury, which can distribute them only according to military rank. The army which alone assures the continuance of this source of income would not tolerate any other method of distribution. And this suggests that the same principle of distribution should be applied to the products of home production, which similarly accrue to citizens as the tribute and yield of serfdom.

In this way the communism of the Hellenic pirates of Lipara and all other robber states can be explained.[16] It is the "communism of robbers and freebooters,"[17] arising from the application of military ideas to all social relationships. Caesar relates of the Suebi, whom he calls *gens longe bellicossima Germanorum omnium* (a people long the most warlike of the German tribes), that they sent warriors over the borders every year for plunder. Those who remained behind carried on economic activity for those in the field; in the following year the roles were exchanged. There was no land in the exclusive ownership of individuals.[18] Only by each sharing in the product of the military and economic activity carried on with a common purpose and subject to a common danger, can the warrior state make every citizen a soldier and every soldier a citizen. Once it allows some to remain soldiers and others to remain citizens working with their own property the two callings will soon stand out in contrast. Either the warriors must subjugate the citizens and in that case it would be doubtful if they could set out on plundering expeditions leaving an oppressed population at home—or the citizens will succeed in gaining the upper hand. In the latter event the warriors will be reduced to mercenaries and forbidden to set out in search of plunder because, as a standing danger, they cannot be allowed to grow
too powerful. In either case the state must lose its purely military character. 251

---

[16] On Lipara see Poehlmann, *Geschichte der sozialen Frage und des Sozialismus in der antiken welt*, Vol. I, pp. 44 ff.

[17] Max Weber, "Der Streit um den Charakter der altgermanischen Sozialverfassung in der deutschen Literatur des letzten Jahrzehnts," (*Jahrbücher für Nationalökonomie und Statistik*, Vol. XXVIII, 1904, p. 445).

[18] Caesar, *De bello Gallico*, IV, 1.

Therefore any weakening of "communistic" institutions involves a weakening of the military nature of the state, and the warrior society is slowly transformed into an industrial one.[19]

The forces driving a military state to Socialism could be clearly observed in the Great War. The longer the war lasted and the more the states of Europe were transformed into armed camps, the more politically untenable seemed the distinction between the fighting man, who had to endure the hardships and danger of the war, and the man who remained at home to profit from the war boom. The burden was distributed too unequally. If the distinction had been allowed to persist and the war had continued longer the countries would infallibly have been split into two factions and the armies would have finally turned their weapons against their own kinsmen. The Socialism of conscript armies demands for its complement the Socialism of conscript labour at home.

The fact that they cannot preserve their military character without a communistic organization does not strengthen the warrior states in the war. Communism is for them an evil which they must accept; it produces a weakness by which they eventually perish. Germany in the first years of the war trod the path to Socialism because the military etatistic spirit, which was responsible for the policy leading to the war, drove it towards State Socialism. Towards the end of the war socialization was more and more energetically carried out because, for the reasons just stated, it was necessary to make conditions at home similar to those at the front. State Socialism did not alleviate the situation in Germany, however, but worsened it; it did not stimulate production but restricted it; it did not improve the provisioning of the army and those at home but made it worse.[20] And needless to say it was the fault of the etatistic spirit that in the tremendous convulsions of the war and the subsequent revolution not one strong individual arose from the German people.

The lesser productivity of communistic methods of economic activity is a disadvantage to the communistic warrior state when it comes into clash with the richer and therefore better armed and provisioned members of nations
252 which acknowledge the principle of private property. The destruction of initiative in the individual, unavoidable under Socialism, deprives it in the decisive hour of battle of leaders who can show the way to victory, and subordinates who can carry out their instructions. The great military com-

[19] Herbert Spencer, *Die Prinzipien der Soziologie*, trans. Vetter, Vol. II (Stuttgart, 1899), pp. 710 ff. Publisher's Note: In English, *The Principles of Sociology* (New York: Appleton, 1897), Vol. II, Part V, pp. 610 ff.

[20] See my *Nation, Staat und Wirtschaft*, pp. 115 ff.; 143 ff.

munist state of the Incas[21] was easily overthrown by a handful of Spaniards.

If the enemy against which the warrior state has to fight is to be found at home then we can speak of a communism of overlords. "Casino communism" was the name given by Max Weber to the social arrangements of the Dorians in Sparta because of their habits of eating together.[22] If the ruling caste, instead of adopting communistic institutions assigns land together with its inhabitants to the ownership of individuals sooner or later it will be ethnically absorbed by the conquered. It becomes transformed into a land-owning nobility, which eventually draws even the conquered into military service. In this way the state loses the character based upon the waging of war. This development took place in the kingdoms of the Langobards, the West Goths and the Franks and in all the regions where the Normans appeared as conquerors.

4

Christian Socialism

A theocratic organization of the state demands either a self-sufficing family economy or the socialist organization of industry. It is incompatible with an economic order which allows the individual free play to develop his powers. Simple faith and economic rationalism cannot dwell together. It is unthinkable that priests should govern entrepreneurs.

Christian Socialism, as it has taken root in the last few decades among countless followers of all Christian churches, is merely a variety of State Socialism. State Socialism and Christian Socialism are so entangled that it is difficult to draw any clear line between them, or to say of individual socialists
whether they belong to the one or the other. Even more than etatism, 253
Christian Socialism is governed by the idea that the economic system would be perfectly stationary if the desire for profit and personal gain by men directing their efforts solely to the satisfaction of material interests did not disturb its smooth course. The advantage of progressive improvements in

[21] Wiener, *Essai sur les Institutions Politiques, Religieuses, Économiques et Sociales de l'Empire des Incas* (Paris, 1874), pp. 64, 90 ff. attributes Pizarro's easy conquest of Peru to the fact that communism had unnerved the people.

[22] Max Weber, "Der Streit um der Charakter der altgermanischen Sozialverfassung in der deutschen Literatur des letzten Jahrzehnts," (*Jahrbücher für Nationalökonomie und Statistik*, Vol. XXVIII, 1904), p. 445.

methods of production is admitted, if only with limitations; but the Christian socialist does not clearly understand that it is just these innovations which disturb the peaceful course of the economic system. In so far as this is recognized, the existing state of affairs is preferred to any further progress. Agriculture and handicraft, with perhaps small shopkeeping, are the only admissible occupations. Trade and speculation are superfluous, injurious, and evil. Factories and large scale industries are a wicked invention of the "Jewish spirit"; they produce only bad goods which are foisted on buyers by the large stores and by other monstrosities of modern trade to the detriment of purchasers. It is the duty of legislation to suppress these excesses of the business spirit and to restore to handicraft the place in production from which it has been displaced by the machinations of big capital.[23] Large transport undertakings that cannot be abolished should be nationalized.

The basic idea of Christian Socialism that runs through all the teachings of its representatives is purely stationary in outlook. In the economic system which they have in mind there is no entrepreneur, no speculation, and no "inordinate" profit. The prices and wages demanded and given are "just." Everyone is satisfied with his lot because dissatisfaction would signify rebellion against divine and human laws. For those incapable of work Christian charity will provide. This ideal it is asserted was achieved in medieval times. Only unbelief could have driven mankind out of this paradise. If it is to be regained mankind must first find the way back to the Church. Enlightenment and liberal thought have created all the evil which afflicts the world today.

The protagonists of Christian social reform as a rule do not regard their ideal Society of Christian Socialism as in any way socialistic. But this is simply
254 self-deception. Christian Socialism appears to be conservative because it desires to maintain the existing order of property, or more properly it appears reactionary because it wishes to restore and then maintain an order of property that prevailed in the past. It is also true that it combats with great energy the plans of socialists of other persuasions for a radical abolition of private property, and in contradistinction to them asserts that not Socialism but social reform is its aim. But Conservatism can only be achieved by Socialism. Where private property in the means of production exists not only in name but in fact, income cannot be distributed according to an historically determined or an any other way permanently established order. Where private property exists, only market prices can determine the formation of

[23] See the criticism of the economic policy of the Austrian Christian Socialist Party in Sigmund Mayer, *Die Aufhebung des Befähigungsnachweises in Österreich* (Leipzig, 1894), especially pp. 124 ff.

income. To the degree in which this is realized, the Christian social reformer is step by step driven to Socialism, which for him can be only State Socialism. He must see that otherwise there cannot be that complete adherence to the traditional state of affairs which his ideal demands. He sees that fixed prices and wages cannot be maintained, unless deviations from them are menaced by threats of punishment from a supreme authority. He must also realize that wages and prices cannot be arbitrarily determined according to the ideas of a world improver, because every deviation from market prices destroys the equilibrium of economic life. He must therefore progressively move from a demand for price regulation to a demand for a supreme control over production and distribution. It is the same path that practical etatism has followed. At the end in both cases, is a rigid Socialism which leaves private property only in name, and in fact transfers all control over the means of production to the State.

Only a part of the Christian socialist movement has openly subscribed to this radical programme. The others have shunned an open declaration. They have anxiously avoided drawing the logical conclusions of their premises. They give one to understand that they are combating only the excrescences and abuses of the capitalist order; they protest that they have not the slightest desire to abolish private property; and they constantly emphasize their opposition to Marxian Socialism. But they characteristically perceive that this opposition mainly consists in differences of opinion as to the way in which the best state of society can be attained. They are not revolutionary and expect everything from an increasing realization that reform is necessary. For the rest they constantly proclaim that they do no wish to attack private
property. But what they would retain is only the name of private property. 255
If the control of private property is transferred to the State the property owner is only an official, a deputy of the economic administration.

It can be seen at once how the Christian Socialism of today corresponds to the economic ideal of the medieval Scholastics. The starting point, the demand for "just" wages and prices, that is, for a definite historically attained distribution of income, is common to both. Only the realization that this is impossible, if the economic system retains private property in the means of production, forces the modern Christian reform movement towards Socialism. In order to achieve their demands, they must advocate measures which, even if formally retaining private property, lead to the complete socialization of society.

It will be shown later that this modern Christian Socialism has nothing to do with the suppositious but often cited Communism of the Early Christians.

The socialist idea is new to the Church. This is not altered by the fact that the most recent development of Christian social theory has led the Church[24] to recognize the fundamental rightfulness of private property in the means of production, whereas the early church teaching, in view of the command of the gospels condemning all economic activity, had avoided unconditionally accepting even the name of private property. For we must understand what the Church has done in recognizing the rightfulness of private property, only as opposition to the efforts of the socialists to overthrow the existing order forcibly. In reality the Church desires nothing but State Socialism of a particular colour.

The nature of socialistic methods of production is independent of the concrete methods involved in the attempt to realize it. Every attempt at Socialism, however brought about, must founder on the impracticability of setting up a purely socialistic economy. For that reason, and not because of deficiencies in the moral character of mankind, Socialism must fail.

256 It may be granted, that the moral qualities required of the members of a socialist community could best be fostered by the Church. The spirit which must prevail in a socialist community is most akin to that of a religious community. But to overcome the difficulties in the way of establishing a socialist community would require a change in human nature or in the laws of the nature by which we are surrounded, and even faith cannot bring this to pass.

5

The Planned Economy

The so-called planned economy (*Planwirtschaft*) is a more recent variety of Socialism.

Every attempt to realize Socialism comes up quickly against insurmountable difficulties. This is what happened to Prussian State Socialism. The failure of nationalization was so striking that it could not be overlooked. Conditions

[24] In the above text we have always spoken only of the Church in general, without considering the differences between the various denominations. This is quite admissible. The evolution towards Socialism is common to all denominations. In Catholicism, Leo XIII's encyclical, "Rerum Novarum," of 1891, has recognized the origin of private property in Natural Law; but simultaneously the Church laid down a series of fundamental ethical principles for the distribution of incomes, which could be put into practice only under State Socialism. On this basis stands also Pius XI's encyclical, "Quadragesimo anno" of 1931. In German Protestantism the Christian Socialist idea is so tied up with State Socialism that the two can hardly be distinguished.

in government undertakings were not such as to encourage further steps along the road to state and municipal control. The blame for this was thrown upon the officials. It had been a mistake to exclude the "business man." In some way or other the abilities of the entrepreneur must be brought to the service of Socialism. From this notion came the arrangement of "mixed" enterprises. Instead of complete nationalization or municipalization we have the private undertaking in which the state or municipality is interested. In this way, on the one side, regard is paid to the demand of those who think it is not right that the state and municipalities should not share in the yield of undertakings carried on under their august sway. (Of course the State might get and gets its share more effectively by taxation without exposing the public finances to the possibility of loss. On the other hand it is thought by this system to bring all the active powers of the entrepreneur into the service of the common enterprise—a gross error. For as soon as representatives of the government take part in administration all the hindrances which cripple the initiative of public officials come into play. The "mixed" form of undertaking makes it possible to exempt employees and workers from the regulations applying to public officials and thereby to mitigate slightly the harmful effects which the official spirit exerts upon the profitability of undertakings. The mixed undertakings have certainly turned out better 257
on the whole than the purely governmental undertakings. But this no more shows that Socialism is practicable than do the good results occasionally shown by individual public undertakings. That it is possible under certain favourable circumstances to carry on a public enterprise with some success in the midst of an economic society otherwise based on private property in the means of production does not prove that a complete socialization of society is practicable.

During the Great War the authorities in Germany and Austria tried, under war Socialism, to leave to the entrepreneurs the direction of nationalized undertakings. The haste with which socialist measures were adopted under very difficult war conditions and the fact that at the outset no one had any clear idea of the fundamental implications of the new policy, nor of the lengths to which it was to be carried, left no other means open. The direction of individual branches of production was made over to compulsory associations of employers, who were put under government supervision. Price regulation on the one hand and drastic taxation of profits on the other hand were to ensure that the employer was no more than an employee sharing the yield.[25] The system worked very badly. Nevertheless it was necessary to

---

[25] On War Socialism and its consequences, see my *Nation, Staat und Wirtschaft*, pp. 140 ff.

adhere to it, unless all attempts at Socialism were to be abandoned, because no one knew anything better to put in its place. The memorandum of the German Economic Ministry (May 7th, 1919), drawn up by Wissell and Moellendorff, states in plain words, that there was nothing else for a socialist government to do but to maintain the system known during the war as "war economy." "A socialist government" it says "cannot ignore the fact that, because of a few abuses, public opinion is being poisoned by interested criticisms against a systematic planned economy; it may improve the planned system; it may reorganize the old bureaucracy; it may even in the form of self-government make over the responsibility to the people concerned in the business; but it must proclaim itself an adherent of the compulsory planned economy: that is to say an adherent of the most unpopular concepts of duty and coercion."[26]

258 Planned economy is a scheme of a socialist community that attempts to solve in a particular way the insoluble problem of the responsibility of the acting organ. Not only is the idea on which this attempt is based deficient, but the solution itself is only a sham, and that the creators and supporters of this scheme should overlook this, is particularly characteristic of the mental attitude of officialdom. The self-government granted to individual areas and to individual branches of production is important only in minor matters, for the centre of gravity of economic activity lies in the adjustment between individual areas and individual branches of production. This adjustment can only proceed uniformly; if this is not provided for, the whole plan would have to be regarded as syndicalist. In fact Wissell and Möllendorff envisage a State Economic Council which has "supreme control of the German economic system in co-operation with the highest competent organs of the State."[27] In essence, therefore, the whole proposal comes to nothing more than that responsibility for the economic administration is to be shared between the ministers and a second authority.

The Socialism of the planned economy is distinguished from the State Socialism of the Prussian State under the Hohenzollerns chiefly by the fact that the privileged position in business control and in the distribution of income, which the latter allotted to the Junkers and the bureaucrats, is here assigned to the ci-devant entrepreneur. This is an innovation dictated by the change in the political situation resulting from the catastrophe which has overwhelmed the Crown, the nobility, the bureaucracy and the officer class; apart from this it is without significance for the problem of Socialism.

[26] *Denkschrift des Reichswirtschaftsministeriums*, reprinted in Wissell, p. 106.

[27] *Denkschrift des Reichswirtschaftsministeriums*, reprinted in Wissell, p. 116.

In the last few years, a new word has been found for that which was covered by the expression "planned economy": *State Capitalism*, and no doubt in the future many more proposals for the salvaging of Socialism will be brought forward. We shall learn many new names for the same old thing. But the thing, not its names, is what matters, and all schemes of this sort will not alter the nature of Socialism.

6

Guild Socialism

In the first years after the World War, people in England and on the Continent looked on Guild Socialism as the panacea. It has long since been 259
forgotten. Nevertheless, we must not pass it over in silence, when discussing socialist projects; for it represents the one contribution to modern socialist plans made by the Anglo-Saxons, in economic matters the most advanced of peoples. Guild Socialism is another attempt to surmount the insoluble problem of a socialist direction of industry. It did not need the failure of state socialistic activities to open the eyes of the English people, preserved by the long reign of liberal ideas from that over-valuation of the State which has been prevalent in modern Germany. Socialism in England has never been able to overcome the mistrust of the government's capacity to regulate all human affairs for the best. The English have always recognized the great problem which other Europeans before 1914 had scarcely grasped.

In Guild Socialism three different things must be distinguished. It establishes the necessity for replacing the capitalist system by a socialist one; this thoroughly eclectic theory need not worry us further. It also provides a way by which Socialism may be realized; this is only important for us inasmuch as it could very easily lead to Syndicalism instead of Socialism. Finally it draws up the programme of a future socialist order of society. It is with this that we are concerned.

The aim of Guild Socialism is the socialization of the means of production. We are therefore justified in calling it socialism. Its unique feature is the particular structure which it gives to the administrative organization of the future socialist state. Production is to be controlled by the workers in individual branches of productions. They elect foremen, managers and other business leaders, and they regulate directly and indirectly the conditions of

labour and order the methods and aims of production.[28] The Guilds as
260 organizations of the producers in the individual branches of industry, face the State as the organization of the consumers. The State has the right to tax the Guilds, and is thus able to regulate their price—and wages-policy.[29]

Guild Socialism greatly deceives itself if it believes that in this way it could create a socialist order of society which would not endanger the freedom of the individual and would avoid all those evils of centralized Socialism which the English detest as Prussianism.[30] Even in a guild socialist society the whole control of production belongs to the State. The State alone sets the aim of production and determines what must be done in order to achieve this aim. Directly or indirectly through its taxation policy, it determines the conditions of labour, moves capital and labour from one branch of industry to another, makes adjustments and acts as intermediary between the guilds themselves and between producers and consumers. These tasks falling to the State are the only important ones and they constitute the essence of economic control.[31] What is left to the individual guilds, and, inside them, to the local unions and individual concerns is the execution of work assigned to them by the

[28] "Guildsmen are opposed to private ownership of industry, and strongly in favour of public ownership. Of course, this does not mean that they desire to see industry bureaucratically administered by State departments. They aim at the control of industry by National Guilds including the whole personnel of the industry. But they do not desire the ownership of any industry by the workers employed in it. Their aim is to establish industrial democracy by placing the administration in the hands of the workers, but at the same time to eliminate profit by placing the ownership in the hands of the public. Thus the workers in a Guild will not be working for profit: the prices of their commodities and, indirectly at least, the level of their remuneration will be subject to a considerable measure of public control. The Guild system is one of industrial partnership between the workers and the public, and is thereby sharply distinguished from the proposals described as 'Syndicalist' . . . The governing idea of National Guilds is that of industrial self-government and democracy. Guildsmen hold that democratic principles are fully as applicable to industry as to politics." Cole, *Chaos and Order in Industry* (London, 1920), p. 58 ff.

[29] Cole, *Self-Government in Industry*, 5th ed. (London, 1920), pp. 235 ff.; also Schuster, "Zum englischen Gildensozialismus" (*Jahrbücher für Nationalökonomie und Statistik*, Vol. CXV), pp. 487 ff.

[30] Cole, *Self-Government in Industry*, p. 255.

[31] "A moment's consideration will show that it is one thing to lay drains, another to decide where drains are to be laid; it is one thing to make bread, another to decide how much bread is to be made; it is one thing to build houses, another to decide where the houses are to be built. This list of opposites can be lengthened indefinitely, and no amount of democratic fervour will destroy them. Faced with these facts, the Guild Socialist says that there is need for local and central authorities whose business it shall be to watch over that important part of life that lies outside production. A builder may think it advisable to be forever building, but the same man lives in some locality and has a right to say whether this purely industrial point of view shall have absolutely free play. Everyone, in fact, is not a producer but also a citizen." G. D. H. Cole and W. Mellor, *The Meaning of Industrial Freedom* (London, 1918), p. 30.

State. The whole system is an attempt to translate the political constitution of the English State into the sphere of production; its model is the relation in which local government stands to central government. Guild Socialism expressly describes itself as economic Federalism. But in the political constitution of a liberal state it is not difficult to concede a certain independence to local government. The necessary co-ordination of the parts within the whole is sufficiently ensured by the compulsion enforced on every territorial unit to manage its affairs in accordance with the laws. But in the case of
production this is far from sufficient. Society cannot leave it to the workers 261
themselves in individual branches of production to determine the amount and the quality of the labour they perform and how the material means of production thereby involved shall be applied.[32] If the workers of a guild work less zealously or use the means of production wastefully, this is a matter which concerns not only them but the whole society. The State entrusted with the direction of production cannot therefore refrain from occupying itself with the internal affairs of the guild. If it is not allowed to exercise direct control by appointing managers and works directors, then in some other way—perhaps by the means which lie at hand in the right of taxation, or the influence it has over the distribution of consumption goods—it must endeavour to reduce the independence of the guilds to a meaningless façade. It is the foremen who are in daily and hourly contact with the individual worker to direct and supervise his work who are hated most by the worker. Social reformers, who take over naively the sentiments of the workers, may believe it possible to replace these organs of control by trustworthy men chosen by the workers themselves. This is not quite as absurd as the belief of the anarchists that everyone would be prepared without compulsion to observe the rules indispensable for communal life; but it is not much better. Social production is a unity in which every part must perform exactly its function in the framework of the whole. It cannot be left to the discretion of the part to determine how it will accommodate itself to the general scheme. If the freely chosen foreman does not display the same zeal and energy in

[32] Tawney, *The Acquisitive Society* (London, 1921), p. 122, considers that the advantage of the Guild System for the worker is that it puts an end to "the odious and degrading system under which he is thrown aside like unused material whenever his services do not happen to be required." But just this reveals the gravest defect of the system recommended. If one needs no more building because relatively sufficient buildings exist, yet must build so as to occupy the workers in the building trades who are unwilling to change over to other branches of production that suffer from a comparative scarcity of labour, the position is uneconomic and wasteful. The very fact that Capitalism forces men to change their occupations is its advantage from the standpoint of the General Best, even though it may directly disadvantage the special interests of small groups.

his supervisory work as one not chosen by the workers, the productivity of labour will fall.

Guild Socialism therefore does not abolish any of the difficulties in the way of establishing a socialist order of society. It makes Socialism more acceptable to the English spirit by replacing the word nationalization, which
262 sounds disagreeable in English ears, by the catchword "Self-Government in Industry." But in essence it does not offer anything different from what continental socialists recommend today, namely, the proposal to leave the direction of production to committees of the workers and employees engaged in production, and of consumers. We have already seen that this brings us no nearer to solving the problem of Socialism.

Guild Socialism owes much of its popularity to the syndicalistic elements which many of its adherents believe are to be found in it. Guild Socialism as its literary representatives conceive it, is doubtless not syndicalistic. But the way in which it proposes to attain its end might very easily lead to Syndicalism. If, to begin with, national guilds were established in certain important branches of production which would have to work in an otherwise capitalist system, this would mean the syndicalization of individual branches of industry. As everywhere else, so here too, what appears to be the road to Socialism can in fact easily prove to be really the path to Syndicalism.

CHAPTER 16

Pseudo-Socialist Systems

1

Solidarism

In recent decades few have managed to remain uninfluenced by the success of the socialist criticism of the capitalist social order. Even those who did not want to capitulate to Socialism, have tried in many ways to act according to its criticism of private ownership in the means of production. Thus they have originated systems, ill-thought-out, eclectic in theory and weak in politics, which attempted to reconcile the contradictions. They were soon forgotten. Only one of these systems has spread—the system which calls itself Solidarism. This is at home above all in France; it has been called, not unjustly, the official social philosophy of the Third Republic. Outside of France, the term "Solidarism" is less well known, but the theories which make Solidarism are everywhere the social-political creed of all those religiously or conservatively inclined who have not joined Christian or State Socialism. Solidarism is distinguished neither by the depth of its theory, nor the number of its adherents. That which gives it a certain importance is its influence on many of the best and finest men and women of our times. 263

Solidarism starts by saying that the interests of all members of society harmonize. Private ownership in the means of production is a social institution the maintenance of which is to the interest of all, not merely of the owners; everyone would be harmed were it replaced by a common ownership endangering the productivity of social labour. So far, Solidarism goes hand in hand with Liberalism. Then, however, their ways separate. For solidarist theory believes that the principle of social solidarity is not realized simply by a social order based on private ownership in the means of production. It denies—without, however, arguing this more closely or bringing to light ideas not put forward before by the socialists, especially the non-Marxists—
that merely acting for one's own property-interests within a legal order 264

guaranteeing liberty and property ensures an interaction of the individual economic actions corresponding to the ends of social co-operation. Men in society, by the very nature of social co-operation, within which alone they can exist, are reciprocally interested in the well-being of their fellow men; their interests are "solidary," and they ought therefore to act with "solidarity." But mere private ownership in the means of production has not achieved solidarity in the society dividing labour. To do so, special provisions must be made. The more etatistically inclined wing of Solidarism wants to bring about "solidary" action by State action: laws shall impose obligations on the possessors in favour of the poorer people and in favour of the public welfare. The more ecclesiastically inclined wing of Solidarism wants to achieve the same thing by appeals to the conscience; not by State laws, but by moral prescriptions: Christian love will make the individual fulfil his social duties.

The representatives of Solidarism have laid down their social-philosophic views in brilliantly written essays, which reveal all the splendour of the French spirit. No one has been better able to paint in beautiful words the mutual dependence of men in society. At the head of them all is Sully Prudhomme. In his famous sonnet he shows the poet on awaking from a bad dream in which he has seen himself, as division of labour has ceased and no one will work for him, *seul, abandonné de tout le genre humain.* (Alone, abandoned by all mankind.) This leads him to the knowledge:

> . . . qu'au siècle où nous sommes
> Nul ne peut se vanter de se passer des hommes;
> Et depuis ce jour-là, je les ai tous aimés,
>
> (. . . *In our century*
> *No one can claim to take the place of men;*
> *And from that day I have loved everyone of them,*)

They have also known well how to state their case firmly, either by theological[1] or juristic arguments.[2] But all this must not blind us to the inner weakness of the theory. Solidarist theory is a foggy eclecticism. It demands no special
265 discussion. It interests us here much less than its social ideal, which claims

[1] Here one must name before all the Jesuit Pesch, *Lehrbuch der Nationalökonomie*, Vol. I, 2nd ed. (Freiburg, 1914), pp. 392–438. In France there is a conflict between catholic and freethinking solidarists—about the relation of the Church to the State and to society, rather than about the real principles of social theory and policy—which makes Church circles suspicious of the term "solidarism." See Haussonville, "Assistance publique et bienfaisance privée" (*Revue des Deux Mondes*, Vol. CLXII, 1900, pp. 773–808); Bouglé, *Le Solidarisme* (Paris, 1907), pp. 8 ff.

[2] Bourgeois, *Solidarité*, 6th ed. (Paris, 1907), pp. 115 ff.; Waha, *Die Nationalökonomie in Frankreich* (Stuttgart, 1910), pp. 432 ff.

"to avoid the faults of the individualist and socialist systems, to maintain that which is right in both."[3]

Solidarism proposes to leave the private ownership in the means of production. But it places above the owner an authority—indifferent whether Law and its creator, the State, or conscience and its counsellor, the Church—which is to see that the owner uses his property correctly. The authority shall prevent the individual from exploiting "unrestrainedly" his position in the economic process; certain restrictions are to be imposed on property. Thus State or Church, law or conscience, become the decisive factor in society. Property is put under their norms, it ceases to be the basic and ultimate element in the social order. It continues to exist only as far as Law or Ethics allow, that is to say, ownership is abolished, since the owner, in administering his property, must follow principles other than those imposed on him by his property interests. To say that, under all circumstances, the owner is bound to follow the prescription of Law and Ethics, and that no legal order recognizes ownership except within limits drawn by the norms, is by no means a reply. For if these norms aim only at free ownership and to prevent the owner from being disturbed in his right to keep his property as long as it does not pass to others on the basis of contracts he has made, then these norms contain merely recognition of private ownership in the means of production. Solidarism, however, does not regard these norms as alone sufficient to bring together fruitfully the labour of members of society. Solidarism wants to put other norms *above* them. These other norms thus become society's fundamental law. No longer private property but legal and moral prescription of a special kind, are society's fundamental law. Solidarism replaces ownership by a "Higher Law;" in other words, it abolishes it.

Of course, the solidarists do not really want to go as far. They want, they say, only to limit property, but to maintain it in principle. But when one has gone so far as to set up for property limits other than those resulting from its own nature, one has already abolished property. If the owner may do with his property only that which is prescribed to him, what directs the national economic activity is not property but that prescribing power.

Solidarism desires, for instance, to regulate competition; it shall not be 266
allowed to lead to "the decay of the middle-class" or to the "oppression of
the weak."[4] This merely means that a given condition of social production
is to be preserved, even though it would vanish under private property. The
owner is told what and how and how much he shall produce and at what

---

[3] Pesch, *op. cit.*, Vol. I, p. 420.

[4] *Ibid.*, p. 422.

conditions and to whom he shall sell. He thus ceases to be owner; he becomes a privileged member of a planned economy, an official drawing a special income.

Who shall decide in every single case, how far Law or Ethics go in limiting the owner's rights? Only the Law or Ethics itself.

Were Solidarism itself clear about the consequences of its postulates, it would certainly have to be called a variety of Socialism. But it is far from clear. It believes itself fundamentally different from State Socialism,[5] and the majority of its supporters would be horrified, were they to recognize what their ideal really was. Therefore its social ideal may still be counted one of the pseudo-socialist systems. But it must be realized that what separates it from Socialism is one single step. Only the mental atmosphere of France, generally more favourable to Liberalism and Capitalism, has prevented the French Solidarists and the Jesuit Pesch, an economist under French influence, from overstepping decisively the boundary between Solidarism and Socialism. Many, however, who still call themselves solidarists, must be counted complete etatists. Charles Gide, for example, is one of these.

2

Various Proposals for Expropriation

Precapitalist movements for the reform of property generally culminate in the demand for equality in wealth. All shall be equally rich; no one shall possess more or less than the others. This equality is to be achieved by redividing the land and to be made lasting by prohibiting sale or mortgage of land. Clearly, this is not Socialism, though it is sometimes called Agrarian Socialism.

Socialism does not want to divide the means of production at all, and wants to do more than merely expropriate; it wants to produce on the basis
267 of common ownership of the means of production. All such proposals, therefore, which aim only to expropriate the means of production are not to be regarded as Socialism; at best, they can be only proposals for a way to Socialism.

If, for example, they proposed a maximum amount to which one and the same person may own private property, they could be regarded as Socialism

---

[5] *Ibid.*, p. 420.

only if they intend to make the wealth thus accruing to the State the basis of socialist production. We should then have before us a proposal for socialization. It is not difficult to see that this proposal is not expedient. Whether the amount of the means of production which could thus be socialized is a greater or smaller one will depend on the extent to which private fortunes are still permitted. If this is fixed low, the proposed system is little different from immediate socialization. If it is fixed high, the action against private property will not do much to socialize the means of production. But anyway a whole series of unintended consequences must occur. For just the most energetic and active entrepreneurs will be prematurely excluded from economic activity, whilst those rich men whose fortunes approach the limit will be tempted to extravagant ways of living. The limitation of individual fortunes may be expected to slow down the formation of capital.

Similar considerations apply to proposals, which one hears in various quarters, to abolish the right of inheritance. To abolish inheritance and the right to make donations intended to circumvent the prohibition, would not bring about complete Socialism, though it would, in a generation, transfer to society a considerable part of all means of production. But it would, above all, slow down the formation of new capital, and a part of the existing capital would be consumed.

3

Profit-Sharing

One school of well-meaning writers and entrepreneurs recommends profit-sharing with wage earners. Profits shall no longer accrue exclusively to the entrepreneur; they shall be divided between the entrepreneurs and the workers. A share in the profits of the undertakings shall supplement the wages of the workers. Engel expects from this no less than "a settlement, satisfying both parties, of the raging fight, and thus, too, a solution of the 268
social question."[6] Most protagonists of the profit-sharing system attach no less importance to it.

[6] Engel, "Der Arbeitsvertrag und die Arbeitsgesellschaft" (in *Arbeiterfreund*, 5 Year, 1867, pp. 129–154). A survey of the German literature on profit sharing is given in the memorandum of the German "Statistisches Reichsamt": *Untersuchungen and Vorschläge zur Beteiligung der Arbeiter an dem Erträge wirtschaftlicher Unternehmungen*, published as a supplement to the *Reichs-Arbeitsblatt* of March 3, 1920.

The proposals to transfer to the worker a part of the entrepreneur's profits proceed from the idea that, under Capitalism, the entrepreneur deprives the worker of a part of that which he could really claim. The basis for the idea is the obscure concept of an inalienable right to the "full" product of labour, the exploitation theory in its popular, most naive, form, here expressed more or less openly. To its advocates the social question appears as a fight for the entrepreneur's profit. The socialists want to give this to the workers; the entrepreneurs claim it for themselves. Somebody comes along and recommends that the fight be ended by a compromise: each party shall have part of his claim. Both will thus fare well: The entrepreneurs, because their claim is obviously unjust, the workers because they get, without fighting, a considerable increase of income. This train of thought, which treats the problem of the social organization of labour as a problem of rights, and tries to settle a historical dispute as if it were a quarrel between two tradesmen, by splitting the difference, is so wrong that there is no purpose in going into it more closely. Either private ownership in the means of production is a necessary institution of human society or it is not. If it is not, one can or must abolish it, and there is no reason to stop half-way out of regard for the entrepreneur's personal interests. If, however, private property is necessary, it needs no other justification for existing, and there is no reason why, by partially abolishing it, its social effectiveness should be weakened.

The friends of profit-sharing think it would spur the worker on to a more zealous fulfilment of his duties than can be expected from a worker not interested in the yield of the undertaking. Here too, they err. Where the efficiency of labour has not been diminished by all kinds of socialist destructionist sabotage, where the worker can be dismissed without difficulty and his wages adjusted to his achievements without regard to collective agreements, no other spur is necessary to make him industrious. There, in such
269 conditions, the worker works fully conscious of the fact that his wages depend on what he does. But where these factors are lacking, the prospect of getting a fraction of the net profit of the undertaking would not induce him to do more than just as much as is formally necessary. Though of a different order of magnitude, it is the same problem we have already considered in examining the inducements in a socialist community to overcome the disutility of labour. Of the product of the extra labour, the burden of which the worker alone has to carry, he receives a fraction not sufficiently large to reward the extra effort.

If the workers' profit-sharing is carried out individually, so that each worker participates in the profits of just that undertaking he happens to be working for, there are created without any evident reason, differences in income, which fulfil no economic function, appear to be utterly unjustifed, and which all must feel unjust. "It is inadmissible that the turner in one works should earn twenty marks and receive ten marks more as a share of profits, while a turner in a competing works, where business is worse, perhaps worse directed, gets only twenty marks." This means either that a "rent" is created and perhaps that jobs connected with this "rent" are sold or that the worker tells his entrepreneur: "I don't care from what fund you pay the thirty marks; if my colleague receives it from the competition I demand it too."[7] Individual profit-sharing must lead straight to Syndicalism, even if it is a Syndicalism where the entrepreneur still keeps part of the entrepreneur's profit.

However, another way could be tried. Not the individual workers participate in the profits, but all the citizens; a part of the profits of all undertakings is distributed to all without distinction. This is already realized in taxation. Long before the war, joint stock companies in Austria had to surrender to the State and to other tax-levying authorities from twenty to forty per cent of their net profits; in the first years of the peace this grew from sixty to ninety per cent and more. The "mixed" public enterprise is the attempt to find a form for the community's participation, which makes the community share the management of the concern, in return for which it has to share in the providing of capital. Here, too, there is no reason why one should be content with half abolishing private property, if society could abolish the 270
institution completely without injuring the productivity of labour. If, however, to abolish private property is disadvantageous, then the half abolition is disadvantageous too. The half-measure may, in fact, be hardly less destructive than the clean sweep. Advocates usually say that the "mixed" undertaking leaves scope for the entrepreneur. However, as we have already shown, state or municipal activity hampers the freedom of the entrepreneur's decisions. An undertaking forced to collaborate with civil servants is not able to utilize the means of production in such ways as profit making demands.[8]

4

Syndicalism

As political tactics Syndicalism presents a particular method of attack by organized labour for the attainment of their political ends. This end may also be the establishment of the true Socialism, that is to say, the socialization of

---

[7] See the arguments of Vogelstein at the Regensburg session of the Verein für Sozialpolitik (*Schriften des Vereins für Sozialpolitik*, Vol. CLIX, pp. 132 ff.).

[8] See pp. 226-227.

the means of production. But the term Syndicalism is also used in a second sense, in which it means a socio-political aim of a special kind. In that sense Syndicalism is to be understood as a movement whose object is to bring about a state of society in which the workers are the owners of the means of production. We are concerned here with Syndicalism only as an aim; with Syndicalism as a movement, as political tactics, we need not deal.

Syndicalism as an aim and Syndicalism as political tactics do not always go hand in hand. Many groups which have adopted the syndicalist "direct action" as the basis of their proceedings are striving for a genuinely socialist community. On the other hand the attempt to realize Syndicalism as an end can be carried on by methods other than those of violence recommended by Sorel.

In the minds of the great bulk of workers who call themselves socialists or communists, Syndicalism presents itself, at least as vividly as Socialism, as the aim of the great revolution. The "petty bourgeois" ideas which Marx thought to overcome are very widespread—even in the ranks of the Marxian socialists. The great mass desire not the genuine Socialism, that is, centralized Socialism but Syndicalism. The worker wishes to be the lord of the means
271 of production which are employed in his particular undertaking. The social movement round about us shows more clearly every day that this and nothing else is what the worker desires. In contradistinction to Socialism which is the result of armchair study, syndicalist ideas spring direct from the mind of the ordinary man, who is always hostile to "unearned" income obtained by someone else. Syndicalism like Socialism aims at the abolition of the separation of worker from the means of production, only it proceeds by another method. Not all the workers will become the owners of all the means of production; those in a particular industry or undertaking or the workers engaged in a complete branch of production will obtain the means of production employed in it. The railways to the railway men, the mines to the miners, the factories to the factory hands—this is the slogan.

We must ignore every freak scheme for enacting Syndicalist ideas and take a thoroughly consistent application of the main principle to the whole economic order as the starting point of our examination. This is not difficult. Every measure which takes the ownership of all the means of production from the entrepreneurs, capitalists, and landlords without transferring it to the *whole* of the citizens of the economic area, is to be regarded as Syndicalism. It makes no difference in this case, whether in such a society more or less of these associations are formed. It is unimportant whether all branches of production are constituted as separate bodies or only single undertakings, just as they happen to have evolved historically, or single factories of even

single workshops. In essence the scheme is hardly affected if the lines drawn through the society are more or less, horizontal or vertical. The only decisive point is that the citizen of such a community is the owner of a share of certain means of production and the non-owner of other means of production, and that in some cases, for example, when he is unable to work, he may own no property at all. The question whether the workers' incomes will, or will not, be noticeably increased, is unimportant here. Most workers have absolutely fantastic ideas about the increase of wealth they could expect under syndicalist arrangements of property. They believe that just the mere distribution of the share which landlords, capitalists and entrepreneurs draw under capitalist industry must considerably increase the income of each of them. Apart from this they expect an important increase in the product of industry, because they, who regard themselves as particularly expert, will themselves conduct the enterprise, and because every worker will be per- 272
sonally interested in the prosperity of the undertaking. The worker will no longer work for a stranger but for himself. The liberal thinks quite differently about all this. He points out that the distribution of rent and profit incomes among the workers would bring them an insignificant increase in incomes. Above all he maintains that enterprises which are no longer directed by the self-interest of entrepreneurs working on their own account but by labour leaders unfitted for the task will yield less, so that the workers will not only earn no more than under a free economy, but considerably less.

If syndicalist reform merely handed over to the workers the ownership of the means of production and left the system of property of the capitalist order otherwise unchanged, the result would be no more than a primitive redistribution of wealth. The redistribution of goods with the object of restoring the equality of property and wealth is at the back of the mind of the ordinary man whenever he thinks of reforming social conditions, and it forms the basis for all popular proposals for socialization. This is not incomprehensible in the case of land workers, to whom the object of all ambition is to acquire a homestead and a piece of land large enough to support him and his family; in the village, redistribution, the popular solution of the social problem, is quite conceivable. In industry, in mining, in communications, in trade and in banking where a physical redistribution of the means of production is quite inconceivable, we get instead a desire for the division of the property rights while preserving the unity of the industry or enterprise. To divide in this simple way would be, at best, a method of abolishing for the moment the inequality in the distribution of income and poverty. But after a short time, some would have squandered their shares, and others would have enriched themselves by acquiring the shares of the less economically efficient. Consequently there would have to be constant redistributions, which would simply serve to reward frivolity and waste—in short every form of uneconomic behaviour. There will be no stimulus to economy if the industrious and thrifty are constantly compelled to hand over the fruits of their industry and thrift to the lazy and extravagant.

Yet even this result—the temporary achievement of equality of income and property—could not be accomplished by syndicalization. For syndicalization is by no means the same for all workers. The value of the means of production in different branches of production is not proportional to the number of workers employed. It is unnecessary to elaborate the fact that there are products which involve more of the productive factor, labour, and less of the productive factor, Nature. Even a division of the means of production at the historical commencement of all human production would have led to inequality; much more so if these means are syndicalized at a highly progressive stage of capital accumulation in which not only natural factors of
273 production but produced means of production are divided. The values of the share falling to individual workers in a redistribution of this kind would be very different: some would obtain more, others less, and as a result some would draw a larger income from property—unearned income—than others. Syndicalization is in no way a means of achieving equality of incomes. It abolishes the existing inequality of incomes and property and replaces it by another. It may be that this syndicalistic inequality is regarded as more just than that of the capitalistic order—but on this point science can give no judgment.

If syndicalist reform is to mean more than the mere redistribution of productive goods, then it cannot allow the property arrangements of Capitalism to persist in regard to the means of production. It must withdraw productive goods from the market. Individual citizens must not dispose of the shares in the means of production which are allotted to them; for under Syndicalism these are bound up with the person of the owner in a much closer way than is the case in the liberal society. How, in different circumstances, they may be separated from the person can be regulated in various ways.

The naive logic of the advocates of Syndicalism assumes without any further ado a completely stationary condition of society, and pays no attention to the problem, how the system will adapt itself to changes of economic conditions. If we assume that no changes occur in the methods of production, in the relations of supply and demand, in technique, or in population, then everything seems to be quite in order. Each worker has only one child, and departs out of this world at the moment his successor and sole heir becomes

capable of work; the son promptly steps into his place. We can perhaps assume that a change of occupation, a transfer from one branch of production to another or from one independent undertaking to another by a voluntary 274
simultaneous exchange of positions and of shares in the means of production will be permitted. But for the rest the syndicalist state of society necessarily assumes a strictly imposed caste system and the complete end of all changes in industry and, therefore, in life. The mere death of a childless citizen disturbs it and opens up problems which are quite insoluble within the logic of the system.

In the syndicalist society the income of a citizen is made up of the yield from his portion of property and of the wages from his labour. If the shares in the property in the means of production can be freely inherited, then in a very short time differences in property holding will arise even if no changes occur among the living. Even if at the beginning of the syndicalist era the separation of the worker from the means of production is overcome, so that every citizen is an enterpreneur as well as a worker in his undertaking, it may so happen that later on citizens who do not belong to a particular undertaking inherit shares in it. This would very quickly drive the syndicalist society to a separation of labour and property, without the advantages of the capitalist order of society.[9]

Every economic change immediately creates problems on which Syndicalism would inevitably be wrecked. If changes in the direction and extent of demand or in the technique of production cause changes in the organization of the industry, which require the transfer of workers from one concern to another or from one branch of production to another, the question immediately arises what is to be done with the shares of these workers in the means of production. Should the workers and their heirs keep the shares in those industries to which they happened to belong at the actual time of syndicalization and enter the new industries as simple workers earning wages, without being allowed to draw any part of the property income? Or should they lose their share on leaving an industry and in return receive a share per head equal to that possessed by the workers already occupied in the new industry? Either solution would quickly violate the principle of Syndicalism. If, in addition, men were permitted to dispose of their shares, conditions would gradually return to the state prevailing before the reform. But if the worker on his departure from an industry loses his share and on entering another industry acquires a share in that, those workers who stood 275

[9] It is misleading, therefore, to call Syndicalism "workers' Capitalism," as I too have done in *Nation, Staat und Wirtschaft*, p. 164.

to lose by the change would, naturally, oppose energetically every change in production. The introduction of a process making for greater productivity of labour would be resisted if it displaced workers or might displace them. On the other hand the workers in an undertaking or branch of industry would oppose any development by the introduction of new workers if it threatened to reduce their income from property. In short, Syndicalism would make every change in production practically impossible. Where it existed there could be no question of economic progress.

As an aim Syndicalism is so absurd, that speaking generally, it has not found any advocates who dared to write openly and clearly in its favour. Those who have dealt with it under the name of co-partnership have never thought out its problems. Syndicalism has never been anything else than the ideal of plundering hordes.

5

Partial Socialism

Natural ownership of the means of production is divisible. In capitalist society, it generally is divided.[10] But the power to dispose which belongs to him who directs production and which alone we call ownership, is indivisible and illimitable. It may belong to several people jointly, but cannot be divided in the sense that the power of disposing itself can be decomposed into separate rights of command. The power to dispose of the use of a commodity in production can only be unitary; that this could in any way be dissolved into elements is unthinkable. Ownership in the natural sense cannot be limited; wherever one speaks of limitation, one means either a curtailment of a too-widely drawn juristic definition or recognition of the fact that ownership in the natural sense belongs concretely to someone other than the person whom the law recognizes as owner.

All attempts to abolish by a compromise the contrast between common property and private ownership in the means of production are therefore
276 mistaken. Ownership is always where the power to dispose resides.[11] Therefore State Socialism and planned economies, which want to maintain private

[10] See pp. 29 ff.

[11] On interventionism see my *Kritik des Interventionismus*, pp. 1 ff. Publisher's Note: In English, *A Critique of Interventionism*, trans. Hans F. Sennholz (New York: Arlington House, 1977), pp. 15 ff.

property in name and in law, but in fact, because they subordinate the power of disposing to State orders, want to socialize property, are socialist systems in the full sense. Private property exists only where the individual can deal with his private ownership in the means of production in the way he considers most advantageous. That in doing so he serves other members of society, because in the society based on division of labour everyone is the servant of all and all the masters of each, in no way alters the fact that he himself looks for the way in which he can best perform this service.

It is not possible to compromise, either, by putting part of the means of production at the disposal of society and leaving the remainder to individuals. Such systems simply stand unconnected, side by side, and operate fully only within the space they occupy. Such mixtures of the social principles of organization must be considered senseless by everyone. No one can believe that the principle which he holds to be right should not be carried through to the end. Nor can anyone assert that one or the other of the systems proves the better only for certain groups of the means of production. Where people seem to be asserting this, they are really asserting that we must demand the one system at least for a group of the means of production or that it should be given at most for a group. Compromise is always only a momentary lull in the fight between the two principles, not the result of a logical thinking-out of the problem. Regarded from the stand-point of each side, half-measures are a temporary halt on the way to complete success.

The best known and most respected of the systems of compromise believes indeed that it can recommend half-measures as a permanent institution. The land-reformers want to socialize the natural factors of production, but for the rest to leave private ownership in the means of production. They hereby proceed from the assumption, regarded as self-evident, that common property in the means of production gives a higher yield than private property. Because they regard land as the most important means of production, they wish to transfer it to society. With the breakdown of the thesis that
public ownership could achieve better results than private ownership, the 277
idea of land reform also falls to the ground. Whoever regards land as the most important means of production must certainly advocate the private ownership of land, if he considers private ownership the superior economic form.

PART III
THE ALLEGED INEVITABILITY OF SOCIALISM

SECTION 1

SOCIAL EVOLUTION

CHAPTER 17

Socialistic Chiliasm

1

The Origin of Chiliasm

Socialism derives its strength from two different sources. On the one hand it is an ethical, political, and economico-political challenge. The socialist order of society, fulfilling the claims of higher morality, is to replace the "immoral" capitalist economy; the "economic rule" of the few over the many is to give way to a co-operative order which alone can make true democracy possible; planned economy, the only rational system working according to uniform principles, is to sweep away the irrational private economic order, the anarchical production for profit. Socialism thus appears as a goal towards which we ought to strive because it is morally and rationally desirable. The task therefore of men of good will is to defeat the resistance to it which is inspired by misunderstanding and prejudice. This is the basic idea of that Socialism which Marx and his school call Utopian. 281

On the other hand, however, Socialism is made to appear as the inevitable goal and end of historical evolution. An obscure force from which we cannot escape leads humanity step by step to higher planes of social and moral being. History is a progressive process of purification, with perfection, in the form of Socialism, at the end. This train of thought does not run counter to the ideas of Utopian Socialism. Rather it includes them, for it presupposes, as obviously self-evident, that the socialist condition would be better, nobler, and more beautiful than the non-socialist. But it goes farther; it sees the change to Socialism—envisioned as progress, an evolution to a higher stage—as something independent of human will. A necessity of Nature, Socialism is the inevitable outcome of the forces underlying social life: this is the fundamental idea of evolutionary socialism, which, in its Marxist form, has taken the proud name of "Scientific" Socialism.

In recent times scholars have been at pains to prove that the main notions

282 of the materialist or economic conception of history had been set forth by pre-Marxian writers, among them some of those whom Marx and his supporters contemptuously call Utopians. These researches and the critique of the materialist conception of history which accompany them, however, tend to set the problem in much too narrow a perspective. They concentrate on the peculiarities of the Marxist theory of evolution, its specifically economic nature, and the importance it gives to the class war, and they forget that it is also a doctrine of perfection, a theory of progress and evolution.

The materialist conception of history contains three elements, which, though they combine to form a closed system, have each a special significance for the Marxian theory. First, it involves a special method of historical and sociological research. As such it tries to explain the relation between the economic structure and the whole life of a period. Secondly, it is a sociological theory, since it sets up a definite concept of class and class war as a sociological element. Finally, it is a theory of progress, a doctrine of the destiny of the human race, of the meaning and nature, purpose and aim of human life. This aspect of the materialist conception of history has been less noticed than the other two, yet this alone concerns socialist theory as such. Merely as a method of research, an heuristic principle for the cognition of social evolution, the materialist conception of history is obviously in no position to talk about the inevitability of a socialistic order of society. The conclusion that our evolution is tending towards Socialism does not of necessity follow from the study of economic history. The same is true of the theory of the class-war. Once the view has been adopted that the history of all previous society is the history of class struggles, it becomes difficult to see why the struggle of classes should suddenly disappear. Might it not be supposed that what had always been the substance of history will continue to be so to the very end? Only as a theory of progress can the materialist conception of history concern itself with the final goal of historical evolution and assert that the decay of Capitalism and the victory of the proletariat are alike inevitable. Nothing has helped the spread of socialist ideas more than this belief that Socialism is inevitable. Even the opponents of Socialism are for the most part bewitched by it: it takes the heart out of their resistance. The educated person is afraid of appearing unmodern if he does not show that he is actuated by the "social"
283 spirit, for already the age of Socialism, the historic day of the Fourth Estate, is supposed to have dawned and everyone who still clings to Liberalism is in consequence a reactionary. Every triumph of the socialist idea which brings us nearer to the socialist way of production is counted as progress; every measure which protects private property is a setback. The one side looks on with sadness or an even deeper emotion, the other with delight,

as the age of private property passes with the changing times, but all are convinced that history has destined it to irrevocable destruction.

Now as a theory of progress, going beyond experience and what can be experienced, the materialist conception of history is not science but metaphysics. The essence of all metaphysics of evolution and history is the doctrine of the beginning and end, the origin and purpose of things. This is conceived either cosmically, embracing the whole universe, or it is anthropocentric and considers man alone. It can be religious or philosophic. The anthropocentric metaphysical theories of evolution are known as the philosophy of history. The theories of evolution which are of a religious character must always be anthropocentric, for the high significance religion attaches to mankind can be justified only by an anthropocentric doctrine. These theories are based generally on the assumption of a paradisiac origin, a Golden Age, from which man is moving farther and farther away, only to return finally to an equally good, or, if possible, even better, age of perfection. This generally includes the idea of Salvation. The return of the Golden Age will save men from the ills which have befallen them in an age of evil. Thus the whole doctrine is a message of earthly salvation. It must not be confused with that supreme refinement of the religious idea of Salvation developed in those doctrines which transfer salvation from Man's earthly life into a better world Beyond. According to these doctrines the earthly life of the individual is never the final end. It is merely preparation for a different, better and painless existence which may even be found in a state of non-existence, in dissolution in the All, or in Destruction.

For our civilization the message of salvation of the Jewish prophets came to have a special importance. The Jewish Prophets promise no salvation in a better world beyond, they proclaim a Kingdom of God on Earth. "Behold, the days come, saith the Lord, that the plowman shall overtake the reaper, and the treader of grapes him that soweth the seed; and the mountains shall drop sweet wine, and all the hills shall melt."[1] "The wolf also shall dwell 284
with the lamb, and the leopard shall lie down with the kid; and the calf and the young lion and the fatling together; and a little child shall lead them. And the cow and the bear shall feed, their young ones shall lie down together: and the lion shall eat straw like the ox. And the suckling child shall play on the hole of the asp, and the weaned child shall put his hand on the cockatrice' den. They shall not hurt or destroy in all my holy mountain, for the earth shall be full of the knowledge of the Lord, as the waters cover the sea."[2] Only when such a message of salvation is prom-

[1] Amos, IX, 13.
[2] Isaiah, XI, 6–9.

ised for the immediate future will it be joyfully accepted. And in fact Isaiah says that only "yet a very little while" separates men from the promised hour.[3] But the longer they have to wait the more impatient must the faithful become. What good to them is a Kingdom of Redemption which they will not live to enjoy! The promise of salvation therefore, must necessarily expand into a doctrine of the Resurrection of the Dead, a Resurrection that brings every individual before the Lord, to be judged good or evil.

Judaism is full of these ideas at the time when Jesus appears among his people as the Messiah. He comes not only to proclaim an imminent salvation but also, in fulfilment of the prophecy, as the bringer of the Kingdom of God.[4] He walks among the people and preaches, but the world goes its way as of old. He dies on the cross, but everything remains as it was. At first this shakes the faith of the disciples profoundly. For the time being they go all to pieces and the first little congregation scatters. Only belief in the Resurrection of Christ crucified reinspires them, filling them with fresh enthusiasm and giving them the strength to win new adherents to their doctrine of salvation.[5] The message of salvation they preach is the same that was preached by Christ: the Lord is near and with him the great Day of Judgment, when the world shall be renewed and the Kingdom of God founded in place of the Kingdoms of the world. But as expectation of an imminent Return of Christ vanished and the growing congregations began to settle down to a longer period of waiting, the belief in salvation had also to undergo a change. No lasting world-religion could have been built up on the belief that the Kingdom
285 of God was imminent. Each day that left the prophecy unfulfilled would have impaired the Church's prestige. The fundamental idea of primitive Christianity that the Kingdom of God was at hand had to be transformed into the Christian cult: into the belief that the heavenly presence of their risen Lord entered into the congregation, and into belief in the salvation of the sinful world by Him. Only thus could the Christian Religious Community be founded. From the moment of this transformation Christian doctrine ceases to expect a Kingdom of God on Earth. The idea of salvation is sublimated into the doctrine that by baptism the faithful become part of the

[3] Isaiah, XXIX, 17.

[4] Whether or not Jesus held Himself to be the Messiah we need not discuss here. The only important thing for us is that He announced the immediate coming of the Kingdom of God and that the first congregation looked on Him as the Messiah.

[5] Pfleiderer, *Das Urchristentum*, 2nd ed. (Berlin, 1902), Vol. I, pp. 7 ff.

Body of Christ. "Already in Apostolic times the Kingdom of God becomes merged in the Church, and all that is left for the Coming of the Kingdom is the glorification of the Church, the shattering of the earthly vessel, and the liberation of the shining treasure from its mortal frame. For the rest, the Kingdom of God is replaced by the eschatology of Heaven, Hell and Purgatory, Immortality and the Beyond—a contrast to the Gospels which is of the highest significance. But even this end recedes, until at last the Millennium came to mean the Church."[6]

There was, however, another way of meeting the difficulties which arose when fulfilment of the promise had been postponed longer than was originally expected. The faithful could take refuge in the belief which had once sustained the Prophets. According to this doctrine an earthly Kingdom of Salvation lasting one thousand years would be set up. Condemned by the Church as heresy, this doctrine of the Visible Return of Christ is continually revived not only as a religious and political belief, but above all as an idea of social and economic revolution.

From Christian Chiliasm, which runs through the centuries constantly renewing its strength, a single step leads to the philosophic Chiliasm which in the eighteenth century was the rationalist reinterpretation of Christianity; and thence, through Saint Simon, Hegel, and Weitling to Marx and Lenin.[7] Curiously enough, it is this particular Socialism, derived in this way from mystical ideas whose origin is lost in the darkness of history, which has called itself scientific Socialism, while it has tried to disqualify as "Utopian" the Socialism that is derived from the rational considerations of the philos- 286
ophers.

The philosophical anthropocentric metaphysics of evolution resembles the religious in every essential. In its prophecy of salvation is found the same strange mixture of ecstatically extravagant phantasy with uninspired commonplace and coarse materialism as is found in the most ancient messianic prophecies. Like Christian literature which seeks to interpret the apocalypse, it tries to prove itself applicable to life by interpreting concrete historical events. In these attempts it often makes itself ridiculous, rushing in on every great occasion with a doctrine which both meets the case and embraces the history of the universe. How many of these philosophies of history arose during the World War!

---

[6] Troeltsch, "Die Soziallehren der christlichen Kirchen und Gruppen" in *Gesammelte Schriften* (Tübingen, 1912), Vol. I, p. 110.

[7] Gerlich, *Der Kommunismus als Lehre vom tausendjährigen Reich* (Munich, 1920), pp. 17 ff.

2

Chiliasm and Social Theory

The metaphysical philosophy of history must be clearly distinguished from the rational. The latter is built up solely on experience, seeking results which are based on logic and empiricism. Wherever rational philosophy has to go beyond this, it tries hypotheses, but it never forgets where experience ceases and hypothetical interpretations begin. Where experience is possible it avoids using conceptual fictions; it never tries to supplant experimental science. Its only aim is to unify our view of social events and of the course of historical evolution. Only thus is it able to establish a law which governs changes in social conditions. By indicating, or attempting to indicate, the force which determines the growth of society, it endeavours to reveal the principle determining social evolution. This principle is assumed to be externally valid, that is, it is active so long as there is any society at all. Were it otherwise, a second principle would have to be placed next to this one, and it would be necessary to show under which conditions the first ruled and under which the second. But this only means that the law governing the interchange of the two principles would be the ultimate Law of Social Life.

To define a principle according to which society grows, and changes in social conditions take place, is a different thing from defining the course
287 which social evolution takes. Such a course is necessarily limited. It has a beginning and an end. The reign of a law is necessarily unlimited, without beginning or end. It is continuity, not an occurrence. The law is imperfect if it defines only a part of social evolution and leaves us in the lurch after a certain point. In this case it would cease to be a law. The end of social evolution can be no other than that of society itself.

The teleological view describes the course of evolution in all its windings and deviations. Thus it is typically a theory of stages. It shows us the successive stages of civilization until one is reached which must necessarily be the last, because no other follows it. When this point has been reached it is impossible to see how history is to proceed.[8]

---

[8] Wundt, *Ethik*, 4th ed. (Stuttgart, 1912), Vol. II, p. 246. One sees in Engels' survey of the history of warfare a characteristic example of how ready the representatives of this movement are to see the end of all evolution attained. Engels there—1878—expresses the opinion that, with the Franco-German war, "a turning point of quite other importance than all previous ones had occurred" in the history of warfare. "Weapons are so perfected that a fresh process of any revolutionary influence is no longer possible. When one has guns which can hit a battalion as far as the eye can see and rifles which can do the same with a single person as aim, with which

The chiliastic philosophy of history takes the "standpoint of Providence, which lies beyond all human wisdom"; it aims at prophesying as only "the eye of a God" could prophesy.[9] Whether we call its teaching Poetry, Prophecy, Faith, Hope or anything else whatever, there are two things it can never be: Science or Knowledge. Nor may it be called hypothesis, any more than the utterances of a clairvoyant or a fortune-teller may be called hypotheses. It was an unusually clever trick on the part of the Marxists to call their chiliastic teachings science. Such a step was bound to be effective in an age when people relied on nothing but science, and rejected metaphysics (though, admittedly, only to surrender themselves uncritically to the native metaphysics of Büchner and Moleschott).

The law of social evolution tells us much less than the metaphysics of evolution. It limits its statements *a priori* in admitting that its sway can be frustrated by the co-existence of forces other than those it describes. On the 288
other hand, it admits no limits to its applicability. It claims eternal validity, it is without beginning and without end. But it does not evoke a dark fate whose "will-less and impotent bearers" we are. It discloses only the inner driving power of our own will, revealing how it conforms to natural laws and why its existence is necessary. This is insight, not into man's destiny, but into man's doings.

In so far as "scientific" Socialism is metaphysics, a chiliastic promise of salvation, it would be vain and superfluous to argue scientifically against it. It serves no useful purpose to fight mystical dogmas with reason. There is no teaching fanatics. They must break their heads against the wall. But Marxism is not merely chiliasm. It is sufficiently influenced by the scientific spirit of the nineteenth century to attempt to justify its doctrine rationally. With these attempts, and these only, we shall deal in the following chapters.

---

loading takes less time than firing, then all further advances are more or less indifferent in field war. Thus the era of evolution on this side is essentially closed." See *Herrn Eugen Dührings Umwälzung der Wissenschaft*, p. 176. Publisher's Note: p. 236 in the English edition. In judging other views, Marx understands well how to find out the weaknesses of the theory of stages. According to their teachings, says Marx, "a history has existed but none exists any longer." See *Das Elend der Philosophie*, German translation by Bernstein and Kautsky, 8th ed. (Stuttgart, 1920), p. 104. He merely does not notice that the same will be true of his teachings on the day when the means of production will have been socialized. Publisher's Note: In English, Marx, *The Poverty of Philosophy: Answer to the "Philosophy of Poverty" by M. Proudhon* (Moscow: Foreign Language Publishing House), p. 112.

[9] Kant, "Der Streit der Fakultäten" (*Collected Works*, Vol. I), p. 636.

CHAPTER 18

Society

1

The Nature of Society

289 The idea of human destiny dominates all the more ancient views of social existence. Society progresses towards a goal fore-ordained by the deity. Whoever thinks in this way is logically correct if, in speaking of progress and retrogression, of revolution and counterrevolution, of action and reaction he lays on these concepts the emphasis adopted by so many historians and politicians. History is judged according as it brings mankind nearer to the goal or carries it farther away.

Social science, however, begins at the point where one frees oneself from such habits, and indeed from all valuation. Social science is indeed teleological in the sense in which every causal study of the will must be. But its concept of purpose is wholly comprised in the causal explanation. For social science causality remains the fundamental principle of cognition, the maintenance of which must not be impaired even by teleology.[1] Since it does not evaluate purposes, it cannot speak of evolution to a higher plane, in the sense let us say, of Hegel and Marx. For it is by no means proved that all evolution leads upwards, or that every later stage is a higher one. No more, of course, can it agree with the pessimistic philosophers of history, who see in the historical process a decline, a progressive approach to a bad end. To ask what are the driving forces of historical evolution is to ask what is the nature of society and the origin and causes of the changes in social conditions. What society is, how it originates, how it changes—these alone can be the problems which scientific sociology sets itself.

---

[1] Cohen, *Logik der reinen Erkenntnis*, 2nd ed. (Berlin, 1914), p. 359.

That the social life of men resembles the biological process is an observation of ancient date. It lies at the basis of the famous legend of Menenius Agrippa, handed down to us by Livy. Social science did itself little good when, inspired by the triumph of Biology in the nineteenth century, voluminous works 290
developed this analogy to the point of absurdity. What is the use of calling the products of human activity "social intercellular substance"?[2] Who was enlightened when scholars disputed which organ of the social body corresponded to the central nervous system? The best comment on this form of sociological study was the remark of an economist, to the effect that anyone who compared money with blood and the circulation of money with the circulation of blood would be making the same contribution to economics as would be made to biology by a man who compared blood with money and the blood-circulation with the circulation of money. Modern biology has borrowed from social science some of its most important concepts—that of evolution, of the division of labour, and of the struggle for existence. But it has not stopped short at metaphorical phrases and conclusions by analogy; rather has it proceeded to make profitable use of what it had gained. On the other hand biological-sociology did nothing but play a futile word-spinning game with the ideas it borrowed back. The romantic movement, with its "organic" theory of the state has done even less to clear up our knowledge of social interrelations. Because it deliberately cold-shouldered the most important achievement of social science up to that date—the system of classical Political Economy—it was unable to utilize the doctrine of the division of labour, that part of the classical system which must be the starting point of all sociology, as it is of modern biology.[3]

Comparison with the biological organism should have taught sociology one thing: that the organism can only be conceived as a system of organs.

---

[2] As is done by Lilienfeld, *La pathologie sociale* (Paris, 1896), p. 95. When a government takes a loan from the House of Rothschild organic sociology conceives the process as follows: "*La maison Rothschild agit, dans cette occasion, parfaitement en analogie avec l'action d'un groupe de cellules qui, dans le corps humain, coopèrent à la production du sang nécessaire à l'alimentation du cerveau dans l'espoir d'en être indemnisées par une réaction des cellules de la substance grise dont ils ont besoin pour s'activer de nouveau et accumuler de nouvelles énergies.*" ("The House of Rothschild's operation, on such an occasion, is precisely similar to the action of a group of human body cells which cooperate in the production of the blood necessary for nourishing the brain, in the hope of being compensated by a reaction of the gray matter cells which they need to reactivate and to accumulate new energies.") (*Ibid.*, p. 104.) This is the method which claims that it stands on "firm ground" and explores "the Becoming of Phenomena step by step, proceeding from the simpler to the more complex." See Lilienfeld, *Zur Verteidigung der organischen Methode in der Soziologie* (Berlin, 1898), p. 75.

[3] It is characteristic that just the romantics stress excessively society's organic character, whereas liberal social philosophy has never done so. Quite understandably. A social theory which was genuinely organic did not need to stress obtrusively this attribute of its system.

This, however, merely means that the essence of the organism is the division of labour. Only division of labour makes the parts become members; it is in
291 the collaboration of the members that we recognize the unity of the system, the organism.[4] This is true of the life of plants and animals as well as of society. As far as the principle of the division of labour is concerned, the social body may be compared with the biological. The division of labour is the *tertium comparationis* (basis for comparison) of the old simile.

The division of labour is a fundamental principle of all forms of life.[5] It was first detected in the sphere of social life when political economists emphasized the meaning of the division of labour in the social economy. Biology then adopted it, at the instigation in the first place of Milne Edwards in 1827. The fact that we can regard the division of labour as a general law must not, however, prevent us from recognizing the fundamental differences between division of labour in the animal and vegetable organism on the one hand and division of labour in the social life of human beings on the other. Whatever we imagine to be the origin, evolution, and meaning of the physiological division of labour, it clearly does not shed any light on the nature of the sociological division of labour. The process that differentiates and integrates homogeneous cells is completely different from that which led to the growth of human society out of self-sufficient individuals. In the second process, reason and will play their part in the coalescence, by which the previously independent units form a larger unit and become parts of a whole, whereas the intervention of such forces in the first process is inconceivable.

Even where creatures such as ants and bees come together in "animal communities," all movements and changes take place instinctively and unconsciously. Instinct may very well have operated at the beginning and in the earliest stages of social formation also. Man is already a member of a social body when he appears as a thinking, willing creature, for the thinking man is inconceivable as a solitary individual. "Only amongst men does man become a man" (Fichte). The development of human reason and the development of human society are one and the same process. All further growth of social relations is entirely a matter of will. Society is the product of thought and will. It does not exist outside thought and will. Its being lies within man, not in the outer world. It is projected from within outwards.

292 Society is co-operation; it is community in action.

To say that Society is an organism, means that society is division of labour.[6]

[4] Cohen, *Logik der reinen Erkenntnis*, p. 349.

[5] Hertwig, *Allgemeine Biologie*, 4th ed. (Jena, 1912), pp. 500 ff; Hertwig, *Zur Abwehr des ethischen, des sozialen und des politischen Darwinismus* (Jena, 1918), pp. 69 ff.

[6] Izoulet, *La cité moderne* (Paris, 1894), pp. 35 ff.

To do justice to this idea we must take into account all the aims which men set themselves and the means by which these are to be attained. It includes every inter-relation of thinking and willing man. Modern man is a social being, not only as one whose material needs could not be supplied in isolation, but also as one who has achieved a development of reason and of the perceptive faculty that would have been impossible except within society. Man is inconceivable as an isolated being, for humanity exists only as a social phenomenon and mankind transcended the stage of animality only in so far as co-operation evolved the social relationships between the individuals. Evolution from the human animal to the human being was made possible by and achieved by means of social cooperation and by that alone. And therein lies the interpretation of Aristotle's dictum that man is the ζῶον πσλιτιχὸν (the living body politic).

2

The Division of Labour as the Principle of Social Development

We are still far from understanding the ultimate and most profound secret of life, the principle of the origin of organisms. Who knows whether we shall ever discover it? All we know today is that when organisms are formed, something which did not exist before is created out of individuals. Vegetable and animal organisms are more than conglomerations of single cells, and society is more than the sum of the individuals of which it is composed. We have not yet grasped the whole significance of this fact. Our thoughts are still limited by the mechanical theory of the conservation of energy and of matter, which is never able to tell us how one can become two. Here again, if we are to extend our knowledge of the nature of life, understanding of the social organization will have to precede that of the biological.

Historically division of labour originates in two facts of nature: the inequality of human abilities and the variety of the external conditions of human life on the earth. These two facts are really one: the diversity of Nature,
which does not repeat itself but creates the universe in infinite, inexhaustible 293
variety. The special nature of our inquiry, however, which is directed towards sociological knowledge, justifies us in treating these two aspects separately.

It is obvious that as soon as human action becomes conscious and logical it must be influenced by these two conditions. They are indeed such as almost to force the division of labour on mankind.[7] Old and young, men and women co-operate by making appropriate use of their various abilities. Here also is the germ of the geographical division of labour; man goes to the hunt and woman to the spring to fetch water. Had the strength and abilities of all individuals and the external conditions of production been everywhere equal the idea of division of labour could never have arisen. Man would never of himself have hit upon the idea of making the struggle for existence easier by co-operation in the division of labour. No social life could have arisen among men of equal natural capacity in a world which was geographically uniform.[8] Perhaps men would have joined together to cope with tasks which were beyond the strength of individuals, but such alliances do not make a society. The relations they create are transient, and endure only for the occasion that brings them about. Their only importance in the origin of social life is that they create a *rapprochement* between men which brings with it mutual recognition of the difference in the natural capacities of individuals and thus in turn gives rise to the division of labour.

Once labour has been divided, the division itself exercises a differentiating influence. The fact that labour is divided makes possible further cultivation of individual talent and thus co-operation becomes more and more produc-
294 tive. Through co-operation men are able to achieve what would have been beyond them as individuals, and even the work which individuals are capable of doing alone is made more productive. But all this can only be grasped fully when the conditions which govern increase of productivity under co-operation are set out with analytical precision.

The theory of the international division of labour is one of the most important contributions of Classical Political Economy. It shows that as long as—for any reasons—movements of capital and labour between countries are prevented, it is the comparative, not the absolute, costs of production

[7] Durkheim, *De la division du travail social* (Paris, 1893), pp. 294 ff. endeavours (following Comte and against Spencer) to prove that the division of labour prevails not because, as the economists think, it increases output but as a result of the struggle for existence. The denser the social mass the sharper the struggle for existence. This forces individuals to specialize in their work, as otherwise they would not be able to maintain themselves. But Durkheim overlooks the fact that the division of labour makes this possible only because it makes labour more productive. Durkheim comes to reject the theory of the importance of the greater productivity in the division of labour through a false conception of the fundamental idea of utilitarianism and of the law of the satiation of wants (*op. cit.*, 218 ff., 257 ff.). His view that civilization is called forth by changes in the volume and density of society is untenable. Population grows because labour becomes more productive and is able to nourish more people, not vice versa.

[8] On the important part played by the local variety of productive conditions in the origin of the division of labour see von den Steinen, *Unter den Naturvölkern Zentralbrasiliens*, 2nd ed. (Berlin, 1897), pp. 196 ff.

which govern the geographical division of labour.[9] When the same principle is applied to the personal division of labour it is found that the individual enjoys an advantage in co-operating not only with people superior to himself in this or that capacity but also with those who are inferior to himself in every relevant way. If, through his superiority to B, A needs three hours' labour for the production of one unit of commodity p compared with B's five, and for the production of commodity q two hours against B's four, then A will gain if he confines his labour to producing q and leaves B to produce p. If each gives sixty hours to producing both p and q, the result of A's labour is $20p + 30q$, of B's $12p + 15q$, and for both together $32p + 45q$. If however, A confines himself to producing q alone he produces sixty units in 120 hours, whilst B, if he confines himself to producing p, produces in the same time twenty-four units. The result of the activity is then $24p + 60q$, which, as p has for A a substitution value of $3:2q$ and for B one of $5:4q$, signifies a larger production than $32p + 45q$. Therefore it is obvious that every expansion of the personal division of labour brings advantages to all who take part in it. He who collaborates with the less talented, less able, and less industrious individuals gains an advantage equally as the man who associated with the more talented, more able, and more industrious. The advantage of the division of labour is mutual; it is not limited to the case where work is done which the solitary individual could never have carried out.

The greater productivity of work under the division of labour is a unifying influence. It leads men to regard each other as comrades in a joint struggle 295
for welfare, rather than as competitors in a struggle for existence. It makes friends out of enemies, peace out of war, society out of individuals.[10]

3

Organism and Organization

Organism and organization are as different from each other as life is from a machine, as a flower which is natural from one which is artificial. In the natural plant each cell lives its own life for itself while functioning reciprocally

[9] Ricardo, *Principles of Political Economy and Taxation*, pp. 76 ff.; Mill, *Principles of Political Economy*, pp. 348 ff.; Bastable, *The Theory of International Trade*, 3rd ed. (London, 1900), pp. 16 ff.

[10] "Trade makes the human race, which originally has only the unity of the species, into a really unitary society." See Steinthal, *Allgemeine Ethik* (Berlin, 1885), p. 208. Trade, however, is nothing more than a technical aid of the division of labour. On the division of labour in the sociology of Thomas Aquinas see Schreiber, *Die volkswirtschaftlichen Anschauungen der Scholastik seit Thomas von Aquin* (Jena, 1913), pp. 19 ff.

with the others. What we call living is just this self-existence and self-maintenance. In the artificial plant the separate parts are members of the whole only as far as the will of him, who united them, has been effective. Only to the extent to which this will is effective are the parts within the organization inter-related. Each part occupies only the place given to it, and leaves that place, so to speak, only on instructions. Within this framework the parts can live, that is, exist for themselves, only in so far as the creator has put them alive into his creation. The horse which the driver has harnessed to the cart lives as a horse. In the organization, the "team," the horse is just as foreign to the vehicle as is an engine to the car it drives. The parts may use their life in opposition to the organization, as, for instance, when the horse runs away with the carriage or the tissue out of which the artificial flower is made disintegrates under chemical action. Human organization is no different. Like society it is a result of will. But in this case the will no more produces a living social organism than the flower-maker produces a living rose. The organization holds together as long as the creating will is effective, no longer. The parts which compose the organization merge into the whole only so far as the will of the creator can impose itself upon them and their life can be fixed in the organization. In the battalion on parade there is one will, the will of the commander. Everything else so far as it functions within the organization is lifeless machinery. In this destruction
296 of the will, or that portion of it which does not serve the purpose of the body of troops, lies the essence of military drill. The soldier in the phalangial order, fighting in line, in which the body of troops must be nothing more than an organization—is drilled. Within the mass there is no life. Whatever life the individual lives is by the side of, or outside the body of troops—against it perhaps, but never in it. Modern warfare, based on the skirmisher's personal enterprise, has to make use of the individual soldier, of his thought and his will. So the army no longer simply drills the soldier. It seeks to educate him.

Organization is an association based on authority, organism is mutuality. The primitive thinker always sees things as having been organized from outside, never as having grown themselves, organically. He sees the arrow which he has carved, he knows how it came into existence and how it was set in motion. So he asks of everything he sees, who made it and who sets it in motion. He inquires after the creation of every form of life, the authors of every change in nature, and discovers an animistic explanation. Thus the Gods are born. Man sees the organized community with its contrast of rulers and ruled, and, accordingly, he tries to understand life as an organization, not as an organism. Hence the ancient conception of the head as the master of the body, and the use of the same term 'head' for the chief of the organization.

In recognizing the nature of the organism and sweeping away the exclusiveness of the concept of organization, science made one of its great steps forward. With all deference to earlier thinkers one may say that in the domain of Social Science this was achieved mainly in the eighteenth century, and that Classical Political Economy and its immediate precursors played the chief part. Biology took up the good work, flinging off all animistic and vitalistic beliefs. For modern biology the head is no longer the crown, the ruler of the body. In the living body there is no longer leader and followers, a contrast of sovereign and subjects, of means and purpose. There are only members, organs.

To seek to organize society is just as crazy as it would be to tear a living plant to bits in order to make a new one out of the dead parts. An organization of mankind can only be conceived after the living social organism has been killed. The collectivist movements are therefore fore-doomed to failure. It may be possible to create an organization embracing all mankind. But this
would always be merely an organization, side by side with which social life 297
would continue. It could be altered and destroyed by the forces of social life, and it certainly would be destroyed from the moment it tried to rebel against these forces. To make Collectivism a fact one must first kill all social life, then build up the collectivist state. The Bolshevists are thus quite logical in wishing to dissolve all traditional social ties, to destroy the social edifice built up through countless centuries, in order to erect a new structure on the ruins. Only they overlook the fact that isolated individuals, between whom no kind of social relations exist, can no longer be organized.

Organizations are possible only as long as they are not directed against the organic or do it any injury. All attempts to coerce the living will of human beings into the service of something they do not want must fail. An organization cannot flourish unless it is founded on the will of those organized and serves their purposes.

4

The Individual and Society

Society is not mere reciprocity. There is reciprocity amongst animals, for example when the wolf eats the lamb or when the wolf and she-wolf mate. Yet we do not speak of animal societies or of a society of wolves. Wolf and lamb, wolf and she-wolf, are indeed members of an organism—the organism of Nature. But this organism lacks the specific characteristic of the social organism: it is beyond the reach of will and action. For the same reason, the relation between the sexes is not, as such, a social relation. When a man and a woman come together they follow the law which assigns to them their place in Nature. Thus far they are ruled by instinct. Society exists only where willing becomes a co-willing and action co-action. To strive jointly towards aims which alone individuals could not reach at all, or not with equal effectiveness—that is society.[11]

Therefore, Society is not an end but a means, the means by which each individual member seeks to attain his own ends. That society is possible at
298 all is due to the fact that the will of one person and the will of another find themselves linked in a joint endeavour. Community of work springs from community of will. Because I can get what I want only if my fellow citizen gets what he wants, his will and action become the means by which I can attain my own end. Because my willing necessarily includes his willing, my intention cannot be to frustrate his will. On this fundamental fact all social life is built up.[12]

---

[11] Therefore, too, one must reject the idea of Guyau, which derives the social bond directly from bi-sexuality. See Guyau, *Sittlichkeit ohne Pflicht,* translated by Schwarz (Leipzig, 1909), p. 113 ff.

[12] Fouillée argues as follows against the utilitarian theory of society, which calls society a *"moyen universal"* ("universal means") (Belot): *"Tout moyen n'a qu'une valeur provisoire; le jour où un instrument dont je me servais me devient inutile ou nuisible, je le mets de côté. Si la société n'est qu'un moyen, le jour où, exceptionellement, elle se trouvera contraire à mes fins, je me delivrerai des lois sociales et moyens sociaux. . . . Aucune considération sociale ne pourra empêcher la révolte de l'individu tant qu'on ne lui aura pas montré que la société est établie pour des fins qui sont d'abord et avant tout ses vraies fins à lui-même et qui, de plus, ne sont pas simplement des fins de plaisir ou d'intérêt, l'intérêt n'étant que le plaisir différé et attendu pour l'avenir . . . L'idée d'intérêt est précisément ce qui divise les hommes, malgré les rapprochements qu'elle peut produire lorsqu'il y a convergence d'intérêts sur certains points."* ("Every means has only a temporary value; the day when a means ceases to serve me or becomes harmful to me, I cast it aside. If society is only a means, the day when, by some special circumstances, it is found to act contrary to my ends, I will free myself from its social laws and social means. . . . No social consideration can prevent an individual from rebelling when it has not been demonstrated to him that society exists for ends which are primarily and above all his own true ends and, further, which are not simply for the ends of pleasure or self-interest, self-interest being only pleasure postponed and expected in the future. . . . The idea of self-interest is precisely what divides men, in spite of the cooperation it can produce when self-interests coincide in certain instances.") Fouillée, *Humanitaires et libertaires au point de vue sociologique et moral* (Paris, 1914), pp. 146 ff.; see also Guyau, *Die englische Ethik der Gegenwart,* translated by Peusner (Leipzig, 1914), pp. 372 ff. Fouillée does not see that the provisional value which society gets as a means, lasts as long as the conditions of human life, given by nature, continue unchanged and as long as man continues to recognize the advantages of human co-operation. The "eternal," not merely provisional, existence of society follows from the eternity of the conditions on which it is built up. Those in power may demand of social theory that it should serve them by preventing the individual from

The principle of the division of labour revealed the nature of the growth of society. Once the significance of the division of labour had been grasped, social knowledge developed at an extraordinary pace, as we see from a comparison between Kant and those who came after him. The doctrine of the division of labour as put forward by eighteenth-century economists, was far from fully developed when Kant wrote. It had yet to be made precise by the Ricardian Theory of International Trade. But the Doctrine of the Harmony of Interests had already anticipated its far-reaching application to social theory. Kant was untouched by these ideas. His only explanation of society, therefore, is that there is an impulse in human beings to form a society, and a second contrary impulse that seeks to split up society. The antagonism of these two tendencies is used by Nature to lead men towards the ultimate goal to which it wishes to lead them.[13] It is difficult to imagine a more threadbare idea than such an attempt to explain society by the interplay of
two impulses, the impulse "to socialize oneself" and the impulse "to isolate 299
oneself." Obviously it goes no farther than the attempt to explain the effects of opium from the *virtus dormitiva, cuius est natura sensus assupire* (the sleep-inducing property whose nature is to dull the senses).

Once it has been perceived that the division of labour is the essence of society, nothing remains of the antithesis between individual and society. The contradiction between individual principle and social principle disappears.

5

The Development of the Division of Labour

In so far as the individual becomes a social being under the influence of blind instinct, before thought and will are fully conscious, the formation of society cannot be the subject of sociological inquiry. But this does not mean that Sociology must shift the task of explaining the origins of society on to another science, accepting the social web of mankind as a given fact. For if

revolting against society, but this is by no means a scientific demand. Besides no social theory could, as easily as the utilitarian, induce the social individual to enrol himself voluntarily in the social union. But when an individual shows that he is an enemy of society there is nothing left for society to do but make him harmless.

[13] Kant, "Idee zu einer allgemeinen Geschichte in weltbürgerlicher Absicht" (*Collected Works*, Vol. I), pp. 227 ff. Publisher's Note: In English pp. 17 ff. in *On History*, ed. Lewis White Beck.

we decide—and this is the immediate consequence of equating society and division of labour—that the structure of society was incomplete at the appearance of the thinking and willing human being and that the constructive process is continuous throughout history, then we must seek a principle which makes this evolution intelligible to us. The economic theory of the division of labour gives us this principle. It has been said that the happy accident which made possible the birth of civilization was the fact that divided labour is more productive than labour without division. The division of labour extends by the spread of the realization that the more labour is divided the more productive it is. In this sense the extension of the division of labour is economic progress: it brings production nearer to its goal—the greatest possible satisfaction of wants, and this progress is sociological progress also, for it involves the intensification of the social relation.

It is only in this sense, and if all teleological or ethical valuation is excluded, that it is legitimate to use the expression "progress" sociologically in historical inquiry. We believe that we can observe a certain tendency in the changes of social conditions and we examine each single change separately, to see whether and how far this assumption is compatible with it. It may be that
300 we make various assumptions of this kind, each of which corresponds in like measure to experience. The problem next arises of the relations between these assumptions, whether they are independent of each other or whether they are connected internally. We should then have to go further, and define the nature of the connection. But all that this amounts to is a study, free from valuation and based on a hypothesis, of the course of successive changes.

If we disregard those theories of evolution that are naively built up on value judgments, we shall find, in the majority of the theories claiming to interpret social evolution, two outstanding defects which render them unsatisfactory. The first is that their evolutionary principle is not connected with society as such. Neither Comte's law of the three stages of the human mind nor Lamprecht's five stages of social-psychical development gives any clue to the inner and necessary connection between evolution of the mind and evolution of society. We are shown how society behaves when it has entered a new stage, but we want to know more, namely by what law society originates and transforms itself. The changes which we see as social changes are treated by such theories as facts acting on society from outside; but we need to understand them as the workings of a constant law. The second defeat is that all these theories are "stage" theories (*Stufentheorien*). For the stage-theories there is really no such thing as evolution, that is, no continuous change in which we can recognize a definite trend. The statements of these theories do not go beyond establishing a definite sequence of events; they give no proof of the causal connection between the stages constituting the sequence. At best they succeed in establishing parallels between the sequence of events in different nations. But it is one thing to divide human life into childhood, youth, maturity, and old age, it is another to reveal the law which governs the growth and decay of the organism. A certain arbitrariness attaches to every theory of stages. The delimitation of the stages always fluctuates.

Modern German economic history has undoubtedly done right in making the division of labour the basis of its theory of evolution. But it has not been able to free itself from the old traditional scheme of development by stages. Its theory is still a stage-theory. Thus Bücher distinguishes the stage of the closed domestic economy (pure production for one's own use, barterless economy), the stage of town economy (production for clients, the stage of direct exchange), and the stage of national economy (production for markets, 301
the stage of the circulation of goods).[14] Schmoller differentiates the periods of village economy, town economy, territorial economy, and state economy.[15] Philippovich distinguishes closed domestic economy and trade economy, and within trade economy he finds the period of the locally limited trade, the period of trade controlled by the state and limited to the state area, and the period of free trade (developed national economy, Capitalism).[16] Against these attempts to force evolution into a general scheme many grave objections have been raised. We need not discuss what value such classification may have in revealing the characteristics of clearly defined historical epochs and how far they may be admitted as aids to description. At any rate they should be used with great discretion. The barren dispute over the economic life of the nations of antiquity shows how easily such classifying may lead to our mistaking the shadow of scholastic word-splitting for the substance of historical reality. For sociological study the stage theories are useless.[17] They mislead us in regard to one of the most important problems of history—that of deciding how far historical evolution is continuous. The solution of this problem usually takes the form either of an assumption, that social evolution—which it should be remembered is the development of the division of

---

[14] Bücher, *Die Entstehung der Volkswirtschaft*, First collection, 10th ed. (Tübingen, 1917), p. 91.

[15] Schmoller, *Grundriss der allgemeinen Volkswirtschaftslehre* (Munich, 1920), Vol. II, pp. 760 ff.

[16] Philippovich, *Grundriss der politischen Ökonomie*, Vol. I, 11th ed. (Tübingen, 1916), pp. 11 ff.

[17] On the stages theory see also my *Grundprobleme der Nationalökonomie* (Jena, 1933), pp. 106 ff. Publisher's Note: In English, *Epistemological Problems of Economics*, trans. George Reisman (Princeton, N.J.: D. Van Nostrand, 1960). The reference to pp. 106 ff. in this footnote in the German book is to the essay "Sociology and History" (pp. 68–129) in the English translation, especially the section starting on p. 108.

labour—has moved in an uninterrupted line, or by the assumption that each nation has progressed step-by-step over the same ground. Both assumptions are beside the point. It is absurd to say that evolution is uninterrupted when we can clearly discern periods of decay in history, periods when the division of labour has retrogressed. On the other hand, the progress achieved by individual nations by reaching a higher stage of the division of labour is never completely lost. It spreads to other nations and hastens their evolution. The fall of the ancient world undoubtedly put back economic evolution for centuries. But more recent historical research has shown that the ties connecting the economic civilization of antiquity with that of the Middle Ages
302 were much stronger than people used to assume. The Exchange Economy certainly suffered badly under the storm of the great migration of peoples, but it survived them. The towns on which it depended, were not entirely ruined, and a link was soon made between the remnants of town-life and the new development of traffic by barter.[18] In the civilization of the towns a fragment of the social achievements of antiquity was preserved and carried over into the life of the Middle Ages.

Progress in the division of labour depends entirely on a realization of its advantages, that is, of its higher productivity. The truth of this first became fully evident through the free-trade doctrines of the physiocrats and the classical eighteenth-century political economy. But in rudiments it is found in all arguments favouring peace, wherever peace is praised, or war condemned. History is a struggle between two principles, the peaceful principle, which advances the development of trade, and the militarist-imperialist principle, which interprets human society not as a friendly division of labour but as the forcible repression of some of its members by others. The imperialistic principle continually regains the upper hand. The liberal principle cannot maintain itself against it until the inclination for peaceful labour inherent in the masses shall have struggled through to full recognition of its own importance as a principle of social evolution. Wherever the imperialistic principle is in force peace can only be local and temporary: it never lasts longer than the facts which created it. The mental atmosphere with which Imperialism surrounds itself is little suited to the promotion of the growth of the division of labour within state frontiers; it practically prohibits the extension of the division of labour beyond the political-military barriers which separate the states. The division of labour needs liberty and peace. Only when the modern liberal thought of the eighteenth century had supplied a

---

[18] Dopsch, *Wirtschaftliche und soziale Grundlagen der europäischen Kulturentwicklung* (Vienna, 1918), Vol. I, pp. 91 ff.

philosophy of peace and social collaboration was the basis laid for the astonishing development of the economic civilization of that age—an age branded by the latest imperialistic and socialistic doctrines as the age of crass materialism, egotism and capitalism.

Nothing could be more perverted than the conclusions drawn in this connection by the materialistic conception of history, which represents the
development of social ideology as dependent on the stage of technical evo- 303
lution which has been attained. Nothing is more erroneous than Marx's well-known saying: "The handmill produces a society with feudal lords, the steam-mill a society with industrial capitalists."[19] It is not even formally correct. To try and explain social evolution through the evolution of technique is merely to side-track the problem without in any way solving it. For on such a conception, how are we to explain technical evolution itself?

Ferguson showed that the development of technique depends on social conditions, and that each age gets as far in technique as is permitted by the stages it has reached in the social division of labour.[20] Technical advances are possible only where the division of labour has prepared the way for their application. The mass manufacturing of shoes presupposes a society in which the production of shoes for hundreds of thousands or millions of human beings can be united in a few enterprises. In a society of self-sufficing peasants there is no possible use for the steam mill. Only the division of labour could inspire the idea of placing mechanical forces at the service of manufacture.[21]

To trace the origin of everything concerned with society in the development of the division of labour has nothing in common with the gross and naive materialism of the technological and other materialistic theories of history. Nor does it by any means signify, as disciples of the idealistic philosophy are apt to maintain, an inadmissible limitation of the concept of social relations. Neither does it restrict society to the specifically material. That part

---

[19] Marx, *Das Elend der Philosophie*, p. 91. In the formulations which Marx later on gave to his conception of history he avoided the rigidity of this earliest version. Behind such indefinite expressions as "productive forces" and "conditions of production" are hidden the critical doubts which Marx may meanwhile have experienced. But obscurity, opening the way to multitudinous interpretations, does not make an untenable theory tenable. Publisher's Note: In the English edition p. 105.

[20] Ferguson, *Abhandlung über die Geschichte der bürgerlichen Gesellschaft*, trans. Dorn (Jena, 1904), pp. 237 ff.; also Barth, *Die Philosophie der Geschichte als Soziologie*, 2nd ed. (Leipzig, 1915), Part I, pp. 578 ff.

[21] All that remains of the materialist conception of history, which appeared with the widest possible claims, is the discovery that all human and social action is decisively influenced by the scarcity of goods and the disutility of labour. But the Marxists can least admit just this, for all they say about the future socialist order of society disregards these two economic conditions.

of social life which lies beyond the economic is indeed the ultimate aim, but the ways which lead to it are governed by the law of all rational action; wherever they come into question there is economic action.

304

6

Changes in the Individual in Society

The most important effect of the division of labour is that it turns the independent individual into a dependent social being. Under the division of labour social man changes, like the cell which adapts itself to be part of an organism. He adapts himself to new ways of life, permits some energies and organs to atrophy and develops others. He becomes one-sided. The whole tribe of romantics, the unbending *laudatores temporis acti* (praisers of time past), have deplored this fact. For them the man of the past who developed his powers "harmoniously" is the ideal: an ideal which alas no longer inspires our degenerate age. They recommend retrogression in the division of labour, hence their praise of agricultural labour, by which they always mean the almost self-sufficing peasant.[22]

Here, again the modern socialist outdoes the rest. Marx promises that in the higher phase of the communist society "the enslaving subjection of individuals under the division of labour, and with this also the contrast between mental and bodily labour, shall have disappeared."[23] Account will

[22] Adam Müller says about "the vicious tendency to divide labour in all branches of private industry and in government business too," that man needs "an all round, I might say a sphere-round field of activity." If the "division of labour in large cities or industrial or mining provinces cuts up man, the completely free man, into wheels, rollers, spokes, shafts, etc., forces on him an utterly one-sided scope in the already one-sided field of the provisioning of one single want, how can one then demand that this fragment should accord with the whole complete life and with its law, or with legality; how should the rhombuses, triangles, and figures of all kinds accord separately with the great sphere of political life and its law?" See Adam Müller, *Ausgewählte Abhandlungen*, ed. Baxa (Jena, 1921), p. 46.

[23] Marx, *Zur Kritik des sozialdemokratischen Parteiprogramms von Gotha*, p. 17. Innumerable passages in his writings show how falsely Marx conceived the nature of labour in industry. Thus he thought also that "the division of labour in the mechanical factory" is characterized by "having lost every specialized character . . . The automatic factory abolishes the specialist and the one-track mind." And he blames Proudhon, "who did not understand even this one revolutionary side of the automatic factory." Marx, *Das Elend der Philosophie*, p. 129. Publisher's Note: p. 138 of the English translation.

be taken of the human "need for change." "Alternation of mental and bodily labour" will "safeguard man's harmonious development."[24]

We have already dealt with this illusion.[25] Were it possible to achieve all human aims with only that amount of labour which does not itself cause any discomfort but at the same time relieves the sensation of displeasure that 305
arises from doing nothing, then labour would not be an economic object at all. To satisfy needs would not be work but play. This, however, is not possible. Even the self-sufficient worker, for the most part, must labour far beyond the point where the effort is agreeable. One may assume that work is less unpleasant to him than to the worker who is tied to a definite task, as he finds at the beginning of each job he tackles fresh sensations of pleasure in the activity itself. If, nevertheless, man has given himself up more and more to the division of labour, it is because he has recognized that the higher productivity of labour thus specialized more than repays him for the loss of pleasure. The extent of the division of labour cannot be curtailed without reducing the productivity of labour. This is true of all kinds of labour. It is an illusion to believe that one can maintain productivity and reduce the division of labour.

Abolition of the division of labour would be no remedy for the injuries inflicted on the individual, body and soul, by specialized labour, unless we are prepared to set back social development. It is for the individual himself to set about becoming a complete human being. The remedy lies in reforming consumption, not in "reforming" labour. Play and sport, the pleasure of art, reading are the obvious way of escape.

It is futile to look for the harmoniously developed man at the outset of economic evolution. The almost self-sufficient economic subject as we know him in the solitary peasant of remote valleys shows none of that noble, harmonious development of body, mind, and feeling which the romantics ascribe to him. Civilization is a product of leisure and the peace of mind that only the division of labour can make possible. Nothing is more false than to assume that man first appeared in history with an independent individuality and that only during the evolution which led to the Great Society did he lose, together with material freedom, his spiritual independence. All history, evidence and observation of the lives of primitive peoples is directly contrary to this view. Primitive man lacks all individuality in our sense. Two South Sea Islanders resemble each other far more closely than two twentieth-century

---

[24] Bebel, *Die Frau und der Sozialismus*, pp. 283 ff. Publisher's Note: In English translation pp. 392–394.
[25] See pp. 144 ff.

Londoners. Personality was not bestowed upon man at the outset. It has been acquired in the course of evolution of society.[26]

306 7

Social Regression

Social evolution—in the sense of evolution of the division of labour—is a will-phenomenon: it depends entirely on the human will. We do not consider whether one is justified in regarding every advance in the division of labour and hence in the intensification of the social bond, as a rise to a higher stage; we must ask whether such a development is a necessary phenomenon. Is an ever greater development of society the content of history? Is it possible for society to stand still or retrogress?

We must reject *a priori* any assumption that historical evolution is provided with a goal by any "intention," or "hidden plan" of Nature, such as Kant imagined and Hegel and Marx had in mind; but we cannot avoid the inquiry whether a principle might not be found to demonstrate that continuous social growth is inevitable. The first principle that offers itself to our attention is the principle of natural selection. More highly developed societies attain greater material wealth than the less highly developed; therefore they have more prospect of preserving their members from misery and poverty. They are also better equipped to defend themselves from the enemy. One must not be misled by the observation that richer and more civilized nations were often crushed in war by nations less wealthy and civilized. Nations in an advanced stage of social evolution have always been able at least to resist a superior force of less developed nations. It is only decaying nations, civilizations inwardly disintegrated, which have fallen a prey to nations on the up grade. Where a more highly organized society has succumbed to the attack of a less developed people, the victors have in the end been culturally submerged, accepting the economic and social order, and even the language and faith of the conquered race.

The superiority of the more highly developed societies lies not only in their material welfare but also quantitatively in the number of their members and qualitatively in the greater solidity of their internal structure. For this, precisely, is the key to higher social development: the widening of the social

[26] Durkheim, *De la division du travail social*, pp. 452 ff.

range, the inclusion in the division of labour of more human beings and its stronger grip on each individual. The more highly developed society differs from the less developed in the closer union of its members; this precludes 307
the violent solution of internal conflict and forms externally a closed defensive front against any enemy. In less developed societies, where the social bond is still weak, and between the separate parts of which there exists a confederation for the purposes of war rather than true solidarity based on joint work and economic co-operation—disagreement breaks out more easily and more quickly than in highly developed societies. For the military confederation has no firm and lasting hold upon its members. By its very nature it is merely a temporary bond which is upheld by the prospect of momentary advantage, but dissolves as soon as the enemy has been defeated and the scramble for the booty sets in. In fighting against the less developed societies the more developed ones have always found that their greatest advantage lay in the lack of unity in the enemy's ranks. Only temporarily do the nations in a lower state of organization manage to co-operate for great military enterprises. Internal disunity has always dispersed their armies quickly. Take for example the Mongol raids on the Central European civilization of the thirteenth century or the efforts of the Turks to penetrate into the West. The superiority of the industrial over the military type of society, to use Herbert Spencer's expression, consists largely in the fact that associations which are merely military always fall to pieces through internal disunity.[27]

But there is another circumstance which advances further social development. It has been shown that it is to the interest of all members of society that the social range should be extended. For a highly developed social organism it is by no means a matter of indifference whether or not nations outside its range continue to lead a self-sufficient existence on a lower plane of social evolution. It is to the interest of the more advanced organism to 308
draw the less advanced into the area of its economic and social community,

[27] The romantic-militarist notion of the military superiority of the nations which have made little progress in Capitalism, completely refuted afresh by the World War, arises from the view that what tells in a fight is man's physical strength alone. This, however, is not completely true, even of the fights of the Homeric Age. Not physical but mental power decides a fight. On these mental powers depend the fighters' tactics and the way he is armed. The A B C of the art of warfare is to have the superiority at the decisive moment, though otherwise one may be numerically weaker than the enemy. The A B C of the preparation for war is to set up armies as strong as possible and to provide them with all war materials in the best way. One has to stress this only because people are again endeavouring to obscure these connections, by trying to differentiate between the military and economic-political causes of victory and defeat in war. It always has been and always will be the fact, that victory or defeat is decided by the whole social position of the combatants before their armies meet in battle.

even though its persistence in remaining on a lower plane makes it politically and militarily innocuous, and even though no immediate advantages are likely to accrue from the occupation of its territory, in which, presumably, the natural conditions of production are unfavourable. We have seen that it is always an advantage to widen the range of workers in a society that divides labour, so that even a more efficient people may have an interest in co-operating with a less efficient. This is what so often drives nations of a high social development to expand their field of economic activity by absorbing hitherto inaccessible territories. The opening up of the backward regions of the Near and Far East, of Africa and America, cleared the way for a world-wide economic community, so that shortly before the World War we were in sight of realizing the dream of an œcumenical society. Has the war merely interrupted this development for a brief period or has it utterly destroyed it? Is it conceivable that this development can cease, that society can even retrogress?

This problem cannot be approached except in connection with another: the problem of the death of nations. It is customary to talk of nations aging and dying, of young and old communities. The comparison is lame—as are all comparisons—and in discussing such things we are well advised to discard metaphorical phrases. What is the core of the problem that here presents itself?

It is clear that we must not confuse it with another not less difficult problem, the problem of the changes of the national quality. A thousand or fifteen hundred years ago the Germans spoke a different language from that of today, but we should not think of saying, on that account, that German medieval culture was "dead." On the contrary we see in the German culture an uninterrupted evolutionary chain, stretching (without mentioning lost monuments of literature) from the "Heliand," and Otfried's *Gospels* to the present day. We do indeed say of the Pomeranians and Prussians, who in the course of centuries have been assimilated by the German colonists, that they have died out, yet we shall hardly maintain that as nations they grew "old." To carry through the simile one would have to talk of nations that had died young. We are not concerned with national transformation; our problem is different. Neither does the decay of states come into the question,
309 for this phenomenon sometimes appears as a sequence to the aging nations and sometimes independently of it. The fall of the ancient state of Poland had nothing to do with any decay of Polish civilization or of the Polish people. It did not stop the social development of Poland.

The facts which are present in practically all the examples brought forward of the aging of a culture are: a decline in population, a diminution of welfare, and the decay of the towns. The historical significance of all these phenomena becomes clear as soon as we conceive of the aging of nations as the retrogression of the social division of labour and of society. The decline of the ancient world for instance, was a social retrogression. The decline of the Roman Empire was only a result of the disintegration of ancient society which after reaching a high level of division of labour sank back into an almost moneyless economy. Thus towns were depopulated and thus, also, did the population of the countryside diminish and want and misery set in simply because an economic order working on a lower level in respect of the social division of labour is less productive. Technical skill was gradually lost, artistic talent decayed, scientific thought was slowly extinguished. The word which most aptly describes this process is disintegration. The Classical culture died because Classical society retrogressed.[28]

The death of nations is the retrogression of the social relation, the retrogression of the division of labour. Whatever may have been the cause in individual cases, it has always been the cessation of the disposition to social co-operation which actually effected the decline. This may once have seemed an incomprehensible riddle to us, but now that we watch with terror the process at work in our own experience we come nearer to understanding it, though we still fail to recognize the deepest, most ultimate causes of the change.

It is the social spirit, the spirit of social co-operation, which forms, develops, and upholds societies. Once it is lost, the society falls apart again. The death of a nation is social retrogression, the decline from the division of labour to self-sufficiency. The social organism disintegrates into the cells from which it began. Man remains, but society dies.[29]

There is no evidence that social evolution must move steadily upwards in 310
a straight line. Social standstill and social retrogression are historical facts which we cannot ignore. World history is the graveyard of dead civilizations, and in India and Eastern Asia we see large-scale examples of civilization at a standstill.

Our literary and artistic cliques whose exaggerated opinion of their own trifling productions contrast so vividly with the modesty and self-criticism of the really great artists, say that it does not matter much whether economic evolution continues so long as inner culture is intensified. But all inner culture requires external means for its realization, and these external means can be attained only by economic effort. When the productivity of labour

[28] On the decline of Ancient Greek Civilization see Pareto, *Les Systèmes Socialistes* (Paris, 1902), Vol. I, pp. 155 ff.

[29] Izoulet, *La Cité moderne*, pp. 488 ff.

decays through the retrogression of social co-operation the decay of inner culture follows.

All the older civilizations were born and grew up without being fully conscious of the basic laws of cultural evolution and the significance of division of labour and co-operation. In the course of their development they had often to combat tendencies and movements inimical to civilization. Often they triumphed over these, but sooner or later they fell. They succumbed to the spirit of disintegration. Through the social philosophy of Liberalism men became conscious of the laws of social evolution for the first time, and for the first time clearly recognized the basis of civilization and cultural progress. Those were days when hopes for the future ran high. Unimagined vistas seemed to be opening up. But it was not to be. Liberalism had to meet the opposition of militaristic-nationalist and, above all, of socialist-communist doctrines which tended to bring about social dissolution. The nationalist theory calls itself organic, the socialist theory calls itself social, but in reality both are disorganizing and anti-social in their effect.

Of all accusations against the system of Free Trade and Private Property, none is more foolish than the statement that it is anti-social and individualistic and that it atomizes the body social. Trade does not disintegrate, as romantic enthusiasts for the autarky of small portions of the earth's surface assert; it unites. The division of labour is what first makes social ties: it is the social element pure and simple. Whoever advocates the economic self-sufficiency of nations and states, seeks to disintegrate the ecumenical society; whoever seeks to destroy the social division of labour within a nation by means of class war is anti-social.

311 A decline of the ecumenical society, which has been slowly forming itself during the last two hundred years under the influence of the gradual germination of the liberal idea, would be a world catastrophe absolutely without parallel in history as we know it. No nation would be spared. Who then would rebuild the shattered world?

8

Private Property and Social Evolution

The division of individuals into owners and non-owners is an outcome of the division of labour.

The second great sociological achievement of Classical Political Economy and the "individualistic" social theory of the eighteenth century was to recognize the social function of private property. From the older point of view property was always considered more or less a privilege of the Few, a raid upon the common stock, an institution regarded ethically as an evil, if sometimes as an inevitable one. Liberalism was the first to recognize that the social function of private ownership in the means of production is to put the goods into the hands of those who know best how to use them, into the hands, that is, of the most expert managers. Nothing therefore is more foreign to the essence of property than special privileges for special property and protection for special producers. Any kind of constraint such as exclusive rights and other privileges of producers, are apt to obstruct the working of the social function of property. Liberalism fights such institutions as vigorously as it opposes every attempt to limit the freedom of the worker.

The owner takes nothing away from anyone. No one can say that he goes short because of another's abundance. It is flattering the envious instincts of the masses to give them a calculation of how much more the poor man would have to dispose of, if property were equally distributed. What is overlooked is the fact that the volume of production and of the social income are not fixed and unchangeable but depend essentially upon the distribution of property. If this is interfered with, there is danger that property may fall into the hands of those not so competent to maintain it, those whose foresight is less, whose disposal of their means is less productive; this would necessarily 312
reduce the amount produced.[30] The ideas of distributive Communism are atavistic, harking back to the times before social relations existed or reached their present stage of development, when the yield of production was correspondingly much lower. The landless man of an economic order based on production without exchange is quite logical in making the redistribution of fields the goal of his ambition. But the modern proletarian misunderstands the nature of social production when he hankers after a similar redistribution.

Liberalism combats the socialist ideal of transferring the means of production to the hands of organized society with the argument that socialist production would give a lower yield. Against this the Socialism of the Hegelian school seeks to prove that the evolution of history leads inevitably to the abolition of private ownership in the means of production.

---

[30] "The laws, in creating property, have created wealth, but with respect to poverty, it is not the work of the laws—it is the primitive condition of the human race. The man who lives only from day to day, is precisely the man in a state of nature. . . . The laws, in creating property, have been benefactors to those who remain in the original poverty. They participate more or less in the pleasures, advantages and resources of civilized society," Bentham, *Principles of the Civil Code*, ed. Bowring (Edinburgh, 1843), Vol. I, p. 309.

It was the view of Lassalle that "the course of all legal history consists, generally speaking, in an ever greater limitation of the property of the individual, and in placing more and more objects outside private ownership." The tendency to enlarge the freedom of property which is read into historical evolution is only apparent. However much the "idea of the increasingly rapid reduction of the sphere of private property as a principle working in the cultural and historical development of law could be held to be paradoxical," yet, according to Lassalle it survived the most detailed examination. Unfortunately Lassalle produced no details of the examination of this idea. According to his own words he "honoured it (the idea) with a few very superficial glances instead."[31] Neither has anyone since Lassalle's time undertaken to provide a proof. But even if the attempt had been made, this fact would by no means have demonstrated the necessity of the development in question. The conceptual constructions of speculative jurisprudence steeped in the Hegelian spirit serve at best to exhibit historical tendencies of evolution in the past. That the evolutionary tendency thus discovered must necessarily
313 continue to develop is a thoroughly arbitrary assumption. Only if it could be shown that the force behind evolution was still active would the hypothetical proof which is needed be adduced. The Hegelian Lassalle did nothing of the kind. For him, the matter is disposed of when he realizes "that this progressive reduction of the sphere of private property is based on nothing else than the positive development of human liberty."[32] Having fitted his law of evolution into the great Hegelian scheme of historical evolution, he had done all that his school could ask.

Marx saw the faults in the Hegelian scheme of evolution. He too holds it to be an indisputable truth that the course of history leads from private property to common property. But unlike Hegel and Lassalle he does not deal with the idea of property and the juristic concept of property. Private property "in its political-economic tendencies" is drifting towards its dissolution, "but only by a development independent of it, of which it is unconscious, which is taking place against its will, and is conditioned by the nature of the question; only by creating the proletariat *qua* proletariat, the misery that is conscious of its spiritual and physical misery, the dehumanization that is conscious of its dehumanization."[33] Thus the doctrine of the class struggle is introduced as the driving element of historical evolution.

---

[31] Lassalle, *Das System der erworbenen Rechte*, 2nd ed. (Leipzig, 1880), Vol. I, pp. 217 ff.

[32] Lassalle, *op. cit.*, Vol. I, pp. 222 ff.

[33] Marx, *Die heilige Familie. Aus dem literarischen Nachlass von Karl Marx, Friedrich Engels und Ferdinand Lassalle*, ed. Mehring, Vol. II (Stuttgart, 1902), p. 132. Publisher's Note: In English, The Holy Family (Moscow: Foreign Language Publishing House, 1956).

CHAPTER 19

Conflict as a Factor in Social Evolution

1

The Cause of Social Evolution

The simplest way to depict the evolution of society is to show the distinction 314
between two evolutionary tendencies which are related to each other in the same way as intension and extension. Society develops subjectively and objectively; subjectively by enlarging its membership, objectively by enlarging the aims of its activities. Originally confined to the narrowest circles of people, to immediate neighbours, the division of labour gradually becomes more general until eventually it includes all mankind. This process, still far from complete and never at any point in history completed, is finite. When all men on earth form a unitary system of division of labour, it will have reached its goal. Side by side with this extension of the social bond goes a process of intensification. Social action embraces more and more aims; the area in which the individual provides for his own consumption becomes constantly narrower. We need not pause at this stage to ask whether this process will eventually result in the specialization of all productive activity.

Social development is always a collaboration for joint action; the social relationship always means peace, never war. Death-dealing actions and war are anti-social.[1] All those theories which regard human progress as an outcome of conflicts between human groups have overlooked this truth.

---

[1] *"La guerre est une dissociation."* ("War is a breakdown of social cooperation.") See Novicow, *La Critique du Darwinisme Social* (Paris, 1910), p. 124. See also the refutation of the struggle theories of Gumplowicz, Ratzenhofer, and Oppenheimer by Holsti, *The Relation of War to the Origin of the State* (Helsingfors, 1913), pp. 276 ff.

2

Darwinism

The individual's fate is determined unequivocally by his Being. Everything that is has necessarily proceeded from his Becoming, and everything that
315 will be results necessarily from that which is. The situation at any given moment is the consummation of history.[2] He who understood it completely would be able to foresee the whole future. For a long time it was thought necessary to exclude human volition and action from the determination of events, for the special significance of "imputation"—that thought-process peculiar to all rational action—had not been grasped. It was believed that causal explanation was incompatible with imputation. This is no longer so. Economics, the Philosophy of Law, and Ethics have cleared up the problem of imputation sufficiently to remove the old misunderstandings.

If, to simplify our study, we analyse the unity we call the individual into certain complexes it must be clearly understood that only the heuristic value of the division can justify our doing so. Attempts to separate, according to external characteristics, what is essentially similar can never survive ultimate examination. Only subject to this admission can we proceed to group the determinants of individual life.

That which man brings into the world at birth, the innate, we call racial inheritance or, for short, the race.[3] The innate in man is the precipitate of the history of all his ancestors, their fate, and all their experiences. The life and fate of the individual do not start at birth, but stretch back into the infinite, unimaginable past. The descendant inherits from the ancestors; this fact is outside the sphere of the dispute over the inheritance of acquired characteristics.

After birth, direct experience begins. The individual begins to be influenced by his environment. Together with what is innate, this influence produces the individual's Being in each moment of his life. The environment is natural in the form of soil, climate, nourishment, fauna, flora, in short, external natural surroundings. It is social in the shape of society. The social forces acting on the individual are language, his position in the process of work and exchange, ideology and the forces of compulsion: unrestrained and ordered coercion. The ordered organization of coercion we call the State.

---

[2] Taine, *Histoire de la littérature anglaise* (Paris, 1863), Vol. I, p. xxv.

[3] *Ibid.*, p. xxiii: "*Ce qu'on appelle la race, ce sont ces dispositions innées et héréditaires que l'homme apporte avec lui à la lumière.*" ("Race is the innate and hereditary characteristics and tendencies with which man is born.")

Since Darwin we have been inclined to regard the dependence of human life on natural environment as a struggle against antagonistic forces. There was no objection to this as long as people did not transfer the figurative 316
expression to a field where it was quite out of place and was bound to cause grave errors. When the formulas of Darwinism, which had sprung from ideas taken over by Biology from Social Science, reverted to Social Science, people forgot what the ideas had originally meant. Thus arose that monstrosity, sociological Darwinism, which, ending in a romantic glorification of war and murder, was peculiarly responsible for the overshadowing of liberal ideas and for creating the mental atmosphere which led to the World War and the social struggles of today.

It is well known that Darwin was under the influence of Malthus's *Essay on the Principle of Population.* But Malthus was far from believing struggle to be a necessary social institution. Even Darwin, when he speaks of the struggle for existence, does not always mean the destructive combat of living creatures, the life or death struggle for feeding places and females. He often uses the expression figuratively to show the dependence of living beings on each other and on their surroundings.[4] It is a misunderstanding to take the phrase quite literally, for it is a metaphor. The confusion is worse confounded when people equate the struggle for existence with the war of extermination between human beings, and proceed to construct a social theory based on the necessity of struggle.

The Malthusian Theory of Population is—what its critics, ignorant of sociology, always overlook—merely a part of the social theory of Liberalism. Only within such a framework can it be understood. The core of liberal social theory is the theory of the division of labour. Only side by side with this can one make use of the Law of Population to interpret social conditions. Society is the union of human beings for the better exploitation of the natural conditions of existence; in its very conception it abolishes the struggle between human beings and substitutes the mutual aid which provides the essential motive of all members united in an organism. Within the limits of society there is no struggle, only peace. Every struggle suspends in effect the social community. Society as a whole, as organism, does fight a struggle for existence against forces inimical to it. But inside, as far as society has absorbed individuals completely, there is only collaboration. For society is nothing but collaboration. Within modern society even war cannot break all social ties. 317
Some remain, though loosened, in a war between states which acknowledge the binding force of International Law. Thus a fragment of peace survives even in wartime.

---

[4] Hertwig, *Zur Abwehr des ethischen, des sozialen und des politischen Darwinismus,* pp. 10 ff.

Private ownership in the means of production is the regulating principle which, within society, balances the limited means of subsistence at society's disposal with the less limited ability of the consumers to increase. By making the share in the social product which falls to each member of society depend on the product economically imputed to him, that is, to his labour and his property, the elimination of surplus human beings by the struggle for existence, as it rages in the vegetable and animal kingdom, is replaced by a reduction in the birth-rate as a result of social forces. "Moral restraint," the limitations of offspring imposed by social positions, replaces the struggle for existence.

In society there is no struggle for existence. It is a grave error to suppose that the logically developed social theory of liberalism could lead to any other conclusion. Certain isolated phrases in Malthus's essay, which might be interpreted otherwise, are easily accounted for by the fact that Malthus composed the original incomplete draft of his famous first work before he had completely absorbed the spirit of Classical Political Economy. As proof that his doctrine permits of no other interpretation, it may be pointed out that, before Spencer and Darwin, no one thought of looking on the struggle for existence (in the modern sense of the expression) as a principle active within human society. Darwinism first suggested the theories which regard the struggle of individuals, races, nations, and classes as the basic social element; and it was in Darwinism, which had originated in the intellectual circle of liberal social theory, that people now found weapons to fight the Liberalism they abhorred. In Darwin's hypothesis, long regarded as irrefutable scientific fact, Marxism,[5] Racial Mysticism,[6] and Nationalism found, as they believed, an unshakable foundation for their teachings. Modern Imperialism especially relies on the catchwords coined by popular science out of Darwinism.

318 The Darwinian—or more correctly, pseudo-Darwinian-social theories have never realized the main difficulty involved in applying to social relations their catchwords about the struggle for existence. In Nature it is individuals who struggle for existence. It is exceptional to find in Nature phenomena which could be interpreted as struggles between animal groups. There are, of course, the fights between groups of ants—though here we may be one

[5] Ferri, *Sozialismus und moderne Wissenschaft*, trans. Kurella (Leipzig, 1895), pp. 65 ff.

[6] Gumplowicz, *Der Rassenkampf* (Innsbruck, 1883), p. 176. On Gumplowicz's dependence on Darwinism see Barth, *Die Philosophie der Geschichte als Soziologie*, p. 253. The "liberal" Darwinism is a badly thought out product of an epoch which could no longer grasp the meaning of the liberal social philosophy.

day obliged to adopt explanations very different from those hitherto accepted.[7] A social theory that was founded on Darwinism would either come to the point of declaring that the war of all against all was the natural and necessary form of human intercourse, thus denying that any social bonds were possible; or it would have, on the one hand, to show why peace does and must reign within certain groups and yet, on the other, to prove that the principle of peaceful union which leads to the formation of these associations is ineffective beyond the circle of the group, so that the groups among themselves must struggle. This is precisely the rock on which all non-liberal social theories founder. If one recognizes a principle which results in the union of all Germans, all Dolichocephalics or all Proletarians and forms a special nation, race, or class out of individuals, then this principle cannot be proved to be effective only *within* the collective groups. The anti-liberal social theories skim over the problem by confining themselves to the assumption that the solidarity of interests within the groups is so self-evident as to be accepted without further discussion, and by taking pains only to prove the existence of the conflict of interests between groups and the necessity of conflict as the sole dynamic force of historical development. But if war is to be the father of all things, the fruitful source of historical progress, it is difficult to see why its fruitful activity should be restricted within states, nations, races, and classes. If Nature needs war, why not the war of all against all, why merely the war of all groups against all groups? The only theory which explains how peace is possible between individuals and how society grows out of individuals is the liberal social theory of the division of labour. But the acceptance of this theory makes it impossible to believe the enmity of collective groups to be necessary. If Brandenburgers and Hanoverians live in society peacefully side by side, why cannot Germans and Frenchmen do so too?

Sociological Darwinism is unable to explain the phenomenon of the rise 319
of society. It is not a social theory, but "a theory of unsociability."[8]

A fact which clearly exposes the decay of sociological thought in recent decades, is that people now begin to combat sociological Darwinism by pointing to examples of mutual aid (symbiosis) which, Biology has only lately discovered in the vegetable and animal kingdoms. Kropotkin, a defiant antagonist of liberal social theory, who never understood what he rejected and combated, found among animals the rudiments of social ties and set these up in opposition to conflict, contrasting the beneficial principle of

[7] Novicow, *La Critique du Darwinisme Social*, p. 45.

[8] Barth, *Die Philosophie der Geschichte als Soziologie*, p. 243.

mutual aid with the harmful principle of war-to-the-knife.[9] Kammerer, a biologist enslaved by the ideas of Marxist Socialism, demonstrated that in addition to conflict the principle of aid dominates life in Nature.[10] At this point Biology returns to its starting-point, Sociology. It hands back the principle of divided labour given it by Sociology. It teaches Sociology nothing new, nothing essential that had not been included in the theory of the division of labour as defined by the despised Classical Political Economy.

3

Conflict and Competition

The social theories which are based on natural law start from the dogma that human beings are equal. Since all men are equal, they are supposed to have a natural claim to be treated as members of society with full rights, and, because everybody has a natural right to live, it would be a violation of right to try to take his life. Thus are formulated the postulates of the all-inclusiveness of society, of equality within society, and of peace. Liberal theory, on the other hand, deduces these principles from utility. To Liberalism the concepts man and social man are the same. Society welcomes as members all who can see the benefit of peace and social collaboration in work. It is to
320 the personal advantage of every individual that he should be treated as a citizen with equal rights. But the man who, ignoring the advantages of peaceful collaboration, prefers to fight and refuses to fit himself into the social order, must be fought like a dangerous animal. It is necessary to take up this attitude against the anti-social criminal and savage tribes. Liberalism can approve of war only as a defence. For the rest it sees in war the anti-social principle by which social co-operation is annihilated.

By confusing the fundamental difference between fighting and competition, the anti-liberal social theories sought to discredit the liberal principle of peace. In the original sense of the word, "fight" means the conflict of men and animals in order to destroy each other. Man's social life begins with the overcoming of instincts and considerations which impel him to fight to the

[9] Kropotkin, *Gegenseitige Hilfe in der Tier und Menschenwelt*, German edition by Landauer (Leipzig, 1908), pp. 69 ff.

[10] Kammerer, *Genossenschaften von Lebewesen auf Grund gegenseitiger Vorteile* (Stuttgart, 1913); Kammerer, *Allgemeine Biologie* (Stuttgart, 1915), p. 306; Kammerer, *Einzeltod, Völkertod, biologische Unsterblichkeit* (Vienna, 1918), pp. 29 ff.

death. History shows us a constant retreat from conflict as a form of human relations. Fights become less intense and less frequent. The defeated opponent is no longer destroyed; if society can find a way of absorbing him, his life is spared. Fighting itself is bound by rules and is thus somewhat mitigated. Nevertheless war and revolution remain the instruments of destruction and annihilation. For this reason Liberalism never ceases to stress the fact that they are anti-social.

It is merely a metaphor to call competition competitive war, or simply, war. The function of battle is destruction; of competition, construction. Economic competition provides that production shall be carried on in the most rational manner. Here, as everywhere else, its task is the selection of the best. It is a fundamental principle of social collaboration which cannot be thought out of the picture. Even a socialist community could not exist without it in some form, though it might be necessary to introduce it in the guise, say, of examinations. The efficiency of a socialist order of life would depend on its ability to make the competition sufficiently ruthless and keen to be properly selective.

There are three points of comparison which serve to explain the metaphorical use of the word "fight" for competition. In the first place it is clear that enmity and conflict of interests exist between the opponents in a fight as they do between competitors. The hate which a small shopkeeper feels for his immediate competitor may be no less in degree than the hate which a Moslem inspired in a Montenegrin. But the feelings responsible for men's actions have no bearing on the social function of these actions. What the
individual feels does not matter as long as the limits set by the social order 321
inhibit his actions.

The second point of comparison is found in the selective function of both fighting and competition. To what extent fighting is capable of making the best selection is open to question; later we shall show that many people ascribe anti-selective effects to wars and revolutions.[11] But because they both fulfil a selective function one must not forget that there is an essential difference between fighting and competition.

The third point of comparison is sought in the consequences which defeat lays on the vanquished. People say that the vanquished are destroyed, not reflecting that they use the word destruction in the one case only figuratively. Whoever is defeated in fight is *killed*; in modern war, even where the surviving vanquished are spared, blood flows. People say that in the competitive struggle, economic lives are destroyed. This, however, merely means that

[11] See p. 290 of this work.

those who succumb are forced to seek in the structure of the social division of labour a position other than the one they would like to occupy. It does not by any means signify that they are to starve. In the capitalist society there is a place and bread for all. Its ability to expand provides sustenance for every worker. Permanent unemployment is not a feature of free capitalism.

Fighting in the actual original sense of the word is anti-social. It renders co-operation, which is the basic element of the social relation, impossible among the fighters, and where the co-operation already exists, destroys it. Competition is an element of social collaboration, the ruling principle within the social body. Viewed sociologically, fighting and competition are extreme contrasts.

The realization of this provides a criterion for judging all those theories which regard social evolution as a fight between conflicting groups. Class struggle, race conflicts, and national wars cannot be the constructive principle. No edifice will ever rise from a foundation of destruction and annihilation.

4

National War

The most important medium for social co-operation is language. Language
322 bridges the chasm between individuals and only with its help can one man communicate to another something at least of what he is feeling. We need not discuss at this point the wider significance of language in relation to thought and will: how it conditions thought and will and how, without it, there could be no thought but only instinct, no will but only impulse.[12] Thought also is a social phenomenon; it is not the product of an isolated mind but of the mutual stimulus of men who strive towards the same aims. The work of the solitary thinker, brooding in retirement over problems which few people trouble to consider, is talk too, is conversation with the residue of thought which generations of mental labour have deposited in language in everyday concepts, and in written tradition. Thought is bound up with speech. The thinker's conceptual edifice is built on the elements of language.

The human mind works only in language; it is by the Word that it first breaks through from the obscurity of uncertainty and the vagueness of

[12] Cohen, *Ethik des reinen Willens* (Berlin, 1904), pp. 183 ff.

instinct to such clarity as it can ever hope to attain. Thinking and that which is thought cannot be detached from the language to which they owe their origin. Some day we may get a universal language, but certainly not by means of the method employed by the inventors of Volapuk, Esperanto, and other similar devices. The difficulties of a universal language and of the mutual understanding of peoples are not to be solved by hatching out identical combinations of syllables for the terms of every day life and for use by those who speak without overmuch thinking. The untranslatable element in ideas, which vibrates in the words expressing them, is what separates languages quite as much as the variety of sounds in words, which can be transposed intact. If everyone, all the world over, used the same words for "waiter" and "doorstep" we should still not have bridged the gap between languages and nations. But suppose everything expressed in one language could be translated into other languages without losing anything in the process, we should then have achieved unity of language, even though we had not found identical sounds for the syllables. Different languages would then be only different tongues, and our inability to translate a word would no longer impede the passage of thought from nation to nation.

Until that day comes—and it is possible that it never will come—political
friction is bound to arise among members of different nations living together 323
with mixed languages, friction that may lead to serious political antagonism.[13]
Directly or indirectly, these disputes are responsible for the *modern* "hate"
between nations, on which Imperialism is based.

Imperialist theory simplifies its task when it limits itself to proving that conflicts between nations exist. To clinch its arguments it would have to show also that there is a solidarity of interests within the nations. The nationalist-imperialist doctrine made its appearance as a reaction against the ecumenical-solidarism of the Free Trade doctrine. At its advent the cosmopolitan idea of world-citizenship and the fraternity of the nations dominated men's minds. All that seemed necessary, therefore, was to prove that there were conflicting interests between the various nations. The fact, that all the arguments it used to prove the incompatibility of national interests could with equal justification be used to prove the incompatibility of regional interests and finally even of the individual's personal interests, was quite overlooked. If the Germans suffer from consuming English cloth and Russian corn, the inhabitants of Berlin must, presumably, suffer from consuming Bavarian beer and Rhine wine. If it is not well to let the division of labour pass the frontiers of the state, it would no doubt be best in the end to return

---

[13] See my *Nation, Staat und Wirtschaft*, pp. 31 ff.

to the self-sufficiency of the closed domestic economy. The slogan "Away with foreign goods!" would lead us, if we accepted all its implications, to abolish the division of labour altogether. For the principle that makes the *international* division of labour seem advantageous is precisely the principle which recommends division of labour in any circumstances.

It is no accident, that of all nations the German people has least sense of national cohesion, and that among all European nations it was the last to understand the idea of a political union in which one state comprises all members of the nation. The idea of national union is a child of Liberalism, of free trade, and of *laissez-faire*. The German nation, of which important parts are living as minorities in areas settled by people of different tongues, was among the first to learn the disadvantages of nationalistic oppression. This experience led to a negative attitude to Liberalism. But without Liberalism, it lacked the intellectual equipment necessary to overcome the regional
324 particularism of separate groups. It is no accident that the sentiment of national cohesion is in no other people so strongly developed as among the Anglo-Saxons, the traditional home of Liberalism.

Imperialists delude themselves fatally when they suppose it possible to strengthen the cohesion of members of a nation by rejecting cosmopolitanism. They overlook the fact that the basic anti-social element of their doctrine must, if logically applied, split up every community.

5

Racial War

Scientific knowledge of the innate qualities of man is still in its infancy. We cannot really say any more about the inherited characteristics of the individual than that some men are more gifted from birth than others. Where the difference between good and bad is to be sought we cannot say. We know that men differ in their physical and psychic qualities. We know that certain families, breeds, and groups of breeds reveal similar traits. We know that we are justified in differentiating between races and in speaking of the different racial qualities of individuals. But so far, attempts to find somatic characteristics of racial relationships have had no result. At one time it was thought that a racial characteristic had been discovered in the cranial index, but now it is clear that those relations between the cranial index and the psychic and mental qualities of the individual on which Lapouge's anthroposociological school based its system do not exist. More recent measurements have shown that long-headed men are not always blond, good, noble, and cultured, and that the short-headed are not always black, evil, common and uncultured. Amongst the most long-headed races are the Australian aborigines, the Eskimos, and the Kaffirs. Many of the greatest geniuses were round-heads. Kant's cranial index was 88.[14] We have learnt that changes in the cranial index very probably can take place without racial mixture—as the result of the mode of life and geographical environment.[15]

It is impossible to condemn too emphatically the procedure of the "race 325 experts." They set up criteria of race in an entirely uncritical spirit. More anxious to coin catchwords than to advance knowledge, they scoff at all the standards demanded by scientific thought. But the critics of such dilettantism take their job too lightly in directing their attention solely to the concrete form which individual writers give their theories and to the content of their statements about particular races, their physical characteristics and psychic qualities. Though Gobineau and Chamberlain's arbitrary and contradictory hypotheses are utterly without foundation and have been pooh-poohed as empty chimeras, there still remains a germ of the race theory which is independent of the specific differentiation between noble and ignoble races.

In Gobineau's theory the race is a beginning; originating in a special act of creation, it is fitted out with special qualities.[16] The influence of environment is estimated to be low: mixture of races creates bastards, in whom the good hereditary qualities of the nobler races deteriorate or are lost. To contest the sociological importance of the race theories, however, it will not suffice to prove that this view is untenable, or to show that race is the outcome of an evolution that has proceeded under the most varied influences. This objection might be overruled by asserting that certain influences, operating over a long period, have bred one race or several, with specially favourable qualities, and that the members of these races had by means of these advantages obtained so long a lead that members of other races could not overtake them within a limited time. In its most modern variations the race theory does, in fact, put forward arguments of this kind. It is necessary to study this form of the race theory and to ask how it stands in relation to the theory of social co-operation which has here been developed.

We see at once that it contains nothing directly inimical to the doctrine of

---

[14] Oppenheimer, "Die rassentheoretische Geschichtsphilosophie" in *Verhandlungen des Zweiten deutschen Soziologentages* (Tübingen, 1913), p. 106; also Hertz, *Rasse und Kultur*, 3rd ed. (Leipzig, 1925), p. 37; Weidenreich, *Rasse und Körperbau* (Berlin, 1927), pp. 133 ff.

[15] Nystrom, "Über die Formenveränderungen des menschlichen Schädels und deren Ursachen" (*Archiv für Anthropologie*, Vol. XXVII, pp. 321 ff., 630 ff., 642).

[16] Oppenheimer, "Die rassentheoretische Geschichtsphilosophie," pp. 110 ff.

the division of labour. The two are quite compatible. It may be assumed that races do differ in intelligence and will power, and that, this being so, they are very unequal in their ability to form society, and further that the better races distinguish themselves precisely by their special aptitude for strengthening social co-operation. This hypothesis throws light on various aspects of social evolution not otherwise easily comprehensible. It enables us to
326 explain the development and regression of the social division of labour and the flowering and decline of civilizations. We leave it open whether the hypothesis itself and the hypothesis erected on it are tenable. At the moment this does not concern us. We are solely concerned to show that the race theory is easily compatible with our theory of social co-operation.

When the race theory combats the natural law postulate of the equality and equal rights of all men, it does not affect the free trade argument of the liberal school. For Liberalism does not advocate the liberty of the workers for reasons of natural law but because it regards unfree labour—the failure to reward the labourer with the whole produce economically imputed to his labour, and the divorce of his income from the productivity of his labour—as being less productive than free labour. In the race theory there are no arguments to refute free trade theory as to the effects of the expanding social division of labour. It may be admitted that the races differ in talent and character and that there is no hope of ever seeing those differences resolved. Still, free trade theory shows that even the more capable races derive an advantage from associating with the less capable and that social co-operation brings them the advantage of higher productivity in the total labour process.[17]

The race theory begins to conflict with the liberal social theory at the point where it begins to preach the struggle between races. But it has no better arguments to advance in this connection than those of other militaristic social theories. The saying of Heraclitus "that war is the father of all things" remains unproven dogma. It, too, fails to demonstrate how the social structure could have grown out of destruction and annihilation. Nay, the race theorists too—in so far as they try to judge unbiased and not simply to follow their sympathy for the ideology of militarism and conflict—have to admit that war has to be condemned precisely from the point of view of selection. Lapouge has pointed out that only in the case of primitive peoples does war lead to the selection of the stronger and more gifted, and that among civilized peoples it leads to a deterioration of the race by unfavourable selection.[18]

---

[17] See p. 260.

[18] *"Chez les peuples modernes, la guerre et le militarisme sont de véritables fléaux dont le résultat définitif est de déprimer la race."* ("For modern people, war and militarism are true calamities, of which the ultimate result is to debase the human race.") Lapouge, *Les sélections sociales* (Paris, 1896), p. 230.

The fit are more likely to be killed than the unfit, who are kept longer, if not
altogether, away from the front. Those who survive the war find their power 327
to produce healthy children impaired by the various injuries they have received in the fight.

The results of the scientific study of races cannot in any way refute the liberal theory of social development. Rather they confirm it. The race theories of Gobineau and many others originated in the resentment of a defeated military and noble caste against bourgeois democracy and capitalist economy. For use in the daily politics of modern Imperialism they have taken a form which re-embodies old theories of violence and war. But their critical strictures are applicable only to the catchwords of the old natural law philosophy. They are irrelevant so far as Liberalism is concerned. Even the race theory cannot shake the assertion that civilization is a work of peaceful co-operation.

CHAPTER 20

The Clash of Class Interests and the Class War

1

The Concept of Class and of Class Conflict

328 At any given moment the position of the individual in the social economy determines his relation to all other members of society. He is related to them in respect of exchange, as giver and receiver, as seller and buyer. His position in the society need not necessarily tie him down to one and the same activity. One man may be simultaneously landlord, wage-earner, and capitalist; another simultaneously entrepreneur, employee, and landlord; a third entrepreneur, capitalist, and landlord, etc. One may produce cheese and baskets and hire himself out occasionally as a day labourer. But even the situation of those who find themselves in approximately equal positions differs according to the special circumstances in which they appear on the market. Even as a buyer for his own consumption every man is situated differently from others according to his special needs. On the market there are always only single individuals. In a free economy the market permits the emergence of individual differences: it "atomizes" as is sometimes said—usually somewhat regretfully. Even Marx had to make a point of explaining that "As purchases and sales are made only between single individuals, it is not admissible to look to them for relations between whole social classes."[1]

[1] Marx, *Das Kapital*, Vol. I, p. 550. The passage from which the above quotation is taken was not in the first edition, published 1867. Marx first inserted it in the French version, published 1873, whence Engels took it over into the fourth German edition. Publisher's Note: p. 643 in the English translation. Masaryk, *Die philosophischen und soziologischen Grundlagen des Marxismus* (Vienna, 1899), p. 299, justly remarks that the alteration is presumably connected with the change Marx made in his theory in Vol. III of *Das Kapital*. It can be regarded as a recantation of the Marxist class theory. Significantly the third volume breaks off after a few sentences in the chapter headed "The Classes." In treating the problem of class Marx got only as far as setting up a dogma without proof, and no further.

If we use the term class to denote all those in approximately equal social positions, it is important to remember that the problem whether classes have any special importance in social life is not thereby solved. Schematization and classification *per se* have no cognitive value. The scientific significance 329
of a concept arises out of its function in the theories to which it belongs; outside the context of these theories it is no more than an intellectual plaything. The usefulness of the class theory is not proved when it is pointed out that since men find themselves in different social positions, the existence of social classes is undeniable. What matters is not the social position of the individual but the significance of this position in the life of society. It has long been recognized that the contrast between rich and poor, like all economic contrasts, plays a great part in politics. Equally well known is the historical importance of differences in rank and caste, that is, differences in legal position, or inequality before the Law. Classical Political Economy did not contest this. But it undertook to show that all these contrasts derived from wrong political institutions. According to Classical Political Economy, correctly understood, the interests of individuals are never incompatible. Belief in conflicts of interest, which formerly was very important, really sprang from ignorance of the natural laws of social life. Once men recognized that, rightly understood, all interests were identical, these issues would cease to influence political discussion.

But Classical Political Economy, which taught the solidarity of interests, itself laid the foundation stone for a new theory of class conflict. The mercantilists had placed goods in the centre of economics, which in their eyes was a theory of objective wealth. It was the great achievement of the Classics in this respect that beside the goods they set up economic man. They thus prepared the way for modern Economics which puts man and his subjective valuations into the centre of its system. A system in which man and goods are placed, so to speak, on an equal footing falls inevitably into two parts, the one treating of the production of wealth, the other of its distribution. The more Economics becomes a strict science, a system of catallactics, the more this conception tends to recede. But the idea of distribution remains for a time. And this gives rise in turn to the idea of a division between the process of production and that of distribution. The goods are first produced, then distributed. However clear it is that, in the capitalist economy, production and "distribution" are indissolubly interconnected, this unhappy conception tends to confuse the issue.[2]

[2] On the history of the concept of distribution, see Cannan, *A History of the Theories of Production and Distribution*, pp. 183 ff.

330 Such misunderstandings are indeed inevitable as soon as this term "distribution" is adopted and the problem of imputation is considered as a problem of distribution. For such a theory of imputation or, to use a term corresponding more closely to the classic setting of the problem, a theory of income, must distinguish between the various categories of factors of production, though in fact the same fundamental principle of value formation are to be applied to all of them. "Labour" is separated from "Capital" and from "Land." Nothing is easier in such a context, than to regard labourers, capitalists, and landowners as separate classes, as Ricardo first did in the preface to his *Principles.* The fact that the classic economists do not split up "profit" into its component parts, only increased this tendency and gave us the picture of society divided into three great classes.

But Ricardo goes still further. By showing how "in different stages of society"[3] the proportions of the total produce which will be allotted to each of the three classes are different, he extends the class conflict to dynamics. His successors follow him here. And it is here that Marx steps in with the economic theory that he puts forward in *Das Kapital.* In his earlier writings, especially in the introductory words of the Communist Manifesto, Marx still conceives class and class conflict in the old sense of a contrast in legal position and the size of fortune. The link between the two notions is provided by a view of modern industrial relations as the domination of capitalists over workers. But even in *Das Kapital* Marx does not delimit precisely the concept of class, although it is of fundamental importance for his theory. He does not define what class is, but limits himself to enumerating the "great classes" into which modern capitalist society is divided.[4] Here he follows Ricardo's division, neglecting the fact that for Ricardo the division of classes is only of importance for the theory of catallactics.

The success of the Marxist theory of class and class conflicts has been tremendous. Today the Marxian distinction of classes within society and the theory of the irreconcilable conflict between these classes is almost universally accepted. Even those who desire, and work for, peace between classes do not as a rule contest the view that there are class contrasts and class struggles.
331 But the concept of class remains as uncertain as before. For the followers of Marx, as for Marx himself, the concept coruscates in all the colours of the rainbow.

If, following the system of *Das Kapital,* this concept is based on the classical division of the factors of production, then a classification that was invented only for purposes of the theory of exchange and is only justifiable there, is

[3] Ricardo, *Principles of Political Economy and Taxation,* p. 5.

[4] Marx, *Das Kapital,* Vol. III, Part 2, 3rd ed., p. 421.

transformed into the basis of general sociological knowledge. The fact is overlooked that the assembling of the factors of production into two, three or four large groups is merely a problem of the arrangement of economic theory, and that it can be valid within this context only. The classification of the factors of production is not a classification of men or groups of men, but of functions; the rationale of the division lies solely in the purpose of the theory of catallactics it is intended to serve. The separation of "Land" for example, owes its special position to the Classical theory of ground-rent. According to this theory, land is that requisite of production which, under certain assumptions, can yield a rent. Similarly, the position of capital as the source of profit, and of labour as the source of wages, is due to the peculiarities of the classical system. In subsequent solutions of the problem of distribution which divided the "profit" of the classical school into entrepreneur's profit and interest on capital, the grouping of the factors of production was entirely different. In the modern imputation theory on the contrary, the grouping of the factors of production according to the scheme of the classical theory is no longer of any importance. What was formerly called the problem of distribution is now the problem of the formation of prices of goods of higher orders. Only conservatism of scientific classification has tended to retain the old terminology. A grouping more in accordance with the spirit of imputation theory would have to proceed on an entirely different basis—for example, the separation of static and dynamic branches of income.

But—and this is the essential point—in no system is the basis for the grouping of factors determined by their natural characteristics. It is the failure to perceive this that constitutes the gravest error of the theory of economic classes. This theory began by naively assuming an inner relation (created by natural economic conditions) between those factors of production which have been grouped together for analytical reasons. It constructs a uniform
land, which can be used for at least all kinds of agriculture, and a uniform 332
labour, which can work at anything. It makes a concession, an attempt to conform to reality, when it distinguishes between land to be used agriculturally, land to be used for mining, and urban land, and when it differentiates between skilled and unskilled labour. But this concession does not improve matters. Skilled labour is just as much an abstraction as "labour" pure and simple, and agricultural land is just as much an abstraction as "land" pure and simple. And—what is important here—they are abstractions which leave out just those characteristics essential to sociological study. When dealing with the peculiarities of price formation we may, in certain circumstances, be permitted to make the contrast between the three groups: land, capital, and labour. But this does not prove at all that such grouping is permissible when we are dealing with a quite different problem.

2

Estates and Classes

The theory of the class war constantly confuses the notions of Estate ("Stand") and class.[5] Estates were legal institutions, not economically determined facts. Every man was born into an estate and generally remained in it until he died. All through life one possessed estate-membership, the quality of being a member of a certain estate. One was master or serf, freeman or slave, lord of the land or tied to it, patrician or plebeian, not because one occupied a certain position in *economic* life, but because one belonged to a certain estate. Admittedly the estates were in their origins an economic
333 institution, in the sense that, like every social order, they had arisen ultimately from the need to safeguard social co-operation. But the social theory underlying this institution was fundamentally different from the liberal theory, for human co-operation was conceived only as a "taking" by some and a "giving" by others. That the give and take could be mutual and all parties gain thereby was utterly incomprehensible to such a theory. A later epoch, seeking to justify the estate system which, in the light of the liberal ideas then slowly dawning in the world, had begun to appear unsocial and also unjust, based on a one-sided burdening of the lower orders, fabricated an artificial reciprocity in the relationship: the higher orders gave the lower protection, sustenance, the use of the land, and so on. But the very existence of this doctrine reveals that the decay of the estate ideology had already begun. Such ideas were alien to the institution in its heyday, when the relationship was frankly one of violence, as may be clearly seen in the first essential distinction drawn by estate—the distinction between free and unfree. The reason why the slave looked on slavery as natural, resigning himself to his lot instead of continuing to rebel and run away as long as there was breath

[5] Cunow, *Die Marxsche Geschichts-,Gesellschafts-und Staatstheorie*, Vol. II (Berlin, 1921), pp. 61 ff., tried to protect Marx from the accusation that he has mixed up the concepts class and estate. But his own remarks and the passages he quotes from Marx and Engels show how justified is this accusation. Read, for example, the first six paragraphs of the first part of the Communist Manifesto, headed "Bourgeois and Proletarians" and you will be convinced that there at least the expressions "Stand" and class are used indiscriminately. We have already said that when, later on in London, Marx became familiar with the Ricardian system, he separated his concept class from the concept "stand" and connected it with the three factors of production of the Ricardian system. But he never developed this new concept of class. Neither has Engels or any other Marxist tried to show what really welds the competitors—for these are the people of whom the "uniformity of incomes and of sources of incomes" makes a conceptual unit—into a class inspired by the same special interests.

in his body, was not that he believed slavery to be a just institution, equally advantageous to master and slave, but simply that he did not want to endanger his life by insubordination.

By stressing the historical role of slavery it has been sought to refute the liberal view of subjection and of the institution of the estate also. Slavery was said to mark an advance in civilization, when men taken in battle were enslaved instead of being killed. Without slavery a society dividing labour, in which trades are separated from primary production, could not have developed until all free soil had been disposed of; for everyone would have preferred to be free master of his own land rather than a landless worker on raw materials produced by others, let alone a propertyless labourer on someone else's land. On this view slavery has an historical justification, as higher civilization is inconceivable without the division of labour which gives part of the population a life of leisure, freed from common worries over daily bread.[6]

It is only for those who study history with the eyes of the moralist that the question of whether an historical institution can be justified or not can arise at all. The fact that it has appeared in history shows that forces were active to bring it about. The only question that can be asked scientifically is whether 334
the institution actually fulfilled the function ascribed to it. In this instance the answer is definitely in the negative. Slavery did not prepare the way for division of labour. On the contrary it blocked the way. Indeed modern industrial society, with its highly developed division of labour, could not begin to grow until slavery had been abolished. Free, ownerless land has continued to exist for settlement without preventing the rise of special trades or of a class of free wage earners. For the free land had first to be made cultivable. Before it yielded its fruits it needed stock and improvements. Often in its fertility and nearly always in its situation, it was worse than land already under cultivation.[7] Private ownership in the means of production is the only necessary condition for the extensive development of the division of labour. The enslavement of the worker was not necessary to create it.

In the relation between estates, two types are characteristic. One is the relation between feudal lord and the cultivator. The feudal lord stands quite outside the process of production. He appears on the stage only when the crop has been harvested and the process of production has been completed. Then he takes his share. To understand the nature of this relationship we

---

[6] Bagehot, *Physics and Politics* (London, 1872), pp. 71 ff.

[7] Even today there is plenty of ownerless land which anyone who wishes can appropriate. Yet the European proletarian does not migrate to the interior of Africa or Brazil, but remains a wage labourer at home.

do not need to know whether it originated in the subjection of formerly free peasants or in the settlement of people on land owned by the lord. The one relevant fact is that the relationship is outside production and cannot, therefore, be dissolved through an economic process, such as commutation of rent and tithes by the cultivator. As soon as the rent is commutable it ceases to be a dependent relationship and becomes a property right. The second typical relation is that of master to slave. Here the master demands labour, not goods, and receives what he demands without any counterservice to the slave. For giving food, clothing, and shelter is not a counterservice, but a necessary expenditure unless he is to lose the slave's labour. Under the strictly developed institution of slavery the slave is fed only so long as his labour brings in a surplus over his subsistence costs.

Nothing is less reasonable than to compare these two relationships with that of entrepreneur and worker in a free economy. Historically, free wage
335 labour grew to a certain extent out of the labour of slaves and serfs, and it was a long time before it cast off all trace of its origin and became what it is in the capitalist economy. But it is a complete misunderstanding of the capitalist economy to equate economically *free* labour for wages with the work done by the unfree. One may draw sociological comparisons between the two systems. For both involve division of labour and social co-operation, and in this reveal common features. But sociological study must not overlook the fact that the economic character of the two systems is quite different. Analysis of the economic character of free labour with arguments derived from the study of slave labour is bound to be worthless. The free worker receives in wages what is economically imputed to his labour. The slave owner expends the same amount—by providing for the sustenance of the slave and by paying the slave dealer a price for the slave that corresponds to the present value of the amounts by which the wages of free labour are or would be higher than the slave's sustenance costs. The surplus of the wages of labour over the workers' sustenance costs thus goes to the man who transforms free men into slaves—to the slave hunter, not to the slave dealer or the slave owner. These two do not derive any specific income in the slave economy. It is clear, therefore, that anyone who tries to support the exploitation theory by referring to conditions of a slave economy completely misunderstands the problem.[8]

[8] "The source of the slave owner's profits," says Lexis (in discussing Wicksell's "Über Wert, Kapital, und Rente" in *Schmoller's Jahrbuch*, Vol. XIX, pp. 335 ff.) "is unmistakable, and this is probably still true of the 'sweater.' In the normal relationship between entrepreneur and worker there is no such exploitation, but rather an economic dependence on the part of the worker, which undeniably influences the distribution of the produce of labour. The propertyless worker

In a society divided into estates all members of the estates who lack complete rights before the law have *one* interest in common with other 336
members: they struggle to improve the legal position of their estate. All who are bound to the soil strive to have the burden of rent lightened; all slaves strive for freedom, that is, for a condition under which they can use their labour for themselves. The community of interest of all the members of an estate is stronger, the less the individual is able to raise himself above the legal sphere of his estate. It does not matter very much here that in some rare cases, especially gifted individuals, aided by happy accidents, are able to rise into higher estates. No mass movements are born of the unsatisfied wishes and hopes of isolated individuals. Desire to renew their own strength rather than a wish to smother social discontent is what causes the privileged estates to clear the way for the rise of the talented. Gifted individuals who have been prevented from rising can become dangerous only if their call to violent action finds an echo in wide strata of discontented men.

3

Class War

The settlement of particular conflicts between estates could not remove the distinction between estates, as long as the idea of dividing society in this way remained. Even when the oppressed shook off the yoke, all differences in status were not abolished. Liberalism alone could overcome the fundamental conflict of estates. It did so by abolishing slavery—on the ground that free labour was more productive than unfree—and by proclaiming

must absolutely procure 'present goods' for himself; otherwise he dies. He can generally realize his labour only by collaborating in the production of 'future goods.' But this is not the decisive factor, for even though he produces, like the baker's labourer, a commodity to be consumed on the day of its production, yet his share in the yield is conditioned by the circumstances disadvantageous to him, that he cannot make an independent use of his labour, but is forced to sell it against more or less sufficient means of life, renouncing his claim to its product. These are trivial propositions, but I believe that they will always have a convincing force for unprejudiced observers because of their direct self-evidence." One agrees with Böhm-Bawerk, *Einige strittige Fragen der Kapitalstheorie* (Vienna and Leipzig, 1900), p. 112; and Engels, Preface to the third volume of *Das Kapital*, p. xii, that in these ideas, which, by the way, only reproduce the views dominant in German "Popular Economics," is to be found a recognition dressed up in careful words, of the socialist theory of exploitation. The economic fallacies of the exploitation theory are nowhere exposed more clearly than in this attempt of Lexis to find a basis for it. Publisher's Note: The reference to page xii in the Engels citation is in Vol. III, pp. 19–21 of the English translation.

freedom of movement and choice of occupation as the fundamental desiderata of a rational policy. Nothing exposes more clearly the inability of anti-liberalism to grasp the historical significance of Liberalism than its attempt to represent this achievement as the product of special group "interests."

In the struggle between estates all members of an estate stand together because they have a common aim. However much their interests otherwise diverge they meet on this one ground. They want a better legal position for their estate. Economic advantages usually accompany this, for the reason why legal differences are maintained between estates is precisely that they confer economic advantages on some to the economic prejudice of others.

337 But the "class" of the theory of the class-war is a different matter altogether. The theory of irreconcilable class conflict is illogical when it stops short at dividing society into three or four large classes. Carried to its logical conclusions, the theory would have to go on dissolving society into groups of interests till it reached groups whose members fulfilled precisely the same function. It is not enough to separate owners into landowners and capitalists. The differentiation must proceed until it reaches such groups as cotton spinners who manufacture the same count of yarn, or the manufacturers of black kid leather, or the brewers of light beer. Such groups have, it is true, *one* common interest as against the mass of others: they are vitally interested in the favourable sale of their products. But this common interest is narrowly limited. In a free economy a single branch of production cannot in the long run obtain more than an average profit and cannot, on the other hand, work at a loss. The common interest of members of a trade does not extend, therefore, beyond the trend of the market within a limited space of time. For the rest, competition, not immediate solidarity of interest, operates between them. This competition is suspended by special interests only when economic liberty is limited in some way. But if the scheme is to retain its usefulness for the critique of the theory of the solidarity of class interests, evidence must be produced that this competition is suspended under a free economy. The class struggle theory cannot be proved to be sound by a reference to the common interests of landowners as being in conflict with the urban population on tariff policy, or to the conflict between landowners and town dwellers on the matter of political government. Liberal theory does not deny that state interference in trade creates special interests, nor that by this means particular groups can extract privileges for themselves. It merely says that such special favours, when they are exceptional privileges of small groups, lead to violent political conflict, to revolts of the non-privileged many against the privileged few, which by constantly disturbing the peace, hold up social development. It explains further that where these special privileges constitute

a general rule, they injure everyone, for they take on the one hand what they give on the other, and leave behind, as a permanent result, only a general decline in the productivity of labour.

In the long run the community of interests among the members of a group and the contrast between their interests and the interests of other groups arise always from limitations of the right of ownership, of the freedom of 338
trade, of the choice of occupation. Only in the short run can they arise from the condition of the market as such. But if among the groups whose members occupy the same position in the economy there is no community of interest which would place them in opposition to all other groups, there can certainly be no such community within the larger groups whose members occupy not the same but merely a similar position. If there is no community of special interests between the cotton-spinners among themselves, neither is there any within the cotton industry or between the spinners and the machine makers. Between spinner and weaver, machine maker and machine user, the direct contrast of interests is as marked as it can possibly be. A community of interests exists only where competition is ruled out, for example, between the owners of land of a certain quality or situation.

The theory that the population is divided into three or four large groups, each with a common interest, errs in regarding land owners as a class with unitary interests. No special common interest unites the owners of arable land, of forests, of vineyards, of mines, or of urban real estate, unless it be that they defend the right of private property in land. But that is not the special interest of the owners. Whoever has recognized the significance of private ownership in the means of production must, whether he possesses property or not, advocate the principle in his own as well as the owner's interest. Landowners have genuine special interests only where the liberty of acquiring property and of trading has been limited.

There are no common interests among labourers either. Homogeneous labour is as non-existent as the universal worker. The work of the spinner is different from the work of the miner and the work of the doctor. The theorists of Socialism and of irreconcilable class conflict talk as though there was some kind of abstract labour which everyone was qualified to perform and as though skilled labour hardly came into the question. In reality no such "absolute" labour exists. Nor is unskilled labour homogeneous. A scavenger is different from a porter. Moreover the role of unskilled labour is much smaller, considered purely numerically, than orthodox class theory assumes.

In deducing the laws of the theory of imputation we are justified in speaking simply of "land" and "labour." For from this point all goods of the

higher order are significant only as economic objects. The reason for sim-
339 plifying the infinite variety of goods of higher orders into a few large groups is convenience in working out the theory which is of course directed towards a definite aim. It is often complained that economic theory works with abstractions; but precisely those who make this complaint themselves forget that the concepts "labour" and "worker," "capital" and "capitalist," and so on, are abstract; and do not hesitate to transplant the "worker" of theoretical Economics into a picture of what is supposed to be actual social life.

The members of a class are competitors. If the number of workers diminishes, and if the marginal productivity of labour grows accordingly, wages rise, and with them the income and standard of living of the worker. Trade unions cannot alter this. When they, who were supposed to be called into being to fight the entrepreneurs, close their membership like guilds, they implicitly recognize the fact.

Competition operates among the workers when they compete for higher positions and for promotion to higher ranks. Members of other classes can afford to remain indifferent as to the precise persons who are numbered among the relative minority which rises from the lower to the higher strata, so long as these are the most capable. But for the workers themselves this is an important matter. Each is in competition with the others. Of course each is interested to see that every *other* foreman's job shall be occupied by the most suitable man and the best. But each is anxious that that *one* job which comes within his reach shall fall to him, even though he is not the most suitable man for the job; and the advantage to him outweighs the fraction of the general disadvantages which may eventually also come his way.

The theory of the solidarity of the interests of all members of society is the only theory which shows how society is possible; and if it is dropped, the social unity dissolves not only into classes, but into individuals confronting each other as opponents. Conflict between individual interests is overcome in society but not in the class. Society knows no components other than individuals. The class united by a community of special interests does not exist; it is the invention of a theory incompletely articulated. The more complicated society is, and the further differentiation has progressed within it, so much the more numerous are the groups of persons similarly placed within the social organism; though necessarily, the number of members in each group diminishes as the number of groups increase. The fact that the
340 members of each group have certain immediate interest in common does not, of itself, create universal equality of interests between them. The equality of position makes them competitors, not people with common aspirations.

Nor can any absolute community of interests arise from the incomplete similarity between the positions of allied groups. As far as their positions are similar, competition will operate between them.

The interests of all cotton mill owners may run parallel in certain directions, but in so far as this is the case, the more are they competitors among themselves. In other respects only those owners of mills who produce the same count of yarn will be in exactly parallel positions. Here again to this extent they are in competition with each other. In other respects however, the common interests are similar over a much wider field; they may comprise all workers in the cotton industry, then, again, all cotton producers, including planters and workers, or further, all industrialists of any kind, etc.: the grouping varies perpetually according to the aim and interests to be pursued. But complete similarity there is rare, and where it does exist, it leads not only to common interests *vis-a-vis* third parties but, simultaneously, to competition between the parties within the group.

A theory which made all social development proceed from class struggles would have to show that the position of each individual in the social organism was unequivocally determined by his class position, that is, by his membership of a certain class and the relation of this class to other classes. The fact that in all political struggles certain social groups are in conflict with each other is by no means a proof of this theory. To be correct it must be capable of demonstrating that the grouping is necessarily directed into a certain path and cannot be influenced by ideologies which are independent of the class position; that the way in which the smaller groups combine to form larger groups, and these again form classes which divide the whole of society, is not a way of compromises and alliances formed for temporary co-operation but results from facts created by social necessities, from an unequivocal community of interests.

Let us consider, for example, the different elements of which an Agrarian Party is composed. In Austria, the wine-growers, the cereal-growers, and the stock-breeders unite to form a common party. But it certainly cannot be asserted that similarity of interest has brought them together. For each of these three groups has different interests. The fusion with a view to securing
certain protective policies is a compromise between conflicting interests. 341
Such a compromise is, however, only possible on the basis of an ideology that goes beyond the interests of the class. The class interest of each of these three groups is opposed to that of the other groups. They can meet only by setting certain special interests wholly or partly aside, though they do this so as to fight all the more effectively for other special interests.

It is the same with the workers, who are contrasted with the owners of the means of production. The special interests of the separate workers' groups are also not unitary. They have quite different interests according to the knowledge and skill of their members. It is certaintly not in virtue of its class position that the proletariat is that homogeneous class the socialist parties imagine it to be. Only adherence to the socialist ideology, which obliges every individual and every group to give up his or its special interests, brings it about that it is so. The daily work of the trade unions consists precisely in effecting compromises between these conflicts of interest.[9]

Coalitions and alliances between group interests, other than existing coalitions and alliances, are always possible. And those which actually exist depend on the *ideology*, not on the *class position*, of the groups. Political aims, not identity of interests, is what determines the coherence of the group. The community of special interests is always restricted to a narrow field and is obliterated or counter-vailed by the conflict of other special interests, unless a certain ideology makes the community of interests seem stronger than the conflict of interests.

The community of class interests does not exist independently of class consciousness, and class consciousness is not merely additional to a community of special interests; it creates such a community. The proletarians are not a special group within the framework of modern society, whose attitude is unequivocally determined by their class position. Individuals are brought together for common political action by the socialist ideology; the unity of the proletariat comes, not from its class position, but from the ideology of the class-war. As a class the proletariat does not exist before Socialism: the
342 socialist idea first created it by combining certain individuals to attain a certain political end. There is nothing in Socialism which makes it especially appropriate to forwarding the real interests of the proletarian classes.

In principle class ideology is no different from national ideology. In fact there is no contrast between the interests of particular nations and races. It is national ideology which first creates the belief in special interests and turns nations into special groups which fight each other. Nationalist ideology divides society vertically; the socialist ideology divides society horizontally. In this sense the two are mutually exclusive. Sometimes the one has the upper hand, sometimes the other. In Germany in 1914 the nationalist ideology shouldered the socialist ideology into the background—and suddenly there

[9] Even the Communist Manifesto has to admit: "The organization of the proletarians into a class, and thus into a political party, is ever and again broken up by competition among the workers themselves." (Marx and Engels: *Das Kommunistische Manifest*, p. 30). See also Marx, *Das Elend der Philosophie*, 8th ed. (Stuttgart, 1920), p. 161. Publisher's Note: pp. 165–166 in the English edition of *The Poverty of Philosophy*.

was a nationalist united front. In 1918 the socialist triumphed over the nationalist.

In a free society no classes are separated by irreconcilably contrasted interests. Society is the solidarity of interests. The union of special groups has always as its safe aim the destruction of this cohesion. Its aim is anti-social. The special community of proletarian interests extends only so far as they pursue one aim—to break up society. It is the same with the special community of interests which is supposed to exist for a whole nation.

Because Marxian theory does not define its notion of class more closely, people have been able to use it for the expression of the most diverse ideas. When they define the decisive conflict as that between owners and non-owners, or between urban and rural interests, or between bourgeois, peasant, and worker; when they speak of the interests of "armament capital," of "alcohol capital," of "finance capital";[10] when at one moment they talk about the Glorious International and in the next breath explain that Imperialism is due to the conflicts of capital, it is easy to see that these are the merest catchwords of the demagogue, devoid of any real sociological interest. Thus in its most fundamental contentions Marxism has never risen above the level of a doctrine for the soap box orator.[11]

4 343

The Forms of Class War

The total national product is divided into wages, rent, interest, and profits. All economic theory considers it definitely settled that this division proceeds, not according to the non-economic power of the individual classes, but according to the importance which the market imputes to individual factors of production. Classical Political Economy and the modern theory of marginal value agree in this. Even Marxian doctrine, which has borrowed its theory of distribution from classical theory, agrees. By deducing in this way the laws according to which the value of labour is determined, it, too, sets up a theory of distribution in which economic elements alone are decisive. The

[10] At which point people quite illogically overlook the fact that the wage-earner too is interested in the prosperity of the branch of production and of the plant in which he is engaged.

[11] Even Cunow, *Die Marxsche Geschichts-, Gesellschafts-und Staatstheorie*, Vol. II, p. 53, in his uncritical Marx apology has to admit that Marx and Engels in their political writings speak not only of the three main classes but differentiate between a whole series of minor and side classes.

Marxian theory of distribution seems to us full of contradictions and absurdities. Nevertheless it is an attempt to find a purely economic explanation for the way in which the prices of the factors of production are formed. Later on, when Marx was moved for political reasons to recognize the advantages of the trade union movement, he did make certain slight concessions on this point. But the fact that he stuck to his system of economics shows that these were only concessions which left his fundamental views untouched.

If we were to describe as a "struggle" the effort of all parties on the market to get the best price obtainable, then we might say that there is a constant war of each against each throughout economic life; but not by any means that there is a class-war. The fight is not between class and class but between individuals. When groups of competitors come together for joint action, class does not confront class, but group opposes group. What a single workers' group has obtained for itself does not benefit all workers; the interests of the workers of different branches of production are as conflicting as those of entrepreneurs and workers. When it speaks of class war, socialist theory cannot have in mind this opposition of the interests of buyers and sellers in the market.[12] What it means by class war takes place outside economic life, though as a result of economic motives. When it considers the class war as being analogous to the war between estates it can only refer to a political
344 fight which takes place outside the market. After all this was the only kind of conflict possible between masters and slaves, landowners and serfs; on the market they had no dealings with each other.

But Marxism goes beyond this. It assumes it to be self-evident that only the owners are interested in maintaining private ownership in the means of production, that the proletarians have the contrary interest, and that both know their interests and act accordingly. We have already seen that this view is acceptable only if we are prepared to swallow the Marxian theory whole. Private ownership in the means of production serves equally the interests of owners and non-owners. It is certainly by no means true that the members of the two great classes into which according to Marxian theory society is divided, are naturally conscious of their interest in the class struggle. The Marxians had to work hard to awaken the class consciousness of the workers, that is, to make the workers support Marxian plans for the socialization of property. What joins the workers for co-operative action against the bourgeois class is precisely the theory of irreconcilable class conflict. Class consciousness, created by the ideology of the class conflict, is the essence of the struggle, and not vice versa. The idea created the class, not the class the idea.

---

[12] See Marx's words quoted on p. 292.

The weapons of the class struggle are no more economic than its origins. Strikes, sabotage, violent action and terrorism of every kind are not economic means. They are destructive means, designed to interrupt the movement of economic life. They are weapons of war which must inevitably lead to the destruction of society.

5

Class War as a Factor in Social Evolution

From the theory of the class-war, Marxians argue that the socialist order of society is the inevitable future of the human race. In any society based on private property, says Marxism, there must of necessity be an irreconcilable conflict between the interests of separate classes: exploiters oppose the exploited. This contrast of interests, it is assumed, determines the historical position of the classes; it prescribes the policy they must follow. Thus history becomes a chain of class struggles, until finally, in the modern proletariat,
there appears a class which can free itself from class rule only by abolishing 345
all class conflicts and all exploitation generally.

The Marxist theory of class war has extended its influence far beyond socialist circles. That the liberal theory of the solidarity of the ultimate interests of all members of society has been thrust into the background was, of course, not due to this theory only, but also to the revival of imperialist and protectionist ideas. But as the liberal idea lost its glamour, the fascinations of the Marxian promises were bound to be more widely felt. For it has one thing in common with the liberal theory which the other anti-liberal theories lack: it affirms the possibility of social life. All other theories which deny the solidarity of interests deny also by implications social life itself. Whoever argues with the nationalists, the race dogmatists, and even the protectionists, that the conflict of interests between nations and races cannot be reconciled, denies the possibility of peaceful co-operation between nations and thereby the possibility of international organization. Those who, with the implacable champions of peasant or petty bourgeois interests, consider the unflinching pursuit of class interests as the essence of politics, would be only logical if they were to deny all advantages of social co-operation. Compared with these theories, which necessarily lead to very pessimistic views of the future of society, Socialism seems to be an optimistic doctrine. At least for the desired coming social order, it claims the solidarity of the interests of all members of society. The desire for a philosophy, which does not altogether deny the advantages of social co-operation is so intensive, that many people have been driven into the arms of Socialism who would otherwise have avoided it altogether. The only oasis they find in the desert of anti-liberal theories is Socialism.

But in their readiness to accept the Marxian dogmas, such people overlook the fact that its promise of a classless future for society rests entirely on the assertion, presented as irrefutable, that the productivity of socialistically organized labour would be higher—indeed, limitless. The argument is well known: "The possibility of giving all members of society, by social production, an existence which shall be not merely materially adequate, increasing in wealth from day to day, but which shall guarantee them also the complete freedom to develop and practice their physical and mental abilities—this possibility now exists for the first time, but it *exists*."[13] Private ownership in
346 the means of production is the Red Sea which bars our path to this Promised Land of general well-being. From being an "evolutionary form of the forces of production" it became their "chains."[14] The liberation of the productive forces from the shackles of capitalism is the "sole presupposition to an uninterrupted development at an ever-increasing pace of the productive forces and, thus, to a practically unlimited increase in production itself."[15] "As the development of modern technique makes possible a sufficient, even abundant, satisfaction of wants for all, on condition that production is directed economically by and for the country, the class conflict now appears, for the first time, not as a condition of social development but as the obstacle to its conscious and planned organization. In the light of this knowledge the class interest of the oppressed proletarians is directed towards abolishing all class interests and setting up a classless society. The old, apparently eternal law of the class struggle practically necessitates by its own logic, by the interest of the last and most numerous class—the proletariat—the abolition of all class contrasts and the creation of a society in which interests are unitary and which is humanly solidary."[16] Ultimately, therefore, the Marxian demonstration is this: Socialism must come, because the socialist way of

[13] Engels, *Herrn Eugen Dührings Umwälzung der Wissenschaft*, p. 305. Publisher's Note: In English translation p. 392.

[14] Marx, *Zur Kritik der politischen Ökonomie*, ed. Kautsky (Stuttgart, 1897), p. xi. Publisher's Note: The quote cited in Marx's *Zur Kritik der politischen Ökonomie (A Contribution to the Critique of Political Economy)* may be found on p. 11 of the Eastman anthology; p. 12 of the Kerr edition.

[15] Engels, *Herrn Eugen Dührings Umwälzung der Wissenschaft*, p. 304. Publisher's Note: In English translation, p. 391.

[16] Max Adler, *Marx als Denker*, 2nd ed. (Vienna, 1921), p. 68.

production is more rational than the capitalist. But in all this the alleged superiority of socialist production is simply taken for granted. Except for a few casual remarks no attempt to prove anything is made.[17]

If one assumes that production under Socialism would be higher than under any other system, how can one limit the assertion by saying that it is true only under certain historical conditions and has not always been so? Why must time ripen for Socialism? It would be understandable if the Marxians were to explain why, before the nineteenth century, people did not hit upon this happy idea or why even if it had been conceived earlier, it could not have been realized. But why must a community, to attain Socialism, go through all the stages of evolution, although it is already familiar with the idea of Socialism? One can understand that "a nation is not ripe for Socialism as long as the majority of the masses oppose Socialism and want to have nothing to do with Socialism." But it is not easy to see why 347
"one cannot say definitely" that the time is ripe "when the proletariat forms the majority of the nation and when the latter in its majority manifests the will to Socialism."[18] Is it not quite illogical, to maintain that the World War* has put back our evolution and thus retarded the coming of the right moment for Socialism? "Socialism, that is, general well-being within modern civilization, becomes possible only through the enormous development of the productive forces brought about by Capitalism, through the enormous wealth Capitalism has created and concentrated in the hands of the capitalist class. A state which has wasted this wealth in senseless policy, such as an unsuccessful war, offers no favourable opportunity for the quickest spread of well-being amongst all classes."[19] But surely those who believe that Socialism will multiply productivity should see in the fact that war has impoverished us one reason more for hastening its coming.

To this Marx answers: "a social order never succumbs until all the productive forces of which it is capable are developed, and new and higher conditions of production never replace it until the old society itself has conceived within its womb the material conditions of their existence."[20] But this answer assumes that what needs to be demonstrated is proved already: that socialist production would be more productive and that socialist production is a "higher" one, that is, on a higher stage of social development.

---

[17] On Kautsky's attempted proofs, pp. 159 ff.

[18] Kautsky, *Die Diktatur des Proletariats*, 2nd ed. (Vienna, 1918), p. 12.

[19] *Ibid.*, p. 40.

[20] Marx, *Zur Kritik der politischen Ökonomie*, p. xii. Publisher's Note: In English, p. 11 of the Eastman anthology; p. 12 of the Kerr edition.

* World War I (Pub.).

6

The Theory of the Class War and the Interpretation of History

The opinion that history leads to Socialism is almost universal today. From Feudalism through Capitalism to Socialism, from the rule of the aristocracy through the rule of the bourgeoisie to proletarian democracy—thus, approximately, people conceive the inevitable evolution. The gospel that Socialism is our inescapable destiny is acclaimed by many with joy, accepted by others with regret, doubted by only the courageous few. This scheme of evolution was known before Marx, but Marx developed it and made it popular. Above all Marx managed to fit it into a philosophic system.

348 Of the great systems of German idealist philosophy only those of Schelling and Hegel have had a direct and lasting influence on the formation of the individual sciences. Out of Schelling's Natural Philosophy grew a speculative school whose achievements, once so much admired, have long been forgotten. Hegel's Philosophy of History mesmerized the German historians of a whole generation. People wrote Universal History, History of Philosophy, History of Religion, History of Law, History of Art, History of Literature according to the Hegelian scheme. These arbitrary and often eccentric evolutionary hypotheses have also vanished. The disrespect into which the schools of Hegel and Schelling brought philosophy led Natural Science to reject everything that went beyond laboratory experiment and analysis, and caused the Moral Sciences to reject everything except the collection and sifting of sources. Science limited itself to mere facts and rejected all synthesis as unscientific. The impulse to permeate science once more with the philosophic spirit had to come from elsewhere—from biology and sociology.

Of all the creations of the Hegelian School only one was fated to a longer lease of life—the Marxian Social Theory. But its place was outside scholarship. Marxian ideas have proved utterly useless as guides to historical research. All attempts to write history according to the Marxian scheme have failed lamentably. The historical works of the orthodox Marxists, such as Kautsky and Mehring, made no progress at all in original and exhaustive research. They produced only expositions based on the researches of others, expositions whose only original feature was an effort to see everything through Marxist spectacles. But the influence of Marxist ideas extends far beyond the circle of orthodox disciples. Many historians, by no means to be classed politically as Marxian socialists, approach them closely in their views on the philosophy of history. In their works the Marxian influence is a disturbing element. The use of such indefinite expressions as "exploitation," "the striving of capital for surplus value," and "proletariat" dulls the vision that should be kept clear for the impartial scrutiny of the material, and the idea that all history is merely a preliminary to the socialist society prompts the historian to do violence in his interpretation of the sources.

The notion that the rule of the proletariat must replace the rule of the bourgeoisie is largely based on that grading of the estates and classes which 349
has become general since the French Revolution. People call the French Revolution and the movement it introduced into the various states of Europe and America the emancipation of the Third Estate and think that now the Fourth Estate must have its turn. We may overlook here the fact that a view which regards the victory of liberal ideas as a class triumph of the bourgeoisie and the Free Trade Period as an epoch of the rule of the bourgeoisie, presupposes that all elements of the socialist theory of society are already proved. But another question immediately occurs to us. Must this Fourth Estate, whose turn is now supposed to come, be sought in the proletariat? Might not one look for it with equal or greater justice in the peasantry? Marx, of course, could have no doubts on the subject. In his view it was a settled thing that in agriculture big-scale concerns would oust small-scale enterprises and the peasant make way for the landless labourer of the latifundia. Now, when the theory of the inability of medium and small-scale agricultural enterprise to compete has long been buried, a problem arises which Marxism cannot answer. The evolution which is going on before our eyes would permit us to suppose that domination was passing into the hands of the peasants rather than that of the proletarians.[21]

But here, too, our decision must rest on our judgment of the efficiency of the two social orders, the capitalist and the socialist. If Capitalism is not the diabolical scheme shown in socialist caricature, if Socialism is not the ideal order which socialists assert it to be, then the whole doctrine collapses. The discussion always returns to the same point—the fundamental question whether the socialist order of society promises a higher productivity than Capitalism.

7

Summary

Race, nationality, citizenship, estate-rights: these things directly affect action. It does not matter whether a party ideology unites all those belonging to the same race or nation, the same state or estate. The fact that races,

[21] Gerhard Hildebrand, *Die Erschütterung der Industrieherrschaft und des Industriesozialismus* (Jena, 1910), pp. 213 ff.

nations, states or estates exist determines human action even when there is
350 no ideology to guide members of a group in a certain direction. A German's thought and actions are influenced by the kind of mind he has acquired as a member of the German language community. Whether or not he is influenced by nationalist party ideology is here unimportant. As a German he thinks and acts differently from the Rumanian whose thought the history of the Rumanian, and not the German, language determines.

The nationalist party ideology is a factor quite independent of one's membership of any given nation. Various mutually contradictory nationalist party ideologies can exist concurrently and fight for the individual's soul; on the other hand there may be no sort of nationalist party ideology in existence. A party ideology is always something specially introduced from outside into the already established membership of a certain social group, and for which it thereafter forms a special source of action. Mere living in a society does not create party doctrine in one's mind. Party attitudes always arise from a theory of what is and is not advantageous. Social life may, under certain circumstances, predispose one to accept a certain ideology, and occasionally party doctrines are so formed that they specially attract members of a particular social group. But the ideology must always be kept separate from the actual social and natural being.

Social being itself is ideological in so far as society is a product of human will, and so of human thought. The materialistic conception of history errs profoundly when it regards social life as independent of thought.

If the position of the individual in the co-operative organism of economic life is considered to be his class position, then what we have said above applies also to the class. But again, one has to differentiate here, too, between the influences to which his class position exposes the individual and the political ideologies which influence him. The fact that he occupies his particular position in society has its influence on the life of the bank clerk. Whether he deduces from this that he ought to advocate the capitalist or the socialist policy depends on the ideas which dominate him.

But if one conceives "class" in the Marxist sense, as a tripartite division of society into capitalists, land owners, and workers, it loses all definiteness. It becomes nothing more than a fiction to justify a concrete party-political ideology. Thus the concepts Bourgeoisie, Working Class, Proletariat are
351 fictions, the cognitive value of which depends on the theory in the service of which they are applied. This theory is the Marxian doctrine that class conflict is irreconcilable. If we consider this theory inadmissible, then no class differences and no class conflicts in the Marxian sense exist. If we prove that, correctly understood, the interests of all members of society are not in

conflict, we have shown not merely that the Marxian idea of a conflict of interests is untenable: we have discarded as valueless the very concept of class as it figures in socialist theory. For only within the framework of this theory has the attempt to classify society into capitalists, landowners, and workers any meaning. Outside this theory it is as purposeless as, for example, any attempt to lump together all fair or all dark people—unless indeed we propose, with certain race theorists, to give special importance to the colour of the hair, whether as an external characteristic or as a constitutive element.

The position of the individual in the division of labour influences his whole way of living, his thought, and his attitude towards the world. This is true in some respects also of the differences in the situations which individuals occupy in social production. Entrepreneurs and workers think differently because the habits of their daily work give them different points of view. The entrepreneur always has in mind the large and the whole, the worker only the near and the small.[22] The first learns to think and act on a large scale, the other remains stuck in the groove of small preoccupations. These facts are certainly of importance in a knowledge of social conditions, but it does not follow that to introduce the concept of the class in the sense of socialist theory would serve any useful purpose. For these differences do not derive simply and solely from differences of position in the process of production. The small entrepreneur's way of thinking is nearer to that of the worker than to that of the large-scale entrepreneur; the salaried manager of large undertakings is more closely allied to the entrepreneur than to the worker. The difference between poor and rich is, in many respects, more helpful to our understanding of the social conditions we are studying than the difference between worker and entrepreneur. The level of income, rather than the individual's relation to the factors of production, determines a man's standard of life. His position as producer becomes important only in so far as it affects the grading of his income.

---

[22] Ehrenberg, *Der Gesichtskreis eines deutschen Fabrikarbeiters* (Thünen-Archiv, Vol. I), pp. 320 ff.

CHAPTER 21

The Materialist Conception of History

1

Thought and Being

352 It was said by Feuerbach: "thought proceeds from being, but not being from thought."[1] This remark, which was intended to express merely the renunciation of Hegelian Idealism, becomes in the famous aphorism, "Man is what he eats" (*"Der Mensch ist was er isst"*)[2], the watchword of Materialism, as represented by Büchner and Moleschott. Vogt stiffened the materialist thesis by defending the statement "that thoughts stand in about the same relation to the brain as the gall to the liver or urine to the kidneys."[3] The same naive materialism, which, ignoring all the difficulties, attempts to solve the basic problem of philosophy simply and completely by referring everything concerned with the mind to a physical phenomenon, is revealed also in the economic conception of history of Marx and Engels. The title "Materialist Conception of History" is true to the nature of the theory; it emphasizes, in the striking manner intended by its founders, the epistemological homogeneity between their belief and the materialism of their time.[4]

According to the materialist conception of history thought depends on social being. This doctrine has two different versions fundamentally contradictory to each other. The one explains thought as a simple and direct development of the economic environment, of the conditions of production, under which men live. According to this version there is no history of science

---

[1] Feuerbach, *Vorläufige Thesen zur Reform der Philosophie*, 1842, Collected Works, Vol. II (Stuttgart, 1904), p. 239.

[2] Feuerbach, *Die Naturwissenschaft und die Revolution*, 1850, Vol. X (Stuttgart, 1911), p. 22.

[3] Vogt, *Köhlerglaube und Wissenschaft*, 2nd ed. (Giessen, 1855), p. 32.

[4] Max Adler, who tries to reconcile Marxism with the Kantian New Criticism, vainly tries to prove that Marxism and philosophic materialism have nothing in common. See especially *Marxistische Probleme* (Stuttgart, 1913), pp. 60 ff., 216 ff., in which he conflicts sharply with other Marxists. See, for example, Plekhanov, *Grundprobleme des Marxismus* (Stuttgart, 1910).

and no history of the individual sciences as independent evolutionary sequences because the setting of problems and their solutions do not represent 353
a progressive intellectual process, but merely reflect the momentary conditions of production. Descartes, says Marx, regarded the animal as a machine, because he "sees with the eyes of the manufacturing period, as distinguished from the eyes of the Middle Ages, when the animal was regarded as the assistant of man—a position assigned to it also at a later date by Herr von Haller in his *Restauration der Staatswissenschaft*."[5] In such a passage it is clear that the conditions of production are regarded as facts independent of human thought. They "correspond" in turn to a "definite stage of development" in the "material productive forces,"[6] or, what is only another way of putting the same thing, to "a definite stage in the development of the means of production and of transport."[7] The productive forces, the means of work, "result in" a definite order of society.[8] "Technology reveals the active conduct of man towards nature, the direct productive process of his life, and consequently his social conditions of life and the spiritual ideas which arise from them."[9] It never seems to have occurred to Marx that the productive forces are themselves a product of human thought, so that one merely moves in a circle when one tries to derive thought from them. He was completely bewitched by the word-fetish, "material production." Material, materialistic, and materialism were the fashionable philosophic catch-words in his time, and he could not escape their influence. He felt that his foremost task as a philosopher was to remove the "deficiencies of the abstract natural-science materialism which exclude the historical process"; those deficiencies which he thought he could perceive "in the abstract and ideological theories of its spokesmen, as soon as they venture beyond their special sphere." And that is why he called his procedure "the only materialistic, hence the only scientific method."[10]

According to the second version of the materialist conception of history, class interest determines thought. Marx says of Locke that he "represented

[5] Marx, *Das Kapital*, Vol. I, p. 354, note. But between Descartes and Haller stands La Mettrie, with his "homme machine," whose philosophy Marx has unfortunately omitted to interpret genetically. Publisher's Note: This is page 426n in the Kerr edition.

[6] Marx, *Zur Kritik der politischen Ökonomie*, p. xi. Publisher's Note: p. 11 in the Eastman anthology, p. 12 in the Kerr edition.

[7] Marx and Engels, *Das Kommunistische Manifest*, p. 27. Publisher's Note: This quote appears on p. 326 of the Eastman anthology.

[8] Marx, *Das Elend der Philosophie, ibid.*, p. 91. See also p. 269 of the present work. Publisher's Note: p. 105 in the English translation.

[9] Marx, *Das Kapital*, Vol. I, p. 336. Publisher's Note: p. 406n in the English translation.

[10] *Ibid.*

the new bourgeoisie in all its forms: the industrialists versus the working
354 classes and paupers, the merchants versus the old-fashioned usurers, high finance versus state debtors, and in one of his own works he even demonstrated the bourgeois intelligence to be the normal human intellect."[11] For Mehring, the most prolific of the Marxian historians, Schopenhauer is "the philosopher of the terrified philistines . . . in his sneaking, selfish, and slandering way the spiritual image of the bourgeoisie which, frightened by the clash of arms, trembling like the aspen, retired to live on its revenues and foreswore the ideals of its epoch like the plague."[12] In Nietzsche he sees "the philosopher of the Upper Bourgeoisie."[13]

His judgments in economics represent this point of view most clearly. Marx was the first to divide economists into bourgeois and proletarian, a division which etatism afterwards made its own. Held explains Ricardo's theory of rent as "dictated simply by the hate of the moneyed capitalists against the landed proprietors," and thinks that Ricardo's whole theory of value can only be looked upon "as the attempt to justify, under the semblance of an endeavour to secure natural rights, the domination and profits of Capitalism."[14] The best way to disprove this view is to point out the obvious fact that Marx's economic theory is nothing more than a product of the Ricardo school. All its essential elements are taken from the Ricardian system, from which it derives also the methodological principle of the separation of theory and politics and the exclusion of the ethical point of view.[15] Politically, classical economics was employed both for defending and for attacking Capitalism, for advocating as well as for rejecting Socialism.

Marxism makes use of the same method with regard to modern subjective economics. Unable to oppose it by a single word of reasonable criticism, the Marxian tries to dispose of it by denouncing it as "bourgeois economics."[16]
355 To show that subjective economics is not "capitalist apologetics" it should be sufficient, surely, to point out that there are socialists who stand firmly

[11] Marx, *Zur Kritik der politischen Ökonomie*, p. 62. Barth, *Die Philosophie der Geschichte als Soziologie*, Vol. I, pp. 658 ff., says rightly that the comparison between the innate privileges of the nobility and the presumably innate ideas can be considered as at most a joke. But the first part of Marx's characterization of Locke is no less untenable than the second. Publisher's Note: p. 93 of the Kerr edition. Please note that this particular quotation is not in the excerpt reprinted in the Eastman anthology.

[12] Mehring, *Die Lessing-Legende*, 3rd ed. (Stuttgart, 1909), p. 422.

[13] *Ibid.*, p. 423.

[14] Held, *Zwei Bücher zur sozialen Geschichte Englands* (Leipzig, 1881), pp. 176, 183.

[15] Schumpeter, "Epochen der Dogmen und Methodengeschichte," *Grundriss der Sozialökonomik*, Pt. I (Tübingen, 1914), pp. 81 ff.

[16] Hilferding, *Böhm-Bawerk's Marx-Kritik* (Vienna, 1904), pp. 1, 61. For the Catholic Marxist Hohoff, *Warenwert und Kapitalprofit* (Paderborn, 1902), p. 57. Böhm-Bawerk is "an indeed well gifted, ordinary economist who could not lift himself out of the capitalistic prejudices among which he

by the theory of subjective value.[17] The evolution of economics is a process of the mind, independent of the supposed class interests of economists, and has nothing to do with supporting or condemning any particular social institutions. Every scientific theory can be misused for political purpose; the politician does not need to construct a theory to support the aims he happens to pursue.[18] The ideas of modern Socialism have not sprung from proletarian brains. They were originated by intellectuals, sons of the bourgeoisie, not of wage-earners.[19] Socialism has captured not only the working class; it has supporters, open and secret, even amongst the propertied classes too.

2

Science and Socialism

Abstract thought is independent of the wishes which move the thinker and of the aims for which he strives.[20] Only this independence qualifies it as thought. Wishes and purposes regulate *action*. When it is said that economic

---

grew up." See my *Grundprobleme der Nationalökonomie* (Jena, 1933), pp. 170 ff. Publisher's Note: The Hilferding essay is available in English in *Karl Marx and the Close of his System by Eugen Böhm-Bawerk & Böhm-Bawerk's Criticism of Marx by Rudolf Hilferding*, ed. Paul M. Sweezy (New York: Augustus M. Kelly, 1949), pp. 121–196. The pages cited here are pp. 121 and 196. Please also note that Mises' book, *Grundprobleme der Nationalökonomie* is in English as *Epistemological Problems of Economics* (Princeton, N.J.: D. Van Nostrand, 1960). The particular citation here is to the essay entitled "The Psychological Basis of the Opposition to Economic Theory," essay VI in this collection, pp. 183–203. This was first published in 1931.

[17] See Bernard Shaw, for example, *Fabian Essays* (1889), pp. 16 ff. In the same way, in sociology and political science, natural law and contract theory have served both to advocate and fight Absolutism.

[18] If one wants to credit the materialist conception of history with having stressed the fact that social relations are dependent on the natural conditions of life and production, one must remember that this can appear as a special merit only in contrast to the excesses of the Hegelian historians and philosophers of history. The liberal philosophy of society and history and the writing of history since the end of the XVIIIth Century (even the German, see Below, *Die deutsche Geschichtsschreibung von den Befreiungskriegen bis zu unseren Tagen* [Leipzig, 1916], pp. 124 ff.,) were beforehand with this knowledge.

[19] Of the chief representatives of French and Italian Syndicalism, Sombart, *Sozialismus und soziale Bewegung*, 7th ed. (Jena, 1919), p. 110, says, "So far as I know them personally—amiable, fine, educated people. Cultured people with clean linen, good manners and elegant wives, whom one meets as gladly as one's own kind of people, and who certainly do not look as if they represented a movement which turns above all against the increasingly bourgeois nature of Socialism and wants to help the wealed fist, the genuine and true only-manual-workers to their rights." And De Man, *Zur Psychologie des Sozialismus*, pp. 16 ff., says, "If one accepted the misleading Marxist expression which connects every social ideology with a definite class attachment, one would have to say that Socialism as a doctrine, even Marxism, is of bourgeois origin."

[20] The wish is father to the *thought*, says a figure of speech. What it means is that the wish is the father of *faith*.

life influences thought the facts are reversed. Economy as rational action is dependent on thought, not thought on economy.

356 Even if it were wished to admit that thought is determined by class-interest, it could only be done by considering recognized class interests. But the recognition of class interest is already a result of thought. Whether such thought shows that special class interests exist or that the interests of all classes in society harmonize, the process of thought itself has taken place before the idea of class influenced thought.

For proletarian thought, it is true, Marxism assumes a truth and eternal value, free of all limitations of class interest. Though itself admittedly a class, the proletariat must, transcending class interests, guard the interests of humanity by abolishing the division of society into classes. In the same way, proletarian thought contains in place of the relativity of class-determined thought, the absolute truth content of the pure science which will come to fruition in the future socialist society. In other words, Marxism alone is science. What preceded Marx historically, may be reckoned the pre-history of science. Marxism gives philosophers before Hegel about the same place which Christianity gives to the prophets, and grants Hegel the same position which Christianity assigns to the Baptist in relation to the Redeemer. Since the appearance of Marx, however, all truth is with the Marxist, and everything else is lies, deception, and capitalist apologetics.

This is a very simple and clear philosophy, and in the hands of Marx's successors it becomes still simpler and clearer. To them science and Marxian Socialism are identical. Science is the exegesis of the words of Marx and Engels. Proofs are demonstrated by the quotation and interpretation of these words. The protagonists exchange accusations of ignorance of the "Writ." Thus a real cult of the proletariat arises. Engels says: "Only in the working class does the German theoretic mind persist unstunted. Here it is not to be exterminated. Here no regard is paid to career, profit-making, gracious patronage from above. On the contrary, the more regardlessly and disinterestedly science proceeds the more it finds itself in unison with the workers' interests and strivings."[21] According to Tönnies "only the proletariat, i.e. its literary spokesmen and leaders," suscribe, "on principle, to the unscientific view and all its consequences."[22]

357 To reveal these presumptuous assertions in their proper light we have only to recall the socialist attitude towards all scientific achievements during recent

[21] Engels, *Ludwig Feuerbach und der Ausgang der klassischen deutschen Philosophie*, 5th ed. (Stuttgart, 1910), p. 58.

[22] Tönnies, *Der Nietzsche-Kultus* (Leipzig, 1897), p. 6.

decades. When about a quarter of a century ago, a number of Marxian writers tried to cleanse the party doctrine of its grossest errors, a heresy hunt was instituted to preserve the purity of the system. Revisionism succumbed to Orthodoxy. Within Marxism there is no place for free thought.

3

The Psychological Presuppositions of Socialism

According to Marxism, the proletariat in capitalist society necessarily think socialistically. But why is this the case? It is easy to see why the socialist idea could not arise before there was large scale enterprise in industry, transport, and mining. As long as one could conceive of redistributing the actual physical property of the wealthy, it occurred to no one to devise any other way of securing equality of income. Only when the development of the division of labour had created large scale enterprise, unmistakably indivisible, did it become necessary to invoke the socialistic way of achieving equality. But although this explains why in the capitalist system there can no longer be any question of "dividing up," it by no means explains why the policy of the proletariat must be Socialism.

In our day we take it for granted that the workman must think and act socialistically. But we arrive at this conclusion only by assuming that the socialist order of society is either the form of social life most advantageous to the proletariat or, at least, that the proletariat thinks it so. The first alternative has already been discussed in these pages. In view of the undoubted fact that Socialism, though it counts numerous supporters in other classes, is most widespread amongst the workers, there remains only the question why the worker, because of the position he occupies, tends to be the more receptive to the socialist ideology.

The demagogic flattering of the socialist parties praises the worker of modern Capitalism as a being distinguished by every excellency of mind and character. A sober and less biased study might perhaps arrive at a very different opinion. But this kind of inquiry may safely be left to the party hacks of the various movements. For knowledge of social conditions in general and the sociology of the party system in particular it is quite valueless. 358
Our problem is simply to discover why the worker's position in production should incline him to the view that the socialist method of production is not only possible in principle, but that it would be more rational than the capitalist method.

The answer is not difficult. The workman in the large or medium scale capitalist enterprise sees and knows nothing of the connections uniting the individual parts of the work to the economic system as a whole. His horizon as worker and producer does not extend beyond the process which is his task. He holds that he alone is a productive member of society, and thinks that everyone, engineer and overseer equally well as entrepreneur, who does not, like himself, stand at the machine or carry loads, is a parasite. Even the bank clerk believes that he alone is actively productive in banking, that he earns the profit of the undertaking, and that the manager who concludes transactions is a superfluity, easily replaceable without loss. Now from where he stands, the worker cannot see how things hang together. He might find out by means of hard thinking and the aid of books, never from the facts of his own working environment. Just as the average man can only conclude from the facts of daily experience that the earth stands still and the sun moves from east to west, so the worker, judging by his own experience can never arrive at a true knowledge of the nature and functioning of economic life.

But when the socialist ideology comes to this economically ignorant man and shouts:

> Working man, awake, awake!
> Of thy strength full measure take,
> All the wheels must needs stand still
> If thy strong arm so doth will, (Herwegh)

is it any wonder if, dizzy with dreams of power, he follows this invitation? Socialism is the expression of the principle of violence crying from the workers' soul, just as Imperialism is the principle of violence speaking from the soul of the official and the soldier.

The masses incline towards Socialism, not because it really tends to their interests but because they believe that it does so.

PART III
THE ALLEGED INEVITABILITY OF SOCIALISM

SECTION 2

THE CONCENTRATION OF CAPITAL AND THE FORMATION OF MONOPOLIES AS PRELIMINARY STEPS TO SOCIALISM

CHAPTER 22

The Problem

1

The Marxian Theory of Concentration

Marx seeks to establish an economic foundation for the thesis that the 361
evolution towards Socialism is inevitable, by demonstrating the progressive concentration of capital. Capitalism has succeeded in depriving the worker of private ownership in the means of production; it has consummated the "expropriation of the direct producers." As soon as this process is completed "the further socialization of labour and the further transformation of land and other agents into socially exploited and therefore collective means of production, together with the ensuing expropriation of private owners, assume a new form. That which is now to be expropriated is no longer the worker labouring independently but the capitalist exploiting the worker. This expropriation is carried out by the play of the inherent forces of capitalist production itself; by the centralization of capital, each individual capitalist deals the death-blow to a number of others." Hand in hand with this goes the socialization of production. The number of the "capitalist magnates" is continually decreasing. "The centralization of the means of production and the socialization of labour reach a point where they become incompatible with their capitalist framework. They burst it. The last hour of capitalist private property has arrived. The expropriators are expropriated." This is the "expropriation of the few usurpers by the mass of the people," through the "transformation of capitalist ownership, which actually rests already on social production, into social ownership," a process much less "lengthy, hard, and difficult" than was, in its own time, the process that transformed the private ownership of individuals doing their own work into capitalist ownership.[1]

[1] Marx, *Das Kapital*, Vol. I, pp. 726 ff. Publisher's Note: p. 837 in the English translation.

Marx gives a dialectical turn to his contentions. "Capitalist private own-
362 ership is the first negation of the individual private ownership created by the workers' toil. But, with the inevitability of a natural process, capitalist production brings forth its own negation. It is the negation of the negation. This does not re-establish private ownership, by only individual ownership based on the achievements of the capitalist era: co-operation and the collective ownership of land and of the means or production produced by labour."[2] Strip these statements of the dialectic accessories and there remains the fact that the concentration of establishments, enterprises, and fortunes is inevitable. (Marx does not distinguish between these three and obviously regards them as identical.) This concentration would eventually lead to Socialism, as the world, once it was transformed into one single gigantic enterprise, could be taken over by society with perfect ease; but before that stage has been reached, the result will have been achieved by "the revolt of the ever-expanding working class which has been schooled, united, and organized by the very mechanism of the capitalist production."[3]

To Kautsky it is clear that "capitalist production tends to unite the means of production, which have become the monopoly of the capitalist class, into fewer and fewer hands. This evolution finally makes all the means of production of a nation, indeed of the whole world economy, the private property of a single individual or company, which disposes of them arbitrarily. The whole economy will be drawn together into one colossal undertaking, in which everything has to serve one master. In capitalist society private ownership in the means of production ends with all except one person being propertyless. It thus leads to its own abolition, to the lack of property by all and to the enslavement of all." This is a condition towards which we are rapidly advancing "more rapidly than most people believe." Of course, we are told, the matter will not go so far. "For the mere approach to this condition must increase the sufferings, conflicts, and contradictions in society to such an extent, that they become intolerable and society bursts its bounds and falls to pieces" unless evolution has previously been given a different direction.[4]

It should be observed that, according to this view, the transition from "High" Capitalism to Socialism is to be effected only by the deliberate action of the Masses. The Masses believe that certain evils are to be ascribed to
363 private ownership in the means of production. They believe that socialist

[2] Marx, *Das Kapital*, Vol. I, pp. 728 ff. Publisher's Note: pp. 837 ff. in the English translation.
[3] *Ibid.*, p. 728. Publisher's Note: pp. 836–837 in the English translation.
[4] Kautsky, *Das Erfurter Programm*, pp. 83 ff.

production is likely to improve their condition. It is therefore a theoretical insight which guides them. According to the materialist conception of history, however, this theory must itself be the inevitable result of a certain organization of production. Here we observe once more how Marxism moves in a circle when it tries to demonstrate its propositions. A certain condition must arise because evolution leads to it; evolution leads there because thought demands it; but thought is determined by being. This being, however, can be nothing more than that of the existing social condition. From the thinking determined by the existing condition the necessity of another condition follows.

There are two objections against which this whole chain of reasoning has no defence. It is unable to refute the contention of anyone who, though arguing on the same lines, regards thought as the cause, and society as that which is caused. And it has similarly no reply to the objection that future conditions may very well be misconceived, and that that which now seems so desirable may prove to be less tolerable than existing conditions. This, however, re-opens discussion on the advantages and disadvantages of types of societies, those existing and those sketched out by would-be reformers. But this is the very discussion which Marxism desired to suppress.

Let no one suppose that the Marxian doctrine of the concentration of capital can be verified by the simple method of consulting the statistics of establishments, incomes, and fortunes. The statistics of incomes and fortunes utterly contradict it. This can be definitely asserted in spite of all the imperfections of present statistical methods and all the difficulties which fluctuations in the value of money place in the way of using the material. With equal confidence one can say that the counterpart of the theory of concentration, the much discussed theory of increasing poverty—in which even orthodox Marxists can hardly continue to believe—is incompatible with the results of statistical investigation.[5] The statistics of agricultural holdings also contradict the Marxian assumptions. Those giving the number of the establishments in industry, mining and transport appear to confirm it. But figures that indicate a particular evolution during a limited period cannot be conclusive. The development in this brief span might run contrary to the long 364
term trend. We shall do better, therefore, to leave statistics on both sides, both for and against. For it must not be forgotten that there is a theory underlying every statistical demonstration. Figures alone prove or disprove nothing. Only the conclusions drawn from the collected material can do this. And these are theoretical.

---

[5] Wolf, *Sozialismus und kapitalistische Gesellschaftsordnung* (Stuttgart, 1892), pp. 149 ff.

2

The Theory of Anti-Monopolistic Policy

The theory of monopoly goes deeper than the Marxian theory of concentration. According to it, free competition, the life blood of a society based on private ownership in the means of production, is weakened by the steady growth of monopoly. The disadvantages bred within the economy by the unlimited rule of private monopolies are, however, so great that society has no choice but to transform private monopoly by socialization into state ownership. However great an evil Socialism might be, it would be less harmful than private monopoly. Should it prove impossible to counteract the tendency towards monopoly in ever widening fields of production, then private ownership in the means of production is already doomed.[6]

It is clear that this doctrine calls for a searching investigation: first, as to whether evolution is really in the direction of monopoly control, and secondly as to what are the economic effects of such monopoly. Here one has to proceed with special care. The time at which this doctrine was first expounded was generally not favourable to the theoretical study of such problems. The emotional judgment of appearances rather than the cool examination of the essence of things was the order of the day. Even the arguments of such an outstanding economist as J. B. Clark are imbued with the popular hatred of the trusts. Utterances typical of contemporary politicians are to be found in the report of the German Socialization Commission of February 15th, 1919, where it was affirmed as "indisputable" that the monopolistic position of the German coal industry "constitutes an independent power which is incompatible with the nature of the modern state, and not merely the socialist
365 one." It was, in the opinion of the Commission, "unnecessary to discuss anew the question whether and to what degree this power is misused to the detriment of the remaining members of society, those to whom it is raw material, the consumers, and the workers; its existence suffices to make evident the necessity for completely abolishing it."[7]

---

[6] Clark, *Essentials of Economic Theory*, pp. 374 ff., 397.

[7] Report of the *Sozialisierungskommission über die Frage der Sozialisierung des Kohlenbergbaus vom 31 Juli 1920* (Appendix: *Vorläufiger Bericht vom 15 Februar 1919*), *op. cit.*, p. 32.

CHAPTER 23

The Concentration of Establishments

1

The Concentration of Establishments as the Complement of the Division of Labour

The concentration of establishments comes automatically with the division 366
of labour. In the shoemaker's workshop the production of footwear, formerly carried on in each individual household, is united in one single establishment. The shoemaking village, the shoe-manufactory, becomes the manufacturing centre for a large area. The shoe factory that is organized for the mass-production of footwear represents a still wider union of establishments, and the basic principle of its internal organization is on the one side, division of labour, and, on the other side, concentration of similar work in special departments. In short, the more the work is split up, the more must similar labour processes be concentrated.

Neither from the results of the census undertaken in various countries to verify the doctrine of the concentration of productive units, nor from other statistical evidence of changes in the number of establishments, can we learn all there is to be known about them. For what appears in these enumerations as a unit is always, in a certain sense, a unit of business, not a unit of production. Only in certain cases do these investigations count separately works which, whilst united in locality, are conducted separately inside a single enterprise. The conception of the establishment and its evolution has to be elaborated from a point of view other than that which lies at the basis of trade statistics.

The higher productivity of the division of labour results, above all, from the specialization of processes which it makes possible. The more often a process has to be repeated the more does it pay to install a specially adapted tool. The splitting up of labour goes farther than the specialization of occupations, or at least than the specialization of enterprises. In the shoe factory shoes are produced by various part processes. It is quite conceivable that 367 each part process might take place in a special establishment and in a special enterprise. In fact, there are factories which make only parts of shoes and supply them to the shoe factories. Nevertheless, we usually consider as one productive unit the sum of part processes combined in a single shoe factory which itself produces all the component parts of shoes. If to the shoe factory is joined also a leather factory or a department for producing the boxes in which the shoes are packed, we speak of the union of several productive units for a common enterprise. This is a purely historical distinction which neither the technical circumstances of production nor the peculiarities of business enterprise suffice by themselves to explain.

When we regard as an establishment that totality of process involved in economic activity which businessmen regard as a unity, we must remember that this unit is by no means an indivisible thing. Each productive unit is itself composed of technical processes already horizontally and vertically combined. The concept of an establishment, therefore, is economic, not technical. Its delimitation in individual cases is determined by economic, not by technical, considerations.

The size of the productive unit is determined by the complementary quality of the factors of production. The aim is the optimal combination of these factors, i.e. that combination by which the greatest return can be produced economically. Economic development drives industry to ever greater division of labour, involving at once an increase in the size and a limiting of the scope of the unit of production. The actual size of the unit is the result of the interaction of these two forces.

2

The Optimal Size of Establishments in Primary Production and in Transport

The Law of Proportionality in combining the factors of production was first formulated in connection with agricultural production, as the Law of Diminishing Returns. For a long time its general character was misunderstood, and it was regarded as a law of agricultural technique. It was contrasted
368 with a Law of Increasing Returns, which was thought to be valid for industrial production. These errors have since been corrected.[1]

[1] Vogelstein, "Die finanzielle Organisation der kapitalistischen Industrie und die Monopolbildungen," *Grundriss der Sozialökonomik*, Pt. VI (Tübingen, 1914), pp. 203 ff. Weiss, "Abnehmender Ertrag," *Handwörterbuch der Staatswissenschaften*, 4th ed., Vol. I, pp. 11 ff.

The Law of the Optimal Combination of the factors of production indicates the most profitable size of the establishment. Net profit is greater according to the degree to which its size permits all factors of production to be employed without residue. In this way alone is to be estimated the superiority which the size of one particular establishment gives it over another establishment—at the given level of productive technique. It was a mistake to think that enlargement of the industrial establishment must always lead to an economy of costs, a mistake of which Marx and his school have been guilty, although occasional remarks betray the fact that he recognized the true state of affairs. For here, too, there is a limit beyond which enlargement of the establishment does not result in a more economical application of the factors of production. In principle, the same may be said of agriculture and mining; the concrete data only differ. It is merely certain peculiarities of the conditions of agricultural production which cause us to regard the Law of Diminishing Returns as primarily affecting land.

The concentration of establishments is primarily concentration in space. As the land suitable to agriculture and forestry extends in space, every effort to enlarge the establishment increases the difficulties that spring from distance. Thus an upper limit is set for the size of the agricultural unit of exploitation. Because agriculture and forestry extend in space it is possible to concentrate the establishment only up to a definite point. It is superfluous to enter into the question—often raised in discussion of this problem—whether large or small scale production is the more economical in agriculture. This has nothing to do with the Law of the Concentration of Establishments. Even supposing large scale production to be superior, one cannot deny that there could be no question of a Law of the Concentration of Establishments in agriculture or forestry. The fact that land is owned on a large scale does not mean that it is worked on a large scale. The great estates are always composed of numerous farms.

This appears even more clearly in a different branch of primary production,
mining. Mining enterprise is tied to the place where the ore is found. The *369*
establishments are as large as these separate places permit. They can be concentrated only to the degree in which the geographical position of the separate beds of ore make concentration seem profitable. In short, one can see nowhere in primary production any tendency to concentrate productive units. This is equally true of transport.

3

The Optimal Size of Establishments in Manufacturing

The process of manufacture out of raw materials is to a certain extent free from the limitations of space. The working of cotton plantations cannot be concentrated, but the spinning and weaving works may be united. But, here too, it would be rash to derive without further consideration a Law of the Concentration of Establishments from the fact that the larger plant generally proves superior to the smaller.

For in industry too localization is of importance, quite apart from the fact that (other things being equal, i.e. at a given level of the division of labour) the economic superiority of the larger productive unit exists only in so far as the Law of the Optimal Combination of Factors of Production demands it and that consequently no advantage is to be gained by enlarging the establishment beyond the point where the instruments are most efficiently utilized. Each type of production has a natural location, which depends ultimately on the geographical distribution of primary production. The fact that primary production cannot be concentrated must influence the subsequent process of manufacture. The power of this influence varies with the importance attaching to the transport of raw materials and finished products in the separate branches of production.

A Law of the Concentration of Establishments operates therefore only in so far as the division of labour leads to progressive division of production into new branches. This concentration is really nothing more than the reverse side of the division of labour. As a result of the division of labour numerous dissimilar establishments, within which uniformity is the rule, replace numerous similar establishments within which various different processes of
370 production are carried out. It causes the number of similar plants to decrease, whilst the circle of persons, for whose needs they work directly or indirectly, grows. If the production of raw materials was not geographically fixed, a circumstance which acts counter to the process initiated by the division of labour, one single plant only would exist for every branch of production.[2]

[2] See Alfred Weber, "Industrielle Standortslehre," *Grundriss der Sozialökonomik*, Pt. VI (Tübingen, 1914), pp. 54 ff. The remaining factors of localization can be passed over, as the present, or the historically transmitted, distribution of primary production ultimately determines them.

CHAPTER 24

The Concentration of Enterprises

1

The Horizontal Concentration of Enterprises

The merger of several similar independent establishments into one enterprise may be called horizontal concentration of production. Here we follow broadly the usage of writers on cartels, though their definition is not in complete accord with ours. If the separate establishments do not remain completely independent, if, for example the management or some departments are amalgamated, there is concentration of establishments. A mere concentration of enterprises occurs only when the individual units remain independent in everything except the taking of decisive economic decisions. The typical example of this is a cartel or a syndicate. Everything stays as it was, but, according to whether it is a buying cartel or a selling cartel or both, decisions about purchases and sales are taken unitarily. 371

When it is not merely the preliminary step to an amalgamation of establishments, the purpose of these unions is monopolistic domination of the market. Horizontal concentration originates only in the efforts of separate entrepreneurs to derive those advantages enjoyed under certain circumstances by the monopolist.

2

The Vertical Concentration of Enterprises

Vertical concentration is the union into one unitary enterprise of independent enterprises, some of which use the products of the others. This terminology follows the usage of modern economic literature. Examples of vertical concentration are the union of weaving, spinning, bleaching and dyeing works; a printing works to which a paper factory and a newspaper enterprise are joined; the mixed works of the iron industry and of coal mining, etc.

372 Each productive unit is a vertical concentration of part processes and of apparatus. Unity of *production* is created by the fact that part of the means of production—certain machines, buildings, the direction of the works—is jointly held. Such joint holding is lacking in the vertical union of *enterprises.* Here the essence of the union lies in the will of the entrepreneur to make one enterprise serve another. The mere fact that one man owns two enterprises is not in itself sufficient if this will does not exist. Where a chocolate manufacturer owns also an iron works there is no vertical concentration. Vertical concentration is usually considered to aim at ensuring an outlet for the product or safeguarding the source of raw materials and half finished goods. This is what entrepreneurs reply when questioned as to the advantages of such combinations. Many economists accept it without question, for apparently they do not think it is their job to scrutinize what is said by "practical men"; and after accepting the statement as final they proceed to examine it from the ethical point of view. Still, even if they avoid thinking about it, closer research into facts should show them the truth. There is the fact that managers of plants attached to a vertical combination often have to make complaints. The manager of the paper-mill says: "I could get much better value for my paper if I did not have to supply it to 'our' printing works." The manager of the weaving-mill: "If I didn't have to get the yarn from 'our' spinning works I could get it cheaper." Such complaints are the order of the day, and it is not difficult to understand why they must accompany every vertical concentration.

If the amalgamated establishments were individually so efficient that they did not have to shun competition, vertical combination would serve no special purpose. A paper factory of the best type never needs to ensure its market. A printing works which is on a level with its competitors does not need to ensure its paper supply. The efficient enterprise sells where it gets the best prices, buys where it can do so most economically. Hence, it does not follow that two enterprises, working at different stages of the same branch of production and held by one owner, must necessarily unite in vertical combination. Only when one or other of them shows itself less able to sustain competition does the entrepreneur conceive the idea of supporting it by tying it to the strong one. He looks to the profits of the prosperous
373 business for a fund to cover the deficits of the non-prosperous. Apart from tax remissions and other special advantages, such as those which the mixed

works in the German iron industry were able to derive from cartel agreements, union achieves nothing but an apparent profit in one enterprise and an apparent loss in the other.

The number and importance of vertical concentrations is extraordinarily overestimated. In modern capitalist economic life on the contrary, new branches of enterprise are constantly forming and parts of those existing are constantly breaking away to become independent.

The progressive tendency to specialization in modern industry shows that development is moving away from vertical concentration, which, except where it is demanded by considerations of productive technique, is always an exceptional phenomenon, generally to be explained by regard for the legal and other political conditions of production. But even here the break-up of such unions and the re-establishment of individual enterprise is to be witnessed over and over again.

CHAPTER 25

The Concentration of Fortunes

1

The Problem

374 A tendency to the concentration of establishments or to the concentration of enterprises is not by any means equivalent to a tendency to the concentration of fortunes. In the same degree in which establishments and enterprises became bigger and bigger modern capitalism has developed forms of enterprise which enable people with small fortunes to undertake big businesses. The proof that there is no tendency to concentrate fortunes lies in the number of these types of enterprises that have come up and are growing daily in importance, while the individual merchant has almost disappeared from large scale industry, mining, and transport. The history of forms of enterprise, from the *societas unius acti* to the modern joint stock company, is a wholesale contradiction of the doctrine of the concentration of capital so arbitrarily set up by Marx.

If we wish to prove that the poor are becoming ever more numerous and poorer, and the rich ever less numerous and richer, it is useless to point out that in a period of remote antiquity, as elusive to us as the Golden Age to Ovid and Virgil, the differences of wealth were less than they are today. We must prove that there is an economic cause which leads imperatively to the concentration of fortunes. The Marxians have not even attempted this. Their theory which ascribes to the capitalist age a special tendency towards the concentration of fortunes, is pure invention. The attempt to give it some sort of historical foundation is hopeless and adduces just the contrary of that which Marx asserts to be demonstrable.

2

The Foundation of Fortunes Outside the Market Economy

The desire for an increase of wealth can be satisfied through exchange, which is the only method possible in a capitalist economy, or by violence 375
and petition as in a militarist society, where the strong acquire by force, the weak by petitioning. In the feudal society ownership of the strong endures only so long as they have the power to hold it; that of the weak is always precarious, for having been acquired by grace of the strong it is always dependent on them. The weak hold their property without legal protection. In a militarist society, therefore, there is nothing but power to hinder the strong from extending their wealth. They can go on enriching themselves as long as no stronger men oppose them.

Nowhere and at no time has the large scale ownership of land come into being through the working of economic forces in the market. It is the result of military and political effort. Founded by violence, it has been upheld by violence and by that alone. As soon as the latifundia are drawn into the sphere of market transactions they begin to crumble, until at last they disappear completely. Neither at their formation nor in their maintenance have economic causes operated. The great landed fortunes did not arise through the economic superiority of large scale ownership, but through violent annexation outside the area of trade. "And they covet fields" complains the prophet Micah,[1] "and take them by violence; and houses, and take them away." Thus comes into existence the property of those who, in the words of Isaiah, "join house to house . . . lay field to field, till there be no place, that they may be placed alone in the midst of the earth."[2]

The non-economic origin of landed fortunes is clearly revealed by the fact that, as a rule, the expropriation by which they have been created in no way alters the manner of production. The old owner remains on the soil under a different legal title and continues to carry on production.

Land ownership may be founded also on gifts. It was in this way that the Church acquired its great possessions in the Frankish kingdom. Not later than the eighth century, these latifundia fell into the hands of the nobility; according to the older theory this was the result of secularizations by Charles Martel and his successors, but recent research is inclined to make "an offensive of the lay aristocrats" responsible.[3]

---

[1] Micah, II, 2.

[2] Isaiah, V, 8.

[3] Schröder, *Lehrbuch der deutschen Rechtsgeschichte*, pp. 159 ff.; Dopsch, *Wirtschaftliche und soziale Grundlagen der europäischen Kulturentwicklung*, Part 2 (Vienna, 1920), pp. 289, 309 ff.

376 That in a market economy it is difficult even now to uphold the latifundia, is shown by the endeavours to create legislation institutions like the "*Fideikommiss*" (feoffment in trust) and related legal institutions such as the English "entail." The purpose of the "*Fideikommiss*" was to maintain large-scale landed proprietorship, because it could not be kept together otherwise. The Law of Inheritance is changed, mortgaging and alienation are made impossible, and the State is appointed guardian of the indivisibility and inalienability of the property, so that the prestige of family tradition shall not be impaired. If economic circumstances had tended towards the continuous concentration of land ownership such laws would have been superfluous. Legislation would have been enacted against the formation of estates rather than for their protection. But of such laws legal history knows nothing. The regulations against "*Bauernlegen*," against enclosing arable land, etc., are directed against movements outside the area of trade, that is, against force. The legal restrictions of mortmain are similar. The lands of the mortmain, which, incidentally, are legally protected in much the same way as the "Fideikommiss," do not increase by force of economic development but through pious donations.

Now the highest concentration of fortunes is to be found just in agriculture, where concentration of establishments is impossible and the concentration of enterprises economically purposeless, where the large property appears to be economically inferior to the small and unable to withstand it in free competition. Never was the ownership of the means of production more closely concentrated than at the time of Pliny, when half the province of Africa was owned by six people, or in the days of the Merovingians, when the Church possessed the greater part of all French soil. And in no part of the world is there less large-scale land ownership than in capitalist North America.

3

The Formation of Fortunes Within the Market Economy

The assertion that wealth on the one hand and poverty on the other are ever increasing was maintained at first without any conscious connection with an economic theory. Its supporters think they have derived it from an
377 observation of social relations. But the observer's judgment is influenced by the idea that the sum of wealth in any society is a given quantity, so that if

some possess more others must possess less.[4] As, however, in every society the growth of new riches and the coming into existence of new poverty are always to be found in a conspicuous manner whilst the slow decline of ancient fortunes and the slow enrichment of less propertied classes easily escape the eye of the inattentive student, it is easy to arrive at the premature conclusion summed up in the socialist catchword "the rich richer, the poor poorer."

No protracted argument is required to prove that the evidence completely fails to substantiate this assertion. It is quite an unfounded hypothesis that in a society based on the division of labour the wealth of some implies the poverty of others. Under certain assumptions it is true of militarist societies, where there is no division of labour. But of a capitalist society it is untrue. Moreover an opinion formed on the basis of casual observations of that narrow section with which the individual is personally acquainted is quite insufficient proof of the theory of concentration.

The foreigner who visits England equipped with good recommendations has opportunities for learning something of the noble and wealthy families, and their manner of living. If he wants to know more or feels it his duty to make his visit more than a mere pleasure trip, he is allowed to make a flying tour of the works of great enterprises. For the layman, there is nothing particularly attractive about this. At first the noise, the bustle, the activity astonish the visitor, but after inspecting two or three factories the spectacle grows monotonous. Such a study of social relations, on the other hand, as can be undertaken during a short visit to England, is more stimulating. A walk through the slums of London or any other large city produces more vivid impressions, and the effect on the traveller who, when not occupied in this study, will be hurrying from one entertainment to another, is twice as powerful. Thus visits to the slums have become a popular item in the itinerary of the Continental's obligatory tour of England. In this way the future statesman and economist gathered an impression of the effects of industry on the masses, which became a basis for the social views of a lifetime. He went home firm in the opinion that industry makes few rich
and many poor. When later he wrote or spoke about industrial conditions 378
he never forgot to describe the misery he had found in the slums, elaborating the most painful details, often with more or less conscious exaggeration. All the same his picture tells us nothing more than that some people are rich and some poor. But to know this, we do not need the report of people who have seen the suffering with their own eyes. Before they wrote we knew

[4] Michels, *Die Verelendungstheorie* (Leipzig, 1928), pp. 19 ff.

that Capitalism has not yet abolished all misery in the world. What they have to set about proving is that the number of wealthy people is decreasing, while the wealthy individual grows richer, and that the number and the poverty of the poor is steadily on the increase. It would, however, take a theory of economic evolution to prove this.

Attempts to demonstrate by statistical research the progressive increase of the misery of the masses and the growth of wealth among a numerically diminishing rich class are no better than these mere appeals to emotion. The estimates of money incomes at the disposal of statistical inquiry are unusable because the purchasing power of money alters. This fact alone is enough to show that we lack any basis for comparing arithmetically the distribution of income over a number of years. For where it is not possible to reduce to a common denominator the various goods and services of which incomes are composed, one cannot form any series for historical comparison from known statistics of income and capital.

The attention of sociologists is often drawn to the fact that mercantile and industrial wealth, that is, wealth not invested in land and mining property, seldom maintains itself in one family for a long period. The bourgeois families rise steadily from poverty to wealth, sometimes so quickly that a man who has been in want a few years previously becomes one of the richest of his time. The history of modern fortunes is full of stories of beggar boys who have made themselves millionaires. Little is said of the decay of fortunes among the well-to-do. This does not usually take place so quickly as to strike the casual observer; closer examination, however, will reveal how unceasing the process is. Seldom does mercantile and industrial wealth maintain itself in one family for more than two or three generations, unless, by investment in land, it has ceased to be wealth of this nature.[5] It becomes property in land, no longer used in the business of active acquisition.

379 Fortunes invested in capital do not, as the naive economic philosophy of the common man imagines, represent eternal sources of income. That capital yields a profit, that it even maintains itself at all, is by no means a self-evident fact following *a priori* from the fact of its existence. The capital goods, of which capital is concretely composed, appear and disappear in production; in their place come other goods, ultimately consumption goods, out of the value of which the value of the capital mass must be reconstituted. This is possible only when the production has been successful, that is when it has produced more value than it absorbed. Not only profits of capital, but the reproduction of capital presupposes a successful process of production. The

---

[5] Hansen, *Die drei Bevölkerungsstufen* (Munich, 1889), pp. 181 ff.

profits of capital and maintenance of capital are always the result of successful enterprise. If this enterprise fails, the investor loses not only the yield on the capital, but his original capital fund as well. One ought carefully to distinguish between produced means of production and the primary factors of production. In agriculture and forestry the original and indestructible forces of the soil are maintained even though production fails, for faulty management cannot dissipate them. They may become valueless through changes in demand, but they cannot lose their inherent capacity to yield produce. This is not so in manufacturing production. There everything can be lost, root and branch. Production must continually replenish capital. The individual capital goods which compose it have a limited life; the existence of capital is prolonged only by the manner in which the owner deliberately reïnvests it in production. To own capital one must earn it afresh day by day. In the long run a capital fortune is not a source of income which can be enjoyed in idleness.

To combat these arguments by pointing to the steady yield from "good" capital investments would be wrong. The point is that the investments must be "*good*," and to be that, they must be the result of successful speculation. Arithmetical jugglers have calculated the amount to which a penny, invested at compound interest at the time of Christ, would have grown by now. The result is so striking that one might very well ask why nobody was clever enough to reap a fortune this way. But quite apart from all the other obstacles to such a course of action, there is the crowning disability that to every capital investment is attached the risk of a total or partial loss of the original capital sum. This is true not only of the entrepreneur's investment, but also
of the investment the capitalist makes in lending to the entrepreneur, for his 380
investment naturally depends completely on the entrepreneur's. His risk is smaller, because the entrepreneur offers him as security that part of his own wealth which is outside the immediate undertaking, but qualitatively the two risks are the same. The moneylender too can, and often does, lose his wealth.[6]

An eternal capital investment is as non-existent as a secure one. Every capital investment is speculative; its success cannot be foreseen with absolute assurance. Not even the idea of an "eternal and secure" capital yield could have arisen if the concepts of capital investment had been taken from the sphere of business and capital enterprise. The ideas of eternity and security come from rents secured on landed property and from the related government securities. It corresponds to actual conditions when the law recognizes as

---

[6] This is quite apart from the effects of currency depreciation.

trustee investments only those which are in land or in incomes secured on land or afforded by the State or by other public corporations. In capitalist enterprise there is no secure income and no security of wealth. It is obvious that an entail invested in enterprises outside agriculture, forestry, and mining would be senseless.

If, then, capital sums do not grow of themselves, if for their maintenance alone, quite apart from their fructification and increase, successful speculation is constantly required, there can be no question whatever of a tendency for fortunes to grow bigger and bigger. Fortunes cannot grow; someone has to increase them.[7] For this the successful activity of an entrepreneur is needed. The capital reproduces itself, bears fruit and increases only so long as a successful and lucky investment endures. The more rapid the change in economic environment the shorter the time in which an investment is to be considered as good. For the making of new investments, for reorganization of production, for innovations in technique, abilities are needed which only a few possess. If under exceptional circumstances these are inherited from generation to generation, the successors are able to maintain the wealth left by their ancestors, even perhaps to increase it, despite the fact that it may have been split up on inheritance. But if, as is generally the case, the heirs
381 are not equal to the demands which life makes on an entrepreneur, the inherited wealth rapidly vanishes.

When rich entrepreneurs wish to perpetuate their wealth in the family they take refuge in land. The descendants of the Fuggers and the Welsers* live even today in considerable affluence, if not luxury, but they have long since ceased to be merchants and have transformed their wealth into landed property. They became members of the German nobility, differing in no way from other South German noble families. Numerous merchant families in other countries have undergone the same development; having become rich in trade and industry they have ceased to be merchants and entrepreneurs and have become landowners, not to increase their fortunes but to maintain them and transmit them to their children and their children's children. The

---

[7] Considerant tries to prove the theory of concentration with a metaphor borrowed from mechanics: "*Les capitaux suivent aujourd'hui sans contrepoids la loi de leur propre gravitation; c'est que, s'attirant en raison de leurs masses, les richesses sociales se concentrent de plus en plus entre les mains des grands possesseurs.*" ("Capital today follows, without any opposing force, the law of its own magnetism. Capital attracts capital to itself, by reason of its very size. Social wealth is concentrated more and more in the hands of the largest owners.") Quoted by Tugan-Baranowsky, *Der moderne Sozialismus in seiner geschichtlichen Entwicklung*, p. 62. That is word play, nothing more.

* The Fuggers and the Welsers were prominent, wealthy German families, descended respectively from Johannes Fugger, a successful weaver of the first half of the 19th century, and Bartholomeus Welser (d.1559), the head of a large banking and commercial firm (Pub.).

families which did otherwise soon disappeared in obscure poverty. There are few banking families whose business has existed for a hundred years or more, and a closer glance at the affairs of these few will show that they are generally commercially active only in administering fortunes really invested in land and mines. There are no ancient fortunes which thrive in the sense that they continually increase.

4

The Theory of Increasing Poverty

The theory of increasing poverty among the masses stands at the centre of Marxist thought as well as of older socialist doctrines. The accumulation of poverty parallels the accumulation of capital. It is the "antagonistic character of capitalist production" that "the accumulation of wealth at one pole" is simultaneously "accumulation of misery, work torture, slavery, ignorance, brutalization, and moral degeneracy at the other."[8] This is the theory of the progressive increase in the absolute poverty of the masses. Based on nothing but the tortuous processes of an abstruse system of thought, it need occupy us all the less in that it is gradually receding into the background, even in the writings of orthodox Marxian disciples and the official programmes of the Social-Democratic parties. Even Kautsky, during the revisionism quarrel,
was reduced to conceding that, according to all the facts, it was precisely in 382
the most advanced capitalist countries that physical misery was on the decline, and that the working classes had a higher standard of life than fifty years ago.[9] The Marxians still cling to the theory of increasing poverty purely on account of its propaganda value, and exploit it today just as much as during the youth of the now aged Party.

But intellectually the theory of the relative growth of poverty, developed by Rodbertus, has replaced the theory of absolute growth. "Poverty," says Rodbertus, "is a social, that is, a relative, concept. Now, I maintain that the justifiable needs of the working classes, since these have attained a higher social position, have become considerably more numerous. It would be as wrong, now that they have attained this position, not to speak, even with unchanged wages, of a deterioration in their material condition as it would

---

[8] Marx, *Das Kapital*, Vol. I, p. 611. Publisher's Note: In the English *Capital*, Vol. I, pp. 736–737.

[9] Kautsky, *Bernstein und das Sozialdemokratische Programm* (Stuttgart, 1899), p. 116.

have been at an earlier stage when their wages fell, and they had not yet attained this position."[10] This thought is derived entirely from the point of view of the State Socialist, which considers a raising of the workers' claims to be "justified" and assigns them a "higher position" in the social order. Against arbitrary judgments of this kind, no argument is possible.

The Marxians have taken over the doctrine of the relative growth of poverty. "If in the course of evolution the grandson of a small master weaver, who had lived with his own journeymen, comes to inhabit a palatial, magnificently furnished villa, while the journeyman's grandson lives in lodgings, which though more comfortable, no doubt, than his grandfather's garret in the master weaver's house, yet serves to widen the social gulf between the two, then the journeyman's grandson will feel his poverty all the more for seeing the comforts that are within his employer's reach. His own position is better than his ancestor's, his standard of living has risen, but relatively his situation has become worse. Social misery becomes greater . . . the workers relatively more wretched."[11] Assuming that this were true, it would be no indictment against the capitalist system. If Capitalism improves the economic position all round, it is of secondary importance that it does not raise all to the same level. A social order is not bad simply because it helps
383 one more than another. If I am doing better, what can it harm me that others are doing better still? Must one destroy Capitalism which better satisfies from day to day the wants of all people, merely because some individuals become rich and a few of them very rich? How, then, can it be asserted as "logically unassailable" that "a growth in the relative poverty of the masses . . . must finally end in catastrophe."[12]

Kautsky tries to make his conception of the Marxian theory of increasing poverty different from that which emerges from an unprejudiced reading of *Das Kapital*. "The word poverty," he says, "may mean physical poverty, but it may also mean social poverty. In the first sense it is measured by man's physiological needs. These are indeed not everywhere and at all times the same, still they do not show differences nearly so great as the social needs, non-satisfaction of which produces social poverty."[13] It is social poverty, says Kautsky, that Marx had in mind. Considering the clarity and precision of Marx's style this interpretation is a masterpiece of sophistry, and it was accordingly rejected by the revisionists. To the person who does not take

---

[10] Rodbertus, "Erster sozialer Brief an v. Kirchmann" (Ausgabe von Zeller, *Zur Erkenntnis unserer staatwirtschaftlichen Zustände*, 2nd ed. (Berlin, 1885), p. 273 n.

[11] Herman Müller, *Karl Marx und die Gewerkschaften* (Berlin, 1918) pp. 82 ff.

[12] As is done by Ballod, *Der Zukunftsstaat*, 2nd ed. (Stuttgart, 1919), p. 12.

[13] Kautsky, *Bernstein und das Sozialdemokratische Programm*, p. 116.

Marx's words as revelation it may, indeed, be a matter of indifference whether the theory of increasing social poverty is contained in the first volume of *Das Kapital* or is taken from Engels or was first put forward by the neo-Marxists. The important questions are whether it is tenable and what conclusions follow from it.

Kautsky holds that the growth of poverty in the social sense is "attested by the bourgeoisie themselves, only they have given the matter a different name; they call it *covetousness* . . . The decisive fact is that the contrast between the wage-earners' needs and the possibility of satisfying them out of wages, the contrast therefore between wage-earning and capital, is becoming greater and greater."[14] Covetousness has always existed, however; it is no new phenomenon. We may even admit that it is more prevalent now than formerly; the general striving after improvement of economic position is a peculiarly characteristic mark of capitalist society. But how one can conclude from this that the capitalist order of society must necessarily change into the socialist, is inexplicable.

The fact is, that the doctrine of increasing relative social poverty is nothing
more than an attempt to give an economic justification to policies based on 384
the resentment of the masses. Growing social poverty means merely growing envy.[15] Mandeville and Hume, two of the greatest observers of human nature, have remarked that the intensity of envy depends on the distance between the envier and the envied. If the distance is great one does not compare oneself with the envied, and, in fact, no envy is felt. The smaller the distance, however, the greater the envy.[16] Thus one can deduce from the growth of resentment in the masses that inequalities of income are diminishing. The increasing "covetousness" is not, as Kautsky thinks, a proof of the relative growth of poverty; on the contrary, it shows that the economic distance between the classes is becoming less and less.

---

[14] *Ibid.*, p. 120.

[15] Compare the remarks of Weitling, quoted in Sombart, *Der proletarische Sozialismus* (Jena, 1924), Vol. I, p. 106.

[16] Hume, *A Treatise of Human Nature*, Philosophical Works, ed. Green and Grose (London, 1874), Vol. II, pp. 162 ff.; Mandeville, *Bienenfabel*, ed. Bobertag (Munich, 1914), p. 123. Publisher's Note: In English, Mandeville, *The Fable of the Bees*, ed. F. B. Kaye (Oxford University Press, 1924), pp. 135–136; Schatz, *L'Individualisme économique et social* (Paris, 1907), p. 73 n2, calls this an "*idée fondamentale pour bien comprendre la cause profonde des antagonismes sociaux.*" ("Fundamental idea for a good understanding of the profound cause of social animosities.")

CHAPTER 26

Monopoly and Its Effects

1

The Nature of Monopoly and its Significance for the Formation of Prices

385 No other part of economic theory has been so much misunderstood as the theory of monopoly. The mere mention of the word monopoly usually stirs up emotions which make clear judgment impossible and provokes, instead of economic arguments, the usual moral indignation evinced in etatistic and other anti-capitalist literature. Even in the United States the controversy raging over the trust problem has supplanted all impartial discussion of the problem of monopoly.

The widespread view that the monopolist can fix prices at will, that—in common phrase—he can dictate prices, is as erroneous as the conclusion, derived from this view, that he has in his hands the power to do whatever he likes. This could only be the case if the commodity monopolized were, by its very essence, completely outside the range of other goods. A man who could monopolize the atmosphere or drinking water could undoubtedly force all other human beings to obey him blindly. Such a monopoly would be unhampered by any competing economic agency. The monopolist would be able to dispose freely of the lives and property of his fellowmen. Such monopolies, however, do not come under our theory of monopoly. Water and air are free goods, and where they are not free—as in the case of water on a mountain top—one can evade the effect of monopoly by moving to a different place. Perhaps the nearest approach to such a monopoly was the power to administer grace to believers, exercised by the medieval Church. Excommunication and interdict were no less terrible than death from thirst or suffocation. In a socialist community the State as organized society would form such a monopoly. All economic goods would be united in its hands and it would therefore be in a position to force the citizen to fulfil its commands, would in fact confront the individual with a choice between obedience and starvation.

The only monopolies which concern us here are trade monopolies. They 386
affect only economic goods which, however important and indispensable they may seem, do not of themselves exert any decisive power over human life. When a commodity of which a definite minimum is essential to everyone who wishes to go on living, falls under a monopoly, then indeed do all those consequences popularly assigned to monopolies inevitably follow. But we need not discuss this hypothesis. It is of no practical importance as it lies outside the range of economics, and therefore of price theory—except in the case of strikes in certain enterprises.[1] A distinction between goods which are essential to life and those which are not, is sometimes made when the effects of monopoly are being considered. But these supposedly indispensable commodities are, strictly speaking, not what they seem. As the whole argument is based on the strict concept of indispensability, we have first of all to consider whether we have to deal with indispensability in the exact and full meaning of the word. Actually we can dispense with the commodities in question, either by renouncing the services we obtain from them or by procuring those services from some alternative commodity. Bread is certainly an important commodity. Yet one can live without it, by living on potatoes, cakes made from maize, and so on. Coal, so important today that it might be called the bread of industry, is not, in the strict sense of the word, indispensable, for power and heat can be produced without coal too. And this is all that matters. The concept "monopoly" which alone concerns us here is that contained in the theory of price monopoly and is the only one which contributes materially to an understanding of economic conditions; it does not demand that a monopolized commodity shall be indispensable, unique, and without substitute. It assumes only the absence of perfect competition on the side of supply.[2]

Such loose concepts of monopoly are, moreover, not merely inappropriate; they are also theoretically misleading. They lead to the supposition that price phenomena can be explained without further investigation by demonstrating a monopolistic condition. Having once laid it down that the monopolist "dictates" prices, that his attempt to raise prices as high as possible could only be restrained by a "power" influencing the market from outside, such 387
theorists proceed to render the concept of monopoly so elastic as to include all commodities not increasable or only increasable with increasing costs. As this already comprises most price phenomena, they are able to avoid the necessity of working out a theory of prices themselves. As a result many

---

[1] See p. 437.

[2] As there cannot be any question here of giving a theory of monopoly price, the monopoly of supply alone is examined.

come to speak of the monopoly ownership of land and believe that they have solved the problem of rent by pointing out that this monopolistic relation exists. Others go further and seek to explain interest, profit, and even wages as monopoly prices and monopoly profits. Quite apart from other defects in these "explanations," their authors fail to perceive that, while alleging that a monopoly exists, they say nothing at all about the nature of price formation and that therefore the catchword monopoly is no substitute for a properly developed theory of prices.[3]

The laws determining monopoly prices are the same as those which determine other prices. The monopolist cannot ask any price he fancies. The price offers with which he enters the market influence the attitude of the buyers. Demand expands or contracts according to the price he demands, and he has to reckon with this like any other seller. The one and only peculiarity of monopoly is that, assuming a certain shape for the demand curve, the maximum net profit lies at a higher price than would have been the case in competition between sellers.[4] If we assume these conditions and if the monopolist cannot so discriminate as to exploit the purchasing power of each class of buyers, it pays him better to sell at the higher monopoly price than at the lower competitive price, even though sales are thereby diminished. Therefore, monopoly under such conditions has three results: the market price is higher, the profit is greater, both the quantity sold and the consumption are smaller than they would have been under free competition.

The last of these results must be examined more closely. If there is more of the monopolized commodity than can be placed at the monopoly price
388 the monopolist must lock up or destroy so many surplus units that the remainder may attain the price needed. Thus the Dutch East India Company, which monopolized the European coffee market in the seventeenth century, destroyed some of its stocks. Other monopolists have done likewise: the Greek Government, for instance, destroyed currants in order to raise the price. Economically only one verdict on these proceedings is possible: they diminish the stock of wealth which serves to satisfy needs, they reduce

[3] Ely, *Monopolies and Trusts* (New York, 1900), pp. 11 ff.; Vogelstein, "Die finanzielle Organisation der kapitalistischen Industrie und die Monopolbildungen" (*op. cit.*, p. 231) too, and following him the German Socialization Commission (*op. cit.*, pp. 31 ff.), start from a concept of monopoly which comes very close to the views criticized by Ely and generally abandoned by the price theory of modern science.

[4] Carl Menger, *Grundsätze der Volkswirtschaftslehre* (Vienna, 1871), p. 195; further Forchheimer, "Theoretisches zum unvollständigen Monopole" (*Schmoller's Jahrbuch* XXXII), pp. 3 ff. Publisher's Note: In English, Menger, *Principles of Economics*, trans. and ed. James Dingwall and Bert F. Hoselitz (Glencoe, Illinois: The Free Press, 1950), pp. 211 ff.

welfare, they diminish riches. That goods which could have satisfied wants, and foodstuffs which could have stilled the hunger of the many, should be destroyed is a state of things which the outraged populace and the discerning economist unite, for once, in condemning.

Even in monopolistic undertakings, however, destruction of economic goods is rare. The far-sighted monopolist does not produce goods for the incinerator. If he wishes to place fewer goods on the market he takes steps to reduce his output. The problem of monopoly must be considered, not from the point of view of goods destroyed, but from that of production restricted.

2

The Economic Effects of Isolated Monopolies

Whether the monopolist can exploit his position at all depends on the shape of the demand curve of the monopolized commodity and on the costs of producing the marginal unit of the commodity at the existing scale of production. Only when the conditions are such that the sale of a smaller quantity at higher prices yields a greater net profit than the sale of a larger quantity at lower prices, is it possible to apply the specific principle of monopolistic policy.[5] But even then it is applied only if the monopolist fails to find a method of securing still higher profits. The monopolist serves his interests best if he can separate buyers into classes according to their purchasing power, for he can then exploit the purchasing power of each class separately and exact the highest prices from its members. Railways and other transport undertakings, which grade their tariffs according to what the traffic will bear are in this class. If, following the general method of monopolists, 389
they treated all users of transport uniformly, those less able to pay would be excluded from transport and for those able to stand higher charges transport would be cheapened. The effect of this on the local distribution of industry is clear; amongst the factors determining the localization of individual industries the transport factor would make itself felt in a different way.

[5] Compare on this important principle the large literature on the monopoly price. For example, Wieser, "Theorie der gesellschaftlichen Wirtschaft," in *Grundriss für Sozialökonomik*, Part I (Tübingen, 1914), p. 276.

In examining the economic effect of monopoly, we must limit investigation to the type which restricts the production of its commodity. Now the result of this restriction is not that less is produced quantitatively. Capital and labour, set free by the restriction of production, must find employment in other production. For in the long run in the free economy there is neither unemployed capital nor unemployed labour. Thus against the smaller production of the monopolized goods one must set the increased production of other goods. But these, of course, are less important goods, which would not have been produced and consumed if the more pressing demands for a larger quantity of the monopolized commodity could have been satisfied. The difference between the value of these goods and the higher value of the quantity of the monopolized commodity not produced represents the loss of welfare which the monopoly has inflicted on the national economy. Here private profit and social productivity are at variance. A social society under such circumstances would act differently from a capitalist society.

It has sometimes been pointed out that although the monopoly can prove harmful to the consumer it might, on the other hand, be turned to his advantage. Monopoly could produce more cheaply because it eliminates all the expenses of competition and because, being adapted to large scale operations it enjoys all advantages of the division of labour. But this in no wise alters the fact that monopoly deflects production from more important products to less important ones. It may be as the defender of trusts is fond of repeating, that the monopolist, unable to increase his profit otherwise, endeavours to improve productive technique, but it is difficult to understand why the urge to this should be greater in him than in the competitive producer. Even if this be admitted, however, it does not alter what we have said about the social effects of monopoly.

390

3

The Limits of Monopoly Formation

The possibility of monopolizing the market varies radically with different goods. Even the producer who is protected from competition need not necessarily be in a position to sell at monopoly prices and obtain monopoly profits. If the quantity sold falls so steeply with the rise of prices that the extra sum obtained does not cover the deficiency in the number sold, then the monopolist is forced to content himself with the price which would have emerged under competitive selling.[6]

[6] According to Wieser, *ibid.*, this is "perhaps even the rule."

Apart from the enjoyment of artificial support—the grant of special legal privileges, for example—we shall find that a monopoly can, as a rule, maintain itself only by the exclusive power to dispose of certain natural factors of production. Similar power over reproducible means of production does not as a rule allow permanent monopolization. New enterprises may always spring up. As already pointed out, the progressive division of labour tends towards a condition in which, at the highest specialization of production, everyone will be the sole producer of one or several articles. But this would by no means necessarily involve a monopolized market for all these articles. The attempts of manufacturers to extract monopoly prices would, apart from other circumstances, be checked by the appearance of new competitors.

Experience of cartels and trusts during the last generation completely confirms this. All enduring monopolistic organizations are built up on the power of the monopoly to dispose of natural resources or of particular land sites. A man who tried to become a monopolist without the control of such resources—and without special legal aids such as tariffs, patents, etc.—had to resort to all sorts of tricks and artifices to secure even a temporary success. The complaints raised against cartels and trusts and investigated by the commissions of inquiry whose published records are so voluminous, deal almost exclusively with these tricks and practices, which aim at creating monopolies artificially where the conditions for them do not exist. Most cartels and trusts would never have been set up had not the governments created the necessary conditions by protectionist measures. Manufacturing and commercial monopolies owe their origin not to a tendency immanent 391
in capitalist economy but to governmental interventionist policy directed against free trade and *laisser-faire*.

Without the special power to dispose of natural resources, or of advantageously situated land, monopolies could arise only where the capital required to erect a competing enterprise was not able to count on an adequate return. A railway company can achieve a monopoly where it would not pay to build a competing line, the traffic being too small for two lines to be profitable. The same may be true in other cases. But while this shows that a few monopolies of this kind are possible it does not reveal a general tendency to their formation.

The effect of such monopolies, e.g. the railway company or the electric power plant, is that the monopolist may be able, according to the circumstances of the case, to absorb a greater or smaller quantity of the ground rents of adjoining properties. The result of this may be a change in the distribution of income and property which is felt to be disagreeable—at least, by those directly affected.

4

The Significance of Monopoly in Primary Production

In an economy based on private ownership in the means of production, specific primary production is the only field liable to monopolization without special protection from the State. Monopolies in certain branches of primary production are possible. Mining, in the widest sense of the word, is their true domain. Where today we have monopolistic structures which do not spring from government intervention, they are—apart from such instances as the railway company and the power works—almost exclusively organizations built up on a power to dispose of certain kinds of natural resources. These natural resources must be such as are found in relatively few places, for this alone makes the monopoly possible. A world monopoly of potato farmers or milk producers is unthinkable.[7] Potatoes and milk, or at least substitutes for them, can be produced over the greater part of the earth's surface. World monopolies of oil, mercury, zinc, nickel, and other materials
392 can occasionally be formed if the owners of the rare places where they exist can combine; examples of this are found in the history of recent years.

When such a monopoly is formed the higher monopoly price replaces the competitive price. The income of mine owners rises, production and consumption of their product fall. A quantity of capital and labour which would otherwise have been active in this branch of production is diverted to other fields. If we consider the effects of monopoly from the standpoint of the separate branches of world economy we see only the rise in the monopolists' income and the corresponding decline in the income of all other branches. Considered, however, from the standpoint of world economy and *subspecie aeternitatis* (from the point of view of eternity), monopolies would appear to economize consumption of irreplaceable natural resources. People come to deal more thriftily with these precious resources when as in mining, the monopoly price occasionally replaces the competitive price and they are driven to do less digging and more working up. Since in every mine in operation nature's irreplaceable gift to man is being used up, the less we touch this stock the better we provide for the supply of coming generations. We see now what it means when people detect in monopoly a conflict between social productivity and private profit. True, a socialist community would have no occasion to restrict production as Capitalism does under

[7] It is different, perhaps, with agricultural productions which flourish only on relatively restricted soils; for example, coffee growing.

monopolies, but this would only mean that Socialism would deal less thriftily with irreplaceable natural treasures, that it would sacrifice the future to the present.

When we find that monopoly causes a conflict between profit and productivity which is not to be found anywhere else, we do not necessarily say that the effects of monopoly are pernicious. The naive assumption that the behavior of the socialist community—as typifying the idea of productivity—constitutes the Absolute Good is quite arbitrary. We have no standard on which to base a valid decision between what is good and what is evil in this context.

If, then, we consider the effects of monopoly without being biased by popular writers on cartels and trusts, we can discover nothing which could justify the assertion that growing monopolization makes the capitalist system intolerable. The monopolist's scope in a capitalist economy free from state interference is much smaller than this type of writer commonly assumes; and the consequences of monopoly must be judged by other standards than the mere catchwords Price Dictation and the Rule of the Trust Magnates.

PART IV
SOCIALISM AS A MORAL IMPERATIVE

CHAPTER 27

Socialism and Ethics

1

The Socialist Attitude to Ethics

For pure Marxism Socialism is not a political programme. It does not 395
demand that society shall be transformed into the socialist order, nor does it condemn the liberal order of society. It presents itself as a scientific theory which claims to have discovered in the dynamic laws of historical development a movement towards the socialization of the means of production. To say that pure Marxism pronounces itself in favour of Socialism or that it desires Socialism or wishes to bring it about would be just as absurd as to say that Astronomy wishes or thought it desirable to bring about a solar eclipse which it had predicted. We know that Marx's life and even many of his writings and sayings sharply contradict his theoretic outlook and that the Socialism of resentment is always showing its cloven hoof. In practical politics at least, his supporters have long since forgotten what they owe strictly to his doctrine. Their words and deeds go far beyond what the "midwife theory" permits.[1] This, however, is of secondary importance for our study, which here deals only with the doctrine pure and undefiled.

Besides the pure Marxist view that Socialism must come of inexorable necessity, there are two other motives which guide the advocates of Communism. They are socialists either because they expect socialist society to increase productivity, or because they believe that a socialist society would be more just. Marxism is unable to reconcile itself to ethical Socialism. But

[1] How little the Social-Democrats have made this fundamental doctrine of Marxism their own, one sees from a glance at their literature. A leader of German Social-Democracy, the former German Minister of National Economy Wissell, confesses succinctly: "I am Socialist and shall remain Socialist, for I see in socialist economy, with its subordination of the Individual to the Whole, the expression of a higher moral principle than that which lies at the basis of individualistic economy." *Praktische Wirtschaftspolitik* (Berlin, 1919), p. 53.

its attitude to economic-rationalist Socialism is quite different: it is possible
396 to interpret the materialistic conception of history as meaning that the trend of economic development naturally leads to the most productive type of economy, that is to say Socialism. Of course, this view is very different from that held by the majority of Marxists. They are for Socialism, firstly because it is bound to come in any case, secondly because it is morally preferable, and finaliy because it involves more rational economic organization.

The two motives of non-Marxian Socialism are mutually exclusive. If a man advocates Socialism because he expects it to increase the productivity of social labour he need not try to bolster up his demands with a higher moral valuation of the socialist order. If he elects to do so, he is open to the question whether he would be prepared to advocate Socialism if he discovered that it was after all not the morally perfect order. On the other hand it is clear that one who advocates the socialistic order for moral reasons would have to go on doing so even if he were convinced that the order based on private ownership in the means of production yielded greater productivity of labour.

2

Eudaemonistic Ethics and Socialism

To eudaemonism, which looks at social phenomena rationalistically, the very way in which ethical Socialism states its problems seems unsatisfactory. Unless Ethics and "Economy" are regarded as two systems of objectivization which have nothing to do with each other, then ethical and economic valuation and judgment cannot appear as mutually independent factors. All ethical ends are merely a part of human aims. This implies that on the one hand the ethical aim is a means, in so far as it assists in the human struggle for happiness, but that on the other hand it is comprised in the process of valuation which unites all intermediate aims into a unitary scale of values and grades them according to their importance. The conception of absolute ethical values, which might be opposed to economic values, cannot therefore be maintained.

Of course one cannot discuss this point with the ethical apriorist or the intuitionist. Those who uphold the Moral as ultimate fact, and who rule out scientific examination of its elements by referring to a transcendental origin, will never be able to agree with those who are dragging down the concept of Right into the dust of scientific analysis. Ethical ideas of duty and conscience demand nothing less than the blindest submission.[2] *A priori* ethics, claiming unconditional validity for its norms, approaches all earthly relations from the outside and aims at transmuting them into its own form with no concern whatever for the consequences. *Fiat iustitia, pereat mundus* (let justice be done even though the world be destroyed) is its motto, and it is when it becomes honestly indignant about the eternally misunderstood plea, "the end justifies the means," that it is most sincere. 397

Isolated man settles all his ends according to his own law. He sees and knows nothing but himself and arranges his actions accordingly. In society, however, he must temper his actions to the fact that he lives in society and that his actions must affirm the existence and progress of society. From the basic law of social life it follows that he does not do this to achieve aims lying outside his own personal system of ends. In making the social ends his own he does not thereby subordinate his personality and his wishes to those of a higher personality or renounce the fulfilment of any of his own desires in favour of those of a mystical universe. For, from the standpoint of his own valuation, social ends are not ultimate but intermediate in his own scale of values. He must accept society because social life helps him to fulfil his own wishes more completely. If he denied it he would be able to create only transitory advantages for himself; by destroying the social body he would in the long run injure himself.

The idea of a dualism of motivation assumed by most ethical theorists, when they distinguish between egoistic and altruistic motives of action, cannot therefore be maintained. This attempt to contrast egoistic and altruistic action springs from a misconception of the social interdependence of individuals. The power to choose whether my actions and conduct shall serve myself or my fellow beings is not given to me—which perhaps may be regarded as fortunate. If it were, human society would not be possible. In the society based on division of labour and co-operation, the interests of all members are in harmony, and it follows from this basic fact of social life that ultimately action in the interests of myself and action in the interest of others do not conflict, since the interests of individuals come together in the end.
Thus the famous scientific dispute as to the possibility of deriving the altruistic 398
from the egoistic motives of action may be regarded as definitely disposed of.

There is no contrast between moral duty and selfish interests. What the individual gives to society to preserve it as society, he gives, not for the sake

[2] Jodl, *Geschichte der Ethik als philosophischer Wissenschaft*, Vol. II, 2nd ed. (Stuttgart, 1921), p. 450.

of aims alien to himself, but in his own interest.[3] The individual, who is a product of society not only as a thinking, willing, sentient man, but also simply as a living creature, cannot deny society without denying himself.

This position of social ends in the system of individual ends is perceived by the individual's reason, which enables him to recognize aright his own interests. But society cannot always trust the individual to see which are his true interests. If it left everyone to judge of his own it would expose itself to the caprice of every foolish, sick, and weak-willed person, leaving him free to put its very existence into question, thus imperilling the continuity of development. This is what led to the creation of powers of social coercion which, *vis-à-vis* the individual, appear as external constraints because they demand imperative obedience. And here we see the social significance of the State and the Law. They are not something outside the individual, demanding from him actions which run counter to his own interests, forcing him to serve alien purposes. They merely prevent the misguided, asocial individual, blind to his own interests, from injuring his fellow men by a revolt against the social order.

It is therefore absurd to maintain that Liberalism, Utilitarianism and Eudaemonism are "inimical to the State." They reject the idea of Etatism, which under the name State adores as God a mysterious being not comprehensible to human understanding; they dissent from Hegel, to whom the State is "divine will"; they reject the Hegelian Marx and his school who have replaced the cult of "State" with the cult of "Society"; they combat all those who want the State or "Society" to perform tasks other than those corresponding to that social order which they themselves believe the most proper to the end in view. Because they favour private ownership in the means of production they demand that the State coercive apparatus shall be directed to maintain this, and they reject all proposals intended to restrict or abolish private property. But never for a moment do they think of "abolishing the State." The liberal conception of society by no means omits the apparatus of the
399 State; it assigns to this the task of safeguarding life and property. Anybody who calls opposition to State railways, State theatres, or State dairies "enmity to the State" must be deeply enmeshed indeed in the realistic (in the scholastic sense) conception of the State.

Occasionally society can prevail against the individual even without coercion. Not every social norm requires that the most extreme coercive measures shall at once be put into force. In many things, morals and custom can wring from the individual a recognition of social aims without assistance from the

[3] Izoulet, *La cité moderne*, pp. 413 ff.

sword of justice. Morals and customs go further than State law in so far as they protect more extensive social aims. In this respect, there may be a difference in extent between them, but no incompatibility of principle. Essential contrasts between the legal order and moral laws occur only where the two derive from different conceptions of the social order, that is, where they appertain to different social systems. The contrast is then dynamic, not static.

The ethical valuation "good" or "evil" can be applied only in respect of ends towards which action strives. As Epicurus said: "Αδιχία οὐ χαθ' ἑαυτην χαχόν" ("Vice without injurious consequences would not be vice.")[4] Since action is never its own end, but rather the means to an end, we call an action good or evil only in respect of the consequences of the action. It is judged according to its place in the system of cause and effect. It is valued as a means. And for the value of the means the valuation of the end is decisive. Ethical, like all other, valuation proceeds from valuation of ends, of the ultimate good. The value of an action is the value of the end it serves. Intention, too, has value in so far as it leads to action.

Unity of action can exist only when all ultimate values can be brought into a unitary scale of values. If this were not possible, man would always be finding himself in a position where he could not act, that is, work as a creature conscious of his striving towards a goal; he would have to abandon the issue to forces beyond his control. Conscious scaling of values precedes every human action. The man who chooses to attain A while renouncing B, C, D, etc., has decided that in the given circumstances the attainment of A is more valuable to him than the attainment of the others.

Philosophers had been arguing about this ultimate Good for a long time 400
before it was settled by modern investigation. At the present day Eudaemonism is no longer open to attack. In the long run all the arguments which philosophers from Kant to Hegel brought against it were unable to dissociate the concept Morality from that of Happiness. Never in history has more intellect and ingenuity been expended in defending an untenable position. We are lost in admiration of the magnificent performance of these philosophers. We might almost say that what they have done to prove the impossible elicits more admiration than the achievements of the great thinkers and sociologists who have made Eudaemonism and Utilitarianism a permanent possession of the human mind. Certainly their efforts were not in vain. Their gigantic struggle for anti-eudaemonistic ethics were necessary to expose the problem in all its wide ramifications and so enable a conclusive solution to be reached.

---

[4] Guyau, *Die englische Ethik der Gegenwart*, trans. Peusner (Leipzig, 1914), p. 20.

Since the tenets of intuitionist ethics, which are irreconcilable with scientific method, have been deprived of their very foundations, anyone who recognizes the eudaemonistic character of all ethical valuation is exempt from further discussion of ethical Socialism. For such a one the Moral does not stand outside the scale of values which comprises all values of life. For him no moral ethic is valid *per se*. He must first be allowed to inquire why it is so rated. He can never reject that which has been recognized as beneficial and reasonable simply because a norm, based on some mysterious intuition, declares it to be immoral—a norm the sense and purpose of which he is not entitled even to investigate.[5] His principle is not *fiat iustitia, pereat mundus*, (let justice be done, though the world perish), but *fiat iustitia, ne pereat mundus* (let justice be done, lest the world perish).

If nevertheless it appears not entirely superfluous to discuss separately the arguments of ethical Socialism, this is not merely because it counts many adherents, but, what is more important, because it provides an opportunity of showing how eudaemonistic ideas lie concealed in every train of aprioristic-intuitive ethical thought, and how this system can be traced back, in every one of its utterances, to untenable notions of economic conduct and of social co-operation. Every ethical system built up on the idea of duty, even though it exhibits itself as strictly as Kant's, is finally obliged to yield so much to
401 Eudaemonism that its principles can no longer be maintained.[6] In the same way every single requirement of aprioristic-intuitive ethics displays ultimately an eudaemonistic character.

3

A Contribution to the Understanding of Eudaemonism

Formalist ethics takes its differences with Eudaemonism altogether too lightly when it interprets the happiness of which the latter speaks as satisfaction of sensual desires. More or less consciously, formalistic ethics foists upon Eudaemonism the assertion that all human striving is directed solely towards filling the belly and the basest forms of sensual enjoyment. It is of course not to be denied that the thoughts and endeavors of many, very many people are concentrated on these things. This, however, is no fault of social

[5] Bentham, *Deontology or the Science of Morality*, ed. Bowring (London, 1834), Vol. I, pp. 8 ff.
[6] Mill, *Utilitarianism* (London, 1863), pp. 5 ff.; Jodl, *Geschichte der Ethik als philosophischer Wissenschaft*, Vol. II, p. 36.

science, which merely points it out as a fact. Eudaemonism does not advise men to strive after happiness; it merely shows that human striving necessarily tends in this direction. And after all, happiness is not to be found only in sexual enjoyment and a good digestion.

The energistic conception of the Moral sees the highest good in fulfilling oneself, in the full exercise of one's own powers, and this is perhaps only another way of saying what eudaemonists have in mind when they speak of happiness. The happiness of the strong and the healthy certainly does not lie in idle dreaming. But when this conception is contrasted with Eudaemonism it becomes untenable. What are we to make of Guyau when he says: "Life is not calculation, but action. In every living being there is a store of strength, a surplus of energy, which strives to spend itself, *not for the sake of the accompanying pleasurable sensations but because it must spend itself . . . Duty* derives from *strength*, which necessarily urges towards action."[7] Action means working with a conscious end, that is, on a basis of reflection and calculation. Guyau is guilty of a lapse into intuitionism, which he otherwise rejects, when he represents a mysterious urge as the guide of moral action. In the *idées-forces* of Fouillée the intuitionist element is still more clearly revealed.[8]
What *was* thought is supposed to urge towards realization. But presumably 402
this is only when the end, which the action serves, seems desirable. To the question why an end appears good or evil, however, Fouillée offers no reply.

Nothing is gained when the teacher of morals constructs an absolute ethic without reference to the nature of man and his life. The declamations of philosophers cannot alter the fact that life strives to live itself out, that the living being seeks pleasure and avoids pain. All one's scruples against acknowledging this as the basic law of human actions fall away as soon as the fundamental principle of social co-operation is recognized. That everyone lives and wishes to live primarily for himself does not disturb social life but promotes it, for the higher fulfilment of the individual's life is possible only in and through society. This is the true meaning of the doctrine that egoism is the basic law of society.

The highest demand that Society makes of the individual is the sacrifice of his life. Though all other restrictions of his action which the individual has to accept from society may be considered ultimately in his own interests, this, says the anti-eudaemonistic ethic, can be explained by no method which smooths over the opposition between individual and general interests. The hero's death may be useful to the community, but that is no great consolation

[7] Guyau, *Sittlichkeit ohne "Pflicht,"* pp. 272 ff.

[8] Fouillée, *Humanitaires et libertaires au point de vue sociologique et moral*, pp. 157 ff.

to him. Only an ethic based on duty could help one over this difficulty. On closer considerations we see that this objection may be easily disproved. When society's existence is threatened, each individual must risk his best to avoid destruction. Even the prospect of perishing in the attempt can no longer deter him. For there is then no choice between either living on as one formerly lived or sacrificing oneself for one's country, for society, or for one's convictions. Rather, must the certainty of death, servitude, or insufferable poverty be set against the chance of returning victorious from the struggle. War carried on *pro aris et focis* (for our altars and our hearths) demands no sacrifice from the individual. One does not engage in it merely to reap benefits for others, but to preserve one's own existence. This of course, is only true of wars in which individuals fight for their very existence. It is not true of wars which are merely a means of enrichment, such as the quarrels of feudal lords or the cabinet wars of princes. Thus Imperialism, ever covetous of conquests, cannot do without an ethic which demands from the individual "sacrifices" for the "good of the State."

403 The long fight carried on by moralists against the convenient eudaemonistic explanation of the Moral finds its counterpart in the efforts of economists to solve the problem of economic value otherwise than through the utility of consumption goods. Economists had nothing nearer to hand than the idea of value as reflecting in some way the significance of a commodity to human welfare, nevertheless the attempt to explain the phenomena of value with the help of this concept has been given up again and again and other theories of value have been persistently sought. This is because of the difficulties presented by the problem of the quantity of value. There was, for instance, the apparent contradiction that precious stones, satisfying an obviously minor want, have a higher value than bread, which satisfies one of the most important needs, and that air and water, without which man simply cannot live, are generally without value. The basis for erecting a theory of value on the utility of goods was laid only when the idea of a scale of importance of *classes* of wants was separated from that of the concrete wants themselves, and the fact recognized that the scale according to which the importance of the wants depending on the power to dispose of goods is judged, is that of the concrete wants themselves.[9]

The difficulty which the utilitarian-eudaemonistic explanation of the Moral had to overcome was not less than that with which economic theory had to fight in the effort to trace economic values back to utility. No one could

---

[9] Böhm-Bawerk, *Kapital und Kapitalzins*, 3rd ed., Part II (Innsbruck, 1909), pp. 233 ff. Publisher's Note: This is pp. 135 ff. in Volume II of the English edition.

discover how to bring eudaemonistic doctrine into harmony with the obvious fact that moral action consists just in the individual's avoiding actions which seem directly useful to him and doing that which seems directly harmful to him. Liberal social philosophy was the first to find the solution. It showed that by maintaining and developing the social bond each individual serves his highest interest, so that the sacrifices made in the fulfilment of social life are only temporary ones. He exchanges a smaller direct advantage for a considerably greater indirect advantage. Thus duty and interest coincide.[10] This is the meaning of the harmony of interests of which the liberal theory of society speaks.

---

[10] Bentham, *Deontology*, Vol. I, p. 87 ff.

CHAPTER 28

Socialism as an Emanation of Asceticism

1

The Ascetic Point of View

404 Withdrawal from the world and denial of life are, even from the religious point of view, not ultimate ends, pursued for their own sakes, but means to the attainment of certain transcendental ends. But though they appear in the believer's universe as means, they must be regarded as ultimate ends by an inquiry which cannot go beyond the limits of this life. In what follows, we shall mean by asceticism only that which is inspired by a philosophy of life or by religious motives. With these restrictions, asceticism is the subject of our study. We must not confuse it with that kind of asceticism which is only a means to certain earthly ends. If he is convinced of the poisonous effects of liquor, a man abstains from it either to protect his health generally or to steel his strength for a special effort. He is no ascetic in the sense defined above.

Nowhere has the idea of withdrawal from the world and denial of life been manifested more logically and completely than in the Indian religion of Jainism, which is able to look back on a history of 2500 years. "Homelessness," said Max Weber, "is the fundamental idea of salvation in Jainism. It means the breaking off of all earthly relations, and therefore, above all, indifference to general impressions and avoidance of all worldly motives, the ceasing to act, to hope, to desire. A man who has only the capacity left to feel and think 'I am I' is homeless in this sense. He wishes neither life nor death—because in either case it would mean desire, and that might wake Karma. He neither has friends nor raises objections to the actions of others towards him (for example, to the usual washing of feet which the pious person performs for the saint). He behaves according to the principle that one should not resist evil and that the individual's state of grace during life must be

tested by his capacity to bear trouble and pain."[1] Jainism prohibits most 405
strictly any killing of living beings. Orthodox Jains burn no light during the dark months because it would burn the moths, make no fire because it would kill insects, strain the water before boiling it, wear a mouth and nose veil to prevent themselves from inhaling insects. It is the highest piety to let oneself be tortured by insects without driving them away.[2]

Only a section of society can realize the ideal of ascetic living, for the ascetic cannot be a worker. The body that is exhausted by penitential exercises and castigations can do nothing but lie in passive contemplation and let things come to it or consume the rest of its strength in ecstatic trances and thus hasten the end. The ascetic who embarks on work and economic activity to earn for himself only the smallest quantity of the necessities of life abandons his principles. The history of monasticism, not only of Christian monasticism, reveals this. From being abodes of asceticism the monasteries sometimes became the seat of a refined enjoyment of life.

The non-working ascetic can only exist if asceticism is not obligatory for all. Since he cannot nourish himself without the labour of others, labourers must exist on whom he may live.[3] He needs tributary laymen. His sexual abstinence requires laymen who will bear successors. If this necessary complement is lacking, the race of ascetics quickly dies out. As a general rule of conduct asceticism would mean the end of the human race. The holocaust of his own life is the end towards which the individual ascetic strives, and though this principle may not include abstinence from all actions necessary to maintain life with the object of putting a premature end to it, it implies, by suppression of the sexual desire, the destruction of society. The ascetic ideal is the ideal of voluntary death. That no society can be built on the ascetic principle is too obvious to need closer explanation. For it is a destroyer of society and life.

This fact can be overlooked only because the ascetic ideal is seldom thought out, and still more seldom carried out, to its logical conclusion. The ascetic
in the forest who lives like the animals on roots and herbs is the only one 406
who lives and acts according to his principles. This strictly logical behaviour is rare; there are, after all, not many people who are prepared to renounce light-heartedly the fruits of culture, however much they may despise them in thought and abuse them in words, few who are willing to return without more ado to the way of life of the deer and the stag. St. Aegidius, one of St.

---

[1] Weber, *Gesammelte Aufsätze zur Religionssoziologie* (Tübingen, 1920), Vol. II, p. 206.

[2] *Ibid.*, p. 211.

[3] Weber, *op. cit.*, Vol. I, p. 262.

Francis's most zealous companions, found fault with the ants because they were too much preoccupied with collecting supplies; he approved only of the birds, because they do not store food in barns. For the birds in the air, the animals on earth, the fish in the sea, are satisfied when they have sufficient nourishment. He himself believed that he lived according to the same ideal when he fed himself with the labour of his hands and the collection of alms. When he went gleaning with the rest of the poor at harvest-time, and people wanted to add to his gleanings, he would refuse saying: "I have no barn for storing. I do not wish for one." Yet this saint did derive advantages from the economic order he condemned. His life in poverty, possibly only in and by this economic order, was infinitely better off than that of the fishes and birds he believed he was imitating. He received income for his labour out of the stores of an ordered economy. If others had not gathered in barns the saint would have gone hungry. Only if everybody else had taken the fish as their example, could he have known what it was to live like a fish. Critically disposed contemporaries recognized this. The English Benedictine, Matthew Paris, reports that Pope Innocent III advised St. Francis, after listening to his rule, to go to the swine, whom he resembled more than men, to roll with them in the mud, and to teach his rule to them.[4]

Ascetic morals can never have universal application as binding principles of life. The ascetic who acts logically passes voluntarily out of the world. Asceticism which seeks to maintain itself on earth does not carry its principles to the logical end; it stops at a certain point. It is immaterial by what sophistry it tries to explain this; it is sufficient that it does so and must do so. Moreover, it is compelled at least to tolerate non-ascetics. By thus developing a double morality, one for saints, one for worldlings, it splits ethics in two. The only truly moral folk are the monks, or whatever else they may be called, who
407 strive for perfection by asceticism. By splitting morality in this way asceticism renounces its claim to rule life. The only demand that it still ventures to make upon laymen is for small donations to keep the saint's body and soul together.

As a strict ideal, asceticism knows no satisfaction of wants at all. It is therefore non-economic in the most literal sense. The watered-down ideal of asceticism, conceived by the laymen of a society that reveres the asceticism of the perfect, or by monks living in a self-sufficient community, may demand only the most primitive hand to mouth production, but it by no means opposes the extreme rationalization of economic activity. On the contrary, it demands this. For, since all preoccupation with worldly matters keeps people away from the only purely moral way of life and is to be tolerated

[4] Glaser, *Die franziskanische Bewegung* (Stuttgart and Berlin, 1903), pp. 53 ff., 59.

at all only as a means to an intermediate—unfortunately unavoidable—purpose, then it is essential that this unholy activity should be as economical as possible, so as to reduce it to a minimum. Rationalization, desirable to the worldling in his efforts to reduce painful and increase pleasant sensations, is imposed upon the ascetic, to whom the painful sensations aroused by work and privation are valuable castigations, because it is his duty to devote himself to the transitory no longer than is absolutely necessary.

From the ascetic point of view too, therefore, socialistic production cannot be preferred to the capitalistic unless it is held to be more rational. Asceticism may recommend its devotees to limit the activities by which they satisfy their wants because it abhors a too comfortable existence. But within the limits which it leaves for the satisfaction of these wants, it cannot regard as right anything but what rational economy demands.

2

Asceticism and Socialism

Socialist thought at first cold-shouldered all principles of asceticism. It harshly rejected any consoling promise of a life after death and aimed at an earthly paradise for everybody. Neither the world to come nor any other religious inducements have any interest for it. Socialism's one aim was to guarantee that everyone should reach the highest standard of well-being attainable. Not self-denial, but enjoyment was its criterion. Socialist leaders *408*
have always definitely opposed all those who show themselves indifferent to the increase in productivity. They have pointed out that, to lessen the hardships of labour and increase the pleasures of enjoyment, the productivity of human labour must be multiplied. The grandiose gestures of degenerate scions of wealthy families in praise of the charms of poverty and the simple life made no appeal to them.

But on looking into this more closely, we may detect a gradual change in their attitude. In proportion as the uneconomic nature of socialistic production becomes apparent, socialists are beginning to transform their views on the desirability of a more abundant satisfaction of human wants. Many of them are even beginning to show some sympathy with writers who praise the Middle Ages and look with contempt on the riches which Capitalism adds to the means of existence.[5]

---

[5] Heichen, "Sozialismus und Ethik" in *Die Neue Zeit*, Vol. 38, Vol. 1, pp. 312 ff. Specially remarkable in this context are also the remarks of Charles Gide, "Le Matérialisme et l'Économie Politique" in *Le Matérialisme actuel* (Paris, 1924).

The assertion that we could be happy, or even happier, with fewer goods can no more be refuted than it can itself be proved. Of course, most people imagine that they have not enough material goods; and, because they value the increase of well-being that greater exertions on their part can bring more than they value the leisure which they would gain by renouncing it, they exhaust themselves by laborious work. But even if we admit the assertions of those semi-ascetics whose outlook we have been discussing, this by no means commits us to giving the socialist method of production precedence over the capitalist. For supposing too many goods are produced under Capitalism, the matter could be remedied quite simply by reducing the quantity of work to be done. The demand that we should reduce the productivity of labour by adopting a less fruitful way of production cannot be justified by such arguments.

CHAPTER 29

Christianity and Socialism

1

Religion and Social Ethics

Religion, not merely as a church but as a philosophy too, is like any other 409
raft of spiritual life, a product of men's social co-operation. Our thinking is by no means an individual phenomenon independent of all social relations and traditions; it has a social character by reason of the very fact that it follows methods of thought formed during millennia of co-operation between innumerable groups. And we, again, are able to take over these methods of thought only because we are members of society. Now, for exactly the same reasons, we cannot imagine religion as an isolated phenomenon. Even the mystic, who forgets his surroundings in awestruck joy as he experiences communion with his God, has not made his religion by his own efforts. The forms of thought which have led him to it are not his own individual creation; they belong to society. A Kaspar Hauser* cannot evolve a religion without help from outside. Religion, like everything else, has grown up historically, and is subject to the constant change that affects every social phenomenon.

But religion is also a social factor in the sense that it regards social relations from a special angle and sets up rules for human conduct in society accordingly. It cannot refuse to state its principles in matters of social ethics. No religion which sets out to give its devotees an answer to the problems of life, and to console them where they most need consolation, can rest content

* The first fact known positively about Kaspar Hauser is that he appeared in Nuremberg in 1828 with a letter purporting to give some of his background. According to the letter, he had been found in 1812, when only a few months old, by a German laborer who had raised him. The boy said that he had been confined in a dark room all his life until he was sent forth into the world. In time he was placed in the care of the German poet and philosopher, Georg Friedrich Daumer (1800–1875). Hauser died in 1833 from a wound inflicted, he said, by a stranger who had promised information about his origin. Many myths and romances developed over the years as to Hauser's true identity and ancestry (Pub.).

with interpreting the relations of man to Nature, to becoming, and to passing away. If it leaves out the relations of man to man, it can produce no rules for earthly conduct but abandons the believer so soon as he starts thinking about the inadequacy of social conditions. Religion must provide him an answer when he asks why there are rich and poor, violence and justice, war and peace, or it will force him to look for an answer elsewhere. This would
410 mean losing its hold on its adherents and its power over the spirit. Without social ethics religion would be dead.

Today the Islamic and Jewish religions are dead. They offer their adherents nothing more than a ritual. They know how to prescribe prayers and fasts, certain foods, circumcision and the rest; but that is all. They offer nothing to the mind. Completely despiritualized, all they teach and preach are legal forms and external rule. They lock their follower into a cage of traditional usages, in which he is often hardly able to breathe; but for his inner soul they have no message. They suppress the soul, instead of elevating and saving it. For many centuries in Islam, for nearly two thousand years in Jewry, there have been no new religious movements. Today the religion of the Jews is just as it was when the Talmud was drawn up. The religion of Islam has not changed since the days of the Arab conquests. Their literature, their philosophies continue to repeat the old ideas and do not penetrate beyond the circle of theology. One looks in vain among them for men and movements such as Western Christianity has produced in each century. They maintain their identity only by rejecting everything foreign and "different," by traditionalism and conservatism. Only their hatred of everything foreign rouses them to great deeds from time to time. All new sects, even the new doctrines which arise with them, are nothing more than echoes of this fight against the foreign, the new, the infidel. Religion has no influence on the spiritual life of the individual, where indeed this is able to develop at all against the stifling pressure of rigid traditionalism. We see this most clearly in the lack of clerical influence. Respect for the clergy is purely superficial. In these religions there is nothing which could be compared to the profound influence which the clergy exercises in the Western Churches—though of a different order in each church; there is nothing to compare to the Jesuit, the Catholic bishop, and the Protestant pastor. There was the same inertia in the polytheistic religions of antiquity and there still is in the Eastern Church. The Greek Church has been dead for over a thousand years.[1] Only in the second half of the nineteenth century did it once more produce a man in

[1] Compare the characterization of the Eastern Church given by Harnack, *Das Mönchtum*, 7th ed. (Giessen, 1907), p. 32 ff.

whom faith and hope flared up like fire. But Tolstoy's Christianity, however
much it may bear a superficially Eastern and Russian hue, is at bottom
founded on Western ideas. It is particularly characteristic of this great Gos- 411
peller that, unlike the Italian merchant's son, Francis of Assisi, or the German
miner's son, Martin Luther, he did not come from the people but from the
nobility which, by upbringing and education, had been completely Wester-
nized. The Russian Church proper has produced at most men like John of
Kronstadt* or Rasputin.

These dead churches lack any special ethics. Harnack says of the Greek Church:[2] "The real sphere of the working life whose morality is to be regulated by the Faith, falls outside its direct observation. This is left to the state and the nation." But it is otherwise in the living Church of the West. Here, where faith is not yet extinct, where it is not merely external form that conceals nothing but the priest's meaningless ritual, where, in a word, it grips the whole man, there is continuous striving after a social ethic. Again and again do its members go back to the Gospels to renew their life in the Lord and His Message.

2

The Gospels as a Source of Christian Ethics

To the believer Holy Writ is the deposit of divine revelation, God's word to humanity, which must forever be the unshakable foundation of all religion and all conduct controlled by it. This is true not only of the Protestant, who accepts the teaching of the pulpit only in so far as it can be reconciled with Holy Writ; it is true also of the Catholics who, on the one hand, derive the authority of Holy Writ from the Church, but, on the other, ascribe Holy Writ itself to divine origin by teaching that it came into being with the help of the Holy Ghost. The dualism here is resolved by entitling the Church alone to make what is the finally authentic—infallible—interpretation of Holy Writ. Both creeds assume the logical and systematic unity of the whole of the sacred writings; to bridge over the difficulties arising from this assumption must, therefore, be one of the most important tasks of ecclesiastical doctrine and science.

---

[2] Harnack, *Das Mönchtum*, p. 33.

* John of Kronstadt (1821–1908), real name Ioann Sergiev, an orthodox Russian priest and popular idol, alleged performer of miracles, carried on charitable work and ministered to the poor, sick and needy.

Scientific research regards the writings of the Old and New Testament as historical sources to be approached in the same manner as all other historical
412 documents. It breaks up the unity of the Bible and tries to give each section its place in the history of literature. Now, modern biblical research of this order is incompatible with theology. The Catholic Church has recognized this fact but the Protestant Church still tries to delude itself. It is senseless to reconstruct the character of an historical Jesus in order to build up a doctrine of faith and morals on the results. Efforts of this kind hamper documentary research of a scientific kind by deflecting it from its real aim and assigning to it tasks which it cannot fulfill without introducing modern scales of value; moreover they are contradictory in themselves. On the one hand they try to explain Christ and the origin of Christianity historically; on the other, to regard these historical phenomena as the eternal source from which spring all the rules of ecclesiastical conduct, even in the totally different world of today. What is it but a contradiction to examine Christianity with the eye of a historian and then to seek a clue to the present in the results of the study. History can never present Christianity in its "pure form," but only in its "original form." To confuse the two is to shut one's eyes to two thousand years of development.[3] The error into which many Protestant theologians fall in this matter is the same as that committed by a section of the historical school of law when it attempted to impose the results of its researches into the history of jurisprudence upon present-day legislation and administration of justice. This is not the procedure of the true historian but rather of one who denies all evolution and all possibility of evolution. Contrasted with the absolutism of this point of view, the absolutism of the much condemned "shallow" eighteenth-century rationalists, who stressed precisely this element of progress and evolution, seems genuinely historical in its outlook.

The relation of Christian ethics to the problem of Socialism must not therefore be viewed through the eyes of Protestant theologians whose research is directed towards an unchangeable and immovable "essence" of Christianity. If one looks on Christianity as a living, and hence a constantly changing, phenomenon—a view not so incompatible with the outlook of the Catholic Church as one might at first imagine—then one must decline *a priori* to inquire whether Socialism or private property is more in keeping with its idea. The best we can do is to pass the history of Christianity in review and
413 consider whether it has ever shown a bias in favour of this or that form of social organization. The attention we pay to the writings of the Old and New

[3] Troeltsch, *Gesammelte Schriften*, Vol. II (Tübingen, 1913), pp. 386 ff.

Testament in the process is justified by their importance even today as sources of ecclesiastical doctrine, but not by the supposition that from them alone can one glean what Christianity really is.

The ultimate aim of research of this kind should be to ascertain whether, both now and in the future, Christianity must necessarily reject an economy based on private property in the means of production. This question cannot be settled merely by establishing the fact, already familiar, that ever since its inception close on two thousand years ago Christianity has found its own ways of coming to terms with private property. For it might happen that either Christianity or "private property" should reach a point in its evolution which renders the compatibility of the two impossible—supposing that it had ever existed.

3

Primitive Christianity and Society

Primitive Christianity was not ascetic. With a joyful acceptance of life it deliberately pushed into the background the ascetic ideals which permeated many contemporary sects. (Even John the Baptist lived as an ascetic.) Only in the third and fourth centuries was ascetisism introduced into Christianity, from this time dates the ascetic re-interpretation and reformation of Gospel teachings. The Christ of the Gospels enjoys life among his disciples, refreshes himself with food and drink and shares the feasts of the people. He is as far removed from asceticism and a desire to flee the world as he is from intemperance and debauchery.[4] Alone his attitude to the relations of the sexes strikes us as ascetic, but we can explain this, as we can explain all practical Gospel Teachings—and they offer no rules of life except practical ones—by the basic conception which gives us our whole idea of Jesus, the conception of the Messiah.

"The Time is fulfilled, and the Kingdom of God is at hand: repent ye, and
believe the gospel." These are the words with which, in the Gospel of Mark,
the Redeemer makes his entry.[5] Jesus regards himself as the prophet of the 414
approaching Kingdom of God, the Kingdom which according to ancient
prophecy shall bring redemption from all earthly insufficiency, and with it
from all economic cares. His followers have nothing to do but to prepare

---

[4] Harnack, *Das Wesen des Christentums* (Leipzig, 1907), pp. 50 ff.

[5] Mark, 1, 15.

themselves for this Day. The time for worrying about earthly matters is past, for now, in expectation of the Kingdom, men must attend to more important things. Jesus offers no rules for earthly action and struggle; his Kingdom is not of this world. Such rules of conduct as he gives his followers are valid only for the short interval of time which has still to be lived while waiting for the great things to come. In the Kingdom of God there will be no economic cares. There the believers will eat and drink at the Lord's table.[6] For this Kingdom therefore, all economic and political counsel would be superfluous. Any preparations made by Jesus must be regarded as merely transitional expedients.[7]

It is only in this way that we can understand why, in the Sermon on the Mount, Jesus recommends his own people to take no thought for food, drink, and clothing; why he exhorts them not to sow or reap or gather in barns, not to labour or spin. It is the only explanation, too, of his and his disciples' "communism." This "communism" is not Socialism; it is not production with means of production belonging to the community. It is nothing more than a distribution of consumption goods among the members of the community—"unto each, according as any one had need."[8] It is a communism of consumption goods, not of the means of production, a community of consumers, not of producers. The primitive Christians do not produce, labour, or gather anything at all. The newly converted realize their possessions and divide the proceeds with the brethren and sisters. Such a way of living is untenable in the long run. It can be looked upon only as a temporary order which is what it was in fact intended to be. Christ's disciples lived in daily expectation of Salvation.

The primitive Christian's idea of imminent fulfilment transforms itself gradually into that conception of the Last Judgment which lies at the root of all ecclesiastical movements that have had any prolonged existence. Hand in hand with this transformation went the entire reconstruction of the Chris-
415 tian rules of life. Expectation of the coming of the Kingdom of God could no longer serve as a basis. When the congregations sought to organize themselves for a prolonged life on earth they had to cease demanding that their members should abstain from work and dedicate themselves to the contemplative life in preparation for the Divine Kingdom. Not only did they have to tolerate their brethren's participation in the world's work, they had to insist upon it, as otherwise they would have destroyed the conditions nec-

---

[6] Luke, xxii, 30.

[7] Harnack, *Aus Wissenschaft und Leben*, Vol. II (Giessen, 1911), pp. 257 ff.; Troeltsch, *Die Soziallehren der christlichen Kirchen und Gruppen*, pp. 31 ff.

[8] Acts of the Apostles, iv, 35.

essary to the existence of their religion. And thus, Christianity, which began with complete indifference to all social conditions, practically canonized the social order of the declining Roman Empire once the process of adapting the Church to that order had begun.

It is an error to speak of the social teachings of primitive Christianity. The historical Christ and his teachings, as the oldest part of the New Testament represents them, are quite indifferent to all social considerations. Not that Christ did not sharply criticize the existing state of affairs, but he did not think it worth while to consider how matters could be improved or even to think about them at all. That was God's affair. He would set up his own glorious and faultless Kingdom, and its coming would be soon. Nobody knew what this Kingdom would look like, but one thing was certain: in it one would live carefree. Jesus omits all minuter details, and they were not needed; for the Jews of his time did not doubt the splendour of life in the Kingdom of God. The Prophets had announced this Kingdom and their words continued to live in the minds of the people, forming indeed the essential content of their religious thought.

The expectation of God's own reorganization when the time came and the exclusive transfer of all action and thought to the future Kingdom of God, made Jesus's teaching utterly negative. He rejects everything that exists without offering anything to replace it. He arrives at dissolving all existing social ties. The disciple shall not merely be indifferent to supporting himself, shall not merely refrain from work and dispossess himself of all goods, but he shall hate "father, and mother, and wife, and children, and brethren, and sisters, yea, and his own life."[9] Jesus is able to tolerate the worldly laws of the Roman Empire and the prescriptions of the Jewish Law because he is indifferent to them, despising them as things important only within the narrow limits of time and not because he acknowledges their value. His zeal 416
in destroying social ties knows no limits. The motive force behind the purity and power of this complete negation is ecstatic inspiration and enthusiastic hope of a new world. Hence his passionate attack upon everything that exists. Everything may be destroyed because God in His omnipotence will rebuild the future order. No need to scrutinize whether anything can be carried over from the old to the new order, because this new order will arise without human aid. It demands therefore from its adherents no system of ethics, no particular conduct in any positive direction. Faith and faith alone, hope, expectation—that is all he needs. He need contribute nothing to the reconstruction of the future, this God Himself has provided for. The clearest

---

[9] Luke, XIV, 26.

modern parallel to the attitude of complete negation of primitive Christianity is Bolshevism. The Bolshevists, too, wish to destroy everything that exists because they regard it as hopelessly bad. But they have in mind ideas, indefinite and contradictory though they may be, of the future social order. They demand not only that their followers shall destroy all that is, but also that they pursue a definite line of conduct leading towards the future Kingdom of which they have dreamt. Jesus teaching in this respect, on the other hand, is merely negation.[10]

Jesus was no social reformer. His teachings had no moral application to life on earth, and his instructions to the disciples only have a meaning in the light of their immediate aim—to await the Lord with girded loins and burning lamps, "that when he cometh and knocketh, they may straightaway open unto him."[11] It is just this that has enabled Christianity to make its triumphant progress through the world. Being neutral to any social system, it was able to traverse the centuries without being destroyed by the tremendous social revolutions which took place. Only for this reason could it become the religion of Roman Emperors and Anglo-Saxon entrepreneurs, of African negroes and European Teutons, medieval feudal lords and modern industrial labourers. Each epoch and every party has been able to take from it what they wanted, because it contains nothing which binds it to a definite social order.

417 4

The Canon Law Prohibition of Interest

Each epoch has found in the Gospels what it sought to find there, and has overlooked what it wished to overlook. This is best proved by reference to the preponderant importance which ecclesiastical social ethics for many centuries attached to the doctrine of usury.[12] The demand made upon Christ's disciples in the Gospels and other writings of the New Testament is something very different from the renunciation of interest on capital lent out. The canonic prohibition of interest is a product of the medieval doctrine of society

---

[10] Pfleiderer, *Das Urchristentum*, Vol. I, pp. 649 ff.

[11] Luke, XII, 35–36.

[12] "The doctrine of the medieval law of trade is rooted in the canonic dogma of the barrenness of money and in the sum of corollaries which are to be understood under the name of the usury law. The history of the trade law of those times cannot be anything except the history of the rule of the doctrine of usury in legal doctrine." Endemann, *Studien in der romanisch-kanonistischen Wirtschafts-und Rechtslehre bis gegen Ende des siebzehnten Jahrhunderts* (Berlin, 1874–83), Vol. I, p. 2.

and trade, and had originally nothing to do with Christianity and its teachings. Moral condemnation of usury and the prohibition of interest preceded Christianity. They were taken over from the writers and the legislators of antiquity and enlarged as the struggle between agriculturists and the rising merchants and tradesmen developed. Only then did the people try to support them with quotations from Holy Writ. The taking of interest was not opposed because Christianity required it, but rather, because the public condemned it, people tried to read into the Christian writings a condemnation of usury. For this purpose the New Testament seemed at first to be useless, and accordingly the Old Testament was drawn on. For centuries no one thought of quoting any passage from the New Testament in support of the prohibition. It was some time before the scholastic art of interpretation succeeded in reading what it sought into that much quoted passage from Luke, and so finding support in the Gospels from the suppression of usury.[13] This was not until the beginning of the twelfth century. Only after the decree of Urban III is that passage quoted as proof of the prohibition.[14] The construction then put on Luke's words was, however, quite untenable. The passage is certainly not concerned with the taking of interest. It is possible that in the context 418
of that passage Μηδὲν ἀπελπίζοντες may mean "do not count on the restitution of what is lent." Or more probably: "you shall lend not only to the well-to-do, who can also lend to you at some time, but also to him from whom there is no prospect of this, to the poor."[15]

The great importance people attached to this passage contrasts sharply with their disregard of other Gospel commands and prohibitions. The medieval Church was intent on carrying the order against usury to its logical conclusion, but it wilfully omitted to enforce many clear and unambiguous commands of the Gospels with a fraction of the energy devoted to stamping out this particular practice. In the very same chapter of Luke other things are ordained or forbidden in precise words. The Church has never, for example, been seriously at pains to forbid a man who has been robbed from demanding back his own, nor has it deprecated resistance to the robber, nor tried to brand an act of judgment as an unchristian act. Other injunctions of the Sermon on the Mount, such as indifference to food and drink, have similarly never been whole-heartedly enforced.[16]

---

[13] Luke, VI, 35.

[14] C. 10. X. *De usuris* (III, 19). See Schaub, *Der Kampf gegen den Zinswucher, ungerechten Preis und unlautern Handel im Mittelalter* (Freiburg, 1905), pp. 61 ff.

[15] The passage is thus interpreted by Knies, *Geld und Kredit,* Part II (Berlin, 1876), pp. 333–5 note.

[16] On the latest legislation of the Church, which in *c.* 1543, *Cod. iur. can.*, has come to acknowledge conditionally the legality of the taking of interest, see Zehentbauer, *Das Zinsproblem nach Moral und Recht* (Vienna, 1920), pp. 138 ff.

5

Christianity and Property

Since the third century Christianity has always served simultaneously those who supported the social order and those who wished to overthrow it. Both parties have taken the same false step of appealing to the Gospels and have found Biblical passages to support them. It is the same today: Christianity fights both for and against Socialism.

But all efforts to find support for the institution of private property generally, and for private ownership in the means of production in particular, in the teachings of Christ are quite vain. No art of interpretation can find a single passage in the New Testament that could be read as upholding private property. Those who look for a Biblical ukase must go back to the Old
419 Testament, or content themselves with disputing the assertion that communism prevailed in the congregation of the early Christians.[17] No one has ever denied that the Jewish community was familiar with private property, but this brings us no further towards defining the attitude towards it of primitive Christianity. There is as little proof that Jesus approved the economic and political ideas of the Jewish Law as that he did not. Christ does say, indeed, that he has not come to destroy the Law but to fulfil it.[18] But this we should try to understand from the standpoint which alone makes Jesus' work intelligible. The words can hardly refer to the rules of the Mosaic Law, made for earthly life before the coming of the Kingdom of God, since several of his commands are in sharp contrast to that Law. We may admit that the reference to the "communism" of the first Christians proves nothing in favour of "the collectivist communism according to modern notions,"[19] and yet not deduce from this that Christ approved of property.[20]

[17] Pesch, *Lehrbuch der Nationalökonomie*, pp. 212 ff.

[18] Matthew v, 17.

[19] Pesch, *op. cit.*, p. 212.

[20] Pfleiderer, *Das Urchristentum*, Vol. I, p. 651, explains Jesus' pessimistic judgment of earthly possessions by the apocalyptic expectation of the near world catastrophe. "Instead of trying to reinterpret and adapt His rigoristic expressions on this subject in the sense of our modern social ethics, one should make oneself familiar, once and for all, with the idea that Jesus did not appear as a rational moralist but as an enthusiastic prophet of the impending Kingdom of God and has only thus become the source of the religion of salvation. He who wants to make the eschatological enthusiasm of the prophet the direct and permanent authority for social ethics does just as wisely as he who would wish to warm his hearth and cook his soup with the flames of a volcano." On May 25th, 1525, Luther wrote to the Danzig Council: "The Gospel is a spiritual law by which one cannot well govern." See Neumann, *Geschichte des Wuchers in Deutschland* (Halle, 1865), p. 618. Also Traub, *Ethik und Kapitalismus*, 2nd ed. (Heilbronn, 1909), p. 71.

One thing of course is clear, and no skilful interpretation can obscure it. Jesus' words are full of resentment against the rich, and the Apostles are no meeker in this respect. The Rich Man is condemned because he is rich, the Beggar praised because he is poor. The only reason why Jesus does not declare war against the rich and preach revenge on them is that God has said: "Revenge is mine." In God's Kingdom the poor shall be rich, but the rich shall be made to suffer. Later revisers have tried to soften the words of Christ against the rich, of which the most complete and powerful version is found in the Gospel of Luke, but there is quite enough left to support those who incite the world to hatred of the rich, revenge, murder and arson. Up to the time of modern Socialism no movement against private poverty which
has arisen in the Christian world has failed to seek authority in Jesus, the 420
Apostles, and the Christian Fathers, not to mention those who, like Tolstoy, made the Gospel resentment against the rich the very heart and soul of their teaching. This is a case in which the Redeemer's words bore evil seed. More harm has been done, and more blood shed, on account of them than by the persecution of heretics and the burning of witches. They have always rendered the Church defenceless against all movements which aim at destroying human society. The Church as an organization has certainly always stood on the side of those who tried to ward off communistic attack. But it could not achieve much in this struggle. For it was continually disarmed by the words: "Blessed be ye poor: for yours is the Kingdom of God."

Nothing, therefore, is less tenable than the constantly repeated assertion that religion, that is, the confession of the Christian Faith, forms a defence against doctrines inimical to property, and that it makes the masses unreceptive to the poison of social incitement. Every church which grows up in a society built on private property must somehow come to terms with private property. But considering the attitude of Jesus to questions of social life, no Christian Church can ever make anything more than a compromise here, a compromise which is effective only as long as nobody insists on a literal interpretation of the words of the Scriptures. It would be foolish to maintain that Enlightenment, by undermining the religious feeling of the masses, had cleared the way for Socialism. On the contrary, it is the resistance which the Church has offered to the spread of liberal ideas which has prepared the soil for the destructive resentment of modern socialist thought. Not only has the Church done nothing to extinguish the fire, it has even blown upon the embers. Christian Socialism grew up in the Catholic and Protestant countries, while the Russian Church witnessed the birth of Tolstoy's teachings, which are unequalled in the bitterness of their antagonism to society. True, the official Church tried at first to resist these movements, but it had to submit in the end, just because it was defenceless against the words of the Scriptures.

The Gospels are not socialistic and not communistic. They are, as we have seen, indifferent to all social questions on the one hand, full of resentment against all property and against all owners on the other. So it is that Christian doctrine, once separated from the context in which Christ preached it—
421 expectation of the imminent Kingdom of God—can be extremely destructive. Never and nowhere can a system of social ethics embracing social co-operation be built up on a doctrine which prohibits any concern for sustenance and work, while it expresses fierce resentment against the rich, preaches hatred of the family, and advocates voluntary castration.

The cultural achievements of the Church in its centuries of development are the work of the Church, not of Christianity. It is an open question how much of this work is due to the civilization inherited from the Roman state and how much to the idea of Christian love completely transformed under the influence of the Stoics and other ancient philosophers. The social ethics of Jesus have no part in this cultural development. The Church's achievement in this case was to render them harmless, but always only for a limited period of time. Since the Church is obliged to maintain the Gospels as its foundation, it must always be prepared for a revolt on the part of those among its members who put on Christ's words an interpretation different from that ordained by the Church.

Social ethics applicable to earthly life can never be derived from the words of the Gospels. It matters little whether they are a true and just report of what, as a matter of history, Jesus taught. For to every Christian Church these, together with the other books of the New Testament, must represent the foundation without which its essential character is destroyed. Even should historical research show, with a high degree of probability, that the historical Jesus thought and spoke about human society otherwise than he is made to do in the New Testament, its doctrines would still remain unaltered for the Church. For the Church, that which is written in the New Testament must forever remain the Word of God. Here, apparently, only two things are possible. Either the Church may renounce, in the manner of the Eastern Church, the responsibility of taking up any attitude to the problems of social ethics, at which point it ceases to be a moral force and limits itself to purely decorative action in life. Or it may follow the other path taken by the Western Church, which has always incorporated in its teachings those social ethics which best served its interests at the moment and its position in state and society. It has allied itself with the feudal lords against the serfs, it has supported the slave-economy of American plantations, but it has also—in
422 the case of Protestantism and especially in Calvinism—made the morals of the rising Rationalism its own. It has promoted the struggle of the Irish

tenants against the English aristocrats, it has fought with the Catholic trade unions against the entrepreneurs, and with the conservative governments against social democracy. And in each case it has been able to justify its attitude by quotations from the Bible. This too amounts in fact to an abdication by Christianity in the field of social ethics, for the Church becomes thus a volitionless tool in the hands of time and fashion. But what is worse: it attempts to base each phase of partisanship on the teaching of the Gospels and in this way encourages every movement to seek scriptural justification for its ends. Considering the character of the scriptural passages so exploited, it is clear that the more destructive doctrines are bound to win.

But even if it is hopeless to try to build up an independent Christian social ethic on the Gospels, might it not be possible to bring Christian doctrines into harmony with a social ethic that promotes social life instead of destroying it, and thus to utilize the great forces of Christianity in the service of Civilization? Such a transformation would not be unprecedented in history. The Church is now reconciled to the fact that modern research has exploded the fallacies of the Old and New Testaments with regard to natural science. It no longer burns at the stake heretics who maintain that the world moves in space, or institutes inquisitional proceedings against the man who dares to doubt the raising of Lazarus and the bodily resurrection of the dead. Even priests of the Church of Rome are today permitted to study astronomy and the history of evolution. Might not the same be possible then in sociology? Might not the Church reconcile itself with the social principle of free co-operation by the division of labour? Might not the very principle of Christian love be interpreted to this end?

These are questions which interest not only the Church. The fate of Civilization is involved. For it is not as if the resistance of the Church to liberal ideas was harmless. The Church is such a tremendous power that its enmity to the forces which bring society into existence would be enough to break our whole culture into fragments. In the last decades we have witnessed with horror its terrible transformation into an enemy of society. For the Church, Catholic as well as Protestant, is not the least of the factors responsible for the prevalence of destructive ideals in the world today; Christian
Socialism has done hardly less than atheist socialism to bring about the 423
present state of confusion.

6

Christian Socialism

Historically it is easy to understand the dislike which the Church has shown for economic liberty and political Liberalism in any form. Liberalism is the flower of that rational enlightenment which dealt a death blow to the regime of the old Church and from which modern historical criticism has sprung. It was Liberalism that undermined the power of the classes that had for centuries been closely bound up with the Church. It transformed the world more than Christianity had ever done. It restored humanity to the world and to life. It awakened forces which shook the foundations of the inert traditionalism on which Church and creed rested. The new outlook caused the Church great uneasiness, and it has not yet adjusted itself to even the externals of the modern epoch. True, the priests in Catholic countries sprinkle holy water on newly laid railways and dynamos of new power stations, but the professed Christian still shudders inwardly at the workings of a civilization which his faith cannot grasp. The Church strongly resented modernity and the modern spirit. What wonder, then, that it allied itself with those whom resentment had driven to wish for the break-up of this wonderful new world, and feverishly explored its well-stocked arsenal for the means to denounce the earthly struggle for work and wealth. The religion which called itself the religion of love became a religion of hatred in a world that seemed ripe for happiness. Any would-be destroyers of the modern social order could count on finding a champion in Christianity.

It is tragic that it should have been just the greatest minds of the Church, those who realized the significance of Christian love and acted on it, who took part in this work of destruction. Priests and monks who practised true Christian charity, ministered and taught in hospitals and prisons and knew all there was to know about suffering and sinning humanity—these were the first to be ensnared by the new gospel of social destruction. Only a firm grasp of liberal philosophy could have innoculated them against the infectious resentment which raged among their protégés and was justified by the
424 Gospels. As it was, they became dangerous enemies of society. From the work of charity sprang hatred of society.

Some of these emotional opponents of the liberal economic orders stopped short at open opposition. Many, however, became socialists—not, of course, atheistical socialists like the proletarian social-democrats, but Christian Socialists. And Christian Socialism is none the less Socialism.

It was no less a mistake for Socialism to seek a parallel with itself in the early centuries of the Christian Era as in the first congregation. Even the "consumers communism" of that early congregation vanished when expectation of the coming of the Kingdom began to recede into the background. Socialist methods of production did not, however, replace it in the community. What the Christians produced, was produced by the individual within his own farm or shop. The revenues which provided for the needy and met the cost of joint activities came from contributions, voluntary or compulsory, of members of the congregation, who produced on their own account with their own means of production. A few isolated instances of socialist production may have occurred in the Christian congregations of the first centuries, but there is no documentary evidence of it. There was never a teacher of Christianity, whose teachings and writings are known to us, who recommended it. We often find the Apostolic Fathers and the Fathers of the Church, exhorting their followers to return to the communism of the first congregation, but this is always a communism of consumption. They never recommend the socialistic organization of production.[21]

The best known of these exhortations in praise of communism is that of John Chrysostom. In the eleventh of his homilies to the Acts of the Apostles the Saint applauds the consumers' communism of the first Christian congregation, and with all his fiery eloquence advocates its revival. Not only does he recommend this form of communism by reference to the example of the Apostles and their contemporaries, but tries to set forth rationally the advantages of communism as he conceives it. If all the Christians of Constantinople were to hand over their possessions to a common ownership, then so much would be amassed that all the Christian poor could be fed and no one would suffer want, for the costs of joint living are far smaller than those of single households. Here St. Chrysostom adduces arguments similar 425
to those brought forward today by people who advocate one-kitchen houses or communal kitchens and try to prove arithmetically the economies which a concentration of cooking and housekeeping would achieve. The costs, says this Father of the Church, would not be large, and the enormous fund which would be amassed by uniting the goods of individuals would be inexhaustible, especially as God's blessings would then be poured yet more lavishly on the faithful. Moreover, every newcomer would have to add something to the general fund.[22] These sober, matter of fact expositions show us that what Chrysostom had in mind was merely joint consumption. His comments on the economic advantages of unification, culminating in the statement that

[21] Seipel, *Die wirtschaftsethischen Lehren der Kirchenväter* (Vienna, 1907), pp. 84 ff.

[22] Migne, *Patrologiae Graecae*, Vol. LX, pp. 96 ff.

division into fragments leads to diminution, while unity and co-operation lead to increase, of well-being, do credit to their author's economic perception. On the whole, however, his proposals reveal a complete lack of understanding of the problem of production. His thoughts are directed exclusively to consumption. That production comes before consumption had never occurred to him. All goods were to be transferred to the community (St. Chrysostom presumably thinks here of their sale, following the example of the Gospels and the Acts of the Apostles) after which the community was to begin consuming in common. He had not realized that this could not go on for ever. He believed that the millions which would be gathered together—he estimates the treasure at between one and three million pounds weight of gold—could never be used up. One notices that the saint's economic insight ends just where the wisdom of our social politicians also tends to end, when they try to reorganize the whole national economy in the light of experience gained in charitable work in the field of consumption.

St. Chrysostom explains that people fear to risk the change to the communism, which he recommends, more than a plunge into the ocean. And so the Church, too, soon dropped the communistic idea.

For monastic economy cannot be regarded as Socialism. Monasteries which could not subsist on private donations usually lived on the tithes and dues of rent-paying peasants and the yields of farms and other property. Very occasionally the monks themselves worked, on a sort of producers' co-operative basis. The whole monastic existence is an ideal of life accessible
426 only to the few, and monastic production can never be taken as a standard for the whole commonwealth. Socialism, on the other hand, is a general economic system.

The roots of Christian Socialism are found neither in the primitive nor in the medieval Church. It was the Christianity that emerged revitalized from the tremendous struggles of faith in the sixteenth century which first adopted it, though only gradually and in the face of strong opposition.

The modern Church differs from the medieval Church in that it has continually to fight for its existence. The medieval Church ruled unchallenged; all that men thought, taught, or wrote emanated from it and eventually returned to it. The spiritual inheritance of classic antiquity could not shake its dominion, for its ultimate meaning was beyond the understanding of a generation cramped by feudal concepts and ideas. But in proportion as social evolution progressed in the direction of rational thought and action, men's efforts to shake off the fetters of traditional thought in respect of ultimate truths became more successful. The Renaissance strikes at the root of Christianity. Based on classical reasoning and classical art, its influence inevitably tended to lead away from the Church or at best to leave it out of account. Far from trying to stem the tide, churchmen became the most zealous protagonists of the new spirit. At the beginning of the sixteenth century no one was further removed from Christianity than the Church itself. The last hour of the old faith seemed to have sounded.

Then came the great revulsion, the Christian counter-revolution. It did not come from above, from the princes of the Church or from the monasteries, in fact it did not come from the Church at all. It was forced upon the Church from outside, springing from the depths of the people where Christianity still survived as an inner force. The assault on the moribund Church with a view to its reformation came thus from outside and below. The Reformation and the Counter-reformation are the two great expressions of this ecclesiastical rebirth. They differ in origin and in method, in their forms of worship and prescribed doctrines, above all in their presuppositions and achievements in political affairs; but they are at one in their ultimate aim: to base the world order once more on the Gospels, to reinstate faith as a power controlling the minds and hearts of men. It is the greatest revolt of faith against thought,
of tradition against philosophy known to history. Its successes were enor- 427
mous, and it created Christianity as we know it today, the religion that has its seat in the heart of the individual, which controls conscience and comforts the soul. But complete victory has been denied it. Though it warded off defeat—the fall of Christianity—it could not destroy the enemy. For ever since the sixteenth century this struggle of ideas has been pursued almost without intermission.

The Church knows that it cannot win unless it can seal the fount from which its opponent continues to draw inspiration. As long as rationalism and the spiritual freedom of the individual are maintained in economic life, the Church will never succeed in fettering thought and shepherding the intellect in the desired direction. To do this it would first have to obtain supremacy over all human activity. Therefore it cannot rest content to live as a free Church in a free state; it must seek to dominate that state. The Papacy of Rome and the Protestant national churches both fight for such dominion as would enable them to order all things temporal according to their ideals. The Church can tolerate no other spiritual power. Every independent spiritual power is a menace to it, a menace which increases in strength as the rationalization of life progresses.

Now independent production does not tolerate any spiritual over-lordship. In our day, dominion over the mind can only be obtained through the control of production. All Churches have long been dimly aware of this, but it was first made clear to them when the socialist idea, rising from an independent source, made itself felt as a powerful and rapidly growing force. It then dawned upon the Churches that theocracy is only possible in a socialist community.

On one occasion this idea was actually realized. This was when the Society of Jesus created that remarkable state in Paraguay, which was not unlike an embodiment of the ideal Republic of Plato. This unique state flourished for more than a century, when it was destroyed by external forces. It is certain that the Jesuits did not found this society with the idea of making a social experiment or of setting up an example for other communities of the world. But ultimately they were aiming in Paraguay at no more than what they have everywhere tried to achieve, but without success, on account of the great resistance encountered. They have tried to bring laymen—as children needing the guardianship of the Church—under the beneficial government of the
428 Church and of their own Order. Neither the Jesuit order nor any other ecclesiastical body has since tried anything like the Paraguayan experiment. But it is plain that all Western Churches, as well as the Roman Catholic Church, are aiming at the same goal. Remove all the obstacles which hamper the Church to-day, and nothing will prevent it from repeating the Paraguayan achievement everywhere.

That the Church, generally speaking, takes up a negative attitude to socialist ideas does not disprove the truth of these arguments. It opposes any Socialism which is to be effected on any other basis than its own. It is against Socialism as conceived by atheists, for this would strike at its very roots; but it has no hesitation in approaching socialist ideals provided this menace is resumed. The Prussian Church stands at the head of Prussian State Socialism and the Roman Catholic Church everywhere pursues its special Christian social ideal.

In face of all this evidence, it would seem that only a negative answer can be made to the question asked above: whether it might not be possible to reconcile Christianity with a free social order based on private ownership in the means of production. A living Christianity cannot, it seems, exist side by side with Capitalism. Just as in the case of Eastern religions, Christianity must either overcome Capitalism or go under. Yet, in the fight against Capitalism today, there is no more effective war-cry than Socialism, now that suggestions of a return to the medieval social order find few supporters.

But there may be an alternative. No one can foresee with certainty how Church and Christianity may change in the future. Papacy and Catholicism now face problems incomparably more difficult than all those they have had to solve for over a thousand years. The world-wide Universal Church is threatened in its very being by Chauvinist nationalism. By refinement of political art it has succeeded in maintaining the principle of Catholicism through all the turmoil of national wars, but it must realize more clearly every day that its continuance is incompatible with nationalist ideas. Unless it is prepared to succumb, and make way for national churches, it must drive out nationalism by an ideology which makes it possible for nations to live and work together in peace. But in so doing the Church would find itself inevitably committed to Liberalism. No other doctrine would serve.

If the Roman Church is to find any way out of the crisis into which 429
nationalism has brought it, then it must be thoroughly transformed. It may be that this transformation and reformation will lead to its unconditional acceptance of the indispensability of private ownership in the means of production. At present it is still far from this, as witness the recent encyclical Quadragesimo anno.*

* Issued in 1931, by Pius XI (Pope, 1922–1939) (Pub.).

CHAPTER 30

Ethical Socialism, Especially That of the New Criticism

1

The Categorical Imperative as a Foundation for Socialism

430 Engels called the German Labour Movement the heir to the German classical philosophy.[1] It would be more correct to say that German (not only Marxian) Socialism represents the decadence of the school of idealist philosophy. Socialism owes the dominion it won over the German mind to the idea of society as conceived by the great German thinkers. Out of Kant's mysticism of duty and Hegel's deification of the State it is easy to trace the development of socialist thought; Fichte is already a socialist.

In recent decades the revival of Kantian criticism, that much praised achievement of German philosophy, has benefited Socialism also. The Neo-Kantians, especially Friedrich Albert Lange and Hermann Cohen, have declared themselves socialists. Simultaneously Marxians have tried to reconcile Marxism with the New Criticism. Ever since the philosophical foundations of Marxism have shown signs of cracking, attempts to find in critical philosophy support for socialist ideas have multiplied.

The weakest part of Kant's system is his ethics. Although they are vitalized by his mighty intellect, the grandeur of individual concepts does not blind us to the fact that his starting-point is unfortunately chosen and his fundamental conception a mistaken one. His desperate attempt to uproot Eudaemonism has failed. In ethics, Bentham, Mill, and Feuerbach triumph over Kant. The social philosophy of his contemporaries, Ferguson and Adam Smith, left him untouched. Economics remained foreign to him. All his perception of social problems suffers from these deficiencies.

In this respect, Neo-Kantians have made no better progress than their

---

[1] Engels, *Ludwig Feuerbach und der Ausgang der klassischen deutschen Philosophie*, 5th ed. (Stuttgart, 1910), p. 58.

master. They, too, lack insight into the fundamental social law of the division 431
of labour. They only see that the distribution of income does not correspond to their ideal, that the largest incomes do not go to those whom they consider the most deserving, but to a class they despise. They see people poor and in want, but do not try to discover whether this is due to the institution of private property or to attempts to restrict it. And they promptly condemn the institution of private ownership itself, for which they—living far away from the troubles of business—never had any sympathies. In social cognition they remain bound to the external and symptomatic. They tackle all other problems without a qualm, but here timidity restrains them. In their embarrassment, they betray their underlying bias. In social philosophy it is often difficult for thinkers who are otherwise quite open-minded to avoid all resentment. Into their thoughts obtrudes the recollection of those more prosperous than themselves; they make comparisons between their own value and the lack of it in others on the one hand, and their own poverty and the wealth of others on the other. In the end anger and envy, rather than reason, guide their pen.

This alone explains why such lucid thinkers as the Neo-Kantians have not yet clearly thought out the only salient problems in social philosophy. Not even the rudiments of a comprehensive social philosophy are to be found in their works. They make numerous unfounded criticisms of certain social conditions, but omit to discuss the most important systems of sociology. They judge, without having first made themselves familiar with the results of economic science.

The starting-point of their Socialism is generally the sentence: "Act in such a way that you use your being, equally with the being of anyone else, always as a purpose, never merely as a means." In these words, says Cohen, "the most profound and powerful meaning of the categoric imperative is expressed; *they contain the moral programme of the modern age and of all future world history*."[2] And from that to Socialism, he seems to infer, is no great distance. "The idea of the purpose preference of humanity becomes transformed into the idea of Socialism by the definition of every individual as ultimate purpose, an end in himself."[3]

It is evident that this ethical argument for Socialism stands or falls by the assertion that in the economic order based on private ownership in the means
of production all men, or some men, are means and not purpose. Cohen 432
considers this to be completely proved. He believes that in such a social order

[2] Cohen, *Ethik des reinen Willens*, Berlin, 1904, pp. 303 ff.

[3] *Ibid.*, p. 304.

two classes of men exist, owners and non-owners, of whom only the first lead an existence worthy of a human being, while the second merely serve. It is easy to see where this notion comes from. It rests on popular ideas on the relations of rich and poor, and is supported by the Marxian social philosophy, for which Cohen professes great sympathy without, however, making his views about it clear.[4] Cohen completely ignores the liberal social theory. He takes it for granted that this is untenable, and thinks that it would be a waste of time to criticize it. Yet only by refuting the liberal views of the nature of society and the function of private property could he justify the assertion that in a society based on private ownership in the means of production men serve as means, not as ends. For liberal social theory proves that each single man sees in all others, first of all, only means to the realization of his purposes, while he himself is to all others a means to the realization of their purposes; that finally, by this reciprocal action, in which each is simultaneously means and end, the highest aim of social life is attained—the achievement of a better existence for everyone. As society is only possible if everyone, while living his own life, at the same time helps others to live, if every individual is simultaneously means and end; if each individual's well-being is simultaneously the condition necessary to the well-being of the others, it is evident that the contrast between I and thou, means and end, automatically is overcome. This, after all, is just what the simile of the biological organism is supposed to make us perceive. In the organic structure no parts are to be regarded only as means and none only as ends. According to Kant the organism is a being "in which everything is end and reciprocally also means."[5] Now Kant was thoroughly familiar with the nature of the organic, but he did not see—and in this he lagged far behind the great sociologists who were his contemporaries—that human society is formed according to the same principle.

433 The teleological view, which differentiates means and end, is permissible

[4] "The direct purpose of capitalist production is not the production of goods but of surplus value, or of profit in its developed form; not of the product but of the surplus product. . . . In this view the workers themselves appear as what, in the capitalist production, they are—mere means of production, not ends in themselves, not purpose of production." Marx, *Theorien über den Mehrwert* (Stuttgart, 1905), Part 2, pp. 333 ff. That the workers play a role in the economic process as consumers also, Marx never understood. Publisher's Note: Only a part of the work by Marx, *Theorien über den Mehrwert* (Stuttgart, 1905) has been translated into English in the book titled *Theories of Surplus Value: Selections,* translated from the German by G. A. Bonner and Emile Burns (New York: International Publishers, 1952), 432 pp.

[5] Kant, *Kritik der Urteilskraft* (Works, Vol. VI), p. 265. Publisher's Note: In English, *Critique of Judgment.* In Immanuel Kant, *The Critique of Judgement. Part II. Critique of Teleological Judgement,* trans. James Creed Meredith (Oxford: Clarendon Press, 1952).

only in so far as we make the will and action of individual men or individual human associations the subject of investigation. It ceases to have any meaning as soon as we go further and look at the effects of this action in society. For every individual who acts there exists an ultimate purpose, the purpose which Eudaemonism enables us to understand; in this sense one may say that every man is an end to himself and an end in himself. But as an observation applied to the whole of society, this mode of expression is without any cognitive value. Here we cannot speak of purpose with more justification than of any other phenomenon of nature. When we ask whether, in society, this or that is end or means, we mentally substitute for society—that is, for the structure of human co-operation held together by the superiority of the division of labour over isolated labour—a structure welded together by *one* will, and then ask what is the aim of this will. This is animistic thought, it is not in any way sociological or scientific.

Cohen's special argument for the abolition of private property reveals the obscurity in which he still labours with regard to this fundamental problem of social life. Things, he says, have value. Persons, however, have no value. They have dignity. The market price of the value of labour is incompatible with the dignity of the person.[6] This leads us into the abyss of Marxian phraseology and the doctrine of the "commodity-character" of labour and its objectionableness. This is the phrase which found its way into the treaties of Versailles and St. Germain in the form of a demand for the acceptance of the basic principle; "that labour should not be regarded merely as an article of commerce."[7] Enough, however, of these scholastic trivialities.

After this we need not be surprised to find repeated in Cohen all those catchwords which for thousands of years have been brought to bear against the institution of private property. He rejects property because the owner, by getting control over an isolated action, becomes in fact the owner of the person.[8] He rejects property because it withdraws from the worker the produce of his labour.[9]

Clearly the argument for Socialism presented by the Kantian school always 434
leads us back to the economic concepts of the various socialistic writers; above all to Marx and the "academic" socialists who followed in his steps. They have no arguments other than economic and sociological arguments, and these prove to be untenable.

---

[6] Cohen, *Ethik des reinen Willens*, p. 305. See also Steinthal, *Allgemeine Ethik*, pp. 266 ff.

[7] *Art.* 427 of the *Treaty of Versailles* and *Art.* 372 of the *Treaty of Saint Germain*.

[8] Cohen, *Ethik des reinen Willens*, p. 572.

[9] *Ibid.*, p. 578.

2

The Duty of Work as a Foundation for Socialism

"If any would not work, neither should he eat," says the Second Epistle of the Thessalonians, which was ascribed to the Apostle Paul.[10] This admonition to work is directed to those who want to live on their Christianity at the expense of the working members of the congregation; they are to support themselves without burdening their fellows.[11] Torn out of its context, this has long been interpreted as a rejection of unearned income.[12] It contains a most succinctly expressed moral precept which is continually being advocated with great vigour.

The train of thought which has led people to this principle can be followed in a saying of Kant: "Man may be as ingenious as he will, yet he cannot force Nature to accept other laws. Either he must work himself or others for him, and his labour will rob others of as much of their happiness as he needs to increase his own above the mean."[13]

It is important to note that Kant cannot base the indirect rejection of private property which lies in these words otherwise than on a utilitarian or eudaemonistic view. The conception from which he proceeds is that through private property more work is laid on some, while others are allowed to idle. This criticism is not proof against the objection that private ownership and
435 the differences in the amount of property do not take anything from anyone, that, rather, in a social order where neither were permitted so much less would be produced, that the per capita quota of the product of labour would amount to less than what the propertyless worker receives as income in a social order based on private property. It collapses as soon as one disproves the statement that the leisure of the possessors is bought by the extra efforts of those without possessions. Such ethical judgments against private property also show clearly that all moral evaluation of economic functions rests ultimately on a view of their economic achievements—on that and nothing else. To reject on "moral grounds" only an institution not considered objectionable

---

[10] II Thessalonians, III, 10. On the letter not being Paul's see Pfleiderer, *Das Urchristentum*, Vol. I, pp. 95 ff.

[11] Against this Paul, in the First Epistle to the Corinthians (IX, 6–14), favours on principle the Apostle's claim to live at the cost of the congregation.

[12] Todt (*Der radikale deutsche Sozialismus und die christliche Gesellschaft*, 2nd ed. (Wittenberg, 1878), pp. 306—19, is a good example of how, out of this and similar passages, people try to justify from the New Testament modern catchwords of the anti-liberal movement.

[13] Kant, "Fragmente aus dem Nachlass," Collected works, ed. Hartenstein, Vol. VIII (Leipzig, 1868), p. 622.

from the utilitarian standpoint is, if we look more closely, not the aim of ethical considerations. Actually, in all such cases the only difference of opinion is a difference of opinion about the economic function of such institutions.

That this fact has been overlooked is because those who tried to refute ethical criticism of private property have used the wrong arguments. Instead of pointing out its social significance they have usually been content to demonstrate the right of ownership or to prove that the owner, too, is not inactive, since he has worked to acquire his property and works to maintain it, and other arguments of this nature. The unsoundness of all this is obvious. It is absurd to refer to existing law when the problem is what the law should be; to refer to work which the owner does or has done when the problem is, not whether a certain kind of work should or should not be paid for, but whether private property in the means of production is to exist at all, and, if it exists, whether inequality of such ownership can be tolerated.

Therefore, from the ethical point of view, one is not permitted to ask whether a certain price is justified or not. Ethical judgment has to choose between a social order resting on private ownership in the means of production and one based on common ownership. Once it has arrived at this decision—which, for eudaemonistic ethics, can be based only upon an opinion of what each of the two imagined forms of society would achieve—it cannot proceed to call immoral single consequences of the order it has selected. That which is necessary to the social order it has chosen is moral, and everything else is immoral.

3 436

The Equality of Incomes as an Ethical Postulate

Against the assertion that all men should have equal incomes, as little can be said scientifically as can be said in support of it. Here is an ethical postulate which can only be evaluated subjectively. All science can do is to show what this aim would cost us, what other aims we should have to forgo in striving to attain this one.

Most people who demand the greatest possible equality of incomes do not realize that what they desire would only be achieved by sacrificing other aims. They imagine that the sum of incomes will remain unchanged and that all they need to do is to distribute it more equally than it is distributed in the social order based on private property. The rich will give as much as they receive over and above the average, and the poor receive as much as is needed to make up their incomes to the average. But the average income itself will remain unchanged. It must be clearly understood, however, that this idea rests on a grave error. It has been shown that, in whatever way one envisages the equalization of incomes this must always and necessarily lead to a very considerable reduction of the total national income and, thus, also, of the average income. On this showing, the matter takes on quite a different complexion. For we have then to decide whether we are in favor of an equal distribution of income at a lower average income, or inequality of incomes at a higher average income.

The decision will depend, of course, essentially, on how high one estimates the reduction which alteration in the social distribution of income will cause. If we conclude that the average income will be lower than that received today by the poorest, our attitude will probably be quite different from the attitude of most socialists of the sentimental type. If we accept what has been said in the second part of the book about how low productivity under Socialism and especially the contention that economic calculation would be quite impossible, then this argument of ethical Socialism also collapses.

437 It is untrue that some are poor because others are rich.[14] If an order of society in which incomes were equal replaced the capitalist order, everyone would become poorer. Paradoxical though it may sound, the poor receive what they do because rich people exist.

And if we reject the argument for the general conscription of labour and for equality of wealth and incomes which is based on the statement that some have their leisure and fortune at the expense of the increased labour and poverty of others, then there remains no basis for these ethical postulates except resentment. No one shall be idle if I have to work; no one shall be rich if I am poor. Thus we see, again and again, that resentment lies behind all socialist ideas.

4

The Ethical-Aesthetic Condemnation of the Profit-Motive

Another reproach which philosophers level against the capitalist economic order is that it encourages rank over-development of the acquisitive instinct.

[14] This, for example, is also how Thomas Aquinas imagines it. See Schreiber, *Die volkswirtschaftlichen Anschauungen der Scholastik seit Thomas von Aquin* (Jena, 1913), p. 18.

Man, they say, is no longer lord of the economic process, but its slave. That economic activity exists merely to satisfy wants and is a means, not an end in itself, has been forgotten. Life wears itself out in the perpetual hurry and scurry to get rich, and men have no time left for inner composure and real enjoyment. They lay waste their best powers in the exhausting daily struggle of free competition. And the ideologists look back into a distant past, where all is romantically transfigured. They see the Roman patrician at his country seat, meditating peacefully on the problems of the stoa, the medieval monk dividing his hours between devotion and the classics; the prince of the Renaissance at whose court artists and scholars meet, the Rococo lady in whose salon the encyclopedists develop their ideas—marvellous pictures, these, which produce in us a deep longing for the past. And our loathing for the present deepens when we turn from these visions to the life led by those who lack culture in our own time.

The weakness of this argument, which appeals to the feelings rather than to the mind, is not only that it contrasts the brightest flowers of all times and peoples with the weeds of modern life. It is clear that one cannot compare the life of a Pericles or Maecenas with the life of the ordinary man in the street. But it is still quite untrue that the haste of modern business life has killed man's sense of the beautiful and the sublime. The wealth of the "bourgeois" civilization is not spent on base enjoyments alone. If argument 438
be necessary, one need only point to the way in which serious music has become popular in the last decades, particularly among that class of the population which is caught in the whirl of business life. There never has been a time when art was closer to the heart of large circles of the people. It is no phenomenon peculiar to our time that coarse and vulgar amusements appeal more to the great mass of the people than nobler forms of enjoyment. It was always so. And we may take it that in the socialist community good taste will not always predominate.

Modern man has always before his eyes the possibility of growing rich by work and enterprise. In the more rigid economy of the past this was less easy. People were rich or poor from birth, and remained so through their lives unless they were given a change of position through some unforeseen accident, which their own work or enterprise could not have caused or avoided. Accordingly, we had the rich walking on the heights and the poor who stayed in the depths. It is not so in capitalistic society. The rich can more easily become poor and the poor can more easily become rich. And because every individual is not born with, as it were, his own or his family fate sealed, he tries to rise as high as he can. He can never be rich enough, because in capitalist society no wealth is eternal. In the past nobody could touch the feudal landlord. When his lands became less fertile he had less to consume, but as long as he did not get into debt he stayed on his property. The capitalist who lends out his capital and the entrepreneur who produces must stand the test of the market. Whoever invests unwisely, or produces too dearly, is ruined. Unhampered seclusion from the market no longer exists. Even landed fortunes cannot escape its influences; agriculture, too, must produce capitalistically. Today a man must earn or become poor.

Let those who wish to eliminate this coercion to work and enterprise understand quite clearly that they are proposing to undermine the foundations of our well-being. That in 1914 the earth nourished far more human beings than ever before, and that they all lived far better than their ancestors, was due entirely to the acquisitive instinct. If the diligence of modern industry were replaced by the contemplative life of the past, unnumbered millions would be doomed to death by starvation.

439 In the socialist society the lordly ease of government offices will take the place of the keen activity of modern financial houses and factories. The civil servant will supplant the energetic entrepreneur. Whether civilization will gain by it, we leave to the self-constituted judges of the world and its institutions to decide. Is the bureaucrat really the ideal human type, and must we aspire to fill the world with his kind at any price?

Many socialists describe with great enthusiasm the advantages of a society of civil servants over a society of profit-seekers.[15] In a society of the latter kind (the Acquisitive Society), every one pursues only his own advantage; in the society of those devoted to their profession (the Functional Society) everyone does his duty in the service of the whole. This higher evaluation of officialdom, in so far as it does not rest on a misconception of the social order based on private ownership in the means of production, is merely a new form of that contempt for the work of the painstaking citizen in which feudal landowners, soldiers, literary men, and bohemians have always indulged.

5

The Cultural Achievements of Capitalism

The inexactness and untruthfulness of ethical Socialism, its logical inconsistencies and its lack of scientific criticism, characterize it as the philosophic

[15] Ruskin, *Unto this last* (Tauchnitz-Ed.), pp. 19 ff.; Steinbach, *Erwerb und Beruf* (Vienna, 1896), pp. 13 ff.; Otto Conrad, *Volkswirtschaftspolitik oder Erwerbspolitik?* (Vienna, 1918), pp. 5 ff.; Tawney, *The Acquisitive Society*, p. 38.

product of a period of decay. It is the spiritual expression of the decline of European civilization at the turn of the nineteenth and twentieth centuries. Under its sway the German people and with them the whole of humanity were swept from the height of their culture to their deepest degradation. It created the mental premises for the World War and for Bolshevism. Its theories of violence were triumphant in the carnage of 1914–18, which brought to a close the finest flowering of civilization that world history has ever known.

In Ethical Socialism imperfect understanding of human social co-operation is combined with the resentment of the ne'er-do-well. It is the inability to
understand the difficult problems of social life which renders ethical socialists 440
so unsophisticated and so certain that they are competent to solve social problems offhand. Resentment strengthens that indignation which is always sure of a response from those of like mind. But the fire of their language comes from a romantic enthusiasm for unrestraint. In every man there is a deep-rooted desire for freedom from social ties; this is combined with a longing for conditions which fully satisfy all imaginable wishes and needs. Reason teaches us not to give way to the first unless we are prepared to sink back into the deepest misery, and reminds us further that the second cannot be fulfilled. Where reason ceases to function the way to romanticism is open. The anti-social in man triumphs over the mind.

The romantic movement, which addresses itself above all to the imagination, is rich in words. The colourful splendour of its dreams cannot be surpassed. Its praises awaken infinite longing, its curses breed loathing and contempt. Its longing is directed towards a past envisaged not soberly, but as a transfigured image, and towards a future which it paints with all the bright colours of desire. Between the two it sees the sober, everyday working life of bourgeois society and for this it feels only hatred and abhorrence. In the bourgeois it sees embodied everything that is shameful and petty. It roams the world at will, praises all ages and all lands; but for the conditions of the present day it has neither understanding nor respect.

The great creative minds, whom we honour above all others as Classics, understood the profound significance of the bourgeois order. The romanticists lack this insight. They are too small to sing the song of bourgeois society. They deride the citizen, despise "shopkeepers' ethics," laugh at the law. They are extraordinarily quick to see all the faults of everyday life and as quick to trace them back to defects in social institutions. No romantic has perceived the grandeur of capitalist society. Compare the results achieved by these "shopkeepers' ethics" with the achievements of Christianity! Christianity has acquiesced in slavery and polygamy, has practically canonized

war, has, in the name of the Lord, burnt heretics and devastated countries. The much abused "shopkeepers" have abolished slavery and serfdom, made woman the companion of man with equal rights, proclaimed equality before the law and freedom of thought and opinion, declared war on war, abolished torture, and mitigated the cruelty of punishment. What cultural force can
441 boast of similar achievements? Bourgeois civilization has created and spread a well-being, compared with which all the court life of the past seems meagre. Before the War, even the less favoured classes of the urban population could not only clothe and nourish themselves respectably but could enjoy genuine art and undertake journeys into distant lands. The romantics, however, saw only those who were not so well-off; the reason for their comparative poverty being that bourgeois civilization had not yet created sufficient wealth to make everybody comfortable. The same romantics had no eyes for those who were already comfortably circumstanced.[16] What they saw was always only invariably the dirt and the misery capitalist civilization had inherited from the past, not the values which it had already achieved.

---

[16] English economic history has destroyed the legend which taxed the rise of factory industry with having made the position of the working classes worse. See Hutt, "The Factory System of the Early 19th Century" in *Economica*, Vol. VI, 1926, p. 78 ff.; Clapham, *An Economic History of Modern Britain*, 2nd ec. (Cambridge, 1930), pp. 548 ff. Publisher's Note: The Hutt article, "The Factory System of the Early 19th Century," was reprinted in *Capitalism and the Historians*, ed. F. A. Hayek, essays by T. S. Ashton, L. M. Hacker, W. H. Hutt, B. de Jouvenel (Chicago: University of Chicago Press, 1954), pp. 160–188.

CHAPTER 31

Economic Democracy

1

The Slogan "Economic Democracy"

One of the more important arguments in favor of Socialism is that contained in the slogan "self-government in industry." As in the political sphere the King's absolutism was broken by the peoples' right to share decisions and later by its sole right to decide, so the absolutism of owners of the means of production and of entrepreneurs is to be abolished by consumers and workers. Democracy is incomplete as long as everyone is obliged to submit to the dictatorship of the owners. The worst part of Capitalism is by no means inequality of income; more unbearable still is the power which it gives the capitalists over their fellow citizens. As long as this state of affairs continues there can be no personal freedom. The People must take the administration of economic matters into their own hands, just as they have taken over the government of the state.[1] 442

There is a double error in this argument. It misconceives on the one hand, the nature and function of political democracy, and on the other, the nature of the social order based on private ownership in the means of production.

We have already shown that the essence of democracy is to be found neither in the electoral system, nor in the discussions and resolutions of national councils, nor in any sort of committee appointed by these councils.

---

[1] "The central wrong of the Capitalist system is neither the poverty of the poor nor the riches of the rich: it is the power which the mere ownership of the instruments of production gives to a relatively small section of the community over the actions of their fellow-citizens and over the mental and physical environment of successive generations. Under such a system personal freedom becomes, for large masses of the people, little better than a mockery. . . . What the Socialist aims at is the substitution, for this Dictatorship of the Capitalist, of government of the people by the people and for the people, in all the industries and services by which the people live." Sidney and Beatrice Webb, *A Constitution for the Socialist Commonwealth of Great Britain* (London, 1920), pp. xiii ff. See also Cole, *Guild Socialism Re-stated* (London, 1920), pp. 12 ff.

These are merely the technical tools of political democracy. Its real function is to make peace. Democratic institutions make the will of the people effective
443 in political matters, by ensuring that its rulers and administrators are elected by the people's votes. Thus are eliminated those dangers to peaceful social development which might result from any clash between the will of the rulers and public opinion. Civil war is averted through the operation of institutions which facilitate a peaceful change of the government. In the economic order based on private ownership in the means of production no special institutions, such as political democracy has created for itself, are needed to achieve corresponding success. Free competition does all that is needed. All production must bend to the consumers' will. From the moment it fails to conform to the consumers' demands it becomes unprofitable. Thus free competition compels the obedience of the producer to the consumer's will and also, in case of need, the transfer of the means of production from the hands of those unwilling or unable to achieve what the consumer demands into the hands of those better able to direct production. The lord of production is the consumer. From this point of view the capitalist society is a democracy in which every penny represents a ballot paper. It is a democracy with an imperative and immediately revocable mandate to its deputies.[2]

It is a consumers' democracy. By themselves the producers, as such, are quite unable to order the direction of production. This is as true of the entrepreneur as of the worker; both must bow ultimately to the consumers' wishes. And it could not well be otherwise. People produce, not for the sake of production, but for the goods that may be consumed. As producer in an economy based on the division of labour, a man is merely the agent of the community and as such has to obey. Only as a consumer can he command.

The entrepreneur is thus no more than an overseer of production. He of course exercises power over the worker. But he cannot exercise it arbitrarily. He must use it in accordance with the requirements of that productive activity which corresponds to the consumers' wishes. To the individual wage-earner whose outlook is enclosed by the narrow horizon of daily work, the entre-
444 preneur's decisions may seem arbitrary and capricious. Seen from too close up the shape of things lose their true significance. If the entrepreneur's disposal of production injures the worker's momentary interest, it is sure to

---

[2] "The market is a democracy where every penny gives a right to vote." Fetter, *The Principles of Economics*, pp. 394, 410. See also Schumpeter, *Theorie der wirtschaftlichen Entwicklung* (Leipzig, 1912), pp. 32 ff. Nothing is more topsy-turvy than a saying such as: "Who is less questioned at the building of a house in a large city than its future tenants?" Lenz, *Macht und Wirtschaft* (Munich, 1915), p. 32. Every builder tries to build in a way that best suits the wishes of the future tenants, so that he may be able to let the dwellings as quickly and profitably as possible. See also the striking remarks in Withers, *The Case for Capitalism* (London, 1920), pp. 41 ff.

seem to him unfounded and arbitrary. He will not realize that the entrepreneur works under the rule of a strict law. True, the entrepreneur is free to give full rein to his whims, to dismiss workers off hand, to cling stubbornly to antiquated processes, deliberately to choose unsuitable methods of production and to allow himself to be guided by motives which conflict with the demands of consumers. But when and in so far as he does this he must pay for it, and if he does not restrain himself in time he will be driven, by the loss of his property, into a position where he can inflict no further damage. Special means of controlling his behaviour are unnecessary. The market controls him more strictly and exactingly than could any government or other organ of society.[3]

Every attempt to replace this rule of the consumers by a rule of producers is absurd. It would run contrary to the very nature of the productive process. We have already treated an example of this in greater detail—the example most important for modern conditions—the example of the syndicalist economy. What is true of it, is true of any producers' policy. All economy must be a consumers' economy. The absurdity of these endeavours to institute "economic democracy" by the creation of syndicalist institutions becomes apparent if we imagine these institutions transferred to the political field. For example, would it be democracy if judges had to decide what laws should be in force and how they should be administered? Or if soldiers had to decide at whose disposal they would place their arms and how to use them? No, judges and soldiers have to conform to law if the state is not to become an arbitrary despotism. The catchword "industrial self-government" is the most blatant of all misconceptions of the nature of democracy.

In the socialist community, too, it is not the workers in separate branches of production who decide what is to be done in their own particular economic territory, but the supreme authority of society. If this were not so, we should have not Socialism but Syndicalism, and between these two there is no possible compromise.

2 445

The Consumer as the Deciding Factor in Production

People sometimes maintain that in guarding their own interests entrepreneurs force production in a direction opposed to the interests of consumers.

---

[3] People overlook this entirely when, like the Webbs, *A Constitution for the Socialist Commonwealth of Great Britain*, p. xii, they say that the workers have to obey the orders "of irresponsible masters intent on their own pleasure or their own gain."

The entrepreneurs have no scruples about "creating or intensifying the public's need for things which provide for merely sensual gratification but inflict harm on health or spiritual welfare." For instance the fight against alcoholism, the dread menace to national health and welfare, is said to be made more difficult because of the opposition "of the vested interests of alcohol capitalism to all attempts to combat it." The habit of smoking would not be "so widespread and so greatly on the increase among the young if economic interests played no role in promoting it." "Luxury articles, baubles and tinsel of all kinds, trashy and obscene publications" are today "forced upon the public because the producers profit by them or hope to do so."[4] It is common knowledge that the large-scale arming of the Powers and therefore, indirectly, war itself are ascribed to the machinations of "armament-capital."

Entrepreneurs and capitalists in search of investments turn towards those branches of production from which they hope to obtain the greatest profit. They try to fathom the future wants of consumers so as to gain a general survey of demand. As Capitalism is constantly creating new wealth for all and extending the satisfaction of wants, consumers are frequently in the position of being able to satisfy wants which formerly remained unsatisfied. Thus it becomes a special task of the capitalist entrepreneur to find out what formerly unsatisfied wants can now be provided for. This is what people have in mind when they say that Capitalism creates wants in order to satisfy them.

The nature of the things demanded by the consumer does not concern the entrepreneur and the capitalist. They are merely the obedient servants of the consumer and it is not their business to prescribe what the consumer shall enjoy. They give him poison and murderous weapons if he wants them. But nothing could be more erroneous than to suppose that products which
446 serve a bad or harmful purpose bring in more than those which serve a good one. The highest profit is obtained from articles for which there is the most urgent demand. The profit-seeker therefore sets about producing those commodities in which there is the greatest disproportion between supply and demand. Of course, once he has invested his capital, it is to his interest to see that the demand for his product increases. He tries to expand sales. But in the long run he cannot prevail against a change of demand. Neither can he obtain much advantage from growth in the demand for his products, for new enterprises turn their attention to his branch of industry and thereby tend to reduce his profits to the average.

---

[4] Messer, *Ethik* (Leipzig, 1918), pp. 111 ff.; Natorp, *Sozialidealismus* (Berlin, 1920), p. 13.

Mankind does not drink alcohol because there are breweries, distilleries, and vineyards; men brew beer, distil spirits, and grow grapes because of the demand for alcoholic drinks. "Alcohol-capital" has not created drinking habits any more than it has created drinking songs. The capitalists who own shares in breweries and distilleries would have preferred shares in publishing firms for devotional books, had the demand been for spiritual and not spirituous sustenance. "Armament capital" did not create wars; wars created "armament capital." It was not Krupp and Schneider who incited the nations to war, but imperialist writers and politicians.

If a man thinks alcohol and nicotine harmful, let him abstain from them. Let him try, if he will, to convert his fellows to his own views on abstinence. What is certain is that he cannot, in a capitalist society, whose basic principle is the self-determination and self-responsibility of each individual, force them against their will to renounce alcohol and nicotine. If this inability to impose his will on others causes him regret, then at least he can console himself with the thought that neither is he at the mercy of the commands of others.

Some socialists reproach the capitalist social order primarily for the rich variety of its goods. Instead of producing uniform products, which could be brought out on the largest scale, people manufacture hundreds and thousands of types of each commodity, and production is made much more expensive thereby. Socialism would put at the comrades' disposal only uniform goods; it would unify production and thereby raise national productivity. Simultaneously Socialism would dissolve separate family households, and in their place provide communal kitchens and hotel-like dwellings; this, too, would increase social wealth by eliminating the waste of labour power in tiny kitchens which serve only a few consumers. Many socialist 447
writings, above all those of Walter Rathenau, have dealt with these ideas in great detail.[5]

Under Capitalism each buyer has to decide whether he prefers the cheaper uniformity of mass production or the greater expense of articles specially manufactured to suit the taste of the individual or the small group. There is unmistakably a tendency towards progressive uniformity of production and consumption through standardization. Commodities used in the productive process itself are daily becoming more standardized. The shrewd entrepreneur soon discovers the advantage of using the standard type—with its lower purchasing cost, its replaceability and adaptability to other productive processes rather than articles produced by a special process. The

[5] Rathenau, *Die neue Wirtschaft* (Berlin, 1918), pp. 41 ff.; also the critique of Wiese, *Freie Wirtschaft* (Leipzig, 1918).

movement to standardize the implements of production is impeded today by the fact that numerous enterprises are indirectly or directly socialized. As they are not rationally controlled, no stress is laid on the advantage of using standard types. Army administrations, municipal building departments, State railways, and similar authorities resist, with bureaucratic obstinacy, the adoption of types in universal use. The unification of the production of machines, factory equipment and semi-finished products does not require a change to Socialism. On the contrary, Capitalism does this more quickly of its own accord.

It is otherwise with goods for use and consumption. If a man satifies his special, personal taste in preference to using the uniform products of mass production and believes that his satisfaction balances the extra cost, then one cannot objectively prove him wrong. If my friend prefers to dress, be housed, and eat as it pleases him and not to do as everyone else does, who can blame him? For his happiness lies in the satisfaction of his wishes; he wants to live as he pleases and not as I or others would live were we in his place. It is his valuation that counts, not mine or other people's. I may be able to prove to him that the judgments on which he bases his values are false. For example I may demonstrate that the foods he consumes have a smaller nutritional value than he assumed. But if his values have been built, not on untenable views about the relation of cause and effect, but on subjective
448 sentiments and feelings, my arguments cannot change his mind. If, notwithstanding the advantages claimed for hotel life and communal kitchens, he still prefers a separate household because such sentiments as "own home" and "own hearth" weigh with him more than arguments in favour of unitary organization, then nothing further remains to be said. If he wishes to furnish his dwelling according to his personal taste and not according to the public taste which guides the furniture manufacturer, there are no arguments with which to refute him. If, knowing the effects of alcohol, he still drinks it, because he is prepared to pay even dearly for the pleasure it gives him, I may certainly, from the standpoint of my values, call him unwise, but it is *his* will, *his* valuation that will decide. If I, as a dictator, or as a member of a despotically ruling majority, prohibit the drinking of alcohol, I do not thus raise the productivity of social production. Those who condemn alcohol would have avoided it without prohibition. For all others, the prohibition of an enjoyment which they value above anything they can obtain by renouncing it means a falling-off in satisfaction.

The contrast of productivity and profitableness, which, as we see from arguments explained in a previous chapter, is valueless for the understanding of the working of production directed to given ends, must lead definitely to false conclusions if applied to the ends of economic action.[6] In dealing with means to a given end, one may call this process or that the more practical, that is, capable of a higher yield. But when we ask whether this or that means gives a greater direct increase of welfare to the individual, we have no objective standards that will serve. Here the subjective will of man is the deciding factor. A man's preference for water, milk, or wine does not depend on the physiological effects of these drinks, but on his valuation of the effects. If a man drinks wine and not water I cannot say he is acting irrationally. At most I can say that in his place I would not do so. But his pursuit of happiness is his own business, not mine.

If the socialist community does not supply the comrades with the goods which they themselves want to enjoy, but with those which the rulers think they ought to enjoy, the sum of satisfactions is not increased, but diminished. One certainly could not call this violation of the individual will "economic democracy."

For it is an essential difference between capitalist and socialist production 449
that under Capitalism men provide for themselves, while under Socialism they are provided for. The socialist wants to feed and house humanity and cover its nakedness. But men prefer to eat, dwell, dress and generally to seek happiness after their own fashion.

3

Socialism as Expression of the Will of the Majority

The number of our contemporaries who decide in favour of Socialism because the majority has already so decided is by no means negligible. "Most people want Socialism; the masses no longer support the capitalist social order, therefore we must socialize." One hears this constantly. But it is not a convincing argument in the eyes of those who reject Socialism. Certainly if the majority want Socialism, Socialism we shall have. Nobody has shown more clearly than the liberal philosophers that there is no resisting public opinion, and that the majority decides, even when it is in error. If the majority makes a mistake, the minority must also suffer the consequences and cannot complain. Has it not been party to the error in having failed to enlighten the majority?

---

[6] See pp. 123 ff., 350 ff.

But in discussing what is to be, the argument that the great mass of people violently demand Socialism would be valid only if Socialism were desired as an ultimate end for its own sake. But this is by no means so. Like all other forms of social organization Socialism is only a means, not an end in itself. Those who want Socialism, like those who reject it, want well-being and happiness, and they are socialists only because they believe that Socialism is the best way to achieve this. If they were convinced that the liberal order of society was better able to fulfill their wishes they would become liberals. Therefore, the argument that one must be socialist because the masses demand Socialism is the worst possible argument against an enemy of Socialism. The will of the people is the highest law for the representatives of the people who have to execute its commands. But those who seek to direct thought must not bend to this will. Only he is a pioneer who speaks out and attempts to bring his fellow citizens to his ways of thinking, even when they differ from those generally held. This argument that one should
450 defer to the masses is nothing else than a demand that those who still oppose Socialism by reasonable criticism should abdicate reason itself. That such an argument can be put forward only shows how far the socialization of intellectual life has already gone. In the very darkest epochs of early history, such arguments have not been used. Those who opposed the prejudices of the greatest number were never told that their opinions were false simply because the majority thought otherwise.

If Socialism is inherently impracticable the fact that everyone desires it will not enable us to accomplish it.

CHAPTER 32

Capitalist Ethics

1

Capitalist Ethics and the Impracticability of Socialism

In the expositions of Ethical Socialism one constantly finds the assertion 451
that it presupposes the moral purification of men. As long as we do not succeed in elevating the masses morally we shall be unable to transfer the socialist order of society from the sphere of ideas to that of reality. The difficulties in the way of Socialism lie exclusively, or predominantly, in men's moral shortcomings. Some writers doubt whether this obstacle will ever be overcome; others are content to say that the world will not be able to achieve Socialism for the present or in the immediate future.

We have been able to show why the socialist economy is impracticable: not because men are morally too base, but because the problems that a socialist order would have to solve present insuperable intellectual difficulties. The impracticability of Socialism is the result of intellectual, not moral, incapacity. Socialism could not achieve its end, because a socialist economy could not calculate value. Even angels, if they were endowed only with human reason, could not form a socialistic community.

If a socialist community were capable of economic calculation, it could be set up without any change in men's moral character. In a socialist society different ethical standards would prevail from those of a society based on private ownership in the means of production. The temporary sacrifices demanded of the individual by society would be different. Yet it would be no more difficult to enforce the code of socialist morals than it is to enforce the code of capitalist morals, if there were any possibility of making objective computations within the socialist society. If a socialist society could ascertain separately the product of the labour of each single member of the society, his share in the social product could be calculated and his reward fixed proportionately to his productive contribution. Under such circumstances

452 the socialist order would have no cause to fear that a comrade would fail to work with the maximum of energy for lack of any incentive to sweeten the toil of labour. Only because this condition is lacking, Socialism will have to construct for its Utopia a type of human being totally different from the race which now walks the earth, one to whom labour is not toil and pain, but joy and pleasure. Because such a calculus is out of the question, the Utopian socialist is obliged to make demands on men which are diametrically opposed to nature. This inadequacy of the human type which would cause the breakdown of Socialism, may appear to be of a moral order; on closer examination it turns out to be a question of intellect.

2

The Alleged Defects of Capitalist Ethics

To act reasonably means to sacrifice the less important to the more important. We make temporary sacrifices when we give up small things to obtain bigger things, as when we cease to indulge in alcohol to avoid its physiological after-effects. Men submit to the effort of labour in order that they may not starve.

Moral behaviour is the name we give to the temporary sacrifices made in the interests of social co-operation, which is the chief means by which human wants and human life generally may be supplied. All ethics are social ethics. (If it be claimed that rational behaviour, directed solely towards one's own good, should be called ethical too, and that we had to deal with individual ethics and with duties to oneself, we could not dispute it; indeed this mode of expression emphasizes perhaps better than ours, that in the last analysis the hygiene of the individual and social ethics are based on the same reasoning.) To behave morally, means to sacrifice the less important to the more important by making social co-operation possible.

The fundamental defect of most of the anti-utilitarian systems of ethics lies in the misconstruction of the meaning of the temporary sacrifices which duty demands. They do not see the purpose of sacrifice and foregoing of pleasure, and they construct the absurd hypothesis that sacrifice and renunciation are morally valuable in themselves. They elevate unselfishness and self-sacrifice and the love of compassion, which lead to them, to absolute moral values. The pain that at first accompanies the sacrifice is defined as
453 moral because it is painful—which is very near asserting that all action painful to the performer is moral.

From the discovery of this confusion we can see why various sentiments and actions which are socially neutral or even harmful come to be called moral. Of course, even reasoning of this sort cannot avoid returning furtively to utilitarian ideas. If we are unwilling to praise the compassion of a doctor who hesitates to undertake a life-saving operation on the ground that he thereby saves the patient pain, and distinguish, therefore, between true and false compassion, we re-introduce the teleological consideration of purpose which we tried to avoid. If we praise unselfish action, then human welfare, as a purpose, cannot be excluded. There thus arises a negative utilitarianism: we are to regard as moral that which benefits, not the person acting, but others. An ethical ideal has been set up which cannot be fitted into the world we live in. Therefore, having condemned the society built up on "self-interest" the moralist proceeds to construct a society in which human beings are to be what his ideal requires. He begins by misunderstanding the world and laws; he then wishes to construct a world corresponding to his false theories, and he calls this the setting up of a moral ideal.

Man is not evil merely because he wants to enjoy pleasure and avoid pain—in other words, to live. Renunciation, abnegation, and self-sacrifice are not good in themselves. To condemn the ethics demanded by social life under Capitalism and to set up in their place standards for moral behaviour which—it is thought—might be adopted under Socialism is a purely arbitrary procedure.

PART V
DESTRUCTIONISM

CHAPTER 33

The Motive Powers of Destructionism

1

The Nature of Destructionism

To the socialist, the coming of Socialism means a transition from an 457
irrational to a rational economy. Under Socialism, planned management of economic life takes the place of anarchy of production; society, which is conceived as the incarnation of reason, takes the place of the conflicting aims of unreasonable and self-interested individuals. A just distribution replaces an unjust distribution of goods. Want and misery vanish and there is wealth for all. A picture of paradise is unfolded before us, a paradise which—so the laws of historical evolution tell us—we, or at least our heirs, must at length inherit. For all history leads to that promised land, and all that has happened in the past has only prepared the way for our salvation.

This is how our contemporaries see Socialism, and they believe in its excellence. It is false to imagine that the socialist ideology dominates only those parties which call themselves socialist or—what is generally intended to mean the same thing—"social." All present-day political parties are saturated with the leading socialistic ideas. Even the stoutest opponents of Socialism fall within its shadow. They, too, are convinced that the socialist economy is more rational than the capitalist, that it guarantees a more just distribution of income, that historical evolution is driving man inexorably in that direction. When they oppose Socialism they do so with the sense that they are defending selfish private interests and that they are combating a development which from the standpoint of public welfare is desirable and is based upon the only ethically acceptable principle. And in their hearts they are convinced that their resistance is hopeless.

Yet the socialist idea is nothing but a grandiose rationalization of petty resentments. Not one of its theories can withstand scientific criticism and all

its deductions are ill-founded. Its conception of the capitalist economy has
458 long been seen to be false; its plan of a future social order proves to be inwardly contradictory, and therefore impracticable. Not only would Socialism fail to make economic life more rational, it would abolish social co-operation outright. That it would bring justice is merely an arbitrary assertion, arising, as we can show, from resentment and the false interpretation of what takes place under Capitalism. And that historical evolution leaves us no alternative but Socialism turns out to be a prophecy which differs from the chiliastic dreams of primitive Christian sectarians only in its claim to the title "science."

In fact Socialism is not in the least what it pretends to be. It is not the pioneer of a better and finer world, but the spoiler of what thousands of years of civilization have created. It does not build; it destroys. For destruction is the essence of it. It produces nothing, it only consumes what the social order based on private ownership in the means of production has created. Since a socialist order of society cannot exist, unless it be as a fragment of Socialism within an economic order resting otherwise on private property, each step leading towards Socialism must exhaust itself in the destruction of what already exists.

Such a policy of destructionism means the consumption of capital. There are few who recognize this fact. Capital consumption can be detected statistically and can be conceived intellectually, but it is not obvious to everyone. To see the weakness of a policy which raises the consumption of the masses at the cost of existing capital wealth, and thus sacrifices the future to the present, and to recognize the nature of this policy, requires deeper insight than that vouchsafed to statesmen and politicians or to the masses who have put them into power. As long as the walls of the factory buildings stand, and the trains continue to run, it is supposed that all is well with the world. The increasing difficulties of maintaining the higher standard of living are ascribed to various causes, but never to the fact that a policy of capital consumption is being followed.

In the problem of the capital consumption of a destructionist society we find one of the key problems of the socialist economic policy. The danger of capital consumption would be particularly great in the socialist community; the demagogue would achieve success most easily by increasing consumption per head at the cost of the formation of additional capital and to the detriment of existing capital.

459 It is in the nature of capitalist society that new capital is continually being formed. The greater the capital fund becomes, the higher does the marginal productivity of labour rise and the higher, therefore, are wages, absolute

and relative. The progressive formation of capital is the only way to increase the quantity of goods which society can consume annually without diminishing production in the future—the only way to increase the workers' consumption without harm to future generations of workers. Therefore, it has been laid down by Liberalism that progressive capital formation is the only means by which the position of the great masses can be permanently improved. Socialism and destructionism seek to attain this end in a different way. They propose to use up capital so as to achieve present wealth at the expense of the future. The policy of Liberalism is the procedure of the prudent father who saves and builds for himself and his successors. The policy of destructionism is the policy of the spendthrift who dissipates his inheritance regardless of the future.

2

Demagogy

To Marxians, Karl Marx's supreme achievement lay in the fact that he roused the proletariat to class-consciousness. Before he wrote, socialist ideas had led an academic existence in the writings of the Utopians and in the narrow circles of their disciples. By connecting these ideas with a revolutionary workers' movement, which till then had only a petty bourgeois aim, Marx created, say the Marxians, the foundations of the proletarian movement. This movement, they believe, will live until it has accomplished its historical mission, the setting up of the socialist order of society.

Marx is supposed to have discovered the dynamic laws of capitalist society and, with the aid of the theory of historical evolution, to have defined the aims of the modern social movement as inevitable consequences of that evolution. He is said to have shown that the proletariat could free itself as a class only by itself abolishing the class conflict, and so making possible a society in which "the free development of each individual is the condition for the free development of all."

Ecstatic enthusiasts see in Marx one of the heroic figures of world history,
and class him among the great economists and sociologists, even among the 460
most eminent philosophers. The unbiased observer looks on Karl Marx's work with different eyes. As an economist Marx entirely lacked originality. He was a follower of the Classical political economists, but he lacked the ability to approach essentially economic problems without a political bias.

He saw everything through the spectacles of the agitator, who considers first and foremost the effect made on the popular mind. Even here he was not really original, for the English socialist defenders of the "right to the full produce of labour," who with their pamphlets in the third and fourth decades of the nineteenth century prepared the way for Chartism, had already anticipated him in all essentials. Moreover, he had the misfortune to be entirely ignorant of the revolution in theoretical economics which was proceeding during the years when he worked out his system, a transformation which made itself known soon after the issue of the first volume of *Das Kapital*. As a result, the later volumes of *Das Kapital*, from the day they were published, were quite out of touch with modern science. This was a piece of bad luck which hit his infatuated followers particularly hard. From the beginning, they had to be content with barren expositions of the master's writings. They have timidly avoided any contact with the modern theory of value. As a sociologist and historical philosopher Marx was never more than an able agitator writing for the daily needs of his party. The materialist conception of history is scientifically worthless; moreover Marx never worked it out exactly but propounded it in various incompatible forms. His philosophic standpoint was that of the Hegelians. He is one of the many writers of his time, now mostly forgotten, who applied the dialectic method to all fields of science. Decades had to pass before people had the face to call him a philosopher and to place him side by side with the great thinkers.

As a scientific writer Marx was dry, pedantic, and heavy. The gift of expressing himself intelligibly had been denied him. In his political writings alone does he produce powerful effects, and these only by means of dazzling antitheses and of phrases which are easy to remember, sentences which by play of words hide their own vacuity. In his polemics he does not hesitate to distort what his own opponent had said. Instead of refuting he tends to
461 abuse.[1] Here, too, his disciples (his school really exists only in Germany and Eastern Europe, especially in Russia) have faithfully imitated the master's example, reviling their opponents but never attempting to refute them by argument.

Marx's originality and historical significance lie entirely in the field of political technique. He recognizes the immense social power that can be achieved by welding out of the great masses of workers, herded together in

[1] See, for instance, in *Das Kapital* the remarks on Bentham: "the most homely platitude," "only copied stupidly," "trash," "a genius of bourgeois stupidity," *op. cit.*, Vol. I, p. 573; on Malthus, "a schoolboyishly superficial and clerically stilted plagiarism," *Ibid.*, Vol. I, p. 580. Publisher's Note: In the English edition of Marx, *Capital*, Volume I, these quotations appear on p. 668 (Bentham) and p. 675 n3 (Malthus).

workshops, a political factor; and he seeks and finds the slogans to unite these masses into a coherent movement. He produces the catchword which leads people otherwise indifferent to politics to attack private property. He preaches a doctrine of salvation which rationalizes their resentment and transfigures their envy and desire for revenge into a mission ordained by world history. He inspires them with consciousness of their mission by greeting them as those who carry in themselves the future of the human race. The rapid expansion of Socialism has been compared to that of Christianity. More appropriate, perhaps, would be a comparison with Islam, which inspired the sons of the desert to lay waste ancient civilizations, cloaked their destructive fury with an ethical ideology and stiffened their courage with rigid fatalism.[2]

At the core of Marxism is the doctrine of the identity of interests of all proletarians. As an individual, however, the worker is daily in sharp competitive conflict with his fellow-workers and with those who are quite ready to take his job from him; together with his own comrades in his own trade he competes with workers in other branches of the trade and with the consumers of the products in the production of which he collaborates. In the face of all these facts, all his passions had to be raised to induce him to seek his salvation in union with other workers. But this was not so very difficult; it always pays to rouse what is evil in the human heart. Yet Marx has done more: he has decked out the resentment of the common man with the nimbus of science, and has thus made it attractive to those who live on a higher intellectual and ethical plane. Every socialist movement has borrowed in this respect from Marx, adapting the doctrine slightly for its special needs.

As a master of demagogic technique Marx was a genius; this cannot be 462
sufficiently emphasized. He found the propitious historical moment for uniting the masses into a single political movement, and was himself on the spot to lead this movement. For him all politics was only the continuation of war by other means; his political art was always political tactics. The socialist parties which trace their origin back to Marx have kept this up, as have those who have taken the Marxist parties for their model. They have elaborated the technique of agitation, the cadging for votes and for souls, the stirring up of electoral excitement, the street demonstrations, and the terrorism. To learn the technique of these things requires years of hard study.

[2] Thus Marxism finds it easy to ally with Islamic zealotism. Full of pride the Marxist Otto Bauer cries: "In Turkestan and Azerbaijan monuments to Marx stand opposite the mosques, and the Mullah in Persia mingles quotations from Marx with passages from the Koran when he calls the people to the Holy War against European Imperialism." See Otto Bauer, "*Marx als Mahnung*" in *Der Kampf*, XVI, 1923, p. 83.

At their party conferences and in their party literature, the Marxians give more attention to questions of organization and of tactics than to the most important basic problems of politics. In fact, if one wished to be more precise one would have to admit that nothing interests them at all except from the point of view of party tactics and that they have no interest to spare for anything else.

This militarist attitude to politics, which reveals the inner affinity of Marxism with Prussian and Russian etatism has quickly found adherents. The modern parties of the continent of Europe have completely accepted the Marxian ideology. Especially the parties which aim to promote particular interests, and which gather together the peasant class, the industrial middle class and the class of employers, make use of the Marxist doctrine of class-war for their own purposes. They have learnt all they know from Marxism.

The defeat of the liberal ideology could not long be postponed. Liberalism has anxiously avoided all political artifice. It has relied entirely upon the inner vitality of its ideas and their power to convince, and has disdained all other means of political conflict. It has never pursued political tactics, never stooped to demagogy. The old Liberalism was honest through and through and faithful to its principles. Its opponents called this being "doctrinaire."

Today the old liberal principles have to be submitted to a thorough re-examination. Science has been completely transformed in the last hundred years, and today the general sociological and economic foundations of the liberal doctrine have to be relaid. On many questions Liberalism did not think logically to the conclusion. There are loose threads to be gathered up.[3]
463 But the mode of political activity of Liberalism cannot alter. It regards all social co-operation as an emanation of rationally recognized utility, in which all power is based on public opinion, and can undertake no course of action that would hinder the free decision of thinking men. Liberalism knows that society can advance to a higher stage only by men recognizing the usefulness of social co-operation; that neither God nor veiled destiny determines the future of the human race, but only man himself. When nations rush blindly towards destruction, Liberalism must try to enlighten them. But even if they do not hear, whether because they are deaf or because the warning voice is too feeble, one must not seek to seduce them to the right mode of conduct by tactical and demagogic artifice. It might be possible to destroy society by demagogy. But it can never be built up by that means.

---

[3] See my *Liberalismus* (Jena, 1927). Publisher's Note: In English as *The Free and Prosperous Commonwealth: An Exposition of the Ideas of Classical Liberalism* (Princeton: Van Nostrand, 1962).

3

The Destructionism of the Literati

The romantic and the social art of the nineteenth century have prepared the way for socialist destructionism. Without the help it got from this direction Socialism would never have gained its hold on people's minds.

Romanticism is man's revolt against reason, as well as against the condition under which nature has compelled him to live. The romantic is a daydreamer; he easily manages in imagination to disregard the laws of logic and of nature. The thinking and rationally acting man tries to rid himself of the discomfort of unsatisfied wants by economic action and work; he produces in order to improve his position. The romantic is too weak—too neurasthenic—for work; he imagines the pleasures of success but he does nothing to achieve them. He does not remove the obstacles; he merely removes them in imagination. He has a grudge against reality because it is not like the dream world he has created. He hates work, economy, and reason.

The romantic takes all the gifts of a social civilization for granted and desires, in addition, everything fine and beatiful that, as he thinks, distant times and countries had or have to offer. Surrounded by the comforts of European town life he longs to be an Indian rajah, Bedouin, corsair, or
troubadour. But he sees only that portion of these people's lives which seems 464
pleasant to him, never their lack of the things he obtains in such abundance. His horsemen gallop over the plains on fiery steeds, his corsairs capture beautiful women, his knights vanquish their enemies between episodes of love and song. The perilous nature of their existence, the comparative poverty of their circumstances, their miseries and their toils—these things his imagination tactfully overlooks: all is transfigured by a rosy gleam. Compared with this dream ideal, reality appears arid and shallow. There are obstacles to overcome which do not exist in the dream. There are very different tasks to be undertaken. Here are no beautiful women to be rescued from the hands of robbers, no lost treasures to be found, no dragons to kill. Here there is work to do, ceaselessly, assiduously, day after day, year after year. Here one must plough and sow if one wishes to reap. The romantic does not choose to admit all this. Obstinate as a child, he refuses to recognize it. He mocks and jeers; he despises and loathes the bourgeois.

The spread of capitalist thought produced an attitude of mind unfriendly to Romanticism. The poetic figures of knights and pirates become objects of mirth. Now that the lives of Bedouins, maharajahs, pirates, and other romantic heroes had been observed at close quarters, any desire to emulate them vanished. The achievements of the capitalist social order made it good to be alive and there was a growing feeling that security of life and liberty, peaceful welfare, and richer satisfaction of wants could be expected only from Capitalism. The romantic contempt for what is bourgeois fell into disrepute.

But the mental attitude from which Romanticism sprang was not so easy to eradicate. The neurasthenic protest against life sought other forms of expression. It found it in the "social" art of the nineteenth century.

The really great poets and novelists of the period were not social-political propagandist writers. Flaubert, Maupassant, Jacobsen, Strindberg, Konrad Ferdinand Meyer, to name only a few, were far from being followers of the fashionable literature. We do not owe the statement of these social and political problems to the writers whose works have given the nineteenth century its lasting place in the history of literature. This was the task assumed by second- or third-rate writers. It was writers of this class who introduced
465 as literary figures the bloodsucking capitalist entrepreneur and the noble proletarian. To them the rich man is in the wrong because he is rich, and the poor in the right because he is poor.[4] "But this is just as if wealth were a crime," Gerhart Hauptmann makes Frau Dreissiger exclaim in *Die Weber*. The literature of this period is full of the condemnation of property.

This is not the place for an aesthetic analysis of these works; our task is to examine their political efforts. They have brought victory to Socialism by enlisting the allegiance of the educated classes. By means of such books Socialism has been carried into the houses of the wealthy, captivating the wives and daughters and causing the sons to turn away from the family business until at last the capitalist entrepreneur himself has begun to believe in the baseness of his activities. Bankers, captains of industry, and merchants have filled the boxes of theatres in which plays of a socialist tendency were given before enthusiastic audiences.

Social art is tendentious art: all social literature has a thesis to demonstrate.[5] It is ever the same thesis: Capitalism is an evil, Socialism is salvation. That such eternal repetition has not led to boredom sooner must be attributed solely to the fact that the various writers have had different forms of Socialism in mind. But they all follow Marx's example in avoiding detailed exposition of the socialist social order they praise; most of them merely indicate by allusion, though clearly enough, that they desire a socialist order. That the

---

[4] Cazamian, *Le roman social en Angleterre, 1830–50* (Paris, 1904), pp. 267 ff.

[5] On the socialist tendency in painting see Muther, *Geschichte der Malerei im 19. Jahrhundert* (Munich, 1893), Vol. II. pp. 186 ff.; Coulin, *Die sozialistische Weltanschauung in der französischen Malerei* (Leipzig, 1909), pp. 85 ff.

logic of their argument is inadequate and that the conclusions are driven home by an appeal to the emotions rather than to reason is hardly surprising, seeing that the same method is followed by *soi-disant* scientific authorities on Socialism. Fiction is a favoured vehicle for this kind of procedure, as there is little fear that anyone will try to refute its assertions in detail by logical criticism. It is not the custom to inquire into the accuracy of particular remarks in novels and plays. Even if it were, the author could still find a way out by denying responsibility for the particular words put into the mouth of a hero. The conclusions forced home by character-drawing cannot be invalidated by logic. Even if the "man of property" is always depicted as bad through and through, one cannot reproach the author on account of a simple example. 466
For the total effect of the literature of his time no single writer is responsible.

In *Hard Times* Dickens puts into the mouth of Sissy Jupe, the deserted little daughter of a circus clown and dancer, remarks designed to shatter Utilitarianism and Liberalism. He makes Mr. M'Choackumchild, teacher in the model school of the Benthamite capitalist Gradgrind, ask how great is the percentage of victims when, out of 100,000 sea travellers, 500 are drowned. The good child answers, that for the relatives and friends of the victims there is no percentage—and so condemns with quiet simplicity the self-complacency of Manchesterism. Leaving aside the far-fetched improbability of the scene, this is of course all very fine and touching. But it does not diminish the satisfaction which members of a capitalist community may feel when they contemplate the great reduction of the dangers of navigation under Capitalism. And if Capitalism has so contrived that out of 1,000,000 people only twenty-five starve each year, while under more ancient economic systems a much greater proportion starved, then our estimation of this achievement is not impaired by Sissy's platitude, that for those who starve the ordeal is just as bitter when a million or a million million others are starving at the same time or not. Moreover, we are offered no proof that in a socialist society fewer people would starve. The third observation which Dickens puts into Sissy's mouth is intended to show that one cannot judge the economic prosperity of a nation by the amount of its wealth, but one must consider also the distribution of that wealth. Dickens was too ignorant of the writings of the utilitarians to know that these views did not contradict the older utilitarianism. Bentham, particularly, maintained with special emphasis that a sum of wealth brings more happiness when it is evenly distributed than when it is so distributed as to endow some richly while others have little.[6]

---

[6] Bentham, *Principles of the Civil Code*, pp. 304 ff.

Sissy's counterpart is the model boy, Bitzer. He gets his mother into the workhouse and then contents himself with giving her half a pound of tea once a year. Even this, says Dickens, is a weakness in the otherwise admirable youth, whom he calls an excellent young economist. For one thing, all almsgiving inevitably tends to pauperize the recipient. Further, Bitzer's only rational action with regard to tea would have been to buy as cheaply, and sell it as dearly as possible. Have not philosophers demonstrated that in this
467 consists the whole duty of man (the whole, not a part of his duty)? Millions who have read these observations have felt the indignation for the baseness of utilitarian thought which the author meant them to feel. Nevertheless, they are quite unjust. It is true that liberal politicians have striven against the encouragement of beggars by means of indiscriminate almsgiving and have shown the futility of any attempt at bettering the situation of the poor which does not proceed by increasing the productivity of labour. They have exposed the danger to the proletarians themselves of proposals for increasing the birth rate by premature marriages between persons not in a position to take care of their children. But they have never protested against support through the Poor Law of people unable to work. Neither have they contested the moral duty of children to support their parents in old age. The liberal social philosophy has never said that it was a "duty," let alone the beginning and end of morality, to buy as cheaply as possible and sell as dearly as possible. It has shown that this is the rational behaviour for the individual seeking (by buying and selling) the means for the *indirect* satisfaction of his wants. But Liberalism has no more called it irrational to give tea to one's aged mother than it has called tea drinking in itself irrational.

One glance into the works of the utilitarians is enough to unmask these sophistical distortions. But there is hardly one in every hundred thousand readers of Dickens who has ever read a line of a utilitarian writer. Dickens, with other romantics less gifted as storytellers but following the same tendencies, has taught millions to hate Liberalism and Capitalism. And yet Dickens was not an open and direct champion of destructionism, any more than were William Morris, Shaw, Wells, Zola, Anatole France, Gerhart Hauptmann, Edmondo de Amicis, and many others. They all reject the capitalist social order and combat private ownership in the means of production, without perhaps always being conscious of it. Between the lines they suggest an inspiring picture of a better state of affairs economically and socially. They are recruiting agents for Socialism and, since Socialism must destroy society, are at the same time paving the way for destructionism. But just as political Socialism became finally, in Bolshevism, an open avowal of destructionism, so too did literary Socialism. Tolstoy is the great prophet of

a destructionism that goes back to the words of the Gospels. He makes the
teachings of Christ, which rested on a belief that the Kingdom of God was 468
imminent, a gospel for all times and all men. Like the communist sects of the Middle Ages and the Reformation he tries to build society on the commands of the Sermon on the Mount. He does not of course go so far as to take literally the exhortation to follow the example of the lilies of the field, which toil not. But in his idea of society there is only room for self-sufficing agriculturists who, with modest means, till a small piece of land, and he is logical enough to demand that everything else shall be destroyed.

And now the peoples which have hailed with the greatest enthusiasm such writings, which call for the destruction of all cultural values, are themselves on the verge of a great social catastrophe.

CHAPTER 34

The Methods of Destructionism

1

The Means of Destructionism

469 Socialist policy employs two methods to accomplish its purposes: the first aims directly at converting society to Socialism; the second aims only indirectly at this conversion by destroying the social order which is based on private ownership. The parties of social reform and the evolutionary wings of the socialist parties prefer the first means; the second is the weapon of revolutionary Socialism, which is primarily concerned to clear the ground for building up a new civilization by liquidating the old one. To the first category belong municipalization and nationalization of enterprises; to the second, sabotage and revolution.

The importance of this division is lessened materially by the fact that the effects achieved by both groups do not greatly differ. As we have shown, even the direct method which aims at the creation of a new society can only destroy; it cannot create. Thus the beginning and end of the socialist policy, which has dominated the world for decades, is destruction. In the policy of the communists the will to destroy is so clear that no one can overlook it. But although destructionism is more easily recognized in the actions of the Bolshevists than in other parties, it is essentially just as strong in all other socialist movements. State interference in economic life, which calls itself "economic policy," has done nothing but destroy economic life. Prohibitions and regulations have by their general obstructive tendency fostered the growth of the spirit of wastefulness. Already during the war period this policy had gained so much ground that practically all economic action of the entrepreneur was branded as violation of the law. That production is still being carried on, even semi-rationally, is to be ascribed only to the fact that destructionist laws and measures have not yet been able to operate completely and effectively. Were they more effective, hunger and mass extinction would be the lot of all civilized nations today.

Our whole life is so given over to destructionism that one can name hardly 470
a field into which it has not penetrated. "Social" art preaches it, schools teach it, the churches disseminate it. In recent decades the legislation of civilized states has created hardly one important law in which at least a few concessions have not been made to destructionism; some laws it completely dominates. To give a comprehensive account of destructionism one would have to write the history of the years in which the catastrophic World War and the Bolshevist Revolution were prepared and consummated. This cannot be undertaken here. We must content ourselves with a few remarks which may contribute to an understanding of destructionist development.

2

Labour Legislation

Amongst the means destructionist policy has employed, the legal protection of labour is, in its direct effects, the most harmless. Yet this aspect of social policy is specially important as an outcome of destructionist thought.

The advocates of the protection of labour like to consider the problem as analogous to the situation which led to the measures taken in the eighteenth and the first half of the nineteenth century to protect tied labourers under the manorial system. Just as at that time the peasant's labour obligations were continually reduced by State intervention in an attempt to free the serf step by step, so labour legislation at the present day is supposed to be no more than the attempt to raise the modern proletarian from wage slavery to an existence worthy of a human being. But this comparison is quite invalid. The restriction of the labour duties of the serf did not diminish, but rather increased the amount of work done in the country. Forced labour, poor in quality and in quantity, was reduced so that the peasant would be free to improve his own bit of land or work for hire. Most of the measures taken in favour of the unfree peasant aimed, on the one hand, at increasing the intensity of agricultural work, and, on the other, at freeing labour power for industrial production. When the peasant-policy finally abolished the forced
labour of agricultural workers it did not abolish work but increased its 471
opportunities. The effect is quite different when modern social policy "regulates" working time by restricting the working day to ten, nine, and eight hours a day, or, as in various categories of public officials, to six hours or even less. For this reduces the amount of work done and thus the yield of production.

The effect of such measures for the limitation of labour have been too obvious to be overlooked. This is why all efforts to extend the legal protection of labour in calling for a radical reconstruction of conditions of work have encountered strong resistance. Etatist writers generally talk as though the general shortening of working time, the gradual elimination of women's and children's labour, and the limitation of night work were to be ascribed exclusively to legislative intervention and the activity of trade unions.[1] This attitude shows that they are still influenced by the views on the character of industrial wage labour held in circles unsympathetic to modern capitalist industry. According to these views *factory industry* has a peculiar aversion to using fully trained labour. It is supposed to prefer the unskilled labourer, the weak woman, and the frail child to the all-round trained expert. For on the one hand it wishes to produce only inferior mass commodities, in the manufacture of which it has no use for the skilled employee; on the other, the simplicity of the movements involved in mechanical production enables industry to employ the undeveloped and the physically weak. As the factories are supposed to be profitable only if they under-pay the workers, it is natural that they should employ unskilled workers, women, and children and try to extend the working day as much as possible. It is supposed that this view can be substantiated by referring to the evolution of large scale industry. But in its beginnings large scale industry had to be content with such labour because at that time it could only employ labour outside the guild organization of handicrafts. It had to take the untrained women and children because they were the only ones available, and was forced to arrange its processes so as to manage with inferior labour. Wages paid in the factories were lower than the earnings of handicraft workers because the labour yield was lower. For the same reason the working-day was longer than in the handicrafts. Only when in time these conditions changed, could large scale industry change the conditions of its labour. The factory had no other alternative than
472 to employ women and children in the beginning, fully trained workers not being available; but when, by competition, it had vanquished the older labour systems and had attracted to itself all the workers there employed, it altered its processes so that skilled male workers became the main labour factor and women and children were forced more and more out of industry. Wages rose, because the production of the efficient worker was higher than the production of the factory girl or child. The worker's family found that the wife and children did not need to earn. Working hours lessened because the more intensive labour of the efficient worker made possible a better exploi-

See the criticism of this legend by Hutt, *Economica*, Vol. VI, pp. 91 ff.

tation of the machinery than could be achieved with the sluggish and unskilled work of inferior labour.[2]

The shorter working day and the limitation of woman and child labour, in so far as these improvements were in operation in Germany about the outbreak of the War, were by no means a victory won by the champions of the legal protection of labour from selfish entrepreneurs. They were the result of an evolution in large scale industry which, being no longer compelled to seek its workers on the fringe of economic life, had to transform its working conditions to suit the better quality of labour. On the whole, legislation has only anticipated changes which were maturing, or simply sanctioned those that had already taken place. Certainly it has always tried to go further than the development of industry allowed, but it has not been able to maintain the struggle. It has been obstructed, not so much by the resistance of entrepreneurs, as by the resistance of the workers themselves, a resistance not the less effective for being unvocal and little advertised. For the workers themselves had to pay for every protective regulation, directly as well as indirectly. A restriction on female and child labour burdened the workers' budget just as much as a limitation of employment in adult labour. The reduction in the supply of labour achieved by such measures does indeed raise the marginal productivity of labour and thus the wage rate corresponding to one unit of production. Whether this rise is sufficient to compensate
the worker for the burden of rising commodity prices is questionable. One 473
would have to examine the data of each individual example before forming any conclusions about this. It is probable that the decline of production cannot bring an absolute rise of real income to the worker. But we need not go into this in detail. For one could only speak of a considerable reduction in the supply of labour, brought about by labour laws, if these laws were valid beyond a single country. As long as this was not so, as long as every state proceeded on its own lines, and those countries, whose recently developed industry took every opportunity to supplant the industry of the older industrial states, were backward in promulgating labour-protection, then the worker's position in the market could not be improved by labour protection. Efforts to generalize labour protection by international treaties were intended to remedy this. But of international labour protection, even

[2] This even Brentano has to admit, who otherwise boundlessly overvalues the effects of labour legislation. "The imperfect machine had replaced the family father with child labour . . . the perfected machine makes the father again the nourisher of family and gives the child back to the school . . . Grown-up workers are now needed again and only those can be used who, by their higher standard of living, are equal to the heightened claims of the machines." Brentano, *Über das Verhältnis von Arbeitslohn und Arbeitszeit zur Arbeitsleistung*, 2nd ed. (Leipzig, 1893), p. 43.

more truly than of the national movement, one may say that the process has not gone beyond the stage which would have been reached in the normal evolution of industry.

This attitude of destructionism emerges more clearly from the theory than from the execution of labour protection, for the danger to industrial development implied in the regulations has to a certain extent limited attempts to carry theory into practice. That the theory of the exploitation of wage earners has spread and been so rapidly accepted is due above all to destructionism, which has not hesitated to use a technique for describing industrial working conditions which can only be called emotional. The popular figures, the hard-hearted entrepreneur and the grasping capitalist on the one side, and the noble poor, the exploited worker on the other side, have, so to speak, been introduced into the presuppositions of the legal system. Legislators have been taught to see in every frustration of the plans of an entrepreneur a victory of public welfare over the selfish interests of parasitic individuals. The worker has been taught to believe that he is toiling thanklessly for the profit of capital, and that it is his duty to his class and to history to perform his work as sluggishly as possible.

The theory of wages assumed by the advocates of legal labour protection has many defects. They treat Senior's arguments against the legal regulation of working hours with contempt, but they produce nothing relevant in refutation of the conclusions he reaches on the assumption of stationary
474 conditions. The inability of the "Socialists of the Chair" ("Kathedersozialist") school to understand economic problems is particularly evident in Brentano. The idea that wages correspond to the efficiency of labour is so far beyond his comprehension that he actually formulates a "law" that a high wage increases the product of labour, whilst a low wage reduces it, although nothing could be more clear than the fact that good work is paid for at a higher rate than bad.[3] This mistake is again obvious when he goes on to say that the shortening of working hours is a cause and not a result of greater efficiency of labour.

Marx and Engels, the fathers of German Socialism, well understood how fundamentally important to the spread of destructionist ideas was the fight for labour legislation. The "Inaugural Address of the International Association of Workers" says that the English ten-hour day was "not only a great practical success; it was the victory of a principle. For the first time the political

[3] Brentano, *Über das Verhältnis von Arbeitslohn und Arbeitszeit zur Arbeitsleistung*, pp. 11, 23 ff.; Brentano, *Arbeitszeit und Arbeitslohn nach dem Kriege* (Jena, 1919), p. 10; Stucken, "Theorie der Lohnsteigerung" (*Schmollers Jahrbuch*, 45th year, pp. 1152 ff.).

economy of the bourgeoisie was openly vanquished by the political economy of the working class."[4] Over twenty years before, Engels had made an even more candid admission of the destructionist nature of the Ten Hour Day Bill. He could not help admitting that the counter-arguments of the entrepreneurs were half true. The Bill would, he thought, depress wages and make English industry unable to compete. But this did not alarm him. "Naturally," he added, "were the Ten Hour Day Bill a final measure, England would be ruined, but because it necessarily involves the passing of subsequent measures, which must lead England into a path quite different from that she has travelled up till now, it will mean progress."[5] If English industry were to succumb to foreign competition the revolution would be unavoidable.[6] In a later essay he said of the Ten Hour Day Bill: "It is no longer an isolated attempt to lame industrial development. It is one link in a long chain of measures which will transform the whole present form of society and gradually destroy the former class conflicts. It is not a reactionary but a revolutionary measure."[7]

The fundamental importance of the fight for labour legislation cannot be 475
overestimated. But Marx and Engels and their liberal opponents both overestimated the immediate destructive effects of the particular measures. Destructionism advanced on other fronts.

3

Compulsory Social Insurance

The essence of the programme of German etatism is social insurance. But people outside the German Empire have also come to look upon social insurance as the highest point to which the insight of the statesman and political wisdom can attain. If some praise the wonderful results of these institutions, others can only reproach them for not going far enough, for not including all classes and for not giving the favoured all that, in their opinion,

---

[4] *Die Inauguraladresse der Internationalen Arbeiterassoziation*, ed. Kautsky (Stuttgart, 1922), p. 27.

[5] Engels, *Die Lage der arbeitenden Klasse in England*, 2nd ed. (Stuttgart, 1892), p. 178. Publisher's Note: In English, *The Condition of the Working Class in England in 1844*, with a Preface written in 1892 (London, George Allen & Unwin, Ltd., 1892), p. 177.

[6] *Ibid.*, p. 297. Publisher's Note: In English edition, p. 295.

[7] Engels, "Die englische Zehnstundenbill" in *Aus dem literarischen Nachlass von Karl Marx, Friedrich Engels und Ferdinand Lassalle*, Vol. III (Stuttgart, 1902), p. 393.

they should have. Social insurance, it was said, ultimately aimed at giving every citizen adequate care and the best medical treatment in sickness and adequate sustenance if he should become incapable of work through accident, sickness or old age, or if he should fail to find work on conditions he considered necessary.

No ordered community has callously allowed the poor and incapacitated to starve. There has always been some sort of institution designed to save from destitution people unable to sustain themselves. As general well-being has increased hand in hand with the development of Capitalism, so too has the relief of the poor improved. Simultaneously the legal basis of this relief has changed. What was formerly a charity on which the poor had no claim is now a duty of the community. Arrangements are made to ensure the support of the poor. But at first people took care not to give the individual poor a legally enforceable claim to support or sustenance. In the same way they did not at once think of removing the slight stigma attaching to all who were thus maintained by the community. This was not callousness. The discussions which grew out of the English Poor Law in particular show that people were fully conscious of the great social dangers involved in every extension of poor relief.

German social insurance and the corresponding institutions of other states
476 are constructed on a very different basis. Maintenance is a claim which the person entitled to it can enforce at law. The claimant suffers no slur on his social standing. He is a State pensioner like the king or his ministers or the receiver of an insurance annuity, like anyone else who has entered into an insurance contract. There is also no doubt that he is entitled to look on what he receives as the equivalent of his own contributions. For the insurance contributions are always at the expense of wages, immaterial of whether they are collected from the entrepreneur or from the workers. What the entrepreneur has to pay for the insurance is a charge on labour's marginal productivity, it thus tends to reduce the wages of labour. When the costs of maintenance are provided out of taxes the worker clearly contributes towards them, directly or indirectly.

To the intellectual champions of social insurance, and to the politicians and statesmen who enacted it, illness and health appeared as two conditions of the human body sharply separated from each other and always recognizable without difficulty or doubt. Any doctor could diagnose the characteristics of "health." "Illness" was a bodily phenomenon which showed itself independently of human will, and was not susceptible to influence by will. There were people who for some reason or other simulated illness, but a doctor could expose the pretence. Only the healthy person was fully efficient.

The efficiency of the sick person was lowered according to the gravity and nature of his illness, and the doctor was able, by means of objectively ascertainable physiological tests, to indicate the degree of the reduction of efficiency.

Now every statement in this theory is false. There is no clearly defined frontier between health and illness. Being ill is not a phenomenon independent of conscious will and of psychic forces working in the subconscious. A man's efficiency is not merely the result of his physical condition; it depends largely on his mind and will. Thus the whole idea of being able to separate, by medical examination, the unfit from the fit and from the malingerers, and those able to work from those unable to work, proves to be untenable. Those who believed that accident and health insurance could be based on completely effective means of ascertaining illnesses and injuries and their consequences were very much mistaken. The destructionist aspect of accident and health insurance lies above all in the fact that such institutions promote accidents and illness, hinder recovery, and very often create, or at 477
any rate intensify and lengthen, the functional disorders which follow illness or accident.

A special disease, traumatic neurosis, which had already appeared in some cases as a result of the legal regulation of claims for compensation for injury, has been thus turned into a national disease by compulsory social insurance. No one any longer denies that traumatic neurosis is a result of social legislation. Overwhelming statistics show that insured persons take much longer time to recover from their injuries than other persons, and that they are liable to more extensions and permanent functional disturbances than those of the uninsured. Insurance against diseases breeds disease. Individual observation by doctors as well as statistics prove that recovery from illnesses and injuries is much slower in officials and permanent employees and people compulsorily insured than in members of the professions and those not insured. The desire and the necessity of becoming well again and ready for work as soon as possible assist recuperation to a degree so great as to be capable of demonstration.[8]

To feel healthy is quite different from being healthy in the medical sense, and a man's ability to work is largely independent of the physiologically ascertainable and measurable performances of his individual organs. The man who does not want to be healthy is not merely a malingerer. He is a sick person. If the will to be well and efficient is weakened, illness and

[8] Liek, *Der Arzt und seine Sendung*, 4th ed. (Munich, 1927), p. 54; Liek, *Die Schaden der sozialen Versicherung*, 2nd ed. (Munich, 1928), pp. 17 ff., and a steadily growing mass of medical writings.

inability to work is caused. By weakening or completely destroying the will to be well and able to work, social insurance creates illness and inability to work; it produces the habit of complaining—which is in itself a neurosis—and neuroses of other kinds. In short, it is an institution which tends to encourage disease, not to say accidents, and to intensify considerably the physical and psychic results of accidents and illnesses. As a social institution it makes a people sick bodily and mentally or at least helps to multiply, lengthen, and intensify disease.

The psychic forces which are active in every living thing, including man, in the form of a will to health and a desire to work, are not independent of social surroundings. Certain circumstances strengthen them; others weaken
478 them. The social environment of an African tribe living by hunting is decidedly calculated to stimulate these forces. The same is true of the quite different environment of the citizens of a capitalist society, based on division of labour and on private property. On the other hand a social order weakens these forces when it promises that if the individual's work is hindered by illness or the effects of a trauma he shall live without work or with little work and suffer no very noticeable reduction in his income. Matters are not so simple as they appear to the naive pathology of the army or prison doctor.

Social insurance has thus made the neurosis of the insured a dangerous public disease. Should the institution be extended and developed the disease will spread. No reform can be of any assistance. We cannot weaken or destroy the will to health without producing illness.

4

Trade Unions

The fundamental problem for the appreciation of the economic and social consequences of the trade unionism is the question whether labour can succeed, within a market economy, by association and by collective bargaining, in getting high wages lastingly and for all workers. To this question, economic theory—both the classic (including its Marxist wing), and the modern (including its socialist wing too)—answers categorically in the negative. Public opinion believes that the facts have proved the efficiency of trade unionism to improve the conditions of labour, because the standard of living of the masses has been steadily rising in the last hundred years. But

economists explain this fact in an absolutely different way. According to them, this improvement is due to the progress of capitalism, to the progressive accumulation of capital and to its corollary, the increase of the marginal productivity of labour. And there is no doubt that we must give more credit to the views of the economists, substantiated as they are by the actual course of events, than to the naive belief of men who simply argue *post hoc ergo propter hoc* (after this, therefore, because of it). It is true that this fundamental point has been entirely misunderstood by many thousands of worthy labour leaders, who have devoted their life work to the organization of trade unions, and by many eminent philanthropists who have advocated trade unionism 479
as the cornerstone of future society. It was the true tragedy of the age of capitalism that this attitude was wrong and that trade unionism developed into the most important weapon of destructionist policy. Socialist ideology has so successfully obscured the nature and peculiarity of the trade union that nowadays it is difficult to envisage what trade unions are and what they do. People are still inclined to treat the problem of workers' associations as if it were a question of the freedom to combine and the right to strike. But there has been no question for decades now of whether the workers shall be granted liberty to form associations or whether they shall have the right to cease work, even in violation of a labour contract. No legislation denies them this right, for the legal damages which might devolve upon individual workers for stopping work in breach of contract have no importance in practice. Thus even the most extreme advocates of destructionism have hardly bothered to claim for the worker the right to break contractual obligations at will. When in recent years some countries, and among them Great Britain, the cradle of modern trade unionism, tried to limit the power of trade union policy, it was not part of their purpose to do away with what they considered the non-political action of trade unionism. The Act of 1927 attempted to outlaw general strikes and sympathetic strikes, but did not in any way interfere either with the freedom of association or with the strike for the sake of obtaining better rates of pay.

The general strike has always been considered, both by its supporters and by its opponents, as a revolutionary measure, or even as the essence of revolution itself. The vital element in the general strike is the more or less complete paralysis of the economic life of the community in order to bring about certain desired ends. How successful a general strike can be was proved when the Kapp Putsch,* supported both by the German legal army

* The Kapp Putsch (March 13, 1920) was both symptom and product of the post World War I revolutionary turmoil in Germany. Gustav Noske's (1868–1946) new army, organized by the post-

and by a great illegal armed force which had compelled the Government to flee from the capital, was defeated in a few days by the general strike. In this case the weapon of the general strike was used to defend democracy. But whether one finds the political attitude of organized labour sympathetic or not, is of no consequence. The fact is that in a country where trade unionism is strong enough to set in motion a general strike, the supreme power is in
480 the hands of trade unions and not in the hands of parliament and the government dependent on it. It was the comprehension of the real meaning of trade unionism and its working which inspired the French Syndicalists with their basic idea that violence is the means which political parties must use if they want to come to power. It should never be forgotten that the philosophy of violence, which replaced the conciliatory teaching of liberalism and democracy, started as a philosophy of trade unionism. Syndicalism is nothing else but the French word for trade unionism. The glorification of violence which characterizes the policy of Russian Sovietism, of Italian Fascism and of German Nazism, and which today seriously threatens all democratic governments, sprang from the teachings of revolutionary syndicalists. The essence of the trade union problem is the compulsion to coalesce and to strike. The unions claim the right to force out of employment all those who refuse to combine with them or those to whom they have refused membership. They claim the right to stop work at will, and to prevent anyone from taking the place of the strikers. They claim the right to prevent and punish by violence the contravention of their decisions, and to take all steps to organize this violent action so that its success shall be assured.

Every association becomes more cumbrous and prudent when the men at its head have grown old. Fighting associations lose the desire to attack and the ability to overcome their opponents by swift action. The armies of military powers, above all the armies of Austria and Prussia have learned over and over again that victory is difficult under old leaders. The Unions are no exception to the rule. So it may come about that some of the older and fully developed trade unions have temporarily lost some of their destructionist lust for attack and readiness for battle. Thus when the aged resist the destructive policy of impetuous youth, an instrument of destruction becomes for the moment an instrument which supports the *status quo*. It is just on this

war Majority Socialist government to crush the left, revolted against the government and Wolfgang Kapp (1868–1922), founder of the Fatherland Party, was placed in office. Karl Legien (1861–1920) leader of the right wing German trade unions, then called a general strike. Response to this right-wing move was tremendous and the Putsch promptly collapsed. The two competing Socialist Parties then came to terms and formed a coalition administration in April 1920, which excluded the extreme leftists and Communists from political power (Pub.).

ground that the radicals have continually reproached the trade unions, and it is just this plea which the trade unions have themselves put forward when they have wanted help from the nonsocialist classes of the community in their work of extending compulsory unionism. These pauses for breath in the trade unions' destructive fights have always been short. Over and over again those who triumphed were those who advocated an uninterrupted continuation of the fight against the capitalist social order. The violent
elements have either pushed out the old trade union leaders or erected new 481
organizations in the place of the old. It could not be otherwise. For, consistently with the idea on which they have developed, the associations of workers in trade unions are only imaginable as a weapon of destruction. We have shown that the solidarity of the members of the trade union can be founded only on the idea of a war to destroy the social order based on private ownership in the means of production. The basic idea and not merely the practice of the trades unions is destructionist.

The cornerstone of trade unionism is compulsory membership. The workers refuse to work with men who belong to an organization not recognized by themselves. They exclude the non-union men by threatening to strike or, ultimately, by striking. Those who refuse to join the union are sometimes compelled to do so by rough handling. It is not necessary to dilate upon the drastic violation of the liberty of the individual which this implies. Even the sophistries of advocates of trade union destructionism have not succeeded in reassuring public opinion on this point. When from time to time specially gross examples of violence against a non-union worker get publicity, even those newspapers which otherwise stand more or less on the side of the destructionist parties are moved to protest.

The weapon of the trade union is the strike. It must be borne in mind that every strike is an act of coercion, a form of extortion, a measure of violence directed against all who might act in opposition to the strikers' intentions. For the purpose of the strike would be defeated if the entrepreneur were able to employ others to do the work of the strikers, or if only a section of the workers joined the strike. The long and the short of trade union rights is in fact the right to proceed against the strike-breaker with primitive violence, and this right the workers have successfully maintained. How this right was established by the trade unions in various countries does not concern us here. It is sufficient to say that in the last decades it has been established everywhere, less by explicit legislative sanction than by the tacit toleration of public authority and the law. For years it has hardly been possible to break a strike in any part of Europe by employing strike-breakers. For a long time it was at least possible to avoid strikes on railways, lighting and water services, and the most important urban food supply enterprises. But here, too, destructionism has at last carried the day.

482 No one has seriously contested the destructionist function of trade unionism. There has never yet been a wage-theory from which one could deduce that association by means of trade unions led to a permanent increase in the real income of the workers. Certainly Marx was far from allowing that trade unions had any effect on wages. In a speech made in 1865 before the General Council of the "International"[9] Marx tried to win over his comrades to joint action with the trade unions. His introductory words reveal his object in doing so. The view that increase of wages could not be obtained by strikes—a view represented in France by the Proudhonists, in Germany by the Lassallians—was, he said, "most unpopular with the working class." But his great qualities as a tactitian, which a year before had enabled him in his "Inaugural Address" to weld into one unitary programme the most diverse opinions upon the nature, aims, and tasks of the labour movement, were now again brought into play, and as he was anxious to link up the trade union movement with the International, he produced everything that can be said in favour of trade unions. Nevertheless he is careful not to commit himself to a statement that the workers' economic position could be directly improved through the trade unions. As he sees it, the foremost task of the trade unions is to lead the fight against Capitalism. The position he assigns to trade unions admits of no doubt as to the results he expects from their intervention. "In place of the conservative motto: 'A just day's wage for a just day's work' they ought to print on their banners, 'Abolition of the wage system'—They generally miss their aim because they limit themselves to carrying on a guerilla war against the consequences of the present system, instead of working at the same time for its transformation and employing their organized power as a lever for the final emancipation of the working classes; that is, for the final abolition of the wage system."[10] Marx could hardly have said more plainly that he could see nothing more in the trade unions than tools for the destruction of the capitalist social order. It remained for the "realistic" economists and revisionist Marxians to assert that the trade unions were able to maintain wages permanently above the level at which they would have stood without trade unionism. There is no need to argue
483 the point, for no attempt was made even to develop a theory from it. It

[9] The speech, translated into German, has been published by Bernstein under the title *Lohn, Preis und Profit*. I quote from the third edition, which appeared in Frankfurt in 1910. Publisher's Note: The speech by Marx was published originally in English as *Value, Price and Profit*, ed. Eleanor Marx Aveling (Chicago: Charles H. Kerr & Co., 1910).

[10] *Ibid.*, p. 46. Publisher's Note: In English edition, pp. 126–128.

remains an assertion which is always made without any reference to the interdependence of economic factors and without any sort of proof.

The policy of strike, violence, and sabotage can claim no merit whatever for any improvement in the workers' position.[11] It has helped to shake to the foundations the skillfully constructed edifice of the capitalist economy, in which the lot of everyone down to the poorest worker has been continually rising. And it has operated not in the interests of Socialism but in that of Syndicalism.

If workers in the so-called non-vital industries succeed in their demand for wages above the level given by the situation on the market, there ensues a dislocation which sets in motion forces that lead finally to a readjustment of the market's disturbed equilibrium. If, however, the workers in vital industries are able to enforce by strikes or threat of strikes their demands for higher wages, and to claim all those rights claimed in the wage struggle by other workers, the position is altogether different. It would be misleading to say that those workers were then virtually monopolists, for the question here lies outside the concept of economic monopoly. If the employees of all transport undertakings strike and circumvent action which might weaken the intended effect of their strike, they are absolute tyrants of the territories under their dominion. One may say, of course, that they make a sober use of their power, but this does not alter the fact that they have the power. That being so, there are only two classes in the country: members of the trade unions for the branches of production essential to life, and the remainder of the people, who are slaves without rights. We arrive at a position where "the indispensable workers dominate the remaining classes by the rule of violence."[12]

And, speaking once again of power it may be well to inquire at this point on what this power, in common with all other power, is based. The power of the workers organized in trade unions, before which the world now trembles, has precisely the same foundations as the power of any other 484
tyrants at any time; it is nothing more than the product of human ideologies. For decades it was impressed upon people that the association of workers

[11] Adolf Weber, *Der Kampf zwischen Kapital und Arbeit*, 3rd and 4th eds. (Tübingen, 1921), pp. 384 ff.; Robbins, *Wages* (London, 1926), pp. 58 ff.; Hutt, *The Theory of Collective Bargaining* (London, 1930), pp. 1 ff.; also my *Kritik des Interventionismus* (Jena, 1929), pp. 12 ff.; 79 ff.; 133 ff. Publisher's Note: Hutt's *The Theory of Collective Bargaining* was reprinted in 1954 by the Free Press of Glencoe, Illinois. Preface to the American edition is by Ludwig von Mises. Please also note that in the English edition of Mises' *A Critique of Interventionism*, the page references are pp. 26 ff., 95 ff., and 148 ff., respectively.

[12] Kautsky, quoted by Dietzel, "Ausbeutung der Arbeiterklasse durch Arbeitergruppen" (*Deutsche Arbeit*, vol. 4, 1919), pp. 145 ff.

in trade unions was necessary and useful to the individual as well as to the community, that only the wicked selfishness of exploiters could think of combating the unions, that in strikes the strikers were always right, that there could hardly be a worse infamy than strike-breaking, and that attempts to protect those willing to work were anti-social. The generations which grew up in the last decades have been taught from childhood that membership in a trade union was a worker's most important social duty. A strike came to mean a sort of holy action, a social ordinance. On this ideology rests the power of the workers' association. It would break down if the theory of its social utility were superseded by other views on the effects of trade unionism. Plainly, therefore, it is precisely the most powerful unions which are obliged to use their power sparingly, since, by putting an undue strain on society, they might cause people to reflect upon the nature and effect of trade unionism and so lead to a re-examination and rejection of these theories. This, of course, is and always has been true of all holders of power and is no peculiarity of the trade unions.

For this surely is clear: that should there ever be a thorough discussion of the right of the workers in vital industries to strike, the whole theory of trade unionism and compulsory strikes would soon collapse and such strike-breaking associations as the "Technische Nothilfe"* would receive the applause which today goes to the strikers. It is possible that in the ensuing conflict society would be destroyed. On the other hand, it is certain that a society which aims at preserving trade unionism on its present lines is in a fair way towards destroying itself.

5

Unemployment Insurance

Assistance of the unemployed has proved to be one of the most effective weapons of destructionism.

The reasoning which brought about unemployment insurance was the same as that which led to the setting up of insurance against sickness and

* *Technische Nothilfe*, established September 1919 to help provide essential services during strikes, lock-outs and natural cataclysms. A voluntary politically neutral association, under the German Ministry of Interior, with 260,000 members in 1928, converted into a public agency in 1939, dissolved by the Allied Occupational Forces in 1945, then replaced by a government institution, *Technisches Hilfswerk*, in 1953 to give assistance during catastrophes (Pub.).

accident. Unemployment was held to be a misfortune which overwhelmed 485
men like an avalanche. It occurred to no one that lack of wages would be a better term than lack of employment, for what the unemployed person misses is not work but the remuneration of work. The point was not that the "unemployed" could not find work, but that they were not willing to work at the wages they could get in the labour market for the particular work they were able and willing to perform.

The value of health and accident insurance becomes problematic by reason of the possibility that the insured person may himself bring about, or at least intensify, the condition insured against. But in the case of unemployment insurance, the condition insured against can never develop unless the insured persons so will. If they did not act as trade unionists, but reduced their demands and changed their locations and occupations according to the requirements of the labour market, they could eventually find work. For as long as we live in the real world and not in the Land of Heart's Desire, labour will be a scarce good, that is, there will be an unsatisfied demand for labour. Unemployment is a problem of wages, not of work. It is just as impossible to insure against unemployment as it would be to insure against, say, the unsaleability of commodities.

Unemployment insurance is definitely a misnomer. There can never be any statistical foundation for such an insurance. Most countries have acknowledged this by dropping the name "insurance," or at least by ignoring its implications. It has now become undisguised "assistance." It enables the trade unions to keep wages up to a rate at which only a part of those seeking work can be employed. Therefore, the assistance of the unemployed is what first creates unemployment as a permanent phenomenon. At present many European states are devoting to the purpose sums that considerably exceed the capacity of their public finances.

The fact that there exists in almost every country permanent mass unemployment is considered by public opinion as conclusive proof that Capitalism is incapable of solving the economic problem, and that therefore government interference, totalitarian planning and Socialism are necessary. And this argument is regarded as irrefutable when people realize that the only big country which does not suffer from the evils of unemployment is communist Russia. The logic of this argument however, is very weak. Unemployment in the capitalist countries is due to the fact that the policy both
of the governments and of the trade unions aims at maintaining a level of 486
wages which is out of harmony with the existing productivity of labour. It is true that as far as we can see there is no large scale unemployment in Russia. But the standard of living of the Russian worker is much lower than

the standard of living of the unemployed dole receiver in the capitalist countries of the West. If the British or Continental workers were ready to accept wages which would indeed be lower than their present wages but which would still be several times higher than the wages of the Russian worker, unemployment would disappear in these countries too. Unemployment in the capitalist countries is not a proof of the insufficiency of the capitalist system, nor is the absence of unemployment in Russia a proof of the efficiency of the communist system. But the fact that there is unemployment as a mass phenomenon in almost every capitalist country is nevertheless the most formidable menace to the continuance of the capitalist system. Permanent mass unemployment destroys the moral foundations of the social order. The young people, who, having finished their training for work, are forced to remain idle, are the ferment out of which the most radical political movements are formed. In their ranks the soldiers of the coming revolutions are recruited.

This indeed is the tragedy of our situation. The friends of trade unionism and of the policy of unemployment doles honestly believe that there is no way to ensure the maintenance of fair conditions of life for the masses other than the policy of the trade unions. They do not see that in the long run all efforts to raise wages above a level corresponding to the market reflection of the marginal productivity of the labour concerned must lead to unemployment, and that in the long run unemployment doles can have no other effect than the perpetuation of unemployment. They do not see that the remedies which they recommend for the relief of the victims—doles and public works—lead to consumption of capital, and that finally capital consumption necessitates a lowering of the wage level still further. Under present conditions it is clear that it would not be feasible to abolish the dole and the other less important provisions for the relief of the unemployed, public works and so on, at one single stroke. It is indeed one of the principal drawbacks of every kind of interventionism that it is so difficult to reverse the process—
487 that its abolition gives rise to problems which it is almost impossible to solve in a completely satisfactory way. At the present day the great problem of statesmanship is how to find a way out of this labyrinth of interventionist measures. For what has been done in recent years has been nothing else than a series of attempts to conceal the effects of an economic policy which has lowered the productivity of labour. What is now needed is first of all a return to a policy which ensures the higher productivity of labour. This includes clearly the abandonment of the whole policy of protectionism, import duties and quotas. It is necessary to restore to labour the possibility to move freely from industry to industry and from country to country.

It is not Capitalism which is responsible for the evils of permanent mass unemployment, but the policy which paralyses its working.

6

Socialization

Under Liberalism, state-owned factories and production by the State were abolished. The postal service was practically the only exception to the general principle that the means of production should be left to private ownership and every economic activity made over to the private citizen. The advocates of etatism have gone to a lot of trouble to set forth the reasons which they suppose to favour the nationalization of the postal and the related telegraph service. In the first place they put forward political arguments. But in such discussions of the pros and cons of state control of the post and telegraph system, two things are generally lumped together which ought to be considered separately: the questions of unifying the service and of transferring it exclusively to the State. No one denies that the post and telegraph systems afford excellent facilities for unification, and that, even if they were left perfectly free, trusts would inevitably be formed, leading to a *de facto* monopoly of individuals over whole territories at least. With no other enterprises are the advantages of concentration more obvious. But to admit this is not by any means to decide whether the State is to be granted a legally assured monopoly for all branches of such services. It could easily be demonstrated
that State management works uneconomically, that it is slow to extend the 488
facilities for the transmission of letters and parcels in accordance with business requirements, and that it can only with difficulty be persuaded to introduce practical improvements. The great progress in this sphere of economic life has been achieved by private enterprise. We owe largely to private enterprise the development on a large scale of overland telegraphy: in England this was nationalized only in 1869, in the U.S.A. it is still in the hands of joint stock companies. Submarine cables are mostly in the hands of private enterprise. Even German etatism showed hesitation in "freeing" the State from collaboration with private enterprise in deep sea telegraphy. The liberals of that time also advocated the principle of full freedom in post and telegraph services and attempted with great success to expose the inadequacy of State enterprise.[13] That nevertheless these branches of production have not been

[13] Millar, "The Evils of State Trading as Illustrated by the Post Office" in *A Plea for Liberty*, ed. Mackay, 2nd ed. (London, 1891), pp. 305 ff.

denationalized is to be ascribed only to the fact that those holding political power need the post and telegraph to control public opinion.

The military powers, everywhere ready to hinder the entrepreneur, have acknowledged his superiority by handing over to him the production of arms and munitions. The great advances in war technique date from the moment when private enterprise began to produce war material. The State has had to recognize that the entrepreneur produces better arms than the civil servant; this was proved on the battlefields in a way that enlightened even the most stubborn advocate of state production. In the nineteenth century arsenals and state shipyards disappeared almost completely, or were transformed into mere magazines, and their place was taken by private enterprises. Literary and parliamentary supporters of the nationalization of industry had scant success with their demand for the nationalization of the armaments industry, even in the most flourishing days of etatism in the years immediately preceding the World War. The general staffs knew well the superiority of the private undertaking.

For reasons of public finance, certain revenue monopolies which had existed from a distant past were not abolished even during the epoch of Liberalism. They remained because they were looked upon as a convenient
489 way of collecting a tax on consumption. But people had no illusions about the uneconomic nature of state enterprise—in the administration of the tobacco monopolies, for example. But before Liberalism could carry its victorious principle into this field, Socialism had already introduced a retrograde movement.

The ideas from which sprang the first modern nationalizations and municipalizations were not altogether inspired by modern Socialism. In the origins of the movement, ideas of the old police state and purely military and political considerations played a great part. But soon the socialist ideology became dominant. It was a conscious socialization that was carried out by states and municipalities. The slogan was: away with uneconomic private enterprise, away with private ownership.

At first the economic inferiority of socialist production did not hinder the progress of nationalization and municipalization. The voice of caution was not heard. It was lost in the shouting of etatists, socialists, and all the elements whose interests were at stake. People did not choose to see the faults of government enterprise, and so overlooked them. Only one circumstance restricted the excessive zeal of the enemies of private property—the financial difficulties with which a large number of public undertakings had to contend. For political reasons the government could not completely pass on to consumers the higher costs of State management, and working losses

were therefore frequent. Its supporters consoled themselves by stating that the general economic and social political advantages of state and municipal enterprise were well worth the sacrifice. All the same, it became necessary to proceed cautiously with the etatistic policy. The embarrassment in which economists writing on these problems found themselves became evident from their reluctance to ascribe the financial failure of public enterprises to the uneconomic methods of this kind of enterprise. They tried instead to account for it by some special circumstance, such as personal mistakes in the management and errors in organization. And they pointed repeatedly to the Prussian State railways as the most brilliant model of a good administration. Of course the Prussian State railways have yielded good working surpluses. But there were special reasons. Prussia acquired the most important part of its State railway system in the first half of the 'eighties, that was at a time of specially low prices, and the whole system was equipped and expanded to a large extent before the rapid growth of German industrial prosperity *490*
which set in during the second half of the 'nineties. Thus there was nothing particularly remarkable in the fact that these railways paid well, for their loads grew from year to year without any solicitation, they ran mostly through plains, they had coal on every hand, and could count on favourable running conditions. Their situation was such that they could yield profits for a while although run by the State. It was the same with the gas, water, and electricity works and with the tramway systems of several large cities. The conclusions generally drawn from this were, however, far from accurate.

Generally speaking, the result of nationalization and municipalization was that taxation had to contribute to running costs. So it may be said that no catchword has ever been made public at so inappropriate a moment as Goldscheid's slogan of "the suppression of the taxation state." Goldscheid thinks that the financial troubles into which the World War and its consequences have landed the State can no longer be remedied by the old methods of public finance. The taxation of private enterprise is failing. Therefore, one must start to "repropriate" the State by expropriating capitalist enterprises, so that the State will be able to cover its expenses out of the profits of its own undertakings.[14] Here we have the cart before the horse. The financial difficulties result from the fact that taxation can no longer pay the large contributions required by socialist enterprises. Were all enterprises socialized, the form of the evil would indeed be changed, but far from being abolished

---

[14] Goldscheid, *Staatssozialismus oder Staatskapitalismus* (Vienna, 1917); *Sozialisierung der Wirtschaft oder Staatsbankerott* (Vienna, 1919); against: Schumpeter, *Die Krise des Steuerstaates* (Graz and Leipzig, 1918).

it would be intensified. The smaller yield of the public enterprises would no longer be visible in a budget deficit, it is true, but the population would be worse off. Distress and misery would increase, not diminish. To remove the State's financial troubles Goldscheid proposes to carry socialization to the bitter end. But this financial trouble has come about because socialization has already gone too far. It will vanish only when socialized enterprises are returned to private ownership. Socialism has arrived at a point where the impossibility of carrying out its technique is apparent to all, where even the blind begin to see that it is hastening the decline of all civilization. The effort made in Central Europe to socialize completely at a single stroke was wrecked
491 not by the resistance of the bourgeoisie, but by the fact that further socialization was quite impossible from a financial point of view. The systematic, cool and deliberate socialization practised by states and municipalities up to the war, came to a standstill because the result to which it was leading became all too clear. The attempt to pass it off under a different name, as the socialization commission in Germany and Austria tried to do, could have no success in these circumstances. If the work of socialization had to be carried on, it was not possible to do so by the old methods. The voice of reason which warned men not to venture any further on this path must be silenced, criticism must be obliterated by the intoxication of enthusiasm and fanaticism, opponents must be killed, as there was no other way of refuting them. Bolshevism and Spartacism were the last weapons of Socialism. In this sense they are the inevitable outcome of the policy of destructionism.

7

Taxation

For classical nineteenth-century Liberalism, which assigns to the State the sole task of safeguarding the citizen's property and person, the problem of raising the means needed for public services is a matter of small importance. The expenditure caused by the apparatus of a liberal community is so small, compared with the total national income, that there is little appreciable difference between meeting it one way or another. If the liberal writers of that period have been concerned to find the best form of taxation, they have done so because they wish to arrange every detail of the social system in the most effective way, not because they think that public finance is one of the main problems of society. They have of course to take into account the fact

that nowhere in the world have their ideas been realized, and that the hope of seeing them *completely* realized in the near future is slender. They see clear evidence of liberal development everywhere, they believe that the distant future belongs to Liberalism; but the forces of the past still seem sufficiently strong to inhibit its progress, though no longer strong enough to stop it completely, let alone suppress it. There still exist schemes for violence and
conquest, there are standing armies, secret diplomatic treaties, wars, tariffs, 492
State interference in trade and industry—in short, interventionism of every kind in home and foreign policy. So, for a considerable time to come, the nations must be prepared to allow considerable sums for governmental expenditure. Though questions of taxation would be of minor importance in the purely liberal state, they call for increased attention in the authoritarian state in which liberal politicians of their time have to work. In the first place, therefore, they recommend that State expenditure shall be restricted. But if they do not completely succeed in this they must decide how the necessary funds are to be raised without more harm than is absolutely necessary.

Liberal taxation proposals must necessarily be misunderstood unless it is realized that liberal politicians look on every tax as an evil—though up to a point an unavoidable one—and that they proceed from the supposition that one must try to keep State expenditure down to a minimum. When they recommend a certain tax, or, to speak more correctly, call it less harmful than other taxes, they always have in mind the raising of only a relatively small sum. A low rate of taxation is an integral part of all liberal programmes of taxation. This alone explains their attitude towards the income tax, which they were the first to introduce into serious discussions on public finance, and their willingness to agree that a modest minimum of subsistence shall be free from taxation and the rate of taxation on small incomes lowered.[15]

The socialist financial policy also is only a temporary one, its validity being limited to the period of transition. For the Socialist State, where all means of production belong to society and all income finds its way in the first place to the State coffers, questions of finance and taxation do not exist at all in the sense in which the social order based on private property has to deal with them. Those forms of the socialist community which, like State Socialism, intend to allow private property to continue in name and in outward form, would not really need to levy taxes either, although they might retain the name and legal form of taxation. They would simply decree how much of the social income obtained in the individual enterprises should remain with

[15] On the negative attitude of the liberals to the idea of progressive taxes see Thiers, *De la Propriété* (Paris, 1848), pp. 352 ff.

the nominal owner and how much should be handed over to the State. There
493 would not be any question here of a taxation which imposes certain obstacles in individual businesses, but leaves the market to deal with its effect upon the prices of commodities and wages, on profits, interest, and rents. Questions of public finance and the policy of taxation exist only where there is private ownership in the means of production.

But for socialists, too, the public finance problems of capitalist society increase in importance as the period of transition becomes more and more prolonged. This is inevitable, seeing that they are continually trying to expand the area of the State's tasks and that there is consequently an increase in expenditure. They thus take over the responsibility of increasing the income of the State. The socialist policy has become the decisive factor in the development of government expenditure, socialist demands regulate the policy of taxation and in the socialist programme itself public finance comes more and more into the foreground. Whilst in the liberal programme the basic principle is a low rate of taxation, the socialists think a tax is better the heavier it is.

Classical economics achieved much in the theory of the incidence of taxes. This must be admitted in spite of all the faults of its basic theory of value. When liberal politicians criticized existing conditions and proposed reforms they started from the masterly propositions of Ricardo's admirable investigations on this subject. Socialist politicians have taken things much more easily. They had no new opinions of their own, and from the Classical writers they took merely what they needed for the politics of the moment—isolated remarks, torn from their context and dealing mainly with the incidence of taxes on consumption. They improvised a rough system which nowhere penetrated to the main problem, but had the virtue of being so simple that the masses could understand it. Taxes were to be paid by the rich, the entrepreneurs, the capitalists, in short, by "the others"; the workers, that is the electors whose votes were what mattered at the moment, should remain tax free. All taxes on mass consumption, even on alcoholic drinks, were to be rejected, because they burdened the people. Direct taxes could be as high as the government wished to make them, as long as the incomes and possessions of the workers were left alone. Not for one moment does it occur to the advocates of this popular taxation policy that direct taxes and taxes on trade may start a chain of events that will force down the standard
494 of living of the very classes whose alleged special interests they claim to represent. Seldom does anyone ask whether the restriction of capital formation, which results from the taxation of property, may not harm the non-

propertied members of society as well. More and more the policy of taxation evolves into a policy of confiscation. The aim on which it concentrates is to tax out of existence every kind of fortune and income from property, in which process property invested in trade and industry, in shares and bonds, is generally treated more ruthlessly than property in land. Taxation becomes the favourite weapon of interventionism. Taxation laws no longer aim exclusively or predominantly at increasing State revenues; they are intended to serve other purposes besides fiscal requirements. Sometimes their relation to public finance vanishes completely and they fulfil an entirely different function. Some taxes seem to be inflicted as punishment for behaviour that is considered injurious; the tax on big stores is intended to make it more difficult for big stores to compete with small shops; the taxes on stock exchange transactions are designed to restrict speculation. The dues become so numerous and varied that in making business transactions a man must first of all consider what the effect on his taxation will be. Innumerable economic projects lie fallow because the load of taxation would make them unprofitable. Thus in many states the high duties on founding, maintaining, amalgamating, and liquidating joint stock companies seriously restrict the development of the system.

Nothing is more calculated to make a demagogue popular than a constantly reiterated demand for heavy taxes on the rich. Capital levies and high income taxes on the larger incomes are extraordinarily popular with the masses, who do not have to pay them. The assessors and collectors go about their business with positive enthusiasm; they are intent upon increasing the taxpayer's liability by the subtleties of legal interpretation.

The destructionist policy of taxation culminates in capital levies. Property is expropriated and then consumed. Capital is transformed into goods for use and for consumption. The effect of all this should be plain to see. Yet the whole popular theory of taxation today leads to the same result.

Confiscations of capital through the legal form of taxation are neither socialistic nor a means to Socialism. They lead, not to socialization of the
means of production, but to consumption of capital. Only when they are set 495
within a socialist system, which retains the name and form of private property, are they a part of Socialism. In "War Socialism" they supplemented the compulsory economic system and were instrumental in determining the evolution of the whole system towards Socialism.[16] In a socialist system where the means of production are totally and formally socialized, there

[16] See my *Nation, Staat und Wirtschaft*, pp. 134 ff.

could in principle be no more taxes on property or income from property. When the socialist community levies dues from its members this in no way alters the disposal of the means of production.

Marx has spoken unfavourably of efforts to alter the social order by measures of taxation. He emphatically insisted that taxation reform alone could not replace Socialism.[17] His views on the effect of taxes within the capitalist order were also different from those of the ordinary run of socialists. He said on one occasion, that to assert that "the income tax does not affect the workers" was "truly absurd." "In our present social order, where entrepreneurs and workers stand opposed, the bourgeoisie generally compensates itself for higher taxation by reducing wages or raising prices."[18] But the Communist Manifesto had already demanded "a heavy progressive tax" and the Social Democratic Party's demands in taxation have always been the most radical. In that field also, therefore, it is moving towards destructionism.

8

Inflation

Inflation is the last word in destructionism. The Bolshevists, with their inimitable gift for rationalizing their resentments and interpreting defeats as victories, have represented their financial policy as an effort to abolish Capitalism by destroying the institution of money. But although inflation does indeed destroy Capitalism, it does not do away with private property. It effects great changes of fortune and income, it destroys the whole finely organized mechanism of production based on division of labour, it can cause a relapse into an economy without trade if the use of metal money or at least
496 of barter trade is not maintained. But it cannot create anything, not even a socialist order of society.

By destroying the basis of reckoning values—the possibility of calculating with a general denominator of prices which, for short periods at least, does not fluctuate too wildly—inflation shakes the system of calculations in terms of money, the most important aid to economic action which thought has evolved. As long as it is kept within certain limits, inflation is an excellent

[17] Mengelberg, *Die Finanzpolitik der sozialdemokratischen Partei in ihren Zusammenhängen mit dem sozialistischen Staatsgedanken* (Mannheim, 1919), pp. 30 ff.

[18] Marx-Engels, *Gesammelte Schriften, 1852–62* (*Collected Writings, 1852–62*), ed. Rjasanoff (Stuttgart, 1917), Vol. I, p. 127.

psychological support of an economic policy which lives on the consumption of capital. In the usual, and indeed the only possible, kind of capitalist book-keeping, inflation creates an illusion of profit where in reality there are only losses. As people start off from the nominal sum of the erstwhile cost price, they allow too little for depreciation on fixed capital, and since they take into account the apparent increases in the value of circulating capital as if these increases were real increases of value, they show profits where accounts in a stable currency would reveal losses.[19] This is certainly not a means of abolishing the effects of an evil etatistic policy, of war and revolution; it merely hides them from the eye of the multitude. People talk of profits, they think they are living in a period of economic progress, and finally they even applaud the wise policy which apparently makes everyone richer.

But the moment inflation passes a certain point the picture changes. It begins to promote destructionism, not merely indirectly by disguising the effects of destructionist policy; it becomes in itself one of the most important tools of destructionism. It leads everyone to consume his fortune; it discourages saving, and thereby prevents the formation of fresh capital. It encourages the confiscatory policy of taxation. The depreciation of money raises the monetary expression of commodity values and this, reacting on the book values of changes in capital—which the tax administration regards as increases in income and capital—becomes a new legal justification for confiscation of part of the owners' fortune. References to the apparently high profits which entrepreneurs can be shown to be making, on a calculation assuming that the value of money remains stable, offers an excellent means of stimulating popular frenzy. In this way, one can easily represent all entrepreneurial activity as profiteering, swindling, and parasitism. And the chaos which follows, the money system collapsing under the avalanche of
continuous issues of additional notes, gives a favourable opportunity for 497
completing the work of destruction.

The destructionist policy of interventionism and Socialism has plunged the world into great misery. Politicians are helpless in the face of the crisis they have conjured up. They cannot recommend any way out except more inflation or, as they call it now, reflation. Economic life is to be "cranked up again" by new bank credits (that is, by additional "circulation" credit) as the moderates demand, or by the issue of fresh government paper money, which is the more radical programme.

But increases in the quantity of money and fiduciary media will not enrich the world or build up what destructionism has torn down. Expansion of

---

[19] See my *Nation, Staat und Wirtschaft,* pp. 129 ff.

credit does lead to a boom at first, it is true, but sooner or later this boom is bound to crash and bring about a new depression. Only apparent and temporary relief can be won by tricks of banking and currency. In the long run they must land the nation in profounder catastrophe. For the damage such methods inflict on national well-being is all the heavier, the longer people have managed to deceive themselves with the illusion of prosperity which the continuous creation of credit has conjured up.[20]

9

Marxism and Destructionism

Socialism has not consciously willed the destruction of society. It believed it was creating a higher form of society. But since a socialist society is not a possibility every step towards it must harm society.

It is the history of Marxian Socialism which shows most clearly that every socialist policy must turn into destructionism. Marxism described Capitalism as the inevitable preliminary to Socialism, and looked forward to the new society only as the result of Capitalism's fruition. If we take our stand on this part of Marx's theory—it is true that he has put forward other theories with which this is completely incompatible—then the policy of all the parties that claim Marx's authority is quite non-Marxian. The Marxians ought to have combated everything that could in any way hinder the development
498 of Capitalism. They should have protested against the trade unions and their methods, against laws protecting labour, against compulsory social insurance, against the taxation of property; they should have fought laws hindering the full working of the stock and produce exchanges, the fixation of prices, the policy which proceeds against cartels and trusts; they should have resisted inflationism. But they have done the reverse of all this, have been content to repeat Marx's condemnation of the "petty bourgeois" policy, without

[20] See my *Theory of Money and Credit* (London, 1934), pp. 339 ff.; also my *Geldwertstabilisierung und Konjunkturpolitik* (Jena, 1928), pp. 43 ff. Publisher's Note: Mises' *Theory of Money and Credit* has been reprinted since the 1934 edition cited here (Yale, 1953), (FEE, 1971), and (Liberty Fund, 1981). Mises' *Geldwertstabilisierung und Konjunkturpolitik* is included in the anthology, *On the Manipulation of Money and Credit*, edited by Percy L. Greaves, Jr., translated by Bettina Bien Graves, under the title "Monetary Stabilization and Cyclical Policy," pp. 57–171. This particular citation is to pp. 118 ff. of the English translation.

however drawing the inevitable conclusions. The Marxians who, in the beginning, wished to dissociate themselves definitely from the policy of all parties looking to the pre-capitalist economic idea, arrived in the end at exactly the same point of view.

The fight between Marxists and the parties calling themselves emphatically anti-Marxists is carried on by both sides with such a violence of expression that one might easily be led into supposing them irreconcilable. But this is by no means the case. Both parties, Marxism and National Socialism, agree in opposing Liberalism and rejecting the capitalist social order. Both desire a socialist order of society. The only difference in their programme lies in slight variations in their respective pictures of the future socialist State; non-essential variations, as we could easily show. The foremost demands of the National Socialist agitation are different from those of the Marxists. While the Marxists speak of abolishing the commodity character of labour, the National Socialists speak of breaking the slavery of interest (*Brechung der Zinsknechtschaft*). While the Marxists hold the "capitalists" responsible for every evil, the National Socialists think to express themselves more concretely by shouting "Death to the Jews" (*Juda verrecke*).[21]

Marxism, National Socialism, and other anti-capitalist parties are indeed separated, not only by clique enmities, and personal resentments, but also by problems of metaphysics and the conduct of life. But they all agree on the decisive problem of reshaping the social order: they reject private ownership in the means of production and desire a socialist order of society. It is true that the paths by which they hope to reach the common goal run parallel only for short stretches, but even where they diverge they remain on adjacent territories.

It is not surprising that in spite of this close relationship they fight out 499
their feud with consuming bitterness. In a socialist community the fate of the political minorities would necessarily become unbearable. How would National Socialists fare under a Bolshevist rule or Bolshevists under National Socialism?

The results of the destructionist policy are not affected by the different slogans and banners employed. Whether the protagonists of the "right" or of the "left" happen to be in power, "tomorrow" is always unhesitatingly

[21] For a criticism of National Socialist doctrine see my *Kritik des Interventionismus* (Jena, 1929), pp. 91 ff.; also Karl Wagner, "Brechung der Zinsknechtschaft?" in *Jahrbücher für Nationalökonomie und Statistik*, Third Series, Vol. LXXIX, pp. 790 ff. Publisher's Note: In the English edition of *Kritik des Interventionismus*, p. 107.

sacrificed to "today." The supporters of the system continue to feed it on capital—as long as a crumb is left.[22]

[22] The best characterization of destructionism is in the words with which Stourm tried to describe the financial policy of the Jacobins: *"L'esprit financier des jacobins consista exclusivement en ceci: epuiser à outrance le présent, en sacrifiant l'avenir. Le lendemain ne compta jamais pour eux: les affaires furent menées chaque jour comme s'il s'agissait du dernier: tel fut le caractère distinctif de tous les actes de la Révolution. Tel est aussi le secret de son étonnante durée: la déprédation quotidienne des réserves accumulées chez une nation riche et puissante fit surgir des ressources inattendues, dépassant toute prévision."* (The financial spirit of the Jacobins consisted exclusively of this: Consume in the present to the utmost at the expense of the future. Tomorrow never counted for them: Activities were conducted each day as if that day were the last: Such was the distinctive spirit of all the actions of the Revolution. Such is also the secret of its surprising duration: The daily plundering of the accumulated reserves of a rich and powerful nation brought forth resources beyond all expectations.) And it applies word for word to the German inflation policy of 1923 when Stourm goes on: *"Les assignats, tant qu'ils valurent quelque chose, si peu que ce fût, inondèrent le pays en quantités sans cesse progressives. La perspective de la faillite n'arrêta pas un seul instant les émissions. Elles ne cessèrent que sur le refus absolu du public d'accepter, même à vil prix, n'importe quelle sorte de papier-monnaie."* (The assignats, so long as they were worth anything, as little as that might be, flooded the country in ever-increasing quantities. The prospect of their collapse did not stop the emissions for a single instant; they stopped issuing them only when the public absolutely refused to accept, even when dirt cheap, any kind of paper money.) Stourm, *Les Finances de l'Ancien Régime et de la Révolution* (Paris, 1885), Vol. II, p. 388.

CHAPTER 35

Overcoming Destructionism

1

The "Interest" as an Obstacle to Destructionism

According to Marx the political faith of the individual depends upon the 500
class to which he belongs; the political faith of his class depends upon its interests as a class. The bourgeoisie is bound to support Capitalism. On the other hand the proletariat can only achieve its purpose, can only free itself from capitalist exploitation, by preparing the way for Socialism. Thus the respective positions of the bourgeoisie and the proletariat in the political arena are defined in advance. Perhaps no doctrine of Marx has made a deeper or more lasting impression on political theory than this. It has found acceptance far beyond the immediate range of Marxism. Liberalism has come to be regarded as the doctrine in which the class interests of the bourgeoisie and of big business find expression. Whoever professes liberal opinions is considered to be a more or less well-meaning representative of the special interests which stand in opposition to the general good. Economists who reject the Marxian doctrine are characterized as the "spiritual bodyguard of the profits of capital—and sometimes also of ground-rents"[1]—a remarkably convenient theory which saves the Marxian the trouble of arguing with them.

Nothing indicates more clearly the widespread recognition which has been accorded to this doctrine of Marx than its acceptance even by the opponents of Socialism. When people suggest that the defeat of socialist effort is a task chiefly or even exclusively for the propertied classes, when they attempt to form a "united front" of all the bourgeois parties in order to oppose Socialism, they then admit that the maintenance of private property in the means of production is the special interest of a certain class, and that it is antagonistic

[1] Thus by Kautsky, quoted by Georg Adler, *Grundlagen der Karl Marxschen Kritik der bestehenden Volkswirtschaft* (Tübingen, 1887), p. 511

to the public welfare. These strangely short-sighted adversaries of Socialism
501 do not realize that any attempt on the part of a class, which is comparatively small when contrasted with the masses, to defend its particular interests must be futile; they do not recognize that private property is doomed when it is regarded as the privilege of its owners. Still less are they able to perceive that their assumption is radically contradicted by the experience of the formation of actual political parties.

Liberalism is not a doctrine which serves the class interests of those in possession of property. Whoever conceives it as such has already admitted one of the leading contentions of Socialism; he is no liberal. Liberalism upholds private property not in the interests of the owners, but in the general interest; it believes that the maintenance of the capitalist system is to the advantage not only of the capitalists but of every member of society. It admits that in the socialist community there will, in all probability, be little or no inequality of income. But it urges that owing to the smaller yield of socialist production, the total amount to be shared will be considerably smaller, so that each individual will receive less than the poorest receives today. Whether this thesis is accepted or rejected is another question. This is precisely the point upon which Socialism and Liberalism are in conflict. Whoever rejects it out of hand, rejects Liberalism. Yet it would be unreasonable to do this without careful consideration of the problem and of the arguments of either sides.

In fact nothing is further from the particular interests of the entrepreneurs, whether as individuals or as a class, than to defend the principle of private property or to resist the principle of Socialism. That the introduction of Socialism must necessarily injure the entrepreneurs and capitalists, or at least their children, cannot be disputed by those who believe that Socialism implies want and distress for all. To this extent, therefore, the propertied classes are admittedly concerned in resisting Socialism. But their interest is no greater than that of any other member of society and is quite independent of their privileged position. If it were possible to imagine that Socialism would be introduced lock stock and barrel overnight, then it might be said that the entrepreneurs and capitalists had special reasons for wishing to maintain the capitalist system. They would have more to lose. Even if the distress which resulted from the reorganization were the same for all, those would suffer more whose fall had been the greater. But it is not possible to
502 imagine that Socialism will be introduced so rapidly; and if it were, it may be assumed that the entrepreneurs, by reason of their expert knowledge and ability to take responsibility, would occupy, at any rate for a time, privileged positions within the socialist organization.

The entrepreneur is unable to provide for his grandchildren and great-grandchildren, for it is characteristic of private property in the means of production under the capitalist system that it creates no permanent source of income. Every fortune must be renewed by effort. When the feudal lord supported the feudal system he was defending not only his own property but that of his descendants. But the entrepreneur in the capitalist system knows that his children and grandchildren will only survive in the face of new competition if they can hold their ground as directors of productive enterprise. If he is concerned for the fate of his successors and wants to consolidate his property for them in a way contrary to the interests of the community, he will have to become an enemy of the capitalist social order and demand every kind of restriction on competition. Even the way to Socialism may strike him as the best means for this, provided the transition does not take place too suddenly, for he may expect compensation against expropriation so that, for a longer or shorter time, the expropriated will enjoy a secure income in place of the uncertainty and insecurity that is the lot of owners of an enterprise. Consideration for his own property and for the property of his successors may, therefore, urge the entrepreneurs rather to support than to oppose Socialism. He must welcome all efforts which aim at suppressing newly created and newly developed fortunes, especially all measures intended to limit anything in the nature of economic freedom, because they make secure the income which otherwise must be earned by daily struggle as long as competition is not restricted—because they exclude new competitors.[2]

Entrepreneurs have an interest in combining to proceed uniformly in wage negotiations with the workers organized in trade unions.[3] And they have an interest in combining to carry through tariff and other restrictions which conflict with the essence and principle of Liberalism or to resist government interference which may injure them. But they have absolutely no special 503
interest in fighting Socialism and socialization as such. They have no special

[2] "*Beaucoup d'ouvriers, et non les meilleurs, préfèrent le travail payé à la journée au travail à la tâche. Beaucoup d'entrepreneurs, et non les meilleurs, préféraient les conditions qu'ils espèrent pouvoir obtenir d'un État socialiste à celles que leur fait un régime de libre concurrence. Sous ce régime les entrepreneurs sont des 'fonctionnaires' payés à la tâche; avec une organisation socialiste ils déviendraient des 'fonctionnaires' payés à la journée.*" (Many workers, and not the best, prefer to be paid by the day and not by the work completed. Many entrepreneurs, and not the best, prefer what they can hope to obtain from a socialist state to that which a free competitive system would award them. Under such a competitive system, entrepreneurs are the "officials" paid for the work completed; under a socialist organization, they would become "officials" paid by the day.) Pareto, *Cours d'Économie Politique*, Vol. II, p. 97n.

[3] Hutt, *The Theory of Collective Bargaining*, pp. 25 ff.

interest in fighting destructionism. The whole purpose of the entrepreneur is to adjust himself to the economic contingencies of any moment. His aim is not to fight Socialism, but to adjust himself to conditions created by a policy directed towards socialization. It is not to be expected that entrepreneurs or any other particular group in the community should, out of self-interest, necessarily make the general principles of well-being the maxim of their own procedure. The necessities of life compel them to make the best of any given circumstances. It is not the business of the entrepreneurs to lead the political fight against Socialism; all that concerns them is to adjust themselves and their enterprises to the situations created by the measures directed towards socialization, so that they will make the greatest profit possible under the conditions prevailing.

It follows, therefore, that neither associations of entrepreneurs, nor those organizations in which the entrepreneurs' support counts, are inclined to fight on principle against Socialism. The entrepreneur, the man who seizes the opportunity of the moment, has little interest in the issue of a *secular* struggle of indefinite duration. His interest is to adjust himself to the circumstances in which he finds himself at the moment. An entrepreneurs' organization aims solely at repulsing some individual encroachment of the trade unions; or it may oppose acts of legislation, such as special forms of taxation. It carries out the tasks assigned to it by parliaments and governments in cases where it is desired that the organized body of entrepreneurs should co-operate with the organized working class in order to give the destructionist element its say in the national economy. To fight on principle for the maintenance of an economy based on private property in the means of production is no part of the programme of organized entrepreneurs. Its attitude towards Liberalism is one of indifference or even, as in the case of tariff policy, of antagonism.

Organized interests, as the socialist doctrine depicts them, correspond not to the entrepreneurs' associations but to the farmers' unions, which advocate tariff duties on agricultural products, or those associations of small producers, which—above all in Austria—press for the exclusion of competition. These clearly are not efforts on behalf of Liberalism.

504 Thus there are no individuals and no classes whose particular interests would lead them to support Capitalism as such. The policy of Liberalism is the policy of the common good, the policy of subjecting particular interests to the public welfare—a process that demands from the individual not so much a renunciation of his own interests as a perception of the harmony of all individual interests. There are, therefore, no individuals and no groups whose interests would ultimately be better guarded by Socialism than by a

society based on private ownership in the means of production. But although ultimately no one's interests would actually be better served by Socialism, there are plenty of people whose particular interests of the moment are better guarded by a policy directed towards socialization than by the maintenance of Liberalism. Liberalism has opposed everything in the nature of a sinecure and has sought to reduce to a minimum the number of public officials. The interventionist policy provides thousands and thousands of people with safe, placid, and not too strenuous jobs at the expense of the rest of society. All nationalization or setting up of a municipal or public enterprise links private interests with the movement against private property. Today Socialism and destructionism find their strongest supporters in the millions for whom a return to a freer economy would be at first and in the short run detrimental to their particular interests.

2

Violence and Authority

The attitude of mind which sees in private property a privilege of the owners is an echo from former periods in the history of property. All property ownership began with appropriation of ownerless things. The history of property passed through a period in which forcible dispossession of the owners was the rule. It is safe to say that the ownership of any piece of ground property can be traced back to seizure by violence. This has of course no application to the social order of Capitalism, as property here is constantly being acquired in the process of market competition. But as the liberal principles have nowhere—in Europe at least—been put into practice in their entirety, and as everywhere, especially in landed property, very much of 505
the old taint of violence survives, the tradition of the feudal owners is still upheld: *"Ich lieg und besitze"* (I occupy and possess). Criticism of property rights is met with violent abuse. This is the policy the German Junkers adopted against Social Democracy—with what success is well known.[4]

Partisans of this order can say nothing in justification of private ownership in the means of production but that it is upheld by force. The right of the strong is the only right they can enforce. They boast of their physical force,

[4] The Junker is not concerned with the maintenance of private property as disposal over the means of production, but rather with maintaining it as title to a special source of income. Therefore State Socialism has easily won him over. It is to secure him his privileged income.

rely on their armed equipment, and consider themselves entitled to despise any other argument. Only when the ground begins to tremble under their feet, do they produce another argument by taking their stand upon acquired rights. Violation of their property becomes an illegality which must be avoided. We need waste no words in exposing the weakness of this point of view in the struggle against a movement that wants to found new rights. It is quite powerless to change public opinion if that opinion has condemned property. Its beneficiaries recognize this with horror and turn in their distress to the Church, with the odd request that the Church shall keep the *misera plebs* (wretched masses) modest and humble, fight covetousness and turn the eyes of the propertyless from earthly goods to heavenly things.[5] Christianity is to be kept alive so that the people shall not become covetous. But the demand thus made to the Church is monstrous. It is asked to serve the interests, generally assumed to be harmful to the community, of a number of privileged persons. It is obvious that the true servants of the Church have revolted against this presumptuous demand, while enemies of the Church have found it an effective weapon in their war of liberation against religion. What is surprising is that ecclesiastical enemies of Socialism, in their efforts to represent Socialism as a child of Liberalism, of the free school, and of atheism, have taken up just the same attitude towards the work which the Church performs in maintaining existing property relations. Thus the Jesuit Cathrein says: "If one assumes that with this life all is finished, that to man is given no greater destiny than to any other mammal that wallows in the
506 mire, who then will ask of the poor and oppressed, whose life is a constant struggle for existence, that they should bear their hard fate with patience and resignation, and look on while others clothe themselves in silk and purple and have regular and ample meals? Does not the worker too carry in his heart the indestructible *impulse towards perfect happiness?* If he is robbed of every hope of a better world beyond, by what right is he prevented from seeking his happiness as far as possible on earth and so demanding imperatively, his share of the earth's riches? Is he not just as much man as his employer? Why should some just manage to exist in want and poverty while others live on the fat of the land, when from their point of view there is no reason why the good things of this world should belong to some rather than to others? If the atheistic-naturalistic standpoint is justified, so also is the Socialist demand: that worldly goods and happiness should be distributed to all as equally as possible, that it is wrong for some to live a life of idle

[5] This, for example, was Bismarck's view. See his speech in the Landtag of June 15th, 1847 in *Fürst Bismarcks Reden*, edited by Stein, Vol. I, p. 24.

enjoyment in palaces while others live in miserable cellars and attics, barely able in spite of the most strenuous efforts to earn their daily bread."[6] Assuming matters to be just as Cathrein imagines them—that private property is a privilege of the owners, that the others are poorer in proportion as these are rich, that some starve because others carouse, that some live in miserable little rooms because others live in lordly places—does he really believe that it could possibly be a work of the Church to maintain such conditions? Whatever one may read into the Church's social teaching, one cannot suppose that its founder or his supporters would have approved of its being used to bolster up unjust social institutions that are obviously disadvantageous to the greater part of humanity. Christianity would long since have vanished from the earth, were it that for which, in common with many of its bitterest enemies, Bismarck and Cathrein mistook it: a bodyguard for a social institution injurious to the masses.

The socialist idea can be suppressed neither by force nor by authority, for both are on the side of Socialism and not of its opponents. If guns and machine-guns are brought into action today they will be in the ranks of Socialism and Syndicalism, and not opposed to them. For the great mass of our contemporaries are imbued with the spirit of Socialism or of Syndicalism.
Whatever system is set in authority at the present time, it can certainly not 507
be Capitalism, for the masses do not believe in it.

3

The Battle of Ideas

It is a mistake to think that the lack of success of experiments in Socialism that have been made can help to overcome Socialism. Facts *per se* can neither prove nor refute anything. Everything is decided by the interpretation and explanation of the facts, by the ideas and the theories.

The man who clings to Socialism will continue to ascribe all the world's evil to private property and to expect salvation from Socialism. Socialists ascribe the failures of Russian Bolshevism to every circumstance except the inadequacy of the system. From the socialist point of view, Capitalism alone is responsible for all the misery the world has had to endure in recent years. Socialists see only what they want to see and are blind to anything that might contradict their theory.

---

[6] Cathrein, *Der Sozialismus*, 12th and 13th eds. (Freiburg, 1920), pp. 347 ff.

Only ideas can overcome ideas and it is only the *ideas* of Capitalism and of Liberalism that can overcome Socialism. Only by a battle of ideas can a decision be reached.

Liberalism and Capitalism address themselves to the cool, well-balanced mind. They proceed by strict logic, eliminating any appeal to the emotions. Socialism, on the contrary, works on the emotions, tries to violate logical considerations by rousing a sense of personal interest and to stifle the voice of reason by awakening primitive instincts.

Even with those of intellectually higher standing, with the few capable of independent reflection, this seems to give Socialism an advantage. With the others, the great masses who are unable to think, the Socialist position is considered unshakable. A speaker who inflames the passions of the masses is supposed to have a better chance of success than one who appeals to their reason. Thus the prospects of Liberalism in the fight with Socialism are accounted very poor.

This pessimistic point of view is completely mistaken in its estimate of the influence which rational and quiet reflection can exercise on the masses. It
508 also exaggerates enormously the importance of the part played by the masses, and consequently mass-psychological elements, in creating and forming the predominant ideas of an epoch.

It is true that the masses do not think. But just for this reason they follow those who do think. The intellectual guidance of humanity belongs to the very few who think for themselves. At first they influence the circle of those capable of grasping and understanding what others have thought; through these intermediaries their ideas reach the masses and there condense themselves into the public opinion of the time. Socialism has not become the ruling idea of our period because the masses first thought out the idea of the socialization of the means of production and then transmitted it to the intellectually higher classes. Even the materialistic conception of history, haunted as it is by "the psyche of the people" as conceived by Romanticism and the historical school of jurisprudence does not risk such an assertion. Of itself the mass psyche has never produced anything but mass crime, devastation, and destruction.[7] Admittedly the idea of Socialism is also in its effects nothing more than destruction, but it is nevertheless an idea. It had to be thought out, and this could only be the work of individual thinkers. Like every other great thought, it has penetrated to the masses only through the intellectual middle class. Neither the people nor the masses were the first socialists. Even today they are agrarian socialist and syndicalist rather

[7] MacIver, *Community*, London, 1924, pp. 79 ff.

than socialist. The first socialists were the intellectuals; they and not the masses are the backbone of Socialism.[8] The power of Socialism too, is like any other power ultimately spiritual; and it finds its support in ideas proceeding from the intellectual leaders, who give them to the people. If the intelligentsia abandoned Socialism its power would end. In the long run the masses cannot withstand the ideas of the leaders. True, individual demagogues may be ready, for the sake of a career and against their better knowledge, to instil into the people ideas which flatter their baser instincts and which are therefore sure to be well received. But in the end, prophets who in their heart know themselves to be false cannot prevail against those filled with the power of sincere conviction. Nothing can corrupt ideas. Neither 509
by money nor by other rewards can one hire men for the fight against ideas.

Human society is an issue of the mind. Social co-operation must first be conceived, then willed, then realized in action. It is ideas that make history, not the "material productive forces," those nebulous and mystical schemata of the materialist conception of history. If we could overcome the *idea* of Socialism, if humanity could be brought to recognize the social necessity of private ownership in the means of production, then Socialism would have to leave the stage. That is the only thing that counts.

The victory of the socialist idea over the Liberal idea has only come about through the displacement of the social attitude, which has regard to the social function of the single institution and the total effect of the whole social apparatus, by an anti-social attitude, which considers the individual parts of the social mechanism as detached units. Socialism sees the individuals—the hungry, the unemployed, and the rich—and finds fault on that account; Liberalism never forgets the whole and the interdependence of every phenomenon. It knows well enough that private ownership in the means of production is not able to transform the world into a paradise; it has never tried to establish anything beyond the simple fact that the socialist order of society is unrealizable, and therefore less able than Capitalism to promote the well-being of all.

No one has understood Liberalism less than those who have joined its ranks during the recent decades. They have felt themselves obliged to fight "excrescences" of Capitalism, thereby taking over without a qualm the characteristic anti-social attitude of the socialists. A social order has no excrescences which can be cut off at will. If a phenomenon results inevitably

---

[8] This, of course, is true also of the German nation. Almost the whole intelligentsia of Germany is socialistic: in national circles it is State or, as one usually says today, National Socialism, in Catholic circles, Church Socialism, in other circles, Social-Democracy or Bolshevism.

from a social system based on private ownership in the means of production, no ethical or aesthetic caprice can condemn it. Speculation, for example, which is inherent in all economic action, in a socialistic society as well as any other, cannot be condemned for the form it takes under Capitalism merely because the censor of morals mistakes its social function. Nor have these disciples of Liberalism been any more fortunate in their criticisms of Socialism. They have constantly declared that Socialism is a beautiful and noble ideal towards which one ought to strive were it realizable, but that, alas, it could not be so, because it presupposed human beings more perfect morally than
510 those with whom we have to deal. It is difficult to see how people can decide that Socialism is in any way better than Capitalism unless they can maintain that it functions better as a social system. With the same justification it might be said that a machine constructed on the basis of perpetual motion would be better than one worked according to the given laws of mechanics—if only it could be made to function reliably. If the concept of Socialism contains an error which prevents that system from doing what it is supposed to do, then Socialism cannot be compared with the Capitalist system, for this has proved itself workable. Neither can it be called nobler, more beautiful or more just.

It is true, Socialism cannot be realized, but it is not because it calls for sublime and altruistic beings. One of the things this book set out to prove was that the socialist commonwealth lacks above all one quality which is indispensable for every economic system which does not live from hand to mouth but works with indirect and roundabout methods of production: that is the ability to calculate, and therefore to proceed rationally. Once this has been generally recognized, all socialist ideas must vanish from the minds of reasonable human beings.

How untenable is the opinion that Socialism must come because social evolution necessarily leads to it, has been shown in earlier sections of this book. The world inclines to Socialism because the great majority of people want it. They want it because they believe that Socialism will guarantee a higher standard of welfare. The loss of this conviction would signify the end of Socialism.

CONCLUSION

THE HISTORICAL SIGNIFICANCE OF MODERN SOCIALISM

CONCLUSION

1

Socialism in History

Nothing is more difficult than to get a clear, historical perspective of a 511
contemporary movement. The proximity of the phenomenon makes it difficult to recognize the whole in true proportion. Historical judgment above all demands distance.

Wherever Europeans or the descendants of European emigrants live, we see Socialism at work today; and in Asia it is the banner round which the antagonists of European civilization gather. If the intellectual dominance of Socialism remains unshaken, then in a short time the whole co-operative system of culture which Europe has built up during thousands of years will be shattered. For a socialist order of society is unrealizable. All efforts to realize Socialism lead only to the destruction of society. Factories, mines, and railways will come to a standstill, towns will be deserted. The population of the industrial territories will die out or migrate elsewhere. The farmer will return to the self-sufficiency of the closed, domestic economy. Without private ownership in the means of production there is, in the long run, no production other than a hand-to-mouth production for one's own needs.

We need not describe in detail the cultural and political consequences of such a transformation. Nomad tribes from the Eastern steppes would again raid and pillage Europe, sweeping across it with swift cavalry. Who could resist them in the thinly populated land left defenceless after the weapons inherited from the higher technique of Capitalism had worn out?

This is one possibility. But there are others. It might so happen that some nations would remain socialistic while others returned to Capitalism. Then the socialist countries alone would proceed towards social decline. The capitalist countries would progress to a higher development of the division
of labour until at last, driven by the fundamental social law to draw the 512

greatest number of human beings into the personal division of labour, and the whole earth's surface into the geographical division of labour, they would impose culture upon the backward nations or destroy them if they resisted. This has always been the historical fate of nations who have eschewed the road of capitalist development or who have halted prematurely upon it.

It may be that we exaggerate enormously the importance of the present-day socialist movement. Perhaps it has no more significance than the outbreaks against private property in the medieval persecution of the Jews, in the Franciscan movement, or in the Reformation period. And the Bolshevism of Lenin and Trotsky is possibly no more important than Knipperdolling's and Bockelson's* anabaptist rule in Münster; it is no greater in proportion to the latter than is modern Capitalism in proportion to the Capitalism of the sixteenth century. Just as civilization overcame those attacks so it may emerge stronger and purer from the upheavals of our time.

2

The Crisis of Civilization

Society is a product of will and action. Only human beings are able to will and act. All the mysticism and symbolism of collectivist philosophy cannot help us over the fact that we can speak only figuratively of the thinking, willing, and acting of communities, and that the conception of sentient thinking, willing, and acting communities is merely anthropomorphism. Society and the individual postulate each other; those collective bodies, which collectivism assumes to have existed logically and historically before individuals, may have been herds and hordes, but they were in no way societies—that is, associations created and existing by means of the collaboration of thinking creatures. Human beings construct society by making their actions a mutually conditioned co-operation.

---

* Johann Bockelson (also spelled Beukelsz, Boockelszoon, Buckholdt or Bockholdt) (c. 1508–1535) was better known as John of Leiden. He and Bernt Knipperdolling (also Bernhardt or Berend Knipperdollinck) (c. 1490–1536) were both Dutch and followers of the Anabaptist Jan, or Johann Matthysz (also Matthisson or Matthyszoon). In 1533 the Anabaptists took over Munster. Bockelson became burgomaster. A charismatic fanatic, Bockelson often engaged in wild excesses, even beheading one of his four wives himself in a fit of frenzy. Anabaptist-held Munster was besieged and Matthysz was killed in 1534. Bockelson succeeded him as "prophet." Knipperdolling, at first a rival of Bockelson's, became an abject follower. Munster was taken from the Anabaptists in 1535. Both Bockelson and Knipperdolling were then cruelly executed (Pub.).

The basis and starting point of social co-operation lie in peace-making, which consists in the mutual recognition of the "state of property." Out of a *de facto having,* maintained by force, arises the legal concept of ownership, and simultaneously, the legal order and the coercive apparatus to maintain it. All this is the result of conscious willing and awareness of the aims willed. 513
But this willing sees and wills only the most immediate and direct result: of the remoter consequences it knows nothing and can know nothing. Men who create peace and standards of conduct are only concerned to provide for the needs of the coming hours, days, years; that they are, at the same time, working to build a great structure like human society, escapes their notice. Therefore the individual institutions, which collectively support the social organism, are created with no other view in mind than the utility of the moment. They seem individually necessary and useful to their creators; their social function remains unknown to them.

The human mind ripens slowly to the recognition of social interdependence. At first, society is so mysterious and incomprehensible a formation to man that, to grasp its origin and nature, he continues to assume a divine will guiding human destinies from outside long after he has renounced this concept in the natural sciences. Kant's *Nature,* which leads humanity towards a special aim, Hegel's *World Spirit,* and the Darwinian *Natural Selection* are the last great expressions of this method. It remained for the liberal social philosophy to explain society through the actions of mankind without having to draw on metaphysics. It alone succeeds in interpreting the social function of private property. It is not content to accept the Just as a given category which cannot be analysed, or to account for it by an inexplicable predilection for just conduct. It bases its conclusions on the considerations of the consequences of acts and from a valuation of these consequences.

Judged from the old standpoint, property was sacred. Liberalism destroyed this nimbus, as it destroys all others. It "debased" property into a utilitarian, worldly matter. Property no longer has absolute value; it is valued as a means, that is, for its utility. In philosophy such a change of views involves no special difficulties; an inadequate doctrine is replaced by one more adequate. But a fundamental revolution of the mind cannot be carried out in life and in the consciousness of the masses with the same lack of friction. It is no trifle when an idol before which humanity has trembled and feared for thousands of years is destroyed and the frightened slave gets his freedom. That which was law because God and conscience so ordained, is now to be law because one can oneself make it so at will. What was certain becomes uncertain; right and wrong, good and evil, all these conceptions begin to 514
totter. The old tables of the law are shattered and man is left to make new

commandments for himself. This cannot be achieved by means of parliamentary debate or in peaceful voting. A revision of the moral code can only be carried through when minds are deeply stirred and passions unloosed. To recognize the social utility of private property one must first be convinced of the perniciousness of every other system.

That this is the substance of the great fight between Capitalism and Socialism becomes evident when we realize that the same process is taking place in other spheres of moral life. The problem of property is not the only one which is being discussed today. It is the same with the problem of bloodshed which, in its many aspects—and particularly in connection with war and peace—agitates the whole world. In sexual morality, too, age-old moral precepts are undergoing transformation. Things which were held to be taboo, rules which have been obeyed for moral and almost sacred reasons, are now prescribed or prohibited according to the importance attached to them in respect of the promotion of public welfare. This revaluation of the grounds on which precepts of conduct have been based has inevitably caused a general revision of standards which have been in force up till now. Men ask: are they really useful or might they not really be abolished?

In the inner life of the individual the fact that the moral equilibrium has not yet been reached causes grave psychological shocks, well known to medicine as neuroses.[1] This is the characteristic malady of our time of moral transition, of the *spiritual adolescence of the nations*. In social life the discord works itself out in conflicts and errors which we witness with horror. Just as it is decisively important in the life of the individual man whether he merges safe and sound from the troubles and fears of adolescence of whether he carries away scars which hinder him permanently from developing his abilities, so is it important in what manner human society will struggle through the vexed problems of organization. A rise to a closer interdependence of individuals and hence to a higher well-being, on the one hand; a decay of co-operation and hence of wealth, on the other: these are the choices before us. There is no third alternative.

515 The great social discussion cannot proceed otherwise than by means of the thought, will, and action of individuals. Society lives and acts only in individuals; it is nothing more than a certain attitude on their part. Everyone carries a part of society on his shoulders; no one is relieved of his share of responsibility by others. And no one can find a safe way out for himself if

[1] Freud, *Totem und Tabu* (Vienna, 1913), pp. 62 ff. Publisher's Note: In English, "Totem and Taboo," in The Standard Edition of *The Complete Psychological Works of Sigmund Freud* (London: Hogarth; New York: Macmillan, 1953).

society is sweeping towards destruction. Therefore everyone, in his own interests, must thrust himself vigorously into the intellectual battle. None can stand aside with unconcern; the interests of everyone hang on the result. Whether he chooses or not, every man is drawn into the great historical struggle, the decisive battle into which our epoch has plunged us.

Neither God nor a mystical "Natural Force" created society; it was created by mankind. Whether society shall continue to evolve or whether it shall decay lies—in the sense in which causal determination of all events permits us to speak of freewill—in the hand of man. Whether Society is good or bad may be a matter of individual judgment; but whoever prefers life to death, happiness to suffering, well-being to misery, must accept society. And whoever desires that society should exist and develop must also accept, without limitation or reserve, private ownership in the means of production.

APPENDIX

A CONTRIBUTION TO THE CRITIQUE OF ATTEMPTS TO CONSTRUCT A SYSTEM OF ECONOMIC CALCULATION FOR THE SOCIALIST COMMUNITY

APPENDIX

We may divide the various attempts, which have been made to think out a system of economic calculation which would work under Socialism, into two main groups. In so doing we leave out of count works based on the labour theory of value which are misleading from the very outset. The first would contain those which may be designated syndicalist constructions, the second those which try to evade the impossibility of solving the problem by assuming that economic data do not change. The error in both groups of proposals should be clear from what we have said above (pp. 97–130). The following criticism, which I have made of two typical constructions of this kind, is intended to add further elucidations.[1] 516

In an article entitled "Sozialistische Rechnungslegung" (Socialist Accounting)[2] Karl Polányi has attempted to solve what he calls "the problem of socialist accounting" which is, according to him, "generally recognized to be the key problem of the socialist economy." Polányi first admits unreservedly that he considers the solution of the problem impossible "in a central administrative economy."[3] His attempt to solve the problem is designed only for "a functionally organized socialist transition-economy." This is the name he gives to a type of society corresponding approximately to the ideal of the English Guild Socialists. But his concept of the nature and possibilities of his system is, unfortunately, no less nebulous and vague than that of the Guild Socialists themselves. The political community "is considered to be 'the owner of the means of production'; but no direct right of disposing of

[1] *Archiv für Sozialwissenschaft*, Vol. LI, pp. 490–95. Publisher's Note: The article Mises cites here is his "Neue Beiträge Zum Problem der sozialistischen Wirtschaftsrechnung."

[2] *Ibid.*, Vol. XLIX, pp. 377–420.

[3] *Ibid.*, pp. 378 and 419.

production is implied by this ownership." This right belongs to associations of producers, elected by workers in the various branches of production. The several individual producers' associations are to be amalgamated as the Congress of producers' associations, which "represents the whole of pro-
517 duction." Confronting this is the "Commune," as the second "functional main association of society." The Commune is not only the political organ, but also the "real bearer of the community's higher aims." Each of these two functional associations exercise "within its own sphere the legislative and executive functions." Agreements between these functional main associations constitute the highest power in society.[4]

Now the defect in this system is the obscurity in which it evades the central problem—Socialism or Syndicalism? With the Guild-Socialists, Polányi expressly assigns to society, to the Commune, ownership of the means of production. In doing so he seems to think he has said enough to save his system from the charge of Syndicalism. But in the next sentence he withdraws what he has said. Ownership is the right of disposal. If the right of disposal belongs not to the Commune, but to the producers' association, these are the owners, and we have before us a syndicalist community. One or the other it must be; between Syndicalism and Socialism there can be no compromise or reconciliation. Polányi does not see this. He says: "Functional representatives (associations) of one and of the same person can never irreconcilably conflict with each other; this is the fundamental idea of every functional constitution. For the settlement of each conflict, as it arises, either joint committees of the Commune and the Producers' Association are provided or a kind of Supreme Constitutional Court (co-ordinating organs), which has, however, no legislative power and only limited executive power (guarding law and order, etc.)."[5] This fundamental idea of the functional form of constitution is, however, wrong. If the political parliament is to be formed by the votes of all citizens, with equal voting rights for each—and this condition is implied by Polányi and all other similar systems—then the parliament and the congress of producers' associations, which is the result of an electoral structure quite differently built up, may, easily, conflict. These conflicts cannot be settled by joint committees or by law courts. The committees can settle the quarrel only if one or other of the main associations preponderates within them. If both are equally strong, the committee can come to no decision. If one of the two associations preponderates the ultimate decision lies with it. A law court cannot settle questions of political or

[4] *Archiv für Sozialwissenschaft*, Vol. XLIX, p. 404.
[5] *Ibid.*, p. 404 n20.

economic practice. Law courts can give judgment only on the basis of already 518
existing norms, which they apply to individual cases. If they are to deal with questions of utility, then they are in reality not law courts but supreme political authorities, and everything we have said about the committee is true of them.

If the final decision rests with neither the Commune nor the Congress of Producers' Associations, the system cannot live at all. If ultimate decision lies with the Commune, we have to deal with a "central administrative economy," and this, as even Polányi admits, could not calculate economically. If the Producers' Associations decide, then we have a syndicalist community.

Polányi's obscurity on this fundamental point allows him to accept a merely apparent solution as an actual workable solution of the problem. His associations and sub-associations maintain a mutual exchange-relationship; they receive and give as if they were owners. Thus a market and market-prices are formed. But because he thinks he has surmounted the unbridgeable gulf between Socialism and Syndicalism, Polányi does not perceive that this is incompatible with Socialism. We might say much more about other errors in the details of Polányi's system. But in view of his fundamental mistake they are of little interest, as they are peculiar to Polányi's train of thought. That fundamental mistake is, however, no peculiarity of Polányi's; all guild socialist systems share it. Polányi has the merit of having worked out this system more clearly than most other writers. He has thus exposed its weakness more clearly. He must also be given due credit for having realized that economic calculation would be impossible in a centralized administrative economy with no markets.

Another contribution to our problem comes from Eduard Heimann.[6] Heimann is a believer in an ethical or religious Socialism. But his political views do not blind him to the problem of economic calculation. In treating this, he follows the arguments of Max Weber. Max Weber had seen that this was the "absolutely central" problem for Socialism, and had shown in a detailed discussion, in which he rejected Otto Neurath's pet dreams of "calculation in kind" ("*Naturalrechnung*") that rational economic action was impossible
without money and money-accounting.[7] Heimann therefore tries to prove 519
that one could calculate in a socialist economy.

Whilst Polányi proceeds from a system allied to the English guild socialists, Heimann develops proposals parallel to the German ideas for a planned

---

[6] Heimann, *Mehrwert und Gemeinwirtschaft, kritische und positive Beiträge zur Theorie des Sozialismus* (Berlin, 1922).

[7] Max Weber, *Wirtschaft und Gesellschaft*, *op. cit.*, pp. 45–9.

economy. It is characteristic that the arguments, nevertheless, resemble Polányi's on the only point that matters: they are regrettably vague just where they ought to be explicit about the relationship between the individual productive groups, into which the society organized according to planned economy is to be divided, and society as a whole. Thus he is able to speak of trade taking place as in a market,[8] without noticing that the planned economy, completely and logically carried through, is tradeless and that what might be called buying and selling should, according to its nature, be described quite otherwise. Heimann makes this mistake because he thinks that the characteristic mark of the planned economy is above all the monopolistic amalgamation of individual branches of production, instead of the dependence of production on the unitary will of a central organ. This mistake is all the more astonishing as the very name "planned economy" and all the arguments brought forward to support it stress particularly that the economic direction would be unitary. Heimann does indeed see the hollowness of the propaganda which works with the catchword "anarchy of production."[9] But this ought never to have allowed him to forget that just this point and nothing else, is what sharply divides Socialism from Capitalism.

Like most writers who have dealt with the planned economy, Heimann does not notice that a planned economy logically carried out is nothing more than pure Socialism and differs from the strictly centrally organized socialist community only in externals. That under the unitary direction of the central authority the administration of individual branches of production is entrusted to seemingly independent departments does not alter the fact that only the central authority directs. The relations between the individual departments are settled, not on the market by the competition of buyers and sellers, but the command of authority. The problem is this: that there is no standard by which one may account and calculate the effects of these authoritarian interventions, because the central authority cannot be guided by exchange-
520 relationships formed on a market. The authority may indeed base its calculations on substitution-relations, which it determines itself. But this decision is arbitrary; it is not based, as are market prices, on the subjective valuations of individuals and imputed to the producers' goods by the cooperation of all those active in production and trade. Rational economic calculation cannot therefore be based upon it.

Heimann achieves an apparent solution of the problem by invoking the theory of costs. Economic calculation is to be based upon cost computations,

---

[8] Heimann, *op. cit.*, pp. 184 ff.

[9] *Ibid.*, p. 174.

prices are to be calculated on the basis of the average costs of production, including wages, of the works attached to the accounting-office.[10] This is a solution which might have satisfied us two or three generations ago. It is not enough nowadays. If by costs we mean the loss of utility which a different use of the factors of production could have avoided, it is easy to see that Heimann is moving in a circle. In the socialist community only an order from the central authority could enable industry to use the factors of production elsewhere, and the problem is just whether this authority could calculate so as to decide upon such an order. The competition of entrepreneurs who, in a social order based on private property, try to use goods and services most profitably, *is replaced* in the planned economy—as in every imaginable form of socialist society—by actions-according-to-plan of the supreme authority. Now it is only by this competition between entrepreneurs, trying to wrest from each other the material means of production and the services of labour, that the prices of the factors of production are formed. Where production is to be carried on "according to plan," that is, by a central authority to whom everything is subject, the basis of calculation of profitability vanishes; only accounting in kind remains. Heimann says: "As soon as real competition exists on the market for consumers' goods, the price-relationships thus determined spread from there through all the stages of production, provided that pricing is effected reasonably; and this happens independently of the constitution of the parties in the markets for producers' goods."[11] This, however, would only be the case if there were genuine competition. Heimann conceives society to be the association of a number of "monopolists," that is, of departments of the socialist community, to each of which is entrusted
the exclusive working of a delimited field of production. If *these* buy producers' 521
goods on the "market," it is not competition, because the central authority has in advance assigned to them the field in which they are to be active and which they must not leave. Competition exists only when everyone produces what seems to promise the best profit. I have tried to show that this can only be ensured by private ownership in the means of production.

Heimann's picture of the socialist community considers only the current transformation of raw materials into consumers' goods; it thus creates the impression that the individual departments could proceed independently. Far more important than this part of the productive process is the renewal of capital and the investment of newly-formed capital. This is the central problem of economic calculation, not the problem of disposing of the cir-

---

[10] Heimann, *op. cit.*, p. 185.

[11] *Ibid.*, pp. 188 ff.

culating capital already in existence. One cannot base decisions of this sort, which are binding for years and decades ahead, on the momentary demand for consumers' goods. One must look to the future, that is, one must be "speculative." Heimann's scheme, which enlarges or restricts production mechanically and automatically, so to speak, according to the present demand for consumers' goods, fails here entirely. For to solve the problem of value by going back to costs would suffice only for a theoretically conceivable state of equilibrium, imaginatively conceivable but empirically non-existent. Only in such an imaginary state of equilibrium do price and costs coincide, not in a changing economy.

For this reason, in my judgment, Heimann's attempt to solve the problem, which I submit I have shown to be unsolvable, breaks down.

EPILOGUE

(Originally published in 1947 as Planned Chaos *by the Foundation for Economic Education, Inc.)*

EPILOGUE

(Originally published in 1947 as Planned Chaos *by the Foundation for Economic Education, Inc.)*

Introductory Remarks

The characteristic mark of this age of dictators, wars and revolutions is its 525
anti-capitalistic bias. Most governments and political parties are eager to restrict the sphere of private initiative and free enterprise. It is an almost unchallenged dogma that capitalism is done for and that the coming of all-round regimentation of economic activities is both inescapable and highly desirable.

None the less capitalism is still very vigorous in the Western Hemisphere. Capitalist production has made very remarkable progress even in these last years. Methods of production were greatly improved. Consumers have been supplied with better and cheaper goods and with many new articles unheard of a short time ago. Many countries have expanded the size and improved the quality of their manufacturing. In spite of the anti-capitalistic policies of all governments and of almost all political parties, the capitalist mode of production is in many countries still fulfilling its social function in supplying the consumers with more, better and cheaper goods.

It is certainly not a merit of governments, politicians and labour union officers that the standard of living is improving in the countries committed to the principle of private ownership of the means of production. Not offices and bureaucrats, but big business deserves credit for the fact that most of the families in the United States own a motor car and a radio set. The increase in per capita consumption in America as compared with conditions a quarter of a century ago is not an achievement of laws and executive orders. It is an accomplishment of business men who enlarged the size of their factories or built new ones.

One must stress this point because our contemporaries are inclined to ignore it. Entangled in the superstitions of statism and government omnipotence, they are exclusively preoccupied with governmental measures. They expect everything from authoritarian action and very little from the initiative of enterprising citizens. Yet, the only means to increase well-being is to increase the quantity of products. This is what business aims at.

It is grotesque that there is much more talk about the achievements of the
526 Tennessee Valley Authority than about all the unprecedented and unparalleled achievements of American privately operated processing industries. However, it was only the latter which enabled the United Nations to win the war and today enable the United States to come to the aid of the Marshall Plan countries.

The dogma that the State or the Government is the embodiment of all that is good and beneficial and that the individuals are wretched underlings, exclusively intent upon inflicting harm upon one another and badly in need of a guardian, is almost unchallenged. It is taboo to question it in the slightest way. He who proclaims the godliness of the State and the infallibility of its priests, the bureaucrats, is considered as an impartial student of the social sciences. All those raising objections are branded as biased and narrow-minded. The supporters of the new religion of statolatry are no less fanatical and intolerant than were the Mohammedan conquerors of Africa and Spain.

History will call our age the age of the dictators and tyrants. We have witnessed in the last years the fall of two of these inflated supermen. But the spirit which raised these knaves to autocratic power survives. It permeates textbooks and periodicals, it speaks through the mouths of teachers and politicians, it manifests itself in party programmes and in plays and novels. As long as this spirit prevails there cannot be any hope of durable peace, of democracy, of the preservation of freedom or of a steady improvement in the nation's economic well-being.

1

The Failure of Interventionism

Nothing is more unpopular today than the free market economy, i.e., 527
capitalism. Everything that is considered unsatisfactory in present-day conditions is charged to capitalism. The atheists make capitalism responsible for the survival of Christianity. But the papal encyclicals blame capitalism for the spread of irreligion and the sins of our contemporaries, and the Protestant churches and sects are no less vigorous in their indictment of capitalist greed. Friends of peace consider our wars as an offshoot of capitalist imperialism. But the adamant nationalist warmongers of Germany and Italy indicted capitalism for its "bourgeois" pacifism, contrary to human nature and to the inescapable laws of history. Sermonizers accuse capitalism of disrupting the family and fostering licentiousness. But the "progressives" blame capitalism for the preservation of allegedly outdated rules of sexual restraint. Almost all men agree that poverty is an outcome of capitalism. On the other hand many deplore the fact that capitalism, in catering lavishly to the wishes of people intent upon getting more amenities and a better living, promotes a crass materialism. These contradictory accusations of capitalism cancel one another. But the fact remains that there are few people left who would not condemn capitalism altogether.

Although capitalism is the economic system of modern Western civilization, the policies of all Western nations are guided by utterly anti-capitalistic ideas. The aim of these interventionist policies is not to preserve capitalism, but to substitute a mixed economy for it. It is assumed that this mixed economy is neither capitalism nor socialism. It is described as a third system, as far from capitalism as it is from socialism. It is alleged that it stands midway between socialism and capitalism, retaining the advantages of both and avoiding the disadvantages inherent in each.

More than half a century ago the outstanding man in the British socialist
528 movement, Sidney Webb, declared that the socialist philosophy is "but the conscious and explicit assertion of principles of social organization which have been already in great part unconsciously adopted." And he added that the economic history of the nineteenth century was "an almost continuous record of the progress of socialism."[1] A few years later an eminent British statesman, Sir William Harcourt, stated: "We are all socialists now."[2] When in 1913 an American, Elmer Roberts, published a book on the economic policies of the Imperial Government of Germany as conducted since the end of the 1870s, he called them "monarchical socialism."[3]

However, it was not correct simply to identify interventionism and socialism. There are many supporters of interventionism who consider it the most appropriate method of realizing—step by step—full socialism. But there are also many interventionists who are not outright socialists; they aim at the establishment of the mixed economy as a permanent system of economic management. They endeavour to restrain, to regulate and to "improve" capitalism by government interference with business and by labour unionism.

In order to comprehend the working of interventionism and of the mixed economy it is necessary to clarify two points:

First: If within a society based on private ownership of the means of production some of these means are owned and operated by the government or by municipalities, this still does not make for a mixed system which would combine socialism and private ownership. As long as only certain individual enterprises are publicly controlled, the characteristics of the market economy determining economic activity remain essentially unimpaired. The publicly owned enterprises, too, as buyers of raw materials, semi-finished goods and labour, and as sellers of goods and services, must fit into the mechanism of the market economy. They are subject to the law of the market; they have to strive after profits or, at least, to avoid losses. When it is attempted to mitigate or to eliminate this dependence by covering the losses of such enterprises with subsidies out of public funds, the only result is a shifting of this dependence somewhere else. This is because the means for the subsidies have to be raised somewhere. They may be raised by collecting taxes. But the burden of such taxes has its effects on the public, not on the
529 government collecting the tax. It is the market, and not the revenue department, which decides upon whom the burden of the tax falls and how

[1] Sidney Webb in *Fabian Essays in Socialism*, first published in 1889 (American edition, New York, 1891, p. 4).

[2] Cf. G. M. Trevelyan, *A Shortened History of England* (London, 1942), p. 510.

[3] Elmer Roberts, *Monarchical Socialism in Germany* (New York, 1913).

it affects production and consumption. The market and its inescapable law are supreme.

Second: There are two different patterns for the realization of socialism. The one pattern—we may call it the Marxian or Russian pattern—is purely bureaucratic. All economic enterprises are departments of the government just as the administration of the army and the navy or the postal system. Every single plant, shop or farm, stands in the same relation to the superior central organization as does a post office to the office of the Postmaster-General. The whole nation forms one single labour army with compulsory service; the commander of this army is the chief of state.

The second pattern—we may call it the German or *Zwangswirtschaft* system[4]—differs from the first one in that it, seemingly and nominally, maintains private ownership of the means of production, entrepreneurship, and market exchange. So-called entrepreneurs do the buying and selling, pay the workers, contract debts and pay interest and amortization. But they are no longer entrepreneurs. In Nazi Germany they were called shop managers or *Betriebsführer*. The government tells these seeming entrepreneurs what and how to produce, at what prices and from whom to buy, at what prices and to whom to sell. The government decrees at what wages labourers should work, and to whom and under what terms the capitalists should entrust their funds. Market exchange is but a sham. As all prices, wages and interest rates are fixed by the authority, they are prices, wages and interest rates in appearance only; in fact they are merely quantitative terms in the authoritarian orders determining each citizen's income, consumption and standard of living. The authority, not the consumers, directs production. The central board of production management is supreme; all citizens are nothing else but civil servants. This is socialism with the outward appearance of capitalism. Some labels of the capitalistic market economy are retained, but they signify here something entirely different from what they mean in the market economy.

It is necessary to point out this fact to prevent a confusion of socialism and interventionism. The system of the hampered market economy, or interven- 530
tionism, differs from socialism by the very fact that it is still market economy. The authority seeks to influence the market by the intervention of its coercive power, but it does not want to eliminate the market altogether. It desires that production and consumption should develop along lines different from those prescribed by the unhindered market, and it wants to achieve its aim

[4] *Zwang* means compulsion, *Wirtschaft* means economy. The English language equivalent for *Zwangswirtschaft* is something like compulsory economy.

by injecting into the working of the market orders, commands and prohibitions for whose enforcement the police power and its apparatus of coercion and compulsion stand ready. But these are isolated interventions; their authors assert that they do not plan to combine these measures into a completely integrated system which regulates all prices, wages and interest rates, and which thus places full control of production and consumption in the hands of the authorities.

However, all the methods of interventionism are doomed to failure. This means: the interventionist measures must needs result in conditions which *from the point of view of their own advocates* are more unsatisfactory than the previous state of affairs they were designed to alter. These policies are therefore contrary to purpose.

Minimum wage rates, whether enforced by government decree or by labour union pressure and compulsion, are useless if they fix wage rates at the market level. But if they try to raise wage rates above the level which the unhampered labour market would have determined, they result in permanent unemployment of a great part of the potential labour force.

Government spending cannot create additional jobs. If the government provides the funds required by taxing the citizens or by borrowing from the public, it abolishes on the one hand as many jobs as it creates on the other. If government spending is financed by borrowing from the commercial banks, it means credit expansion and inflation. If in the course of such an inflation the rise in commodity prices exceeds the rise in nominal wage rates, unemployment will drop. But what makes unemployment shrink is precisely the fact that real wage rates are falling.

The inherent tendency of capitalist evolution is to raise real wage rates steadily. This is the effect of the progressive accumulation of capital by means of which technological methods of production are improved. There is no means by which the height of wage rates can be raised for all those eager to earn wages other than through the increase of the per capita quota of
531 capital invested. Whenever the accumulation of additional capital stops, the tendency towards a further increase in real wage rates comes to a standstill. If capital consumption is substituted for an increase in capital available, real wage rates must drop temporarily until the checks on a further increase in capital are removed. Government measures which retard capital accumulation or lead to capital consumption—such as confiscatory taxation—are therefore detrimental to the vital interests of the workers.

Credit expansion can bring about a temporary boom. But such a fictitious prosperity must end in a general depression of trade, a slump.

It can hardly be asserted that the economic history of the last decades has run counter to the pessimistic predictions of the economists. Our age has to face great economic troubles. But this is not a crisis of capitalism. It is the crisis of interventionism, of policies designed to improve capitalism and to substitute a better system for it.

No economist ever dared to assert that interventionism could result in anything else than in disaster and chaos. The advocates of interventionism—foremost among them the Prussian Historical School and the American Institutionalists—were not economists. On the contrary. In order to promote their plans they flatly denied that there is any such thing as economic law. In their opinion governments are free to achieve all they aim at without being restrained by an inexorable regularity in the sequence of economic phenomena. Like the German socialist Ferdinand Lassalle, they maintain that the State is God.

The interventionists do not approach the study of economic matters with scientific disinterestedness. Most of them are driven by an envious resentment against those whose incomes are larger than their own. This bias makes it impossible for them to see things as they really are. For them the main thing is not to improve the conditions of the masses, but to harm the entrepreneurs and capitalists even if this policy victimizes the immense majority of the people.

In the eyes of the interventionists the mere existence of profits is objectionable. They speak of profit without dealing with its corollary, loss. They do not comprehend that profit and loss are the instruments by means of which the consumers keep a tight rein on all entrepreneurial activities. It is profit and loss that make the consumers supreme in the direction of business. 532
It is absurd to contrast production for profit and production for use. On the unhampered market a man can earn profits only by supplying the consumers in the best and cheapest way with the goods they want to use. Profit and loss withdraw the material factors of production from the hands of the inefficient and place them in the hands of the more efficient. It is their social function to make a man the more influential in the conduct of business the better he succeeds in producing commodities for which people scramble. The consumers suffer when the laws of the country prevent the most efficient entrepreneurs from expanding the sphere of their activities. What made some enterprises develop into "big business" was precisely their success in filling best the demand of the masses.

Anti-capitalistic policies sabotage the operation of the capitalist system of the market economy. The failure of interventionism does not demonstrate the necessity of adopting socialism. It merely exposes the futility of interventionism. All those evils which the self-styled "progressives" interpret as evidence of the failure of capitalism are the outcome of their allegedly beneficial interference with the market. Only the ignorant, wrongly identifying interventionism and capitalism, believe that the remedy for these evils is socialism.

2

The Dictatorial, Anti-Democratic and Socialist Character of Interventionism

Many advocates of interventionism are bewildered when one tells them that in recommending interventionism they themselves are fostering anti-democratic and dictatorial tendencies and the establishment of totalitarian socialism. They protest that they are sincere believers and opposed to tyranny and socialism. What they aim at is only the improvement of the conditions of the poor. They say that they are driven by considerations of social justice, and favour a fairer distribution of income precisely because they are intent upon preserving capitalism and its political corollary or superstructure, viz., democratic government.

533 What these people fail to realize is that the various measures they suggest are not capable of bringing about the beneficial results aimed at. On the contrary they produce a state of affairs which from the point of view of their advocates is worse than the previous state which they were designed to alter. If the government, faced with this failure of its first intervention, is not prepared to undo its interference with the market and to return to a free economy, it must add to its first measure more and more regulations and restrictions. Proceeding step by step on this way it finally reaches a point in which all economic freedom of individuals has disappeared. Then socialism of the German pattern, the *Zwangswirtschaft* of the Nazis, emerges.

We have already mentioned the case of minimum wage rates. Let us illustrate the matter further by an analysis of a typical case of price control.

If the government wants to make it possible for poor parents to give more milk to their children, it must buy milk at the market price and sell it to those poor people with a loss at a cheaper rate; the loss may be covered from the means collected by taxation. But if the government simply fixes the price of milk at a lower rate than the market, the results obtained will be contrary to the aims of the government. The marginal producers will, in order to avoid losses, go out of the business of producing and selling milk. There will be less milk available for the consumers, not more. This outcome is contrary to the government's intentions. The government interfered because it considered milk as a vital necessity. It did not want to restrict its supply.

Now the government has to face the alternative: either to refrain from any endeavours to control prices, or to add to its first measure a second one, i.e., to fix the prices of the factors of production necessary for the production of milk. Then the same story repeats itself on a remoter plane: the government has again to fix the prices of the factors of production necessary for the production of those factors of production which are needed for the production of milk. Thus the government has to go further and further, fixing the prices of all the factors of production—both human (labour) and material—and forcing every entrepreneur and every worker to continue work at these prices and wages. No branch of production can be omitted from this all-round fixing of prices and wages and this general order to continue production. If some branches of production were left free, the result would be a shifting
of capital and labour to them and a corresponding fall of the supply of the 534
goods whose prices the government had fixed. However, it is precisely these goods which the government considers as especially important for the satisfaction of the needs of the masses.

But when this state of all-round control of business is achieved, the market economy has been replaced by a system of planned economy, by socialism. Of course, this is not the socialism of immediate state management of every plant by the government as in Russia, but the socialism of the German or Nazi pattern.

Many people were fascinated by the alleged success of German price control. They said: You have only to be as brutal and ruthless as the Nazis and you will succeed in controlling prices. What these people, eager to fight Nazism by adopting its methods, did not see was that the Nazis did not enforce price control within a market society, but they established a full socialist system, a totalitarian commonwealth.

Price control is contrary to purpose if it is limited to some commodities only. It cannot work satisfactorily within a market economy. If the government does not draw from this failure the conclusion that it must abandon all attempts to control prices, it must go further and further until it substitutes socialist all-round planning for the market economy.

Production can either be directed by the prices fixed on the market by the buying and by the abstention from buying on the part of the public. Or it can be directed by the government's central board of production management. There is no third solution available. There is no third social system feasible which would be neither market economy nor socialism. Government control of only a part of prices must result in a state of affairs which—without any exception—everybody considers as absurd and contrary to purpose. Its inevitable result is chaos and social unrest.

It is this that the economists have in mind in referring to economic law and asserting that interventionism is contrary to economic law.

In the market economy the consumers are supreme. Their buying and their abstention from buying ultimately determine what the entrepreneurs produce and in what quantity and quality. It determines directly the prices of the consumers' goods and indirectly the prices of all producers' goods, viz., labour and material factors of production. It determines the emergence
535 of profits and losses and the formation of the rate of interest. It determines every individual's income. The focal point of the market economy is the market, i.e., the process of the formation of commodity prices, wage rates and interest rates and their derivatives, profits and losses. It makes all men in their capacity as producers responsible to the consumers. This dependence is direct with entrepreneurs, capitalists, farmers and professional men, and indirect with people working for salaries and wages. The market adjusts the efforts of all those engaged in supplying the needs of the consumers to the wishes of those for whom they produce, the consumers. It subjects production to consumption.

The market is a democracy in which every penny gives a right to vote. It is true that the various individuals have not the same power to vote. The richer man casts more ballots than the poorer fellow. But to be rich and to earn a higher income is, in the market economy, already the outcome of a previous election. The only means to acquire wealth and to preserve it, in a market economy not adulterated by government-made privileges and restrictions, is to serve the consumers in the best and cheapest way. Capitalists and landowners who fail in this regard suffer losses. If they do not change their procedure, they lose their wealth and become poor. It is consumers who make poor people rich and rich people poor. It is the consumers who fix the wages of a movie star and an opera singer at a higher level than those of a welder or an accountant.

Every individual is free to disagree with the outcome of an election campaign or of the market process. But in a democracy he has no other means to alter things than persuasion. If a man were to say: "I do not like the mayor elected by majority vote; therefore I ask the government to replace him by the man I prefer," one would hardly call him a democrat. But if the same claims are raised with regard to the market, most people are too dull to discover the dictatorial aspirations involved.

The consumers have made their choices and determined the income of the shoe manufacturer, the movie star and the welder. Who is Professor X to arrogate to himself the privilege of overthrowing their decision? If he were not a potential dictator, he would not ask the government to interfere. He would try to persuade his fellow-citizens to increase their demand for the products of the welders and to reduce their demand for shoes and pictures.

The consumers are not prepared to pay for cotton prices which would 536
render the marginal farms, i.e., those producing under the least favourable conditions, profitable. This is very unfortunate indeed for the farmers concerned; they must discontinue growing cotton and try to integrate themselves in another way into the whole of production.

But what shall we think of the statesman who interferes by compulsion in order to raise the price of cotton above the level it would reach on the free market? What the interventionist aims at is the substitution of police pressure for the choice of the consumers. All this talk: the state should do this or that, ultimately means: the police should force consumers to behave otherwise than they would behave spontaneously. In such proposals as: let *us* raise farm prices, let *us* raise wage rates, let *us* lower profits, let *us* curtail the salaries of executives, the *us* ultimately refers to the police. Yet the authors of these projects protest that they are planning for freedom and industrial democracy.

In most non-socialist countries the labour unions are granted special rights. They are permitted to prevent non-members from working. They are allowed to call a strike and, when on strike, are virtually free to employ violence against all those who are prepared to continue working, viz., the strike-breakers. This system assigns an unlimited privilege to those engaged in vital branches of industry. Those workers whose strike cuts off the supply of water, light, food and other necessities are in a position to obtain all they want at the expense of the rest of the population. It is true that in the United States their unions have up to now exercised some moderation in taking advantage of this opportunity. Other American unions and many European unions have been less cautious. They are intent upon enforcing wage increases without bothering about the disaster inevitably resulting.

The interventionists are not shrewd enough to realize that labour union pressure and compulsion are absolutely incompatible with any system of social organization. The union problem has no reference whatsoever to the right of citizens to associate with one another in assemblies and associations; no democratic country denies its citizens this right. Neither does anybody dispute a man's right to stop work and to go on strike. The only question is whether or not the unions should be granted the privilege of resorting
with impunity to violence. This privilege is no less incompatible with socialism 537
than with capitalism. No social co-operation under the division of labour is

possible when some people or unions of people are granted the right to prevent by violence and the threat of violence other people from working. When enforced by violence, a strike in vital branches of production or a general strike are tantamount to a revolutionary destruction of society.

A government abdicates if it tolerates any non-governmental agency's use of violence. If the government forsakes its monopoly of coercion and compulsion, anarchic conditions result. If it were true that a democratic system of government is unfit to protect unconditionally every individual's right to work in defiance of the orders of a union, democracy would be doomed. Then dictatorship would be the only means to preserve the division of labour and to avoid anarchy. What generated dictatorship in Russia and Germany was precisely the fact that the mentality of these nations made suppression of union violence unfeasible under democratic conditions. The dictators abolished strikes and thus broke the spine of labour unionism. There is no question of strikes in the Soviet empire.

It is illusory to believe that arbitration of labour disputes could bring the unions into the framework of the market economy and make their functioning compatible with the preservation of domestic peace. Judicial settlement of controversies is feasible if there is a set of rules available, according to which individual cases can be judged. But if such a code is valid and its provisions are applied to the determination of the height of wage rates, it is no longer the market which fixes them, but the code and those who legislate with regard to it. Then the government is supreme and no longer the consumers buying and selling on the market. If no such code exists, a standard according to which a controversy between employers and employees could be decided is lacking. It is vain to speak of "fair" wages in the absence of such a code. The notion of fairness is nonsensical if not related to an established standard. In practice, if the employers do not yield to the threats of the unions, arbitration is tantamount to the determination of wage rates by the government-appointed arbitrator. Peremptory authoritarian decision is substituted for the market price. The issue is always the same: the government *or* the market. There is no third solution.

Metaphors are often very useful in elucidating complicated problems and
538 in making them comprehensible to less intelligent minds. But they become misleading and result in nonsense if people forget that every comparison is imperfect. It is silly to take metaphorical idioms literally and to deduce from their interpretation features of the object one wished to make more easily understandable by their use. There is no harm in the economists' description of the operation of the market as *automatic* and in their custom of speaking of the *anonymous* forces operating on the market. They could not anticipate that anybody would be so stupid as to take these metaphors literally.

No "automatic" and "anonymous" forces actuate the "mechanism" of the market. The only factors directing the market and determining prices are purposive acts of men. There is no automatism; there are men consciously aiming at ends chosen and deliberately resorting to definite means for the attainment of these ends. There are no mysterious mechanical forces; there is only the will of every individual to satisfy his demand for various goods. There is no anonymity; there are you and I and Bill and Joe and all the rest. And each of us is engaged both in production and consumption. Each contributes his share to the determination of prices.

The dilemma is not between automatic forces and planned action. It is between the democratic process of the market, in which every individual has his share, and the exclusive rule of a dictatorial body. Whatever people do in the market economy, is the execution of their own plans. In this sense every human action means planning. What those calling themselves planners advocate is not the substitution of planned action for letting things go. It is the substitution of the planner's own plan for the plans of his fellow-men. The planner is a potential dictator who wants to deprive all other people of the power to plan and act according to their own plans. He aims at one thing only: the exclusive absolute pre-eminence of his own plan.

It is no less erroneous to declare that a government that is not socialistic has no plan. Whatever a government does is the execution of a plan, i.e., of a design. One may disagree with such a plan. But one must not say that it is not a plan at all. Professor Wesley C. Mitchell maintained that the British liberal government "planned to have no plan."[5] However, the British government in the liberal age certainly had a definite plan. Its plan was private ownership of the means of production, free initiative and market economy. Great Britain was very prosperous indeed under this plan which according *539*
to Professor Mitchell is "no plan."

The planners pretend that their plans are scientific and that there cannot be disagreement with regard to them among well-intentioned and decent people. However, there is no such thing as a scientific *ought*. Science is competent to establish what *is*. It can never dictate what ought to be and what ends people should aim at. It is a fact that men disagree in their value judgments. It is insolent to arrogate to oneself the right to overrule the plans of other people and to force them to submit to the plan of the planner. Whose plan should be executed? The plan of the CIO or those of any other group? The plan of Trotsky or that of Stalin? The plan of Hitler or that of Strasser?

When people were committed to the idea that in the field of religion only

---

[5] Wesley C. Mitchell, "The Social Sciences and National Planning" in *Planned Society*, ed. Findlay Mackenzie (New York, 1937), p. 112

one plan must be adopted, bloody wars resulted. With the acknowledgment of the principle of religious freedom these wars ceased. The market economy safeguards peaceful economic co-operation because it does not use force upon the economic plans of the citizens. If one master plan is to be substituted for the plans of each citizen, endless fighting must emerge. Those who disagree with the dictator's plan have no other means to carry on than to defeat the despot by force of arms.

It is an illusion to believe that a system of planned socialism could be operated according to democratic methods of government. Democracy is inextricably linked with capitalism. It cannot exist where there is planning. Let us refer to the words of the most eminent of the contemporary advocates of socialism. Professor Harold Laski declared that the attainment of power by the British Labour Party in the normal parliamentary fashion must result in a radical transformation of parliamentary government. A socialist administration needs "guarantees" that its work of transformation would not be "disrupted" by repeal in event of its defeat at the polls. Therefore the suspension of the Constitution is "inevitable."[6] How pleased would Charles I and George III have been if they had known the books of Professor Laski!

Sidney and Beatrice Webb (Lord and Lady Passfield) tell us that "in any corporate action a loyal unity of thought is so important that, if anything is
540 to be achieved, public discussion must be suspended between the promulgation of the decision and the accomplishment of the task." Whilst "the work is in progress" any expression of doubt, or even of fear that the plan will not be successful, is "an act of disloyalty, or even of treachery."[7] Now as the process of production never ceases and some work is always in progress and there is always something to be achieved, it follows that a socialist government must never concede any freedom of speech and the press. "A loyal unity of thought," what a high-sounding circumlocution for the ideals of Philip II and the Inquisition! In this regard another eminent admirer of the Soviets, Mr. T. G. Crowther, speaks without any reserve. He plainly declares that inquisition is "beneficial to science when it protects a rising class,"[8] i.e., when Mr. Crowther's friends resort to it. Hundreds of similar dicta could be quoted.

In the Victorian age, when John Stuart Mill wrote his essay *On Liberty*, such views as those held by Professor Laski, Mr. and Mrs. Webb and Mr. Crowther were called reactionary. Today they are called "progressive" and

---

[6] Laski, *Democracy in Crisis* (Chapel Hill, 1933), pp. 87–8.

[7] Sidney and Beatrice Webb, *Soviet Communism: A New Civilization?* (New York, 1936), Vol. II, pp. 1038–39.

[8] T. G. Crowther, *Social Relations of Science* (London, 1941), p. 333.

"liberal." On the other hand people who oppose the suspension of parliamentary government and of the freedom of speech and the press and the establishment of inquisition are scorned as "reactionaries," as "economic royalists" and as "Fascists."

Those interventionists who consider interventionism as a method of bringing about full socialism step by step are at least consistent. If the measures adopted fail to achieve the beneficial results expected and end in disaster, they ask for more and more government interference until the government has taken over the direction of all economic activities. But those interventionists who look at interventionism as a means of improving capitalism and thereby preserving it are utterly confused.

In the eyes of these people all the undesired and undesirable effects of government interference with business are caused by capitalism. The very fact that a governmental measure has brought about a state of affairs which they dislike is for them a justification of further measures. They fail, for instance, to realize that the role monopolistic schemes play in our time is the effect of government interference such as tariffs and patents. They advocate government action for the prevention of monopoly. One could hardly imagine a more unrealistic idea. For the governments whom they ask to fight mo- 541
nopoly are the same governments who are devoted to the principle of monopoly. Thus, the American New Deal Government embarked upon a thorough-going monopolistic organization of every branch of American business, by the NRA, and aimed at organizing American farming as a vast monopolistic scheme, restricting farm output for the sake of substituting monopoly prices for the lower market prices. It was a party to various international commodity control agreements the undisguised aim of which was to establish international monopolies of various commodities. The same is true of all other governments. The Union of Soviet Socialist Republics was also a party to some of these intergovernmental monopolistic conventions.[9] Its repugnance for collaboration with the capitalistic countries was not so great as to cause it to miss any opportunity for fostering monopoly.

The programme of this self-contradictory interventionism is dictatorship, supposedly to make people free. But the liberty its supporters advocate is liberty to do the "right" things, i.e., the things they themselves want to be done. They are not only ignorant of the economic problem involved. They lack the faculty of logical thinking.

The most absurd justification of interventionism is provided by those who

---

[9] The collection of these conventions, published by The International Labour Office under the title *Intergovernmental Commodity Control Agreements* (Montreal, 1943).

look upon the conflict between capitalism and socialism as if it were a contest over the distribution of income. Why should not the propertied classes be more compliant? Why should they not accord to the poor workers a part of their ample revenues? Why should they oppose the government's design to raise the share of the underprivileged by decreeing minimum wage rates and maximum prices and by cutting profits and interest rates down to a "fairer" level? Pliability in such matters, they say, would take the wind from the sails of the radical revolutionaries and preserve capitalism. The worst enemies of capitalism, they say, are those intransigent doctrinaires whose excessive advocacy of economic freedom, of *laisser-faire* and Manchesterism renders vain all attempts to come to a compromise with the claims of labour. These adamant reactionaries are alone responsible for the bitterness of contemporary party strife and the implacable hatred it generates. What is needed
542 is the substitution of a constructive programme for the purely negative attitude of the economic royalists. And, of course, "constructive" is in the eyes of these people only interventionism.

However, this mode of reasoning is entirely vicious. It takes for granted that the various measures of government interference with business will attain those beneficial results which their advocates expect from them. It blithely disregards all that economics says about their futility in attaining the ends sought, and their unavoidable and undesirable consequences. The question is not whether minimum wage rates are fair or unfair, but whether or not they bring about unemployment of a part of those eager to work. By calling these measures just, the interventionist does not refute the objections raised against their expediency by the economists. He merely displays ignorance of the question at issue.

The conflict between capitalism and socialism is not a contest between two groups of claimants concerning the size of the portions to be allotted to each of them out of a definite supply of goods. It is a dispute concerning what system of social organization best serves human welfare. Those fighting socialism do not reject socialism because they envy the workers the benefits they (the workers) could allegedly derive from the socialist mode of production. They fight socialism precisely because they are convinced that it would harm the masses in reducing them to the status of poor serfs entirely at the mercy of irresponsible dictators.

In this conflict of opinions everybody must make up his mind and take a definite stand. Everybody must side either with the advocates of economic freedom or with those of totalitarian socialism. One cannot evade this dilemma by adopting an allegedly middle-of-the-road position, namely interventionism. For interventionism is neither a middle way nor a compromise between capitalism and socialism. It is a third system. It is a system the absurdity and futility of which is agreed upon not only by all economists but even by the Marxians.

There is no such thing as an "excessive" advocacy of economic freedom. On the one hand, production can be directed by the efforts of each individual to adjust his conduct so as to fill the most urgent wants of the consumers in the most appropriate way. This is the market economy. On the other hand, production can be directed by authoritarian decree. If these decrees concern only some isolated items of the economic structure, they fail to attain 543
the ends sought, and their own advocates do not like their outcome. If they come up to all-round regimentation, they mean totalitarian socialism.

Men must choose between the market economy and socialism. The state can preserve the market economy in protecting life, health and private property against violent or fraudulent aggression; or it can itself control the conduct of all production activities. Some agency must determine what should be produced. If it is not the consumers by means of demand and supply on the market, it must be the government by compulsion.

3

Socialism and Communism

In the terminology of Marx and Engels the words communism and socialism are synonymous. They are alternately applied without any distinction between them. The same was true for the practice of all Marxian groups and sects until 1917. The political parties of Marxism which considered the *Communist Manifesto* as the unalterable gospel of their doctrine called themselves *socialist* parties. The most influential and most numerous of these parties, the German party, adopted the name Social Democratic Party. In Italy, in France and in all other countries in which Marxian parties already played a role in political life before 1917, the term *socialist* likewise superseded the term *communist*. No Marxian ever ventured, before 1917, to distinguish between communism and socialism.

In 1875, in his Criticism of the Gotha Programme of the German Social Democratic Party, Marx distinguished between a lower (earlier) and a higher (later) phase of the future communist society. But he did not reserve the name of communism to the higher phase, and did not call the lower phase socialism as differentiated from communism.

One of the fundamental dogmas of Marx is that socialism is bound to come "with the inexorability of a law of nature." Capitalist production begets its own negation and establishes the socialist system of public ownership of the means of production. This process "executes itself through the operation of
544 the inherent laws of capitalist production."[10] It is independent of the wills of people.[11] It is impossible for men to accelerate it, to delay it or to hinder it. For "no social system ever disappears before all the productive forces are developed for the development of which it is broad enough, and new higher methods of production never appear before the material conditions of their existence have been hatched out in the womb of previous society."[12]

This doctrine is, of course, irreconcilable with Marx's own political activities and with the teachings he advanced for the justification of these activities. Marx tried to organize a political party which by means of revolution and civil war should accomplish the transition from capitalism to socialism. The characteristic feature of their parties was, in the eyes of Marx and all Marxian doctrinaires, that they were revolutionary parties invariably committed to the idea of violent action. Their aim was to rise in rebellion, to establish the dictatorship of the proletarians and to exterminate mercilessly all bourgeois. The deeds of the Paris Communards in 1871 were considered as the perfect model of such a civil war. The Paris revolt, of course, had lamentably failed. But later uprisings were expected to succeed.[13]

However, the tactics applied by the Marxian parties in various European countries were irreconcilably opposed to each of these two contradictory varieties of the teachings of Karl Marx. They did not place confidence in the inevitability of the coming of socialism. Neither did they trust in the success of a revolutionary upheaval. They adopted the methods of parliamentary action. They solicited votes in election campaigns and sent their delegates into the parliaments. They "degenerated" into democratic parties. In the parliaments they behaved like other parties of the opposition. In some countries they entered into temporary alliances with other parties, and occasionally socialist members sat in the cabinets. Later, after the end of the first World War, the socialist parties became paramount in many parliaments. In some countries they ruled exclusively, in others in close co-operation with "bourgeois" parties.

---

[10] Marx, *Das Kapital*, 7th ed. (Hamburg, 1914), Vol. I, p. 728. Publisher's Note: In English edition, p. 836.

[11] Marx, *Zur Kritik der politischen Ökonomie*, ed. Kautsky (Stuttgart, 1897), p. xi. Publisher's Note: In English edition by Kerr, pp. 11–12; by Eastman, p. 10.

[12] *Ibid.*, p. xii. Publisher's Note: In English edition by Kerr, p. 12; by Eastman, p. 11.

[13] Marx, *Der Bürgerkrieg in Frankreich*, ed. Pfemfert (Berlin, 1919), *passim*. Publisher's Note: In English, "The Civil War in France." Reprinted in Eastman anthology, pp. 367–429.

It is true that these domesticated socialists before 1917 never abandoned lip service to the rigid principles of orthodox Marxism. They repeated again 545 and again that the coming of socialism is unavoidable. They emphasized the inherent revolutionary character of their parties. Nothing could arouse their anger more than when somebody dared to dispute their adamant revolutionary spirit. However, in fact they were parliamentary parties like all other parties.

From a correct Marxian point of view, as expressed in the later writings of Marx and Engels (but not yet in the Communist Manifesto), all measures designed to restrain, to regulate and to improve capitalism were simply "petty-bourgeois" nonsense stemming from an ignorance of the immanent laws of capitalist evolution. True socialists should not place any obstacles in the way of capitalist evolution. For only the full maturity of capitalism could bring about socialism. It is not only vain, but harmful to the interests of the proletarians to resort to such measures. Even labour-unionism is not an adequate means for the improvement of the conditions of the workers.[14] Marx did not believe that interventionism could benefit the masses. He violently rejected the idea that such measures as minimum wage rates, price ceilings, restriction of interest rates, social security and so on are preliminary steps in bringing about socialism. He aimed at the radical abolition of the wages system which can be accomplished only by communism in its higher phase. He would have sarcastically ridiculed the idea of abolishing the "commodity character" of labour within the frame of a capitalist society by the enactment of a law.

But the socialist parties as they operated in the European countries were virtually no less committed to interventionism than the *Sozialpolitik* of the Kaiser's Germany and the American New Deal. It was against this policy that George Sorel and Syndicalism directed their attacks. Sorel, a timid intellectual of a bourgeois background, deprecated the "degeneration" of the socialist parties for which he blamed their penetration by bourgeois intellectuals. He wanted to see the spirit of ruthless aggressiveness, inherent in the masses, revived and freed from the guardianship of intellectual cowards. For Sorel nothing counted but riots. He advocated *action directe*, i.e., sabotage and the general strike, as initiatory steps towards the final great revolution.

Sorel had success mostly among snobbish and idle intellectuals and no 546 less snobbish and idle heirs of wealthy entrepreneurs. He did not perceptibly move the masses. For the Marxian parties in Western and Central Europe his passionate criticism was hardly more than a nuisance. His historical

[14] Marx, *Value, Price and Profit*, ed. Eleanor Marx Aveling (New York, 1901), pp. 72–74.

importance consisted mainly in the role his ideas played in the evolution of Russian Bolshevism and Italian Fascism.

In order to understand the mentality of the Bolshevists we must again refer to the dogmas of Karl Marx. Marx was fully convinced that capitalism is a stage of economic history which is not limited to a few advanced countries only. Capitalism has the tendency to convert all parts of the world into capitalist countries. The bourgeoisie forces all nations to become capitalist nations. When the final hour of capitalism sounds, the whole world will be uniformly in the stage of mature capitalism, ripe for the transition to socialism. Socialism will emerge at the same time in all parts of the world.

Marx erred on this point no less than in all his other statements. Today even the Marxians cannot and do not deny that there still prevail enormous differences in the development of capitalism in various countries. They realize that there are many countries which, from the point of view of the Marxian interpretation of history, must be described as precapitalistic. In these countries the bourgeoisie has not yet attained a ruling position and has not yet set the historical stage of capitalism which is the necessary prerequisite of the appearance of socialism. These countries therefore must first accomplish their "bourgeois revolution" and must go through all phases of capitalism before there can be any question of transforming them into socialist countries. The only policy which Marxians could adopt in such countries would be to support the bourgeois unconditionally, first in their endeavours to seize power and then in their capitalistic ventures. A Marxian party could for a very long time have no other task than to be subservient to bourgeois liberalism. This alone is the mission which historical materialism, if consistently applied, could assign to Russian Marxians. They would be forced to wait quietly until capitalism should have made their nation ripe for socialism.

But the Russian Marxians did not want to wait. They resorted to a new modification of Marxism according to which it was possible for a nation to
547 skip one of the stages of historical evolution. They shut their eyes to the fact that this new doctrine was not a modification of Marxism, but rather the denial of the last remnant which was left of it. It was an undisguised return to the pre-Marxian and anti-Marxian socialist teachings according to which men are free to adopt socialism at any time if they consider it as a system more beneficial to the commonweal than capitalism. It utterly exploded all the mysticism inwrought into dialectical materialism and in the alleged Marxian discovery of the inexorable laws of mankind's economic evolution.

Having emancipated themselves from Marxian determinism, the Russian Marxians were free to discuss the most appropriate tactics for the realization of socialism in their country. They were no longer bothered with economic problems. They had no longer to investigate whether or not the time had come. They had only one task to accomplish, the seizure of the reins of government.

One group maintained that lasting success could be expected only if the support of a sufficient number of the people, though not necessarily of the majority, could be won. Another group did not favour such a time-consuming procedure. They suggested a bold stroke. A small group of fanatics should be organized as the vanguard of the revolution. Strict discipline and unconditional obedience to the chief should make these professional revolutionists fit for a sudden attack. They should supplant the Czarist government and then rule the country according to the traditional methods of the Czar's police.

The terms used to signify these two groups—Bolshevists (majority) for the latter and Mensheviks (minority) for the former—refer to a vote taken in 1903 at a meeting held for the discussion of these tactical issues. The only difference dividing the two groups from one another was this matter of tactical methods. They both agreed with regard to the ultimate end: socialism.

Both sects tried to justify their respective points of view by quoting passages from Marx's and Engels's writings. This is, of course, the Marxian custom. And each sect was in a position to discover in these sacred books dicta confirming its own stand.

Lenin, the Bolshevist chief, knew his countrymen much better than his adversaries and their leader, Plekhanov, did. He did not, like Plekhanov, make the mistake of applying to Russians the standards of the Western nations. He remembered how foreign women had twice simply usurped *548*
supreme power and quietly ruled for a life-time. He was aware of the fact that the terrorist methods of the Czar's secret police were successful and he was confident that he could considerably improve on these methods. He was a ruthless dictator and he knew that the Russians lacked the courage to resist oppression. Like Cromwell, Robespierre and Napoleon, he was an ambitious usurper and fully trusted the absence of revolutionary spirit in the immense majority. The autocracy of the Romanovs was doomed because the unfortunate Nicholas II was a weakling. The socialist lawyer Kerensky failed because he was committed to the principle of parliamentary government. Lenin succeeded because he never aimed at anything else than his own dictatorship. And the Russians yearned for a dictator, for a successor of the Terrible Ivan.

The rule of Nicholas II was not ended by a real revolutionary upheaval. It collapsed on the battlefields. Anarchy resulted which Kerensky could not master. A skirmish in the streets of Saint Petersburg removed Kerensky. A short time later Lenin had his eighteenth Brumaire. In spite of all the terror practised by the Bolshevists the Constituent Assembly, elected by universal franchise for men and women, had only about twenty per cent Bolshevist members. Lenin dispelled by force of arms the Constituent Assembly. The short-lived "liberal" interlude was liquidated. Russia passed from the hands of the inept Romanovs into those of a real autocrat.

Lenin did not content himself with the conquest of Russia. He was fully convinced that he was destined to bring the bliss of socialism to all nations, not only to Russia. The official name which he chose for his government—Union of the Soviet Socialist Republics—does not contain any reference to Russia. It was designed as the nucleus of a world government. It was implied that all foreign comrades by rights owed allegiance to this government and that all foreign bourgeois who dared to resist were guilty of high treason and deserved capital punishment. Lenin did not doubt in the least that all Western countries were on the eve of the great final revolution. He daily expected its outbreak.

There was in the opinion of Lenin only one group in Europe that might—although without any prospect of success—try to prevent the revolutionary upheaval: the depraved members of the intelligentsia who had usurped the leadership of the socialist parties. Lenin had long hated these men for their
549 addiction to parliamentary procedure and their reluctance to endorse his dictatorial aspirations. He raged against them because he held them responsible for the fact that the socialist parties had supported the war effort of their countries. Already in his Swiss exile, which ended in 1917, Lenin began to split the European socialist parties. Now he set up a new, a Third International which he controlled in the same dictatorial manner in which he directed the Russian Bolshevists. For this new party Lenin chose the name Communist Party. The communists were to fight unto death the various European socialist parties, these "social traitors," and they were to arrange the immediate liquidation of the bourgeoisie and seizure of power by the armed workers. Lenin did not differentiate between socialism and communism as social systems. The goal which he aimed at was not called communism as opposed to socialism. The official name of the Soviet government is Union of the *Socialist* (not of the *Communist*) Soviet Republics. In this regard he did not want to alter the traditional terminology which considered the terms as synonymous. He merely called his partisans, the only sincere and consistent supporters of the revolutionary principles of orthodox Marxism, *communists* and their tactical methods *communism* because he wanted to distinguish them from the "treacherous hirelings of the capitalist exploiters," the wicked Social Democratic leaders like Kautsky and Albert Thomas. These traitors, he

emphasized, were anxious to preserve capitalism. They were not true socialists. The only genuine Marxians were those who rejected the name of socialists, irremediably fallen into disrepute.

Thus the distinction between communists and socialists came into being. Those Marxians who did not surrender to the dictator in Moscow called themselves social democrats or, in short, socialists. What characterized them was the belief that the most appropriate method for the realization of their plans to establish socialism, the final goal common to them as well as to the communists, was to win the support of the majority of their fellow-citizens. They abandoned the revolutionary slogans and tried to adopt democratic methods for the seizure of power. They did not bother about the problem whether or not a socialist regime is compatible with democracy. But for the attainment of socialism they were resolved to apply democratic procedures.

The communists, on the other hand, were in the early years of the Third 550
International firmly committed to the principle of revolution and civil war. They were loyal only to their Russian chief. They expelled from their ranks everybody who was suspected of feeling himself bound by any of his country's laws. They plotted unceasingly and squandered blood in unsuccessful riots.

Lenin could not understand why the communists failed everywhere outside Russia. He did not expect much from the American workers. In the United States, the communists agreed, the workers lacked the revolutionary spirit because they were spoiled by well-being and steeped in the vice of money-making. But Lenin did not doubt that the European masses were class-conscious and therefore fully committed to revolutionary ideas. The only reason why the revolution had not been realized was in his opinion the inadequacy and cowardice of the communist officials. Again and again he deposed his vicars and appointed new men. But he did not succeed any better.

In the Anglo-Saxon and in the Latin-American countries the socialist voters place confidence in democratic methods. Here the number of people who seriously aim at a communist revolution is very small. Most of those who publicly proclaim their adherence to the principles of communism would feel extremely unhappy if the revolution were to arise and expose their lives and their property to danger. If the Russian armies were to march into their countries or if domestic communists were to seize power without engaging them in the fight, they would probably rejoice in the hope of being rewarded for their Marxian orthodoxy. But they themselves do not long for revolutionary laurels.

It is a fact that in all these thirty years of passionate pro-Soviet agitation not a single country outside Russia went communist of its citizens' own accord. Eastern Europe turned to communism only when the diplomatic arrangements of international power politics had converted it into a sphere of exclusive Russian influence and hegemony. It is unlikely that Western Germany, France, Italy and Spain will espouse communism if the United States and Great Britain do not adopt a policy of absolute diplomatic "*désintéressement*." What gives strength to the communist movement in these and in some other countries is the belief that Russia is driven by an unflinching "dynamism" while the Anglo-Saxon powers are indifferent and not very much interested in their fate.

551 Marx and the Marxians erred lamentably when they assumed that the masses long for a revolutionary overthrow of the "bourgeois" order of society. The militant communists are to be found only in the ranks of those who make a living from their communism or expect that a revolution would further their personal ambitions. The subversive activities of these professional plotters are dangerous precisely on account of the naivety of those who are merely flirting with the revolutionary idea. Those confused and misguided sympathizers who call themselves "liberals" and whom the communists call "useful innocents," the fellow-travellers and even the majority of the officially registered party members, would be terribly frightened if they were to discover one day that their chiefs mean business when preaching sedition. But then it may be too late to avert disaster.

For the time being, the ominous peril of the communist parties in the West lies in their stand on foreign affairs. The distinctive mark of all present-day communist parties is their devotion to the aggressive foreign policy of the Soviets. Whenever they must choose between Russia and their own country, they do not hesitate to prefer Russia. Their principle is: Right or wrong, my Russia. They strictly obey all orders issued from Moscow. When Russia was an ally of Hitler, the French communists sabotaged their own country's war effort and the American communists passionately opposed President Roosevelt's plans to aid England and France in their struggle against the Nazis. The communists all over the world branded all those who defended themselves against the German invaders as "imperialist warmongers." But as soon as Hitler attacked Russia, the imperialist war of the capitalists changed over-night into a just war of defence. Whenever Stalin conquers one more country, the communists justify this aggression as an act of self-defence against "Fascists."

In their blind worship of everything that is Russian, the communists of Western Europe and the United States by far surpass the worst excesses ever committed by chauvinists. They wax rapturous about Russian movies, Rus-

sian music and the alleged discoveries of Russian science. They speak in ecstatic words about the economic achievements of the Soviets. They ascribe the victory of the United Nations to the deeds of the Russian armed forces. Russia, they contend, has saved the world from the Fascist menace. Russia is the only free country while all other nations are subject to the dictatorship 552
of the capitalists. The Russians alone are happy and enjoy the bliss of living a full life; in the capitalist countries the immense majority are suffering from frustration and unfulfilled desires. Just as the pious Muslim yearns for a pilgrimage to the Prophet's tomb at Mecca, so the communist intellectual deems a pilgrimage to the holy shrines of Moscow as the event of his life.

However, the distinction in the use of the terms communists and socialists did not affect the meaning of the terms communism and socialism as applied to the final goal of the policies common to them both. It was only in 1928 that the programme of the Communist International, adopted by the sixth congress in Moscow,[15] began to differentiate between communism and socialism (and not merely between communists and socialists).

According to this new doctrine there is, in the economic evolution of mankind, between the historical stage of capitalism and that of communism, a third stage, namely that of socialism. Socialism is a social system based on public control of the means of production and full management of all processes of production and distribution by a planning central authority. In this regard it is equal to communism. But it differs from communism in so far as there is no equality of the portions allotted to each individual for his own consumption. There are still wages paid to the comrades and these wage rates are graduated according to economic expediency as far as the central authority deems it necessary for securing the greatest possible output of products. What Stalin calls socialism corresponds by and large to Marx's concept of the "early phase" of communism. Stalin reserves the term communism exclusively for what Marx called the "higher phase" of communism. Socialism, in the sense in which Stalin has lately used the term, is moving towards communism, but is in itself not yet communism. Socialism will turn into communism as soon as the increase in wealth to be expected from the operation of the socialist methods of production has raised the lower standard of living of the Russian masses to the higher standard which the distinguished holders of important offices enjoy in present-day Russia.[16]

The apologetical character of this new terminological practice is obvious. 553

[15] *Blueprint for World Conquest as Outlined by the Communist International,* Human Events (Washington and Chicago, 1946), pp. 181–82.
[16] David J. Dallin, *The Real Soviet Russia* (Yale University Press, 1944), pp. 88–95.

Stalin finds it necessary to explain to the vast majority of his subjects why their standard of living is extremely low, much lower than that of the masses in the capitalist countries and even lower than that of the Russian proletarians in the days of Czarist rule. He wants to justify the fact that salaries and wages are unequal, that a small group of Soviet officials enjoys all the luxuries modern technique can provide, that a second group, more numerous than the first one, but less numerous than the middle class in imperial Russia, lives in "bourgeois" style, while the masses, ragged and barefooted, subsist in congested slums and are poorly fed. He can no longer blame capitalism for this state of affairs. Thus he was compelled to resort to a new ideological makeshift.

Stalin's problem was the more burning as the Russian communists in the early days of their rule had passionately proclaimed income equality as a principle to be enforced from the first instant of the proletarians' seizure of power. Moreover, in the capitalist countries the most powerful demagogic trick applied by the Russia-sponsored communist parties is to excite the envy of those with lower incomes against all those with higher incomes. The main argument advanced by the communists for the support of their thesis that Hitler's National Socialism was not genuine socialism, but, on the contrary, the worst variety of capitalism, was that there was in Nazi Germany inequality in the standard of living.

Stalin's new distinction between socialism and communism is in open contradiction to the policy of Lenin, and no less to the tenets of the propaganda of the communist parties outside the Russian frontiers. But such contradictions do not matter in the realm of the Soviets. The word of the dictator is the ultimate decision, and nobody is so foolhardy as to venture opposition.

It is important to realize that Stalin's semantical innovation affects merely the terms communism and socialism. He did not alter the meaning of the terms socialist and communist. The Bolshevist party is just as before called communist. The Russophile parties beyond the borders of the Soviet Union call themselves communist parties and are violently fighting the socialist parties which, in their eyes, are simply social traitors. But the official name of the Union of Soviet *Socialist* Republics remains unchanged.

554

4

Russia's Aggressiveness

The German, Italian and Japanese nationalists justified their aggressive policies by their lack of *Lebensraum*. Their countries are comparatively overpopulated. They are poorly endowed by nature and depend on the import of foodstuffs and raw materials from abroad. They must export manufactures to pay for these badly needed imports. But the protectionist policies espoused by the countries producing a surplus of foodstuffs and raw materials close their frontiers to import of manufactures. The world is manifestly tending towards a state of full economic autarky of each nation. In such a world, what fate is in store for those nations who can neither feed nor clothe their citizens out of domestic resources?

The *Lebensraum* doctrine of the self-styled "have-not" peoples emphasizes that there are in America and in Australia millions of acres of unused land much more fertile than the barren soil which the farmers of the have-not nations are tilling. Natural conditions for mining and manufacturing are likewise much more propitious than in the countries of the have-nots. But the German, Italian and Japanese peasants and workers are barred from access to these areas favoured by nature. The immigration laws of the comparatively underpopulated countries prevent their migration. These laws raise the marginal productivity of labour and thereby wage rates in the underpopulated countries and lower them in the overpopulated countries. The high standard of living in the United States and the British Dominions is paid for by a lowering of the standard of living in the congested countries of Europe and Asia.

The true aggressors, say these German, Italian and Japanese nationalists, are those nations who by means of trade and migration barriers have arrogated to themselves the lion's share of the natural riches of the earth. Has not the Pope* himself declared that the root causes of the World Wars are "that cold and calculating egoism which tends to hoard the economic resources and materials destined for the use of all to such an extent that the nations less favoured by nature are not permitted access to them"?[17] The war that Hitler, Mussolini and Hirohito kindled was from this point of view a
just war, for its only aim was to give to the have-nots what, by virtue of 555
natural and divine right, belongs to them.

The Russians cannot venture to justify their aggressive policy by such arguments. Russia is a comparatively underpopulated country. Its soil is much better endowed by nature than that of any other nation. It offers the most advantageous conditions for the growing of all kinds of cereals, fruits, seeds and plants. Russia owns immense pastures and almost inexhaustible forests. It has the richest resources for the production of gold, silver, platinum, iron, copper, nickel, manganese and all other metals, and of oil. But for the

---

[17] Christmas Eve broadcast, *New York Times*, December 25, 1941.

* Pius XII (pope, 1939–1958) (Pub.).

despotism of the Czars and the lamentable inadequacy of the communist system, its population could long since have enjoyed the highest standard of living. It is certainly not lack of natural resources that pushes Russia towards conquest.

Lenin's aggressiveness was an outgrowth of his conviction that he was the leader of the final world revolution. He considered himself as the legitimate successor of the First International, destined to accomplish the task in which Marx and Engels had failed. The knell of capitalism had sounded, and no capitalist machinations could delay the expropriation of the expropriators any longer. What was needed was only the dictator of the new social order. Lenin was ready to take the burden upon his shoulders.

Since the days of the Mongol invasions mankind has not had to face such an unflinching and thorough-going aspiration for unlimited world supremacy. In every country the Russian emissaries and the communist fifth columns were fanatically working for the "Anschluss" to Russia. But Lenin lacked the first four columns. Russia's military forces were at that time contemptible. When they crossed the Russian borders, they were stopped by the Poles. They could not march further West. The great campaign for world conquest petered out.

It was just idle talk to discuss the problems whether communism in one country only is possible or desirable. The communists had failed utterly outside the Russian frontiers. They were forced to stay at home.

Stalin devoted all his energy to the organization of a standing army of a size the world had never seen before. But he was not more successful than Lenin and Trotsky had been. The Nazis easily defeated this army and occupied the most important part of Russia's territory. Russia was saved by
556 the British and, above all, by the American forces. American Lend-Lease enabled the Russians to follow on the heels of the Germans when the scarcity of equipment and the threatening American invasion forced them to withdraw from Russia. They could even occasionally defeat the rearguards of the retreating Nazis. They could conquer Berlin and Vienna when the American airplanes had smashed the German defences. When the Americans had crushed the Japanese, the Russians could quietly stab them in the back.

Of course, the communists inside and outside of Russia and the fellow-travellers passionately contend that it was Russia that defeated the Nazis and liberated Europe. They pass over in silence the fact that the only reason why the Nazis could not capture Moscow, Leningrad and Stalingrad was their lack of munitions, airplanes and gasoline. It was the blockade that made it impossible for the Nazis to provide their armies with the equipment needed, and to construct in the occupied Russian territory a transport system that could ship this equipment to the far distant front line. The decisive battle of the war was the battle of the Atlantic. The great strategical events in the war against Germany were the conquest of Africa and Sicily and the victory in Normandy. Stalingrad was, when measured by the gigantic standards of this war, hardly more than a tactical success. In the struggle against the Italians and the Japanese, Russia's share was nil.

But the spoils of the victory go to Russia alone. While the other United Nations do not seek for territorial aggrandizement, the Russians are in full swing. They have annexed the three Baltic Republics, Bessarabia, Czechoslovakia's province of Carpatho-Russia,[18] a part of Finland, a great part of Poland and huge territories in the Far East. They claim the rest of Poland, Rumania, Hungary, Yugoslavia, Bulgaria, Korea and China as their exclusive sphere of influence. They are anxious to establish in these countries "friendly" governments, i.e. puppet governments. But for the opposition raised by the United States and Great Britain they would rule today in the whole of continental Europe, continental Asia and Northern Africa. Only the American and British garrisons in Germany bar the Russians' way to the shores of the Atlantic.

Today, no less than after the first World War, the real menace for the West 557
does not lie in the military power of Russia. Great Britain could easily repel a Russian attack and it would be sheer lunacy for the Russians to undertake a war against the United States. Not the Russian armies, but the communist ideologies threaten the West. The Russians know it very well and place confidence not in their own army, but in their foreign partisans. They want to overthrow the democracies from within, not from without. Their main weapon is the pro-Russian machinations of their Fifth Columns. These are the crack divisions of Bolshevism.

The communist writers and politicians inside and outside of Russia explain Russia's aggressive policies as mere self-defence. It is, they say, not Russia that plans aggression but, on the contrary, the decaying capitalist democracies. Russia wants merely to defend its own independence. This is an old and well-tried method of justifying aggression. Louis XIV and Napoleon I, Wilhelm II and Hitler were the most peace-loving of all men. When they invaded foreign countries, they did so only in just self-defence. Russia was as much menaced by Esthonia or Latvia as Germany was by Luxemburg or Denmark.

An outgrowth of this fable of self-defence is the legend of the *cordon*

---

[18] The annexation of Carpatho-Russia utterly explodes their hypocritical indignation about the Munich agreements of 1938.

sanitaire. The political independence of the small neighbour countries of Russia, it is maintained, is merely a capitalist makeshift designed to prevent the European democracies from being infected with the germ of communism. Hence, it is concluded, these small nations have forfeited their right to independence. For Russia has the inalienable right to claim that its neighbours—and likewise its neighbours' neighbours—should only be ruled by "friendly," i.e., strictly communist, governments. What would happen to the world if all great powers were to make the same pretension?

The truth is that it is not the governments of the democratic nations that aim at overthrowing the present Russian system. They do not foster pro-democratic fifth columns in Russia and they do not incite the Russian masses against their rulers. But the Russians are busy day and night fomenting unrest in every country.

The very lame and hesitant intervention of the Allied Nations in the Russian Civil War was not a pro-capitalist and anti-communist venture. For the Allied Nations, involved in their struggle for life and death with the Germans, Lenin was at that time merely a tool of their deadly foes. Ludendorff
558 had dispatched Lenin to Russia in order to overthrow the Kerensky regime and to bring about the defection of Russia. The Bolshevists fought by force of arms all those Russians who wanted to continue the alliance with France, Great Britain and the United States. From a military point of view it was impossible for the Western nations to stay neutral while their Russian allies were desperately defending themselves against the Bolshevists. For the Allied Nations the Eastern Front was at stake. The cause of the "White" generals was their own cause.

As soon as the war against Germany came to an end in 1918, the Allies lost interest in Russian affairs. There was no longer any need for an Eastern Front. They did not care a whit about the internal problems of Russia. They longed for peace and were anxious to withdraw from the fighting. They were, of course, embarrassed because they did not know how to liquidate their venture with propriety. Their generals were ashamed of abandoning companions in arms who had fought to the best of their abilities in a common cause. To leave these men in the lurch was in their opinion nothing short of cowardice and desertion. Such considerations of military honour delayed for some time the withdrawal of the inconspicuous Allied detachments and the termination of deliveries to the Whites. When this was finally accomplished, the Allied statesmen felt relief. From then on they adopted a policy of strict neutrality with regard to Russian affairs.

It was very unfortunate indeed that the Allied Nations had been willynilly entangled in the Russian Civil War. It would have been better if the military

situation of 1917 and 1918 had not compelled them to interfere. But one must not overlook the fact that the abandonment of intervention in Russia was tantamount to the final failure of President Wilson's policy. The United States had entered the war in order to make "the world safe for democracy." The victory had crushed the Kaiser and substituted in Germany a republican government for the comparatively mild and limited imperial autocracy. On the other hand, it had resulted in Russia in establishing a dictatorship compared with which the despotism of the Czars could be called liberal. But the Allies were not eager to make Russia safe for democracy as they had tried to do with Germany. After all, the Kaiser's Germany had parliaments, ministers responsible to the parliaments, trial by jury, freedom of thought, of religion and of the press not much more limited than in the West, and many other democratic institutions. But Soviet Russia was an unlimited 559
despotism.

The Americans, the French and the British failed to see things from this angle. But the anti-democratic forces in Germany, Italy, Poland, Hungary and the Balkans thought differently. As the nationalists of these countries interpreted it, the neutrality of the Allied Powers with regard to Russia was evidence of the fact that their concern for democracy had been a mere blind. The Allies, they argued, had fought Germany because they envied Germany's economic prosperity and they spared the new Russian autocracy because they were not afraid of Russian economic power. Democracy, these nationalists concluded, was nothing else than a convenient catchword to delude gullible people. And they became frightened that the emotional appeal of this slogan would one day be used as a disguise for insidious assaults against their own independence.

Since the abandonment of the intervention Russia had certainly no longer any reason to fear the great Western powers. Neither were the Soviets afraid of a Nazi aggression. The assertions to the contrary, very popular in Western Europe and in America, resulted from complete ignorance of German affairs. But the Russians knew Germany and the Nazis. They had read *Mein Kampf*. They learned from this book not only that Hitler coveted the Ukraine, but also that Hitler's fundamental strategical idea was to embark upon the conquest of Russia only after having definitely and forever annihilated France. The Russians were fully convinced that Hitler's expectation, as expressed in *Mein Kampf*, that Great Britain and the United States would keep out of this war and would quietly let France be destroyed, was vain. They were certain that such a new world war, in which they themselves planned to stay neutral, would result in a new German defeat. And this defeat, they argued, would make Germany—if not the whole of Europe—

safe for Bolshevism. Guided by this opinion, Stalin already in the time of the Weimar Republic aided the then secret German rearmament. The German communists helped the Nazis as much as they could in their endeavours to undermine the Weimar regime. Finally Stalin entered in August 1939 into an open alliance with Hitler, in order to give him a free hand against the West.

What Stalin—like all other people—did not anticipate was the overwhelm-
560 ing success of the German armies in 1940. Hitler attacked Russia in 1941 because he was fully convinced that not only France but also Great Britain was done for, and that the United States, menaced in the rear by Japan, would not be strong enough to interfere successfully with European affairs.

The disintegration of the Hapsburg Empire in 1918 and the Nazi defeat in 1945 have opened the gates of Europe to Russia. Russia is today the only military power on the European continent. But why are the Russians so intent upon conquering and annexing? They certainly do not need the resources of these countries. Neither is Stalin driven by the idea that such conquests could increase his popularity with the Russian masses. His subjects are indifferent to military glory.

It is not the masses whom Stalin wants to placate by his aggressive policy, but the intellectuals. For their Marxian orthodoxy is at stake, the very foundation of the Soviet might.

These Russian intellectuals were narrow-minded enough to absorb modifications of the Marxian creed which were in fact an abandonment of the essential teachings of dialectical materialism, provided that these modifications flattered their Russian chauvinism. They swallowed the doctrine that their holy Russia could skip one of the inextricable stages of economic evolution as described by Marx. They prided themselves on being the vanguard of the proletariat and the world revolution who, by realizing socialism first in one country only, set up a glorious example for all other nations. But it is impossible to explain to them why the other nations do not finally catch up with Russia. In the writings of Marx and Engels, which one cannot keep out of their hands, they discover that the fathers of Marxism considered Great Britain and France and even Germany as the countries most advanced in civilization and in the evolution of capitalism. These students of the Marxian universities may be too dull to comprehend the philosophical and economic doctrines of the Marxian gospel. But they are not too dull to see that Marx considered those Western countries as much more advanced than Russia.

Then some of these students of economic policies and statistics begin to suspect that the standard of living of the masses is much higher in the capitalist countries than in their own country. How can this be? Why are conditions much more propitious in the United States which—although foremost in capitalist production—is most backward in awakening class-consciousness in the proletarians?

The inference from these facts seems inescapable. If the most advanced 561
countries do not adopt communism and fare rather well under capitalism, if communism is limited to a country which Marx considered as backward and does not bring about riches for all, is not perhaps the correct interpretation that communism is a feature of backward countries and results in general poverty? Must not a Russian patriot be ashamed of the fact that his country is committed to this system?

Such thoughts are very dangerous in a despotic country. Whoever dared to express them would be mercilessly liquidated by the G.P.U. But, even unspoken, they are on the tip of every intelligent man's tongue. They trouble the sleep of the supreme officials and perhaps even that of the great dictator. He certainly has the power to crush every opponent. But considerations of expediency make it inadvisable to eradicate all somewhat judicious people and to run the country only with stupid blockheads.

This is the real crisis of Russian Marxism. Every day that passes without bringing the world revolution aggravates it. The Soviets must conquer the world or else they are menaced in their own country by a defection of the intelligentsia. It is concern about the ideological state of Russia's shrewdest minds that pushes Stalin's Russia towards unflinching aggression.

5

Trotsky's Heresy

The dictatorial doctrine as taught by the Russian Bolshevists, the Italian Fascists and the German Nazis tacitly implies that there cannot arise any disagreement with regard to the question who shall be the dictator. The mystical forces directing the course of historical events designate the providential leader. All righteous people are bound to submit to the unfathomable decrees of history and to bend their knees before the throne of the man of destiny. Those who decline to do so are heretics, abject scoundrels who must be "liquidated."

In reality the dictatorial power is seized by that candidate who succeeds
in exterminating in time all his rivals and their helpers. The dictator paves 562

his way to supreme power by slaughtering all his competitors. He preserves his eminent position by butchering all those who could possibly dispute it. The history of all oriental despotisms bears witness to this, as well as the experience of contemporary dictatorship.

When Lenin died in 1924, Stalin supplanted his most dangerous rival, Trotsky. Trotsky escaped, spent years abroad in various countries of Europe, Asia and America and was finally assassinated in Mexico City. Stalin remained the absolute ruler of Russia.

Trotsky was an intellectual of the orthodox Marxian type. As such he tried to represent his personal feud with Stalin as a conflict of principles. He tried to construct a Trotsky doctrine as distinguished from the Stalin doctrine. He branded Stalin's policies as an apostasy from the sacred legacy of Marx and Lenin. Stalin retorted in the same way. In fact, however, the conflict was a rivalry of two men, not a conflict of antagonistic ideas and principles. There was some minor dissent with regard to tactical methods. But in all essential matters Stalin and Trotsky were in agreement.

Trotsky had lived, before 1917, many years in foreign countries and was to some degree familiar with the main languages of the Western peoples. He posed as an expert in international affairs. Actually he did not know anything about Western civilization, political ideas and economic conditions. As a wandering exile he had moved almost exclusively in the circles of his fellow-exiles. The only foreigners whom he had met occasionally in coffee-houses and club-rooms of Western and Central Europe were radical doctrinaires, by their Marxian prepossessions precluded from reality. His main reading was Marxian books and periodicals. He scorned all other writings as "bourgeois" literature. He was absolutely unfitted to see events from any other angle than that of Marxism. Like Marx he was ready to interpret every great strike and every small riot as the sign of the outbreak of the final great revolution.

Stalin is a poorly educated Georgian. He has not the slightest knowledge of any Western language. He does not know Europe or America. Even his achievements as a Marxian author are questionable. But it was precisely the fact that, although an adamant supporter of communism, he was not indoctrinated with Marxian dogmas that made him superior to Trotsky. Stalin was not deluded by the spurious tenets of dialectical materialism. When
563 faced with a problem, he did not search for an interpretation in the writings of Marx and Engels. He trusted his common sense. He was judicious enough to discern the fact that the policy of world revolution as inaugurated by Lenin and Trotsky in 1917 had failed completely outside the borders of Russia.

In Germany the communists, led by Karl Liebknecht and Rosa Luxemburg, were crushed by detachments of the regular army and by nationalist volunteers in a bloody battle fought in January 1919 in the streets of Berlin. The communist seizure of power in Munich in spring 1919 and the Hölz riot* in March 1921 ended likewise in disaster. In Hungary, in 1919, the communists were defeated by Horthy and Gömbös and the Rumanian army. In Austria various communist plots failed in 1918 and 1919; a violent upheaval in July 1927 was easily quelled by the Vienna police. In Italy, in 1920, the occupation of the factories was a complete miscarriage. In France and in Switzerland the communist propaganda seemed to be very powerful in the first years following the Armistice of 1918; but it evaporated very soon. In Great Britain, in 1926, the general strike called by the labour unions resulted in lamentable failure.

Trotsky was so blinded by his orthodoxy that he refused to admit that the Bolshevist methods had failed. But Stalin realized it very well. He did not abandon the idea of instigating revolutionary outbreaks in all foreign countries and of conquering the whole world for the Soviets. But he was fully aware of the fact that it was necessary to postpone the aggression for a few years and to resort to new methods for its execution. Trotsky was wrong in accusing Stalin of strangling the communist movement outside of Russia. What Stalin really did was to apply other means for the attainment of ends which are common to him and all other Marxians.

As an exegetic of Marxian dogmas Stalin was certainly inferior to Trotsky. But he surpassed his rival by far as a politician. Bolshevism owes its successes in world policies to Stalin, not to Trotsky.

In the field of domestic policies, Trotsky resorted to the well-tried traditional tricks which Marxians had always applied in criticizing socialist measures adopted by other parties. Whatever Stalin did was not true socialism and communism, but, on the contrary, the very opposite of it, a monstrous perversion of the lofty principles of Marx and Lenin. All the disastrous features of public control of production and distribution as they appeared
in Russia were, in Trotsky's interpretation, brought about by Stalin's policies. 564
They were not unavoidable consequences of communist methods. They were attendant phenomena of Stalinism, not of communism. It was exclusively Stalin's fault that an absolutist irresponsible bureaucracy was supreme, that a class of privileged oligarchs enjoyed luxuries while the masses lived on the verge of starvation, that a terrorist regime executed the old guard of revolutionaries and condemned millions to slave labour in concentration camps,

* The Hölz riot was a communist uprising in Germany (March 1921 in Mansfeldischen), led by World War I veteran Max Hölz (1889–1933). Hölz was sentenced to life imprisonment as a result, granted amnesty in 1928, and then left Germany for the Soviet Union (Pub.).

that the secret police was omnipotent, that the labour unions were powerless, that the masses were deprived of all rights and liberties. Stalin was not a champion of the egalitarian classless society. He was the pioneer of a return to the worst methods of class rule and exploitation. A new ruling class of about 10 per cent of the population ruthlessly oppressed and exploited the immense majority of toiling proletarians.

Trotsky was at a loss to explain how all this could be achieved by only one man and his few sycophants. Where were the "material productive forces," much talked about in Marxian historical materialism, which—"independent of the wills of individuals"—determine the course of human events "with the inexorability of a law of nature"? How could it happen that one man was in a position to alter the "juridical and political superstructure" which is uniquely and inalterably fixed by the economic structure of society? Even Trotsky agreed that there was no longer any private ownership of the means of production in Russia. In Stalin's empire, production and distribution are entirely controlled by "society." It is a fundamental dogma of Marxism that the superstructure of such a system must necessarily be the bliss of the earthly paradise. There is in Marxian doctrines no room for an interpretation blaming individuals for a degenerative process which could convert the blessing of public control of business into evil. A consistent Marxian—if consistency were compatible with Marxism—would have to admit that Stalin's political system was the necessary superstructure of communism.

All essential items in Trotsky's programme were in perfect agreement with the policies of Stalin. Trotsky advocated the industrialization of Russia. It was this that Stalin's Five-Year Plans aimed at. Trotsky advocated the collectivization of agriculture. Stalin established the Kolkhoz and liquidated the Kulaks. Trotsky favoured the organization of a big army. Stalin organized
565 such an army. Neither was Trotsky when still in power a friend of democracy. He was, on the contrary, a fanatical supporter of dictatorial oppression of all "saboteurs." It is true, he did not anticipate that the dictator could consider him, Trotsky, author of Marxian tracts and veteran of the glorious extermination of the Romanovs, as the most wicked saboteur. Like all other advocates of dictatorship, he assumed that he himself or one of his intimate friends would be the dictator.

Trotsky was a critic of bureaucratism. But he did not suggest any other method for the conduct of affairs in a socialist system. There is no other alternative to profit-seeking private business than bureaucratic management.[19]

---

[19] Mises, *Bureaucracy* (Yale University Press, 1944).

The truth is that Trotsky found only one fault with Stalin: that he, Stalin, was the dictator and not himself, Trotsky. In their feud they both were right. Stalin was right in maintaining that his regime was the embodiment of socialist principles. Trotsky was right in asserting that Stalin's regime had made Russia a hell.

Trotskyism did not entirely disappear with Trotsky's death. Boulangerism in France, too, survived for some time the end of General Boulanger. There are still Carlists left in Spain although the line of Don Carlos died out. Such posthumous movements are, of course, doomed.

But in all countries there are people who, although themselves fanatically committed to the idea of all-round planning, i.e. public ownership of the means of production, become frightened when they are confronted with the real face of communism. These people are disappointed. They dream of a Garden of Eden. For them communism, or socialism, means an easy life in riches and the full enjoyment of all liberties and pleasures. They fail to realize the contradictions inherent in their image of the communist society. They have uncritically swallowed all the lunatic fantasies of Charles Fourier and all the absurdities of Veblen. They firmly believe in Engels's assertion that socialism will be a realm of unlimited freedom. They indict capitalism for everything they dislike, and are fully convinced that socialism will deliver them from all evil. They ascribe their own failures and frustrations to the unfairness of this "mad" competitive system and expect that socialism will assign them that eminent position and high income which by right are due to them. They are Cinderellas yearning for the prince-saviour who will
recognize their merits and virtues. The loathing of capitalism and the worship 566
of communism are consolations for them. They help them to disguise to themselves their own inferiority, and to blame the "system" for their own shortcomings.

In advocating dictatorship such people always advocate the dictatorship of their own clique. In asking for planning, what they have in mind is always their own plan, not that of others. They will never admit that a socialist or communist regime is true and genuine socialism or communism, if it does not assign to themselves the most eminent position and the highest income. For them the essential feature of true and genuine communism is that all affairs are precisely conducted according to their own will, and that all those who disagree are beaten into submission.

It is a fact that the majority of our contemporaries are imbued with socialist and communist ideas. However, this does not mean that they are unanimous in their proposals for socialization of the means of production and public control of production and distribution. On the contrary. Each socialist coterie is fanatically opposed to the plans of all other socialist groups. The various socialist sects fight one another most bitterly.

If the case of Trotsky and the analogous case of Gregor Strasser in Nazi Germany were isolated cases, there would be no need to deal with them. But they are not casual incidents. They are typical. Study of them reveals the psychological causes both of the popularity of socialism and of its unfeasibility.

6

The Liberation of the Demons

The history of mankind is the history of ideas. For it is ideas, theories and doctrines that guide human action, determine the ultimate ends men aim at, and the choice of the means employed for the attainment of these ends. The sensational events which stir the emotions and catch the interest of superficial observers are merely the consummation of ideological changes. There are no such things as abrupt sweeping transformations of human affairs. What is called, in rather misleading terms, a "turning point in history" is the coming
567 on the scene of forces which were already for a long time at work behind the scene. New ideologies, which had already long since superseded the old ones, throw off their last veil and even the dullest people become aware of the changes which they did not notice before.

In this sense Lenin's seizure of power in October 1917 was certainly a turning point. But its meaning was very different from that which the communists attribute to it.

The Soviet victory played only a minor role in the evolution towards socialism. The pro-socialist policies of the industrial countries of Central and Western Europe were of much greater consequence in this regard. Bismarck's social security scheme was a more momentous pioneering on the way towards socialism than was the expropriation of the backward Russian manufactures. The Prussian National Railways had provided the only instance of a government-operated business which, for some time at least, had avoided manifest financial failure. The British had already before 1914 adopted essential parts of the German social security system. In all industrial countries, the governments were committed to interventionist policies which were bound to result ultimately in socialism. During the war most of them embarked upon what was called war socialism. The German Hindenburg Programme which, of course, could not be executed completely on account of Germany's defeat, was no less radical but much better designed than the much talked-about Russian Five-Year Plans.

For the socialists in the predominantly industrial countries of the West, the Russian methods could not be of any use. For these countries, production of manufactures for export was indispensable. They could not adopt the Russian system of economic autarky. Russia had never exported manufactures in quantities worth mentioning. Under the Soviet system it withdrew almost entirely from the world market of cereals and raw materials. Even fanatical socialists could not help admitting that the West could not learn anything from Russia. It is obvious that the technological achievements in which the Bolshevist gloried were merely clumsy imitations of things accomplished in the West. Lenin defined communism as: "the Soviet power plus electrification." Now, electrification was certainly not of Russian origin, and the Western nations surpass Russia in the field of electrification no less than in every other branch of industry.

The real significance of the Lenin revolution is to be seen in the fact that 568
it was the bursting forth of the principle of unrestricted violence and oppression. It was the negation of all the political ideals that had for three thousand years guided the evolution of Western civilization.

State and government are the social apparatus of violent coercion and repression. Such an apparatus, the police power, is indispensable in order to prevent anti-social individuals and bands from destroying social co-operation. Violent prevention and suppression of anti-social activities benefit the whole of society and each of its members. But violence and oppression are none the less evils and corrupt those in charge of their application. It is necessary to restrict the power of those in office lest they become absolute despots. Society cannot exist without an apparatus of violent coercion. But neither can it exist if the office holders are irresponsible tyrants free to inflict harm upon those they dislike.

It is the social function of the laws to curb the arbitrariness of the police. The rule of law restricts the arbitrariness of the officers as much as possible. It strictly limits their discretion, and thus assigns to the citizens a sphere in which they are free to act without being frustrated by government interference.

Freedom and liberty always mean freedom from police interference. In nature there are no such things as liberty and freedom. There is only the adamant rigidity of the laws of nature to which man must unconditionally submit if he wants to attain any ends at all. Neither was there liberty in the imaginary paradisaical conditions which, according to the fantastic prattle of many writers, preceded the establishment of societal bonds. Where there is no government, everybody is at the mercy of his stronger neighbour. Liberty can be realized only within an established state ready to prevent a gangster from killing and robbing his weaker fellows. But it is the rule of law alone which hinders the rulers from turning themselves into the worst gangsters.

The laws establish norms of legitimate action. They fix the procedures required for the repeal or alteration of existing laws and for the enactment of new laws. They likewise fix the procedures required for the application of the laws in definite cases, the due process of law. They establish courts and tribunals. Thus they are intent upon avoiding a situation in which the individuals are at the mercy of the rulers.

569 Mortal men are liable to error, and legislators and judges are mortal men. It may happen again and again that the valid laws or their interpretation by the courts prevent the executive organs from resorting to some measures which could be beneficial. No great harm, however, can result. If the legislators recognize the deficiency of the valid laws, they can alter them. It is certainly a bad thing that a criminal may sometimes evade punishment because there is a loophole left in the law, or because the prosecutor has neglected some formalities. But it is the minor evil when compared with the consequences of unlimited discretionary power on the part of the "benevolent" despot.

It is precisely this point which anti-social individuals fail to see. Such people condemn the formalism of the due process of law. Why should the laws hinder the government from resorting to beneficial measures? Is it not fetishism to make supreme the laws, and not expediency? They advocate the substitution of the welfare state (*Wohlfahrtsstaat*) for the state governed by the rule of law (*Rechtsstaat*). In this welfare state, paternal government should be free to accomplish all things it considers beneficial to the commonweal. No "scraps of paper" should restrain an enlightened ruler in his endeavours to promote the general welfare. All opponents must be crushed mercilessly lest they frustrate the beneficial action of the government. No empty formalities must protect them any longer against their well-deserved punishment.

It is customary to call the point of view of the advocates of the welfare state the "social" point of view as distinguished from the "individualistic" and "selfish" point of view of the champions of the rule of law. In fact, however, the supporters of the welfare state are utterly anti-social and intolerant zealots. For their ideology tacitly implies that the government will exactly execute what they themselves deem right and beneficial. They entirely disregard the possibility

that there could arise disagreement with regard to the question of what is right
and expedient and what is not. They advocate enlightened despotism, but they
are convinced that the enlightened despot will in every detail comply with their
own opinion concerning the measures to be adopted. They favour planning,
but what they have in mind is exclusively their own plan, not those of other
people. They want to exterminate all opponents, that is, all those who disagree
with them. They are utterly intolerant and are not prepared to allow any dis- 570
cussion. Every advocate of the welfare state and of planning is a potential
dictator. What he plans is to deprive all other men of all their rights, and to
establish his own and his friends' unrestricted omnipotence. He refuses to
convince his fellow-citizens. He prefers to "liquidate" them. He scorns the
"bourgeois" society that worships law and legal procedure. He himself
worships violence and bloodshed.

The irreconcilable conflict of these two doctrines, rule of law versus welfare state, was at issue in all the struggles which men fought for liberty. It was a long and hard evolution. Again and again the champions of absolutism triumphed. But finally the rule of law predominated in the realm of Western civilization. The rule of law, or limited government, as safeguarded by constitutions and bills of rights, is the characteristic mark of this civilization. It was the rule of law that brought about the marvelous achievements of modern capitalism and of its—as consistent Marxians should say—"superstructure," democracy. It secured for a steadily increasing population unprecedented well-being. The masses in the capitalist countries enjoy today a standard of living far above that of the well-to-do of earlier ages.

All these accomplishments have not restrained the advocates of despotism and planning. However, it would have been preposterous for the champions of totalitarianism to disclose the inextricable dictatorial consequences of their endeavours openly. In the nineteenth century the ideas of liberty and the rule of law had won such a prestige that it seemed crazy to attack them frankly. Public opinion was firmly convinced that despotism was done for and could never be restored. Was not even the Czar of barbarian Russia forced to abolish serfdom, to establish trial by jury, to grant a limited freedom to the press and to respect the laws?

Thus the socialists resorted to a trick. They continued to discuss the coming dictatorship of the proletariat, i.e., the dictatorship of each socialist author's own ideas, in their esoteric circles. But to the broad public they spoke in a different way. Socialism, they asserted, will bring true and full liberty and democracy. It will remove all kinds of compulsion and coercion. The state will "wither away." In the socialist commonwealth of the future there will be neither judges and policemen nor prisons and gallows.

571 But the Bolshevists took off the mask. They were fully convinced that the day of their final and unshakable victory had dawned. Further dissimulation was neither possible nor required. The gospel of bloodshed could be preached openly. It found an enthusiastic response among all the degenerate literati and parlour intellectuals who for many years already had raved about the writings of Sorel and Nietzsche. The fruits of the "treason of the intellectuals"[20] mellowed to maturity. The youths who had been fed on the ideas of Carlyle and Ruskin were ready to seize the reins.

Lenin was not the first usurper. Many tyrants had preceded him. But his predecessors were in conflict with the ideas held by their most eminent contemporaries. They were opposed by public opinion because their principles of government were at variance with the accepted principles of right and legality. They were scorned and detested as usurpers. But Lenin's usurpation was seen in a different light. He was the brutal superman for whose coming the pseudo-philosophers had yearned. He was the counterfeit saviour whom history had elected to bring salvation through bloodshed. Was he not the most orthodox adept of Marxian "scientific" socialism? Was he not the man destined to realize the socialist plans for whose execution the weak statesmen of the decaying democracies were too timid? All well-intentioned people asked for socialism; science, through the mouths of the infallible professors, recommended it; the churches preached Christian socialism; the workers longed for the abolition of the wage system. Here was the man to fulfil all these wishes. He was judicious enough to know that you cannot make an omelet without breaking eggs.

Half a century ago all civilized people had censured Bismarck when he declared that history's great problems must be solved by blood and iron. Now the majority of quasi-civilized men bowed to the dictator who was prepared to shed much more blood than Bismarck ever did.

This was the true meaning of the Lenin revolution. All the traditional ideas of right and legality were overthrown. The rule of unrestrained violence and usurpation was substituted for the rule of law. The "narrow horizon of bourgeois legality," as Marx had dubbed it, was abandoned. Henceforth no laws could any longer limit the power of the elect. They were free to kill *ad libitum*. Man's innate impulses towards violent extermination of all whom
572 he dislikes, repressed by a long and wearisome evolution, burst forth. The demons were unfettered. A new age, the age of the usurpers, dawned. The gangsters were called to action, and they listened to the Voice.

---

[20] Benda, *La trahison des clercs* (Paris, 1927). Publisher's Note: In English, *The Treason of the Intellectuals* (New York: William Morrow, 1928) and *The Betrayal of the Intellectuals* (Boston: Beacon Press, 1955).

Of course, Lenin did not mean this. He did not want to concede to other people the prerogatives which he claimed for himself. He did not want to assign to other men the privilege of liquidating their adversaries. Him alone had history elected and entrusted with the dictatorial power. He was the only "legitimate" dictator because—an inner voice had told him so. Lenin was not bright enough to anticipate that other people, imbued with other creeds, could be bold enough to pretend that they also were called by an inner voice. Yet, within a few years two such men, Mussolini and Hitler, became quite conspicuous.

It is important to realize that Fascism and Nazism were socialist dictatorships. The communists, both the registered members of the communist parties and the fellow-travellers, stigmatize Fascism and Nazism as the highest and last and most depraved stage of capitalism. This is in perfect agreement with their habit of calling every party which does not unconditionally surrender to the dictates of Moscow—even the German Social Democrats, the classical party of Marxism—hirelings of capitalism.

It is of much greater consequence that the communists have succeeded in changing the semantic connotation of the term Fascism. Fascism, as will be shown later, was a variety of Italian socialism. It was adjusted to the particular conditions of the masses in overpopulated Italy. It was not a product of Mussolini's mind and will survive the fall of Mussolini. The foreign policies of Fascism and Nazism, from their early beginnings, were rather opposed to one another. The fact that the Nazis and the Fascists closely co-operated after the Ethiopian war, and were allies in the second World War, did not eradicate the differences between these two tenets any more than did the alliance between Russia and the United States eradicate the differences between Sovietism and the American economic system. Fascism and Nazism were both committed to the Soviet principle of dictatorship and violent oppression of dissenters. If one wants to assign Fascism and Nazism to the same class of political systems, one must call this class *dictatorial regime* and one must not neglect to assign the Soviets to the same class.

In recent years the communists' semantic innovations have gone even 573
further. They call everybody whom they dislike, every advocate of the free enterprise system, a Fascist. Bolshevism, they say, is the only really democratic system. All non-communist countries and parties are essentially undemocratic and Fascist.

It is true that sometimes also non-socialists—the last vestiges of the old aristocracy—toyed with the idea of an aristocratic revolution modelled according to the pattern of Soviet dictatorship. Lenin had opened their eyes. What dupes, they moaned, have we been! We have let ourselves be deluded by the spurious catchwords of the liberal bourgeoisie. We believed that it was not permissible to deviate from the rule of law and to crush mercilessly those challenging our rights. How silly were these Romanovs in granting to their deadly foes the benefits of a fair legal trial! If somebody arouses the suspicion of Lenin, he is done for. Lenin does not hesitate to exterminate, without any trial, not only every suspect, but all his kin and friends too. But the Czars were superstitiously afraid of infringing the rules established by those scraps of paper called laws. When Alexander Ulyanov conspired against the Czar's life, he alone was executed; his brother Vladimir was spared. Thus Alexander III himself preserved the life of Ulyanov-Lenin, the man who ruthlessly exterminated his son, his daughter-in-law and their children and with them all the other members of the family he could catch. Was this not the most stupid and suicidal policy?

However, no action could result from the day dreams of these old Tories. They were a small group of powerless grumblers. They were not backed by any ideological forces and they had no followers.

The idea of such an aristocratic revolution motivated the German *Stahlhelm* and the French *Cagoulards.** The Stahlhelm was simply dispelled by order of Hitler. The French Government could easily imprison the Cagoulards before they had any opportunity to do harm.

The nearest approach to an aristocratic dictatorship is Franco's regime. But Franco was merely a puppet of Mussolini and Hitler, who wanted to secure Spanish aid for the impending war against France or at least Spanish "friendly" neutrality. With his protectors gone, he will either have to adopt Western methods of government or face removal.

Dictatorship and violent oppression of all dissenters are today exclusively socialist institutions. This becomes clear as we take a closer look at Fascism and Nazism.

574 7

Fascism

When the war broke out in 1914, the Italian socialist party was divided as to the policy to be adopted.

* Stahlhelm was an association of German World War veterans, established 1918. Cagoulards were members of a secret French extreme rightist, terrorist organization, the Cagoule. It was responsible for several assassinations of socialists and Italian anti-fascists and it collaborated with the Nazis and the French Vichy government during WWII (Pub.).

One group clung to the rigid principles of Marxism. This war, they maintained, is a war of the capitalists. It is not seemly for the proletarians to side with any of the belligerent parties. The proletarians must wait for the great revolution, the civil war of the united socialists against the united exploiters. They must stand for Italian neutrality.

The second group was deeply affected by the traditional hatred of Austria. In their opinion the first task of the Italians was to free their unredeemed brethren. Only then would the day of the socialist revolution appear.

In this conflict Benito Mussolini, the outstanding man in Italian socialism, chose at first the orthodox Marxian position. Nobody could surpass Mussolini in Marxian zeal. He was the intransigent champion of the pure creed, the unyielding defender of the rights of the exploited proletarians, the eloquent prophet of the socialist bliss to come. He was an adamant adversary of patriotism, nationalism, imperialism, monarchical rule and all religious creeds. When Italy in 1911 opened the great series of wars by an insidious assault upon Turkey, Mussolini organized violent demonstrations against the departure of troops for Libya. Now, in 1914, he branded the war against Germany and Austria as an imperialist war. He was then still under the dominating influence of Angelica Balabanoff, the daughter of a wealthy Russian landowner. Miss Balabanoff had initiated him into the subtleties of Marxism. In her eyes the defeat of the Romanovs counted more than the defeat of the Habsburgs. She had no sympathy for the ideals of the Risorgimento.

But the Italian intellectuals were first of all nationalists. As in all other European countries, most of the Marxians longed for war and conquest. Mussolini was not prepared to lose his popularity. The thing he hated most was not to be on the side of the victorious faction. He changed his mind and became the most fanatical advocate of Italy's attack on Austria. With French financial aid he founded a newspaper to fight for the cause of the war.

The anti-Fascists blame Mussolini for this defection from the teachings of 575
rigid Marxism. He was bribed, they say, by the French. Now, even these people should know that the publication of a newspaper requires funds. They themselves do not speak of bribery if a wealthy American provides a man with the money needed for the publication of a fellow-traveller newspaper, or if funds mysteriously flow into the communist publishing firms. It is a fact that Mussolini entered the scene of world politics as an ally of the democracies, while Lenin entered it as a virtual ally of imperial Germany.

More than anybody else Mussolini was instrumental in achieving Italy's entry into the first World War. His journalistic propaganda made it possible for the government to declare war on Austria. Only those few people have a right to find fault with his attitude in the years 1914 to 1918 who realize that the disintegration of the Austro-Hungarian Empire spelled the doom of Europe. Only those Italians are free to blame Mussolini who begin to understand that the only means of protecting the Italian-speaking minorities in the littoral districts of Austria against the threatening annihilation by the Slavonic majorities was to preserve the integrity of the Austrian state, whose constitution guaranteed equal rights to all linguistic groups. Mussolini was one of the most wretched figures of history. But the fact remains that his first great political deed still meets with the approval of all his countrymen and of the immense majority of his foreign detractors.

When the war came to an end, Mussolini's popularity dwindled. The communists, swept into popularity by events in Russia, carried on. But the great communist venture, the occupation of the factories in 1920, ended in complete failure, and the disappointed masses remembered the former leader of the socialist party. They flocked to Mussolini's new party, the Fascists. The youth greeted with turbulent enthusiasm the self-styled successor of the Caesars. Mussolini boasted in later years that he had saved Italy from the danger of communism. His foes passionately dispute his claims. Communism, they say, was no longer a real factor in Italy when Mussolini seized power. The truth is that the frustration of communism swelled the ranks of the Fascists and made it possible for them to destroy all other parties. The overwhelming victory of the Fascists was not the cause, but the consequence, of the communist fiasco.

576 The programme of the Fascists, as drafted in 1919, was vehemently anticapitalistic.[21] The most radical New Dealers and even communists could agree with it. When the Fascists came to power, they had forgotten those points of their programme which referred to the liberty of thought and the press and the right of assembly. In this respect they were conscientious disciples of Bukharin and Lenin. Moreover they did not suppress, as they had promised, the industrial and financial corporations. Italy badly needed foreign credits for the development of its industries. The main problem for Fascism, in the first years of its rule, was to win the confidence of the foreign bankers. It would have been suicidal to destroy the Italian corporations.

Fascist economic policy did not—at the beginning—essentially differ from those of all other Western nations. It was a policy of interventionism. As the years went on, it more and more approached the Nazi pattern of socialism. When Italy, after the defeat of France, entered the second World War, its

---

[21] This programme is reprinted in English in Count Carlo Sforza's book, *Contemporary Italy*, translated by Drake and Denise de Kay (New York, 1944), pp. 295–6.

economy was by and large already shaped according to the Nazi pattern. The main difference was that the Fascists were less efficient and even more corrupt than the Nazis.

But Mussolini could not long remain without an economic philosophy of his own invention. Fascism posed as a new philosophy, unheard of before and unknown to all other nations. It claimed to be the gospel which the resurrected spirit of ancient Rome brought to the decaying democratic peoples whose barbarian ancestors had once destroyed the Roman empire. It was the consummation both of the Rinascimento and the Risorgimento in every respect, the final liberation of the Latin genius from the yoke of foreign ideologies. Its shining leader, the peerless Duce, was called to find the ultimate solution for the burning problems of society's economic organization and of social justice.

From the dust-heap of discarded socialist utopias, the Fascist scholars salvaged the scheme of guild socialism. Guild socialism was very popular with British socialists in the last years of the first World War and in the first years following the Armistice. It was so impracticable that it disappeared very soon from socialist literature. No serious statesman ever paid any attention to contradictory and confused plans of guild socialism. It was 577
almost forgotten when the Fascists attached it to a new label, and flamboyantly proclaimed *corporativism* as the new social panacea. The public inside and outside of Italy was captivated. Innumerable books, pamphlets and articles were written in praise of the *stato corporativo.* The governments of Austria and Portugal very soon declared that they were committed to the noble principles of corporativism. The papal encyclical *Quadragesimo Anno* (1931) contained some paragraphs which could be interpreted—but need not be—as an approval of corporativism. In France its ideas found many eloquent supporters.

It was mere idle talk. Never did the Fascists make any attempt to realize the corporativist programme, industrial self-government. They changed the name of the chambers of commerce into corporative councils. They called *corporazione* the compulsory organizations of the various branches of industry which were the administrative units for the execution of the German pattern of socialism they had adopted. But there was no question of the *corporazione's* self-government. The Fascist cabinet did not tolerate anybody's interference with its absolute authoritarian control of production. All the plans for the establishment of the corporative system remained a dead letter.

Italy's main problem is its comparative overpopulation. In this age of barriers to trade and migration, the Italians are condemned to subsist permanently on a lower standard of living than that of the inhabitants of the countries more favoured by nature. The Fascists saw only one means to remedy this unfortunate situation: conquest. They were too narrow-minded to comprehend that the redress they recommended was spurious and worse than the evil. They were moreover so entirely blinded by self-conceit and vain-glory that they failed to realize that their provocative speeches were simply ridiculous. The foreigners whom they insolently challenged knew very well how negligible Italy's military forces were.

Fascism was not, as its advocates boasted, an original product of the Italian mind. It began with a split in the ranks of Marxian socialism, which certainly was an imported doctrine. Its economic programme was borrowed from German non-Marxian socialism and its aggressiveness was likewise copied from Germans, the *All-deutsche* or Pan-German forerunners of the Nazis. Its conduct of government affairs was a replica of Lenin's dictatorship. Cor-
578 porativism, its much advertised ideological adornment, was of British origin. The only home-grown ingredient of Fascism was the theatrical style of its processions, shows and festivals.

The shortlived Fascist episode ended in blood, misery and ignominy. But the forces which generated Fascism are not dead. Fanatical nationalism is a feature common to all present-day Italians. The communists are certainly not prepared to renounce their principle of dictatorial oppression of all dissenters. Neither do the Catholic parties advocate freedom of thought, of the press or of religion. There are in Italy only very few people indeed who comprehend that the indispensable prerequisite of democracy and the rights of men is economic freedom.

It may happen that Fascism will be resurrected under a new label and with new slogans and symbols. But if this happens, the consequences will be detrimental. For Fascism is not as the Fascists trumpeted a "new way to life,"[22] it is a rather old way towards destruction and death.

8

Nazism

The philosophy of the Nazis, the *German National Socialist Labour Party*, is the purest and most consistent manifestation of the anticapitalistic and socialistic spirit of our age. Its essential ideas are not German or "Aryan" in

---

[22] For instance Mario Palmieri, *The Philosophy of Fascism* (Chicago, 1936), p. 248.

origin, nor are they peculiar to the present day Germans. In the genealogical tree of the Nazi doctrine such Latins as Sismondi and Georges Sorel, and such Anglo-Saxons as Carlyle, Ruskin and Houston Stewart Chamberlain, were more conspicuous than any German. Even the best known ideological attire of Nazism, the fable of the superiority of the Aryan master race, was not of German provenance; its author was a Frenchman, Gobineau. Germans of Jewish descent, like Lassalle, Lasson, Stahl and Walter Rathenau, contributed more to the essential tenets of Nazism than such men as Sombart, Spann and Ferdinand Fried. The slogan into which the Nazis condensed their economic philosophy, viz., *Gemeinnutz geht vor Eigennutz* (i.e., the commonweal ranks above private profit), is likewise the idea underlying the 579
American New Deal and the Soviet management of economic affairs. It implies that profit-seeking business harms the vital interests of the immense majority, and that it is the sacred duty of popular government to prevent the emergence of profits by public control of production and distribution.

The only specifically German ingredient in Nazism was its striving after the conquest of *Lebensraum*. And this, too, was an outcome of their agreement with the ideas guiding the policies of the most influential political parties of all other countries. These parties proclaim income equality as the main thing. The Nazis do the same. What characterizes the Nazis is the fact that they are not prepared to acquiesce in a state of affairs in which the Germans are doomed forever to be "imprisoned," as they say, in a comparatively small and overpopulated area in which the productivity of labour must be smaller than in the comparatively underpopulated countries, which are better endowed with natural resources and capital goods. They aim at a fairer distribution of earth's natural resources. As a "have-not" nation they look at the wealth of the richer nations with the same feelings with which many people in the Western countries look at the higher incomes of some of their countrymen. The "progressives" in the Anglo-Saxon countries assert that "liberty is not worth having" for those who are wronged by the comparative smallness of their incomes. The Nazis say the same with regard to international relations. In their opinion the only freedom that matters is *Nahrungsfreiheit* (viz., freedom from importing food). They aim at the acquisition of a territory so large and rich in natural resources that they could live in economic self-sufficiency at a standard not lower than that of any other nation. They consider themselves as revolutionaries fighting for their inalienable natural rights against the vested interests of a host of reactionary nations.

It is easy for economists to explode the fallacies involved in the Nazi doctrines. But those who disparage economics as "orthodox and reactionary," and fantically support the spurious creeds of socialism and economic nationalism, were at a loss to refute them. For Nazism was nothing but the logical application of their own tenets to the particular conditions of comparatively overpopulated Germany.

580 For more than seventy years the German professors of political science, history, law, geography and philosophy eagerly imbued their disciples with a hysterical hatred of capitalism, and preached the war of "liberation" against the capitalistic West. The German "socialists of the chair," much admired in all foreign countries, were the pacemakers of the two World Wars. At the turn of the century the immense majority of the Germans were already radical supporters of socialism and aggressive nationalism. They were then already firmly committed to the principles of Nazism. What was lacking and was added later was only a new term to signify their doctrine.

When the Soviet policies of mass extermination of all dissenters and of ruthless violence removed the inhibitions against wholesale murder, which still troubled some of the Germans, nothing could any longer stop the advance of Nazism. The Nazis were quick to adopt the Soviet methods. They imported from Russia: the one-party system and the pre-eminence of this party in political life; the paramount position assigned to the secret police; the concentration camps; the administrative execution or imprisonment of all opponents; the extermination of the families of suspects and of exiles; the methods of propaganda; the organization of affiliated parties abroad and their employment for fighting their domestic governments and espionage and sabotage; the use of the diplomatic and consular service for fomenting revolution; and many other things besides. There were nowhere more docile disciples of Lenin, Trotsky and Stalin than the Nazis were.

Hitler was not the founder of Nazism; he was its product. He was, like most of his collaborators, a sadistic gangster. He was uneducated and ignorant; he had failed even in the lower grades of high school. He never had any honest job. It is a fable that he had ever been a paperhanger. His military career in the first World War was rather mediocre. The First Class Iron Cross was given to him after the end of the war as a reward for his activities as a political agent. He was a maniac obsessed by megalomania. But learned professors nourished his self-conceit. Werner Sombart, who once had boasted that his life was devoted to the task of fighting for the ideas of Marx,[23] Sombart, whom the American Economic Association had elected to Honorary membership and many non-German universities to honorary degrees, can-
581 didly declared that *Führertum* means a permanent revelation and that the

[23] Sombart, *Das Lebenswerk von Karl Marx* (Jena, 1909), p. 3.

Führer received his orders directly from God, the supreme *Führer* of the Universe.[24]

The Nazi plan was more comprehensive and therefore more pernicious than that of the Marxians. It aimed at abolishing *laisser-faire* not only in the production of material goods, but no less in the production of men. The Führer was not only the general manager of all industries; he was also the general manager of the breeding-farm intent upon rearing superior men and eliminating inferior stock. A grandiose scheme of eugenics was to be put into effect according to "scientific" principles.

It is vain for the champions of eugenics to protest that they did not mean what the Nazis executed. Eugenics aims at placing some men, backed by the police power, in complete control of human reproduction. It suggests that the methods applied to domestic animals be applied to men. This is precisely what the Nazis tried to do. The only objection which a consistent eugenist can raise is that his own plan differs from that of the Nazi scholars and that he wants to rear another type of men than the Nazis. As every supporter of economic planning aims at the execution of his own plan only, so every advocate of eugenic planning aims at the execution of his own plan and wants himself to act as the breeder of human stock.

The eugenists pretend that they want to eliminate criminal individuals. But the qualification of a man as a criminal depends upon the prevailing laws of the country and varies with the change in social and political ideologies. John Huss, Giordano Bruno and Galileo Galilei were criminals from the point of view of the laws which their judges applied. When Stalin robbed the Russian State Bank of several million rubles, he committed a crime. Today it is an offence in Russia to disagree with Stalin. In Nazi Germany sexual intercourse between "Aryans" and the members of an "inferior" race was a crime. Whom do the eugenists want to eliminate, Brutus or Caesar? Both violated the laws of their country. If eighteenth-century eugenists had prevented alcohol addicts from generating children, their planning would have eliminated Beethoven.

It must be emphasized again: there is no such thing as a scientific *ought*.
Which men are superior and which are inferior can only be decided by 582
personal value judgments not liable to verification or falsification. The eugenists delude themselves in assuming that they themselves will be called to decide what qualities are to be conserved in the human stock. They are too dull to take into account the possibility that other people might make the

[24] Sombart, *A New Social Philosophy*, trans. and ed. K. F. Geiser (Princeton University Press, 1937), p. 194.

choice according to their own value judgments.[25] In the eyes of the Nazis the brutal killer, the "fair-haired beast," is the most perfect specimen of mankind.

The mass slaughters perpetrated in the Nazi horror camps are too horrible to be adequately described by words. But they were the logical and consistent application of doctrines and policies parading as applied science and approved by some men who in a sector of the natural sciences have displayed acumen and technical skill in laboratory research.

9

The Teachings of Soviet Experience

Many people all over the world assert that the Soviet "experiment" has supplied conclusive evidence in favour of socialism and disproved all, or at least most, of the objections raised against it. The facts, they say, speak for themselves. It is no longer permissible to pay any attention to the spurious aprioristic reasoning of armchair economists criticizing the socialist plans. A crucial experiment has exploded their fallacies.

It is, first of all, necessary to comprehend that in the field of purposive human action and social relations no experiments can be made and no experiments have ever been made. The experimental method to which the natural sciences owe all their achievements is inapplicable in the social sciences. The natural sciences are in a position to observe in the laboratory experiment the consequences of the isolated change in one element only, while other elements remain unchanged. Their experimental observation refers ultimately to certain isolable elements in sense experience. What the natural sciences call facts are the causal relations shown in such experiments. Their theories and hypotheses must be in agreement with these facts.

583 But the experience with which the sciences of human action have to deal is essentially different. It is historical experience. It is an experience of complex phenomena, of the joint effects brought about by the co-operation of a multiplicity of elements. The social sciences are never in a position to control the conditions of change and to isolate them from one another in the way in which the experimenter proceeds in arranging his experiments. They never enjoy the advantage of observing the consequences of a change in one

---

[25] The devastating critique of eugenics by H. S. Jennings, *The Biological Basis of Human Nature* (New York, 1930), pp. 223–52.

element only, other conditions being equal. They are never faced with facts in the sense in which the natural sciences employ this term. Every fact and every experience with which the social sciences have to deal is open to various interpretations. Historical facts and historical experience can never prove or disprove a statement in the way in which an experiment proves or disproves.

Historical experience never comments upon itself. It needs to be interpreted from the point of view of theories constructed without the aid of experimental observations. There is no need to enter into an epistemological analysis of the logical and philosophical problems involved. It is enough to refer to the fact that nobody—whether scientist or layman—ever proceeds otherwise when dealing with historical experience. Every discussion of the relevance and meaning of historical facts falls back very soon on a discussion of abstract general principles, logically antecedent to the facts to be elucidated and interpreted. Reference to historical experience can never solve any problem or answer any question. The same historical events and the same statistical figures are claimed as confirmations of contradictory theories.

If history could prove and teach us anything, it would be that private ownership of the means of production is a necessary requisite of civilization and material well-being. All civilizations have up to now been based on private property. Only nations committed to the principle of private property have risen above penury and produced science, art and literature. There is no experience to show that any other social system could provide mankind with any of the achievements of civilization. Nevertheless, only few people consider this as a sufficient and incontestable refutation of the socialist programme.

On the contrary, there are even people who argue the other way round.
It is frequently asserted that the system of private property is done for *584*
precisely because it was the system that men applied in the past. However beneficial a social system may have been in the past, they say, it cannot be so in the future too; a new age requires a new mode of social organization. Mankind has reached maturity; it would be pernicious for it to cling to the principles to which it resorted in the earlier stages of its evolution. This is certainly the most radical abandonment of experimentalism. The experimental method may assert: because *a* produced in the past the result *b*, it will produce it in the future also. It must never assert: because *a* produced in the past the result *b*, it is proved that it cannot produce it any longer.

In spite of the fact that mankind has had no experience with the socialist mode of production, the socialist writers have constructed various schemes of socialist systems based on aprioristic reasoning. But as soon as anybody dares to analyse these projects and to scrutinize them with regard to their feasibility and their ability to further human welfare, the socialists vehemently object. These analyses, they say, are merely idle aprioristic speculations. They cannot disprove the correctness of our statements and the expediency of our plans. They are not experimental. One must try socialism and then the results will speak for themselves.

What these socialists ask for is absurd. Carried to its ultimate logical consequences, their idea implies that men are not free to refute by reasoning any scheme, however nonsensical, self-contradictory and impracticable, that any reformer is pleased to suggest. According to their view, the only method permissible for the refutation of such a—necessarily abstract and aprioristic—plan is to test it by reorganizing the whole of society according to its designs. As soon as a man sketches the plan for a better social order, all nations are bound to try it and to see what will happen.

Even the most stubborn socialists cannot fail to admit that there are various plans for the construction of the future utopia, incompatible with one another. There is the Soviet pattern of all-round socialization of all enterprises and their outright bureaucratic management; there is the German pattern of *Zwangswirtschaft*, towards the complete adoption of which the Anglo-Saxon countries are manifestly tending; there is guild socialism, under the name of corporativism still very popular in some Catholic countries. There are
585 many other varieties. The supporters of most of these competing schemes assert that the beneficial results to be expected from their own scheme will appear only when all nations will have adopted it; they deny that socialism in one country only can already bring the blessings they ascribe to socialism. The Marxians declare that the bliss of socialism will emerge only in its "higher phase" which, as they hint, will appear only after the working class will have passed "through long struggles, through a whole series of historical processes, wholly transforming both circumstances and men."[26] The inference from all this is that one must realize socialism and quietly wait for a very long time until its promised benefits come. No unpleasant experiences in the period of transition, no matter how long this period may be, can disprove the assertion that socialism is the best of all conceivable modes of social organization. He that believeth shall be saved.

But which of the many socialist plans, contradicting one another, should be adopted? Every socialist sect passionately proclaims that its own brand is alone genuine socialism and that all other sects advocate counterfeit,

---

[26] Marx, *Der Bürgerkrieg in Frankreich*, ed. Pfemfert (Berlin, 1919), p. 54. Publisher's Note: In English, "The Civil War in France," p. 408.

entirely pernicious measures. In fighting one another, the various socialist factions resort to the same methods of abstract reasoning which they stigmatize as vain apriorism whenever they are applied against the correctness of their own statements and the expediency and practicability of their own schemes. There is, of course, no other method available. The fallacies implied in a system of abstract reasoning—such as socialism is—cannot be smashed otherwise than by abstract reasoning.

The fundamental objection advanced against the practicability of socialism refers to the impossibility of economic calculation. It has been demonstrated in an irrefutable way that a socialist commonwealth would not be in a position to apply economic calculation. Where there are no market prices for the factors of production because they are neither bought nor sold, it is impossible to resort to calculation in planning future action and in determining the result of past action. A socialist management of production would simply not know whether or not what it plans and executes is the most appropriate means to attain the ends sought. It will operate in the dark, as it were. It will squander the scarce factors of production both material and human (labour). Chaos and poverty for all will unavoidably result.

All earlier socialists were too narrow-minded to see this essential point. *586*
Neither did the earlier economists conceive its full importance. When the present writer in 1920 showed the impossibility of economic calculation under socialism, the apologists of socialism embarked upon the search for a method of calculation applicable to a socialist system. They utterly failed in these endeavours. The futility of the schemes they produced could easily be shown. Those communists who were not entirely intimidated by the fear of the Soviet executioners, for instance Trotsky, freely admitted that economic accounting is unthinkable without market relations.[27] The intellectual bankruptcy of the socialist doctrine can no longer be disguised. In spite of its unprecedented popularity, socialism is done for. No economist can any longer question its impracticability. The avowal of socialist ideas is today the proof of a complete ignorance of the basic problems of economics. The socialist's claims are as vain as those of the astrologers and the magicians.

With regard to this essential problem of socialism, viz., economic calculation, the Russian "experiment" is of no avail. The Soviets are operating within a world the greater part of which still clings to a market economy. They base the calculations on which they make their decisions on the prices established abroad. Without the help of these prices their actions would be aimless and planless. Only as far as they refer to this foreign price system

[27] Hayek, *Individualism and the Economic Order* (Chicago University Press, 1948), pp. 89–91.

are they able to calculate, keep books and prepare their plans. In this respect one may agree with the statement of various socialist and communist authors that socialism in one or a few countries only is not yet true socialism. Of course, these authors attach a quite different meaning to their assertion. They want to say that the full blessings of socialism can be reaped only in a world-embracing socialist community. Those familiar with the teachings of economics must, on the contrary, recognize that socialism will result in full chaos precisely if it is applied in the greater part of the world.

The second main objection raised against socialism is that it is a less efficient mode of production than is capitalism and that it will impair the productivity of labour. Consequently, in a socialist commonwealth the standard of living of the masses will be low when compared with conditions prevailing under capitalism. There is no doubt that this objection has not
587 been disproved by the Soviet experience. The only certain fact about Russian affairs under the Soviet regime with regard to which all people agree is: that the standard of living of the Russian masses is much lower than that of the masses in the country which is universally considered as the paragon of capitalism, the United States of America. If we were to regard the Soviet regime as an experiment, we would have to say that the experiment has clearly demonstrated the superiority of capitalism and the inferiority of socialism.

It is true that the advocates of socialism are intent upon interpreting the lowness of the Russian standard of living in a different way. As they see things, it was not caused by socialism, but was—in spite of socialism—brought about by other agencies. They refer to various factors, e.g., the poverty of Russia under the Czars, the disastrous effects of the wars, the alleged hostility of the capitalist democratic nations, the alleged sabotage of the remnants of the Russian aristocracy and bourgeoisie and of the Kulaks. There is no need to enter into an examination of these matters. For we do not contend that any historical experience could prove or disprove a theoretical statement in the way in which a crucial experiment can verify or falsify a statement concerning natural events. It is not the critics of socialism, but its fanatical advocates, who maintain that the Soviet "experiment" proves something with regard to the effects of socialism. However, what they are really doing in dealing with the manifest and undisputed facts of Russian experience is to push them aside by impermissible tricks and fallacious syllogisms. They disavow the obvious facts by commenting upon them in such a way as to deny their bearing and their significance upon the question to be answered.

Let us, for the sake of argument, assume that their interpretation is correct. But then it would still be absurd to assert that the Soviet experiment has evidenced the superiority of socialism. All that could be said is: the fact that the masses' standard of living is low in Russia does not provide conclusive evidence that socialism is inferior to capitalism.

A comparison with experimentation in the field of the natural sciences may clarify the issue. A biologist wants to test a new patent food. He feeds it to a number of guinea pigs. They all lose weight and finally die. The experimenter believes that their decline and death were not caused by the patent food, but by merely accidental affliction with pneumonia. It would never- 588
theless be absurd for him to proclaim that his experiment had evidenced the nutritive value of the compound because the unfavourable result is to be ascribed to accidental occurrences, not causally linked with the experimental arrangement. The best he could contend is that the outcome of the experiment was not conclusive, that it does not prove anything *against* the nutritive value of the food tested. Things are, he could assert, as if no experiment had been tried at all.

Even if the Russian masses' standard of living were much higher than that of the capitalist countries, this still would not be conclusive proof of the superiority of socialism. It may be admitted that the undisputed fact that the standard of living in Russia is lower than that in the capitalist West does not conclusively prove the inferiority of socialism. But it is nothing short of idiocy to announce that the experience of Russia has demonstrated the superiority of public control of production.

Neither does the fact that the Russian armies, after having suffered many defeats, finally—with armament manufactured by American big business and donated to them by the American taxpayers—could aid the Americans in the conquest of Germany prove the pre-eminence of communism. When the British forces had to sustain a temporary reverse in North Africa, Professor Harold Laski, that most radical advocate of socialism, was quick to announce the final failure of capitalism. He was not consistent enough to interpret the German conquest of the Ukraine as the final failure of Russian communism. Neither did he retract his condemnation of the British system when his country emerged victorious from the war. If the military events are to be considered as the proof of any social system's excellence, it is rather the American than the Russian system for which they bear witness.

Nothing that has happened in Russia since 1917 contradicts any of the statements of the critics of socialism and communism. Even if one bases one's judgment exclusively on the writings of communists and fellow-travellers, one cannot discover any feature in Russian conditions that tells in favour of the Soviet's social and political system. All the technological improvements of the last decades originated in the capitalistic countries. It is true that the Russians have tried to copy some of these innovations. But so did all backward oriental peoples too.

589 Some communists are eager to have us believe that the ruthless oppression of dissenters and the radical abolition of the freedom of thought, speech and the press are not inherent marks of the public control of business. They are, they argue, only accidental phenomena of communism, its signature in a country which—as was the case with Russia—never enjoyed freedom of thought and conscience. However, these apologists for totalitarian despotism are at a loss to explain how the rights of man could be safeguarded under government omnipotence.

Freedom of thought and conscience is a sham in a country in which the authorities are free to exile everybody whom they dislike into the Arctic or the desert, and to assign him hard labour for life. The autocrat may always try to justify such arbitrary acts by pretending that they are motivated exclusively by considerations of public welfare and economic expediency. He alone is the supreme arbiter to decide all matters referring to the execution of the plan. Freedom of the press is illusory when the government owns and operates all paper mills, printing offices and publishing houses, and ultimately decides what is to be printed and what not. The right of assembly is vain if the government owns all assembly halls and determines for what purposes they shall be used. And so it is with all other liberties too. In one of his lucid intervals Trotsky—of course Trotsky the hunted exile, not the ruthless commander of the Red army—saw things realistically and declared: "In a country where the sole employer is the State, opposition means death by slow starvation. The old principle: who does not work shall not eat, has been replaced by a new one: who does not obey shall not eat."[28] This confession settles the issue.

What the Russian experience shows is a very low level of the standard of living of the masses and unlimited dictatorial despotism. The apologists of communism are intent upon explaining these uncontested facts as accidental only; they are, they say, not the fruit of communism, but occurred in spite of communism. But even if one were to accept these excuses for the sake of argument, it would be nonsensical to maintain that the Soviet "experiment" has demonstrated anything *in favour* of communism and socialism.

---

[28] Quoted by Hayek, *The Road to Serfdom* (1944), Chapter IX, p. 119.

10 590

The Alleged Inevitability of Socialism

Many people believe that the coming of totalitarianism is inevitable. The "wave of the future," they say, "carries mankind inexorably towards a system under which all human affairs are managed by omnipotent dictators. It is useless to fight against the unfathomable decrees of history."

The truth is that most people lack the intellectual ability and courage to resist a popular movement, however pernicious and ill-considered. Bismarck once deplored the lack of what he called civilian courage, i.e., bravery in dealing with civic affairs, on the part of his countrymen. But neither did the citizens of other nations display more courage and judiciousness when faced with the menace of communist dictatorship. They either yielded silently, or timidly raised some trifling objections.

One does not fight socialism by criticizing only some accidental features of its schemes. In attacking many socialists' stand on divorce and birth control, or their ideas about art and literature, one does not refute socialism. It is not enough to disapprove of the Marxian assertions that the theory of relativity or the philosophy of Bergson or psycho-analysis is "bourgeois" moonshine. Those who find fault with Bolshevism and Nazism only for their anti-Christian leanings implicitly endorse all the rest of these bloody schemes.

On the other hand, it is sheer stupidity to praise the totalitarian regimes for alleged achievements which have no reference whatever to their political and economic principles. It is questionable whether the observations that in Fascist Italy the railway trains ran on schedule and the bug population of second-rate hotel beds was decreasing, were correct or not; but it is in any case of no importance for the problem of Fascism. The fellow-travellers are enraptured by Russian films, Russian music and Russian caviar. But there lived greater musicians in other countries and under other social systems; good pictures were produced in other countries too; and it is certainly not a merit of Generalissimo Stalin that the taste of caviar is delicious. Neither does the prettiness of Russian ballet dancers or the construction of a great power station on the Dnieper expiate for the mass slaughter of the Kulaks.

The readers of picture magazines and the movie-fans long for the pictur- 591
esque. The operatic pageants of the Fascists and the Nazis and the parading of the girl-battalions of the Red army are after their heart. It is more fun to listen to the radio speeches of a dictator than to study economic treatises. The entrepreneurs and technologists who pave the way for economic improvement work in seclusion; their work is not suitable to be visualized on

the screen. But the dictators, intent upon spreading death and destruction, are spectacularly in sight of the public. Dressed in military garb they eclipse in the eyes of the movie-goers the colourless bourgeois in plain clothes.

The problems of society's economic organization are not suitable for light talk at fashionable cocktail parties. Neither can they be dealt with adequately by demagogues haranguing mass assemblies. They are serious things. They require painstaking study. They must not be taken lightly.

The socialist propaganda never encountered any decided opposition. The devastating critique by which the economists exploded the futility and impracticability of the socialist schemes and doctrines did not reach the moulders of public opinion. The universities were mostly dominated by socialist or interventionist pedants not only in continental Europe, where they were owned and operated by the governments, but even in the Anglo-Saxon countries. The politicians and the statesmen, anxious not to lose popularity, were lukewarm in their defence of freedom. The policy of appeasement, so much criticized when applied in the case of the Nazis and the Fascists, was practised universally for many decades with regard to all other brands of socialism. It was this defeatism that made the rising generation believe that the victory of socialism is inevitable.

It is not true that the masses are vehemently asking for socialism and that there is no means to resist them. The masses favour socialism because they trust the socialist propaganda of the intellectuals. The intellectuals, not the populace, are moulding public opinion. It is a lame excuse of the intellectuals that they must yield to the masses. They themselves have generated the socialist ideas and indoctrinated the masses with them. No proletarian or son of a proletarian has contributed to the elaboration of the interventionist and socialist programmes. Their authors were all of bourgeois background.
592 The esoteric writings of dialectical materialism, of Hegel, the father both of Marxism and of German aggressive nationalism, the books of Georges Sorel, of Gentile and of Spengler were not read by the average man; they did not move the masses directly. It was the intellectuals who popularized them.

The intellectual leaders of the peoples have produced and propagated the fallacies which are on the point of destroying liberty and Western civilization. The intellectuals alone are responsible for the mass slaughters which are the characteristic mark of our century. They alone can reverse the trend and pave the way for a resurrection of freedom.

Not mythical "material productive forces," but reason and ideas determine the course of human affairs. What is needed to stop the trend towards socialism and despotism is common sense and moral courage.

INDEX TO WORKS CITED

All books and articles cited in text and footnotes have been arranged alphabetically by author and indexed here to the page on which each is mentioned. Data about the specific editions referred to, and authors' dates as available, have also been supplied.

Whenever possible, the compiler of this index has included, in parentheses, information about English-language editions of a work. To give an indication of the subject matter treated in a foreign language work, when no English translation is known, the foreign language title is followed immediately, in square brackets, by a literal English translation of that title.

INDEX TO WORKS CITED

INDEX TO SUBJECTS AND NAMES

In preparing this completely new index, the specific terms, phrases, ideas and concepts used in chapter titles, section headings and text of this particular British-English language translation have been taken into consideration. Some recognition has also been given to terms and ideas that have come into more general usage in the United States during the decades since 1936.

If the discussion of a particular topic appears clearly delineated in the text, opening and closing pages are indicated. However, when a discussion is more or less open ended, the page reference is followed by "ff." inviting the reader to keep on reading beyond the specific page cited for further insight into the indexed category.

This "Index to Subjects and Names" includes all the names of persons mentioned and/or quoted in the text, as well as those whose ideas are referred to in footnotes. The "Index to Works Cited" (pp. 543–554 above) lists and identifies all authors and works cited.

INDEX TO SUBJECTS AND NAMES

BIOGRAPHICAL NOTE

Ludwig von Mises (1881–1973) was the acknowledged leader of the Austrian School of economic thought, a prodigious originator in economic theory, and a prolific author. A library of his books would total twenty-one volumes if confined to first editions, forty-eight volumes if all revised editions and translations were included, and still more if the *Festschriften* and other volumes containing contributions by him were added.

Von Mises' writings and lectures encompassed economic theory, history, epistemology, government, and political philosophy. His contributions to economic theory include important clarifications on the quantity theory of money, the theory of the trade cycle, the integration of monetary theory with economic theory in general, and a demonstration that socialism must fail because it cannot solve the problem of economic calculation. Mises was the first scholar to recognize that economics is part of a larger science in human action, a science which Mises called "praxeology."

Ludwig von Mises received doctorates in law and economics from the University of Vienna in 1906. In 1909 he became Economic Advisor to the Austrian Chamber of Commerce (comparable to the U.S. Department of Commerce). After serving in World War I, he became Professor of Economics at the University of Vienna and, in 1934, Professor of International Relations at the Graduate Institute of International Studies in Geneva. In 1945 he became Visiting Professor at New York University where he remained until his retirement in 1969. In a lecturing and teaching career that spanned many continents and more than half a century, Mises numbered among his students one Nobel Laureate, F.A. Hayek, two presidents of the American Economic Association, Gottfried Haberler and Fritz Machlup, and many other economists of international reputation.

His major works are *The Theory of Money and Credit* (1912), *Socialism* (1922), *Human Action* (1949), *Theory and History* (1957), *Epistemological Problems of Economics* (1960), and *The Ultimate Foundations of Economic Science* (1962).

The Palatino typeface used in this volume is the work of Hermann Zapf, the noted European type designer and master calligrapher. Palatino is basically an "old style" letterform, yet it is strongly endowed with Zapf's distinctive exquisiteness. With concern not solely for the individual letter but also for the working visual relationship in a page of text, Zapf's edged pen has given this type a brisk, natural motion.

This book is printed on paper that is acid-free and meets the requirements of the American National Standard for Permanence of Paper for Printed Library Materials, Z39.48-1992 ♾

Text Design by JMH Corporation, Indianapolis, Indiana
Cover Design by Erin Kirk New, Watkinsville, Georgia
Typography by Monotype Composition Co., Inc., Baltimore, Maryland
Printed and bound by Sheridan Books, Chelsea, Michigan